Sixth Edition

Volume I: To 1877
Chapters 1–17

NATION OF NATIONS

A Narrative History of the American Republic

James West Davidson

Brian DeLay
University of Colorado

Christine Leigh Heyrman
University of Delaware

Mark H. Lytle
Bard College

Michael B. Stoff
University of Texas, Austin

Here is not merely a nation but a teeming nation of nations
Walt Whitman

 McGraw-Hill
Higher Education

Boston   Burr Ridge, IL   Dubuque, IA   New York   San Francisco   St. Louis
Bangkok   Bogotá   Caracas   Kuala Lumpur   Lisbon   London   Madrid   Mexico City
Milan   Montreal   New Delhi   Santiago   Seoul   Singapore   Sydney   Taipei   Toronto

NATION OF NATIONS: A NARRATIVE HISTORY OF THE AMERICAN REPUBLIC, VOLUME I: TO 1877

Published by McGraw-Hill, a business unit of The McGraw-Hill Companies, Inc., 1221 Avenue of the Americas, New York, NY 10020. Copyright © 2008 by The McGraw-Hill Companies, Inc. All rights reserved. No part of this publication may be reproduced or distributed in any form or by any means, or stored in a database or retrieval system, without the prior written consent of The McGraw-Hill Companies, Inc., including, but not limited to, any network or other electronic storage or transmission, or broadcast for distance learning.

Some ancillaries, including electronic and print components, may not be available to customers outside the United States.

1 2 3 4 5 6 7 8 9 0 DOW/DOW 0 9 8

ISBN: 978-0-07-333015-0
MHID: 0-07-333015-9

Vice president and editor-in-chief: *Michael Ryan*
Publisher: *Lisa Moore*
Sponsoring editor: *Jon-David Hague*
Development editors: *Barbara Conover,*
    Nicole Caddigan-Bridge
Editorial coordinator: *Sora Lisa Kim*
Marketing manager: *Pamela Cooper*
Marketing Specialist: *Clare Cashen*
Media Project Manager: *Jessalyn Clark*
Production editor: *Mel Valentín*
Production assistant: *Rachel J. Castillo*

Manuscript editor: *Stacey Sawyer*
Art director: *Jeanne M. Schreiber*
Design manager: *Violeta Díaz*
Cover designer: *Laurie Entringer*
Interior designer: *Kiera Pohl*
Art manager: *Robin Mouat*
Photo research coordinator: *Nora Agbayani*
Photo researcher: *PhotoSearch, Inc.*
Illustrators: *Mapping Specialists, Patti Isaacs*
Production supervisor: *Richard DeVitto*

The text was set in 10/12 ITC Galliard Std Roman by Aptara-York, and printed on acid-free 45# Publisher's Matte Plus by R.R. Donnelley & Sons.

Cover image: Library of Congress, Prints & Photographs Division, Civil War Photographs, LC-DIG-cwpb-01109.

Page 244-45 From Charles A. Johnson, *Frontier Camp Meeting*, pp. 43 and 47, copyright 1955, 1985. SMU Press. Reprinted with permission; **435** "Resources of the Union and the Confederacy, 1861", Adapted from THE CIVIL WAR DAY BY DAY by E.B. Long, copyright © 1971 by E.B. Long. Used by permission of Doubleday, a division of Random House, Inc.; **506** "Spending on Education in the South before and after Disfranchisement", Robert A. Margo, Disfranchisement, School Finance, and the Economics of Segregated Schools in the U.S. South, 1890–1910 (New York: Garland Press, 1985). Table 1-1; **718** Charles P. Kindleberg, "Declining World Trade, 1929–1933", *The World in Depression, 1929–1939* (revised ed., 1986) p. 170. copyright © 1986. The Regents of the University of California; **831** Levy, Frank. Figure 6.1, "Major U.S. Migration Flows in the late 1940s and 1950s." In *Dollars and Dreams: The Changing American Income Distribution.* © 1987 Russell Sage Foundation, 112 East 64th St., New York, NY 10021. Reprinted with Permission.

Because this page cannot legibly accommodate all acknowledgements for copyrighted material, credits appear at the end of the book, and constitute an extension of this copyright page.

Library of Congress Cataloging-in-Publication Data
Nation of nations : a history of the American Republic / James West Davidson . . . [et al.]. —6th ed.
    p. cm.
Includes bibliographical references and index.
    ISBN-13: 978-0-07-340684-8 (alk. paper)
    ISBN-10: 0-07-340684-8 (alk. paper)
1. United States—History—Textbooks. 2. United States—History—Sources. I. Davidson, James West.
E178.1.N346 2007
973—dc22   2007042451

www.mhhe.com

Contents in Brief

Contents

Chapter 1
The First Civilizations of North America

Chapter 2
Old Worlds, New Worlds
1400–1600

Chapter 10
The Opening of America
1815–1850

Chapter 11
The Rise of Democracy
1824–1840

Chapter 14

Western Expansion and the Rise of Slavery 1820–1850

Chapter 15

The Union Broken 1850–1861

List of Maps and Charts

Preface to the Sixth Edition

This revision is the most comprehensive one undertaken since the book was conceived more than two decades ago. Our touchstone remains the same—that all good history begins with a good story. But the shape of that story continues to change, enriched by stimulating recent scholarship. We have sought to place the history of this "nation of nations"—Walt Whitman's phrase—within a broader context of communities and environments, from the earliest peopling of the continent to our ongoing complex relationship with its resources. *Nation of Nations* has always been characterized by our attention to a global perspective, and we have made an even stronger effort to establish both continental and international frameworks for such topics as the trans-Atlantic communities created in the wake of first contact between Europe, Africa, and the Americas; the economic and cultural systems created by the spread of slavery and plantation agricultures; the dispersion of democratic and industrial revolutions and a consumer culture in the eighteenth and nineteenth centuries; the imperial and colonial conflicts of the late nineteenth and twentieth centuries; and the tightly linked information networks and global terrorism of the twenty-first century.

The addition of a new author to the *Nation of Nations* team, Brian DeLay of the University of Colorado, sparks our continued effort to incorporate perspectives that are both continental and global. DeLay's transnational study of how native peoples shaped the era of the U.S.-Mexican War, *The War of a Thousand Deserts* (2008), takes just such a continental perspective, integrating Indians and their politics into the narrative of both nation's histories during the first half of the nineteenth century. Especially in Volume I, *Nation of Nations* provides expanded coverage of the dynamics of white-Indian relations, and greater emphasis on the southwestern and western United States than in previous editions.

While adding to our scholarship, we have also streamlined and trimmed our existing narrative, maintaining sensitivity to length and the oft mentioned demands of "too much material and too little time."

Changes to the Sixth Edition

New Features:

- **Chapter Outlines:** For quick and easy reference, brief outlines appear at the beginning of each chapter, mapping out the organization and objectives of the reading material.

- *After the Fact in Brief:* In addition to the longer essays, every chapter of the text now includes a shorter feature, *After the Fact in Brief,* showcasing the variety of evidence historians consult when piecing together the past. Beyond the traditional primary sources, such evidence can include cartoons, maps, material culture—everything from a grisly skull pendant (Chapter 2) to a starched collar (Chapter 19) or an atomic blaster ring (Chapter 27).

- **Global conclusions:** Each chapter ends with a thematic conclusion that steps back to place events in American history in a continental or global context.

- **Map program:** All of the maps have been completely redesigned and updated to provide an exceptional visual presentation and clarity that supports the narrative.

The following list represents a few of the many instances of new and expanded coverage:

- An expanded **Chapter 1:** The First Civilizations of North America surveys the development of cities, agriculture, and civilizations in the pre-Contact Americas, placing greater emphasis on native North American cultures. It also explores how environmental constraints shaped the spread of culture between North and South America and how early American cultures shaped their own landscapes.

- In **Chapter 2,** the section "Eurasia and Africa in the Fifteenth Century" places Europe within the wider international economy in which China was central and the Islamic empires loomed large. The narrative treatment of Africa firmly places slavery in its broader historical context. A new section, "French Huguenots and the Birth of Spanish Florida," illuminates the religious and international rivalries between France and Spain.

- Reorganized **Chapter 3** includes an expanded section on Spanish colonization, beginning chronologically in 1598 with Oñate's Spanish settlements in New Mexico; the system of Indian alliances and Franciscan missions in Florida; and Indian slavery and the Pueblo Revolt. The section "From the Caribbean to the Carolinas" includes new material describing the extensive Indian slave trade and the effect of trading and raiding on Spanish Florida and Indian tribes as far west as the Mississippi.

- In **Chapter 4** expanded material on New France emphasizes French and Dutch interrelations with a host of Indian tribes. A new section, "The People in the Way," compares Indian and Puritan social and political structures and the pressure on Indian societies of English demands for land and of epidemic disease. A fuller discussion of the English "praying towns" for Christian Indians leads into expanded coverage of Metacom's war.

- **Chapter 7** provides a broader context of how Indian peoples were affected by the Revolution as the United States, Britain, Spain, and France sought Indian allies. It also charts the effects of the smallpox pandemic of 1775–1782.

- **Chapters 8 and 9** of the previous edition are streamlined into a new chapter, The Early Republic (1789–1824). A new section, "The Political Culture of the Early Republic," incorporates recent scholarship on the violence of the nation's new party politics, popular participation in political festivals, the rise of partisan newspapers, and the participation of women and African Americans. Global coverage in Chapter 9 stresses the influence of the French Revolution and European wars as well as the instabilities of western lands beyond the Appalachians. We have added a more complex discussion of the War of 1812 and the ramifications for western Indians and the continent as a whole.

- **Chapter 11** includes discussion of the democratic reforms of Jacksonian America in the broader perspective of the American and French Revolutions, the revolutions of 1830 in Europe, and the Latin American movements for independence from Spain. Chapter 12 then sets the ferment of reform within the transatlantic context of the spread of a market economy and industrialization. Chapter 11 also now discusses how free African Americans in the North resisted the deepening racism in Jacksonian America, including a nationalist movement that emphasized racial unity, self-help, and for some, the renewal of ties with Africa.

- New material in **Chapter 13** reveals how the South was affected by the two broad transformations in the nineteenth century: the Industrial Revolution and the democratic revolutions in Europe, Latin America, and in the United States. A new section in Chapter 13 discusses the sometimes blurry lines between slavery and freedom in the Old South. This material explores work settings on the water, where individual initiative was essential, and where both free and enslaved African Americans were able to find more freedom.

- **Chapter 14** includes expanded material on the Mexican borderlands, on the native peoples of the region, and on the regional context and national politics of the U.S.-Mexican War, in which ongoing wars with Indians impoverished and distracted Mexico prior to its conflict with the United States.

- **Chapter 15** ties the American abolition movement arising from western expansion with the push for abolition of slavery across the globe.

Information about Supplements

For Students

Online Learning Center The Online Learning Center, at www.mhhe.com/davidsonnation6, provides them a wide range of tools that will help students test their understanding of the book. It includes chapter overviews, interactive maps, quizzes, and primary source indexes.

Primary Source Investigator Now Available Online.

McGraw-Hill's Primary Source Investigator (PSI), now available online at www.mhhe.com/psi, is designed to support and enrich the text discussion in *Nation of Nations*. PSI gives instructors and students access to more than 650 primary and secondary sources including documents, images, maps, and videos. Students can use these resources to formulate and defend their arguments as well as further their understanding of the topics discussed in each chapter. All assets are indexed alphabetically as well as by type, subject, place, and time period, allowing students and instructors to locate resources quickly and easily.

- **Online Reader:** The Online Reader gives students an opportunity to try their hand at historical analysis. Based on sources found in PSI, the reader's modules ask students to evaluate sources and formulate their own interpretations and analysis.
- **Writing Guide:** The online Writing Guide offers both general assistance for writing college papers, as well as specific tips for history papers. Topics include research, paragraph and argument creation, a comparison of style guides, information on plagiarism and source citation, and much more.

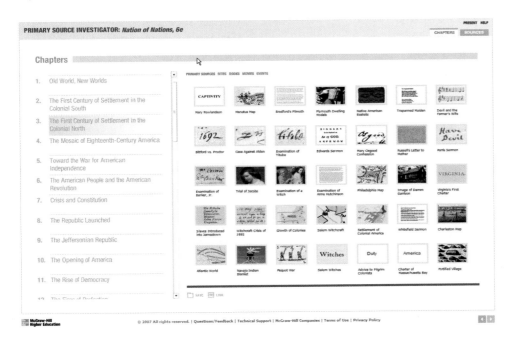

For the Instructor

Online Learning Center for Instructors The Online Learning Center located at www.mhhe.com/davidsonnation6 includes the computerized test bank and power point presentations. The annotated Faculty Guide provides a list of themes, lecture strategies, and easy reference to all learning assets, both in the text and on PSI. Each chapter is accompanied by a rich list of resources, including PowerPoint slides, image bank, outline maps, book maps, and test bank questions, all keyed to the chapter. Resources are organized within chapters by A-Heads to streamline lecture and assignment preparation. Icons allow users to quickly differentiate between text and PSI sources.

Classroom Performance System (CPS) The Classroom Performance System brings ultimate interactivity to *Nation of Nations*. CPS is a wireless response system that gives you immediate feedback from every student in the class. With CPS you can ask subjective and objective questions during your lecture, prompting every student to respond with their individual, wireless response pad, and providing you with instant results. A complete CPS Tutorial is available at www.einstruction.com.

Acknowledgments

We are grateful to the many reviewers who generously offered comments and suggestions at various stages in our development of this manuscript. Our thanks go to:

Keith J. Alexander
Jefferson Community College,
Indiana-Purdue University

Jonathan M. Atkins
Berry College

Mario A.J. Bennekin
Georgia Perimeter College

Jamie Bronstein
New Mexico State University

Kathleen S. Carter
High Point University

Douglas W. Dodd
CSU Bakersfield

Hal Friedman
Henry Ford Community College

David J. Gerleman
George Mason University,
Marymount University

Reid Holland
Midlands Technical College

Carol A. Keller
San Antonio College

Andrew S. Moore
Saint Anselm College

Robert Olwell
University of Texas at Austin

Jaako Puisto
California State University, Stanislaus

Jonathan Rees
Colorado State University–Pueblo

Philip Rubio
Duke University

Mark Meltzer Sawin
Eastern Mennonite University

John E. Semonche
UNC–Chapel Hill

Steven Schultz
Mesa State College

Michael Shepherd
Mid-South Community College

Susan Strauss
Santa Fe Community College

Richard A. Straw
Radford University

Paul D. Travis
Texas Women's University

Paul Toro
Alamo Community College

Richard A. Voeltz
Cameron University

David White
McHenry County College

William Woodward
Seattle Pacific University

One acknowledgment we can never make too often is to the work of our co-author, colleague, and friend, William E. Gienapp. Bill traveled with us on this journey from the book's earliest conception up until his untimely passing in 2003. His insight, erudition and good humor made him a pleasure to work with, and his contribution to the book will endure no matter how many new revisions appear. We would like also to thank Bill's wife, Erica Gienapp, for her unstinting assistance over the years, as she provided suggestions for new illustrations, patient reminders about misplaced modifiers, and substantive contributions to the text. Our families have continued to lend their encouragement but in particular our new member of the team, Brian DeLay, would like to thank his wife, Diliana Angelova, for her support. And as always, we appreciate any suggestions, corrections, or comments from our readers.

James West Davidson
Brian DeLay
Christine Leigh Heyrman
Mark H. Lytle
Michael B. Stoff

Additional Features

Chapter Table of Contents

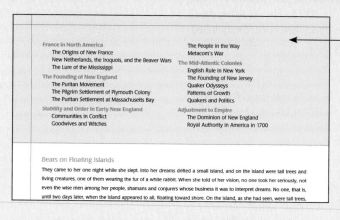

Bears on Floating Islands

They came to her one night while she slept. Into her dreams drifted a small island, and on the island were tall trees and living creatures, one of them wearing the fur of a white rabbit. When she told of her vision, no one took her seriously, not even the wise men among her people, shamans and conjurers whose business it was to interpret dreams. No one, that is, until two days later, when the island appeared to all, floating toward shore. On the island, as she had seen, were tall trees,

Brief outlines appear at the beginning of each chapter, mapping out the organization and chapter reading objectives.

After the Fact

Each chapter in the text includes a brief essay presenting the detective work and research strategies used by historians as they go about reconstructing the past. A wide variety of methods are showcased, from demographic analysis to the deconstruction of cartoons and songs to the exploration of material culture, films, diaries, murals, and statues. The topics under discussion include skull pendants, starched collars, Indian blankets, the Cuyahoga river fire, Ku Klux Klan costumes, minie balls and repeating rifles, phonographs, Scopes trial songs, and the "Great Wall" mural of Tujunga Wash. In addition to these brief features, eight longer essays examine topics in more detail, including the relationship between Thomas Jefferson and Sally Hemings, the causes of the New York draft riots, the demise of the bison and the decision to drop two atomic bombs on Japan.

AFTER THE FACT in Brief

"His Master's Voice"

Assessing the Technologies of Imperialism

How do historians measure the reach and influence of imperialism? Clearly technology played an important role in the conquests of the "Great Powers," most obviously the technology of force, including rifles, explosives, battleships with cannons and armor-plated hulls. But in subduing native peoples, western nations also depended on less blunt instruments such as trade (of goods eagerly desired) and religion (which preached a salvation-embracing western culture along with the westerners' god). Imperialism's reach was also extended by another force, which might be referred to as the technology of culture.

When Edison invented the phonograph in 1877, few people would have thought of it as a weapon of conquest. Instead, it was considered an instrument of entertainment and a civilizing force. But when Americans and Europeans brought the machine with them to less technologically advanced societies, native peoples were awestruck by the sounds it made and sometimes cowed by those who controlled it. These white men, it appeared, had the power to conjure up the voices of invisible speakers and summon music from thin air. The RCA Victrola Company for many years used the painting of a dog sitting attentively in front of an old-fashioned phonograph, with the slogan, "His Master's Voice." Historians have come to see Edison's talking machine as one element (can you think of others?) of the technology of culture that helped make the Great Powers masters.

Daily Lives

DAILY LIVES   Play Ball

Heavy padding protects the internal organs of this Aztec ball player from being injured by the heavy, dangerous rubber ball; the player's head dress is a vulture painted brilliant Mayan blue.

The band strikes up—trumpets blaring, drums pounding, flutes trilling. Dancers whirl and gymnasts cavort. Then the players parade into the stadium, and the

crowd goes wild, cheering their favorites. So many magnificent athletes trained to win, looking all the more formidable in their heavily padded gear. Which team will carry the day? A great deal is at stake for both players and spectators—honor, wealth, perhaps even life itself. The outcome hangs on the arc of a ball.

The Super Bowl? The World Series? Good guesses, because those present-day athletic spectacles bear striking resemblances to the scene described above: the beginning of a ball game in pre-Columbian Mesoamerica. Those contests, with all their accompanying fanfare, consumed the attention of both elites and commoners for many centuries.

It was the Olmecs who got the ball rolling (and flying) around 1500 B.C.E. In the main plazas of their cities, they built ornate stone ballcourts for teams to compete and celebrated star athletes with towering stone sculptures. Even as civilizations rose and fell in Mesoamerica, the passion for playing ball, following the games, and gambling on their outcome not only endured but even spread to the Hohokam in the American Southwest. Archaeological digs have revealed that nearly every city built by the Maya, Toltecs, and Aztecs boasted its own ball court: the most impressive were larger than present-day football fields, painted in vivid colors, and decorated with intricately carved birds, jaguars, and skeletal heads. Renowned players inspired artists to paint murals or to fashion clay figurines depicting ballplayers in full

athletic regalia—kneepads, gloves, and belts festooned with images of their gods or skeletal heads.

In most cultures, the rules of the game dictated that players could use only their hips, buttocks, or knees to bounce the ball against the parallel walls of the court and the alley lying between. And after about A.D. 800, the game became even more challenging: teams earned the most points by shooting hoops—that is, by sending the ball through a stone ring set in the center of the side walls. No mean feat, since players could not use their hands or feet, and the impact of a flying ball—about six pounds of solid rubber—could inflict serious and even fatal injuries.

But it was the ritual significance of these competitions that made for greater danger. In the Southwest, ball games often figured as friendly rivalries, festive occasions intended to strengthen military or trading alliances among neighboring peoples. In Mesoamerica, however, the games typically celebrated military conquests: during postgame rituals, the captain of the losing team—a captive taken in war—was beheaded with an obsidian knife by the winning captain. That practice seems to have stemmed from the religious significance invested in the ball games, which both the winning players and spectators understood as a religious ceremony celebrating their main deity, the Sun, an orb greater than any other celestial body, and encouraging the soil's fertility with a sacrifice of human blood.

Each chapter contains an essay focusing on the lives of ordinary Americans. Topics like food, fashion, and entertainment establish a greater context for each time period in history.

Marginal Headings

Succinct notes in the margins highlight key terms and concepts

The Los Angeles riots of 1992 revealed divisions in the city's multicultural communities of African Americans, Latinos, and Asian Americans.

candidate. Although the situation of African Americans had improved vastly compared with their position in the 1950s, race still mattered—as the case of Rodney King, a black motorist, showed.

Rodney King and the
Los Angeles Riots

In 1991 Los Angeles police arrested King for speeding and drunken driving. As he lay on the ground, the four white officers proceeded to beat him with nightsticks more than 50 times. When blacks complained about such brutality at the hands of largely white police, public officials often dismissed their complaints. This case was different. A man in a nearby apartment videotaped the beating, which the news media repeatedly broadcast to the entire nation. But the following year, an all-white suburban jury acquitted the officers, concluding that King had been threatening and that the officers had acted within their authority.

The verdict enraged the African American community in Los Angeles, where widespread riots erupted for three days, making the violence the worst civil disturbance in Los Angeles history. By the time police and the National Guard restored order, nearly 2,000 people had been injured, 40 people had died, over 4,500 fires burned, and $500 million of property had been looted, damaged, or destroyed.

Complexity of the Riots

At first glance the riot appeared to be much like the one that had decimated Watts, a poor area of Los Angeles, in 1965 (see page 863). Poor African Americans had lashed out in frustration at white racism. In fact, the 1992 riots were multiracial in character,

Chapter Summary

A bulleted summary reinforces each chapter's main points

Chapter Summary

During the eighteenth century, Spain, France, and Great Britain competed for power and influence in North America. Native peoples too played off these shifting alliances, as their cultures were disrupted by epidemics, European settlement, and the arrival of new plants, animals, and technologies. British North Americans grew increasingly diverse, which made the prospect of any future colonial political union appear remote.

- Differences became more pronounced among whites because of the immigration of larger numbers of non-English settlers, the spread of settlement to the backcountry, and the growth of major seaports.

- Although disorder was not uncommon either on the frontier or in cities, the most serious social and political conflict drew its strength from sectional controversies between East and West.

- The South became more embattled, too, as a result of the massive importation of slaves directly from Africa during the first half of the eighteenth century and a rising tide of black resistance to slavery.

- After about 1750 the growth of a native-born population strengthened black communal and family life.

- Religious conflict among colonials was intensified by the spread of Enlightenment ideas and the influence of the first Great Awakening.

- Despite their many differences, a majority of white colonials took pride in their common English ancestry and in belonging to a powerful empire.

- Although the British colonies seemed reluctant in 1754 to unite politically to protect themselves against their French rivals, the looming war for empire eventually created a situation in which British colonials would begin to think themselves better off united and independent.

Additional Readings

Annotated references to both classic studies and recent scholarship encourage further pursuit of the topics and events covered in the chapter.

Additional Reading

Understanding the effects of ethnic and racial diversity is essential to appreciating the dynamism of eighteenth-century colonial society. Some vivid accounts include Bernard Bailyn, *Voyagers to the West* (1986), and Bernard Bailyn and Philip Morgan, eds., *Strangers within the Realm* (1991). Philip Morgan's *Slave Counterpoint* (1998) offers a state-of-the-art overview of African American cultures in the early South. For mounting class, ethnic, and racial tensions in American seaports, consult Jill Lepore, *New York Burning* (2005), and Gary Nash, *The Urban Crucible* (1979).

Nancy Shoemaker, *A Strange Likeness* (2004) and James M. Merrell, *Into the American Woods* (1999), are two compelling accounts of how Indians and white Americans came to perceive one another as different peoples. For the expansion of colonial settlement into the eighteenth-century backcountry, begin with Eric Hinderaker and Peter C. Mancall, *At the Edge of Empire* (2003), and Rachel Klein, *The Unification of a Slave State* (1990). Among the best studies of religion in eighteenth-century society are Rhys Isaac, *The Transformation of Virginia, 1740–1790* (1982); Patricia Bonomi, *Under the Cope of Heaven* (1986); and George Marsden, *Jonathan Edwards* (2003).

For a fuller list of readings, see the Bibliography at www.mhhe.com/davidsonnation6.

Significant Events

A chronology at the end of each chapter gives a brief list of important dates and events.

Significant Events

1790	Slater's textile mill opens
1793	Eli Whitney invents the cotton gin
1798	Whitney begins work on a system of interchangeable parts
1807	Fulton's *Clermont* begins regular steamboat service on the Hudson River
1810	*Fletcher v. Peck*
1810–1820	Cotton boom begins in the South
1811	First steamboat trip from Pittsburgh to New Orleans
1816	Second Bank of the United States chartered; protective tariff enacted
1819	*Dartmouth College v. Woodward; McCulloch v. Maryland*
1819–1823	Panic and depression
1820	Lowell mills established
1824	*Gibbons v. Ogden*
1825	Erie Canal opened
1825–1850	Canal era
1830	Baltimore and Ohio Railroad begins passenger service
1834	National Trades' Union founded
1837	Panic
1839–1843	Depression
1844	Samuel F. B. Morse sends first intercity telegraphic message
1847	Rotary printing press invented

About the Authors

James West Davidson   received his Ph.D. from Yale University. A historian who has pursued a full-time writing career, he is the author of numerous books, among them *After the Fact: The Art of Historical Detection* (with Mark H. Lytle), *The Logic of Millennial Thought: Eighteenth-Century New England*, and *Great Heart: The History of a Labrador Adventure* (with John Rugge). He is co-editor with Michael Stoff of the *Oxford New Narratives in American History*, in which his own most recent book appears: *'They Say': Ida B. Wells and the Reconstruction of Race* (2007).

Brian DeLay   is Assistant Professor of History at the University of Colorado, where he has taught since receiving his Ph.D. from Harvard University. He has published articles in the *American Historical Review* and the *Journal of the Early Republic*. His book *The War of a Thousand Deserts: How Indians Shaped the Era of the U.S.–Mexican War* will be published by Yale University Press in 2008.

Christine Leigh Heyrman   is the Robert W. and Shirley P. Grimble Professor of American History at the University of Delaware. She received a Ph.D. in American Studies from Yale University and is the author of *Commerce and Culture: The Maritime Communities of Colonial Massachusetts, 1690–1750*. Her book *Southern Cross: The Beginnings of the Bible Belt* was awarded the Bancroft Prize in 1998.

Mark H. Lytle,   a Ph.D. from Yale University, is Professor of History and Chair of the Environmental Studies Program at Bard College. He has served two years as Mary Ball Washington Professor of American History at University College, Dublin, in Ireland. His publications include *The Origins of the Iranian-American Alliance, 1941–1953, After the Fact: The Art of Historical Detection* (with James West Davidson), *America's Uncivil Wars: The Sixties Era from Elvis to the Fall of Richard Nixon*, and most recently, *The Gentle Subversive: Rachel Carson, Silent Spring, and the Rise of the Environmental Movement*. He is also co-editor of a joint issue of the journals *Diplomatic History* and *Environmental History* dedicated to the field of environmental diplomacy.

Michael B. Stoff   is Associate Professor of History and Director of the Plan II Honors Program at the University of Texas at Austin. The recipient of a Ph.D. from Yale University, he has been honored many times for his teaching, most recently with election to the Academy of Distinguished Teachers. He is the author of *Oil, War, and American Security: The Search for a National Policy on Foreign Oil, 1941–1947*, co-editor (with Jonathan Fanton and R. Hall Williams) of *The Manhattan Project: A Documentary Introduction to the Atomic Age*, and series co-editor (with James West Davidson) of the *Oxford New Narratives in American History*. He is currently working on a narrative of the bombing of Nagasaki.

Introduction

History is both a discipline of rigor, bound by rules and scholarly methods, and something more: the unique, compelling, even strange way in which we humans define ourselves. We are all the sum of the tales of thousands of people, great and small, whose actions have etched their lines upon us. History supplies our very identity—a sense of the social groups to which we belong, whether family, ethnic group, race, class, or gender. It reveals to us the foundations of our deepest religious beliefs and traces the roots of our economic and political systems. It explores how we celebrate and grieve, how we sing the songs we sing, how we weather the illnesses to which time and chance subject us. It commands our attention for all these good reasons and for no good reason at all, other than a fascination with the way the myriad tales play out. Strange that we should come to care about a host of men and women so many centuries gone, some with names eminent and familiar, others unknown but for a chance scrap of information left behind in an obscure letter.

Yet we do care. We care about Sir Humphrey Gilbert, "devoured and swallowed up of the Sea" one black Atlantic night in 1583; we care about George Washington at Kips Bay, red with fury as he takes a riding crop to his retreating soldiers. We care about Octave Johnson, a slave fleeing through Louisiana swamps trying to decide whether to stand and fight the approaching hounds or take his chances with the bayou alligators; we care about Clara Barton, her nurse's skirts so heavy with blood from the wounded, that she must wring them out before tending to the next soldier. We are drawn to the fate of Chinese laborers, chipping away at the Sierras' looming granite; of a Georgian named Tom Watson seeking to forge a colorblind political alliance; and of desperate immigrant mothers, kerosene lamps in hand, storming Brooklyn butcher shops that had again raised prices. We follow, with a mix of awe and amusement, the fortunes of the quirky Henry Ford ("Everybody wants to be somewhere he ain't"), turning out identical automobiles, insisting his factory workers wear identical expressions ("Fordization of the Face"). We trace the career of young Thurgood Marshall, crisscrossing the South in his own "little old beat-up '29 Ford," typing legal briefs in the back seat, trying to get black teachers to sue for equal pay, hoping to get his people somewhere they weren't. The list could go on and on, spilling out as it did in Walt Whitman's *Leaves of Grass:* "A southerner soon as a northerner, a planter nonchalant and hospitable, / A Yankee bound my own way . . . a Hoosier, a Badger, a Buckeye, a Louisianian or Georgian . . . " Whitman embraced and celebrated them all, inseparable strands of what made him an American and what made him human:

> In all people I see myself, none more and not one a barleycorn less; And the good or bad I say of myself, I say of them.

To encompass so expansive an America, Whitman turned to poetry; historians have traditionally chosen *narrative* as their means of giving life to the past. That mode of explanation permits them to interweave the strands of economic, political, and social history in a coherent chronological framework. By choosing narrative, historians affirm the multicausal nature of historical explanation—the insistence that events be portrayed in context. By choosing narrative, they are also acknowledging that, although long-term economic and social trends shape societies in significant ways, events often take on a logic (or an illogic) of their own, jostling one another, being deflected by unpredictable personal decisions, sudden deaths, natural catastrophes, and chance. There are literary reasons, too, for preferring a narrative approach, because it supplies a dramatic force usually missing from more structural analyses of the past.

In some ways, surveys such as this text are the natural antithesis of narrative history. They strive, by definition, to be comprehensive: to furnish a broad, orderly exposition of their chosen field. Yet to cover so much ground in so limited a space necessarily deprives readers of the context of more detailed accounts. Then, too, the resurgence of social history—with its concern for class and race, patterns of rural and urban life, the spread of market and industrial economies—lends itself to more analytic, less chronological treatments. The challenge facing historians is to incorporate these areas of research without losing the story's narrative drive or the chronological flow that orients readers to the more familiar events of our past.

In the end, the best tale recognizes that the political and the social aspects of the tale are intimately intertwined. It is impossible to separate the marketplace of boom and bust or the vectors of a flu pandemic from the corridors of political maneuvering and the pomp of a presidential inauguration. The primary question of this narrative—how the fledgling, often tumultuous confederation of these United States managed to transform itself into an enduring republic—must grapple with the environmental effects of deforestation or global warming as well as with minimum wages or wars in the Persian Gulf.

In order to survive, a republic must resolve conflicts between citizens of different geographic regions and economic classes, of diverse racial and ethnic origins, of competing religions and ideologies. The resolution of these conflicts has produced tragic consequences, perhaps, as often as noble, ones. But tragic or noble the destiny of these states cannot be understood without comprehending both the social and the political dimensions of the story.

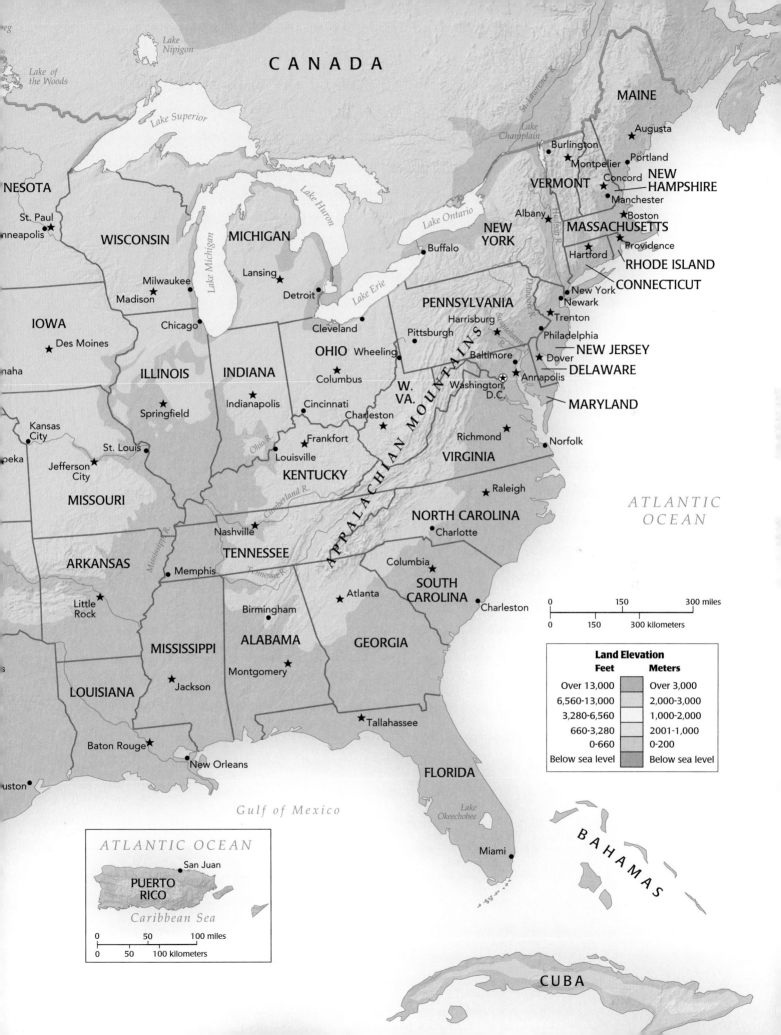

CANADA

Lake of
the Woods

Lake Nipigon

Lake Superior

MINNESOTA
St. Paul
Minneapolis

WISCONSIN

Milwaukee
Madison

Lake Michigan

MICHIGAN
Lansing

Detroit

Lake Huron

Lake Erie

Cleveland

IOWA
Des Moines

Omaha

ILLINOIS
Springfield

Chicago

INDIANA
Indianapolis

OHIO
Columbus

Wheeling

Cincinnati

Kansas City

St. Louis

Topeka

Jefferson City

MISSOURI

Ohio R.

Frankfort
Louisville

KENTUCKY

Cumberland R.

Nashville

TENNESSEE

Tennessee R.

Mississippi R.

Memphis

ARKANSAS

Little Rock

MISSISSIPPI

Jackson

ALABAMA

Montgomery

Birmingham

LOUISIANA

Baton Rouge

New Orleans

Houston

Gulf of Mexico

Charleston

W. VA.

Charleston

VIRGINIA

Richmond

Norfolk

Lake Ontario

Buffalo

NEW YORK

Albany

PENNSYLVANIA

Harrisburg

Pittsburgh

St. Lawrence R.

Lake Champlain

MAINE

Augusta

Burlington
Montpelier

VERMONT

Portland

Concord

NEW HAMPSHIRE

Manchester

Hudson R.

Boston

MASSACHUSETTS

Providence

Hartford

RHODE ISLAND

CONNECTICUT

Delaware R.

New York

Newark

Trenton

Philadelphia

NEW JERSEY

Susquehanna R.

Baltimore

Dover

DELAWARE

Annapolis

Washington, D.C.

MARYLAND

APPALACHIAN MOUNTAINS

Raleigh

NORTH CAROLINA

Charlotte

GEORGIA

Columbia

SOUTH CAROLINA

Charleston

Atlanta

ATLANTIC OCEAN

Tallahassee

FLORIDA

Lake Okeechobee

Miami

BAHAMAS

CUBA

| 0 | 150 | 300 miles |

| 0 | 150 | 300 kilometers |

Land Elevation

Feet	Meters
Over 13,000	Over 3,000
6,560–13,000	2,000–3,000
3,280–6,560	1,000–2,000
660–3,280	2001–1,000
0–660	0–200
Below sea level	Below sea level

ATLANTIC OCEAN

San Juan

PUERTO RICO

Caribbean Sea

| 0 | 50 | 100 miles |

| 0 | 50 | 100 kilometers |

NATION OF NATIONS

A Narrative History of the American Republic

Volume I: To 1877
Chapters 1–17

CHAPTER 1
The First Civilizations of North America

The Power of a Hidden Past

Stories told about the past have power over both the present and the future. Until recently, most students were taught that American history began several centuries ago—with the "discovery" of America by Columbus, or with the English colonization of Jamestown and Plymouth. History books ignored or trivialized the continent's precontact history. But the reminders of that hidden past are everywhere. Scattered across the United States are thousands of ancient archaeological sites and hundreds of examples of monumental architecture, still imposing even after centuries of erosion, looting, and destruction.

Man-made earthen mounds, some nearly 5,000 years old, exist throughout eastern North America in a bewildering variety of shapes and sizes. Many are easily mistaken for modest hills, but others evoke wonder. In present-day Louisiana an ancient town with earthworks took laborers an estimated 5 million work hours to construct. In Ohio a massive serpent effigy snakes for a quarter-mile across the countryside, its head aligned to the summer solstice. In Illinois a vast, earthen building covers 16 acres at its base and once reached as high as a 10-story building.

Observers in the colonial and revolutionary eras looked on such sites as curiosities and marvels. George Washington, Thomas Jefferson, and other prominent Americans collected ancient artifacts, took a keen interest in the excavation of mounds, and speculated about the Indian civilizations that created them. Travelers explored these strange mounds, trying to imagine in their mind's eye the peoples who had built them. In 1795 the Reverend James Smith traced the boundaries of a mound wall that was strategically placed to protect a neck of land along a looping river bend in the Ohio valley. "The wall at present is so mouldered down that a man could easily ride over it. It is however about 10 feet, as near as I can judge, in perpendicular height. . . . In one place I observe a breach in the wall about 60 feet wide, where I suppose the gate formerly stood through which the people passed in and out of this stronghold." Smith was astonished by the size of the project. "Compared with this," he exclaimed, "what feeble and insignificant works are those of Fort Hamilton or Fort Washington! They are no more in comparison to it than a rail fence is to a brick wall."

From the air, this serpentine mound fashioned thousands of years ago still stands out in bold relief. Located in southern Ohio, it extends from the snake's coiled tail at the left of the photo to the open mouth at the top right, which is pointed in the direction of the summer solstice sunset. The snake's tail points toward the winter solstice sunrise.

3

But in the 1830s and 1840s, as Americans sought to drive Indians west of the Mississippi and then confine them on smaller and smaller reservations, many began thinking differently about the continent's ancient sites. Surely the simple and "savage" people just then being expelled from American life could not have constructed such inspiring monuments. Politicians, writers, and even some influential scientists dismissed the claim that North America's ancient architecture had been built by the ancestors of contemporary Indians, and instead attributed the mounds to peoples of Europe, Africa, or Asia—Hindus, perhaps, or Israelites, Egyptians, or Japanese. Many nineteenth-century Americans found special comfort in a tale about King Madoc from Wales who, supposedly shipwrecked in the Americas in the twelfth century, had left behind a small but ingenious population of Welsh pioneers who built the mysterious mounds before being overrun by Indians. The Welsh hypothesis seemed to offer poetic justice, because it implied that nineteenth-century Indians were only receiving a fitting punishment for what their ancestors had done to the remarkable mound builders from Wales.

These fanciful tales were discredited in the late nineteenth and twentieth centuries. In recent decades archaeologists working across the Americas have discovered in more detail how native peoples built the hemisphere's ancient architecture. They have also helped to make clear the degree to which prejudice and politics have blinded European-Americans to the complexity, wonder, and significance of America's history before 1492. Fifteen thousand years of human habitation in North America allowed a broad range of cultures to develop, based on agriculture as well as hunting and gathering. In North America a population in the millions spoke hundreds of languages. Cities evolved as well as towns and farms, exhibiting great diversity in their cultural, political, economic, and religious organization.

A Continent of Cultures

Hunters Cross the Bering Strait

Most archaeologists agree that the Western Hemisphere's first human inhabitants came from northeastern Asia. At least 15,000 years ago B.P.* during the most recent Ice Age, small groups of people began crossing the Bering Strait, then a narrow bridge of land connecting Siberia to Alaska. Gradually these **nomads** filtered southward, some following the Pacific coastline in small boats, but most making their way down a narrow, glacier-free corridor along the eastern base of the Rocky Mountains and onto the northern Great Plains. There they found and hunted a stunning array of huge mammals, so-called megafauna. These animals included mammoths that were twice as heavy as elephants, giant bison, sloths that were taller than giraffes, several kinds of camels, and terrifying, 8-foot long lions. Within a few thousand years the descendants of these Siberians, people whom Columbus would wishfully dub "Indians," had spread throughout the length and breadth of the Americas.

As the new world of the Americas was settled, it was changing dramatically. The last Ice Age literally melted away as warmer global temperatures freed the great reservoirs of water once locked in glaciers. A rise in sea levels inundated the Bering Strait, submerging the land bridge, and creating new lakes and river systems. The emergence of

---

*Before the Present, used most commonly by archaeologists when the time spans are in multiple thousands of years. This text will also use C.E. for Common Era, equivalent to the Christian Era or A.D.; B.C.E. is Before the Common Era, equivalent to B.C.

new **ecosystems**—climates, waterways, and land environments in which humans interacted with other animals and plants—made for ever greater diversity. The first human inhabitants of the Americas had fed, clothed, warmed, and armed themselves by hunting megafauna, and few of these giants survived the end of the Ice Age. As the glaciers receded, later generations had to adapt to changing conditions. They adjusted by hunting smaller animals with new, more specialized kinds of stone tools and by learning to exploit particular places more efficiently.

So it was that between 10,000 and 2,500 years ago, distinctive regional cultures developed among the peoples of the Americas. Those who remained in the Great Plains turned to hunting the much smaller descendants of the now-extinct giant bison; those in the deserts of the Great Basin survived on small game, seeds, and edible plants; those in the Pacific Northwest relied mainly on fishing; and those east of the Mississippi, besides fishing and gathering, tracked deer and bear and trapped smaller game animals and birds. Over these same centuries, distinct groups developed their own languages, social organizations, governments, and religious beliefs and practices. Technological and cultural unity gave way to regional diversity as the first Americans learned how to best exploit their particular environments.

Diversified Societies

Cultures of Ancient Mexico

To the south, pioneers in **Mesoamerica** began domesticating squash 10,000 years ago. Over the next several thousand years farmers added other crops including beans, tomatoes, and especially corn to an agricultural revolution that would transform life through much of the Americas. Because many crops could be dried and stored, agriculture allowed these first farmers to settle in one place.

Agricultural Revolution

By about 1500 B.C.E., farming villages began giving way to larger societies, to richer and more advanced cultures. As the abundant food supply steadily expanded their populations, people began specializing in certain kinds of work. While most continued to labor on the land, others became craftworkers and merchants, architects and artists, warriors and priests. Their built environment reflected this social change as humble villages expanded into skillfully planned urban sites that were centers of trade, government, artistic display, and religious ceremony.

The Olmecs, the first city builders in the Americas, constructed large plazas, pyramidal structures, and sculpted enormous heads chiseled from basalt. The Olmec cultural influence gradually spread throughout Mesoamerica, perhaps as a result of their trade with neighboring peoples. By about 100 B.C.E., the Olmecs' example had inspired the flowering of Teotihuacán from a small town in central Mexico into a metropolis of towering pyramids. The city had bustling marketplaces, palaces decorated with mural paintings that housed an elite of warriors and priests, schools for their children, and sprawling suburbs for commoners. At its height, around 650 C.E., Teotihuacán spanned 15 square miles and had a population of nearly 200,000—making it the sixth largest city in the world.

Olmec City-Builders

More impressive still were the achievements of the Mayas, who benefited from their contacts with both the Olmecs and Teotihuacán. In the lowland jungles of Mesoamerica they built cities filled with palaces, bridges, aqueducts, baths, astronomical observatories, and pyramids topped with temples. Their priests developed a written language, their mathematicians discovered the zero, and their astronomers devised a calendar more accurate than any then existing. In its glory, between the third and ninth century C.E., the Mayan empire boasted some 50 urban centers scattered throughout the Yucatán Peninsula, Belize, Guatemala, and Honduras.

Mayan Civilization

But neither the earliest urban centers of the Olmecs nor the glittering city-state of Teotihuacán survived. Even the enduring kingdom of the Mayas had collapsed by 900 C.E. Like the ancient civilizations of Greece and Rome, they thrived for centuries and then declined. Scholars still debate the reasons for their collapse. Military attack may have brought about their ruin, or perhaps their large populations exhausted local resources.

Heavy padding protects the internal organs of this Aztec ball player from being injured by the heavy, dangerous rubber ball; the player's head dress is a vulture painted brilliant Mayan blue.

The band strikes up—trumpets blaring, drums pounding, flutes trilling. Dancers whirl and gymnasts cavort. Then the players parade into the stadium, and the crowd goes wild, cheering their favorites. So many magnificent athletes trained to win, looking all the more formidable in their heavily padded gear. Which team will carry the day? A great deal is at stake for both players and spectators—honor, wealth, perhaps even life itself. The outcome hangs on the arc of a ball.

The Super Bowl? The World Series? Good guesses, because those present-day athletic spectacles bear striking resemblances to the scene described above: the beginning of a ball game in pre-Columbian Mesoamerica. Those contests, with all their accompanying fanfare, consumed the attention of both elites and commoners for many centuries.

It was the Olmecs who got the ball rolling (and flying) around 1500 B.C.E. In the main plazas of their cities, they built ornate stone ballcourts for teams to compete and celebrated star athletes with towering stone sculptures. Even as civilizations rose and fell in Mesoamerica, the passion for playing ball, following the games, and gambling on their outcome not only endured but even spread to the Hohokam in the American Southwest. Archaeological digs have revealed that nearly every city built by the Maya, Toltecs, and Aztecs boasted its own ball court: the most impressive were larger than present-day football fields, painted in vivid colors, and decorated with intricately carved birds, jaguars, and skeletal heads. Renowned players inspired artists to paint murals or to fashion clay figurines depicting ballplayers in full athletic regalia—kneepads, gloves, and belts festooned with images of their gods or skeletal heads.

In most cultures, the rules of the game dictated that players could use only their hips, buttocks, or knees to bounce the ball against the parallel walls of the court and the alley lying between. And after about A.D. 800, the game became even more challenging: teams earned the most points by shooting hoops—that is, by sending the ball through a stone ring set in the center of the side walls. No mean feat, since players could not use their hands or feet, and the impact of a flying ball—about six pounds of solid rubber—could inflict serious and even fatal injuries.

But it was the ritual significance of these competitions that made for greater danger. In the Southwest, ball games often figured as friendly rivalries, festive occasions intended to strengthen military or trading alliances among neighboring peoples. In Mesoamerica, however, the games typically celebrated military conquests: during postgame rituals, the captain of the losing team—a captive taken in war—was beheaded with an obsidian knife by the winning captain. That practice seems to have stemmed from the religious significance invested in the ball games, which both the winning players and spectators understood as a religious ceremony celebrating their main deity, the Sun, an orb greater than any other celestial body, and encouraging the soil's fertility with a sacrifice of human blood.

Aztec Empire

Mayan grandeur was eventually outdone in the Valley of Mexico. In the middle of the thirteenth century, the Aztecs, a people who had originally lived on Mesoamerica's northern frontiers, swept south and settled in central Mexico. By the end of the fifteenth century, they ruled over a vast empire from their capital at Tenochtitlán, an island metropolis of perhaps a quarter of a million people. At its center lay a large plaza bordered by sumptuous palaces and the Great Temple of the Sun. Beyond stood three broad causeways connecting the island to the mainland, many other tall temples adorned with brightly painted carved images of the gods, zoological and botanical gardens, and well-stocked marketplaces. Through Tenochtitlán's canals flowed gold, silver, exotic feathers and jewels, cocoa, and millions of pounds of maize—all trade goods and tribute from the several million other peoples in the region subjugated by the Aztecs.

Aztec merchants, or pochtecas, spoke many languages and traveled on foot great distances throughout Mesoamerica and parts of North America. This one carries a cane and bears a sack of trade goods, topped off by a parrot.

Unsurpassed in power and wealth, in technological and artistic attainments, theirs was also a highly stratified society. The Aztec ruler, or Chief Speaker, shared governing power with the aristocrats who monopolized all positions of religious, military, and political leadership, while the commoners—merchants, farmers, and craftworkers—performed all manual labor. There were slaves as well, some captives taken in war, others from the ranks of commoners forced by poverty to sell themselves or their children.

Cultures of the Southwest

Mesoamerican crops and farming techniques began making their way north to the American Southwest by 1000 B.C.E. At first the most successful farmers in the region were the Mogollon and Hohokam peoples, two cultures that flourished in New Mexico and southern Arizona during the first millennium C.E. Both tended to cluster their dwellings near streams, relying either on flood-plain irrigation or a system of floodgates and canals to sustain their crops. The Mogollon came to be the master potters of the Southwest. The Hohokam pioneered vast and complex irrigation systems in arid southern Arizona that allowed them to support one of the largest populations in precontact North America.

Mogollon and
Hohokam Peoples

Their neighbors to the north, in what is now known as the Four Corners of Arizona, Colorado, New Mexico, and Utah, are known as the Anasazi. The Anasazi adapted corn, beans, and squash to the relatively high altitude of the Colorado Plateau and soon parlayed their growing surplus and prosperity into societies of considerable complexity. Their most stunning achievements were villages of exquisitely executed masonry buildings—apartment-like structures up to four stories high and containing hundreds of rooms at places such as Mesa Verde (Colorado) and Canyon de Chelly (Arizona). Hundreds of villages in Chaco Canyon (New Mexico), the largest center of Anasazi settlement, were linked to the wider region by hundreds of miles of wide, straight roads.

The Anasazi

Besides their impressive dwellings, the Anasazi filled their towns with religious shrines, astronomical observatories, and stations for sending signals to other villages. Their craftworkers fashioned delicate woven baskets, beautiful feather and hide sashes, decorated pottery, and turquoise jewelry that they traded throughout the region and beyond. For more than a thousand years, Anasazi civilization prospered, reaching its

*The remains of Pueblo Bonito,
one of the nine Great Houses
built by Anasazis in Chaco
Canyon. By the end of the
eleventh century, Pueblo
Bonito stood four stories high
at the rear and contained 800
rooms as well as many towers,
terraces, a large central plaza,
and several round "Kivas"
for religious and ceremonial
purposes.*

zenith between about 900 and 1100 C.E. During those three centuries, the population grew to approximately 30,000 spread over 50,000 square miles, a total area larger than present-day California.

Cultures of the Eastern Woodlands

East of the Mississippi, Indian societies prospered in valleys near great rivers (Mississippi, Ohio, Tennessee, and Cumberland), the shores of the Great Lakes, and the coast of the Atlantic. Everywhere the earliest inhabitants depended on a combination of fishing, gathering, and hunting—mainly deer but also bear, raccoon, and a variety of birds. Around 2000 B.C.E., some groups in the temperate, fertile Southeast began growing the gourds and pumpkins first cultivated by Mesoamerican farmers, and later they also adopted the cultivation of maize. But unlike the ancient peoples of the Southwest, most Eastern Woodland peoples continued to subsist largely on animals, fish, and nuts, all of which were abundant enough to meet their needs and even to expand their numbers.

Indeed, many of the mysterious earthen mounds that would so fascinate Europeans were built by peoples who did not farm. About 1000 B.C.E., residents of a place now known as Poverty Point in northeastern Louisiana fashioned spectacular earthworks—six semicircular rings that rose nine feet in height and covered more than half a mile in diameter. Although these structures might have been sites for studying the planets and stars, hundreds of other mounds—built about 2000 years ago by the Adena and the Hopewell cultures of the Ohio and Mississippi valleys—served as the burial places of their leading men and women. Alongside the corpses mourners heaped their richest goods—headdresses of antlers, necklaces of copper, troves of shells and pearls—rare and precious items imported from as far north as Canada, as far west as Wyoming, and as far east as Florida. All these mounds attest powerfully not only to the skill and sheer numbers of their builders but also to the complexity of these ancient societies, their elaborate religious practices, and the wide scope of their trading networks.

*Adena and
Hopewell Cultures*

Mississippian Culture

Even so, the most magnificent culture of the ancient Eastern Woodlands, the Mississippian, owed much of its prominence to farming. By the twelfth century C.E.,

An artist's reconstruction of the city of Cahokia, c. 1100 C.E., the hearth of Mississippian culture. Note how tiny the human figures are in comparison to the temples.

these peoples had emerged as the premier city-builders of North America, and their towns radiated for hundreds of miles in every direction from the hub of their trading network at Cahokia, a port city of perhaps 30,000 located directly across from present-day St. Louis at the confluence of the Missouri and the Mississippi rivers. Cahokia's many broad plazas teemed with farmers hawking their corn, squash, and beans and with craftworkers and merchants displaying their wares. But what commanded every eye were the structures surrounding the plazas—more than 100 flat-topped pyramidal mounds crowned by religious temples and the palaces of rulers.

Cultures of the Great Plains

Cahokia's size and power depended on consistent agricultural surpluses. Outside the Southwest and the river valleys of the East, agriculture played a smaller role in shaping North American societies. On the Great Plains, for example, some people did cultivate corn, beans, squash, and sunflowers, near reliable rivers and streams. But more typically plains communities relied on hunting and foraging, migrating to exploit seasonally variable resources. Plains hunters pursued game on foot; the horses that had once roamed the Americas became extinct after the last Ice Age. Sometimes large groups of people worked together to drive the buffalos over cliffs or to trap them in corrals. The aridity of the plains made it a dynamic and unpredictable place to live. During times of reliable rainfall, bison populations boomed and hunters flocked to the region. But sometimes centuries passed with lower-than-average precipitation, and families abandoned the plains for eastern river valleys or the foothills of the Rocky Mountains.

Migratory Peoples

Cultures of the Great Basin

Some peoples west of the Great Plains also kept to older ways of subsistence. Among them were the Numic-speaking peoples of the Great Basin, which includes present-day

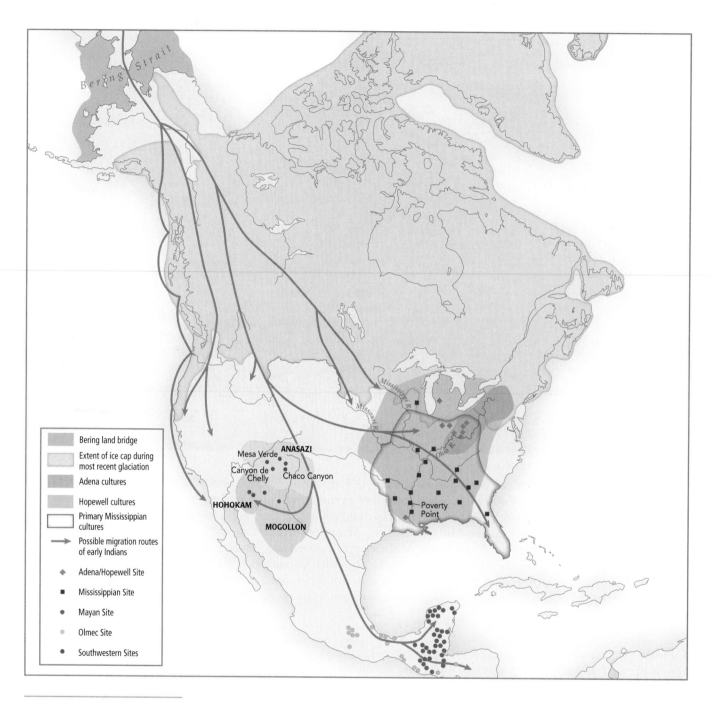

Early Peoples of North America *Migration routes across the Bering Strait from Asia were taken by peoples whose descendants created the major civilizations of ancient America. The influence of Mesoamerica is most striking among the cultures of the Southwest and the Mississippians.*

Nevada and Utah, eastern California, and western Wyoming and Colorado. Small family groups scoured their stark, arid landscape for the limited supplies of food it yielded, moving with each passing season to make the most of their environment. Men tracked elk and antelope and trapped smaller animals, birds, even toads, rattlesnakes, and insects. But the staples of their diet were edible seeds, nuts, and plants, which women gathered and stored in woven baskets to consume in times of scarcity. Several families occasionally hunted together or wintered in common quarters, but because the desert heat and soil defied farming, these bands usually numbered no more than about 50 people.

Cultures of the Pacific Northwest

The rugged stretch of coast from the southern banks of present-day British Columbia to northern California has always been an extraordinarily rich natural environment.

The Numbers Game

Counting the Earliest Americans

Lacking any statistical records of precontact populations, how can historians estimate the population of North America? For much of the twentieth century scholars suggested that North America contained about 1 million inhabitants and Central and South America about 10 million. Over the past several decades, however, archaeologists and historians have increased those projections by a factor of 5 or 10, to as many as 50–100 million inhabitants of the Americas. A variety of methods have produced these revisions.

Small-scale analysis. Archaeologists examine the surviving layout of a single town such as Paquime (right). How many people could have lived in each room? Multiplying the result by the number of rooms in the village and then again by the number of villages within a larger area gives one estimate for a region.

Die-off ratios and epidemic disease. Although death tolls varied regionally, European diseases such as smallpox killed 90 to 95 percent of native American populations. Starting with census records dating from after Europeans had arrived, historians use the ratios to calculate backward toward larger precontact totals.

Ecological carrying capacity. Some scholars have estimated how dense a population could be supported by Native American

The rooms of Paquime, divided by adobe mud walls, help archaeologists estimate population.

farming techniques, given climate and soils. Comparing and combining such different methods provide a range of intelligent estimates, but they remain just that: estimates.

Its mild climate and abundant rainfall yield forests lush with plants and game; its bays and rivers teem with salmon and halibut, its oceans with whales and porpoises, and its rocky beaches with seals, otters, abalone, mussels, and clams. Agriculture was unnecessary in such a bountiful place. From their villages on the banks of rivers, the shores of bays, and the beaches of low-lying offshore islands, the ancestors of the Nootkans, Makahs, Tlingits, Tshimshians, and Kwakiutls speared or netted salmon, trapped sea mammals, gathered shellfish, and launched canoes. The largest of these craft, from which they harpooned whales, measured 45 feet bow to stern and nearly 6 feet wide.

By the fifteenth century these fecund lands supported a population of perhaps 130,000. They also permitted a culture with the leisure time needed to create works of art as well as an elaborate social and ceremonial life. The peoples of the Northwest built houses and canoes from red cedar; carved bowls and dishes from red alder; crafted paddles and harpoon shafts, bows, and clubs from Pacific yew; and wove baskets from bark and blankets from mountain goat wool. They evolved a society with sharp distinctions among nobles, commoners, and slaves, the latter being mainly women and children captured in raids on other villages. Those who were free devoted their lives to accumulating and then redistributing their wealth among other villagers in elaborate potlatch ceremonies in order to confirm or enhance their social prestige.

Social and Ceremonial Distinctions

This ornately carved and painted house post once supported the main beams of a dwelling belonging to a Kwakiutl whaler in the Pacific Northwest. Depicting a man of wealth and high rank, the figure has a whale painted on his chest and copper ornaments on his arms. Two smaller figures, in shadow by the whaler's knees, each support one end of a plank seat. These were his household slaves, most likely children captured in an attack on rival tribes.

Cultures of the Subarctic and Arctic

Most of present-day Canada and Alaska were equally inhospitable to agriculture. In the farthest northern reaches—a treeless belt of Arctic tundra—temperatures fell below freezing for most of the year. The Subarctic, although densely forested, had only about 100 frost-free days each year. As a result, the peoples of both regions survived by fishing and hunting. The Inuit, or Eskimos, of northern Alaska harvested whales from their umiaks, boats made by stretching walrus skin over a driftwood frame and that could bear more than a ton of weight. In the central Arctic, they tracked seals. The inhabitants of the Subarctic, both Algonquian-speaking peoples in the East and Athapaskan speakers of the West, moved from their summer fishing camps to berry patches in the fall to moose and caribou hunting grounds in the winter.

Innovations and Limitations

The first Americans therefore expressed, governed, and supported themselves in a broad variety of ways. And yet they shared certain core characteristics, including the desire and ability to reshape their world. Whether they lived in forests, coastal regions, jungles, or prairies, whether they inhabited high mountains or low deserts, native communities experimented constantly with the resources around them. Over the course of millennia, nearly all the hemisphere's peoples found ways to change the natural world in order to improve and enrich their lives.

America's Agricultural Gifts

Rise of Agriculture

No innovation proved more crucial to human history than native manipulation of individual plants. Like all first farmers, agricultural pioneers in the Americas began experimenting accidentally. Modern-day species of corn, for example, probably derive from a Mesoamerican grass known as teosinte. It seems that ancient peoples gathered teosinte to collect its small grains. By selecting the grains that best suited them and bringing them back to their settlements, and by returning the grains to the soil through spillage or waste disposal, they unintentionally began the process of domestic cultivation. Soon these first farmers began deliberately saving seeds from the best plants and sowing them in gardens. In this way, over hundreds of generations, American farmers transformed the modest teosinte grass into a staple crop that would give rise to the hemisphere's mightiest civilizations.

Worldwide Spread of American Crops

Indeed, ever since contact with Europe, the great breakthroughs in Native American farming have sustained peoples around the world. In addition to corn, the first Americans gave humanity scores of varieties of squash, potatoes, beans, and other basic foods. Today, plants domesticated by indigenous Americans account for three-fifths of the world's crops, including many that have revolutionized the global diet. For good or ill, a handful of corn species occupies the center of the contemporary American diet. In addition to its traditional forms, corn is consumed in chips, breads, and breakfast cereals; corn syrup sweeteners are added to many of our processed foods and nearly all soft drinks; and corn is fed to almost all animals grown to be consumed, even farmed fish.

Theodor de Bry, Florida Indians Planting Maize. Both men and women were portrayed as involved in agriculture. Except for the digging stick at the center rear, however, the farming implements drawn by the artist are European in origin.

Other Native American crops have become integral to diets all over the world. Potatoes revolutionized northern European life in the centuries after contact, helping to avert famine and boost populations in several countries. Ireland's population tripled in the century after the introduction of potatoes. Beans and peanuts became prized for their protein content in Asia. And in Africa, corn, manioc, and other new-world crops so improved diets and overall health that the resulting rise in population may have offset the population lost to the Atlantic slave trade.

Landscapers

Plant domestication requires the smallest of changes, changes farmers slowly encourage at the genetic level. But native peoples in the precontact Americas transformed their world on grand scales as well. In the Andes, Peruvian engineers put people to work by the tens of thousands creating an astonishing patchwork of terraces, dykes, and canals designed to maximize agricultural productivity. Similar public-works projects transformed large parts of central Mexico and the Yucatan. Even today, after several centuries of disuse, overgrowth, and even deliberate destruction, human-shaped landscapes dating from the precontact period still cover thousands of square miles of the Americas.

Recently, scholars have begun to find evidence of incredible manipulation of landscapes and environments in the least likely of places. The vast Amazon rainforest has long been seen by westerners as an imposing symbol of untouched nature. But it now seems that much of the Amazon was in fact made by people. Whereas farmers elsewhere in the world domesticated plants for their gardens and fields, farmers in the Amazon cultivated food-bearing trees for thousands of years, cutting down less useful species and replacing them with ones that better suited human needs. All told there are more than 70 different species of domesticated trees throughout the Amazon. At least one-eighth of the nonflooded rainforest was directly or indirectly created by humans. Likewise, native peoples laboriously improved the soil across as much as a tenth of the Amazon, mixing it with charcoal and a variety of organic materials. These managed soils are more than 10 times as productive as untreated soils in the Amazon. Today, farmers in the region still eagerly search for the places where precontact peoples enriched the earth.

Cultivated Trees of the Amazon

Native North Americans likewise transformed their local environments. Sometimes they moved forests. Anasazis cut down and transported more than 200,000 trees to construct the floors and the roofs of the monumental buildings in Chaco Canyon. Sometimes they moved rivers. By taming the waters of the Salt and Gila Rivers in present-day Arizona with the most extensive system of irrigation canals anywhere in precontact North America, the Hohokam were able to support large populations in a desert environment. And sometimes they moved the land itself. Twenty-two million cubic feet of earth were moved to construct just one building in the Mississippian city of Cahokia.

Fire as a Tool

Indians also employed fire to systematically reshape landscapes across the continent. Throughout North America's great eastern and western forests, native peoples periodically set low fires to consume undergrowth and fallen trees. In this way the continent's first inhabitants managed forests and also animals. Burning enriched the soil and encouraged the growth of grasses and bushes prized by game animals such as deer, elk, beaver, rabbit, grouse, and turkey. The systematic use of fire to reshape forests helped hunters in multiple ways: it increased the overall food supply for grazing animals, it attracted those animal species hunters valued most, and, by clearing forests of ground debris, fire made it easier to track, kill, and transport game. Deliberate burns transformed forests in eastern North America to such an extent that bison migrated from their original ranges on the plains and thrived far to the east. Thus, when native hunters from New York to Georgia brought down a buffalo, they were harvesting a resource that they themselves had helped to create.

The Shape of a Problem

No matter how great their ingenuity, the first Americans were constrained by certain natural realities. One of the most important is so basic that it is easy to overlook. Unlike Eurasia, which stretches across the northern hemisphere along an east-west axis, the Americas fall along a north-south axis, stretching nearly pole to pole. Consequently, the Americas are broken up by tremendous geographic and climactic diversity, making communication and technology transfer far more difficult than it was in the Old World.

Consider the agricultural revolution in Eurasia. Once plants and animals were first domesticated in the Fertile Crescent around 10,000 years ago, they quickly began spreading east and west. Within 1,500 years these innovations had been adopted in Greece and India. A thousand years later the domesticated plants and animals of the Fertile Crescent had reached central Europe, and, from there, it took perhaps 200 years for them to be embraced in present-day Spain. Eurasia's east-west axis facilitated these transfers. Locations at roughly the same latitude share the same seasonal variation, have days of the same length, and often have similar habitats and rates of precipitation, making it relatively easy for plants and animals to move from one place to the next.

In contrast, the north-south orientation of the Americas erected natural barriers to plant and animal transfer. Mesoamerica and South America, for example, are about as far apart as the Balkans and Mesopotamia. It took roughly 2,000 years for plants and animals domesticated in Mesopotamia to reach the Balkans. But because Mesoamerica and South America are separated by tropical, equatorial lowlands, it took domesticated plants such as corn several thousand years to jump between the two regions. Sometimes the transfer never happened at all before European contact. South American potatoes would have thrived in central Mexico, but the tropics stopped their northward migration. Equatorial jungles also denied Mesoamerican societies the llama and the alpaca, domesticated more than 5,000 years ago in the Andes. One wonders what even greater heights the Olmec, Toltec, Mayan, and Aztec civilizations would have achieved if they had had access to these large creatures as draft animals and reliable sources of protein.

Transfer of Technology, Crop, and Animals

Dramatic variations in climate likewise delayed the transfer of agriculture from Mexico to regions north of the Rio Grande. Archaeologists have recently discovered evidence of 10,000-year-old domesticated squash in a cave in southern Mexico, an indication that agriculture began in the Americas nearly as early as anywhere else in the world. Yet squash and corn were not cultivated in the present-day American Southwest for another 7,000 years, and the region's peoples did not embrace a fully sedentary, agricultural lifestyle until the start of the Common Era. Major differences in the length of days, the growing season, average temperatures, and rainfall between the Southwest and central Mexico meant that farmers north of the Rio Grande had to experiment for scores of generations before they had perfected crops suited to their particular environments. Corn took even longer to become a staple crop in eastern North America, which is why major urban centers did not arise there until approximately 1000 C.E.

By erecting barriers to communication and the spread of technology, then, the predominantly north-south orientation of Americas made it more difficult for the hemisphere's inhabitants to build on one another's successes. Had American innovations spread as quickly as innovations in Eurasia, the peoples of the Western Hemisphere would likely have been healthier, more numerous, and more powerful than they were when Europeans first encountered them in 1492.

Animals and Illness

One other profound difference between the Eurasian world and the Americas concerned animals and disease. Most diseases affecting humans originated from domesticated animals, which came naturally into frequent and close contact with the humans who raised them. As people across Eurasia embraced agriculture and started living with one another and with domesticated animals in crowded villages, towns, and cities, they created ideal environments for the evolution and transmission of infectious disease. For example, measles, tuberculosis, and smallpox all seem to have derived from diseases afflicting cattle.

Eurasians therefore paid a heavy price for living closely with animals. Yet in the long run, the continent's terrible illnesses hardened its population. Victims who survived into adulthood enjoyed acquired immunity to the most common diseases: that is, if they had already encountered a particular illness as children, their immune systems would recognize and combat the disease more effectively in the event of reinfection. By the fifteenth century, then, Eurasian bodies had learned to live with a host of deadly communicable diseases.

Eurasia's Deadly Advantage

But Native American bodies had not. With a few important exceptions, including tuberculosis, pneumonia, and possibly herpes and syphilis, human populations in the western hemisphere seem to have been relatively free from major communicable pathogens. Insofar as most major diseases emerge from domesticated animals, it is easy enough to see why. Indigenous Americans domesticated turkeys, dogs, Muscovy ducks, and Guinea pigs but raised only one large mammal—the llama or alpaca (breeds of the same species).

This scarcity of domestic animals had more to do with available supply than with the interest or ability of their would-be breeders. The extinction of most species of megafauna soon after humans arrived in the Americas deprived the hemisphere of 80 percent of its large mammals. Those that remained, including modern-day bison, elk, deer, and moose, were more or less immune to domestication because of peculiarities in their dispositions, diets, rates of growth, mating habits, and social characteristics. In fact, of the world's 148 species of large mammals, only 14 were successfully domesticated before the twentieth century. Of those 14, only one—the ancestor to the llama/alpaca—remained in the Americas following the mass extinctions. Eurasia, in contrast, was home to 13—including the five most common and adaptable domestic mammals: sheep, goats, horses, cows, and pigs.

With virtually no large mammals to domesticate, Native Americans were spared the nightmarish effects of most of the world's major communicable diseases—until 1492.

After that date, European colonizers discovered the grim advantage of their millennia-long dance with disease. Old-world infections that most colonizers had experienced as children raged through indigenous communities, usually doing greatest damages to adults whose robust immune systems reacted violently to the novel pathogens. Often native communities came under attack from multiple diseases at the same time. Combined with the wars that attended colonization and the malnutrition, dislocation, and despair that attend wars, disease would kill native peoples by the millions while European colonizers increased and spread over the land. Despite their ingenuity and genius at reshaping plants and environments to their advantage, native peoples in the Americas labored under crucial disadvantages compared to Europe—disadvantages that would contribute to disaster after contact.

Crisis and Transformation

With its coastal plains, arid deserts, broad forests, and vast grasslands, North America has always been a place of tremendous diversity and constant change. Indeed, many of the continent's most dramatic changes took place in the few centuries before European contact. Because of a complex and still poorly understood combination of ecological and social factors, the continent's most impressive civilizations collapsed as suddenly and mysteriously as had those of the Olmecs and the Mayas of Mesoamerica. In the Southwest, the Mogollon culture went into eclipse around the twelfth century, the Hohokam and the Anasazi by about the fourteenth. In the Eastern Woodlands, the story was strikingly similar. Most of the great Mississippian population centers, including the magnificent city of Cahokia, had faded by the fourteenth century.

Sudden Declines

Enduring Cultures

The survivors of these crises struggled to construct new communities, societies, and political systems. In the Southwest, descendents of the Hohokam withdrew to small farming villages that relied on simpler modes of irrigation. Anasazi refugees embarked on a massive, coordinated exodus from the Four Corners region and established new, permanent villages in Arizona and New Mexico that the Spaniards would collectively call the Pueblos. The Mogollons have a more mysterious legacy, but some of their number may have helped establish the remarkable trading city of Paquime in present-day Chihuahua. Built around 1300, Paquime contained more than 2,000 rooms and had a sophisticated water and sewage system unlike any other in the Americas. The city included 18 large mounds, all shaped differently from one another, and three ballcourts reminiscent of those found elsewhere in Mexico. Until its demise sometime in the fifteenth century Paquime was the center of a massive trading network, breeding macaws and turkeys for export and channeling prized feathers, turquoise, sea shells, and worked copper throughout a huge region.

Trading City of Paquime

The dramatic transformations remaking the Southwest involved tremendous suffering. Southwesterners had to rebuild in unfamiliar and oftentimes less productive places. Although some of their new settlements endure even to this day, many failed. Skeletal analysis from an abandoned pueblo on the Rio Grande, for example, indicates that the average life expectancy was only 16.5 years. Moreover, drought and migrations increased conflict over scarce resources. The most successful new settlements were large, containing several hundred people, and constructed in doorless, defensible blocks, or else set on high mesas to ward off enemy attacks. These changes were only compounded by the arrival of Athapaskan-speaking peoples (known to the Spanish as Apaches and Navajos) in the century or two before contact with Europeans. These hunters and foragers from western Canada and Alaska moved in small bands, were sometimes friendly, sometimes hostile toward different Pueblos, and eventually became key figures in the postcontact Southwest.

In the Eastern Woodlands, the great Mississippian chieftainships never again attained the glory of Cahokia, but key traditions endured in the Southeast. In the lower Mississippi valley, the Natchez maintained both the temple mound–building tradition and the rigid social distinctions of Mississippian civilization. Below the chief, or "Great Sun," of the Natchez stood a hereditary nobility of lesser "Suns" who demanded respect from the lowly "Stinkards," the common people. Other Muskogean-speakers rejected this rigid and hierarchical social model and gradually embraced a new, more flexible system of independent and relatively **egalitarian** villages that forged confederacies to better cope with outsiders. These groupings would eventually mature into three of the great southeastern Indian confederacies: Creek, Choctaw, and Chickasaw.

To the North lived speakers of Iroquoian languages, roughly divided into a southern faction including Cherokees and Tuscaroras, and a northern faction including the powerful Iroquois and Hurons. Like Muskogeans to the South, these Iroquoian communities mixed farming with a hunting/gathering economy and lived in semipermanent towns. The distinctive feature of Iroquois and Huron architecture was not the temple mound but rather the longhouse (some stretching up to 100 feet in length). Each sheltered as many as 10 families.

The Algonquins were the third major group of Eastern Woodlands people. They lived along the Atlantic seaboard and the Great Lakes in communities smaller than those of either the Muskogeans or the Iroquois. By the fifteenth century, the coastal communities from southern New England to Virginia had adopted agriculture to supplement their diets, but those in the colder northern climates with shorter growing seasons depended entirely on hunting, fishing, and gathering plants such as wild rice.

Cultures of equal and even greater resources persisted and flourished during the fifteenth century in the Caribbean, particularly on the Greater Antilles—the islands of present-day Cuba, Haiti and the Dominican Republic, Jamaica, and Puerto Rico. Although the earliest inhabitants of the ancient Caribbean, the Ciboneys, probably came from the Florida peninsula, it was the Tainos, later emigrants from northern South America, who expanded throughout the Greater Antilles and the Bahamas. Taino chiefs known as caciques, along with a small number of noble families, ruled island tribes, controlling the production and distribution of food and tools and exacting tribute from the great mass of commoners, farmers, and fisherfolk. Attending to these elites were the poorest Taino peoples—servants who bedecked their masters and mistresses in brilliant diadems of feathers, fine woven textiles, and gold nose and ear pieces and then shouldered the litters on which the rulers sat and paraded their finery.

Muskogean Peoples

Iroquoians

Algonquins

Caribbean Cultures

North America on the Eve of Contact

By the end of the fifteenth century, North America's peoples numbered between 5 and 10 million—with perhaps another million living on the islands of the Caribbean—and they were spread among more than 350 societies speaking nearly as many distinct languages. (The total precontact population for all of the Americas is estimated at between 57 and 112 million.)

These millions lived in remarkably diverse ways. Some peoples relied entirely on farming; others on hunting, fishing, and gathering; still others on a combination of the two. Some, like the Natchez and the Iroquois, practiced matrilineal forms of kinship, in which women owned land, tools, and even children. Among others, such as the Algonquins, patrilineal kinship prevailed, and all property and prestige descended in the male line. Some societies, like those of the Great Plains and the Great Basin in the West, the Inuit in the Arctic, and the Iroquois and Algonquins in the East, were roughly egalitarian, whereas others, like many in the Caribbean and the Pacific Northwest, were rigidly divided into nobles and commoners and servants or slaves. Some, such as the Natchez and the Arawaks, were ruled by powerful chiefs; others, such as the Algonquins and the

Diverse Life-Ways

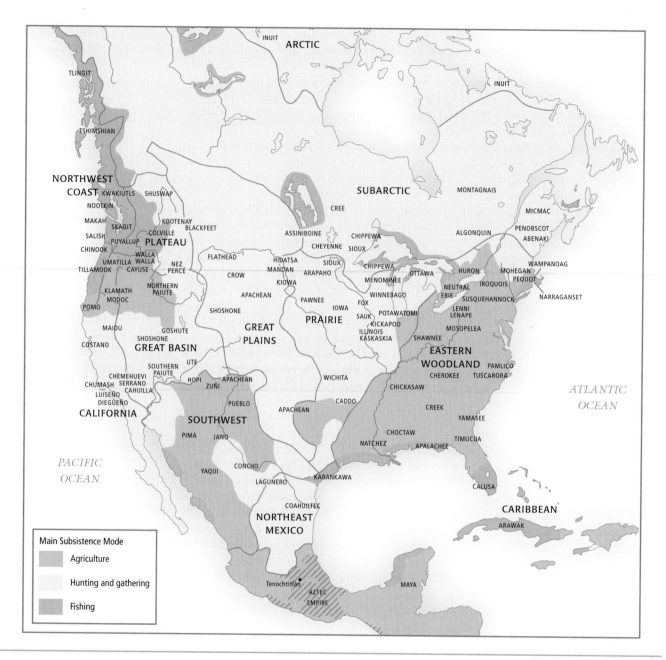

Indians of North America, circa 1500 *The map shows approximate locations of some Native groups.*

Pueblos, by councils of village elders or heads of family clans; still others in the Great Basin, the Great Plains, and the far North by the most skillful hunter or the most powerful shaman in their band. Those people who relied on hunting practiced religions that celebrated their kinship with animals and solicited their aid as guardian spirits, while predominantly agricultural peoples sought the assistance of their gods to make the rain fall and the crops ripen.

When Europeans first arrived in North America, the continent north of present-day Mexico boasted an ancient, rich, and dynamic history marked by cities, towns, and prosperous farms. At contact it was a land occupied by several million men, women, and children speaking hundreds of languages and characterized by tremendous political, cultural, economic, and religious diversity.

But for most of our nation's short history, we have not wanted to remember things this way. European Americans have had a variety of reasons to minimize and belittle the past, the works, even the size of the native populations that ruled North America for 99 percent of its human history. In 1830, for example, President Andrew Jackson delivered an address before Congress in which he tried to answer the many critics of his Indian removal policies. Although "humanity has often wept over the fate of the aborigines of this country," Jackson said, the Indians' fate was as natural and inevitable "as the extinction of one generation to make room for another." He reminded his listeners of the mysterious mounds that had so captivated the founding fathers. "In the monuments and fortresses of an unknown people, spread over the extensive regions of the West, we behold the memorials of a once powerful race, which was exterminated, or has disappeared, to make room for the existing savage tribes." Just as the architects of the mounds supposedly met their end at the hands of these "savage tribes," the president concluded, so too must Indians pass away before the descendents of Europe. "What good man would prefer a country covered with forests and ranged by a few thousand savages, to our extensive republic, studded with cities, towns, and prosperous farms; embellished with all the improvements which art can devise, or industry execute; occupied by more than twelve millions of happy people, and filled with all the blessings of liberty, civilization, and religion!"

Indeed, stories told about the past have power over both the present and the future. Jackson and many others of his era preferred a national history that contained only a few thousand ranging "savages" to one shaped by millions of indigenous hunters, farmers, builders, and inventors. Yet every generation rewrites its history, and what seems clear from this latest draft is the rich diversity of American cultures on the eve of contact between the peoples of Eurasia, Africa, and the Americas. We are still struggling to find stories big enough to encompass not only Indians but all those who have forged this complex, tragic, and marvelous nation of nations.

Significant Events

at least 15,000 B.C.E.	First humans arrive in the Americas
ca. 10,000–2500	Distinctive regional cultures develop in the Americas
ca. 10,000–7000	Agriculture begins in the Western Hemisphere
ca. 2000	Agriculture spreads from Mesoamerica to the present-day Southeast
ca. 1700–700	Poverty Point flourishes in present-day Louisiana
ca. 1500	The Olmecs begin to build the first Mesoamerican cities
ca. 1000	Agriculture spreads from Mesoamerica to the present-day Southwest
ca. 500–100	Adena culture reaches its height in North America
ca. 100	The classical civilization of Teotihuacán emerges in the highlands of central Mexico

ca. 100 B.C.E.–400 C.E.	Hopewell culture thrives in the Ohio and Mississippi valleys
ca. 200–800 C.E.	The Mayan empire flourishes on the Yucatán Peninsula
ca. 200–900	Mogollon culture flourishes in present-day New Mexico
ca. 650–950	The Olmecs, the Mayan empire, and Teotihuacán decline
ca. 800–1200	Mississippian civilization reaches its height
ca. 900–1100	Anasazi civilization reaches its height
ca. 1100	Mogollon culture declines
ca. 1300	Hohokam, Anasazi, and Mississippian civilizations decline; Apache and Navajo peoples enter the Southwest from Canada
ca. 1325–1500	Aztec empire rises in Mesoamerica

Chapter Summary

During the thousands of years after bands of Siberian nomads migrated across the Bering Strait to Alaska, their descendants spread throughout the Americas, creating civilizations that rivaled those of ancient Europe, Asia, and Africa.

- Around 1500 B.C.E. Mesoamerica emerged as the hearth of civilization in the Western Hemisphere, a process started by the Olmecs and brought to its height by the Mayans.

  - These Mesoamerican peoples devised complex ways of organizing society, government, and religious worship and built cities remarkable for their art, architecture, and trade.
  - Both commerce and migration spread cultural influences throughout the hemisphere, notably to the islands of the Caribbean basin and to North America, an influence that endured long after these empires declined.

- The adoption of agriculture gave peoples in the Southwest and the Eastern Woodlands the resource security necessary to develop sedentary cultures of increasing complexity. These cultures eventually enjoyed great achievements in culture, architecture, and agriculture.

- Inhabitants of the Great Plains, the Great Basin, the Arctic, and the Subarctic evolved their own diverse cultures, relying for subsistence on fishing, hunting, and gathering.

- Peoples of the Pacific Northwest boasted large populations and prosperous economies as well as an elaborate social, ceremonial, and artistic life.

- The native inhabitants of the Americas transformed their environments in a variety of ways, from pioneering crops that would eventually feed the world to terraforming mountains and jungles.

- Nonetheless, natural constraints would leave Native Americans at a disadvantage compared to Europe. The continent's north-south orientation inhibited the spread of agriculture and technology, and a lack of domesticatable animals compared to Europe would leave Native Americans with little protection against disease.

- For reasons that remain unclear, many of North America's most impressive early civilizations had collapsed by the end of the fifteenth century. In their wake a diverse array of cultures evolved across the continent.

  - In the Southwest, Pueblo Indians were joined by Athapaskan-speaking hunters and foragers in an arid landscape.
  - In much of eastern North America, stratified chiefdoms of the Mississippian era gave way to more egalitarian confederacies of independent villages subsisting on farming and hunting.

- Although Americans in the nineteenth and even twentieth centuries have been slow to recognize the fact, the societies of precontact America were remarkably populous, complex, and diverse. Their influence would continue to be felt in the centuries after contact.

Additional Reading

The best descriptions of ancient American civilizations are offered by Brian M. Fagan, *Kingdoms of Gold, Kingdoms of Jade: The Americas before Columbus* (1991); and, especially, Charles C. Mann, *1491: New Revelations of the Americas before Columbus* (2005). For North America specifically, see Alice Beck Kehoe, *America before the European Invasions* (2002). For the Southwest, see Stephen Plog, *Ancient Peoples of the Southwest* (1997). For the Eastern Woodlands, see George R. Milner, *The Moundbuilders: Ancient Peoples of Eastern North America* (2005). Roger G. Kennedy, *Hidden Cities: The Discovery and Loss of Ancient North American Civilization* (1994), gives a fascinating account of how white Americans responded to the ruins of ancient American cultures. For the consequences of axis alignment and of domesticated animals, see the captivating work by Jared Diamond, *Guns, Germs, and Steel: The Fates of Human Societies* (1998).

For the cultures of precontact Mexico, see Michael D. Coe and Rex Koontz, *Mexico: From the Olmecs to the Aztecs* (5th ed., 2002). For exhaustive surveys of all regional cultures in North America, see William C. Sturtevant, general editor, *Handbook of North American Indians,* 20 volumes projected (1978–). Carl Waldman, *Atlas of the North American Indian* (1985), is also an excellent source of information, offering much more than good maps.

For a fuller list of readings, see the Bibliography at www.mhhe.com/davidsonnation6.

Historians Reconstruct the Past

Tracking the First Americans

What methods do historians use to discover the history of a past thousands of years before any humans knew how to write? Archaeological research is key; and by carefully unearthing layer after layer of soil, analyzing artifacts and their relation to these layers, scientists and historians have been able to discover a remarkable amount of information about the first immigrants to the Americas over 10,000 years ago.

But the deductions and inferences made—about a past without words and barren of historical documents—are often contested. Archaeologists have continually argued with one another over the scant available evidence. Even today the debate continues over the nature of the earliest migrations. And progress often depends on accidental discoveries, such as the one made by an African American cowboy, George McJunkin. McJunkin, a former slave, was a talented rancher, not to mention a capable fiddler, amateur astronomer, and surveyor. Old fossils also fascinated him, and he collected them.

The Clovis Discoveries

Riding his horse one day in 1908 near Folsom, New Mexico, McJunkin looked down and saw some very old and very large bison bones eroding from a slope. He took some of the

Stone artifacts known as Clovis points found with the skeleton of a mammoth.

bones home and soon realized that they must have belonged to an extinct bison species. McJunkin failed to interest any professional archaeologists in his find, and only after his death did New Mexican locals manage to convince scholars from the University of Colorado to come and investigate. When the team finally began excavations in 1926, they found something that changed the course of modern archaeology: an exquisitely crafted stone spear-point embedded in the bison's ribs.

The discovery rocked the scientific community, which for the previous century had confidently declared that Indians had first arrived in the Americas only about 4,000 years before. Eleven years later another shock wave followed when archaeologists digging near Clovis, New Mexico, found a different sort of projectile point near butchered mammoth bones. Finally, in 1949, scientists confirmed the great antiquity of both finds by using "radiocarbon dating," a method for measuring decay rates of the radioactive isotope of carbon, which exists in organic matter such as bone and starts to break down immediately after an organism dies. Tests revealed that the Indians whose hunting grounds were now called Folsom and Clovis had been turning ancient mammals into bones between 10,800 and 11,500 years ago.

Those conclusions pointedly raised the question of exactly how much earlier the first American ancestors of such hunters had come to the New World. This tantalizing mystery puzzles (and divides) archaeologists and anthropologists, geologists and historians, right down to the present. Such men and women devote their lives to the hard work of digging in remote sites or exploring the ocean's floor, to the harder work of analyzing their finds in laboratories, and to the hardest work of all—trying to make sense of what it all means. Their efforts have yielded much new evidence and increasingly sophisticated techniques for understanding its significance, but many important questions remain unanswered.

Even so, almost all of them agree on a number of points. First, whoever the first inhabitants of the New World were, they came, originally, from Eurasia: scientists have found no fossil remains to support the view that human beings evolved into modern men and women in the Americas. Second, these first Americans were almost certainly fully evolved human beings, known as *Homo sapiens sapiens*—not their less-developed forerunners, the Neanderthals, or even earlier ancestors. These *Homo sapiens sapiens* excelled at surviving anywhere, armed as they were with the intellectual ability to plan and cooperate and with the technology to sew warm clothing, hunt large animals, and store food. About 35,000 years ago, these resourceful adapters came to predominate, edging out the Neanderthals, whose more limited skills had restricted their settlements to the tropical and temperate parts of the world.

Evidence of Migration from Siberia to North America

The new species multiplied rapidly, and the pressure of its growing population pushed many into settling in less hospitable regions—including the Arctic frontier of Siberia in northeastern Asia. Indeed, a third point of general agreement among scholars is that the descendants of these migrants to Siberia continued the wandering ways of their ancestors and somehow, at some time, wandered into North America by way of Alaska. The research of physical anthropologists documents key biological similarities between Siberians and most American Indians. Both groups share not only certain genetic variants that suggest their descent from common ancient ancestors but also distinctive formations of the roots and crowns of their teeth known as sinodonty.

But how did Asians get to Alaska—a region now separated from Siberia by 50 miles of ocean known as the Bering Strait? It is not impossible that they sailed across, for some *Homo sapiens sapiens* could build boats sturdy enough to navigate short stretches of open ocean. Archaeologists have discovered that Southeast Asians floated across 55 miles of ocean on rafts to reach Australia some 35,000 years ago. Could their contemporaries in northeast Asia, using bark canoes, have made a voyage of similar length over the Bering Strait? Not impossible, scientists conclude, but not likely either, if only because navigating calm, tropical waters of the southern Pacific is far less difficult than mastering the Bering Strait, which even in summer is choked with ice floes. Such an undertaking would have been even more daunting to the earliest Siberians, who, as anthropologists have discovered, were land-based hunters, not seafaring folk. So most scientists now believe that Siberians did not sail to the New World: instead, they walked.

They were able to do that because the Bering Strait is not a timeless feature of Arctic geography. On the contrary, geologists have discovered, submerged far below the Bering Strait lie traces of a landmass that once connected Siberia to Alaska. Even in the late nineteenth century, some naturalists suspected that such a land bridge had once existed after noting that the vegetation and wildlife of Siberia were nearly identical to those in Alaska. By the 1930s, scientists had enough information to speculate that what turned a waterway into an exposed, inhabitable lowland plain was the coldest phase of the last Ice Age, which began about 30,000 years earlier, when plunging temperatures caused the world's oceans to drop in depth by freezing great expanses of seawater into sheets of ice. Those climatic changes formed "Beringia," a land bridge between Siberia and Alaska that existed from about 25,000 B.P. until about 15,000 B.P. During those millennia, most scientists now believe, Siberians gradually settled the length of this link to the Americas. Thereafter, when

23

temperatures began to warm again and the seas rose and closed over Beringia, some of its inhabitants strayed into Alaska.

An Even Earlier Arrival?

But even today, some scientists doubt this account. True, no one has yet discovered an archaeological site in Alaska that can be positively dated to earlier than about 13,200 B.P. Yet two different archaeological teams claim to have found artifacts in rock shelters whose settlements, they assert, reach back 16,000 years—and perhaps even to 30,000 years ago, though this evidence is less conclusive. One site, known as the Meadowcroft Rockshelter, is located in southwest Pennsylvania. The other is in the far reaches of southern Chile at a site known as Monte Verde.

The debates over the evidence produced from these excavations and its proponents have been harsh. When a team of independent experts visited Monte Verde in 1997 to assess the evidence, the two sides got into a hot argument at the local bar before the defenders of Monte Verde walked out in a huff. (Or perhaps they did not; even this assertion was contradicted by one of the skeptics.)

Beyond the operatic tales of bickering lie serious issues. The advocates for the Clovis people as the first Americans are persuaded partly because of the deadly spearpoints they made. As one pro-Clovis advocate remarked, the spearpoints reminded him "of the deadly beauty of the Colt pistol and Winchester rifle. Just as production of these weapons coincided with the demise of the buffalo and passenger pigeon, so does the Clovis period coincide with the extinction of America's megafauna—the mammoth, mastodon, and other ice-age giants." However, advocates of an earlier human presence in North America posit

To the left of the tag "F-9" is a fragment of deer antler from excavations at Meadowcroft Rock shelter. Does this and other evidence suggest that hunters were present in Pennsylvania more than 16,000 years ago? Archaeologists hotly debate the point.

a less aggressive culture as arriving first, whose gentle people left little evidence of their presence. But they must also assume that because these newcomers came earlier, they could not have walked across the Beringia land bridge. They must have sailed across the Bering Strait.

A discovery in the state of Washington is also prompting scientists to wonder whether the first inhabitants of the Americas might have included peoples other than Asians. In 1996, the sheriff of a small desert town, puzzled by a half-buried human skeleton found along the shores of the Columbia River, showed the bones to an anthropologist, James Chatters. Like McJunkin's find of almost a century earlier, this skeleton encased a stone spear point, and radiocarbon dating revealed it to be nearly as old (9,300 years) as the Folsom bones. Also like McJunkin's specimen, this one has sparked debate within the scientific community. Chatters and others who measured the skull discovered that it was far narrower than any Indian skull of similar antiquity. They concluded—astonishingly—that the Kennewick Man, as he came to be known, was Caucasoid in appearance. It seemed to be evidence that in addition to the Siberian migrations, some people of European stock may have somehow crossed to the Americas.

But comparisons of the skull with all other known ethnic groups led a panel of scientists to conclude that the Kennewick Man is not a distant relative either of present-day Indians or of Caucasians. The closest resemblance is to the Ainu people of Japan's Sakhalin Islands and to Polynesians of the South Pacific. If such a link were established, it would strengthen the hypothesis that some of the earliest Americans reached the continent by boat, either hopscotching along the Bering Strait or even sailing across the Pacific. Both the Ainu and the Polynesians were maritime peoples.

So the debates about America's first colonizers continue, and if recent history is any guide, so too will the discoveries. This part of the past, like every other, holds in store many surprises for those in the present determined to probe its secrets.

Bibliography Keeping up with recent discoveries in this field poses many challenges. New discoveries turn up frequently, and most reports of those findings are written in a highly technical language. Fortunately, a few well-written books provide a guide to both the early Asian migration to and throughout the Americas and the evolution of scholarly debate. Brian M. Fagan, *The Great Journey* (London, 1987), is lucid, and the same author has also written a more detailed textbook on both ancient Native American archaeology and history, *Ancient North America* (1991). Recent debates are explored in Charles C. Mann's *1491: New Revelations of the Americas before*

Columbus (2005). The long and tense relationship between archaeologists and Americas' native peoples is the subject of David Hearst Thomas's excellent book *Skull Wars: Kennewick Man, Archaeology, and the Battle for Native American Identity* (2000). Students seeking more advanced and specialized information should consult Stuart J. Fiedel, *Prehistory of the Americas* (2nd ed., Cambridge, 1992).

Fiedel is one of the skeptics of earlier claims of human entry into North America. He is treated with something less than cordiality by J. M. Adovasio, the archaeologist who led the excavations at Meadowcroft Rockshelter, in his account (with Jake Page), *The First Americans: In Pursuit of Archaeology's Greatest Mystery* (2002). Adovasio's book is also of interest to outsiders because it presents an unvarnished description of the actual practice of archaeology. "After twelve hours of troweling thin layers of dirt and dust," Adovasio notes, "you go crazy at night. Running, weight lifting, drinking, fornicating, staring off into space and babbling incoherently—you do almost anything for relief. It takes a truly bizarre person to live that way for months on end, and we had tents full of them."

CHAPTER 2
Old Worlds, New Worlds
1400~1600

Fishing Nets and Far Horizons

All the world lay before them. Or so it seemed to mariners from England's seafaring coasts, pushing westward toward unknown lands in the far Atlantic.

The scent of the new land came first—not the sight of it, but the smells, wafted from beyond the horizon, delicious to sailors who had felt nothing but the rolling sea for weeks on end. In northerly latitudes around June, it would be the scent of fir trees or the sight of shore birds wheeling about the masts. Straightaway the captain would call for a lead to be thrown overboard to sound the depths. At its end was a hollowed-out socket with a bit of tallow in it, so that some of the sea bottom would stick when the lead was hauled up. Even out of sight of land, a good sailing master could tell where he was by what came up—"oosy sand" or perhaps "soft worms" or "popplestones as big as beans." If the ship were approaching unknown shores, the captain would hope to sight land early in the day, allowing time to work cautiously toward an untried harbor on uncharted tides.

Through much of the fifteenth century the search for cod had drawn West Country sailors north and west, toward Iceland. In the 1480s and 1490s a few English tried their luck farther west. Old maps, after all, claimed that the bountiful *Hy-Brasil*—Gaelic for "Isle of the Blessed"—lay somewhere west of Ireland. These western ventures returned with little to show for their daring until the coming of an Italian named Giovanni Caboto, called John Cabot by the English. Cabot, who hailed from Venice, obtained the blessing of King Henry VII to hunt for unknown lands. From the port of Bristol his lone ship set out to the west in the spring of 1497.

This time the return voyage brought news of a "new-found" island where the trees were tall enough to make fine masts and the codfish were plentiful. After returning to Bristol, Cabot marched off to London to inform His Majesty, received 10 pounds as his reward, and with the proceeds dressed himself in dashing silks. The multitudes of London flocked after him, wondering over "the Admiral"; then Cabot returned triumphantly to Bristol to undertake a more ambitious search for a northwest passage to Asia. He set sail with five ships in 1498 and was never heard from again.

With sails bellying in a gale, the Dutch ship in this painting has furled the rest of its canvas. Sailors from western Europe risked much as they crossed the Atlantic in search of fish, silver, gold, and other commodities of trade.

By the 1550s Cabot's island, now known as Newfoundland, attracted 400 vessels annually, fishermen not only from England but also from France, Portugal, and Spain. The harbor of present-day St. John's, Newfoundland, served as the informal hub of the North Atlantic fishery. Sailors from three kingdoms dropped anchor there, to take on supplies in the spring, trade with native peoples, or to prepare for the homeward voyage in autumn. There was much talking at this meeting place, for these seafarers knew as much as anyone else—if not more—about the new world of wonders that was opening to Europeans. They were acquainted with names like Cristoforo Colombo, the Italian from Genoa whom Cabot might have known as a boy. They listened to Portuguese tales of sailing around the Horn of Africa in pursuit of spices and to stories of Indian empires to the south, rich in gold and silver that Spanish treasure ships were bringing home.

Indeed, Newfoundland was one of the few places in the world where so many ordinary folk of different nations could gather and talk, crammed aboard dank ships moored in St. John's harbor, huddled before blazing fires on its beaches, or crowded into smoky makeshift taverns. When the ships sailed home in autumn, the tales went with them, repeated in the tiniest coastal villages by those pleased to have cheated the sea and death one more time. Eager to fish, talk, trade, and take profits, West Country mariners were almost giddy at the prospect of Europe's expanding horizons.

Most seafarers who fished the waters of Newfoundland's Grand Banks remain unknown today. Yet it is well to begin with these ordinary fisherfolk, for the European discovery of the Americas cannot be looked on simply as the voyages of a few bold explorers. Adventurers such as Christopher Columbus and John Cabot were only the most visible representatives of a much larger expansion of European peoples and culture that began in the 1450s. That expansion arose out of a series of gradual but telling changes in the fabric of European society—changes that were reflected in the lives of ordinary seafarers as much as in the careers of explorers decked out in silks.

Changes in Europe

Some of these changes were technological, arising out of advances in the arts of navigating and shipbuilding and the use of gunpowder. Some were economic, involving the development of trade networks like those linking Bristol with ports in Iceland and Spain. Some were **demographic,** bringing about a rise in Europe's population after a devastating century of plague. Other changes were religious, adding a dimension of devout belief to the political rivalries that fueled discoveries in the Americas. Yet others were political, making it possible for kingdoms to centralize and extend their influence across the ocean. Portugal, Spain, France, and England—all possessing coasts along the Atlantic—led the way in exploration, spurred on by Italian "admirals" such as Caboto and Colombo, Spanish *conquistadores*—"conquerors"—such as Hernán Cortés and Francisco Pizarro, and English sea dogs such as Humphrey Gilbert and Walter Raleigh. Ordinary folk rode these currents too. The great and the small alike were propelled by forces that were remolding the face of Europe—and were beginning to remold the face of the world.

Eurasia and Africa in the Fifteenth Century

China's Glory

In 1450, however, the Western European kingdoms that would one day dominate much of the world still sat at the fringe of an international economy that revolved around China. By a variety of measures Ming China was the richest, most powerful, and most advanced society in the world. All Eurasia sought Chinese goods, especially spices, ceramics, and silks, and Chinese ships sped these goods to faraway ports. Seven times between 1405 and 1433, China's "treasure fleet"—300 ships manned by 28,000 sailors and commanded by Zheng He (pronounced "Jung Huh")—unfurled its red silk sails off the south China coast and traveled as far as the kingdoms of eastern Africa. The treasure fleet's largest craft were nine-masted junks measuring 400 feet long. They boasted multiple decks and luxury cabins with balconies. (By comparison, Columbus's largest ship in 1492 was a mere 85 feet long, and the crew aboard all three of his ships totaled just 90 men.) Chinese leaders soon grounded their trading fleet and put a stop to the long-distance voyages that might eventually have made Zheng He a forerunner to Columbus. But Chinese luxuries, most transported overland, continued to be Eurasia's most sought-after commodities.

The next mightiest powers in the Old World were not European kingdoms but rather huge Islamic empires, especially the Ottomans in the eastern Mediterranean. The Ottomans rose to prominence during the fourteenth and fifteenth centuries and expanded aggressively in every direction. Muslim rulers gained control of critical trade routes and centers of commerce between Asia and Europe. The Ottomans' greatest triumph came in 1453, when the sultan Mehmed II conquered Constantinople (now Istanbul), the ancient and supposedly impregnable Christian city that straddled Europe and Asia and was one of the world's premier trading hubs. Mehmet's stunning victory sounded alarms throughout Europe.

Islamic Kingdoms

Europe's Place in the World

Europe's rulers had good reason for alarm. Distant from Asia's profitable trade and threatened both economically and militarily by the Ottomans, most of the continent remained fractious and vulnerable. During the fourteenth and the fifteenth centuries, 90 percent of Europe's people, widely dispersed in small villages, made their living from the land. But warfare, poor transportation, and low grain yields all created food shortages, and undernourishment produced a population prone to disease. Under these circumstances life was nasty, brutish, and usually short. One-quarter of

During the sixteenth century, West Country fisherfolk from England sailed from harbors like Plymouth, shown here. Such seaports were small; the fortifications dotting the coastline and a wall around the town itself were used to defend against invaders.

Early Modern Goth

Opening a Window on Death

As bubonic plague swept across Europe during the mid-fourteenth century, it brought the possibility of sudden death closer than ever. But with or without the plague, death was a much closer companion for most people in early modern times. Historians can trace a preoccupation with death not merely in written sources, such as sermons and diaries, but also in material culture, such as this skull pendant, dating from the 1600s. This decorative piece hung at the wearer's breast and could be opened to reveal a skeleton in a coffin. Scholars have noted that in England, funeral monuments changed with the coming of the Black Death. Before its devastation, deceased lords and ladies were often portrayed in brass, dressed in their finest clothing. Afterward, the monuments increasingly featured death masks, contorted corpses or skeletons with serpents slinking among their bones. To make yet another contrast, if one does a Google Image Search today of the phrase "skull

Skull pendant both closed and open.

pendant," a host of modern jewelry comes up. In what ways do such fashions reflect their modern culture in the way that the skull pendants of the sixteenth and seventeenth century reflected theirs?

all children died in the first year of life. People who reached the age of 40 counted themselves fortunate.

It was also a world of sharp inequalities, where nobles and aristocrats enjoyed several hundred times the income of peasants or craftworkers. It was a world with no strong, centralized political authority, where kings were weak and warrior lords held sway over small towns and tiny fiefdoms. It was a world of violence and sudden death, where homicide, robbery, and rape occurred with brutal frequency. It was a world where security and order of any kind seemed so fragile that most people clung to tradition and feared change.

The Black Death

But Europe was changing, in part because of a great calamity. Between the late 1340s and the early 1350s, bubonic plague—known as the Black Death—swept away one-quarter of Europe's population. Some urban areas lost 70 percent of their people to the disease. The Black Death disrupted both agriculture and commerce, and provoked a spiritual crisis that resulted in violent, unsanctioned religious movements, scapegoating of marginal groups, even massacres of Jews. Although Europeans seem to have met recurrent outbreaks of the disease with less panic, the sickness continued to disrupt social and economic life nonetheless.

Yet the sudden drop in population relieved pressure on scarce resources. Survivors of the Black Death found that the relative scarcity of workers and consumers made for better wages, lower prices, and more land. These changes intersected in an overall expansion of trade. In earlier centuries Italian merchants had begun building wealth by encouraging commerce across Europe and by tapping into trade from Africa, the Middle East, and, when able, from Asia. By the late fifteenth century Europe's merchants and bankers had devised more efficient ways of transferring the money generated from manufacturing and trade, and established credit in order to support commerce across longer distances. Wealth flowed into the coffers of fifteenth-century traders, financiers, and landlords, creating a pool of capital that those investors could plow into new technologies, trading ventures, and, eventually, colonial enterprises.

The direction of Europe's political development also laid the groundwork for overseas colonization. After 1450 strong monarchs in Europe steadily enlarged the sphere of royal power at the expense of warrior lords. Henry VII, the founder of England's Tudor dynasty, Francis I of France, and Ferdinand and Isabella of Spain began the trend, forging modern nation-states by extending their political control over more territory, people, and resources. Such larger, more centrally organized states were able to marshal the resources necessary to support colonial outposts and to sustain the professional armies and navies capable of creating and protecting overseas empires. By the mid-fourteenth century western Europe had commercial networks, private fortunes, strong kingdoms, and ambitions that would lead to a transformative period of expansion.

Monarchs Forge Nation-States

Africa and the Portuguese Wave

European expansion began with Africa. For centuries, African spices, ivory, and gold had entered the Eurasian market either westward, through ports on the Indian Ocean, or northward, through the Sahara Desert and into the Mediterranean Sea. Powerful African kingdoms controlled the routes through which these prized commodities moved, and prices ballooned by the time the goods reached cities in Europe. Islamic expansion in the fifteenth century made competition all the more intense. Merchants throughout the continent yearned to access West African markets directly, by ship. But navigational and shipbuilding technology was not yet up to the challenge of the Atlantic's prevailing currents, which sped ships south along Africa's coast but made the return voyage virtually impossible.

Improved Navigation and Sailing Techniques

Portugal was the first to solve this problem and tap directly into West African markets, thanks in large part to the vision and tenacity of one man. Prince Henry "the Navigator," as he became known, was a passionate advocate for Portugal's maritime interests, an ardent Catholic, and a man who dreamed of turning back Islam's rising tide. He understood that direct commerce with West Africa would allow his kingdom to circumvent the costly trans-Sahara trade. To forward his vision, Henry funded exploratory voyages, established a maritime school, and challenged sailors and engineers to conquer the problem of the current. His advocacy helped the Portuguese develop the caravel, a lighter, more maneuverable ship that could sail better against contrary winds and in rough seas. More seaworthy than the lumbering galleys of the Middle Ages, caravels combined longer, narrower hulls—a shape built for speed—with triangular lateen sails, which allowed for more flexible steering. The caravel allowed the Portuguese to regularly do what few Europeans had ever done, sail down Africa's west coast and return home. Other advances, including a sturdier version of the Islamic world's astrolabe, enabled Portugal's vessels to calculate their position at sea with unprecedented accuracy.

This stately ivory mask made by an African artist in the early sixteenth century for the Court of Benin (present-day Nigeria) is adorned with 10 bearded heads of white men, representing Portuguese explorers and traders who had first arrived in Benin in 1472.

The farther south the Portuguese extended their influence along the Atlantic rim of sub-Saharan Africa, the more likely they were to meet with peoples who had had no earlier encounters with Europeans and, indeed, had no knowledge of the existence of other continents. On catching their first sight of a Portuguese expedition in 1455, the inhabitants of one village on the Senegal River marveled at the strangers' clothing and their white skin. As an Italian member of that expedition recounted, some Africans "rubbed me with their spittle to discover whether my whiteness was dye or flesh."

West African States

But the Portuguese were wrong to mistake such acts of innocence for economic or political naïveté. As they made their way south in stages, the newcomers found mature commercial networks and formidible African states, states eager to trade but intent on protecting their interests. Portugal could not simply take what it wanted from West Africa. With few exceptions, it proved impossible for European powers to colonize

This African fortune-teller reads the palm of her white client in this seventeenth-century painting by a Franco-Flemish artist, Nicolas Regnier. In early modern Europe, class and religion were more important in defining social divisions than color and ethnicity. Slaves, servants, and free workers of all races often worked and socialized together.

territory in West Africa before the nineteenth century because the region's people were too many and too organized. Furthermore, its disease environment was too dangerous. Malaria would kill between one-fourth and one-half of all Portuguese unwise and unlucky enough to try and stay. Hence the newcomers had to seek partners, to forge trading relationships with coastal elites. The Portuguese established forts and trading houses on the coast. They gave tribute or taxes to local powers in return for trading privileges and exchanged textiles, especially, but also raw and worked metal goods, currency (in the form of cowry shells), and beads for prized commodities such as gold, ivory, and malaguetta pepper. Portuguese traders also expressed interest in another commodity, one that would reshape the wider Atlantic world: slaves.

Sugar and the Origins of the Atlantic Slave Trade

Unfree labor has existed in nearly all human societies. Although the norms, characteristics, and economic importance of slavery have varied widely over time and place, men, women, and children have been held as slaves from before recorded history to the present. (U.S. and international organizations estimate that today there are as many as 27 million people held in some form of labor bondage and that nearly 1 million unfree people are sold across international borders every year.)

By the Middle Ages, elites in Europe had largely abandoned the slave culture of the Roman Empire and relied instead on serfs or peasants for labor. Slaves became more important as status symbols than as workers, and most were young white women. Indeed, the word "slave" comes originally from "Slav"; Slavic girls and women from the Balkans and the coasts of the Black Sea were frequent targets of slave raids.

Changes in European Slavery

But European slavery began to change again following the Crusades. In 1099 Christian forces captured Jerusalem from the Seljuk Turks (forerunners to the Ottomans). In the Holy Land the crusaders discovered sugar plantations that the Turks had cultivated. At that time some sugar was being produced by Moors in North Africa and Iberia, yet it remained an expensive luxury item coveted by merchants and elites as a medicine and preservative. Crusaders recognized sugar's economic potential, but because it was so labor-intensive they found it a difficult commodity to produce. It required intense work during planting and close tending

The rich, volcanic soils of the Azores, the Canaries, and Madeira proved ideal for growing sugar. These islands in the eastern Atlantic were a stepping-stone to later plantations in the Americas, such as the one pictured in this engraving by Theodore de Bry in 1596.

during the growing season. On maturity the crop had to be harvested and processed 24 hours a day to avoid being spoiled. In short, sugar demanded cheap, pliable labor. The newly arrived crusaders relied in part on slave labor to make their plantations turn a profit.

Once Islamic forces under the famed leader Saladin reconquered Jerusalem in the twelfth century, European investors established new plantations on eastern Mediterranean islands. In addition to being labor intensive, though, sugar was a crop that quickly exhausted soils and forced planters to move operations regularly. Plantations spread to new islands, and by the early 1400s sugar was even being grown in Portugal. As production expanded, planters had to work harder than ever to obtain the necessary labor because of the Black Death and because Ottoman conquests restricted European access to the traditional slaving grounds of the eastern Mediterranean and the Balkans.

Spread of Sugar

Thus by the fifteenth century the Portuguese were already producing sugar on slave-run plantations, but they were seeking new crop land and new sources of slaves. Once again Prince Henry's vision enhanced his kingdom's economic interests. While Portugal's merchants were establishing trading posts along the west coast of Africa, Iberian mariners were discovering or rediscovering islands in the eastern Atlantic: the Canaries, Madeira, and the Azores, islands with rich, volcanic soils ideally suited to sugarcane. By the late fifteenth century sugar plantations were booming on the Atlantic islands, staffed by West African slaves. By the middle of the sixteenth century, people of African descent accounted for 10 percent of the population of Lisbon, Portugal's capital city.

Portugal was growing great in wealth and in ambition. Convinced that they could reach coveted Asian markets by sea, bold mariners sailed their caravels farther and farther south. In 1488 Bartolomeu Dias rounded the Cape of Good Hope on the southern tip of Africa, sailing far enough up that continent's eastern coast to claim discovery of a sea route to India. Ten years later Vasco da Gama reached India itself, and Portugal's interests ultimately extended to Indochina and China.

Dias and da Gama

Portuguese geographers had long felt certain that travel around Africa was the shortest route to the Orient, but an Italian sailor disagreed. Cristoforo Colombo was 25 years old when he shipwrecked on the Portuguese coast in 1476. The ambitious young man spent the next 10 years learning from the world's master mariners. He also threw himself into research, devouring Lisbon's books on geography and cartography. Columbus (the Latinized version of his name) became convinced that the fastest route from Portugal to China lay west, across the uncharted Atlantic Ocean. He appealed to Portugal's king to support an exploratory voyage, but royal geographers scoffed at the idea. They agreed that the world was round but insisted (correctly, as it turns out) that the globe was far larger than Columbus had calculated; hence the proposed westward route was too distant to be practical. Almost a decade of rejection had grayed Columbus's red hair, but—undaunted—he packed up in 1485 and took his audacious idea to Spain.

Spain in the Americas

But Columbus arrived a few years too early. Spain's monarchs, Ferdinand and Isabella, were then engaged in a campaign to drive the Muslims out of their last stronghold on the Iberian peninsula, the Moorish kingdom of Granada. At first the monarchs rejected Columbus's offer, leading him to make other (failed) overtures to the kings of England, France, and even Portugal again. Then in 1492 Ferdinand and Isabella took Granada and completed their reconquest of Spain, or *reconquista.* Flush with victory and ready to expand their horizons, the pair granted Columbus another audience. The mariner insisted that a westward route to Asia would allow Spain to compete with Portugal and generate sufficient revenue to continue the reconquest, even into the holy land itself. Ignoring the advice of their geographers, the monarchs agreed to his proposal.

Columbus Reaches America

Columbus's first voyage across the Atlantic could only have confirmed his conviction that he was destiny's darling. His three ships, no bigger than fishing vessels that sailed to Newfoundland, plied their course over placid seas, south from Seville to the Canary Islands and then due west. On October 11, a little more than two months after leaving Spain, branches, leaves, and flowers floated by their hulls, signals that land lay near. Just after midnight, a sailor spied cliffs shining white in the moonlight. On the morning of October 12, the *Niña*, the *Pinta*, and the *Santa Maria* set anchor in a shallow sapphire bay, and their crews knelt on the white coral beach. Columbus christened the place San Salvador (Holy Savior).

The Spanish Beachhead in the Caribbean

Like many men of destiny, Columbus mistook his true destination. At first he confused his actual location, the Bahamas, with an island off the coast of Japan. He coasted along Cuba and Hispaniola (today's Haiti and Dominican Republic), expecting at any moment to catch sight of gold-roofed Japanese temples or fleets of Chinese junks. He encountered instead a gentle, generous people who knew nothing of the Great Khan but who welcomed the newcomers profusely. Columbus's journals note that they wore little clothing (see Daily Lives: "Barbaric" Dress—Indian and European, pages 34–35), but they did wear jewelry—tiny pendants of gold suspended from the nose. He dubbed the Taino people "Indians"—inhabitants of the Indies.

Columbus would long insist that he had indeed reached the Indies, and it would take some years before other mariners and geographers understood clearly that these newfound islands and the landmasses beyond them lay between Europe and Asia. One of the earliest geographers to do so was the Florentine Amerigo Vespucci, who first described Columbus's Indies as *Mundus Novus,* a "New World." Rather than dub the new lands "Columbia," a German mapmaker called them "America" in Vespucci's honor. The German's maps proved wildly successful, and the name stuck.

West Africa and the Caribbean Compared

Whether Columbus had found Asian isles or a new world, Europeans seemed to agree that the simple societies he encountered were better suited to be ruled than

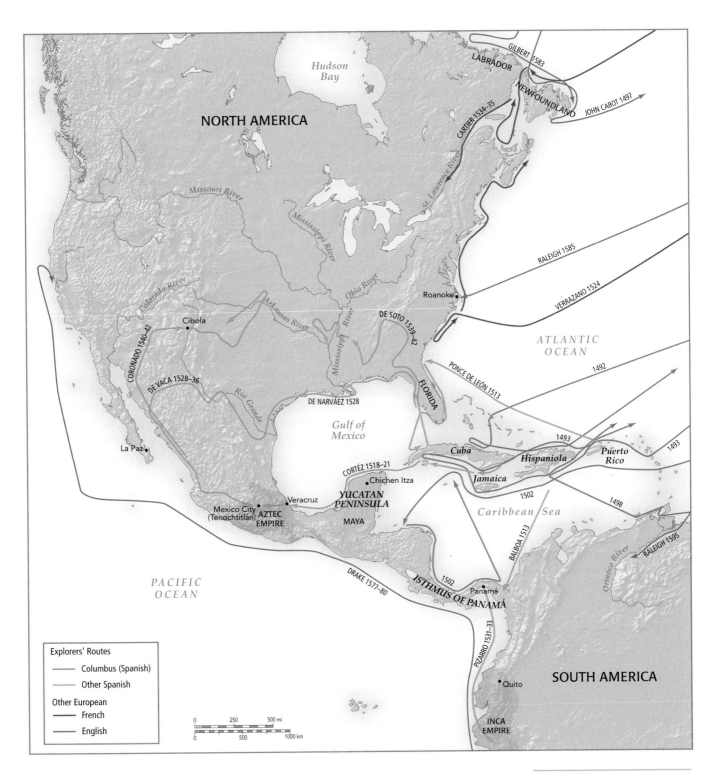

**Principal Routes of
European Exploration**

partnered with. Unlike the kingdoms of West Africa, the Taino chiefdoms lacked the military power to resist European aggression. Moreover, while the newfound islands would eventually present their own threats to European health, they seemed a good deal more inviting than the deadly coast of West Africa. Hints of gold, a seemingly weak and docile population, and a relatively healthy climate all insured that Columbus's second voyage would be one of colonization rather than commerce. During the 1490s and early 1500s, Spanish colonizers imposed a terrifically brutal

It was remarkable to sixteenth-century Europeans how many things seemed to be missing from Indian culture. Even more remarkable, the Indians themselves did not seem to notice. Michel de Montaigne, a French philosopher who had never been to America but liked to talk with explorers and read their accounts, managed to compile quite a list. According to Montaigne, Indians had "no kind of traffic [trade], no knowledge of letters, no intelligence of numbers, no name of magistrate, nor of politics, no use of service [servants], of riches, or of poverty, no contracts, no successions, no partitions, no occupation but idle, no apparel but natural. . . ." That last item—clothing—was crucial. European woodcuts, engravings, and paintings regularly showed native peoples either entirely nude or clad in skimpy loincloths or grass skirts.

Some Europeans interpreted the lack of clothing as evidence of "barbarism." André Thevet, a shocked French visitor to Brazil in 1557, voiced this point of view when he attributed nakedness to simple lust. If the Indians could weave hammocks, he sniffed, why not shirts? But other Europeans viewed unashamed nakedness as a badge of innocence. As remnants of a bygone "golden age," they believed, Indians needed clothing no more than government, laws, regular employment, or other corruptions of civilization.

In fact, Indians were no more "naked" than they were without trade, politics, employment, or religion. While the simplest peoples of the Caribbean and Brazil wore little, the members of more advanced Indian cultures in South, Central, and North America clothed themselves with animal pelts sewn into mantles and robes, breechclouts, leggings, and moccasins. They wrought bird feathers into headdresses and ear decorations and fashioned reptile skins into belts and pouches. Even more formidably clad were the Inuits of the far North, who dressed head to foot in sealskin suits with waterproofed seams.

If natives struck whites as underdressed, Europeans seemed, by the Indians' standards, grotesquely overdressed. Indeed, European fashion was ill suited to the environment between the Chesapeake and the Caribbean. Elizabethan gentlemen strutted in silk stockings attached with garters to padded, puffed knee breeches, topped by long-sleeved shirts and tight quilted jackets called "doublets." Men of lesser status wore coarse woolen hose, canvas breeches, shirts, and fitted vests known as "jerkins." Women wore gowns with long, full skirts, low-cut bodices, aprons, and hosiery held up by garters. Ladies went about in silk and wore hoods and mantles to ward off the sun, while the rest dressed in flannels or canvas and covered their heads with linen caps or coifs.

Such fashions complicated life in the American environment, since heavy clothing and even shoes rotted rapidly from sweat and humidity. The pungent aroma of Europeans also compounded the discomfort of natives who came in contact with them—for the whites who swaddled themselves in woolens also disdained regular bathing. To them,

regime upon the Tainos, slaughtering native leaders and forcing survivors to toil in mines and fields.

Only a few Spaniards spoke out against the exploitation. Among them was Bartolomé de Las Casas, a man who spent several years in the Caribbean, participating in conquests and profiting from native labor. Eventually las Casas had an epiphany, renounced his role in the conquest, and, as a Dominican friar, became a tireless foe of Spanish cruelties toward Indians. He railed against the "unjust, cruel, and tyrannical warfare" waged on Indians, war waged in order to disrupt native societies and force their people into "the hardest, harshest, and most heinous bondage to which men or beasts might ever be bound into." Las Casas's writings, translated throughout Europe and illustrated with gruesome drawings, helped give rise to the "Black Legend" of Spanish oppression in the Americas.

Native Depopulation

The warnings had some effect, but not for decades. Within a generation of Columbus's landfall, the Taino population had nearly collapsed from war, overwork, malnutition, despair, and strange new Eurasian diseases. Ambitious Spaniards began scouring the Caribbean basin, discovering new lands and searching for new populations of Indians to subjugate or enslave in place of the vanishing Tainos. Soon the Bahamas were depopulated by Spanish slavers, and conquests had done to present-day Cuba, Jamaica, and Puerto Rico what they had done to Hispaniola.

indian devotion to daily washing seemed just another uncivilized oddity.

It would have been natural for Indians to wonder why the barbaric newcomers did not adapt their dress to a new setting. The answer may be that for Europeans the psychological risk of shedding familiar apparel was simply too great. However inappropriate or even unhealthy, heavy, elaborate dress afforded the comfort of familiarity and distinguished "civilized" newcomer from "savage" native in America.

Columbus meeting the natives on Hispaniola.

Conquest of the Aztecs

Would-be conquistadors turned their eyes to the mainland. Spanish sailors surveyed the Yucatán Peninsula and clashed with the formidable Maya. In 1519 an expedition led by the impetuous Hernán Cortés made contact with native peoples on Mexico's gulf coast. They spoke of an oppressive imperial people who occupied a fantastic city to the West. These were the Aztecs.

Aztecs had much in common with Spaniards. Both societies were predominantly rural, with most inhabitants living in small villages and engaging in agriculture. In both places, merchants and specialized craftworkers clustered in cities, organized themselves into guilds, and clamored for protection from the government. Aztec noble and priestly classes, like those in Europe, took the lead in politics and religion, demanding tribute from the common people. Finally, both societies were robustly expansionist, bent on bringing new lands and peoples under their control.

Yet critical differences between these two peoples shaped the outcome of their meeting. The Aztecs lacked the knowledge of ocean navigation, metal tools and weaponry, and firearms. Equally important, the relatively young Aztec empire had not yet established total control over central Mexico. Formidable peoples remained outside Aztec domination, and conquered city-states within the empire

Spanish and Aztec Societies

Both the Aztecs and the Spanish tried to understand the new in terms of the familiar. Hence an Aztec artist portrayed Cortés as an Indian with strange clothes and stranger beard (left), *whereas a European artist depicted Moctezuma in the style of a Greco-Roman warrior* (right).

Disease and Defeat

bitterly resented Aztec rule. It was a weakness that Cortés exploited ably. Massing an army of disgruntled native warriors, Cortés and his men marched inland to the mighty Aztec capitol Tenochtitlán, home to more people (roughly a quarter million) than any city then existing in Europe. When the emperor Moctezuma's ambassadors met Cortés on the road and attempted to appease him with gold ornaments and other gifts, an Indian witness noted that "the Spaniards . . . picked up the gold and fingered it like monkeys. . . . Their bodies swelled with greed." The newcomers were welcomed into the city as honored guests but soon siezed Moctezuma and took him captive. For months Cortés ruled the empire indirectly, but the Aztecs drove the Spanish out after Moctezuma's death.

In the midst of this victory the city encountered another foe—smallpox. Geographically isolated from Eurasia and its complex disease environment, the Aztecs and all other native peoples in the Americas lacked the acquired immunity that gave Europeans a degree of protection against Old-World pathogens. The resulting **virgin soil epidemics**—so called because the victims had no prior exposure—took a nightmarish toll. Smallpox claimed millions in central Mexico between 1520 and 1521. This too presented Cortés with opportunities. Supported by a massive Indian force, he put Tenochtitlán to siege, killing tens of thousands before the ragged, starving survivors surrendered in August of 1521. The feared Aztec empire lay in ruins. Conquistadors fanned out from central Mexico, overwhelming new populations and eventually learning of another mighty kingdom to the South. Again relying on political faction, disease, technological advantages, and luck, by 1532 Spaniards under Francisco Pizzaro and his brothers had conquered the Incan empire in South America, which in certain regards rivaled even the Aztecs.

The Columbian Exchange

Virgin soil epidemics, which contributed to the devastation of the Indian populations, were only one aspect of a complex web of interactions between the flora and fauna of the Americas on the one hand and that of Eurasia and Africa on the other. Just as germs migrated along with humans, so did plants and animals. These transfers, begun in the decades after Columbus first landed in the Caribbean, are known by historians as the **Columbian exchange,** and they had far-reaching effects on either side of the Atlantic. Europeans brought a host of American crops home with them, as seen in Chapter 1 (pages 12–13). They also most likely brought syphillis, an American disease that broke out across Europe in more virulent form than ever before. Europeans brought to the Americas the horses and large dogs that intimidated the Aztecs; they brought oranges, lemons, figs, and bananas from Africa and the Canary Islands. Escaped hogs multiplied so rapidly that they overran some Caribbean islands, as did European rats.

The Columbian exchange was not a short-lived event. In a host of different ways it continued to reshape the globe over the next half millennium as travel, exploration, and colonization brought cultures ever closer. Instead of smallpox, today bird flu from Asia or the West Nile virus threatens populations worldwide. But the exchanges of the sixteenth century were often more extreme, unpredictable, and far-reaching because of the previous isolation of the two hemispheres.

Ongoing Exchanges

The Crown Steps In

The proud conquistadors did not long enjoy their mastery in the Americas. Spain's monarchs, who had just tamed an aristocracy at home, were not about to allow a colonial nobility to arise across the Atlantic. The Crown bribed the conquistadors into retirement— or was saved the expense when men such as Francisco Pizarro were assassinated by their own followers. The task of governing Spain's new colonies passed from the conquerors to a small army of officials, soldiers, lawyers, and Catholic bishops, all appointed by the Crown, reporting to the Crown, and loyal to the Crown. Headquartered in urban centers such as Mexico City (formerly Tenochtitlán), an elaborate, centralized bureaucracy administered the Spanish empire, regulating nearly every aspect of economic and social life.

Few Spaniards besides imperial officials settled in the Americas. By 1600, only about 5 percent of the colonial population was of Spanish descent, the other 95 percent being either Indian or African. Even by 1800 only 300,000 Spanish immigrants had come to Central and South America. Indians often remained on the lands that they had farmed under the Aztecs and the Incas, now paying Spanish overlords their taxes and producing livestock for export. More importantly, Indians paid for the new order through their labor, sometimes as slaves but more often through an evolving administrative system channeling native workers to public and private enterprises throughout New Spain. The Spanish also established sugar plantations in the West Indies; these were worked by black slaves who by 1520 were being imported from Africa in large numbers.

Spanish and Indian Populations

Spain's colonies returned even more spectacular profits to the mother country by the 1540s—the result of silver discoveries of epic proportions in both Mexico and Peru. Silver mining developed into a large-scale capitalist enterprise requiring substantial investment. European investors and Spanish immigrants who had profited from cattle raising and sugar planting poured their capital into equipment and supplies that would mine the silver deposits more efficiently: stamp mills, water-powered crushing equipment, pumps, and mercury. Whole villages of Indians were pressed into service in the mines, joining black slaves and free white workers employed there.

Silver Bonanza

In the last decades of the sixteenth century the economies of Mexico and Peru revolved around the mines. By 1570 the town of Potosí, the site of a veritable mountain of silver, had become larger than any city in either Spain or its American empire, with a population of 120,000. Local farmers who supplied mining centers with food and Spanish merchants in Seville who exported European goods to Potosí profited handsomely. So, too, did the Spanish Crown, which claimed one-fifth of all extracted silver. During the sixteenth century, some 16,000 tons of the precious metal were exported from Spanish America to Europe.

The Search for North America's Indian Empires

Riches and glory radicalized Spanish expectations. Would-be conquistadors embarked on an urgent race to discover and topple the next Aztec or Incan Empire, a race to become the next Cortés or Pizarro. The prevailing mood was captured by the portrait of a Spanish soldier that adorns the frontispiece of his book about the West Indies. He stands with one hand on his sword and the other holding a pair of compasses on top of a globe. Beneath is inscribed the motto "By compasses and the sword/More and more and more and more."

Some of the most ambitious adventurers felt certain that more lands and riches would be found in the North. Spanish slavers had been the first to skirt the North American mainland, going as far north as present-day South Carolina. These voyages likely inspired Juan Ponce de León, conquerer of Puerto Rico, to make the first official expedition to the mainland, which he named Florida to mark the day of his landfall, *Pascua Florida* (Easter). Everywhere he went he met armed resistance from Florida's native inhabitants, people who had come to know and despise Spaniards as slave raiders. Ponce de León sailed back to Puerto Rico and then returned for some years to Spain, until Cortés's early exploits in Mexico rekindled his ambitions. Filled with visions of glory, he returned to Florida in 1521 only to be mortally wounded in a battle with Calusa Indians.

Ponce de León died miserably, yet his countrymen still believed that wealthy Indian empires remained undiscovered in the North. In 1526 Spain established a settlement in present-day Georgia, but the endeavor soon collapsed. Two years later Pánfilo de Narváez, a red-bearded veteran from the conquest of Cuba, led a major expedition back to Florida. Ignoring advice from his second-in-command, Alvar Núñez Cabeza de Vaca, Narváez separated from his main force near Tampa Bay and led 300 men on a harrowing march in search of riches. For months the force plundered its way through Florida, while the men fell ill or fell victim to Indian archers, whose longbows could bury an arrow six inches into a tree. Disillusioned and desperate, 242 survivors lashed together makeshift rafts and tried to sail along the Gulf Coast to Mexico. Weeks later proud Narváez and most of his men had disappeared at sea, whereas Cabeza de Vaca and a handful of survivors washed up on islands off the Texas coast.

Local Indian groups then turned the tables and made slaves of the Spaniards. Cabeza de Vaca later recalled that his captors were appalled to learn that the starving castaways had eaten their dead. After years as prisoners, Cabeza de Vaca and three others, including a black slave named Esteban, escaped to make an extraordinary trek across Texas and northern Mexico. Somewhere in present-day Chihuahua they passed through what had been the trading hinterland of Paquime, and Cabeza de Vaca noted an enduring regional commerce in feathers and "green stones"—turquoise. Finally, in July 1536 a shocked party of Spanish slavers stumbled across the four rag-tag castaways and brought them to Mexico City.

The stories the four men told of their trek inspired two more massive expeditions to discover and conquer North America's elusive Indian empires. The first was led by Hernán de Soto, who had grown wealthy helping to conquer Peru. Confident that Florida held similar riches, de Soto scoured the southeast's agricultural villages searching for gold and taking whatever he wanted: food, clothing, luxury goods, even young women whom he and his men "desired both as servants and for their foul uses. . . ." As they raped, stole, and killed their way through the Southeast, de Soto and his men unwittingly had the honor of being the first and last Europeans to glimpse several declining Mississippian chiefdoms, echoes of Cahokia's ancient majesty. Some native communities resisted, inflicting huge losses on de Soto's men. Others shrewdly feigned friendship and insisted that gold and glory could be found in this or that nearby village, thus ridding themselves of a great danger and directing it at enemies instead. De Soto's men ravaged Indian societies through parts of present-day Florida, Georgia, North and

Ponce de León

Pánfilo de Narváez and Cabeza de Vaca

Hernán de Soto

Spanish America, ca. 1600
By 1600, Spain was extracting large amounts of gold and silver from Mexico and South America, as well as profits from sugar plantations in the Caribbean. Each year Spanish treasure ships ferried bullion from mines such as the one at Potosí to the Isthmus of Panama, where it was transported by land to the Caribbean coast, and from there to Spain. An expedition from Acapulco sailed annually to the Philippines as well, returning with Asian spices and other trade goods.

South Carolina, Tennessee, Alabama, Mississippi, Arkansas, Louisiana, and Texas. The expedition never found the treasures it sought, but it did hasten the transformation of the southeastern chiefdoms into decentralized confederacies.

Spanish ambition met a similar fate in the West. In 1539, 29 year old Francisco Vázquez de Coronado led 300 Spaniards and 1,000 Mexican Indian warriors north into the present-day American Southwest. Emboldened by tales of cities more wondrous even than Tenochtitlán, Coronado's brash confidence began to fail him when instead he found only mud and straw pueblos inhabited by modest farmers. Determined to turn his hugely expensive expedition to advantage, Coronado sent men in all directions. Some went west, until they ran into the vastness of the Grand Canyon and had to turn back. Others traveled east, taking up temporary residence among the Pueblo peoples of the Upper Rio Grande. The increasingly abusive visitors soon provoked battles with their hosts, forcing them to abandon 13 villages, which the Spaniards then destroyed. Desperate to redeem his reputation and investment, Coronado followed an Indian he dubbed the Turk out onto the Great Plains in search of a rumored kingdom called Quivira. Perhaps the Turk had in mind one of the easternmost Mississippian chiefdoms, but the frustrated conquistador became convinced he had been deceived. He had the Turk strangled somewhere in present-day Kansas and in 1542 returned to Mexico where crown authorities brought him to trial for inflicting "great cruelties" upon Indians.

Conquistadors such as Coronado might be ruined by their unfulfilled ambitions, but Spain could afford its failed North American excursions. It had taken vast wealth from the Americas, conquered the hemisphere's mightiest peoples, and laid claim

Vázquez de Coronado

Spain's Dominance in the Americas

to most of the new world. Spaniards warily expected competition, and yet for most of the sixteenth century rival European powers took little interest in the Americas. England's fishermen continued to explore the North Sea, Labrador, and Newfoundland. Portugal discovered and laid claim to Brazil. France sent expeditions to explore North America's eastern shoreline (Giovanni da Verrazano, 1524) and the St. Lawrence River Valley (Jacques Cartier, 1534, 1535, and 1541). These efforts proved important in the long run, but for most of the century Spain could treat the Americas as their own. They owed that luxury, in part, to religious upheaval in Europe. During the second decade of the sixteenth century—the same decade in which Cortés laid siege to Tenochtitlán—religious changes of enormous significance began spreading through Europe. That revolution in Christianity, known as the Protestant Reformation, occupied European attentions and eventually figured as a crucial force in shaping the history of the Americas.

Religious Reform Divides Europe

During the Middle Ages, the Roman Catholic church defined what it meant to be a Christian in western Europe. Like other institutions of medieval society the Catholic church was a hierarchy. At the top was the pope in Rome, and under him were the descending ranks of other church officials—cardinals, archbishops, bishops. At the bottom of the Catholic hierarchy were parish priests, each serving his own village, as well as monks and nuns living in monasteries and convents. But medieval popes were weak, and their power was felt little in the lives of most Europeans. Like political units of the era, religious institutions of the Middle Ages were local and decentralized.

Rise of the Papacy   Between about 1100 and 1500, however, as the monarchs of Europe grew more powerful so too did the popes. The Catholic church acquired land throughout Europe, and its swelling bureaucracy added to church income from tithing (taxes contributed by church members) and from fees paid by those appointed to church offices. In the thirteenth century, church officials also began to sell "indulgences." For ordinary believers who expected to spend time after death purging their sins in purgatory, the purchase of an indulgence promised to shorten that punishment by drawing on a "treasury of merit" amassed by the good works of Christ and the saints.

By the fifteenth century the Catholic church and the papacy had become enormously powerful but increasingly indifferent to popular religious concerns. Church officials meddled in secular politics. Popes and bishops flaunted their wealth, while poorly educated parish priests neglected their pastoral duties. At the same time, popular demands for religious assurance grew increasingly intense.

The Teachings of Martin Luther

Into this climate of heightened spirituality stepped Martin Luther, who abandoned studying the law to enter a monastery. Like many of his contemporaries, Luther was consumed by fears over his eternal fate. He was convinced that he was damned, and he could not find any consolation in the Catholic church. Catholic doctrine taught that a person could be saved by faith in God and by his or her own good works—by leading a virtuous life, observing the sacraments (such as baptism, the Mass, and penance), making pilgrimages to holy places, and praying to Christ and the saints. Because Luther believed that human nature was innately evil, he despaired of being able to lead a life that "merited" salvation. If men and women are so bad, he reasoned, how could they ever win their way to heaven with good works?

Justification by Faith Alone   Luther finally broke through his despair with Bible. It convinced him that God did not require fallen humankind to earn salvation. Salvation, he concluded, came by faith alone, the "free gift" of God to undeserving sinners. The ability to live a good life could not be the *cause* of salvation but its *consequence:* once men and women believed that they had saving faith, moral behavior was possible. Luther elaborated that idea, known as "justification by faith alone," between 1513 and 1517.

Luther was ordained a priest and then assigned to teach at a university in Wittenberg, Germany. He became increasingly critical, however, of the Catholic church as an institution. In 1517 he posted on the door of a local church 95 theses attacking the Catholic hierarchy for selling salvation in the form of indulgences.

The novelty of this attack was not Luther's open break with Catholic teaching. Challenges to the church had cropped up throughout the Middle Ages. What was new were the passion and force behind Luther's protest. Using the blunt, earthy Germanic tongue, he expressed the anxieties of many devout laypeople and their outrage at the church hierarchy's neglect. The "gross, ignorant asses and knaves at Rome," he warned, should keep their distance from Germany, or else "jump into the Rhine or the nearest river, and take . . . a cold bath."

The pope and his representatives in Germany at first tried to silence Martin Luther, then excommunicated him. But opposition only pushed Luther toward more radical positions. He asserted that the church and its officials were not infallible; only the Scriptures were without error. Every person, he said, should read and interpret the Bible for himself or herself. In an even more direct assault on church authority, he advanced an idea known as "the priesthood of all believers." Catholic doctrine held that salvation came only through the church and its clergy, a privileged group that possessed special access to God. Luther asserted that every person had the power claimed by priests.

Although Luther had not intended to start a schism within Catholicism, independent Lutheran churches were forming in Germany by the 1520s. And, during the 1530s, Luther's ideas spread throughout Europe, where they were eagerly taken up by other reformers.

Protestants such as Luther and Calvin placed greater emphasis on the Word of Scripture rather than church rituals controlled by priests and bishops. In this seventeenth-century portrait of John Calvin, sacred words from scripture literally help define him.

The Contribution of John Calvin

The most influential of Luther's successors was John Calvin, a French lawyer turned theologian. Calvin agreed with Luther that men and women could not merit their salvation. But, whereas Luther's God was a loving deity who extended his mercy to sinful humankind, Calvin conceived of God as awesome, all-knowing and all-powerful—the controlling force in human history that would ultimately triumph over Satan. To bring about that final victory, to usher in his heavenly kingdom, God had selected certain people as his agents, Calvin believed. These people—"the saints," or "the **elect**"—had been "predestined" by God for eternal salvation in heaven.

The Elect

Calvin's emphasis on predestination led him to another distinctively Protestant notion—the doctrine of calling. How could a person learn whether he or she belonged to the elect who were saved? Calvin answered: strive to behave like a saint. God expected his elect to serve the good of society by unrelenting work in a "calling," or occupation, in the world. In place of the Catholic belief in the importance of good works, Calvin emphasized the goodness of work itself. Success in attaining discipline and self-control, in bringing order into one's own life and the entire society, revealed that a person might be among the elect.

Calvin fashioned a religion to change the world. Whereas Luther believed that Christians should accept the existing social order, Calvin called on Christians to become activists, reshaping society and government to conform with God's laws laid down in the Bible. He wanted all Europe to become like Geneva, the Swiss city that he had converted into a holy commonwealth in which the elect regulated the behavior and morals of everyone else. And unlike Luther, who wrote primarily for a German audience, Calvin addressed his most important book, *The Institutes of the Christian Religion* (1536), to Christians throughout Europe. Reformers from every country flocked to Geneva to learn more about Calvin's ideas.

French Huguenots and the Birth of Spanish Florida

The Protestant Reformation shattered the unity of Christendom in western Europe. Spain, Portugal, Ireland, and Italy remained firmly Catholic. England, Scotland, the Netherlands, Switzerland, and France developed either dominant or substantial Calvinist constituencies. Much of Germany and Scandinavia opted for Lutheranism. As religious groups competed for political power and the loyalties of believers, brutal wars swept sixteenth-century Europe, and France experienced some of the worst violence. An influential group of Huguenots (Calvin's French followers) saw in North America a potential refuge from religious persecution. Under the leadership of Jean Ribault, 150 Huguenots from Normandy in 1562 established a simple village on Parris Island off present-day South Carolina. That experiment ended in desperation and cannibalism, but two years later Ribault led another, larger group to a site south of present-day Jacksonville, Florida. Here the Huguenots constructed a settlement they named Fort Caroline and nurtured a cordial relationship with the local Timucua Indians. It seemed a promising start.

Huguenots as a Threat to Spain

But Spanish authorities in the Caribbean took the Huguenots for a triple threat. First, French pirates had long sought to siphon silver from the Americas by waylaying Spanish galleons. Silver shipments rode the Gulf Stream past the Bahamas and up the southeastern coast of North America before turning east toward Spain. In only four years, from 1556 to 1560, French ships preying on this vulnerable route had helped cut Spain's colonial revenues in half. With good reason, Spanish administrators feared that Fort Caroline would entrench the threat of piracy. Second, Spain had to worry that France would plant successful colonies and take a broader interest in the Americas, perhaps eventually making claims on all of North America. Finally, many Spanish Catholics saw Protestantism as a loathsome contagion, to be expunged from Europe and barred from the Americas.

These interlocking concerns prompted Spain to found a permanent colony in Florida. To do so the Crown turned to a focused and unforgiving man named Pedro Menéndez de Avilés. In 1565 Menéndez established a settlement on the coast called Saint Augustine (still the United States' oldest continuously occupied, non-Indian settlement) and immediately marched north to destory Fort Caroline. He and 500 soldiers slogged through the rain and marsh until they found the simple fort. In battle and through later executions, the attackers killed Ribault and about 500 of his Huguenots. Flush with victory, Menéndez established several more outposts on Florida's Atlantic and Gulf coasts, and in 1570 even encouraged a short-lived Jesuit mission just miles from where English colonists would establish Jamestown a generation later. As for the Huguenots, the calamity at Fort Caroline dashed hope that the New World would be their haven. Most had to resign themselves to intensifying persecution in France.

The English Reformation

While the Reformation racked northern Europe, King Henry VIII of England labored at a goal more worldly than those of Luther and Calvin. He wanted a son, a male heir to continue the Tudor dynasty. When his wife, Catherine of Aragon, gave birth to a daughter, Mary, Henry petitioned the Pope to have his marriage annulled in the hope that a new wife would give him a son. This move enraged the king of Spain, who also happened to be Catherine's nephew. He persuaded the pope to refuse Henry's request. Defiantly, England's king proceeded with the divorce nonetheless and quickly married his mistress, Anne Boleyn. He then went further, making himself, not the pope, the head of the Church of England. Henry was an audacious but practical man, and he had little interest in promoting reformist doctrine. Apart from discarding the Pope, the Church of England remained essentially Catholic in its teachings and rituals.

England's Protestants gained ground during the six-year reign of Henry's son Edward VI but then found themselves persecuted when Edward's Catholic half-sister Mary became queen in 1553. Five years later the situation turned again, when Elizabeth I (Anne Boleyn's daughter) took the throne, proclaiming herself the defender of Protestantism. Elizabeth was no radical Calvinist, however. A vocal minority of her subjects were reformers of that stripe, calling for the English church to purge itself of bishops, elaborate ceremonies, and other Catholic "impurities." Because of the austerity and zeal of such Calvinist radicals, their opponents proclaimed them **"Puritans."**

English Puritans

Radical Protestants might annoy Elizabeth as she pursued her careful, moderate policies, but radical Catholics frightened her. She had reason to worry that Spain might try and employ English Catholics to undermine her rule. More ominously, Elizabeth's advisors cautioned that Catholic Ireland to the west would be an ideal base from which Spain or France could launch an invasion of England. Beginning in 1565 the queen encouraged a number of her elite subjects to sponsor private ventures for subduing the native Irish and settling loyal English Protestants on their land. As events fell out, this Irish venture proved to be a prelude to England's bolder attempt to found colonies across the Atlantic.

Elizabeth's Fears

England's Entry into America

Among the gentlemen eager to win fame and fortune were Humphrey Gilbert and Walter Raleigh, two adventurers with conquistador appetites for more and more. The pair were like most of the English who went to Ireland, ardent Protestants who viewed the native Catholic inhabitants as superstitious, pagan savages: "They blaspheme, they murder, commit whoredome," complained one Englishman, "hold no wedlocke, ravish, steal and commit all abomination without scruple." Thus the English found it easy enough to justify their conquest. They proclaimed it their duty to teach the Irish the discipline of hard work, the rule of law, and the truth of Protestant Christianity. And, while the Irish were learning these civilized, English ways, they would not be allowed to buy land or hold office or serve on juries or give testimony in courts or learn a trade or bear arms.

When the Irish rebelled at that program of "liberation," the English ruthlessly repressed them, slaughtering not only combatants but civilians as well. Most English in Ireland, like most Spaniards in America, believed that native peoples who resisted civilization and proper Christianity should be subdued at any cost. No scruples stopped Gilbert, in an insurgent country, from planting the path to his camp with the severed heads of Irish rebels.

The struggle to colonize and subdue Ireland would serve as a rough model for later English efforts at expansion. The approach was essentially military, like that of the conquistadors. It also set the ominous precedent that Englishmen could treat "savage" peoples with a level of brutal cruelty that would have been inappropriate in wars between "civilized" Europeans. But the campaigns in Ireland seemed to leave the Queen's men with little more than lessons. "Neither reputation, or profytt is to be wonne" in Ireland, concluded Gilbert. He, Raleigh, and many other West County gentry wanted to take their ambition and their Irish education to North America.

The Irish Experience as a Model

The Ambitions of Gilbert, Raleigh, and Wingina

In 1578 Gilbert was the first to get his chance for glory when Elizabeth granted him a royal patent—the first English colonial **charter**—to explore, occupy, and govern any territory in America "not actually possessed of any Christian prince or people." The vague, wildly unrealistic charter matched Gilbert's vast ego. It ignored the Indian possession of North America and made him lord and proprietor of all the land lying between Florida and Labrador. In many ways his dreams looked backward. Gilbert hoped to set up a kind of medieval kingdom of his own, where loyal tenant farmers would work the lands of manors, paying rent to feudal lords. Yet his vision also looked forward to a utopian society. He planned to encourage England's poor to emigrate by providing them free land and a government "to be chosen by consent of the people." Elizabeth had high hopes for her haughty champion, but a fierce storm got the better of his ship, and the Atlantic swallowed him before he ever set foot in his American dominions.

Gilbert's Utopian Dreams

Walter Raleigh

Meanwhile Gilbert's stepbrother Raleigh had been working more industriously to lay the groundwork for a British American empire. Raleigh enlisted the talents of Richard Hakluyt, a clergyman with a passion for spreading knowledge of overseas discoveries. At Raleigh's bidding, Hakluyt wrote an eloquent plea to Elizabeth for the English settlement of America, titled *A Discourse Concerning Westerne Planting*. The temperate and fertile lands of North America, Hakluyt argued, would prove ideal for growing tropical commodities and would be an excellent base from which to harry the Spanish, search for a Northwest Passage to the Orient, and extend the influence of Protestantism. He also stressed the advantages of colonies as potential markets for English goods and as havens for the poor and unemployed. Finally, Hakluyt predicted that because the "Spaniardes have executed most outragious and more then Turkishe cruelties in all the west Indies," that Indians would greet Englishmen as liberators.

First Roanoke Settlement

Raleigh's chance to test the prediction finally came in 1584, when Elizabeth granted him a patent nearly identical to Gilbert's. By the summer Raleigh had dispatched an exploratory voyage to the Outer Banks of present-day North Carolina. Expedition leaders reported making friendly contact with a people known as the Roanoke and ruled by a "weroance," or chief, named Wingina. The enthusiastic Hakluyt envisioned a colony that would become the Mexico of England, full of plantations producing sugar and silk and mountains yielding gold. Elizabeth knighted Raleigh and allowed him to name the new land "Virginia," after his virgin queen.

Wingina's Plans

But Raleigh was not the only one with grand plans. Almost certainly Wingina had encountered or at least heard of Europeans before 1584. Like most coastal groups in the region, his people would have obtained prized European tools and commodities through indirect trade or by scouring wrecked ships. Preoccupied with the political geography of his own region and eager to fortify his own and his people's power, Wingina recognized that friendly relations with the English would give him privileged access to their trade and influence. Perhaps he believed he would act as patron to the newcomers. After all, they knew little of the region, spoke no Indian languages, and even lacked the basic skills necessary to survive in the area without native assistance. In short, Wingina seems to have welcomed the English and encouraged their return because he believed that they could be useful and that they could be controlled. It was a tragic if understandable miscalculation—one that Indian leaders would make again and again in colonial America.

Raleigh apparently aimed to establish on Roanoke a mining camp and a military garrison. In a stroke of genius, he included in the company of 108 men a scientist, Thomas Hariot, to study the country's natural resources and an artist, John White, to make drawings of the Virginia Indians. *A Briefe and True Reporte of the New Found Land of Virginia* (1588), written by Hariot and illustrated by White, served as one of the principal sources about North America and its Indian inhabitants for more than a century. Far less inspired was Raleigh's choice to lead the expedition—two veterans of the Irish campaigns, Sir Richard Grenville and Ralph Lane. Even his fellow conquistadors in Ireland considered Lane proud and greedy. As for Grenville, he was given to breaking wineglasses between his teeth and then swallowing the shards to show that he could stand the sight of blood, even his own.

The bullying ways of both men quickly alienated the natives of Roanoke. Wingina found the newcomers disrespectful, haughty, and cruel: when a local stole a cup, the English tried to teach everyone a lesson by torching his village and destroying its corn stores. As winter arrived and supplies ran low, the hungry colonists made greater and greater demands. The Roanokes' resentment fueled English anxiety that a revolt was brewing, and these anxieties led only to more brutality and more resentment. The following summer Wingina made a final attempt to regain control of the situation. He had agreed to parlay with Lane about improving relations. But the meeting was a ruse. Lane's men opened fire at the Indian envoys, killed Wingina, and hacked the head from his body. All that averted a massive counterattack was the arrival of England's preeminent privateer, Sir Francis Drake, fresh from freebooting up and down the Caribbean. The settlement's 102 survivors piled onto Drake's ships and put an ocean between themselves and the avenging Roanokes.

A Second Roanoke—and Croatoan

Undaunted, Raleigh organized a second expedition to plant a colony farther north, in Chesapeake Bay. He now projected an agricultural community of manors, much like those in England. He recruited 119 men, women, and children, members of the English middle class, and granted each person an estate of 500 acres. He also appointed as governor the artist John White, who brought along a suit of armor for ceremonial occasions.

White deplored Lane's treachery toward Wingina and hated the brazen, senseless violence that had characterized the entire endeavor. The artist had spent his time on Roanoke closely observing native peoples, their material cultures, and their customs. His sensitive watercolors, especially those featuring women and children, indicate a genuine respect and affection. White felt strongly that under prudent, moral leaders an English colony could indeed coexist peacefully with American Indians.

Despite his best intentions, everything went wrong. In July of 1587 the expedition's pilot, Simon Ferdinando, insisted on leaving the colonists at Roanoke Island rather than along Chesapeake Bay. Understandably, the Roanokes took no pleasure in seeing the English return, and even before Ferdinando weighed anchor the settlers began skirmishing with Indians. Sensing that the situation on Roanoke could quickly become desperate, the colonists prevailed on White to sail back with Ferdinando and bring reinforcements.

But White returned home in 1588 just as the massive Spanish navy, the Armada, was marshaling for an assault on England. Elizabeth enlisted every seaworthy ship and able-bodied sailor in her realm to stave off invasion. The Armada was defeated, but Raleigh left the Roanoke colonists to fend for themselves. When White finally returned to Roanoke Island in 1590, he found only an empty fort and a few cottages in a clearing. The sole clue to the colony's fate was carved on a post: CROATOAN. It was the name of a nearby island off Cape Hatteras.

Had the Roanoke colonists fled to Croatoan for safety? Had they moved to the mainland and joined Indian communities? Had they been killed by Wingina's people? The fate of the "lost colony" remains a mystery, though later rumors suggest that the missing colonists merged with native societies in the interior. His dream of a tolerant, cooperative colony dashed, White sailed back to England, leaving behind the little cluster of cottages, which would soon be overgrown with vines, and his suit of armor, which was already "almost eaten through with rust."

All the world lay before them. Or so it had seemed to the young men from England's West Country who dreamed of gold and glory, conquest and colonization. True, they lived on the fringe of the civilized world in the fifteenth and sixteenth centuries. China remained the distant, exotic kingdom of power and wealth, supplying silks and spices and other luxurious goods. Islamic empires stood astride the land routes from Europe to the east. Nations on the western edge of Europe thus took to the seas. Portugal sent slave and gold traders to Africa, as well as merchants to trade with the civilizations of the Indies. Spanish conquerors such as Cortés toppled Indian empires and brought home mountains of silver. But England's West County sea dogs—would-be conquistadors—met only with frustration. In 1600, more than a century after Columbus's first crossing, not a single English settlement existed in the Americas. The Atlantic had devoured Humphrey Gilbert before he even reached America; Raleigh's Roanoke ventures lay in ruins.

What was left of the freebooting world of West Country adventurers? Raleigh, his ambition unquenchable, sailed to South America in quest of a rich city named El Dorado. In 1603, however, Elizabeth's death brought to the English throne her cousin James I, the

John White's sensitive watercolor Indian Elder or Chief *may well be of Wingina. The portrayal includes the copper ornament worn hanging from his neck, indicating high social status and the presence of an active trade network, since copper is not found on the island. Just as Raleigh had to gauge his strategy in dealing with the Indians, Wingina had to decide how to treat the strange newcomers from across the Atlantic.*

founder of the Stuart dynasty. The new king arrested the old queen's favorite for treason and imprisoned him for 15 years in the Tower of London. Set free in 1618 at the age of 64, Raleigh returned to South America, his lust for El Dorado undiminished. Along the way he plundered some Spanish silver ships, defying King James's orders. It was a fatal mistake, for England had made peace with Spain. Raleigh lost his head.

James I did not want to harass the king of Spain; he wanted to imitate him. The Stuarts were even more determined than the Tudors had been to enlarge the sphere of royal power. There would be no room in America for a warrior nobility of conquistadors, no room for a feudal fiefdom ruled by the likes of Raleigh or Gilbert. Instead, there would be English colonies in America like the new outpost of Jamestown, planted on the Chesapeake Bay in Virginia in 1607. There would be profitable plantations and other bold enterprises, enriching English royalty and managed by loyal, efficient bureaucrats. Colonizing America would strengthen English monarchs, paving their path to greater power, just as the dominions of Mexico and Peru had enlarged the authority of the Spanish Crown. America would be the making of kings and queens.

Or would it? For some Europeans, weary of freebooting conquistadors and sea rovers, the order and security that Crown rule and centralized states promoted in western Europe would be enough. But others, men and women who were often desperate and sometimes idealistic, would cast their eyes west across the Atlantic and want more.

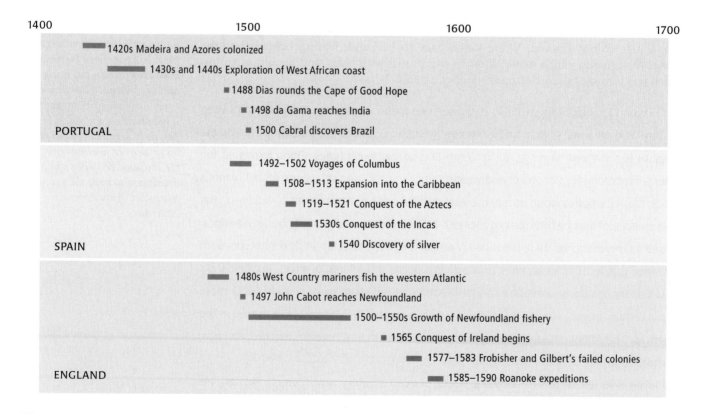

1400   1500   1600   1700

PORTUGAL
- 1420s Madeira and Azores colonized
- 1430s and 1440s Exploration of West African coast
- 1488 Dias rounds the Cape of Good Hope
- 1498 da Gama reaches India
- 1500 Cabral discovers Brazil

SPAIN
- 1492–1502 Voyages of Columbus
- 1508–1513 Expansion into the Caribbean
- 1519–1521 Conquest of the Aztecs
- 1530s Conquest of the Incas
- 1540 Discovery of silver

ENGLAND
- 1480s West Country mariners fish the western Atlantic
- 1497 John Cabot reaches Newfoundland
- 1500–1550s Growth of Newfoundland fishery
- 1565 Conquest of Ireland begins
- 1577–1583 Frobisher and Gilbert's failed colonies
- 1585–1590 Roanoke expeditions

European Exploration: Fifteenth and Sixteenth Centuries

Significant Events

ca. 1300	Rise of the Aztec empire
1347	First outbreak of the Black Death in Europe
1420s	Portuguese settlements in the Atlantic islands
1488	Dias rounds the tip of Africa
1492	Columbus discovers America
1497	John Cabot discovers Newfoundland
1498	da Gama reaches India
1517	Luther posts his 95 theses
1519–1522	Magellan circumnavigates the globe
1521	Tenochtitlán surrenders to Cortés
1528	Narváez leads expedition to Florida
1539	Coronado begins exploration of present-day Southwest
1540	Discovery of silver in Mexico and Peru
1558	Elizabeth I becomes queen of England
1565	England begins its conquest of Ireland
1583	Gilbert's quest for a North American colony
1584–1590	Roanoke voyages

Chapter Summary

During the late fifteenth century, Europeans and Africans made their first contact with the Americas, where native cultures were numerous and diverse.

- During the fourteenth and early fifteenth centuries, Western Europeans were on the fringes of an international economy drawn together by Chinese goods such as spices, ceramics, and silks.

- A combination of technological advances, the rise of new trade networks and techniques, and increased political centralization made Europe's expansion overseas possible.

- Led by Portugal, European expansion began with a push southward along the West African coast, in pursuit of spices, ivory, and gold. As sugar plantations were established in the islands of the eastern Atlantic, a slave trade in Africans became a part of this expansive commerce.

- Spain took the lead in exploring and colonizing the Americas, consolidating a vast and profitable empire of its own in the place of Aztec and Inca empires. Divisions within Indian empires and the devastating effects of European diseases made Spanish conquest possible.

- The conquistadors who led the Spanish occupation were soon replaced by an elaborate, centralized royal bureaucracy, which regulated nearly every aspect of economic and social life. The discovery of silver provided Spain with immense wealth, while leading to sharply increased mortality among the native population.

- Spanish conquistadors also explored much of the present-day southeastern and southwestern United States. They found no cities, silver mines, or rich empires and were thwarted by the Indian peoples they encountered.

- The Protestant Reformation was inaugurated by Martin Luther in 1517 and carried on by John Calvin, whose more activist theology spread from his headquarters in Geneva outward to England, Scotland, the Netherlands, and the Huguenots in France.

- England, apprehensive of Spain's power, did not turn its attention to exploration and colonization until the 1570s and 1580s. By the time it did, European rivalries were heightened by splits arising out of the Protestant Reformation.

- England's merchants and gentry lent support to colonizing ventures, although early efforts, such as those at Roanoke, failed.

Additional Reading

For a description of the entrepreneurs, mariners, and ordinary folk who participated in the era of exploration and discovery, see Kenneth R. Andrews, *Trade, Plunder, and Settlement: Maritime Enterprise and the Genesis of the British Empire, 1480–1630* (1985). For Portugal's initial expansion, see Malyn Newitt, *A History of Portuguese Overseas Expansion, 1400–1668* (2004). John Thornton's *Africa and Africans in the Making of the Atlantic World 1400–1680* (1992) is a detailed analysis of West Africa's role in the changing international economy. For sugar as an engine of expansion, see Philip D. Curtin, *The Rise and Fall of the Plantation Complex: Essays in Atlantic History* (2nd ed., 1998). The demographic catastrophe that followed contact is explored in Noble David Cook, *Born to Die: Disease and New World Conquests* (1998). For a contemporary classic that puts European expansion in global perspective, see *Jared Diamond, Guns, Germs, and Steel: The Fates of Human Societies* (1998).

For Spain in the Caribbean, see Carl Ortwin Sauer, *The Early Spanish Main* (1966). For a scholarly overview of Indians in central Mexico after Cortés, rooted in native language sources, see James Lockhart, *The Nahuas after Conquest: A Social and Cultural History of the Indians of Central Mexico, Sixteenth through Eighteenth Centuries* (1992).

For a magisterial narrative of Spain's activities in North America, see David J. Weber, *The Spanish Frontier in North America* (1992). Rolena Adorno and Patrick Charles Pautz's translation of *The Narrative of Cabeza de Vaca* (2003) is unsurpassed, and Coronado's sojourn is the subject of the exacting work by Richard Flint and Shirley Cushing Flint, *Documents of the Coronado Expedition, 1539–1542* (2005). For the Southeast, see Charles Hudson, *Knights of Spain, Warriors of the Sun: Hernando de Soto and the South's Ancient Chiefdoms* (1997).

For a good introduction to the Reformation in England, see Patrick Collinson, *The Birthpangs of Protestant England* (1988) and Christopher Haigh, *English Revolutions* (1993); Eamon Duffy's *The Voices of Morebath* (2001) offers a vivid depiction of how the Reformation transformed the lives of ordinary people. For early English attempts at colonization, in both Ireland and the Americas, consult the works of Nicholas Canny in the Bibliography, as well as David Beers Quinn, *Set Fair for Roanoke* (1985) and Karen Kupperman, *Roanoake* (1984).

For a fuller list of readings, see the Bibliography at www.mhhe.com/davidsonnation6.

CHAPTER 3
Colonization and Conflict in the South
1600~1750

When the English attempted to crown Powhatan as a subject king, he may have sent King James I this cloak as a reciprocal present. Made from four tanned deerskins, the mantle is decorated with many small marine shells sewn into designs. In addition to human and animal figures, the cloak has 34 roundlets that may represent the Indian districts under Powhatan's control.

Outlandish Strangers

In the year 1617, European time, on a bay Europeans called the Chesapeake, in a land they named Virginia, the mighty weroance Powhatan surveyed his domain. It had all worked according to plan, and Powhatan, leader of the Pamunkeys, had laid his plans carefully. While in his prime, the tall, robust man had drawn some 30 villages along the Virginia coast into a powerful confederacy. As tribute for his protection and leadership, Powhatan collected food, furs, and skins. He forged alliances with communities too distant or too powerful for him to dominate. He married the daughters of prominent men, dozens in all, to solidify his network of patronage and power.

By 1607 Powhatan's confederacy numbered nearly 9,000 souls, a political alliance that had overcome formidable obstacles. The natives of the Chesapeake, like the peoples who inhabited the length of eastern North America, lived for most of the year in small agricultural villages. During certain seasons, though, they ranged over hunting and fishing grounds, following the game from one season to the next. Rivalries over trade, territorial boundaries, and leadership had often erupted into armed conflict. Some coastal villages had fiercely resisted Powhatan's efforts to incorporate them; some peoples to the west still threatened the security of his confederacy.

After 1607 Powhatan was forced to take into account yet another group. The English, as this new people called themselves, came by sea, crammed into three ships. They were 100 men and 4 boys, all clad in heavy, outlandish clothing, many dressed in gaudy colors. The ships followed a river deep into Powhatan's territory and built a fort on a swampy, mosquito-infested site that they called Jamestown.

Powhatan was not frightened. He knew of these strangers from across the waters. The English had larger boats and louder, more deadly weapons than his people did. But the Indians quickly learned how to use guns, and they vastly outnumbered the English, a clumsy, unprepared, and inferior race who seemed unlikely to live long and prosper in Powhatan's land. Even amidst the bounty of the Chesapeake they failed to feed themselves. With bows and arrows, spears and nets, Indian men brought in an abundance of meat and fish. Fields tended by Indian women yielded generous crops of corn, beans, squash, and melon, and edible nuts and fruits grew wild. Still the English starved, and not just during the first few months of their settlement but for several years afterward.

Powhatan could understand why the English refused to grow food. Cultivating crops was women's work—like building houses; or making clothing, pottery, and baskets; or caring for children. And the English settlement included no women until two arrived in the fall of 1608. Yet even after more women came, the English still starved, and they expected—no, they demanded—that Powhatan's people feed them.

And yet these hapless folk put on such airs. They boasted about the power of their god—they had only one—and denounced the Indians' "devil-worship" of "false gods." They crowed endlessly about the power of their king, James I, who expected Powhatan to become his vassal. The English had even planned a "coronation" to crown Powhatan as a "subject king." He was unimpressed. "If your king has sent me presents," he responded, "I also am a king, and this is my land. . . . Your father is to come to me, not I to him." In the end the English did come to Powhatan, only to find what "a fowle trouble there was to make him kneele to receave his crowne. . . . [he] indured so many perswasions, examples and instructions as tired them all. At last by leaning hard on his shoulders, he a little stooped, and . . . put the Crowne on his head."

Inconceivable to Powhatan—that he should willingly bow before this King James, the ruler of so small and savage a race! When the Indians made war, they killed the male warriors of rival communities but adopted their women and children. But when Powhatan's people withheld food or defended their land from these invaders, the English retaliated by murdering Indian women and children. Worse, the English could not even keep order among themselves. Too many of them wanted to lead, and they squabbled constantly among themselves.

Only one man, a brash fellow called Captain John Smith, had briefly brought order to the English settlement. Powhatan granted him a grudging respect, though Smith's boasts made the other English seem modest by comparison. Smith bragged endlessly of his earlier exploits across the ocean, where he had fought as a soldier of fortune. He told fanciful tales of his irresistible appeal to beautiful women who had rescued him from harrowing perils. A rough man, he bullied the Indians for food and would have enslaved them if it had been in his power. Even so, Smith took a genuine interest in Indian ways.

Those are the Lines that shew thy Face but those
That shew thy Grace and Glory, brighter bee
Thy Faire-Discoueries and Fowle - Over throwes
Of Salvages, much Ciuiliz'd by thee
Best shew thy Spirit and to it Glory Wyn
So, thou art Brasse without but Golde within.

No stranger to self-promotion, Captain John Smith included this portrait of himself and verses celebrating his ennobling exploits at the beginning of his Description of New England *(1616). As the military armor and knightly bearing suggest (note Smith on horseback,* lower right*), the outspoken captain stood in the tradition of West Country adventurers and Spanish conquistadors.*

But the fellow returned to England in 1609 after being injured when some English gunpowder blew up by mistake. Thereafter the newcomers returned to squabbling and starving. Small wonder that some English had deserted their settlement to live among Powhatan's people. Anyone could see the superiority of Indian culture to English ways.

The temptation to wipe out the helpless, troublesome, arrogant tribe of English—or simply to let them starve to death—had been almost overwhelming. But Powhatan allowed the English to survive. Like Wingina before him, he decided that even these barbaric people had their uses. English labor, English trading goods, and, most important, English guns would help quell resistance within his confederacy and subdue his Indian rivals to the west.

In 1614 Powhatan cemented his claim on the English and their weapons with the marriage between his favorite child, Pocahontas, and an ambitious Englishman, John Rolfe.

By 1617 events had vindicated Powhatan's strategy of tolerating the English. His chiefdom flourished, ready to be passed on to his brother. Powhatan's people still outnumbered the English, who seldom starved outright now but continued to fight among themselves and sicken and die. Only one thing had changed in the Chesapeake by 1617: the English were clearing woodland along the rivers and planting tobacco.

That was the doing of Powhatan's son-in-law, Rolfe, a man as strange as the rest of the newcomers, all of them eager to store up wealth and worldly goods. Rolfe had been obsessed with finding a crop that could be grown in Virginia and then sold for gain across the sea. When he succeeded by growing tobacco, other English followed his lead. Odder still, not women but men tended the tobacco fields. Here was more evidence of English inferiority. Men wasted long hours laboring when they might supply their needs with far less effort.

In 1617 Powhatan, ruler of the Pamunkeys, surveyed his domain, and sometime in that year, he looked no longer. He had lived long enough to see the tobacco fields lining the riverbanks, straddling the charred stumps of felled trees. But perhaps he went to his grave believing that he had done what Wingina had failed to do: bend the English to his purposes. He died before those stinking tobacco weeds spread over the length of his land and sent his hard-won dominion up in smoke.

Wingina and Powhattan were not the only native leaders that dreamed of turning Europeans to their advantage. Across North America, the fleeting if destructive encounters of the sixteenth century gave way to sustained colonialism in the seventeenth. As Europeans began to settle the edges of North America in earnest, Indian peoples struggled not only to survive and adapt to new realities but also, when possible, to profit from the rapid changes swirling around them.

Those often dramatic changes reflected upheavals underway all across the globe. The tobacco John Rolfe had begun to cultivate was only one of several plantation **monocultures** that Europeans began to establish in their far-flung colonies. Sugar, already flourishing in the Atlantic islands off the coast of West Africa, was gaining a foothold in the islands of the Caribbean. Rice, long a staple in Asia and grown also in Africa, made its way into South Carolina toward the end of the seventeenth century. Because these crops were grown most efficiently on plantations and required intensive labor, African slavery spread during these years, fueled by an expanding international slave trade. Whites, blacks, and Indians were all, in different ways, caught up in the wrenching transformations.

The Rise of Plantation
Monocultures and Slave
Labor Systems

Spain's North American Colonies

Just as Spain had been the first European power to explore North America's interior, so too it led the way in establishing lasting colonies north of Mexico. But while France and especially England would eventually colonize territory ideally suited to European-style agriculture, territory capable of sustaining large colonial populations, Spain confined its North American ventures to the ecologically challenging regions of the upper Rio Grande and coastal Florida. Because economic opportunities and quality farmland existed in abundance elsewhere in Spanish America, relatively few Spaniards chose to eke out an existence in distant and difficult northern outposts. Nonetheless, Spain's colonial endeavors would have tremendous implications for North America's native peoples and for the geopolitics of the continent as a whole.

The Founding of a "New" Mexico

By the 1590s Coronado's dismal expedition a half-century earlier had been all but forgotten. Again, rumors were circulating in Mexico about great riches in the North. New Spain's viceroy began casting about for a champion of means to establish a "new" Mexico, one perhaps as magnificent and profitable as its namesake. He chose Juan de Oñate, son of one of New Spain's richest miners and husband to Isabel de Tolosa Cortés Moctezuma, granddaughter of Hernán Cortés and great-granddaughter of Moctezuma. Oñate needed wealthy connections. Colonizing New Mexico would eventually cost him and his backers more than half a million pesos. But the would-be conquistador expected to recoup the investment with ease. Ignorant of North America's geography and overestimating New Mexico's riches, Oñate even requested and received permission to sail ships up the Pacific to Pueblo country, so that twice a year he could resupply his would-be colony and export its expected treasures.

The magnitude of his mistaken assumptions began coming into focus in 1598, when he led 500 colonists, soldiers, and slaves to the Upper Rio Grande and, like Coronado before him, found modest villages, no ocean, and no evidence of significant mineral wealth. But, whatever the disappointments, Oñate had come with women and children, with livestock and tools, with artisans and tradesmen, with seeds and books and bibles. He had come to stay. Eager to avoid the violence of earlier encounters, and perhaps hopeful of a mutually beneficial relationship, Tewa-speaking Pueblos evacuated a village for the newcomers to use. Many native leaders pledged Oñate their allegience, Pueblo artisans labored on irrigation systems and other public works for the Spaniards, and Indian women (traditionally the builders in Pueblo society) constructed the region's first Catholic church.

Cautious Relations

The colonizers mistook this cautious courtesy for subservience. Oñate's oldest nephew, Juan de Zaldivar, was bolder and cruder than most. At Acoma Pueblo, known today as "Sky City" because of its position high atop a majestic mesa, he brazenly siezed several sacred turkeys to kill and eat, answering Indian protests with insults. Outraged, Acoma's men fell upon Zaldivar, killing him and several of his companions. Oñate responded by putting Zaldivar's younger brother Vicente in command of a punitive expedition. Fueled by grief and rage, Vicente de Zaldivar and his men laid siege to the Pueblo, killed perhaps 800 of its people, and made slaves of several hundred more. Following up on these punishments, Oñate decreed that all adult male survivors were to have one foot chopped off, so that they might spend their lives as limping advertisements for Spanish power. Scholars now doubt that this sentence was actually carried

The Acoma Siege

Like many other Pueblo peoples, the founders of Acoma built their village atop a sandstone mesa to gain protection from enemies. Constructed in the 12th century C.E., Acoma may be the oldest continuously occupied settlement in the present-day United States.

The Mystery of the Sawed-Off Foot

Estevan Arrellano, the director of New Mexico's Juan de Oñate Monument Visitor's Center, couldn't understand it. One January morning in 1998 Arrellano had arrived at work to find that someone had sawed off the right foot of a new bronze statue of Oñate, the man who founded New Mexico's first Spanish colony in 1598. The vandals soon released a statement. "We took the liberty of removing Oñate's right foot on behalf of our brothers and sisters of Acoma Pueblo," they wrote.

Anyone familiar with the region's brutal colonial history understood the connection. In response to an uprising at Acoma Peublo, Oñate had destroyed the village, condemned its women and children to slavery, and ordered that every Acoma man twenty-five and older have his right foot chopped off. Thus, an explanation for the vandalized statue, which Arrellano had to have repaired. "Give me a break," he complained. "It was 400 years ago. It's O.K. to hold a grudge, but for 400 years?"

In fact, monuments to and celebrations of the "distant" past often provoke passionate disagreements in the present. Some Anglo New Mexicans resent the fact that more is not done to memorialize Stephen W. Kearny and other military figures that seized New Mexico for the United States in 1846. New Mexico recently sent a statue of Popé, the leader of the Pueblo Revolt, to represent the state in the Hall of Statues in the U.S. Capitol, despite the protests of some Hispanics that Popé and his followers had massacred Spanish men, women, and children. And, although many Hispanic New Mexicans want to celebrate Oñate as a way to insist on their own centrality to New Mexico's

history – a desire all the more intense now that Hispanics are no longer the majority population in the state – many native peoples insist that celebrations of conquistadors implicitly denigrate the suffering and even the humanity of their own ancestors.

As long as history is relevant to contemporary politics, economics, and culture, partisans will continue to fight over the past with memorials, petitions, marches, statues, and even electric saws.

out, but even today, many Pueblos still consider Oñate's harsh edict as emblematic of Spanish cruelty. (For one recent reaction, see After the Fact in Brief above). Whether or not Oñate executed his cruel judgment, the savagery of the Acoma siege and the brutal repression of other acts of defiance educated all of the region's native communities about the risks of resistance.

Impoverished New Mexico

But it was easier to instill terror than grow rich. Desperate to salvage their enterprise and turn their investments to account, Oñate and key followers toiled on long, fruitless expeditions in search of gold, silver, and cities, and a place to dock those biannual ships. Some more practical entreprenuers decided to exploit the resources they could see. The younger Zaldívar, headstrong conquerer of Acoma, spent time with Apache hunters and decided it would be more efficent to domesticate bison than search for them on the plains. He and his men labored for three days to build a sprawling cottonwood corral, only to discover that bison were "stubborn animals, brave beyond praise," dangerous to catch, and virtually impossible to hold. With varying degrees of enthusiasm, most Spaniards had to turn to more mundane and less hazardous pursuits, to farming and husbandry, in order to support themselves and their families. Others despaired of even securing a living in arid New Mexico, let alone getting rich. The Spanish crown had promised to make minor nobles of those who stayed at least five years, but many spurned even this incentive and fled back into New Spain.

They were not the only ones losing confidence. In 1606, royal authorities removed Oñate from his position, brought him up on charges of mismanagement, and, as they had with Coronado, accused him of abusing Indians. Ruined, the would-be conquerer spent the rest of his days struggling to rebuild his fortune and clear his name. Meanwhile a new viceroy decided that the colonization of "worthless" New Mexico had been an expensive mistake and began planning for its evacuation. The colony would have been abandoned but for the Franciscan religious order. Arguing that it would be a crime and a sin to forsake the many thousands of Indians they claimed to have baptised since 1598, the Franciscans convinced a skeptical King Philip III to continue supporting his outpost on the upper Rio Grande.

The Growth of Spanish Florida

Franciscans Renew Spain's Efforts

Franciscans would become key actors in Spanish North America. Members of a medieval religious order founded by St. Francis of Assisi, Franciscan monks foreswore property, remained **celibate,** and survived by begging for alms or accepting donations from wealthy patrons. Like their peers and occasional rivals the Jesuits, Franciscans wore only sandals, simple robes, and a rope belt and took it as their charge to live with and minister to the poor. Contact with the Americas reinvigorated their mission. Franciscans accompanied Columbus on his second voyage, and they began ministering to the Indians of central Mexico soon after Tenochtitlán fell. By the 1570s, Spanish authorities started secularizing central Mexico's missions, transforming them into self-supporting parishes, and the friars looked to the frontiers for new fields of conversion. Jesuits established several missions in present-day Arizona, and Franciscans went on to become powerful figures in colonial New Mexico.

Florida's Strategic Importance

The Crown needed them, nowhere more so than in Florida. Seventeenth-century New Mexico was a Catholic obligation for Spain's monarchs but a small worry compared with the strategic importance of Florida. As long as pirates or rival colonies on the Atlantic seaboard threatened Spanish shipping, the king had to control Florida.

Artist Jacques Le Moyne recorded this scene of Florida Indians holding council in the 1560s. Observers from Jean Ribaut's French expedition can be seen in the foreground.

Pedro Menéndez de Avilés did much to secure the peninsula in the 1560s when he destroyed France's Fort Caroline and established several Spanish posts on the coast (see Chapter 2). By the 1580s, however, the energetic Menéndez was dead and nearly all his coastal establishments destroyed by Indians or privateers. Only St. Augustine endured, with a population of perhaps 500 in 1600. Spanish Florida needed something more than a beachhead along the coast if it was to survive.

The king turned to the Franciscans, as part of a two-stage policy to consolidate his influence over Florida's interior. First, royal administrators enticed or menaced the peninsula's many native peoples into alliances. In return for trade privileges and regular diplomatic presents, native leaders promised to trade with no other European power, support the Spanish in war, and tax their people on behalf of the Spaniards. Second, allied Indian communities were made to accept Franciscan missions and a few resident soldiers, a policy that would be critical to molding and monitoring native villages. Franciscans set about their work with characteristic determination. By 1675, 40 missions were ministering to as many as 26,000 baptized Indians. That same year, the bishop of Cuba toured Florida and spoke enthusiastically of converts who embraced "with devotion the mysteries of our holy faith."

Spain's plan for Florida seemed to be working, barely. St. Augustine had grown to a settlement of 1,500 by the time of the bishop's tour. Still, Florida's mission system and network of Indian alliances convinced Spanish authorities that they could maintain their grip on this crucial peninsula.

Franciscan Florida

Popé and the Pueblo Revolt

As the seventeenth century progressed, Spain's colony in New Mexico also seemed to stabilize. Although more than a few desperate colonists fled south, enough remained to establish a separate Spanish town, El Villa Real de Santa Fe, in 1610. Santa Fe (the second-oldest European town in the United States after St. Augustine) became the hub of Spanish life in New Mexico. The demands of agriculture and stock raising forced many families to settle elsewhere on the Rio Grande, on well-watered lands near Pueblo villages. Economic and political life revolved around a dozen prominent families. By 1675 New Mexico had a colonial population of perhaps 2,500. It was a diverse

This Native American drawing on a canyon wall in present-day Arizona represents the progress of the Spanish into the Southwest. The prominence of horses underscores their novelty to the Indians, an initial advantage enjoyed by the invaders. "The most essential thing in new lands is horses," one of Coronado's men emphasized. "They instill the greatest fear in the enemy and make the Indians respect the leaders of the army." Many Indian peoples soon put the horse to their own uses, however, and even outshone the Spanish in their riding skills.

community, including Spaniards, Africans, Mexican Indians, mestizos (persons of mixed Spanish-Indian heritage), and mulattos (of Spanish-African heritage).

Indian Captives

This population of 2,500 also included large numbers of Indian captives. Occasionally captives came to Spanish households through war, as after the siege of Acoma. In addition, Spaniards purchased enslaved women and children from other Indians and regularly launched slave raids against so-called enemy Indians such as Utes, Apaches, and Navajos. By 1680 half of all New Mexican households included at least one Indian captive, someone who, depending on age, gender, and the master's disposition, could be treated affectionately as a low-status family member or terrorized and abused as disposable human property.

The colonists also extracted labor from Pueblo Indians. Officially Pueblo households had to surrender three bushels of corn and one processed hide or large cotton blanket each year. Pueblos were also sometimes made to labor on public works, and elite Spaniards often exploited their privileges by insisting on more tribute and labor than legally allowed. Still, the populous Pueblos would have been able to satisfy Spanish demands with little difficulty but for other changes in their world. First and most importantly, colonialism meant epidemics. Smallpox arrived in the early 1620s. In less than a generation the Pueblo population plumeted by 70 percent, to about 30,000. Whereas New Mexico had approximately 100 native villages at contact, by 1680 only 30 remained inhabited. Infestations of locusts, severe droughts, and crop failures compounded the crisis. By 1667 a distraught Franciscan reported widespread famine, with native men, women, and children "lying dead along the roads, in the ravines, and in their hovels." Mounted Utes, Apaches, and Navajos, embittered by New Mexican slaving and barred from their customary trade in the pueblos, launched punishing raids against the most vulnerable Pueblo villages.

Pueblo Suffering

In their deepening misery Pueblos turned to religion—their own. Since 1598, the Franciscans had worked tirelessly to supress the dances, idols, and ceremonies that long mediated Pueblo relationships with the divine. By the 1670s Pueblo elders could

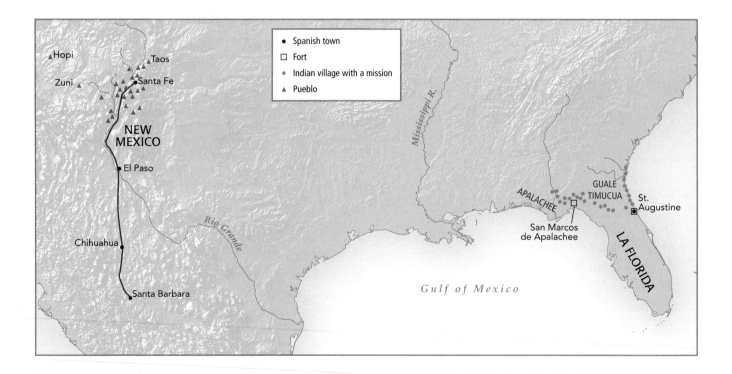

Spanish Missions in North America, ca. 1675   *From St. Augustine, Spanish missionaries spread north into Guale Indian villages in present-day Georgia and westward among the Indians of Timucua, Apalachee, and Apalachicola. In New Mexico, missions radiated outward from the Rio Grande, as distant as Hopi Pueblo in the west.*

argue convincingly that the calamities of the past decades could be reversed only by a rejection of Christianity and a return to the old faith. Such revivalist sentiments threw the friars into a panic. Franciscans and civil authorities scrambled to extinguish the movement, arresting key Pueblo leaders, executing two and whipping 43 others in front of large crowds.

One of the 43, a prominent Tewa man known to history as Popé, nursed his wounds in Taos and laid the groundwork for a general uprising against the Spaniards. Appealing to headmen throughout the Pueblo world, Popé called for a war to purify the land. Many individuals and some entire villages refused to participate. But on August 10, 1680, Indians from across New Mexico rose up and began killing Spaniards. Astonished survivors fled to Santa Fe, followed by Popé and his army, who put the town to siege. Weeks later the desperate Spanish governor, wounded by an arrow in the face and a gunshot to the chest, gathered the remainder of the colonial population and fled south out of New Mexico. The most successful pan-Indian uprising in North American history, the Pueblo Revolt sent shock waves throughout Spanish America and left the Catholic devout agonizing over what they might have done to provoke God's wrath.

English Society on the Chesapeake

By 1700, then, Spain viewed its situation in the Americas from a very different perspective than it had 100 years earlier. The Pueblo Revolt had checked its power at the northern reach of its American possessions. Equally disturbing was the progress of Spain's European rivals in the Americas during the seventeenth century. During the sixteenth, both France and England had envied the wealth Spain reaped from its American conquests. But neither nation did much to check Spain's power, beyond preying on Spanish ships and fishing for cod. During the seventeenth century, this would change.

In fact, by 1600 other European kingdoms were beginning to view overseas colonies as essential to a nation's power and prosperity. They did so in part because of an economic model known as **mercantilism,** which guided Europe's commercial expansion for 200 years. (The theory was so named by the eighteenth-century economist Adam Smith.) Mercantilists called for the state to regulate and protect industry and commerce. Their primary objective was to enrich the nation by fostering a favorable balance of trade. Once the value of exports exceeded the cost of imports, they theorized, gold and silver would flow into home ports.

Mercantilism

If a nation could make do without any imports from other countries, so much the better. It was here that the idea of colonies entered the mercantilist scheme. Colonial producers would supply raw materials that the mother country could not produce, while colonial consumers swelled demand for the finished goods and financial services that the mother country could provide. Convinced that colonies would enhance national self-sufficiency, mercantilists urged states to sponsor overseas settlements.

Mercantilist notions appealed to Europe's monarchs. A thriving trade meant that more taxes and customs duties would fill royal coffers, increasing royal power. That logic led England's King James I to approve a private venture to colonize the Chesapeake Bay, a sprawling inlet of the Atlantic Ocean fed by over 100 rivers and streams.

The Virginia Company

In 1606, the king granted a charter to a number of English merchants, gentlemen, and aristocrats, incorporating them as the Virginia Company of London. The members of the new **joint stock company** sold stock in their venture to English investors, as well as awarding a share to those willing to settle in Virginia at their own expense. With the proceeds from the sale of stock, the company planned to send to Virginia hundreds of poor and unemployed people as well as scores of skilled craftworkers. These laborers were to serve the company for seven years in return for their passage, pooling

In Jamestown's early years its military orientation was clear. The fort's heavy palisades and its strategic location upriver and some distance inland underscore the colonists' concern for defense—as does the imposing figure of Powhatan seated at the right.

their efforts to produce any commodities that would return a profit to stockholders. If gold and silver could not be found, perhaps North America would yield other valuable commodities—furs, pitch, tar, or lumber. In the spring of 1607—nearly a decade after Oñate had launched Spain's colonies in New Mexico—the first expedition dispatched by the Virginia Company founded Jamestown.

Jamestown's Problems

Making the first of many mistakes, Jamestown's 104 men and boys pitched their fort on an inland peninsula in order to prevent a surprise attack from the Spanish. Unfortunately, the marshy, thickly wooded site served as an ideal breeding ground for malaria. The settlers, as well as those who followed them, were weakened by bouts of the disease and beset by dysentery, typhoid, and yellow fever. They died by the scores.

Even before sickness took its toll, many of Jamestown's colonists had little taste for labor. The gentlemen of the expedition expected to lead rather than to work, while most of the other early settlers were gentlemen's servants and craftworkers who knew nothing about growing crops. As did the colonists on Roanoke, Jamestown's settlers resorted to bullying native people for food. Many colonists suffered from malnutrition, which heightened their susceptibility to disease. Only 60 of Jamestown's 500 inhabitants lived through the winter of 1609–1610, known as the "starving time." Some desperate colonists unearthed and ate corpses; one settler even butchered his wife. De facto martial law failed to turn the situation around, and skirmishes with the Indians became more brutal and frequent as rows of tobacco plants steadily invaded tribal lands.

Reform and a Boom in Tobacco

Key Reforms

Determined to salvage their investment, Virginia Company managers in 1618 set in place sweeping reforms. To attract more capital and colonists, the company established a "headright" system for granting land to individuals. Those already settled in the colony received 100 acres apiece. New settlers each received 50 acres, and anyone who paid the passage of other immigrants to Virginia—either family members or servants—received 50 acres per "head." The company also abolished martial law, allowing the planters to elect a representative assembly. Along with a governor and an advisory council appointed by the company, the House of Burgesses had the authority to make laws for the colony. It met for the first time in 1619, beginning what would become a strong tradition of representative government in the English colonies.

The new measures met with immediate success. The free and unfree laborers who poured into Virginia during the 1620s made up the first wave of an English migration to the Chesapeake that numbered between 130,000 and 150,000 over the seventeenth century. Drawn from the ranks of ordinary English working people, the immigrants were largely men, outnumbering women by six to one. Most were young, ranging in age from 15 to 24. Because of their youth, most lacked skills or wealth. Some of those who came to the Chesapeake as free immigrants prospered as Virginia's tobacco economy took off. When in the 1620s demand soared and prices peaked in European markets, colonists with an eye for profit planted every inch of their farms in tobacco and reaped windfalls.

Indentured servants accounted for three-quarters of all immigrants to Virginia. For most of them, the crossing was simply the last of many moves made in the hope of finding work. Although England's population had been rising since the middle of the fifteenth century, the demand for farm laborers was falling because many landowners were converting croplands into pastures for sheep. The search for work pushed young men and women out of their villages, sending them through the countryside and then into the cities. Down and out in London, Bristol, or Liverpool, some decided to make their next move across the Atlantic and signed **indentures.** Pamphlets promoting immigration promised abundant land and quick riches once servants had finished their terms of four to seven years.

Indentured Servants

Even the most skeptical immigrants were shocked at what they found. The death rate in Virginia during the 1620s was higher than that of England during times of epidemic disease. The life expectancy for Chesapeake men who reached the age of 20 was a mere 48 years; for women it was lower still. Servants fared worst of all, because malnutrition, overwork, and abuse made them vulnerable to disease. As masters scrambled to make quick profits, they extracted the maximum amount of work before death carried off their laborers. An estimated 40 percent of servants did not survive to the end of their indentured terms.

The expanding cultivation of tobacco also claimed many lives by putting unbearable pressure on Indian land. After Powhatan's death in 1617, leadership of the confederacy passed to Opechancanough, who watched, year after year, as the tobacco mania grew. In March 1622 he coordinated a sweeping attack on white settlements that killed about a quarter of Virginia's colonial population. English retaliation over the next decade cut down an entire generation of young Indian men, drove the remaining Powhatans to the west, and won the colonists hundreds of thousands more acres for tobacco.

War with the Confederacy

News of the ongoing Indian war jolted English investors into determining the true state of their Virginia venture. It came to light that, despite the tobacco boom, the Virginia Company was plunging toward bankruptcy. Nor was that the worst news. Stockholders discovered that more than 3,000 immigrants had not survived the brutal conditions of Chesapeake life. An investigation by James I revealed the grisly truth, causing the king to dissolve the Virginia Company and take control of the colony himself in 1624. Henceforth Virginia would be governed as a royal colony.

As the tobacco boom broke in the 1630s and 1640s, Virginians began producing more corn and cattle. Nutrition and overall health improved as a result. More and more poor colonists began surviving their indenture and establishing modest farms of their own. For women who survived servitude, prospects were even better. With wives at a premium, single women stood a good chance of improving their status by marriage. Even so, high mortality rates still fractured families: one out of every four children born in the Chesapeake did not survive to maturity, and among those children who reached their 18th birthday, one-third had lost both parents to death.

Decline in Mortality Rates

By 1650 Virginia could boast about 15,000 colonists, although much of that increase resulted from servants and free immigrants arriving in the colony every year. But Virginians looking to expand into more northerly bays of the Chesapeake found their way blocked by a newer English colony.

Colonies of the Chesapeake
Settlements in Virginia and Maryland spread out along the many bays of the Chesapeake, where tobacco could easily be loaded from plantation wharves. The "fall line" on rivers, dividing Tidewater and Piedmont regions, determined the extent of commercial agriculture, since ships could not pick up exports beyond that point.

The Founding of Maryland and the Renewal of Indian Wars

Unlike Virginia, established by a private corporation and later converted into a royal colony, Maryland was founded in 1632 by a single aristocratic family, the Calverts. They held absolute authority to dispose of 10 million acres of land, administer justice, and establish a civil government. All these powers they exercised, granting estates, or "manors," to their friends and dividing other holdings into smaller farms for ordinary immigrants. From all these "tenants"—that is, every settler in the colony—the family collected "quitrents" every year, fees for use of the land. The Calverts appointed a governor and a council to oversee their own interests while allowing the largest landowners to dispense local justice in manorial courts and make laws for the entire colony in a representative assembly.

Virginians liked nothing about Maryland. To begin with, the Calvert family was Catholic and had extended complete religious freedom to all Christians, making

Maryland a haven for Catholics. Worse still, the Marylanders were a source of economic competition. Two thousand inhabitants had settled on Calvert holdings by 1640, virtually all of them planting tobacco on land coveted by the Virginians.

Another obstacle to Virginia's expansion was the remnant of the Powhatan confederacy. Hounded for corn and supplies (most colonial fields grew tobacco rather than food), and constantly pressured by the expanding plantation economy, Virginia's native peoples became desperate and angry enough to risk yet another war. Aged Opechancanough led a new generation of Indians into battle in 1644 against the encroaching Virginia planters. Though his warriors killed several hundred English and brought the frontier to a standstill, Opechancanough was eventually captured and summarily shot through the head. The Powhatan confederacy died with him. Virginia's Indians would never again be in a position to resist the colony militarily. Over the next decades and centuries, many Indians fled the region altogether. But whole communities remained, quietly determined to continue their lives and traditions in their homeland.

Merchant samples of silk thread from Iran. The East India Company, with its network of trade routes from across Asia, Africa, and Europe, was one English firm that benefited from England's Navigation Acts when it imported goods to America.

Changes in English Policy in the Chesapeake

Throughout the 1630s and 1640s colonial affairs drew little concern from royal officials. England itself had become engulfed first by a political crisis and then by a civil war.

Outraged at the contempt that King Charles I had shown toward Parliament, disaffected **elites** and radical Puritans overthrew the king and executed him in 1649. When the "republic" of Oliver Cromwell turned out to be something closer to a military dictatorship, most English were happy to see their throne restored in 1660 to Charles II, the son of the beheaded king. The new monarch was determined to ensure that not only his subjects at home but also his American colonies abroad contributed to England's prosperity. His colonial policy was reflected in a series of regulations known as the Navigation Acts.

The English Civil War

Navigation Acts

The first, passed by Parliament in 1660, gave England and English colonial merchants a monopoly on the shipping and marketing of all colonial goods. It also ordered that the colonies could export certain "enumerated commodities" only to England or other British ports. These goods included sugar, tobacco, cotton, ginger, indigo (a blue dye), and eventually rice. In 1663 Parliament added another regulation, giving British merchants a virtual monopoly on the sale of European manufactured goods to Americans by requiring that most imports going to the colonies pass through England. In 1673 a third Navigation Act placed duties on the coastal trade of the American colonies and provided for customs officials to collect tariffs and enforce commercial regulations.

These acts were mercantilistic, insofar as they were designed to ensure that England—and no foreign nations or their merchants—would profit from colonial production and trade. Chesapeake planters chafed under the Navigation Acts. They were used to conducting their affairs as they pleased—and they were often pleased to trade with the Dutch. What was worse, the new restrictions came at the same time as a downturn in tobacco prices. In the effort to consolidate its empire, England had unintentionally worsened the economic and social difficulties of Chesapeake society.

Chesapeake Society in Crisis

By the 1660s, overproduction was depressing tobacco prices, and wealthy planters reacted by putting even more prime coastal land into production. Newly freed servants had either to become tenants, or try to establish farms to the west in Indian country. Meanwhile, export duties on tobacco paid under the Navigation Acts helped plunge

Diminishing Opportunities

many small planters into crushing debt, and some were forced back into servitude. By 1676 one-quarter of Virginia's free white men remained landless and frustrated.

Diminishing opportunities in the 1660s and 1670s provided the tinder for unrest in Virginia. As the discontent of the poor mounted, so did the worries of big planters. The assembly of the colony lengthened terms of servitude, hoping to limit the number of servants entering the free population. It curbed the political rights of landless men, hoping to stifle opposition by depriving them of the vote. But these measures only set off a spate of mutinies among servants and protests over rising taxes among small planters.

Bacon's Rebellion and Coode's Rebellion

Those tensions came to a head in 1676. The immediate spark to the rebellion was renewed fighting between desperate Indians and the expanding colonial population. Virginia's royal governor, William Berkeley, favored building forts to guard against Indians, but frontier farmers opposed his plan as an expensive and ineffective way to defend their scattered plantations. As they clamored for an expedition to punish the Indians, Nathaniel Bacon stepped forward to lead it.

Nathaniel Bacon

Wealthy and well connected, Bacon had arrived recently from England, expecting to receive every favor from the governor—including permission to trade with the Indians from his frontier plantation. But Berkeley and a few select friends already held a monopoly on the Indian trade. When they declined to include Bacon, he took up the cause of his poorer frontier neighbors against their common enemy, the governor. Other recent, well-to-do immigrants who resented being excluded from Berkeley's circle of power and patronage also joined Bacon.

In the summer of 1676, Bacon marched into Jamestown with a body of armed men and bullied the assembly into approving his expedition to kill Indians. While Bacon carried out that grisly business, slaughtering friendly as well as hostile Indians, Berkeley rallied his supporters and declared Bacon a rebel. Bacon retaliated by turning his forces against those led by the governor. Both sides sought allies by offering freedom to servants and slaves willing to join their ranks. Many were willing: for months the followers of Bacon and Berkeley plundered one another's plantations. In September 1676 Bacon reduced Jamestown itself to a mound of ashes. It was only his death from dysentery a month later that snuffed out the rebellion.

Political upheaval also shook Maryland, where colonists had long resented the sway of the Calvert family. As proprietors, the Calverts and their favorites monopolized political offices, just as Berkeley's circle had in Virginia. Well-to-do planters wanted a share of the Calverts' power. Smaller farmers, like those in Virginia, wanted a less expensive and more representative government. Compounding the tensions were religious differences: the Calverts and their friends were Catholic, but other colonists, including Maryland's most successful planters, were Protestant.

The unrest among Maryland's discontented planters peaked in July 1689. A former member of the assembly, John Coode, gathered an army, captured the proprietary governor, and then took grievances to authorities in England. There Coode received a sympathetic hearing. The Calverts' charter was revoked and not restored until 1715, by which time the family had become Protestant.

Growing Stability

After 1690 rich planters in both Chesapeake colonies fought among themselves less and cooperated more. In Virginia older leaders and newer arrivals divided the spoils of political office. In Maryland Protestants and Catholics shared power and privilege. Those arrangements ensured that no future Bacon or Coode would mobilize restless gentlemen against the government. By acting together in legislative assemblies, the planter elite managed to curb the power of royal and proprietary governors for decades.

But the greater unity among the Chesapeake's leading families did little to ease that region's most fundamental problem—the sharp inequality of white society. The gulf between rich and poor planters, which had been etched ever more deeply by the troubled tobacco economy, persisted long after the rebellions of Bacon and Coode.

All that saved white society in the Chesapeake from renewed crisis and conflict was the growth of black slavery.

From Servitude to Slavery

Like the tobacco plants that spread across Powhatan's land, a labor system based on African slavery was an on-the-ground innovation. Both early promoters and planters preferred paying for English servants to importing alien African slaves. Black slaves, because they served for life, were more expensive than white workers, who served only for several years. Because neither white nor black immigrants lived long, cheaper servant labor was the logical choice. The black population of the Chesapeake remained small for most of the seventeenth century, constituting just 5 percent of all inhabitants in 1675.

Africans had arrived in Virginia by 1619, most likely via the Dutch, who dominated the slave trade until the middle of the eighteenth century. The lives of those newcomers resembled the lot of white servants, with whom they shared harsh work routines and living conditions. White and black bound laborers socialized with one another and formed sexual liaisons. They conspired to steal from their masters and ran away together; if caught, they endured similar punishments. There was more common ground: many of the first black settlers did not arrive directly from Africa but came from the Caribbean, where some had learned English and had adopted Christian beliefs. And not all were slaves: some were indentured servants. A handful were free.

The Lives of Servants and Slaves

A number of changes after 1680 caused planters to invest more heavily in slaves than in servants. First, as death rates in the Chesapeake began to drop, slaves became a more profitable investment. Although they were more expensive to buy than servants, planters could now expect to get many years of work from their bondspeople. Equally important, masters would have title to the children that slaves were now living long enough to have. At the same time, the influx of white servants was falling off just as the pool of available black labor was expanding. When the Royal African Company lost its monopoly on the English slave trade in 1698, other merchants entered the market. The number of Africans sold by British dealers swelled to 20,000 annually.

Africa and the Atlantic Slave Trade

From 1492 to 1820, enslaved African migrants outnumbered European migrants to the new world by nearly five to one. Put differently, before the twentieth-century, African workers did most of the heavy lifting in the economies of the Americas.

For a century after Columbus's arrival, the traffic in slaves to the Americas had numbered a few thousand annually. But as sugar cultivation steadily prospered after 1600, slave imports rose to 19,000 a year during the seventeenth century and mushroomed to 60,000 a year in the eighteenth century. All told, as many as 21 million people were captured in West Africa between 1700 and 1850: some 9 million among them entered the Americas as slaves, but millions died before or during the Atlantic crossing, and as many as 7 million remained slaves in Africa. Although slavery became indispensible to its economy, British North America played a relatively small role in the Atlantic slave trade. Nine-tenths of all Africans brought to the New World landed in Brazil or the Caribbean islands.

Dimensions of the Slave Trade

The rapid growth of the trade transformed not only the Americas but also Africa. Slavery became more widespread within African society, and slave trading more central to its domestic and international commerce. Most important, the African merchants and political leaders most deeply invested in the slave trade used their profits for political advantage—to build new chiefdoms and states such as Dahomey, Asante, and the Lunda Empire. Their ambitions and the greed of European slave dealers drew an increasingly large number of Africans, particularly people living in the interior, into slavery's web. By the late seventeenth century, Africans being sold into slavery were no longer only those who had put themselves at risk by committing crimes, running into debt, or voicing unpopular political and religious views. The larger number were

Transformation of West African Society

African Transatlantic Slave Trade, 1450–1760 *Toward the end of the seventeenth century, Chesapeake and Carolina planters began importing increasing numbers of slaves. In Africa, the center of that trade lay along a mountainous region known as the Gold Coast, where more than a hundred European trading posts and forts funneled the trade. Unlike most of the rest of West Africa's shoreline, the Gold Coast had very little dense rain forest. Despite the heavy trade, only about 4 percent of the total transatlantic slave trade went to North America.*

Katharina, sketched by Albrecht Dürer in 1521, was a servant of a Portuguese diplomat living in Antwerp. She was probably one of the increasing number of Africans being brought to Europe owing to the growing slave trade along the West African coast.

Slaves captured in the African interior were marched out in slave "coffles," a forced march in which captives were linked either by chains or by wooden yoke restraints linking two slaves together as they walked.

Africans found themselves in a variety of conditions in the Americas. Most toiled on plantations. Some, however, like these "watermen" along the James River in Virginia (lower right), claimed more independence. Still others ran away to Maroon communities in the interior. This armed Maroon (a runaway slave; lower left) is from Dutch Guiana, where conditions on the plantations were particularly harsh. ▶

Slaves were often bought and sold on the decks of the ship they traveled on, as in this painting from the 1770s (top). Note that the ship has put up a barricade (left side of the illustration) to keep slaves separate from the rest of the ship while the selling is proceeding.

ATLANTIC OCEAN

ENGLAND
3%

EUROPE

NORTH AMERICA

BRITISH COLONIES

ASIA

ARAB

BERBER

ARAB

SAHARA DESERT

WEST INDIES
4%

French 17%

KAARTA

ARAB

British 24%

SEGU

KANEM-BORNU

Spanish 13%

HAUSA

CENTRAL AMERICA

DAHOMEY

Dutch 7%

ASHANTE

BENIN

AFRICA

GUIANAS

OYO

The Middle Passage

Portuguese 32%

62%

TEKE

Equator

NSUNDI

BRAZIL

36%

KONGO

SWAHILI CITY-STATES

MBUNDU

SOUTH AMERICA

2%

ANGOLA

MOZAMBIQUE

MADAGASCAR

| Main slave sources 1450 to 1760 | |
| SUSU | Ethnic groups |

instead captives taken by soldiers or kidnappers in raids launched specifically to acquire prisoners for the slave trade, or else desperate refugees captured while fleeing war, famine, and disease. During the decades after 1680, captives coming directly from Africa made up more than 80 percent of all new slaves entering the Chesapeake and the rest of mainland North America. Many were shipped from the coast of Africa that Portuguese explorers had first probed, between the Senegal and Niger rivers. Most of the rest came from Angola, farther south.

Seized by other Africans, captives were yoked together at the neck and marched hundreds of miles through the interior to coastal forts or other outposts along the Atlantic. There, they were penned in hundreds of prisons, in lots of anywhere from 20 or 30 to more than 1,000. They might be forced to wait for slaving vessels in French *captiveries* below the fine houses of traders on the island of Goree, or herded into "outfactories" on the Banana Islands upstream on the Sierra Leone River, or perhaps marched into the dank underground slaveholds at the English fort at Cape Coast. Farther south, captives were held in marshy, fever-ridden lowlands along the Bight of Benin, waiting for a slaver to drop anchor. One African, Ottobah Cugoano, recalled finally being taken aboard ship:

> There was nothing to be heard but the rattling of chains, smacking of whips, and the groans and cries of our fellow-men. Some would not stir from the ground, when they were lashed and beat in the most horrible manner. . . . And when we found ourselves at last taken away, death was more preferable than life, and a plan was concerted amongst us that we might burn and blow up the ship and to perish altogether in the flames.

The Middle Passage   Worse than the imprisonment was the voyage itself: the so-called Middle Passage, a nightmarish journey across the Atlantic that could take anywhere between three weeks and three months, depending on currents, weather, and where ships disembarked and landed. Often several hundred black men, women, and children were packed belowdecks, squeezed onto platforms built in tiers spaced so close that sitting upright was impossible. It was difficult to know whether the days or the nights were more hellish. Slaves were taken out and forced to exercise for their health for a few hours each day; the rest of the day, the sun beat down and the heat below the decks was "so excessive," one voyager recalled, that the doctors who went below to examine slaves "would faint away, and the candles would not burn." At night, the slaves "were often heard making a howling melancholy kind of noise, something expressive of extreme anguish," noted a doctor aboard another ship. When he made inquiries, he discovered it was because the slaves, in sleeping, had dreamed "they were back in their own country again, amongst their families and friends" and "when they woke up to find themselves in reality on a slave ship they began to bay and shriek." Historians estimate that for every 85 enslaved Africans that set foot in the Americas, 15 died during the middle passage.

"Seasoning"   After the numb, exhausted survivors reached American ports, they faced more challenges to staying alive. The first year in the colonies was the most deadly for new, "unseasoned" slaves. The sickle cell genetic trait gave them a greater immunity to malaria than Europeans, but Africans were highly susceptible to respiratory infections. One-quarter of all Africans died during their first year in the Chesapeake, and among Carolina and Caribbean slaves, mortality rates were far higher. In addition to the new disease environment, Africans had to adapt to lives without freedom in a wholly unfamiliar country and culture.

A Changing Chesapeake Society

Exchanging a labor system based on servitude for one based on slavery transformed the character of Chesapeake society. Most obviously, the number of Afro-Virginians rose sharply. By 1740, 40 percent of all Virginians were black, and most of those were African-born. Unlike many African men and women who had arrived earlier from the Caribbean, these new inhabitants had little familiarity with English language and culture. This larger, more distinctively African community was also locked into a slave system that was becoming ever more rigid and demeaning. By the late decades of the seventeenth century, new laws made it more difficult for masters to free slaves. Other legislation systematically separated the races by prohibiting free black settlers from having white servants and outlawing interracial marriages and sexual relationships. The legal code encouraged white contempt for black Virginians in a variety of other ways. While masters were prohibited from whipping their white servants on the bare back, slaves had no such protection. And "any Negro that shall presume to strike any white" was to receive 30 lashes for that rash act.

The new laws both reflected and encouraged **racism** among white colonists of all classes. Deepening racial hatred, in turn, made it unlikely that poor white planters, tenants, and servants would ever join with poor black slaves to challenge the privilege of great planters. Instead of identifying with the plight of the slaves, the Chesapeake's poorer white residents considered black Virginians their natural inferiors. They could pride themselves on sharing with wealthy white gentlemen the same skin color and on being their equals in the eyes of the law.

Growing Racism

The leaders of the Chesapeake colonies cultivated unity among white inhabitants by improving economic prospects for freed servants and lesser planters. The Virginia assembly made provisions for freed servants to get a better start as independent farmers. It lowered taxes, allowing small planters to keep more of their earnings. New laws also gave most white male Virginians a vote in elections, allowing them an outlet to express their grievances. Economic trends toward the end of the seventeenth century contributed to the greater prosperity of small planters, because tobacco prices rose slightly and then stabilized. As a result of Bacon's savage campaign against the Virginia Indians, new land on the frontier became available. Even the domestic lives of ordinary people became more secure as mortality rates declined and the numbers of men and women in the white population evened out. As a result, virtually all men were now able to marry, and families were fragmented less often by the premature deaths of spouses and parents.

Opportunities for White Settlers

After 1700 the Chesapeake evolved into a more stable society. Gone were the bands of wild, landless, young bachelors one step ahead of the law, the small body of struggling lesser planters one step ahead of ruin, and the great mass of exploited servants one step away from rebellion. Virginia and Maryland became colonies of farming families, most of them small planters who owned between 50 and 200 acres. These families held no slaves, or at most two or three. And they accepted, usually without question, the social and political leadership of their acknowledged "superiors," great planters who styled themselves the "gentry."

The gentry's fortunes rested in part on the cultivation of tobacco on thousands of acres by hundreds of slaves. But the leading planters made even more money by marketing the tobacco of their humbler neighbors, selling them manufactured goods, supplying them with medical and legal services, lending money, and hiring out slaves. Unlike the rough-hewn barons of the early tobacco boom, the gentry did not owe their wealth to wringing work from poor whites. Instead they amassed great estates by wringing work from black slaves while converting their white "inferiors" into modestly prosperous small planters and paying clients. But the gentry wanted more than money: they wanted the respect of lesser whites. And they received it. On court days, gentlemen served as justices of the peace, bedecked in wigs and robes and seated on raised benches. On Sundays, worshipers filed into the Anglican chapel in order of social rank, with gentlemen heading the procession. When the local militia trained, it did so at the head of gentlemen officers. The courthouse, the church, and the training field all served as theaters in which the new Chesapeake gentry dramatized their superiority and lesser men deferred.

George Booth, the son of a wealthy planter family in Gloucester County, Virginia, was being raised for mastery. The young man's self-assured stance, the bow and arrows, the dog at his feet clutching the kill, the classical busts of women flanking his figure, and his family estate in the distance all suggest the gentry's concern for controlling the natural and social worlds.

It is said that shortly before his death in 735 C.E., the Venerable Bede, an English abbot, bequeathed a precious treasure to his brother monks. It consisted of a cache of spices, including a little stock of sugar. What separated Bede's world, in which sugar was a costly luxury, from twentieth-century Americans' world of ever-present sweetness was the discovery of America and the establishment of plantation economies in the Caribbean and Brazil.

Until the fourteenth century, Europe's merchants imported only small quantities of sugar at great expense from North Africa as well as from distant Persia and India, countries that had produced sugar since 500 C.E.

Throughout the Middle Ages and the early modern era, only the royal and the rich of Europe could indulge their desire for sugar, and even those classes partook sparingly. Europeans classified sugar as a spice, like the equally scarce and exotic pepper, nutmeg, ginger, and saffron. Nobility valued sugar as a medicine for sore throats, stomach disorders, and infertility. The cooks of castle kitchens seasoned food and sauces with a pinch of sugar or sprinkled it on meat, fish, fowl, and fruit to preserve freshness—or to conceal rot. Only on great occasions did the confectioners of noble families splurge, fashioning for courtly feasts great baked sugar sculptures of knights and kings, horses and apes, called "subtleties."

For the ordinary folk of Europe, life was not as sweet. Their diets consisted of bread, peas, beans, and, in good years, a little milk, butter, and cheese. The occasional pig slaughtered, rabbit trapped, or fish caught supplied stray protein for the poor.

That pattern of consumption changed as Europeans turned to African slave labor to grow sugar for them. The early sugar plantations of Madeira and the Canary Islands (see Chapter 2) were a foretaste of veritable sugar factories created in the Caribbean colonies of England and France.

By the sixteenth and seventeenth centuries, Europe's merchant classes could imitate elite patterns of eating by pouring sugar into pastries and puddings. And by the middle of the eighteenth century, an increasingly large supply from the Caribbean was making sugar essential to the poorest Europeans. Among England's laboring classes, another colonial import—Indian tea, laced heavily with sugar—began to accompany an otherwise cold supper of bread. Cheaper, warmer, and more stimulating than milk or beer (its prime competitors), sugared

From the Caribbean to the Carolinas

Transformation of the Caribbean

During the same decade that the English invaded Powhatan's land, they began to colonize the Caribbean, whose islands extended north and west, like beads on a string, from the Lesser Antilles toward the more substantial lands of Puerto Rico, Hispaniola, Jamaica, and Cuba (see map, page 75). At their long journey's end English sailors found what seemed a paradise: shores rimmed with white sand beaches that rose sharply to coral terraces, then to broad plateaus or mountain peaks shrouded in rain forests. The earliest arrivals came intending not to colonize but to steal from the Spanish. Even after 1604 when some English settled on the islands, few intended to stay.

Yet the English did establish permanent plantation colonies in the West Indies. Beyond that, their Caribbean settlements became the jumping-off points for a new colony on the North American mainland—South Carolina. Because of the strong West Indian influence, South Carolina developed a social order in some ways distinct from that of the Chesapeake colonies. In other ways, however, the development paralleled Virginia and Maryland's path. In both regions, extreme violence, high mortality, and uncertainty gave way to relative stability only over the course of many decades.

Paradise Lost

The English had traded and battled with the Spanish in the Caribbean since the 1560s. From those island bases English buccaneers conducted an illegal trade with Spanish settlements, sacked the coastal towns, and plundered silver ships bound for Seville. Weakened by decades of warfare, Spain could not hold the West Indies. The Dutch drove a wedge into Caribbean trade routes, and the French and the English began to colonize the islands.

The Sugar Mill.

Once harvested, sugarcane in the West Indies was crushed, as in this sugar mill. The juice was collected and channeled to the sugar works, where it was concentrated through boiling and evaporation. This neat diagrammatic picture belies the harsh conditions of labor and the high mortality that slaves experienced: sweetness came at a steep price.

tea won the loyalty of England's mass market and ranked as the nonalcoholic beverage of national choice. By the nineteenth century, English working families were also combining sugar and starch by pouring treacle (molasses) over porridge and spreading jams or marmalades on their bread.

Europe and America affected each other in many ways, but diet figured among the more fundamental conditions of life altered by colonization. More than coffee, chocolate, rum, or tobacco—indeed, more than any of the other "drug foods" produced by the colonies except tea—sugar provided a major addition to the diet of the English and other Europeans.

Even though sugar became a mass-marketed basic foodstuff, its association with power persisted. But it was no longer the consumption of sugar that bestowed status. Instead, after 1700 it was the production of sugar that conferred power. Planters who grew it, merchants who shipped and sold it, industrialists who refined it, and politicians who taxed it discovered in sugar sources of profit and distinction less perishable than sweetness on the tongue.

In the 40 years after 1604, some 30,000 immigrants from the British Isles planted crude frontier outposts on St. Kitts, Barbados, Nevis, Montserrat, and Antigua. The settlers—some free, many others indentured servants, and almost all young men—devoted themselves to working as little as possible, drinking as much as possible, and returning to England as soon as possible. They cultivated for export a poor quality of tobacco, which returned just enough profit to maintain straggling settlements of small farms.

Then, nearly overnight, sugar cultivation transformed the Caribbean. In the 1640s Barbados planters learned from the Dutch how to process sugarcane. The Dutch also supplied African slaves to work the cane fields and marketed the sugar for high prices in the Netherlands. Sugar plantations and slave labor rapidly spread to other English and French islands as Europeans developed an insatiable sweet tooth for the once scarce commodity. Caribbean sugar made more money for England than the total volume of commodities exported by all the mainland American colonies.

Even though its great planters became the richest people in English America, they could not have confused the West Indies with paradise. Throughout the seventeenth century, disease took a fearful toll, and island populations grew only because of immigration. In the scramble for land, small farmers were pushed onto tiny plots that barely allowed them to survive.

The desperation of bound laborers posed another threat. After the Caribbean's conversion to cultivating sugar, African slaves gradually replaced indentured servants in the cane fields. By the beginning of the eighteenth century, resident Africans outnumbered English by four to one. Fear of servant mutinies and slave rebellions frayed the nerves of island masters. They tried to contain the danger by imposing harsh slave codes and inflicting brutal punishments on all laborers. But planters lived under a constant state of siege. One visitor to Barbados observed that whites fortified their homes with parapets from which they could pour scalding water on attacking servants and slaves. During the first century of settlement, seven major slave uprisings shook the English islands.

Caribbean Sugar

Slavery in the Caribbean

This scene from Barbados shows several wind-powered sugar mills, used to crush the cane and extract the sweet juice. Houses also spread across the hilly landscape. A white surveyor and his two black assistants work in the foreground.

As more people, both white and black, squeezed onto the islands, some settlers looked for a way out. With all the land in use, the Caribbean no longer offered opportunity to freed servants or even planters' sons. It was then that the West Indies started to shape the history of the American South.

The Founding of the Carolinas

The colonization of the Carolinas began with the schemes of Virginia's royal governor, William Berkeley, and Sir John Colleton, a supporter of Charles I who had been exiled to the Caribbean at the end of England's civil war. Colleton saw that the Caribbean had a surplus of white settlers, and Berkeley knew that Virginians needed room to expand as well. Together the two men set their sights on the area south of Virginia. Along with a number of other aristocrats, they convinced Charles II to make them joint proprietors in 1663 of a place they called the Carolinas, in honor of the king.

North Carolina

A few hardy souls from Virginia had already squatted around Albemarle Sound in the northern part of the Carolina grant. The proprietors provided them with a governor and a representative assembly. About 40 years later, in 1701, they set off North Carolina as a separate colony. The desolate region quickly proved a disappointment. Lacking good harbors and navigable rivers, the colony had no convenient way of marketing its produce. North Carolina remained a poor colony, its sparse population engaged in general farming and the production of masts, pitch, tar, and turpentine.

South Carolina

The southern portion of the Carolina grant held far more promise, especially in the eyes of one of its proprietors, Sir Anthony Ashley Cooper, Earl of Shaftesbury. In 1669 he sponsored an expedition of a few hundred English and Barbadian immigrants, who planted the first permanent settlement in South Carolina. By 1680 the colonists had established the center of economic, social, and political life at the confluence of the Ashley and the Cooper rivers, naming the site Charles Town (later Charleston) after the king. Like others before him, Cooper hoped to create an ideal society in America. His utopia was a place where a few landed aristocrats and gentlemen would rule with the consent of many smaller property holders. With his personal secretary, the renowned philosopher John Locke, Cooper drew up an intricate scheme of government, the Fundamental Constitutions. The design provided Carolina with a proprietary governor and a hereditary nobility who, as a Council of Lords, would recommend all laws to a Parliament elected by lesser landowners.

The Carolinas and the Caribbean *The map underscores the geographic link between West Indian and Carolina settlements. Emigrants from Barbados dominated politics in early South Carolina, while Carolinians provided foodstuffs, grain, and cattle to the West Indies. As South Carolinians began growing rice, Caribbean slave ships found it an easy sail north and west to unload their cargoes in Charleston.*

The Fundamental Constitutions met the same fate as other lordly dreams for America. Instead of peacefully observing its provisions, most of the Carolinians, immigrants from Barbados, plunged into the economic and political wrangling that had plagued Maryland's first government. They challenged proprietary rule, protested or ignored laws and regulations imposed on them, and rejected the proprietors' relatively benevolent vision of Indian relations. Instead of forging genuine alliances with regional Indians, Carolina's colonists fomented a series of Indian slave wars that would nearly destroy the colony altogether.

Carolina, Florida, and the Southeastern Slave Wars

Taking wealthy Barbados as the model, the colonists intended from the start to grow Carolina's economy around cash crops tended by African slaves. But before they could afford to establish such a regime, the newcomers needed to raise capital through trade with Indians. Colonists gave textiles, metal goods, guns, and alcohol in exchange for hundreds of thousands of deer skins, which they then exported.

Growth of the Indian Slave Trade

But the trade soon came to revolve around a commodity dearer still. As did most peoples throughout history, southeastern Indians sometimes made slaves of their enemies. Carolina's traders vastly expanded this existing slave culture by turning captives into prized commodities. Convinced that local Indians were physically weaker than Africans and more likely to rebel or flee, colonial traders bought slaves from Indian allies and then exported them to other mainland colonies or to the Caribbean. They found eager native partners in this business. Contact with Europe had unleashed phenomenal changes in interior North America; epidemics ruined one people and gave advantage to another, new commercial opportunities sparked fierce wars over hunting and trading territories, and many thousands of Indian families became displaced and had to rebuild their lives somewhere new. The chaos, conflict, and movement gave enterprising Indians ample opportunity to enslave weak neighbors and stock Carolina's slave pens.

Raids into Spanish Florida

To ensure a steady supply of slaves and maximize profits, Carolinian merchants courted a variety of Indian allies during the late seventeenth and early eighteenth centuries and encouraged them to raid mission Indians in Spanish Florida. By 1700 Florida's Indian peoples were in sharp decline, and Charles Town's slave traders turned to the large and powerful Creek, Choctaw, Chickasaw, and Cherokee confederacies of the interior, encouraging them to raid one another. Before long the slave wars had a momentum all their own, extending as far west as the Mississippi River. Even native peoples who deplored the violence and despised the English felt compelled to participate, lest they too become victims. One small Indian community elected an elder representative to travel to Charles Town and discover what his people needed to do to stay safe. The town's traders seized the man and sold him into slavery. The trade had become central to Carolina's growing economy, and colonists high and low sought to profit from it. In 1702 Governor James Moore, one of the colony's chief slave traders, launched an audicious raid against Spanish St. Augustine and Florida's missions, returning with hundreds of Indian captives. His campaign inspired still more raids, and over the next few years Creeks, Yamasees, and Englishmen laid waste to 29 Spanish missions, shattering thousands of lives and destroying Spain's precarious system of Indian alliances in Florida. By 1706 Spanish authority was once again confined to St. Augustine and its immediate vicinity, and within another 10 years most of Florida had been depopulated of Indians.

It seemed a double victory from Charles Town's perspective. The English had bested a European rival for the Crown, and had reaped enormous profits besides. The fragmentary evidence suggests that Carolinians had purchased or captured between 30,000 and 50,000 Indian slaves before 1715. Indeed, before that date South Carolina was a net exporter of slaves: it exported more slaves than it imported from Africa or the Caribbean. But in 1715 Carolina's merchants finally paid a price for the wars that they had cynically fomented for over 40 years.

With Florida virtually exhausted of slaves, the Yamasees grew nervous. Convinced that Carolina would soon turn on them as it had on other one-time allies, the Yamasees

Mulberry Plantation in South Carolina was first carved from coastal swamps in 1714. This painting, done half a century later, shows the Great House visible in the distance, flanked by slave quarters. African slaves skilled in rice cultivation oversaw the arduous task of properly planting and irrigating the crop.

struck first. They attacked traders, posts, and plantations on the outskirts of Charles Town, killing hundreds of colonists and dragging scores more to Florida to sell as slaves in St. Augustine. Panicked authorities turned to other Indian peoples in the region but found most had either joined the Yamasee or were too hostile and suspicious to help. Though it lasted only a few months, the Yamasee War finally put an end to the destructive regional slave trade. Animal skins again dominated regional commerce. The powerful southern confederacies grew wary of aligning too closely with any single European power and henceforth sought to play colonies and empires off each other. It was a strategy that would bring them relative peace and prosperity for generations.

Yamasee War

White, Red, and Black: The Search for Order.

As for South Carolina, the Yamasee War set it back 20 years. In its aftermath, colonists invested more and more of their resources in African slaves and in the cultivation of rice, a crop that eventually made South Carolina's planters the richest social group in mainland North America. Unfortunately, South Carolina's swampy coast, so perfectly suited to growing rice, was less suited for human habitation. Weakened by chronic malaria, settlers died in epic numbers from yellow fever, smallpox, and respiratory infections. The white population grew slowly, through immigration rather than natural increase, and numbered only 10,000 by 1730.

Early South Carolinians had little in common but the harsh conditions of frontier existence. Most colonists lived on isolated plantations; early deaths fragmented families and neighborhoods. Immigration after 1700 further intensified the colony's ethnic and religious diversity, adding Swiss and German Lutherans, Scots-Irish Presbyterians, Welsh Baptists, and Spanish Jews. The colony's only courts were in Charles Town; churches and clergy of any denomination were scarce. On those rare occasions when early Carolinians came together, they gathered at Charles Town to escape the pestilential air of their plantations, to sue one another for debt and haggle over prices, or to fight over religious differences and proprietary politics.

Finally, in 1729, the Crown formally established royal government; by 1730 economic recovery had done much to ease the strife. Even more important in bringing greater political stability, the white colonists of South Carolina came to realize that they must unite if they were to counter the Spanish in Florida and the French and their Indian allies on the Gulf Coast.

The growing black population gave white Carolinians another reason to maintain a united front. During the first decades of settlement, frontier conditions and the scarcity

Slavery in South Carolina

of labor had forced masters to allow enslaved Africans greater freedom within bondage. White and black laborers shared chores on small farms. On stock-raising plantations, called "cowpens," black cowboys ranged freely over the countryside. African contributions to the defense of the colony also reinforced racial interdependence and muted white domination. Whenever threats arose—during the Yamasee War, for example— black Carolinians were enlisted in the militia.

White Carolinians depended on black labor even more after turning to rice as their cash crop. In fact, planters began to import slaves in larger numbers partly because of West African skill in rice cultivation. But whites harbored deepening fears of the black workers whose labor built planter fortunes. As early as 1708 black men and women had become a majority in the colony, and by 1730 they outnumbered white settlers by two to one. As their colony recovered and began to prosper, white Carolinians put into effect strict slave codes like those in the Caribbean that converted their colony into an armed camp and snuffed out the marginal freedoms that African settlers once enjoyed.

The Founding of Georgia

After 1730 white South Carolinians could take comfort not only in newfound prosperity and new political harmony but also in the founding of a new colony on their southern border. South Carolinians liked Georgia a great deal more than the Virginians had liked Maryland, because the colony formed a buffer between British North America and Spanish Florida in much the same way that Yamasees and Shawnees had, before the war.

James Oglethorpe

Enhancing the military security of South Carolina was only one reason for the founding of Georgia. More important to General James Oglethorpe and other idealistic English gentlemen was the aim of aiding the "worthy poor" by providing them with land, employment, and a new start. They envisioned a colony of hardworking small farmers who would produce silk and wine, sparing England the need to import those commodities. That dream seemed within reach when George II made Oglethorpe and his friends the trustees of the new colony in 1732, granting them a charter for 21 years. At the end of that time Georgia would revert to royal control.

The trustees did not, as legend has it, empty England's debtors' prisons to populate Georgia. They freed few debtors but recruited from every country in Europe paupers who seemed willing to work hard—and who professed Protestantism. Trustees paid the paupers' passage and provided each with 50 acres of land, tools, and a year's worth of supplies. Settlers who could pay their own way were encouraged to come by being granted larger tracts of land. Much to the trustees' dismay, that generous offer was taken up not only by many hoped-for Protestants but also by several hundred Ashkenazim (German Jews) and Sephardim (Spanish and Portuguese Jews), who established a thriving community in early Savannah.

The trustees were determined to ensure that Georgia became a small farmers' utopia. Rather than selling land, the trustees gave it away, but none of the colony's settlers could own more than 500 acres. The trustees also outlawed slavery and hard liquor in order to cultivate habits of industry and sustain equality among whites. This design for a virtuous and egalitarian utopia was greeted with little enthusiasm by Georgians. They pressed for a free market in land and argued that the colony could never prosper until the trustees revoked their ban on slavery. Because the trustees had provided for no elective assembly, settlers could express their discontent only by moving to South Carolina—which many did during the early decades.

Plantation Colonies of the Americas

As mounting opposition threatened to depopulate the colony, the trustees caved in. They revoked their restrictions on land, slavery, and liquor a few years before the king assumed control of the colony in 1752. Under royal control, Georgia continued to develop an ethnically and religiously diverse society, akin to that of South Carolina. Similarly, its economy was based on rice cultivation and the Indian trade.

Although South Carolina and the English West Indies were both more opulent and more embattled societies than Virginia and Maryland, the plantation colonies stretching from the Chesapeake to the Caribbean had much in common. Indeed, a similar

The Yuchi were neighbors of one of Georgia's early settlements; one of the newly emigrated German colonists painted this watercolor of a Yuchi celebration. Judging from the guns hanging at the back of the shelter, these Indians were already trading with white settlers in the area.

pattern extended into South America, whether in the sugar and coffee plantations of the Guianas or the extensive sugar plantations of Brazil. As Europeans put down colonies in the Americas, Indian farmers and hunters had to be enslaved or expelled to accommodate growing plantation economies. Everywhere planters depended on a single staple crop, which brought both wealth and political power to those commanding the most land and the most labor. Everywhere the biggest planters relied for their success on the very people whom they deeply feared—enslaved African Americans. Everywhere, that fear was reflected in the development of repressive slave codes and the spread of racism throughout all classes of white society.

Empire . . . utopia . . . independence. . . . For more than a century after the founding of Oñate's colony on the upper Rio Grande in 1598, those dreams inspired residents of New Mexico, Florida, the Chesapeake, the English Caribbean, the Carolinas, and Georgia. Each of these regions served as staging grounds where kings and commoners, free and unfree, men and women, red, white, and black played out their hopes. Most met only disappointment, and many met disaster and death in the painful decades before the new colonies achieved a measure of stability.

The dream of an expanding empire faltered for the Spanish, who found few riches in the Southwest and eventually found rebellion. The dream of empire failed, too, when James I and Charles I, England's early Stuart kings, found their power checked by Parliament. And the dream foundered fatally for Indians—for Powhatan's successors, who were unable to resist white diseases and land-hungry tobacco planters, and for Westos, Shawnees, and the many Indian peoples of Florida who sought to survive, accommodate, or exploit colonialism, but fell to ruin in the end.

English lords had dreamed of establishing feudal utopias in America. But proprietors such as the Calvert family in Maryland and Cooper in the Carolinas found themselves hounded by frontier planters and farmers who sought economic and political power.

Empires . . .

The Dream of Utopias

Georgia's trustees struggled in vain to nurture their dream of a utopia for the poor. The dream of a Spanish Catholic utopia brought by missionaries to the American Southwest dimmed with Indian resistance.

Independence and Dependence

The dream of independence proved the most deceptive of all, especially for the inhabitants of England's colonies. Just a bare majority of the white servant immigrants to the Chesapeake survived to enjoy freedom. The rest were struck down by disease or worn down at the hands of tobacco barons eager for profit. Not only in the Chesapeake but also in the Caribbean and the Carolinas, real independence eluded the English planters. Poorer folk—dependent on richer settlers for land and leadership—deferred to them at church and on election days and depended on them to buy crops or to extend credit. Even the richest planters were dependent on the English and Scottish merchants who supplied them with credit and marketed their crops, as well as on the English officials who made colonial policy.

And everywhere in the American Southeast and Southwest, the lingering dreams of Europeans were realized only through the labor of the least free members of colonial America. That stubborn reality would haunt Americans of all colors who continued to dream of freedom and independence.

Significant Events

Late 1500s	Formation of Powhatan's paramount chiefdom
1598	Oñate colonizes New Mexico
1603	James I becomes king of England; beginning of Stuart Dynasty
1604	First English settlements in the Caribbean
1607	English establish Jamestown
1610	Founding of Santa Fe in New Mexico
1619	First record of Africans in Virginia
1620s	Tobacco boom in Virginia; epidemics in New Mexico reduce Pueblo population by nearly 70%
1622	War between Powhatans and English Colonists
1624	Virginia becomes a royal colony
1625	Charles I becomes king of England
1632	Calvert founds Maryland
1640s	Sugar boom begins in Caribbean
1660	Parliament passes the first of the Navigation Acts
1669	First permanent English settlement in South Carolina
1675	Height of Spanish mission system in Florida
1676	Bacon's Rebellion in Virginia
1680	Pueblo Revolt in New Mexico
1689	Coode's Rebellion in Maryland
ca. 1700	Rice boom begins in South Carolina
early 1700s	Indian slave wars devastate much of the Southeast, especially Florida
1700s	Average of 60,000 enslaved Africans cross the Atlantic annually.
1715	Yamasee War in South Carolina
1732	Chartering of Georgia

Chapter Summary

During the seventeenth century, Spain and England moved to colonize critical regions of southern North America.

- Native peoples everywhere in the American South resisted colonization, despite losses from warfare, disease, and enslavement.

- Spanish colonies in New Mexico and Florida grew slowly and faced a variety of threats. By the late seventeenth century Spanish New Mexico had been lost to the Pueblo Revolt, and Florida's delicate mission system was under siege from English Carolina and its Indian allies.

- Thriving monocultures were established in all of England's southern colonies—tobacco in the Chesapeake, rice in the Carolinas, and sugar in the Caribbean.

- Despite a period of intense enslavement of native peoples, African slavery emerged as the dominant labor system throughout these regions.

- Instability and conflict characterized both Spanish and English colonies in the South for most of the first century of their existence.

Additional Reading

David J. Weber's *Spanish Frontier in North America* (1992) remains far the best overview of Spain's colonies north of Mexico. For the southwest more specifically, see also Ramón Gutiérrez, *When Jesus Came, The Corn Mothers Went Away* (1991), John L. Kessell's *Spain in the Southwest* (2002), and James F. Brook's pathbreaking monograph *Captives and Cousins* (2002). For Spain in the Southeast, see Paul E. Hoffman's *Florida's Frontiers* (2002).

For enduring treatments of early Virginia, see Edmund S. Morgan, *American Slavery, American Freedom* (1975), and Rhys Isaac, *The Transformation of Virginia* (1982). For a more recent account, pivoting on ideas about gender, see Kathleen Brown, *Good Wives, Nasty Wenches, and Anxious Patriarchs* (1996). Karen Kupperman offers an excellent overview of relations between whites and Indians not only in the early South but throughout British North America in *Settling with the Indians* (1980). For native Virginia, see also Hellen C. Rountree, *Pocahontas's People* (1990).

In recent years there has been a surge in scholarship on African slavery in the New World. For a new and magisterial overview, see David Brion Davis, *Inhuman Bondage* (2006). For British North America, see Ira Berlin, *Many Thousands Gone* (1998), and Philip D. Morgan, *Slave Counterpoint* (1998). The classic account of the British Caribbean remains Richard Dunn's *Sugar and Slaves* (1972).

The Chesapeake has always drawn more notice from early American historians than South Carolina has, but in recent years some important studies have redressed that neglect. The best overview of that colony's development remains Robert Weir, *Colonial South Carolina* (1982). The complexities of Carolina's slave wars are explored in Alan Gallay, *The Indian Slave Trade* (2002). For fine explorations of more specialized topics, see Peter Colclanis, *The Shadow of a Dream* (1989), and Timothy Silver, *A New Face on the Countryside* (1990).

For a fuller list of readings, see the Bibliography at www.mhhe.com/davidsonnation6.

CHAPTER 4
Colonization and Conflict in the North
1600~1700

This painted chest proudly displays its owner's initials, SW, a bride from the area around Hadley, Massachusetts who married sometime in the late seventeenth or early eighteenth century. Such chests held goods that women traditionally possessed—linens, napkins, embroidered samplers—and were passed down from mother to daughter through the years.

Bears on Floating Islands

They came to her one night while she slept. Into her dreams drifted a small island, and on the island were tall trees and living creatures, one of them wearing the fur of a white rabbit. When she told of her vision, no one took her seriously, not even the wise men among her people, shamans and conjurers whose business it was to interpret dreams. No one, that is, until two days later, when the island appeared to all, floating toward shore. On the island, as she had seen, were tall trees, and on their branches—bears. Or creatures that looked so much like bears that the men grabbed their weapons and raced to the beach, eager for the good hunt sent by the gods. They were disappointed. The island was not an island at all but a strange wooden ship planted with the trunks of trees. And the bears were not bears at all but a strange sort of men whose bodies were covered with hair. Strangest among them, as she had somehow known, was a man dressed all in white. He commanded great respect among the bearlike men as their "shaman," or priest.

In that way, foretold by the dreams of a young woman, the Micmac Indians in 1869 recounted their people's first encounter with Europeans more than two centuries earlier. Uncannily, the traditions of other northern tribes record similar dreams predicting the European arrival: "large canoes with great white wings like those of a giant bird," filled with pale bearded men bearing "long black tubes." Perhaps the dreamers gave shape in their sleep to stories heard from other peoples who had actually seen white strangers and ships. Or perhaps, long before they ever encountered the newcomers, these Indians imagined them, just as Europeans fantasized about a new world.

However Micmacs and other northern Indians first imagined and idealized Europeans, they quickly came to see them as fully human. Traders might bring seemingly wondrous goods, goods that could transform the way labor, commerce, politics, and war functioned in native communities. And yet the traders themselves hardly seemed magical. They could be by turns generous and miserly, brave and frightful, confident and confused, kind and cruel. Moreover it soon became clear that these newcomers hailed from different nations, spoke different languages, and often seemed to have different goals. English colonists, it seemed, were every day more numerous and wanted nothing so much as land. The French, in contrast, were relatively few and seemed to care for nothing so much as trade—unless it was their Christian God they brought with them from across the waters. Strange to say, the Europeans argued over their deity as they did over so many other things. The English, the French, and the Dutch were all rivals, and the Micmacs and others who encountered these new peoples studied them closely, and began to make alliances.

As northern Indians became more and more aware of Europeans and their ways, they came also to realize that whatever their attitudes and intentions, the newcomers provoked dramatic changes everywhere they went. Thousands of English migrants coming into the land founded villages and towns that multiplied throughout the seventeenth century. They not only took up land but brought animals and plants that changed the way Indians lived. The Dutch, Europe's most powerful commercial nation, established no more than a handful of trading settlements up and down the Hudson River, but they encouraged the Iroquois confederacy to push into rival Indian territories in a quest for furs to trade. Even the French, who styled themselves loyal allies to many Indian peoples and claimed to want little more than beaver pelts, even they brought with them profound, sometimes cataclysmic changes—changes that would upend the world that natives knew when Frenchmen were but bears on floating islands.

France in North America

The first official expedition to the land the French would call Canada took place in 1535, when Jacques Cartier sailed through the Gulf of St. Lawrence. But not until 1605 did the French plant a permanent colony, at Port Royal in Acadia (Nova Scotia). Three years later, Samuel de Champlain established Québec farther up the St. Lawrence valley, where he could pursue the fur trade with less competition from rival Europeans. Champlain soon aligned himself with local Montagnais, Algonquins, and, especially, the mighty Hurons—a confederacy of farmers 20,000 strong whose towns near the Georgian Bay straddled a vast trading network.

Cartier and Champlain

The Origins of New France

French-Indian Alliances

These allied peoples had reason to embrace Champlain. Like Europeans elsewhere in North America, the Frenchman came with wondrous goods, such as textiles, glass, copper, and ironware. In the early years of contact such things would have been treated as exotic commodities rather than utilitarian items. Copper kettles, for instance, might be cut into strips for jewlery. But before long, metal tools, especially, began transforming native life. Metal knives made it far easier to butcher animals; trees could be felled and buildings built far more easily with iron than stone axes; cooking became more efficient with brass kettles that could be placed directly on the fire; flint strike-a-lights eliminated the cumbersome need for transporting hot coals in bounded shells; beads, cloth, needles, and thread made possible a new level of creative and visual expression; and, because metal arrowheads traveled farther and truer than stone, they would make hunters and warriors more deadly than they had ever been.

French women as well as men in religious orders dedicated their lives to missionary work in Canada. Marguerite Bourgeoys founded a religious community dedicated to the education of young girls.

Champlain found a warm welcome for all these reasons. But native peoples in North America seldom viewed exchange as a simple market transaction. All exchanges were bound up in complex social relations, and the Montagnais, Algonquins, and Hurons wanted assurance that Champlain would be a good friend as well as a good merchant. To satisfy his hosts, he agreed to accompany them on a campaign against their mutual enemies the Mohawks, one of the five confederated tribes of the Iroquois. The Frenchman proved his friendship, and his worth, in the spring of 1609 when he and his Indian companions confronted two hundred Mohawk warriors in what is now upstate New York. According to Champlain himself, he strode to the front as the battle was about to begin, raised his musket, and shot dead two Mohawk chiefs. Few if any of the assembled warriors had ever seen a gun fired in combat. Chaplain's allies let out a joyous cry, so loud "one could not have heard it thunder," attacked the astonished Mohawks, and drove the survivors from the field. It was not the last time that European newcomers would alter the balance of power in North America.

Satisfied with their new ally, the Montagnais, Algonquins, and Hurons became eager trading partners over the next generation. In return for European goods, they provided tens of thousands of otter, raccoon, and especially beaver pelts. These furs went to make fashionable European hats, whereas mink and marten were sent to adorn the robes of high-ranking European officials and churchmen. Some in France derided the colonial endeavor, dismissing New France as a *comptoir*, a storehouse for the skins of dead animals. And yet Champlain wanted more. He struggled to encourage more immigration to Canada, to convince those who came to settle permanently, and, above all, to bind his native allies closer and closer to the colonial project. To that end, Champlain encouraged certain French men and boys to live with Indian families, to learn their language and become conversant in their customs. *The Fur Trade*

Along with these *couriers de bois*, or "runners in the woods," French authorities engaged Jesuits, members of the Society of Jesus, to establish missions among the region's Indians. Just as devout but often more culturally flexible than Franciscan missionaries, Jesuit friars came to New France in the 1610s determined to master Indian languages and make inroads into native culture. They were also fired with the passions of the **Counter-Reformation** in Europe, a movement by devout Catholics to correct those abuses that had prompted the Protestant Reformation. Initially Jesuit missionaries were tolerated more than listened to. But by the 1630s Champlain began pressing the Indians, insisting that trading partners accept resident Jesuits. More importantly, Christianized Indians got better prices for furs than did their unconverted counterparts. Such policies helped the French pursue what they saw as interlocked economic, strategic, and religious objectives. French pressure also caused friction in native communities, among the Huron in particular. Should they accept European customs and religion? Converts remained relatively few into the 1640s, and the debate over Huron cultural identity provoked internal quarrels that eventually left the confederacy fragmented and vulnerable to enemies. *Jesuit Missions*

New Netherlands, the Iroquois, and the Beaver Wars

If Canada was merely a *comptoir*, it was a profitable one. Potential revenues from the fur trade drew the attention of rival European powers, including the Dutch. By the early seventeenth century the Netherlands had the greatest manufacturing capacity in the world and had become the key economic power in Europe. Intent especially on trade, the Dutch had little desire to plant permanent colonies abroad because they enjoyed prosperity and religious freedom at home. But they did want to tap directly into the wealth flowing out of North America and therefore explored and laid claim to a number of sites around the Connecticut, Delaware, and Hudson Rivers (the last named for the Englishman Henry Hudson, who first explored it for the Dutch in 1609). Most of New Netherlands' few settlers would cluster in the village of New Amsterdam on Manhattan Island at the mouth of the Hudson. *The Dutch Strength in Trade*

Assessing a Contemporary Drawing

To what degree were Indians willing converts to European culture and religion? One view is that Indians readily took to European teachings when they were exposed to them. A very different view is that Europeans exerted pressure to influence Indians to embrace European ways. This image leaves room for both interpretations. A French missionary, Claude Chauchetière, depicted this Indian council at Kahnawake, a mission village along the St. Lawrence River sometime after 1678. The council had convened to ban alcohol, Chauchetière reported. On the one hand, his drawing, dominated by native men, raises the possibility that the decision to outlaw liquor arose from a consensus among the Indians and not merely the insistence of the missionaries. Having witnessed the ravages of alcohol among their peoples, the Indians who sought refuge in Christian communities such as Kahnawake had good reason to initiate such a policy. It is also possible to argue that the drawing accurately portrays the Indians' active role because there are other historically accurate elements in the picture, including the fur robes worn by the Indian men and the crude log chapel in the background.

On the other hand, the only standing figure, a man waving (or emptying) a bottle, appears to be European—most likely a Jesuit. This suggests that Europeans may well be leading the Indians on this issue. And Chauchetière's Christian view is evident in his giving free rein to his imagination by placing front and center the figure of a devil pinned down by a cross. The prominence of both images suggests that he might have

A French missionary's sketch.

seen the council as following the missionaries' lead and as signifying the Indians' cultural accommodation to the teachings of Roman Catholicism.

More importantly for the geopolitics of the continent, the Dutch West India Company also established a trading outpost 150 miles upriver known as Fort Orange (present-day Albany). Initially the traders at Fort Orange hoped to obtain cheap furs by fostering competition among rival Indian customers. But by 1630 the powerful Mohawks had displaced their competitors and come to dominate the fort's commerce. Ever since their encounter with Champlain's musket the Mohawks and the other four members of the **Iroquois League** (the Oneidas, Onondagas, Cayugas, and Senecas) had suffered from their lack of direct access to European goods. With Mohawk ascendancy around Fort Orange, the Iroquois finally had reliable access to the tools and weapons necessary to go on the offensive against their northern enemies. They felt compelled to do so because the beaver population, always fragile, had collapsed within their own territory. To maintain their trading position, they began preying on Huron convoys on their way to Quebec and then selling the plundered pelts to the Dutch.

Collapse of the Beaver
Population

Just as this old rivalry revived, and soon after the aging Champlain died of a stroke, two things happened to help plunge the region into catastrophe. First, waves of disease afflicted the settlements in the northeast in the 1630s and took a nightmarish toll on nearly all the region's native peoples, especially agricultural communities in their densely populated towns. Between 1634 and 1640 smallpox killed more than 10,000 Hurons, reducing their total population by half and precipitating a spate of conversions to Christianity that divided the community all the more. The Iroquois likewise suffered greatly, but, unlike the Huron, they reacted by waging war in an effort to obtain captives that could formally replace dead kin. The second transformative event was a dramatic expansion in the regional arms trade. Initally reluctant to deal in guns, by the late 1630s the Dutch at Fort Orange relaxed their policy in order to obtain more furs. Before long the Iroquois had many times more muskets than the Hurons, whom the French had traditionally refused to arm so long as they remained unconverted.

Reeling from disease and internal division, the Huron saw their world collapsing. In 1648, well-armed Iroquois warriors destroyed three Huron towns. The attacks continued into the next year. At one town under siege, the Jesuit Paul Ragueneau saw desperate Hurons seek baptism and Christian consolation. "Never was their faith more alive, nor their love for their good fathers and pastors more keenly felt." The Hurons made the wrenching decision to burn their remaining towns and abandon their lands for good. As many as 2,000 became Iroquois, either as war-captives or humble refugees. Others merged with neighboring peoples, while thousands more fled in desperation and starved to death or died of exposure in the harsh winter of 1649–1650.

So began the Beaver Wars, a series of conflicts at least as profoundly transformative for the colonial north as the Indian slave wars were for the south. Seeking new hunting grounds and new captives to replenish their diminishing population, Iroquois raiders attacked peoples near and far. After the Hurons, they struck and scattered the nearby Petuns, Eries, and Neutrals—peoples who, like the Hurons, were all Iroquoian speakers and could thus be integrated into Iroquois communities with relative ease. Iroquois warriors next moved against non-Iroquoian groups, including Delawares and Shawnees in the Ohio Valley, and even extended their raids south to the Carolinas. To the North they attacked Algonquins in the Canadian Shield, and Abenakis and others in New England.

The Lure of the Mississippi

The Beaver Wars continued in fits and starts for the rest of the seventeenth century, bringing dozens of Indian nations to grief and provoking a massive refugee crisis as families fled their traditional territories and tried to rebuild their lives in peace. The wars also very nearly led to the ruin of New France. About three hundred Frenchmen were killed or captured in the wars, cutting the colony's meager population in half by 1666. The survivors saw Champlain's carefully managed trading system thrown into disarray. French authorities scrambled to find reliable new partners in the fur trade and henceforth were less reluctant to trade guns to Indian allies. More broadly, the scope of the conflict

Smallpox Epidemic

The Hurons who became infected with smallpox in the 1630s would have experienced fevers, aches, and vomiting before the tell-tale spots emerged on their skin. Agonizing pustules would have soon covered them from head to toe, as in the picture above, and sometimes the pustules merged into oozing sheets that caused large sections of the victims' skin to peel away from their bodies. This horrible disease claimed millions of lives in the Americas after 1492.

This undated French engraving depicts something often overlooked or trivialized by European observers: native women's work. Two Iroquois women grind corn into meal while a swaddled infant rests in a backboard.

and the far-flung movement of refugees compelled the French to take a more expansive view of the continent and their place in it.

By the 1660s, French traders, priests, and officers were making inroads among diverse refugee villages in the Western Great Lakes, a region the French referred to as the *pays d'en haut*. These peoples sought trade, assistance against the Iroquois, and mediation of their own disputes. While the French set about building alliances in the *pays d'en haut*, they became aware of and began exploring the greatest watercourse in North America.

La Salle Descends Mississippi

The Mississipi River travels nearly 2,500 miles from its source in present-day Minnesota to the Gulf of Mexico, carrying water from several other major rivers and dominating a drainage area larger than the Indian subcontinent in Asia. As the French began exploring the river in earnest in the 1670s, it dawned on them that the Mississippi Valley could be the strategic key to success in North America. French officials set out courting Indian peoples along the river and its tributaries, employing their hard-won insights into native diplomatic culture along the way. The region's peoples—the Illinois, Shawnees, Quapaws, and others—expressed keen interest in French trade, as well as fear and hatred of their common Iroquois enemies. When René Robert Cavelier, Sieur de La Salle became the first European to descend the river to the Gulf in 1682, he encountered the Natchez, Chickasaws, and others who had not seen Europeans since De Soto and his maniacal march nearly a century and a half before. Other Frenchmen went further, erecting trading posts and simple missions, and even making contact and tentative alliances with Osages, Arkansas, Ottos, Pawnees, and others west of the great river.

By the early eighteenth century, New France had helped broker an uneasy peace between the Iroquois and Indian nations to the west, extended its influence over a vast area, and fortified its colonial core along the St. Lawrence. In 1700 the colony had scores of simple missions and three modest cities—Quebec, Montreal, and Trois-Rivières—containing a population of approximately 15,000. Most immigrants to New France eventually returned to Europe, and short-sighted French monarchs insisted that Canada be a Catholic colony, off limits to France's most obvious emigrants, the Protestant Huguenots. But even with its small colonial population, New France emerged as a powerful player in North America, given its strategic and economic alliances with native peoples. The French had reason to hope that their native allies could help contain the Spanish to the West and limit English expansion from the east.

The Founding of New England

At first, the English regarded the northern part of North America as a place in which only the mad French could see possibility. English fisherfolk who strayed from Newfoundland to the coast of Acadia and New England carried home descriptions of the long, lonely coast, rockbound and rugged. Long winters of numbing cold melted into short summers of steamy heat. There were no minerals to mine, no crops suitable for export, no large native population available for enslaving. The Chesapeake, with its temperate climate and long growing season, seemed a much likelier spot.

But by 1620, worsening conditions at home had instilled in some English men and women the mixture of desperation and idealism needed to settle an uninviting, unknown world. Religious differences among English Protestants became a matter of sharper controversy during the seventeenth century. Along with the religious crisis came mounting political tensions and continuing problems of unemployment and recession. Times were bad—so bad that the anticipation of worse times to come swept English men and women to the shores of New England.

The Puritan Movement

The colonization of New England started with a king who chose his enemies unwisely. James I, shortly after succeeding Elizabeth I in 1603, vowed to purge England of all radical Protestant reformers. The radicals James had in mind were the **Puritans,** most of whom were either Presbyterians or Congregationalists. Although both groups of Puritan reformers embraced Calvin's ideas, they differed on the best form of church organization. Individual **Presbyterian** churches (or congregations) were guided by higher governing bodies of ministers and laypersons. Those in the **Congregationalist** churches, in contrast, believed that each congregation should conduct its own affairs independently, answering to no other authority.

Like all Christians, Protestant and Catholic, the Puritans believed that God was all-knowing and all-powerful. And, like all Calvinists, the Puritans emphasized that idea of divine sovereignty known as **predestination.** At the center of their thinking was the belief that God had ordained the outcome of history, including the eternal fate of every human being. The Puritans found comfort in their belief in predestination because it provided their lives with meaning and purpose. They felt assured that a sovereign God was directing the fate of individuals, nations, and all of creation. The Puritans strove to play their parts in that divine drama of history and to discover in their performances some signs of personal salvation.

The divine plan, as the Puritans understood it, called for reforming both church and society along the lines laid down by John Calvin. It seemed to the Puritans that England's government hampered rather than promoted religious purity and social order. It tolerated drunkenness, theatergoing, gambling, extravagance, public swearing, and Sabbath-breaking. It permitted popular recreations rooted in pagan custom and superstition—sports such as bear baiting and maypole dancing and festivals such as the celebration of Christmas and saints' days.

Even worse, the state had not done enough to purify the English church of the "corruptions" of Roman Catholicism. The Church of England counted as its members everyone in the nation, saint and sinner alike. To the Puritans, belonging to a church was no birthright. They wished to limit membership and the privileges of baptism and communion to godly men and women. The Puritans also deplored the hierarchy of bishops and archbishops in the Church of England, as well as its elaborate ceremonies in which priests wore ornate vestments. Too many Anglican clergy were "dumb dogges" in Puritan eyes, too poorly educated to instruct churchgoers in the truths of Scripture or to deliver a decent sermon. In reformer John Foxe's vision of good and evil (page 88), Anglican priests on the right side of the drawing are shown in vestments and headdresses worshiping Satan before an altar. Anglican worshipers (bottom right) superstitiously count rosary beads and follow a priestly procession like so many dumb sheep. In contrast, Puritan worshipers (bottom left) conspicuously hold their Bibles and attend only to the word of God.

Puritan Calls for Reform

Because English monarchs had refused to take stronger measures to reform church and society, the Puritans became their outspoken critics. Elizabeth I had tolerated this opposition, but James I would not endure it and intended to rid England of these radicals. With some of the Puritans, known as the Separatists, he seemed to succeed.

The Pilgrim Settlement at Plymouth Colony

The Separatists were devout Congregationalists who concluded that the Church of England was too corrupt to be reformed. They abandoned Anglican worship and met secretly in small congregations. From their first appearance in England during the 1570s, the Separatists suffered persecution from the government—fines, imprisonment, and, in a few cases, execution. Always a tiny minority within the Puritan movement, the Separatists were people from humble backgrounds: craftworkers and farmers without influence to challenge the state. By 1608 some had become so discouraged that they migrated to Holland, where the Dutch government permitted complete freedom of religion. But when their children began to adopt Dutch customs and other religions, some Separatists decided to move again, this time to Virginia.

It can only be imagined what fate would have befallen the unworldly Separatists had they actually settled in the Chesapeake during the tobacco boom. But a series

Early Difficulties

John Foxe's Actes and Monuments *(1563), a book revered by the Puritan founders of New England, arrayed the forces of righteousness* (left side of the page) *against a host of devils, priests, and their sheeplike followers within the Church of England at right. Under the Catholic Queen Mary, Protestants were regarded as heretics and some were burned at the stake* (middle left).

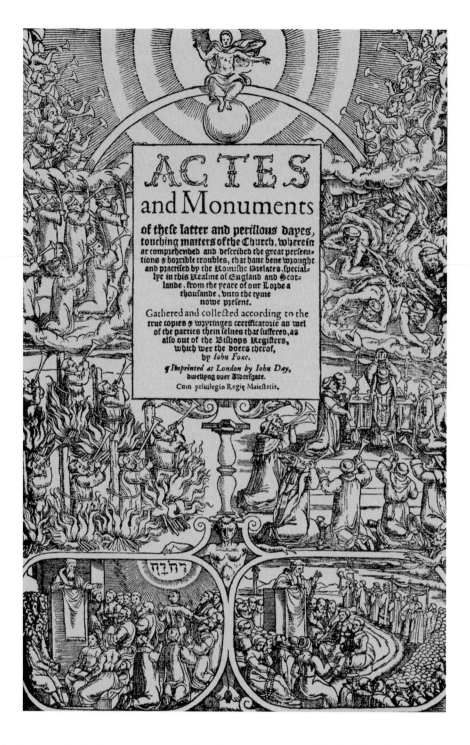

of mistakes—including an error in charting the course of their ship, the *Mayflower*—brought the little band far to the North, to a region Captain John Smith had earlier dubbed "New England." In November 1620, some 88 Separatist "Pilgrims" set anchor at a place they called Plymouth on the coast of present-day southeastern Massachusetts. They were sick with scurvy, weak from malnutrition, and shaken by a shipboard mutiny, and neither the site nor the season invited settlement. As one of their leaders, William Bradford, later remembered:

> For summer being done, all things stand upon them with a weatherbeaten face, and the whole country, full of woods and thickets represented a savage hue. If they looked behind them, there was the mighty ocean which they had passed and was now as a main bar and gulf to separate them from all the civil parts of the world.

For some, the shock was too great. Dorothy Bradford, William's wife, is said to have fallen overboard from the *Mayflower* as it lay anchored off Plymouth. It is more likely that she jumped to her death.

Few Pilgrims could have foreseen founding the first permanent European settlement in New England, and many did not live long enough to enjoy the distinction. They had arrived too late to plant crops and had failed to bring an adequate supply of food. By the spring of 1621, half the immigrants had died. English merchants who had financed the *Mayflower* voyage failed to send supplies to the struggling settlement. Plymouth might have become another doomed colony had the Pilgrims not received better treatment from native inhabitants than they did from their English backers.

Though they understood it only dimly, the Pilgrims were, in one historian's memorable phrase, the "beneficiaries of catastrophe." Only four years before their arrival, coastal New England had been devastated by a massive epidemic, possibly the plague. Losses varied locally, but overall the native coastal population may have been reduced by as much as 90 percent. Abandoned villages lay in ruins up and down the coast, including the village of Patuxet, where the Pilgrims established Plymouth. Years later visitors would still marvel at heaps of unburied human remains dating from the epidemic.

Effect of Epidemic Disease

The Wampanoags dominated the lands around Plymouth. Still reeling from loss in 1620 and eager to obtain trade goods and assistance against native enemies, Masasoit, their chief, agreed to help the starving colonists. Intially, the peoples communicated through a remarkable Wampanoag named Squanto, who had been kidnapped by English sailors prior to the epidemic. Taken to Europe, Squanto learned English and eventually returned to America in time to play a crucial intermediary role between Masasoit and the newcomers. The Pilgrims accepted Wampanoag hospitality and instruction, and invited native leaders to a feast in honor of their first successful harvest in 1621 (the genesis of the "First Thanksgiving" story).

The Pilgrims set up a government for their colony, the framework of which was the Mayflower Compact, drawn up on board ship before landing. That agreement provided for a governor and several assistants to advise him, all to be elected annually by Plymouth's adult males. In the eyes of English law, the Plymouth settlers had no clear basis for their land claims or their government, for they had neither a royal charter nor approval from the Crown. But English authorities, distracted by problems closer to home, left the tiny colony of farmers alone.

The Mayflower Compact

The Puritan Settlement at Massachusetts Bay

Among the Crown's distractions were two groups of Puritans more numerous and influential than the Pilgrims. They included both the Presbyterians and the majority of Congregationalists who, unlike the Pilgrim Separatists, still considered the Church of England capable of being reformed. But the 1620s brought these Puritans only fresh discouragements. In 1625 Charles I inherited his father's throne and all his enemies. When Parliament attempted to limit the king's power, Charles simply dissolved it, in 1629, and proceeded to rule without it. When Puritans pressed for reform, the king began to move against them.

This persecution swelled a second wave of Puritan migration that also drew from the ranks of Congregationalists. Unlike the humble Separatists, these emigrants included merchants, landed gentlemen, and lawyers who organized the Massachusetts Bay Company in 1629. Those able Puritan leaders aimed to build a better society in America, an example to the rest of the world. Unlike the Separatists, they had a strong sense of mission and destiny. They were not abandoning the English church, they insisted, but merely regrouping across the Atlantic for another assault on corruption.

Despite the company's Puritan leanings, it somehow obtained a royal charter confirming its title to most of present-day Massachusetts and New Hampshire. Advance parties in 1629 established the town of Salem on the coast well north of Plymouth. In

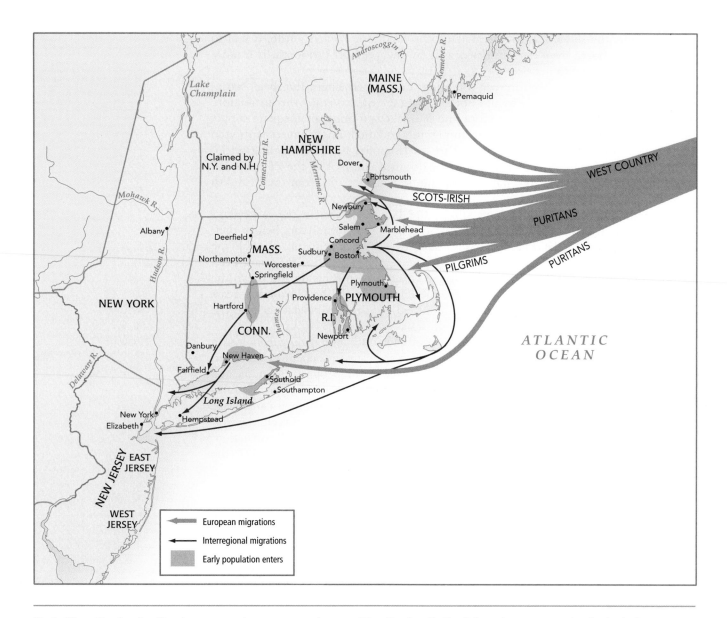

Early New England   *Despite some variety among emigrants, New England's English settlements remained relatively homogeneous and stable. Over the years, groups of settlers "hived off" from the settlements around Massachusetts Bay, beginning new towns along the Connecticut River, southern and western Connecticut, Long Island, and East Jersey.*

1630 the company's first governor, a tough-minded and visionary lawyer named John Winthrop, sailed from England with a dozen other company stockholders and a fleet of men and women to establish the town of Boston. The newcomers intended to build a godly "city on a hill" that would serve as an example to the world.

Establishing the Colony's Government

Once established in the Bay Colony, Winthrop and the other stockholders transformed the charter for their trading company into the framework of government for a colony. The company's governor became the colony's chief executive, and the company's other officers became the governor's assistants. The charter provided for annual elections of the governor and his assistants by company stockholders, known as the freemen. But to create a broad base of support for the new government, Winthrop and his assistants expanded the freemanship in 1631 to include every adult male church member.

The governor, his assistants, and the freemen together made up the General Court of the colony, which passed all laws, levied taxes, established courts, and made war and peace. In 1634 the whole body of the freemen stopped meeting and instead each town

Sudbury, Massachusetts
Everyday life in New England centered in small towns such as Sudbury, west of Boston. Families lived in houses clustered around the meeting house, in contrast to the decentralized plantations of the south. The privately held farm lots were mixed together as well, so that neighbors worked and lived in close contact with one another.

elected representatives or deputies to the General Court. Ten years later, the deputies formed themselves into the lower house of the Bay Colony legislature, and the assistants formed the upper house. By refashioning a company charter into a civil constitution, Massachusetts Bay Puritans were well on the way to shaping society, church, and state to their liking.

Contrary to expectations, New England proved more hospitable to the English than did the Chesapeake. The character of the migration itself gave New England settlers an advantage, for most arrived in family groups—not as young, single, indentured servants of the sort whose discontents unsettled Virginia society. The heads of New England's first households were typically free men—farmers, artisans, and merchants. Most were skilled and literate. Since husbands usually migrated with their wives and children, the ratio of men to women within the population was fairly evenly balanced.

Most of the immigrants, some 21,000, came in a cluster between 1630 and 1642. Thereafter new arrivals tapered off because of the outbreak of the English Civil War. This relatively rapid colonization fostered solidarity because immigrants shared a common past of persecution and a strong desire to create an ordered society modeled on Scripture.

The "Great Migration"

Stability and Order in Early New England

Puritan emigrants and their descendants thrived in New England's bracing but healthy climate. The first generation of colonists lived to an average age of 70, nearly twice as long as Virginians and 10 years longer than men and women living in England. With 90 percent of all children reaching adulthood, the typical family consisted of seven or eight children who came to maturity. Because of low death rates and high birthrates, the number of New Englanders doubled about every 27 years—while the populations of Europe and the Chesapeake barely reproduced themselves. By 1700, New England and the Chesapeake would both have populations of approximately 100,000. But, whereas the southern population grew because of continuing immigration and the importation of slaves, New England's expanded primarily through natural increase.

Long-Lived New Englanders

As immigrants arrived in the Bay Colony after 1630, they carved out an arc of villages around Massachusetts Bay. Within a decade settlers pressed into Connecticut, Rhode Island, and New Hampshire. Connecticut and Rhode Island received separate charters from Charles II in the 1660s, guaranteeing their residents the rights to land and government. New Hampshire, to which Massachusetts laid claim in the 1640s, did not become a separate colony until 1679. The handful of hardy souls settled along the coast of present-day Maine had also accepted the Massachusetts Bay Colony's authority.

Susan Gill, an English maid-servant from the 1670s.

Early New Englanders established most of their settlements with an eye to stability and order. Unlike the Virginians, who scattered across the Chesapeake to isolated plantations, most New Englanders established tightly knit communities like those they had left behind in England. Each family received a lot for a house along with about 150 acres of land in nearby fields. Farmers left many of their acres uncultivated as a legacy for future generations, for most had only the labor of their own families to work their land. While the Chesapeake abounded with servants, tenant farmers, and slaves, almost every adult male in rural New England owned property. With little hope of prospering through commercial agriculture, New England farmers also had no incentive to import large numbers of servants and slaves or to create large plantations.

Strong family institutions contributed to New England's order and stability. While the early deaths of parents regularly splintered Chesapeake families, two adult generations were often on hand to encourage order within New England households. Husbands and fathers exacted submission from wives and strict obedience from children. Land gave New England's long-lived fathers great authority over even their grown children; sons and daughters relied on paternal legacies of farms in order to marry and establish their own families.

Whereas churches were few and far between in seventeenth-century Virginia, they constituted the center of community life in colonial New England. Individual congregations ran their own affairs and regulated their own membership. Those wishing to join had to convince ministers and church members that they had experienced a genuine spiritual rebirth or "conversion." Most New Englanders sought and won membership. As majority institutions supported by public taxes, churches had the reach and the resources to oversee public morality, often censuring or expelling wayward neighbors. Still, ministers enjoyed less public power in New England than in the old country. New England's ministers did not serve as officers in the civil government, and the Congregational churches owned no property. In contrast, Catholic and Anglican church officials wielded real temporal power in European states, and the churches held extensive tracts of land.

Finally, New Englanders governed themselves more democratically than did their counterparts in England. Communities throughout the region held regular town meetings of all resident white men. The town fathers generally set the meeting's agenda and offered advice, but the unanimous consent of townsmen determined all decisions. Colony governments in early New England also evolved into representative and responsive institutions. Typically the central government of each colony, such as the General Court of Massachusetts Bay, consisted of a governor and a bicameral legislature, including an upper house, or council, and a lower house, or assembly. All officials were elected annually by the freemen—white adult men entitled to vote in colony elections. Voting qualifications varied, but the number of men enfranchised made up a much broader segment of society than that in seventeenth-century England.

Communities in Conflict

Although most New Englanders called themselves Puritans and Congregationalists, the very fervency of their convictions often led them to disagree about how best to carry out the teachings of the Bible and the ideas of John Calvin. During the first

The interior of the Old Ship Meetinghouse, built in Hingham, Massachusetts, in 1681, expresses the importance of hierarchy among New England Puritans. Families with wealth and influence enjoyed the comfort of enclosed wooden pews on the ground floor, whereas those with slimmer means sat on rows of benches on the second-floor gallery. The raised pulpit at the front of the meetinghouse bespeaks the congregation's respect for the authority and learning of the clergy.

decades of colonization, such disagreements led to the founding of breakaway colonies. In 1636 Thomas Hooker, the minister of Cambridge, Massachusetts, led part of his congregation to Connecticut, where they established the first English settlement. Somewhat more liberal than other Bay Puritans, Hooker favored more lenient standards for church membership. He also opposed the Bay's policy of limiting voting in colony elections to church members. In contrast, New Haven (a separate colony until it became part of Connecticut in 1662) was begun in 1638 by strict Congregationalists who found Massachusetts too liberal.

While Connecticut and New Haven emerged from voluntary migration, enforced exile filled Rhode Island with men and women whose radical ideas unsettled the rest of Massachusetts. Roger Williams, Rhode Island's founder, had come to New England in 1631, serving as a respected minister of Salem. But soon Williams announced that he was a Separatist, like the Pilgrims of Plymouth. He encouraged the Bay Colony to break all ties to the corrupt Church of England. He also urged a more complete **separation of church and state** than most New Englanders were prepared to accept, and later in his career he endorsed full religious toleration. Finally, Williams denounced the Bay's charter—the legal document that justified Massachusetts's existence—on the grounds that the king had no right to grant land that he had not purchased from the Indians. When Williams boldly suggested that Massachusetts actually inform the king of his mistake, angry authorities prepared to deport him. Instead Williams fled the colony in the dead of winter to live with the Indians. In 1636, he became the founder and first citizen of Providence, later to be part of Rhode Island.

Another charismatic heretic from Massachusetts arrived soon after. Anne Hutchinson, a skilled midwife and the spouse of a wealthy merchant, came to Boston in 1634. Enthusiasm for her minister, John Cotton, started her on a course of explaining his sermons to gatherings of her neighbors—and then to elaborating ideas of her own. The fact that a woman would do such things made the authorities uneasy; but they became alarmed when they learned that Hutchinson embraced controversial positions on doctrine. Soon a majority of the Bay's ministers accused the troublesomely popular Hutchinson of holding heretical views. She in turn denounced her detractors, and the controversy escalated. In 1638 the Bay Colony government expelled Hutchinson and

Roger Williams

Anne Hutchinson

Witchcraft trials and executions took place throughout Europe in the sixteenth and seventeenth centuries, occurring far more frequently and claiming many more victims than in colonial America. But, as this engraving of an English hanging of witches indicates, women composed a majority of those charged and executed on both sides of the Atlantic.

In 1684 the Reverend Increase Mather, a learned Boston minister, proudly issued a plump book entitled *Remarkable Providence*. The work was packed with fantastic occurrences that had taken place during the first 50 years of New England's settlement. Those occurrences dealt with "wonders"—interventions of the supernatural in the normal order of things. Ministers throughout New England contributed marvels of all sorts: a "Conjuring Book" from Salem, which filled readers with "a strange kind of Horror" and caused their hair to stand on end; a house in Newbury inhabited by evil spirits and a "monstrous birth"; a phantom ship sighted sailing into New Haven harbor that suddenly disappeared.

Mather's book of wonders became one of many available to New England readers—a numerous group, for literacy was almost universal. Accounts of marvelous events poured from presses in England, the Continent, and the colonies. The authors drew their reports of visions and voices, untimely deaths and natural disasters from ancient and early Christian authors, medieval chronicles, the Bible, and local lore collected by contemporaries.

Most seventeenth-century New Englanders preferred to read religious books: the Bible, psalmbooks, sermons. Even so, authors such as Increase Mather recognized that a wider audience might be reached by volumes blending godly messages with sensational topics. Ministers recounted wonders to make the religious argument that the world was shot through with mystery and miracle and that men and women were at the mercy of God's will and the devil's wiles. At the same time, these books titillated readers with accounts of witches, apparitions, and

her followers for sedition. She settled briefly in Rhode Island before moving on to Long Island, where she died in an Indian attack.

Goodwives and Witches

If Anne Hutchinson had been a man, her ideas would still have been deemed heretical. However, if she had been a man, she might have found other ways to express her intelligence and magnetism. But life in colonial New England offered women, especially married women, little scope for their talents.

Most adult women were hardworking farm wives who cared for large households of children. Between marriage and middle age, most New England wives were pregnant except when breast-feeding. When they were not nursing or minding children, mothers were producing and preparing much of what was consumed and worn by their families. They planted vegetable gardens and pruned fruit trees, salted beef and pork and pressed cider, milked cows and churned butter, kept bees and tended poultry, cooked and baked, washed and ironed, spun, wove, and sewed. While husbands and sons engaged in farm work that changed with the seasons, took trips to taverns and mills, and went off to hunt or fish, housebound wives and daughters were locked into a humdrum routine with little time for themselves.

Legal Barriers for Women

Women suffered legal disadvantages as well. In contrast to Spanish New Mexico and Florida with their Spanish civil law traditions, English common law and colonial legal codes accorded married women no control over property. Wives could not sue or be sued, they could not make contracts, and they surrendered to their husbands any property that they possessed before marriage. Divorce was almost impossible to obtain until the late eighteenth century. Only widows and a few single women had the same property rights as men, but they could not vote in colony elections.

freaks of nature. Published narratives of New Englanders taken captive by the Indians and the confessions of convicted murderers combined the same mixture of religion and sensationalism.

Knowing what early New Englanders liked to read offers a glimpse not only of their entertainments but of their inner world. Especially significant was their enduring fascination with wonders, which were believed to be true both by learned folks and by humble farmers and their wives. The popularity of wonder lore is powerful proof that all New Englanders inhabited an enchanted universe. Their world brimmed with invisible forces and supernatural beings that could interrupt the order of nature.

That widely shared belief made witchcraft a crime punishable by death and allowed for the unfolding of the notorious witchcraft trials in Salem Village. There,

in the early months of 1692, a group of adolescent girls used the white of a raw egg suspended in a glass of water as a kind of crude crystal ball to divine what sorts of men their future husbands might be. Somehow, the seance went sour, and the frightened adolescents began behaving in ways that other villagers took to be signs of bewitchment. Crying out in pain and terror, the afflicted girls claimed to see taunting specters of witches, whom they recognized as fellow villagers. In the hysteria that ensued, hundreds of accusations of witchcraft led to the trial and execution of 20 innocent women and men. Only when Increase Mather and 14 other Massachusetts ministers publicly warned against the trials' excesses did the killings stop.

Many historians have tried to explain the deeper causes behind the Salem episode. Some point to the Puritan mistrust

of independent women, others to the bitter rivalries among Salem Village families. Still others have noted ties between accused witches and heretical groups such as the Quakers, or deep communal traumas stemming from conflicts with Indians and the French. Whatever the source of Salem's particular troubles, the witchcraft charges there and elsewhere in seventeenth-century New England were rooted in the widespread belief in a world of wonders, at once terrible and fascinating. Witchcraft trials and executions took place throughout Europe in the sixteenth and seventeenth centuries, occurring far more frequently and claiming many more victims than in colonial America. But, as this engraving of an English hanging of witches indicates, women composed a majority of those charged and executed on both sides of the Atlantic.

The one arena in which women could attain something approaching equal standing with men was the churches. Puritan women could not become ministers, but after the 1660s they made up the majority of church members. In some churches membership enabled them to vote for ministerial candidates and to voice opinions about

The artist who sketched this Quaker meeting called attention to one of that sect's most controversial practices by placing a woman at the center of his composition. Women were allowed to speak in Quaker worship services and to preach and proselytize at public gatherings of non-Quakers. The Puritans roundly condemned this liberty as contrary to the teachings of St. Paul.

admitting and disciplining members. Puritan doctrine itself rejected the medieval Catholic suspicion of women as "a necessary evil," seeing them instead as "a necessary good." Even so, the Puritan ideal of the virtuous woman was a chaste, submissive "helpmeet," a wife and mother who served God by serving men.

Witchcraft

Communities sometimes responded to assertive women with accusations of witchcraft. Like most early modern Europeans, New Englanders believed in wizards and witches, men and women who were said to acquire supernatural powers by signing a compact with Satan. A total of 344 New Englanders were charged with witchcraft during the first colonial century, with the Salem Village episode of 1692 producing the largest outpouring of accusations after 20 executions. More than three-quarters of all accused witches were women, usually middle-aged and older, and most of those accused were regarded as unduly independent. Before they were charged with witchcraft, many had been suspected of heretical religious beliefs, others of sexual impropriety. Still others had inherited or stood to inherit property.

The People in the Way

Similarities between Puritans and Indians

Whatever their political battles, doctrinal disputes, and inequalities, New Englanders were all participants in a colonial project that depended on taking land from other people. Perhaps 100,000 Algonquin men and women lived in the area reaching from the Kennebec River in Maine to Cape Cod at contact. Like the Puritans, they relied on fishing in spring and summer, hunting year round, and cultivating and harvesting corn and other crops in spring and fall. And, to an even greater degree than among the colonists, Indian political authority was local. Within each village, a single leader known as the "sachem" or "sagamore" directed economic life, administered justice, and negotiated with other tribes and English settlers. As with New England's town fathers, a sachem's power was contingent on keeping the trust and consent of his people.

Thus the newcomers had more in common with their hosts than they cared to admit. But English expansion in the region had to come at someone's expense, and colonists obtained Indian lands in one of three ways. Sometimes they purchased it. Sales varied—they might be free and fair, fraudulent, subtly coerced, or forced through intimidation and violence. Second, colonists eagerly expanded into lands emptied by epidemics. The English often saw God's hand in such events. Following a terrible smallpox epidemic in 1633–1634, for example, one observer exclaimed that "without this remarkable and terrible stroke of God upon the natives, [we] would with much more difficulty have found room, and at far greater charge have obtained and purchased land."

Third and finally, colonists commonly encouraged and participated in regional wars to obtain native lands. This proved easy enough to do, because, like Europeans, the Indians of New England quarreled frequently with neighboring nations. The antagonism among the English, Spanish, Dutch, and French was matched by the hostilities among the Abenakis, Pawtuckets, Massachusetts, Narragansetts, and Wampanoags of the north Atlantic coast. Epidemics often intensified existing rivalries. Affecting some villages and nations more than others, outbreaks of Old-World disease opened up new opportunities for stronger neighbors to press the advantage. New England settlers, like those in the Chesapeake, studied Indian feuds to better exploit them.

The English began by aligning with Masasoit and his Wampanoags against other coastal peoples in New England. In 1637 colonial forces joined the Narragansetts in a campaign against the formidable Pequots, who controlled coveted territory in present-day Connecticut. The colonists shocked even their Indian allies when they set fire to the main Pequot village, killing hundreds of men, women, and children. Plymouth's William Bradford recalled that "it was a fearful sight to see them thus frying in the fire, and the streams of blood quenching the same, and horrible was the stink and scent thereof; but the victory seemed a sweet sacrifice, and they gave the praise therof to God, who had wrought so wonderfully for them." Several years later the colonists turned against their former allies, joining forces with the Mohegans to intimidate the Narragansetts into ceding much of their territory. Only a few colonists objected to those ruthless policies, among them Roger Williams. "God Land," he warned one Connecticut leader, "will be (as it now is) as great a God with us English as God Gold was with the Spainards."

Metacom's War

Throughout these wars, the colonists more or less nurtured their original alliance with Masasoit and his Wampanoags. As long as regional enemies bore the brunt of English expansion, Masasoit and his people could live in relative safety. Indeed, certain colonists tried to bring the two societies closer together. While the impulse to convert was not nearly as strong in New England as in New Spain or New France, a few Englishmen worked tirelessly to bring the word of their God to Indians.

Most famously, Puritan minister John Eliot began preaching in Algonquian in the 1640s. Over the next two decades he oversaw a project to publish the scriptures in Algonquian using the Latin alphabet. He also trained scores of native ministers (many of whom became literate), and established seven villages or "praying towns" exclusively for Christian Indians. Eliot was not alone. According to its charter of 1650, for example, Harvard College defined its mission as "the education of English & Indian youth of this Country in knowledge and godliness." In 1655 Harvard established an Indian college and dormitory on campus specifically to instruct Wampanoag youth in the English language and in Protestantism. None of these efforts embodied respect for Indian culture or religion. But some in New England, at least, wanted to assimilate Indians rather than drive them away.

Missions to the Indians

And yet the colony always grasped for more land. By the time Masasoit died and was succeeded by his son in the 1660s, the partnership had become a relationship of subordination and suspicion. Colonial authorities reacted to rumors of pending native rebellion with humiliating interrogations and increasingly severe rules and restrictions. The colonists' cows and pigs invaded and destroyed Indian fields, provoking innumerable conflicts as white pressures on Indian lands increased. When Indians themselves tried to adapt by raising their own cows and pigs, colonial authorities barred them from using common pasture or selling meat in Boston. At the same time, as many as half the dwindling Wampanoags had followed Eliot into the praying towns, threatening tribal unity in a time of mounting crisis.

By 1675 these and other pressures convinced Masasoit's son, Metacom, whom the English called King Philip, that his nation could be preserved only by chancing war. Complaining that the English were plotting to kill him and other sachems and replace them with Christian Indians more willing to sell land, Metacom rallied most of southern New England's native peoples and laid waste to Plymouth Colony. Metacom's forces destroyed more than two dozen colonial towns. By the spring of 1676, they were closing in on the coast, raiding settlements within 20 miles of Boston.

But the momentum could not be sustained. Faced with shortages of food and ammunition, Metacom called for assistance from the Abenakis of Maine and the Mahicans of New York. Both refused his plea, and the English even recruited the powerful Mohawks to their cause. In the summer of 1676 Metacom met his death in battle; colonial forces dismembered his body and brought his severed head to Boston and his hands to Plymouth as trophies. The Indian offensive collapsed, but not before threatening New England's very existence. In proportion to population, "King Philip's War" inflicted twice the casualties on New England that the United States as a whole would suffer in the American Civil War. And Metacom's desperate gamble exhuasted native military power in southern New England, virtually destroyed the Wampanoags as a coherent people, and consigned the region's surviving Indians, Christian or not, to quiet and often desperate lives on the margins of colonial life.

The Mid-Atlantic Colonies

The inhabitants of the mid-Atlantic colonies—New York, New Jersey, Pennsylvania, and Delaware—enjoyed more secure lives than most southern colonials. But they lacked the common bonds that lent stability to early New England. Instead, throughout the mid-Atlantic region a variety of ethnic and religious groups vied for wealth from farming and the fur trade and contended bitterly against governments that commanded little popular support.

English Rule in New York

By the 1660s, the Dutch experiment on the mid-Atlantic coast was faltering. While Fort Orange continued to secure furs for the Dutch West India company, the colonial population remained small and fractious. The company made matters worse by appointing corrupt, dictatorial governors who ruled without an elective assembly. It also provided little protection for outlying Dutch settlements; when it did attack neighboring Indian nations, it did so savagely, triggering terrible retaliations. By the time the company went bankrupt in 1654, it had virtually abandoned its American colony.

Taking advantage of the disarray in New Netherlands, Charles II ignored Dutch claims in North America and granted his brother, James, the Duke of York, a proprietary charter there. The charter granted James all of New Netherlands to Delaware Bay as well as Maine, Martha's Vineyard, and Nantucket Island. In 1664 James sent an invading fleet, whose mere arrival caused the Dutch to surrender.

New York's dizzying diversity would make it difficult to govern. The Duke inherited 9,000 or so colonists: Dutch, Belgians, French, English, Portuguese, Swedes, Finns, and Africans—some enslaved, others free. The colony's ethnic diversity ensured a variety of religions. Although the Dutch Reformed church predominated, other early New Netherlanders included Lutherans, Quakers, and Catholics. There were Jews as well, refugees from Portuguese Brazil, who were required by law to live in a ghetto in New Amsterdam. The Dutch resented English rule, and only after a generation of intermarriage and acculturation did that resentment fade. James also failed to win friends among New Englanders who had come to Long Island seeking autonomy and cheap land during the 1640s. He grudgingly gave in to their demand for an elective assembly in 1683 but rejected its first act, the Charter of Liberties, which would have guaranteed basic political rights. The chronic political strife discouraged prospective settlers. By 1698 the colony numbered only 18,000 inhabitants, and New York City, the former New Amsterdam, was an overgrown village of a few thousand.

Ethnic and Religious Diversity

The Founding of New Jersey

Confusion attended New Jersey's beginnings. The lands lying west of the Hudson and east of the Delaware River had been part of the Duke of York's proprietary grant. But in 1664 he gave about 5 million of these acres to Lord Berkeley and Sir George Carteret, two of his favorites who were already involved in the proprietary colonies of the Carolinas. New Jersey's new owners guaranteed settlers land, religious freedom, and a representative assembly in exchange for a small quitrent, an annual fee for the use of the land. The proprietors' terms promptly drew Puritan settlers from New Haven, Connecticut. At the same time, unaware that James had already given New Jersey to Berkeley and Carteret, New York's Governor Richard Nicolls granted Long Island Puritans land there.

More complications ensued when Berkeley and Carteret decided to divide New Jersey into east and west and sell both halves to **Quaker** investors—a prospect that outraged New Jersey's Puritans. Although some English Quakers migrated to West Jersey, the investors quickly decided that two Jerseys were less desirable than one Pennsylvania and resold both East and West Jersey to speculators. In the end the Jerseys became a patchwork of religious and ethnic groups. Settlers who shared a common religion or national origin formed communities and established small family farms. When the Crown finally reunited east and west as a single royal colony in 1702, New Jersey was overshadowed by settlements not only to the north but now, also, to the south and west.

Quaker Odysseys

Religious and political idealism similar to that of the Puritans inspired the colonization of Pennsylvania, making it an oddity among the mid-Atlantic colonies. The oddity began with an improbable founder, William Penn. Young Penn devoted his early years to disappointing his distinguished father, Sir William Penn, an admiral in the Royal Navy. Several years after being expelled from college, young Penn finally chose a career that may have made the admiral yearn for mere disappointment: he undertook a lifelong commitment to put into practice Quaker teachings. By the 1670s he had emerged as an acknowledged leader of the Society of Friends, as the Quakers formally called themselves.

Quaker Beliefs

The Quakers behaved in ways and believed in ideas that most people regarded as odd. They dressed in a deliberately plain and severe manner. They withheld from their social superiors the customary marks of respect, such as bowing, kneeling, and removing their hats. They refused to swear oaths or to make war. They allowed women public roles of religious leadership. That pattern of behavior reflected their egalitarian ideals, the belief that all men and women shared equally in the "Light Within." Some 40,000 English merchants, artisans, and farmers embraced Quakerism by 1660, and many suffered fines, imprisonment, and corporal punishment.

Since the English upper class has always prized eccentricity among its members, it is not surprising that Penn, despite his Quakerism, remained a favorite of Charles II. More surprising is that the king's favor took the extravagant form of presenting Penn in 1681 with all the land between New Jersey and Maryland. Perhaps the king was repaying Penn for the large sum that his father had lent the Stuarts. Or perhaps the king was hoping to export England's Quakers to an American colony governed by his trusted personal friend.

Pennsylvania Established

Penn envisioned that his proprietary colony would provide a refuge for Quakers while producing quitrents for himself. To publicize his colony, he distributed pamphlets praising its attractions throughout the British Isles and Europe. The response was overwhelming: by 1700 its population stood at 21,000. The only early migration of equal magnitude was the Puritan colonization of New England.

Patterns of Growth

Perhaps half of Pennsylvania's settlers arrived as indentured servants, while the families of free farmers and artisans made up the rest. The majority were Quakers from Britain, Holland, and Germany, but the colonists also included Catholics, Lutherans, Baptists, Anglicans, and Presbyterians. In 1682 when Penn purchased and annexed the Three Lower Counties (later the colony of Delaware), his colony included the 1,000 or so Dutch, Swedes, and Finns living there.

Quakers from other colonies—West Jersey, Maryland, and New England—also flocked to the new homeland. Those experienced settlers brought skills and connections that contributed to Pennsylvania's rapid economic growth. Farmers sowed their rich lands into a sea of wheat, which merchants exported to the Caribbean. The center of the colony's trade was Philadelphia, a superb natural harbor situated at the confluence of the Delaware and Schuylkill rivers.

In contrast to New England's landscape of villages, the Pennsylvania countryside beyond Philadelphia was dotted with dispersed farmsteads. Commercial agriculture required larger farms, which kept settlers at greater distances from one another. As a result, the county rather than the town became the basic unit of local government in Pennsylvania.

Quakers and Indians

Another reason that farmers did not need to cluster their homes within a central village was that they were at peace with the coastal Indians, the Lenni Lenapes (also called Delawares by the English). Thanks to two Quaker beliefs—their commitment to pacifism and their conviction that the Indians rightfully owned their land—peace prevailed between native inhabitants and newcomers. Before Penn sold any land to colonists, he purchased it from the Indians. He also prohibited the sale of alcohol to the tribe, strictly regulated the fur trade, and learned the language of the Lenni Lenapes. "Not a language spoken in Europe," he remarked, "hath words of more sweetness in Accent and Emphasis than theirs."

"Our Wildernesse flourishes as a Garden," Penn declared late in 1683, and in fact, his colony lived up to its promises. New arrivals readily acquired good land on liberal terms, while Penn's Frame of Government instituted a representative assembly and guaranteed all inhabitants the basic English civil liberties and complete freedom of worship.

The tidy, productive farmsteads of the Pennsylvania countryside were the basis of that colony's prosperity during the eighteenth century. Their produce fueled the growth of Philadelphia and sustained the expansion of sugar plantations on England's Caribbean islands.

Quakers and Politics

Even so, Penn's colony suffered constant political strife. Rich investors whom he had rewarded with large tracts of land and trade monopolies dominated the council, which held the sole power to initiate legislation. That power and Penn's own claims as proprietor set the stage for controversy. Members of the representative assembly battled for the right to initiate legislation. Farmers opposed Penn's efforts to collect quitrents. The Three Lower Counties agitated for separation, their inhabitants feeling no loyalty to Penn or Quakerism.

Penn finally bought peace at the price of approving a complete revision of his original Frame of Government. In 1701 the Charter of Privileges, Pennsylvania's new constitution, stripped the council of its legislative power, leaving it only the role of advising the governor. The charter also limited Penn's privileges as proprietor to the ownership of ungranted land and the power to veto legislation. Thereafter an elective unicameral assembly, the only single-house legislature in the colonies, dominated Pennsylvania's government.

Penn's Compromises

As Pennsylvania prospered, Philadelphia became the commercial and cultural center of England's North American empire. Gradually the interior of Pennsylvania filled with immigrants—mainly Germans and Scots-Irish—who harbored no "odd" ideas about Indian rights, and the Lenni Lenapes and other native peoples were bullied into moving farther west. As for William Penn, he returned to England and spent time in a debtors' prison after being defrauded by his unscrupulous colonial agents. He died in 1718, an ocean away from his American utopia.

Adjustment to Empire

Whatever his personal disappointments, Penn's colony had enjoyed spectacular growth—as indeed had British North America more generally. And yet by the 1680s England's king had reason to complain. Although North America now abounded in places named in honor of English monarchs, the colonies themselves lacked any strong ties to the English state. Until Parliament passed the first Navigation Acts in 1660, England had not even set in place a coherent policy for regulating colonial trade. And the acts had not produced the desired sense of patriotism in the colonies. While Chesapeake planters grumbled over the customs duties levied on tobacco, New Englanders, the worst of the lot, ignored the Navigation Acts altogether and traded openly with the Dutch. Royally appointed proprietors increasingly met defiance in New York, New Jersey, the Carolinas, and Pennsylvania. If England were to prosper from colonies as Spain's monarchs had, the crown needed to take matters in hand.

The Dominion of New England

And the crown did so in 1686. At the urging of the new King James II (formerly the Duke of York), the Lords of Trade consolidated the colonies of Connecticut, Plymouth, Massachusetts Bay, Rhode Island, and New Hampshire into a single entity to be ruled by a royal governor and a royally appointed council. By 1688 James had added New York and New Jersey to that domain, now called the Dominion of New England. Showing the typical Stuart distaste for representative government, James also abolished all northern colonial assemblies. The king's aim to centralize authority over such a large territory made the Dominion not only a royal dream but a radical experiment in English colonial administration.

The experiment proved to be short-lived. In England James II had revealed himself to be yet another Stuart who tried to dispense with Parliament and who had embraced Catholicism besides. Parliament dispensed with the king just as it had with Charles I during the English Civil War of the 1640s. In a quick, bloodless coup d'état known as the Glorious Revolution, Parliament forced James into exile in 1688. In his place it elevated to the throne his daughter, Mary, and her Dutch husband, William of Orange.

The Glorious Revolution

England, in an effort to regulate colonial trade, required all ships bound from America to pass through British ports and pay customs duties. Places such as Plymouth, Liverpool, and Bristol (shown here) thrived as a result. Contrast this large, bustling commercial center with the modest size of Plymouth 200 years earlier (illustration, page 29).

Mary was a distinctly better sort of Stuart—a staunch Protestant—and she agreed to rule with Parliament.

William and Mary officially dismembered the Dominion of New England and reinstated representative assemblies everywhere in the northern colonies. Connecticut and Rhode Island were restored their old charters, but Massachusetts received a new charter in 1691. Under its terms Massachusetts, Plymouth, and present-day Maine were combined into a single royal colony headed by a governor appointed by the Crown rather than elected by the people. The charter also imposed religious toleration and made property ownership rather than church membership the basis of voting rights.

Royal Authority in America in 1700

Closer Regulation of Trade

William and Mary were more politic than James II, but no less interested in revenue. In 1696 Parliament enlarged the number of customs officials stationed in each colony to enforce the Navigation Acts. To help prosecute smugglers, Parliament established colonial vice-admiralty courts, tribunals without juries presided over by royally appointed justices. To keep current on all colonial matters, the king appointed a new Board of Trade to replace the old Lords of Trade. The new enforcement procedures generally succeeded in discouraging smuggling and channeling colonial trade through England.

These changes were enough for England and its monarchs for half a century thereafter. English kings and queens gave up any dreams of imposing the kind of centralized administration of colonial life represented by the Dominion of New England. Clearly, royal control had increased over the previous half century. By 1700 royal governments had been established in Virginia, New York, Massachusetts, and New Hampshire. New Jersey, the Carolinas, and Georgia would shortly be added to the list. Royal rule meant that the monarch appointed governors and (everywhere except Massachusetts) also appointed their councils. Royally appointed councils could veto any law passed by a colony's representative assembly, royally appointed governors could veto any law passed by both houses, and the Crown could veto any law passed by both houses and approved by the governor.

The Limits of Royal Power

Nonetheless, the sway of royal power remained more apparent than real after 1700. The Glorious Revolution asserted once and for all that Parliament's authority—rule by the legislative branch of government—would be supreme in the governing of England. In the colonies members of representative assemblies grew more skilled at dealing with royal governors and more protective of their rights. They guarded most jealously their strongest lever of power—the right of the lower houses to levy taxes.

The political reality of the assemblies' power reflected a social reality as well. No longer mere outposts along the Atlantic, the colonies of 1700 were becoming more firmly rooted societies. Their laws and traditions were based not only on what they had brought from England but also on the conditions of life in America. That social reality had already blocked Stuart ambitions to shape the future of North America, just as it had thwarted the designs of lordly proprietors and the dreams of religious reformers.

Still, the dream of empire would revive among England's rulers in the middle of the eighteenth century—in part because the rulers of France had never abandoned their own imperial visions. France had long been Europe's largest kingdom in terms of land and overall population. By the 1660s, bureaucratic, financial, and political reforms had left the French with the mightiest military as well. Determined to have more territory, France's ambitious king, Louis XIV, unleashed this titanic war machine against his neighbors on four different occasions between 1667–1714.

Even after 1714, France, England and, to a lesser extent, Spain waged a kind of cold war for a quarter of a century, jockeying for position and influence. Western European monarchs had come to realize that confrontations in North America's vast and distant interior could influence the outcome of their feuds closer to home. In this global chess game, the British had the advantage of numbers: nearly 400,000 subjects in the colonies in 1720, compared with only about 25,000 French spread along a thin line of fishing stations and fur-trading posts, and a meager 5,000 or so Spaniards in New Mexico, Texas, and Florida combined. But by a considerable margin, native peoples still represented the majority population in North America. Moreover, they still controlled more than 90 percent of its territory. If events in North America could affect the balance of power in Europe, then French and Spanish administrators could still believe and hope that their Indian alliances might yet help them prevail against each other, and, especially, against Britain's booming colonies.

Significant Events

late 1500s	Formation of the Iroquois League
1535	Cartier makes first voyage to the Gulf of St. Lawrence
1608	Champlain founds Québec
1616–1618	Epidemic devastates native peoples of the coastal Northeast
1620	Puritans settle at abandoned village of Patuxet and rename it Plymouth
1624	Dutch found New Netherlands
1630	Winthrop fleet arrives in Massachusetts Bay; Boston established
1637	Pequot War
1642–1648	English Civil War
1649	Charles I executed

1660	English monarchy restored; Charles II becomes king
1664	New Netherlands becomes English New York; founding of New Jersey
1675–1676	Metacom's War
1681	Founding of Pennsylvania
1682	La Salle becomes European to descend the Mississippi to its mouth
1685	James II becomes king of England
1686–1690	Dominion of New England
1688	Glorious Revolution; William and Mary become monarchs of England
1692	Witchcraft trials in Salem
1696	Creation of Board of Trade and Plantation

Chapter Summary

While the French colonized Canada, the Protestant Reformation in England spurred the colonization of New England and Pennsylvania.

- During the seventeenth century, the French slowly established a fur trade, agricultural communities, and religious institutions in Canada while building Indian alliances throughout the Mississippi drainage.

- Competition over the fur trade in New France and New Netherlands contributed to a devastating series of wars between Iroquois, Hurons, and dozens of other Indian groups.

- Over the same period, English Puritans planted more populous settlements between Maine and Long Island.

- The migration of family groups and a rough equality of wealth lent stability to early New England society, reinforced by the settlers' shared commitment to Puritanism and a strong tradition of self-government.

- The mid-Atlantic colonies also enjoyed a rapid growth of people and wealth, but political wrangling as well as ethnic and religious diversity made for a higher level of social conflict.

- Whereas New Englanders attempted to subdue native peoples, colonists in the mid-Atlantic enjoyed more harmonious relations with the region's original inhabitants, thanks to William Penn's Quaker principles.

- The efforts of the later Stuart kings to centralize England's empire ended with the Glorious Revolution in 1688, which greatly reduced tensions between the colonies and the parent country.

Additional Reading

For introductions to French and Indian encounters, see Olive Patricia Dickason, *Canada's First Nations* (1992) and Bruce G. Trigger, *Natives and Newcomers* (1995). Colin G. Calloway's *One Vast Winter Count* (2003) masterfully synthesizes the history of natives and Europeans in early North America west of the Appalachians, and Daniel K. Richter does the same for Eastern North America in *Facing East from Indian Country* (2001). For a recent history of Dutch America, see Jaap Jacobs, *New Netherland* (2005). Daniel K. Richter's *Ordeal of the Longhouse* (1992) presents a powerful portrait of the Iroquois before, during, and after the Beaver Wars. To understand the appeal of Puritanism, the best book to read is Charles Cohen, *God's Caress* (1986). To learn more about how English influences shaped the evolution of Puritanism in New England, read Stephen Foster's masterly study, *The Long Argument* (1991). And to learn more about the diversity of religious and supernatural views in New England, consult Philip Gura, *A Glimpse of Sion's Glory* (1984), and David Hall, *Worlds of Wonder, Days of Judgment* (1989).

For the everyday lives of northern colonists in New England and New York, rely on Virginia Dejohn Anderson's *New England's Generation* (1991), and Joyce Goodfriend's *Before the Melting Pot* (1991). The best assessment of British imperial policy in the late seventeenth century is Richard R. Johnson, *Adjustment to Empire* (1981). For the complex interplay among English colonialism, environmental change, and Indian power in the Northeast, see William Cronon's classic *Changes in the Land* (1983). The event and memory of "King Philip's War" is the subject of Jill Lepore's *The Name of War* (1998).

For a fuller list of readings, see the Bibliography at www.mhhe.com/davidsonnation6.

CHAPTER 5
The Mosaic of Eighteenth-Century America
1689~1771

The Tale of a Tattooed Traveler

August 13, 1720: Morning sunlight breaks over the confluence of the Platte and Loup Rivers in what today is Nebraska. Jean L'Archevêque rises stiffly from where he slept and looks about camp at his companions emerging from their tents. A few dozen Spanish soldiers mill about in the early light, donning their long, leather vests and their wide-brimmed hats. At another end of the encampment the Pueblo Indian men who have accompanied the expedition speak softly to one another, making less noise than the soldiers, though double their number. A friar in his habit makes his way around the tents. Don Pedro de Villasur, lieutenant governor of New Mexico and leader of the party, threads his arms through a bright, red officer's coat and orders the soldiers to bring in their horses.

Most of these men had known L'Archevêque for years—had come to appreciate his sly humor and grown accustomed to his thick accent. But on this morning, as they set about the king's business in an alien land some 600 miles from their homes and families, there must have been something unnerving about the dark, swirling tattoos that covered the Frenchman's face. They had been put there years earlier by a steady Indian hand, in the aftermath of a Texas expedition that had ended in calamity. One had only to look at L'Archevêque to be reminded that things sometimes go badly for both kings and their servants.

It was a tangled path that led the Frenchman to spend that summer morning in the company of Spaniards and Pueblo Indians. Born in 1672 in Bayonne, France, L'Archevêque was only a boy when he boarded ship to the French Caribbean, fleeing his family's financial troubles. Soon the eager 12-year-old indentured himself to a wealthy merchant, and in 1684 master and servant enlisted in a colonization scheme led by the French explorer René Robert Cavelier, Sieur de La Salle. Three years earlier La Salle had been the first to navigate the immense Mississippi River from the Great Lakes to the Gulf of Mexico. He was famous and respected. The nearly 300 colonists in his care had reason to put confidence in their leader.

Their confidence was misplaced. Try as he might, La Salle could not find the mouth of the Mississippi when he approached this time from the Gulf of Mexico. Instead he landed on the coast of present-day Texas, threw up some ramshackle buildings, and embarked on months-long forays in search of Indian allies. As the months stretched into years, the expedition lost its ships to pirates, desertion, and the sea. Meanwhile, the colonists sickened, starved, and died. Weakened

In this detail from a remarkable painting, Don Pedro de Villasur lies dead outside his tent and the Spanish just below (wearing hats) form a circle to fend off the attack of Pawnee warriors. Jean L'Archevêque stands bareheaded to the right side of the circle, wearing blue clothing. The shadow across his face likely represents his tattoos.

17 feet long by 4½ feet high, this exquisite painting on bison or elk hide was likely executed by a mission-trained Indian artist in the aftermath of Villasur's debacle. The vivid detail suggests that the artist knew many of the participants personally. Decades after the painting was finished it came into the possession of a Jesuit missionary in Sonora, who then shipped it to his family in Switzerland. It now resides on permanent display in the Governor's Palace in Santa Fe.

survivors blamed their leader and in 1687 hatched a plan to be rid of him. Young L'Archevêque played a part, distracting the great explorer while an accomplice blew his head apart with a musket shot.

The murder hardly improved L'Archevêque's situation. He and a few desperate companions soon found themselves unhappy guests among Caddo Indians in east Texas. These were the people who tattooed the young man's face, carefully inserting a dye made from walnuts into countless tiny cuts. Liberation eventually came from an unexpected quarter. Jumano Indians had carried news of La Salle's efforts to Spanish authorities in Mexico, and these authorities decided to destroy the French colony lest it become a genuine threat. It was 1690 before Spanish explorers located the remains of the French fort and learned definitively that La Salle's colony had self-destructed. They stumbled across L'Archevêque and a companion, ransomed the grateful pair from the Caddos, and took them to Mexico City for interrogation. Soon after the men were chained and shipped off to Spain for two and a half years, only to return afterward to Mexico City.

L'Archevêque had become a pawn in a high-stakes game. News of La Salle's stillborn colony convinced Spanish officials to take more energetic measures to secure their claims on the North American West, to prevent France from using the region as a base for threatening New Spain and its all too famous silver mines. Accordingly, Spain decided to build missions among the Indians of Texas. The project began haltingly, but by the early 1720s it had fortified its claim on Texas with ten missions, four presidios (military garrisons), and one civilian settlement—San Antonio. Spain also expanded its power in the North by reconquering New Mexico. Popé's Pueblo Revolt of 1680 had driven out the Spanish (see Chapter 3), but the determined unity of the diverse Pueblo villages collapsed within a dozen years. When Spanish colonists returned in earnest in 1692 under Diego de Vargas, they met only fragmented resistance.

It was in reconquered New Mexico that L'Archevêque found his first real home since boyhood. Sent north perhaps because of his facility not only with French but also Indian languages, L'Archevêque quickly became a fixture in Santa Fe, prospering, marrying well, and gaining the trust and esteem of his neighbors. The Spanish had not long returned to New Mexico before they began hearing complaints from the Plains Apaches about Pawnee raiders armed with French guns. By 1719, with Spain and France at war in Europe, New Mexico's governor heard that the French had built two large towns to the north where they dispensed weapons to Pawnees and mocked the Spanish, calling them "women." This was too much to bear. The governor ordered his lieutenant Villasur to take L'Archevêque and a mixed group of Indian and Spanish fighters to confront the French—hence the long trek to the Platte River the following summer, where the men awoke at daybreak on August 13 to do the king's business.

But things sometimes go badly for kings and their servants. Moments after ordering his men to bring in their horses, Villasur heard wild screams and saw dozens of painted Pawnee warriors rush the camp. The lieutenant governor was one of the first to die, killed with mouth agape just outside his tent; the well-traveled L'Archevêque fell soon after. In the end only 13 Spaniards and 40 Pueblo warriors escaped to bring the doleful news back to Santa Fe, where residents would long remember the ambush as one of the great calamities of their history.

That a merchant's boy from Bayonne, France, could be shipwrecked, recruited to murder, and tattooed in Texas, imprisoned in Mexico and Spain, married and made respectable on the Upper Rio Grande, and finally killed and buried alongside Spanish and Indian companions somewhere in Nebraska, testifies in a very personal way to the unpredictable changes unleashed by contact between European and American civilizations. As Europeans established colonies and began competing with one another across the far reaches of the continent, individuals throughout North America, especially native peoples, found life changing at astonishing speed. Europeans, with their animals, plants, technologies, diseases, and designs, drove the existing dynamism in the Americas to a fever pitch of transformation. But Europeans could not predict and did not control the process. Despite their grand ambitions, colonial newcomers often found their plans upended and their lives reordered by the very same forces reworking native life across the North.

As the saga of L'Archevêque illustrates, Spain contended with France for power and influence in Indian lands along the Mississippi and farther west. But France also found itself in conflict with the English in the backcountry beyond the Appalachian Mountains.

Imperial Rivalries in Europe and America

Patterns of European Settlement in the Eighteenth Century *The French, English, and Indian nations all jockeyed for power and position across North America during the eighteenth century. The French expanded their fur trade through the interior while the English at midcentury began to press the barrier of the Appalachians. But native peoples still controlled the vast majority of the continent and often held the balance of power in inter-imperial struggles.*

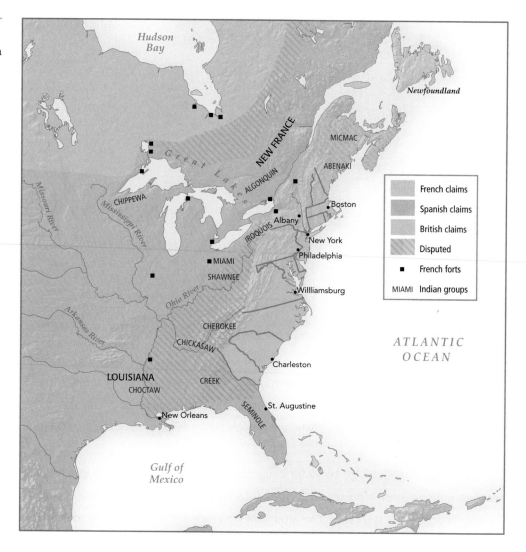

The rivalries had their beginnings in Europe and flared regularly throughout the late seventeenth century and into the eighteenth. In 1689 England joined the Netherlands and the League of Augsburg (several German-speaking states) in a war against France. While the main struggle raged in Europe, French and English colonials, joined by their Indian allies, skirmished in what was known as King William's War. Peace returned in 1697, but only until the Anglo-French struggle resumed with Queen Anne's War, from 1702–1713.

For a quarter of a century thereafter, the two nations waged a kind of cold war, competing for advantage. At stake was not so much control over people or even territory as control over trade. In North America, France and England vied for access to the sugar islands of the Caribbean, a monopoly on supplying manufactured goods to New Spain, and dominance of the fur trade. The British had the advantage of numbers: nearly 400,000 subjects in the colonies in 1720, the year of L'Archevêque's death, compared with only about 25,000 French spread along a thin line of fishing stations and fur-trading posts. Yet the French steadily strengthened their chain of forts, stretching from the mouth of the Mississippi north through the Illinois country and into Canada. The forts helped channel the flow of furs from the Great Lakes and the Mississippi River valley into Canada, thus keeping them out of the clutches of English traders. And the forts neatly encircled England's colonies, confining their settlement to the eastern seaboard.

Forces of Division

British colonials from Maine to the Carolinas distrusted the French and resented their empire of fish and furs. But the English were preoccupied with their own affairs and, by and large, uninterested in uniting against the French. Indeed a traveler during the first half of the eighteenth century would have been struck by how hopelessly divided and disunited England's mainland colonies were, split not only by ethnic and regional differences but also by racial and religious prejudices. Year after year small wooden ships brought a bewildering variety of immigrants to American seaports, aggravating those divisions. Colonials were also separated by vast distances, poor transportation, and slow communications. The frontier districts distrusted seaboard communities and the eastern seabord disdained the backcountry. Taken all in all, the British settlement in America were a diverse and divided lot.

Immigration and Natural Increase

One of the largest immigrant groups—250,000 black men, women, and children—had come to the colonies from Africa not by choice but in chains. White arrivals included many English immigrants but also a quarter of a million Scots-Irish, the descendants of seventeenth-century Scots who had regretted settling in northern Ireland; perhaps 135,000 Germans; and a sprinkling of Swiss, Swedes, Highland Scots, and Spanish Jews. Most non-English white immigrants were fleeing lives torn by famine, warfare, and religious persecution. All the voyagers, English and non-English, risked the hazardous Atlantic crossing (see Daily Lives, pages 114–115). Many had paid for passage by signing indentures to work as servants in America.

The immigrants and slaves who arrived in the colonies between 1700 and 1775 swelled an American population that was already growing dramatically from natural increase. The birthrate in eighteenth-century America was triple what it is today. Most women bore between five and eight children, and most children survived to maturity.

High Birthrate

This astonishing population explosion was quite possibly the fastest in the world at the time. Even so, the surge was merely one part of a more general global acceleration of population in the second half of the eighteenth century. China's population of 150 million in 1700 had doubled to more than 313 million by the end of the century. Europe's total rose from about 118 million to 187 million over the same period. The worldwide rise in population was unprecedented and occurred for a variety of reasons. Europe's climate, for one, had become warmer and drier, allowing for generally better harvests. Health and nutrition improved globally with the spread of Native American crops. Irish farmers discovered that a single acre planted with the American potato could support an entire family. The tomato added crucial vitamins to the Mediterranean diet, and in China the American sweet potato thrived in hilly regions where rice would not grow.

North America Leads a Global Rise in Population

The population explosion in the British colonies, fed by the importation of slaves, immigration, and natural increase, made it hard for colonials to share any common identity. Far from fostering political unity, almost every aspect of social development set Americans at odds with one another. And that process of division and disunity was reflected in the outpouring of new settlers into the backcountry.

Settlement of the Backcountry

To white immigrants from Europe weary of war or worn by want, the seaboard's established communities must have seemed havens of order and stability. But by the beginning of the eighteenth century, even the children of longtime settlers could not acquire land along the coast. In older New England towns, three and four generations were putting pressure on a limited supply of land, while wasteful farming practices had depleted the soil of its fertility. Farther south, earlier settlers had already snatched

A mountain of water swelled from the Atlantic, towered over the *Jamaica Packet,* then toppled onto the small wooden passenger ship. The impact hurled Janet Schaw and her maid about their cabin like rag dolls. As seawater surged in, the ship pitched wildly, "one moment mounted to the clouds and whirled on the pointed wave," the next plunging into the heaving ocean. The ship's provisions—hogsheads of water, coops of chickens, and barrels of salted meat—snapped from their fastenings and careened across the deck before bouncing overboard.

For more than two days the *Jamaica Packet* hurtled in the gale's grip. Then its foremast splintered, and the ship flipped onto its side. Schaw found herself "swimming amongst joint-stools, chests, [and] tables" in her cabin and listening to the sound of "our sails fluttering into rags." It would have been the end of the *Jamaica Packet* if, at that moment, its masts had not washed overboard. With the weight of the masts gone, the ship righted itself.

Schaw, "a lady of quality," as she described herself, was traveling by the finest accommodations from Great Britain to America in the age of sail. For passengers who could not pay for a private cabin, the storm was worse. Twenty-two or more indentured servants from Scotland in that year of 1774 were

bound aboard ship for the West Indies. Like thousands of others who came to America in the eighteenth century, they

up the farmland of Philadelphia's outlying counties, the prime Chesapeake tobacco property, and low-country rice swamps.

With older rural communities offering few opportunities to either native-born or newly arrived white families, both groups were forced to create new communities on the frontier. The peopling of New England's frontier—Maine, New Hampshire, and Vermont—was left mainly to the descendants of old Yankee families. Better opportunities for new immigrants to acquire land at cheaper prices lay south of New York. By the

This log cabin, built in the North Carolina backcountry in 1782, would have been dark inside, given its lack of windows. The spaces between the logs in such cabins were usually chinked with thin stones or wedges of wood and then daubed with mortar.

were consigned to steerage, the between-decks area or "upper hold."

Perhaps four to five feet high, that space was crowded with narrow wooden bunks arranged in tiers about two feet apart. It was impossible for most people to stand in steerage or to sit up in a bunk, where as many as four people huddled together at night. Sanitary facilities consisted of a few wooden buckets filled with seawater; candles and fish-oil lanterns supplied the only light. The sole source of air was the hatch opening onto the deck.

When the storm struck, the hatch was fastened tightly to keep the holds from filling with water. But as waves dashed over the decks, water streamed into steerage, forcing its occupants to stand, clutching their children to keep them from being crushed, drowned, or suffocated. For nine days they stood in water, without a fire or any food except raw potatoes and moldy biscuits. And they were without light or fresh air, except for one young man and his pregnant wife. During the storm the woman miscarried, and her "absolutely distracted" husband, Schaw reported, somehow forced open the hatch and carried her up to the deck, reviving the unconscious woman and saving her life.

Luckily, the *Jamaica Packet* escaped not only shipwreck but epidemic disease. Passengers on other transatlantic voyages were not so fortunate. Outbreaks of epidemic disease—smallpox, influenza, typhus, and diphtheria—were common. Although there are no reliable statistics for shipboard mortality during the eighteenth century, estimates range from 3 percent of all passengers to as high as 10 to 15 percent, a rate nearly comparable to that for slave ships during the Middle Passage across the Atlantic.

For all who ventured abroad, transatlantic travel was tedious and dirty at best, hazardous and horrific at worst. With good reason, those who risked the crossing routinely made out wills and sought the prayers of loved ones. On the high seas, disease and misfortune took a heavy toll.

1720s German and Scots-Irish immigrants as well as native-born settlers were pouring into western Pennsylvania. Some settled permanently, but others streamed southward into the backcountry of Virginia and the Carolinas, where they encountered native-born southerners pressing westward.

Backcountry settlers endured greater isolation than did other colonials. From many farmsteads it was a day's ride to the nearest courthouse; taverns and churches were often just as distant. Isolation hindered the formation of strong social bonds, as did the rapid rate at which people came to and left western communities. Many families pulled up stakes three or four times before settling permanently. Houses reflected that transience: most families crowded into one-room shacks walled with mud, turf, or crude logs.

Isolation of the Backcountry

The backcountry meant economic isolation as well. Large portions of the interior were cut off from water transport because they were located above the fall line, where rivers flowing to the Atlantic became unnavigable. By 1755 several crude wagon roads linked western Pennsylvania and Virginia to towns farther east, including Philadelphia, but transporting crops and driving livestock overland proved prohibitively expensive. Cut off from outside markets, farmers grew only enough to feed their households. Most backcountry inhabitants could not afford to invest in a slave or even a servant. Those conditions made the frontier, more than anywhere else in America, a society of equals.

What the frontier gained in equality it may have lost in stability. In the backcountry there were no southern gentlemen or northern town fathers to supply continuous, experienced local leadership. Nor were the churches much help in promoting law and order, because few frontier communities could afford them. Most western families, although often deeply pious, had only occasional contact with organized religion.

Hard work dominated the lives of backcountry settlers. Besides doing the usual chores of farm women, western wives and daughters joined male family members in the fields. One traveler from the East expressed his astonishment at seeing German women in western Pennsylvania "at work abroad on the Farm mowing, Hoeing Loading Dung into a Cart." Perhaps even more difficult to endure than the hard labor was the loneliness of many women's lives. The reactions of women to being resettled on the frontier can be imagined from the promise that one Scottish husband offered his wife: "We would get all these trees cut down ... [so] that we would see from house to house."

Frontier Women

Social Conflict on the Frontier

Despite the discomforts of frontier life, cheap land lured many families to the West. Benjamin Franklin, Pennsylvania's most successful entrepreneur, inventor, and politician, had observed the hordes of Scots-Irish and German immigrants lingering in Philadelphia just long enough to scrape together the purchase price of a frontier farm. From Franklin's point of view, the backcountry performed a valuable service by siphoning off surplus people from congested eastern settlements. But he knew, too, that the opened frontier unleashed discord, especially between the eastern seaboard and the backcountry.

The Paxton Boys

In Pennsylvania, Franklin himself mediated one such contest between East and West. In 1763 a band of Scots-Irish farmers known as "the Paxton Boys" protested the government's inadequate protection of frontier settlers by killing a number of Indians. Then the Paxton Boys took their protests and their guns to Philadelphia, marching as far as Lancaster before Franklin intervened and promised redress of their grievances.

Strife between East and West was even deadlier and more enduring in North and South Carolina. In both colonies legislatures dominated by coastal planters refused to grant inland settlers equitable political representation or even basic legal institutions. In response to those injustices, two protest movements emerged in the Carolina interior, each known as the Regulation.

Regulation Movements

Farmers in the South Carolina backcountry organized their Regulation in the 1760s, after that colony's assembly refused to set up courts in the backcountry. Westerners were desperate for protection from outlaws who stole livestock, kidnapped and raped women, and tortured and murdered men. In the absence of courts the Regulators acted as vigilantes, meting out their own grisly frontier justice. Only when they threatened to march on Charleston did eastern political leaders extend the court system westward.

This cartoon supported the Paxton Boys by branding Quakers as treacherously sympathetic to frontier Indians. One Quaker, on the left, eagerly supplies Indians with tomahawks, while on the right another makes sexual advances to an Indian woman. Meanwhile Benjamin Franklin, center, offers a sack of money to buy off hostile Indians.

Western North Carolinians organized their Regulation to protest not the absence of a legal system but the corruption of local government. Lawyers and merchants, backed by wealthy eastern planters, moved into the western parts of that colony and seized control of politics. Then they used those local offices to exploit frontier settlers, charging exorbitant fees for legal services, imposing high taxes, and manipulating debt laws. Western farmers responded by seizing county courts and finally squared off against an eastern militia led by the governor. Easterners crushed these Regulators at the Battle of Alamance in 1771 but left frontier North Carolinians with an enduring hostility to the seaboard.

Ethnic differences heightened sectional tensions between East and West. People of English descent predominated along the Atlantic coast, whereas Germans, Scots-Irish, and other white minorities were concentrated in the interior. Many English colonials regarded these new immigrants as culturally inferior and politically subversive. Charles Woodmason, an Anglican missionary in the Carolina backcountry, lamented the arrival of "5 or 6,000 Ignorant, mean, worthless, beggarly Irish Presbyterians, the Scum of the Earth', the Refuse of Mankind," who "delighted in a low, lazy, sluttish, heathenish, hellish life."

Ethnic Conflicts

Non-English Settlements in Eighteenth-Century British North America   *Many non-English settlers spilled into the backcountry: the Scots-Irish and Germans followed the Great Wagon Road through the western parts of the middle colonies and southern colonies while the Dutch and other Germans moved up the Hudson River valley.*

ATLANTIC OCEAN

Philadelphia

Camden

Non-English Settlements
- Scots-Irish
- German
- Dutch
- Great Wagon Road

0   200 mi
0   200   400 km

German immigrants were generally credited with steadier work habits, as well as higher standards of sexual morality and personal hygiene. But like the clannish Scots-Irish, the Germans preferred to live, trade, and worship among themselves. By 1751 Franklin was warning that the Germans would retain their separate language and customs: the Pennsylvania English would be overrun by "the Palatine Boors."

Boundary Disputes and Tenant Wars

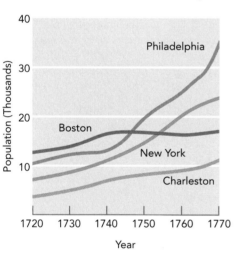

Green Mountain Boys

The settlement of the frontier also triggered disputes between colonies over their boundaries. Colonial charters, with their vague definitions of western borders, often allowed settlers and speculators from different colonies to claim the same tract of land. The most serious of these border wars pitted New York against some farmers from New England who had settled in present-day Vermont: Ethan Allen and the Green Mountain Boys. When New York tried to extend its rule over Vermont in the 1760s, Allen led a successful guerrilla resistance, harassing Yorker settlers and officials, occupying Yorker courthouses, and setting up a competing judicial system in the Green Mountains.

The spread of settlement also set the stage for mass revolts by tenants in areas where proprietors controlled vast amounts of land. In eastern New Jersey, proprietors insisted that squatters pay quitrents on land that had become increasingly valuable. When the squatters, many of them migrants from New England, refused to pay rents, the proprietors began evictions, touching off riots in the 1740s. Tenant unrest also raged in New York's Hudson River valley, where about 30 manors around New York City and Albany dominated the region. The estates encompassed some 2 million acres, worked by several thousand tenants. Newcomers from New England, however, demanded to own land and preached their ideas to Dutch and German tenants. Armed insurrection exploded in 1757 and again, more violently, in 1766. Tenants refused to pay rents, formed mobs, and stormed the homes of landlords.

Eighteenth-Century Seaports

While most Americans on the move settled on the frontier, others swelled the populations of colonial cities. By present-day standards such cities were small, harboring from 8,000 to 22,000 citizens by 1750. The scale of seaports remained intimate, too: all of New York City was clustered at the southern tip of Manhattan island, and the length of Boston or Charleston could be walked in less than half an hour.

All major colonial cities were seaports, their waterfronts fringed with wharves and shipyards. A jumble of shops, taverns, and homes crowded their streets; the spires of churches studded their skylines. By the 1750s, the grandest and most populous was Philadelphia, which boasted straight, neatly paved streets, flagstone sidewalks, and three-story brick buildings. Older cities such as Boston and New York had a more medieval aspect: most of their dwellings and shops were wooden structures with tiny windows and low ceilings, rising no higher than two stories to steeply pitched roofs. The narrow cobblestone streets of Boston and New York also challenged pedestrians, who competed for space with livestock being driven to the butcher, roaming herds of swine and packs of dogs, clattering carts, carriages, and horses.

Commerce, the lifeblood of seaport economies, was managed by merchants who tapped the wealth of surrounding regions. Traders in New York and Philadelphia shipped the Hudson and Delaware valleys' surplus of grain and livestock to the West Indies. Boston's merchants sent fish to the Caribbean and Catholic Europe, masts to England, and rum to West Africa. Charlestonians exported indigo to English dyemakers and rice to southern Europe. Other merchants specialized in the import trade,

Estimated Population of Colonial Cities, 1720–1770
Although Boston's population remained stable after 1740, it was surpassed owing to the sharp growth of New York and, especially, Philadelphia.

The Commercial Classes

selling luxuries and manufactured goods produced in England—fine fabrics, ceramics, tea, and farming implements. Wealth brought many merchants political power: they dominated city governments and shared power in colonial assemblies with lawyers and the richest farmers and planters.

Skilled craftworkers or **artisans** made up the middling classes of colonial cities. The households of master craftworkers usually included a few younger and less skilled journeymen working in other artisans' shops. Unskilled boy apprentices not only worked but also lived under the watchful eye of their masters. No large-scale domestic industry produced goods for a mass market: instead craft shops filled orders for specific items placed by individual purchasers. Some artisans specialized in the maritime trades as shipbuilders, blacksmiths, and sailmakers. Others, such as butchers, millers, and distillers, processed and packed raw materials for export. Still others served the basic needs of city dwellers—the men and, occasionally, women who baked bread, mended shoes, combed and powdered wigs, and tended shops and taverns.

On the lowest rung of a seaport's social hierarchy were free and bound workers. Free laborers were mainly young white men and women—journeyman artisans, sailors, fishermen, domestic workers, seamstresses, and prostitutes. The ranks of unfree workers included apprentices and indentured servants doing menial labor in shops and on the docks.

Black men and women also made up a substantial part of the bound labor force of colonial seaports, but the character of slavery in northern seaports changed decisively during the mid-eighteenth century. When wars raging in Europe reduced the supply of white indentured servants, colonial cities imported a larger number of Africans. In the two decades after 1730, one-third of all immigrants arriving in New York harbor were black; by 1760, blacks constituted more than three-quarters of all bound laborers in

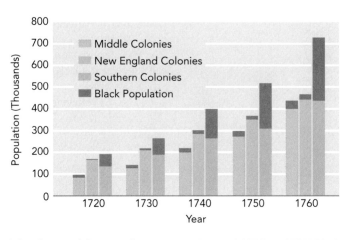

Estimated Population by Region, 1720–1760

Increase of Africans in Northern Seaports

In the mid-eighteenth century, Philadelphia became the largest city in the colonies and the second largest in all the British empire. Its busy harbor served not only as a commercial hub but also as the disembarkation point for thousands of immigrants.

Philadelphia. The preference for importing African men upset what had been an equal balance of black men and women in colonial seaports, making it difficult for the newcomers to establish families. Slaves from Africa also lacked immunity to American diseases, and many did not survive their first winter; the death rate among urban blacks was double that for whites.

But the survivors brought to urban black culture a new awareness of a common West African past. The influence of African traditions appeared most vividly in an annual event known as "Negro election day," celebrated in northern seaports. During the festival, similar to ones held in West Africa, some black men and women paraded in their masters' clothes or mounted on their horses. An election followed to choose black kings, governors, and judges who then held court and settled minor disputes among white and black members of the community. Negro election day did not challenge the established racial order with its temporary reversal of roles. but it did allow the black communities of seaports to honor their own leaders.

Women in Cities

The availability of domestic workers, both black and white, made for leisured lives among women from wealthy white families. Even those city women who could not afford household help spent less time on domestic work than did farming wives and daughters. Although some housewives grew vegetables in backyard gardens or kept a few chickens, large markets stocked by outlying farmers supplied most of the food for urban families.

For women who had to support themselves, seaports offered a number of employments. Young single women from poor families worked in wealthier households as maids, cooks, laundresses, seamstresses, or nurses. The highest-paying occupations for women, midwifery and dressmaking, both required long apprenticeships and expert skills. The wives of artisans and traders sometimes assisted their husbands and, as widows, often continued to manage groceries, taverns, and print shops. But most women were confined to caring for households, husbands, and children; less than 10 percent of women in seaports worked outside their own homes.

Urban Diversions and Hazards

All seaport dwellers—perhaps 1 out of every 20 Americans—enjoyed a more stimulating environment than other colonials did. The wealthiest could attend an occasional ball or concert; those living in New York or Charleston might even see a play performed by touring English actors. The middling classes could converse with other trades-people at private social clubs and fraternal societies. Men of every class found diversion in drink and cockfighting. Crowds of men, women, and children swarmed to

During the eighteenth century in both England and America, portraits of prominent white families and individuals sometimes included black slaves who served wealthy households. This portrait depicts a young child of New York's Van Rensselaer family and foretells his future mastery of both the young black male slave and, in the background, a fine estate in the Hudson River valley.

tavern exhibitions of trained dogs and horses or the spectacular waxworks of one John Dyer, featuring "a lively Representation of Margaret, Countess of Herrinburg, who had 365 Children at one Birth."

But city dwellers, then as now, paid a price for their pleasures. Commerce was riddled with risk: ships sank and wars disrupted trade. When such disasters struck, the lower classes suffered most. The ups and downs of seaport economies, combined with the influx of immigrants, swelled the ranks of the poor in all cities by the mid–eighteenth century. Although the major seaports established workhouses to employ the able-bodied poor, city governments continued to aid most of the dependent with small subsidies of money, food, and firewood. Furthermore, epidemics and catastrophic fires occurred with greater frequency and produced higher mortality rates in congested seaports than in the countryside.

Social Conflict in Seaports

The swelling of seaport populations, like the westward movement of whites, often churned up trouble. English, Scots-Irish, Germans, Swiss, Dutch, French, and Spanish jostled uneasily against one another in the close quarters of Philadelphia and New York. To make matters worse, religious differences heightened ethnic divisions. Jewish funerals in New York, for example, drew crowds of hostile and curious Protestants, who heckled the mourners.

Class resentment also stirred unrest. Some merchant families flaunted their wealth, building imposing town mansions and dressing in the finest imported fashions. During hard times, symbols of merchant wealth such as expensive coaches and full warehouses became targets of mob vandalism. Crowds also gathered to intimidate and punish other groups who provoked popular hostility—politicians, prostitutes, and "press gangs." Impressment, attempts to force colonials to serve in the British navy, triggered some of the most violent urban riots.

Slave Societies in the Eighteenth-Century South

Far starker than the inequalities and divisions among seaport dwellers were those between white and black in the South. By 1775 one out of every five Americans was of African ancestry, and more than 90 percent of all black Americans lived in the South, most along the seaboard. Here, on tobacco and rice plantations, slaves fashioned a distinctive African American society and culture. But they were able to build stable families and communities only late in the eighteenth century and against enormous odds.

Whether a slave was auctioned off to the Chesapeake or to the Lower South shaped his or her future in important ways. Slaves in the low country of South Carolina and Georgia lived on large plantations with as many as 50 other black workers, about half

The Chesapeake and the Lower South Compared

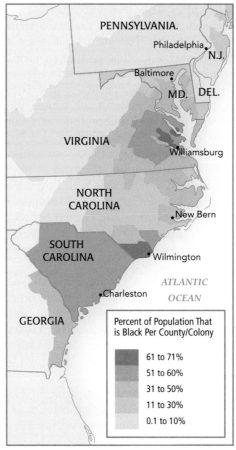

Distribution of the British Colonial Population, 1775
The African American population expanded dramatically during the eighteenth century, especially in the southern colonies. The high volume of slave imports accounts for most of the growth in the first half of the century, but natural increase was responsible for the rising black population during later decades.

of whom were African-born. They had infrequent contact with either their masters or the rest of the sparse white population. "They are as 'twere, a Nation within a Nation," observed Francis LeJau, an Anglican priest in the low country. And their work was arduous, for rice required constant cultivation. Black laborers tended young plants and hoed fields in the sweltering summer heat of the mosquito-infested lowlands. During the winter and early spring, they built dams and canals to regulate the flow of water into the rice fields. But the use of the **"task system"** rather than gang labor widened the window of freedom within slavery. When a slave had completed his assigned task for the day, one planter explained, "his master feels no right to call upon him."

Many Chesapeake slaves, such as those in the Lower South, were African-born, but most lived on smaller plantations with fewer than 20 fellow slaves. Less densely concentrated than in the low country, Chesapeake slaves also had more contact with whites. Unlike Carolina's absentee owners, who left white overseers and black drivers to run their plantations, Chesapeake masters actively managed their estates and subjected their slaves to closer scrutiny.

The Slave Family and Community

The four decades following 1700 marked the heaviest years of slave importation into the Chesapeake and Carolina regions. Those Africans had survived the trauma of captivity, the Middle Passage, and sale at slave auctions only to be thrust into a bewildering new world: a sea of unfamiliar faces, a clamor of different languages, a host of demands from men and women who called themselves masters.

African Slaves versus
American-Born Slaves

The newcomers also had to adjust to their fellow slaves. The "new Negroes" hailed from a number of diverse West African tribes, each with a separate language or dialect and distinctive cultures and kinship systems. Often, they had little in common with one another and even less in common with the American-born black minority. Native-born African Americans enjoyed better health, command of English, and experience in dealing with whites. They were also more likely to enjoy a family life, because their advantages probably made them the preferred partners of black women, who were outnumbered two to one by black men. And, since immigrant women waited two or three years before marrying, some immigrant men died before they could find a wife, and many never married. Africans resented native-born men as rivals in the competition for wives, and some immigrants held in particular contempt native converts to Christianity.

After the middle of the eighteenth century, a number of changes fostered the growth of black families and the vitality of slave communities. As slave importations began to taper off, the rate of natural reproduction among blacks started to climb. As the proportion of new Africans dropped and the number of native-born black Americans grew, the ratio of men to women in the slave community became more equal. Those changes and the appearance of more large plantations, even in the Chesapeake, created more opportunities for black men and women to find partners and form families. Elaborate kinship networks gradually developed, often extending over several plantations in a single neighborhood. And, as the immigrant generations were replaced by native-born offspring, earlier sources of tension and division within the slave community disappeared.

Even so, black families remained vulnerable. If a planter fell on hard times, members of black families might be sold off to different buyers to meet his debts. When an owner died, black spouses, parents, and children might be divided among surviving heirs. Even under the best circumstances, fathers might be hired out to other planters for long periods or sent to work in distant quarters. The migration of slaveholders from the coast to the interior also disrupted black efforts to fashion domestic and communal bonds. Between 1755 and 1782, masters on the move resettled fully one-third of all adult African Americans living in Tidewater, Virginia. Most slaves forced to journey west were men and women in their teens and early 20s, who had to begin again the long process of establishing families and neighborhood networks far from kin and friends.

The Old Plantation *affords a rare glimpse of life in the slave quarters. At this festive gathering, both men and women dance to the music of a molo (a stringed instrument similar to a banjo) and drums. Below is a gudugudu drum, an instrument common throughout West Africa and similar to the drum depicted* (left) *in the painting.*

Black families struggling with terrible uncertainties were sustained by the distinctive African American culture evolving in the slave community. The high percentage of native Africans among the eighteenth-century American black population made it easier for slaves to retain the ways of their lost homeland. Christianity won few converts, in part because white masters feared that baptizing slaves might make them more rebellious but also because African Americans preferred their traditional religions. African influence appeared as well in the slaves' agricultural skills and practices, folktales, music, and dances.

An African gudugudu drum.

Slavery and Colonial Society in French Louisiana

The experience of Africans unfolded differently in the lower Mississippi Valley, France's southernmost outpost in eighteenth-century North America. Louisiana's earliest colonial settlements were begun by a few thousand French soldiers, indentured servants, and free settlers who had straggled down from Canada, and by immigrants who came from France and Germany. When they founded New Orleans in 1718 the colonists, hoping to create prosperous plantations in the surrounding Mississippi delta, immediately clamored for bound laborers. A year later, French authorities bent to their demands, and the Company of the Indies, which managed France's slave trade, brought nearly 6,000 slaves, overwhelmingly men, directly from Africa to Louisiana. Unfortunately for white planters, Louisiana tobacco and, later, indigo proved inferior to the varieties exported from Britains colonies.

Instead of providing the formula for economic success, the sudden influx of Africans challenged French control. In 1729, with blacks already constituting a majority of the population, some newly arrived slaves joined forces with the Natchez Indians, who feared the expansion of white settlement. Their rebellion, the Natchez Revolt, left 200 French planters dead—more than 10 percent of the European population of Louisiana. The French retaliated in a devastating counterattack, enlisting both the Choctaw Indians, who were rivals of the Natchez, and other enslaved blacks, who were promised freedom in return for their support.

Natchez Revolt

The planters' costly victory persuaded French authorities to stop importing slaves into Louisiana, which helped to ensure that the colony did not develop a plantation economy until the end of the eighteenth century, when the cotton boom transformed its culture. In the meantime, blacks continued to make up a majority of all Louisianans, and by the middle of the eighteenth century, nearly all were native-born. The vast majority were slaves, but their work routines—tending cattle, cutting timber, producing

Greater Freedom for Blacks in Louisiana

Louisiana's socially mixed society is evident from this market scene: the buyers and sellers include Indians as well as colonials of French, Spanish, and African descent.

naval stores, manning boats—afforded them greater freedom of movement than most slaves enjoyed elsewhere in the American South. They were also encouraged to market the produce of their gardens, hunts, and handicrafts, which became the basis of a thriving trade with both white settlers and the dwindling numbers of Native Americans. But the greatest prize—freedom—was awarded those black men who served in the French militia, defending the colony from the English and Indians as well as capturing slave runaways. The descendants of these black militiamen would become the core of Louisiana's free black community.

Slave Resistance in Eighteenth-Century British North America

British North America had no comparable group of black soldiers, but it also had no shortage of African Americans who both resisted captivity and developed strategies for survival. Among newly arrived Africans, collective attempts at escape were most common. Groups of slaves, often made up of newcomers from the same tribe, fled inland and formed **"Maroon"** communities of runaways. These efforts were usually unsuccessful because the Maroon settlements were large enough to be easily detected.

More acculturated blacks adopted subtler ways of subverting slavery. Domestics and field hands alike faked illness, feigned stupidity and laziness, broke tools, pilfered from storehouses, hid in the woods for weeks at a time, or simply took off to visit other plantations. Other slaves, usually escaping bondage as solitary individuals, found a new life as craftworkers, dock laborers, or sailors in the relative anonymity of colonial seaports.

More infrequently, black rebellion took direct and violent form. Whites in communities with large numbers of blacks lived in gnawing dread of arson, poisoning, and insurrection. Four slave conspiracies were reported in Virginia during the first half of the eighteenth century. In South Carolina, more than two decades of abortive uprisings and insurrection scares culminated in the Stono Rebellion of 1739, the largest slave revolt of the colonial period. Nearly 100 African Americans, led by a slave named Jemmy, seized arms from a store in the coastal district of Stono and killed several white neighbors before they were caught and killed by the white militia.

The Stono Rebellion

But throughout the eighteenth century, slave rebellions occurred far less frequently on the mainland of North America than in the Caribbean or Brazil. Whites outnumbered blacks in all of Britain's mainland colonies except South Carolina, and only there did rebels have a haven for a quick escape—Spanish Florida. Faced with those odds, most slaves reasoned that the risks of rebellion outweighed the prospects for success—and most sought opportunities for greater personal freedom within the slave system itself.

Enlightenment and Awakening in America

The differences among eighteenth-century colonials resulted in more than clashes between regions, races, classes, and ethnic groups. Those differences also made for diversity in the ways that Americans thought and believed. City dwellers were more attuned

Enlightened Witchcraft? Dissecting a Physician's Scribbled Note

Despite the influence of the Enlightenment and the effects of the Great Awakening, beliefs in witchcraft and magic persisted among many ordinary colonials and even some educated elites throughout the eighteenth century. A telling bit of evidence comes from the medical records left by one Joseph Stafford, a prominent justice of the peace and physician in rural Rhode Island. Stafford not only practiced medicine but as a "Student of Astronomy and Astrology" also cast horoscopes and told his neighbors' fortunes. A curious slip of paper, tucked into one of his medical texts, reveals Stafford's thoughts about a patient: "...God bless and prosper Susan[n]a and deliver her from the false accusations brought against Her who was delivered by God's blessing from their craft and suptiltey [subtlety]."

From John Brook. The Refiner's Fire *(1994)*

Although its purpose is unclear, what does the language of the note mean? Susanna may have sought Stafford's help either because she feared being bewitched or even because she stood accused of practicing witchcraft. Whatever her motives, even more intriguing is that Stafford, a well-educated community leader, saw no contradiction in practicing medicine, making use of magic, and asking God's blessing.

---

to European culture than were people living in small villages or on the frontier. White males from well-to-do families of English ancestry were far more likely to receive college educations than were those from poor or immigrant households. White women of every class and background were excluded from higher education, and slaves received no formal education at all. Where they lived, how well they lived, whether they were male or female, native-born or immigrant, slave or free—all these variables fostered among colonials distinctive worldviews, differing attitudes and assumptions about the individual's relationship to nature, society, and God.

The Enlightenment in America

The diversity of colonials' inner lives became even more pronounced during the eighteenth century because of the **Enlightenment,** an intellectual movement that started in Europe during the seventeenth century. The leading figures of the Enlightenment, the philosophes, stressed the power of human reason to promote progress by revealing the laws that governed both nature and society. In the American colonies the Enlightenment influenced some curious artisans in major seaports and some wealthy merchants, lawyers, and landowners with the leisure and education to read the latest books from Europe.

Like many devotees of the Enlightenment, Benjamin Franklin of Philadelphia was most impressed by its emphasis on useful knowledge and experimentation. He pondered air currents and then invented a stove that heated houses more efficiently. He toyed with electricity and then invented lightning rods to protect buildings in thunderstorms. Other amateur colonial scientists constructed simple telescopes, classified animal species native to North America, or sought to explain epidemics in terms of natural causes.

Higher education helped spread Enlightenment ideas among young colonials from affluent families. Although many Americans were still educated at English universities, six colleges had been established in the colonies by 1763. The founders of some of these institutions, such as Harvard (1636) and Yale (1701), had intended them primarily to train ministers, but by the eighteenth century their graduates included lawyers, merchants, doctors, and scientists. Most offered courses in mathematics and the natural sciences that taught students algebra and such advanced theories as Copernican astronomy and Newtonian physics.

Rational versus Traditional Christianity

Some clergy educated at American colleges were influenced by the Enlightenment, adopting a more liberal theology that stressed the reasonableness of Christian beliefs. By the middle of the eighteenth century this "rational Christianity" commanded a small following among colonials, usually Anglicans or liberal Congregationalists. Their God was not the Calvinists' awesome deity but a benevolent creator who offered salvation to all, not just to a small, predestined elite. They believed that God's greatest gift to humankind was reason, which enabled all human beings to follow the moral teachings of Jesus. They muted the Calvinist emphasis on human sinfulness and the need for a soul-shattering conversion.

Enlightenment philosophy and rational Christianity did not affect the outlook of most colonials. By the middle of the eighteenth century, more than half of all white men (and a smaller percentage of white women) were literate, but most colonial readers were not equipped to tackle the learned writings of Enlightenment philosophes. As a result, the outlook of most colonials contrasted sharply with that of the cosmopolitan few. The great majority of Americans still looked for ultimate truth in biblical revelation rather than human reason and explained the workings of the world in terms of divine providence rather than natural law.

Widespread attachment to traditional Christian beliefs was strengthened by the hundreds of new churches built during the first half of the eighteenth century. Church attendance ran highest in the northern colonies, where some 80 percent of the population turned out for public worship on the Sabbath. In the South, because of the greater distances involved and the shortage of clergy, about half of all colonials regularly attended Sunday services.

Despite the prevalence of traditional religious beliefs, many ministers expressed concern about the dangerous influence of rational Christianity. They also worried that the lack of churches might tempt many frontier families to abandon Christianity altogether. Exaggerated as these fears may have been, the consequence was a major religious revival that swept the colonies during the middle decades of the eighteenth century.

The First Great Awakening

The **Great Awakening,** as the revival came to be called, first appeared in the 1730s among Presbyterians and Congregationalists in the Middle Colonies and New England. Many ministers in these churches preached an "evangelical" message, emphasizing the need for individuals to experience "a new birth" through religious conversion. Among them was Jonathan Edwards the pastor of a Congregational church in Northampton, Massachusetts. Edwards's Calvinist preaching combined moving descriptions of God's grace with terrifying portrayals of eternal damnation. "The God that holds you over the pit of hell, much as one holds a spider or some loathsome insect over the fire, abhors you and is dreadfully provoked," he declaimed to one congregation. "There is no other reason to be given, why you have not dropped into hell since you arise in the morning, but that God's hand has held you up."

These local revivals of the 1730s were mere tremors compared to the earthquake of religious enthusiasm that shook the colonies

George Whitefield drew critics as well as admirers in both England and America. In this satirical English cartoon, he is depicted as a moneygrubbing evangelist who uncharitably condemns other ministers. His audience, which consists mostly of women, is taken in by his pose of sanctity and his youthful good looks.

with the arrival in the fall of 1739 of George Whitefield. This handsome, cross-eyed "boy preacher" from England electrified crowds from Georgia to New Hampshire during his two-year tour of the colonies. He and his many imitators among colonial ministers turned the church into a theater, enlivening sermons with dramatic gestures, flowing tears, and gruesome depictions of hell. The drama of such performances appealed to people of all classes, ethnic groups, and races. By the time Whitefield sailed back to England in 1741, thousands of awakened souls were joining older churches or forming new ones.

The Aftermath of the Great Awakening

Whitefield also left behind a raging storm of controversy. Many "awakened" church members now openly criticized their ministers as cold, unconverted, and uninspiring. To supply the missing fire, some laymen—"and even Women and Common Negroes"—took to "exhorting" any audience willing to listen. The most popular ministers became **"itinerants,"** traveling like Whitefield from one town to another. Throughout the colonies the more rationalist and moderate clergy questioned the unrestrained emotionalism and the disorder that attended the gatherings of lay exhorters and itinerants.

Although Americans had been fighting over religion well before the Great Awakening, the new revivals left colonials even more divided along religious lines. The largest single group of churchgoers in the northern colonies remained within the Congregational and Presbyterian denominations. But both these groups split into factions that either supported or condemned the revivals. Quakers and Anglicans shunned the revivals. In contrast, the most radical converts joined forces with the warmest champions of the Awakening, the Baptists.

Religious Divisions

While northern churches splintered and bickered, the fires of revivalism spread to the South and its backcountry. From the mid-1740s until the 1770s, scores of new Presbyterian and Baptist churches were formed, sparking conflict as they did. Ardent Presbyterians in the Carolina backcountry disrupted Anglican worship by loosing packs of dogs in local chapels. In northern Virginia, Anglicans look the offensive against the Baptists, whose strict moral code sounded a silent reproach to the hard-drinking, high-stepping, horse-racing, slaveholding gentry. County officials, prodded by resentful Anglican parsons, harassed, fined, and imprisoned Baptist ministers.

Evangelicalism on the Frontier

And so a diverse lot of Americans found themselves continually at odds with one another. Because of differences in religion and education, colonials quarreled over whether rational Christianity enlightened the world or emotional revivalists destroyed its order. Because of ethnic and racial tensions, Spanish Jews found themselves persecuted, and African Americans searched for ways to resist their white masters. Because of westward expansion, Carolina Regulators waged war against coastal planters while colonial legislatures from Massachusetts to Virginia quarreled over western boundaries.

Colonial Diversity: a Summary

Benjamin Franklin, a man who made it his business to know, surely understood the depth of those divisions. Even he had brooded over the boatloads of non-English newcomers. He had lived in two booming seaports and felt the explosive force of the frontier. He personified the Enlightenment—and he had heard George Whitefield himself preach from the steps of the Philadelphia courthouse.

Oddly enough, even though he knew how little held colonials together, Franklin had come to harbor hopes for their political unity. After all, the majority were of English descent. And these free, white Americans liked being English. That much they had in common.

Anglo-American Worlds of the Eighteenth Century

Most Americans prided themselves on being English. When colonials named their towns and counties, they named them after places in their parent country. When colonials established governments, they turned to England for their political models. They frequently

Coffeehouses such as this establishment in London were favorite gathering places for eighteenth-century Americans visiting Britain. Here merchants and mariners, ministers and students, lobbyists and tourists warmed themselves, read newspapers, and exchanged gossip about commerce, politics, and social life.

claimed "the liberties of freeborn Englishmen" as their birthright. Even in diet, dress, furniture, architecture, and literature, colonists adopted English standards of taste.

Yet American society had developed in ways significantly different from that of Great Britain.* Some differences made colonials feel inferior, ashamed of their simplicity when compared with London's sophistication. But colonials also came to appreciate the greater equality of their society and the more representative character of their governments. If it was good to be English, it was better still to be English in America.

English Economic and Social Development

The differences between England and America began with their economies. Large financial institutions such as the Bank of England and influential corporations like the East India Company were driving England's commercial development. A growing number of textile factories and mines were deepening its industrial development. Although most English men and women worked at agriculture, it, too, had become a business. Members of the gentry rented their estates to tenants, members of the rural middle class. In turn, these tenants hired men and women from the swollen ranks of England's landless to perform the farm labor. In contrast, most colonial farmers owned their land, and most family farms were a few hundred acres. The scale of commerce and manufacturing was equally modest, limited by the preference of colonials to farm instead.

England's more developed economy fostered the growth of cities, especially London, a teeming colossus of 675,000 in 1750. In contrast, 90 percent of all eighteenth-century colonials lived in towns of fewer than 2,000.

The Consumer Revolution

But in another respect, England's more advanced economy drew the colonies and the parent country together, as a consumer revolution transformed the everyday lives of people on both sides of the Atlantic. By the beginning of the eighteenth century, small manufacturers throughout England had begun to produce an enticing array of consumer goods—fine textiles and hats, ceramics and glassware, carpets and furniture.

---

*When England and Scotland were unified in 1707, the nation as a whole became known officially as Great Britain; its citizens, as British.

Americans were so eager to acquire these commodities that the per capita consumption of imported manufactures among colonials rose 120 percent between 1750 and 1773. Only the wealthy could afford goods of the highest quality, but people of all classes demanded and indulged in small luxuries such as a tin of tea, a pair of gloves, and a bar of Irish soap. In both England and its colonies, the spare and simple material life of earlier centuries was giving way to a new order in which even people of ordinary means owned a wider variety of things.

Inequality in England and America

Then there were people of no means, and in England, they were legion. London seethed with filth, crime, and desperate poverty. The poor and the unemployed as well as pickpockets and prostitutes crowded into its gin-soaked slums, taverns, and brothels. The contrast between the luxuries enjoyed by a wealthy few Londoners and the misery of the many disquieted colonial observers. Ebenezer Hazard, an American Quaker visiting London, knew for certain that he was not in Philadelphia, but instead in "a Sink of Sin."

The opportunities for wealth provided by England's developed economy created deep class distinctions, as did the inherited privileges of its landed aristocracy. The members of the upper class made up less than 2 percent of England's population but owned 70 percent of its land. By right of birth, English aristocrats claimed membership in the House of Lords; by custom, certain powerful gentry families dominated the other branch of Parliament, the House of Commons. England's titled gentlemen shared power and wealth and often family ties with the rich men of the city—major merchants, successful lawyers, and lucky financiers. They too exerted political influence through the House of Commons.

The colonies had their own prominent families but no titled ruling class holding political privilege by hereditary right. And even the wealthiest colonial families lived in far less magnificence than did their English counterparts. Probably the finest mansion in eighteenth-century America, William Byrd's Westover, Virginia, plantation, was scarcely a tenth the size of the Marquis of Rockingham's country house, which was longer than two football fields.

If England's upper classes lived more splendidly, its lower classes were larger and worse off than those in the colonies. Less than a third of England's inhabitants belonged to the "middling sort" of traders, professionals, artisans, and tenant farmers. More than two-thirds struggled for survival at the bottom of society. In contrast, the colonial middle class counted for nearly three-quarters of the white population. With land cheap, labor scarce, and wages for both urban and rural workers 100 percent higher in America than in England, it was much easier for colonials to accumulate savings and then buy a farm of their own.

This tea caddy, owned by a Massachusetts colonial, was a new consumer luxury, as was the tea it held.

Class Distinctions

This portrait of John Stuart, the third Earl of Bute (1713–1792), wearing the ceremonial robes of the House of Lords, epitomizes the opulence of Britain's ruling class in the eighteenth century.

Ambivalent Americans

Colonials were both fascinated and repelled by English society. Benjamin Rush, a Philadelphia physician, felt in the House of Lords as if he "walked on sacred ground." He begged his guide for permission to sit on the throne therein and then sat "for a considerable time." Other colonials gushed over the grandeur of aristocratic estates and imported suits of livery for their servants, tea services for their wives, and wallpaper for their drawing rooms. They exported their sons to Britain for college educations at Oxford and Cambridge, medical school at Edinburgh, and legal training at London's Inns of Court.

But the aping of English ways made colonials uneasy, too. One Philadelphia Quaker ordered an elegant English coach complete with coat of arms—but then reconsidered and removed the crest. Second thoughts also plagued colonial parents when sons educated in England came home wearing dandified silks, affecting foppish manners, and spouting fashionable slang—"Split me, Madam!" "By Gad!" and "Dam me!"

Colonials recognized that England's ruling classes purchased their luxury and leisure at the cost of the rest of the nation. In his *Autobiography,* Benjamin Franklin painted a devastating portrait of the degraded lives of his fellow workers in a London printshop, who drowned their disappointments by drinking throughout the workday, even more excessively on the Sabbath, and then faithfully observing the holiday of "St. Monday's" to nurse their hangovers. Like Franklin, many colonials believed that gross inequalities of wealth would endanger liberty. They regarded the idle among England's rich and poor alike as ominous signs of a degenerate nation.

Politics in England and America

England's Balanced Constitution

Colonials were also of two minds about England's government. While they praised the English constitution as the basis of all liberties, they were alarmed by the actual workings of English politics. In theory, England's **"balanced constitution"** was designed to give every order of English society some voice in the workings of government. Whereas the Crown represented the monarchy and the House of Lords the aristocracy, the House of Commons represented the democracy, the people of England. In fact, the monarch's executive ministers had become dominant by creating support for their policies in Parliament through patronage—or, put more bluntly, bribery.

Tools for "Managing" Parliament

Over the course of the eighteenth century, a large executive bureaucracy had evolved in order to enforce laws, collect taxes, and wage the nearly constant wars in Europe and America. The power to appoint all military and treasury officials, customs and tax collectors, judges and justices of the peace lay with the monarch and his or her ministers. By the middle of the eighteenth century, almost half of all members of Parliament held such Crown offices or government contracts. Royal patronage was also used to manipulate parliamentary elections. The executive branch used money or liquor to bribe local voters into selecting their candidates. The small size of England's electorate fostered executive influence. Perhaps one-fourth of all adult males could vote, and many electoral districts were not adjusted to keep pace with population growth and resettlement. The notorious "rotten boroughs" each elected a member of Parliament to represent fewer than 500 easily bribable voters, whereas some large cities like Manchester and Leeds, newly populous because of industrial growth, had no representation in Parliament at all.

Colonial Governments

Americans liked to think that their colonial governments mirrored the ideal English constitution. In terms of formal structure, there were similarities. Most colonies had a royal governor who represented the monarch in America and a bicameral (two-house) legislature made up of a lower house (the assembly) and an upper house (or council). The democratically elected assembly, like the House of Commons, stood for popular interests, whereas the council, some of which were elected and others appointed, more roughly approximated the House of Lords.

But these formal similarities masked real differences between English and colonial governments. On the face of it, royal governors had much more power than the English Crown. Unlike kings and queens, royal governors could veto laws passed by assemblies; they could dissolve those bodies at will; they could create courts and dismiss judges.

This satirical rendering of an English election, by the English artist William Hogarth, mirrored the reservations of many Americans about the political culture of the mother country. The man seated in the foreground of the jostling crowd represents Hogarth's dark view of the typical English voter: much incapacitated by drink, he is being told for whom to vote by the man standing and whispering in his ear. In the background, the overturned carriage suggests that political corruption threatens the stability of England.

However, governors who asserted their full powers quickly met opposition from their assemblies, who objected that such overwhelming authority endangered popular liberty. In any showdown with their assemblies, most royal governors had to give way, for they lacked the government offices and contracts that bought loyalty. The colonial legislatures possessed additional leverage, since all of them retained the sole authority to levy taxes.

Even if the governors had enjoyed greater patronage powers, their efforts to influence colonial legislatures would have been frustrated by the sheer size of the American electorate. There were too many voters in America to bribe. More than half and possibly as many as 70 percent of all white adult colonial men were enfranchised. Property requirements were the same in America as in England, but widespread ownership of land in the colonies allowed most men to meet the qualifications easily.

The colonial electorate was also more watchful. Representatives were required to reside in the districts that they served, and a few even received binding instructions from their constituents about how to vote. Representation was also apportioned according to population far more equitably than in England. Because they were so closely tied to their constituents' wishes, colonial legislators were far less likely than members of Parliament to be swayed by executive pressure.

Most Americans were as pleased with their inexpensive and representative colonial governments as they were horrified by the conduct of politics in England. John Dickinson, a young Pennsylvanian training as a lawyer in London, was scandalized by a parliamentary election he witnessed in 1754. The king and his ministers had spent over 100,000 pounds sterling to buy support for their candidates, he wrote his father, and "if a man cannot be brought to vote as he is desired, he is made dead drunk and kept in that state, never heard of by his family and friends, till all is over and he can do no harm."

The Imperial System before 1760

Colonials such as Dickinson thought long and hard about the condition of England's society and politics. Meanwhile, the English thought about their colonies little, understood them less, and wished neither to think about them more nor to understand them better. It would be hard to exaggerate just how insignificant North America was in the English scheme of things. Those few Britons who thought about America at all believed that colonials resembled the "savage" Indians more than the "civilized" English. As a London acquaintance remarked to Thomas Hancock, it was a pity Mrs. Hancock had to remain in Boston when he could "take her to England and make her happy with Christians."

The same indifference contributed to England's haphazard administration of its colonies. The Board of Trade and Plantations, created in 1696, gathered commercial information, reviewed laws and petitions from colonial assemblies, and exchanged letters and instructions with royal governors. But the Board of Trade was only an advisory body. Real authority over the colonies was divided among an array of other agencies. The Treasury oversaw customs and gathered other royal revenues; the Admiralty Board enforced regulations of trade; the War Office orchestrated colonial defense. In practice, none of these departments spent much time on colonial affairs. Most British officials in America seemed equally indifferent.

The branch of England's government most indifferent to America was Parliament. Aside from passing an occasional law to regulate trade, restrict manufacturing, or direct monetary policy, Parliament made no effort to assert its authority in America. Its members assumed that Parliament's sovereignty extended over the entire empire, and nothing had occurred to make them think otherwise.

Benefits of Benign Neglect

For the colonies, this chaotic and inefficient system of colonial administration worked well enough. The very weakness of imperial oversight left Americans with a great deal of freedom. Even England's regulation of trade rested lightly on the shoulders of most Americans. Southern planters were obliged to send their rice, indigo, and tobacco to Britain only, but they enjoyed favorable credit terms and knowledgeable marketing from English merchants. Colonials were prohibited from finishing iron products and exporting hats and textiles, but they had scant interest in developing domestic industries. Americans were required to import all manufactured goods through England, but by doing so, they acquired high-quality goods at low prices. At little

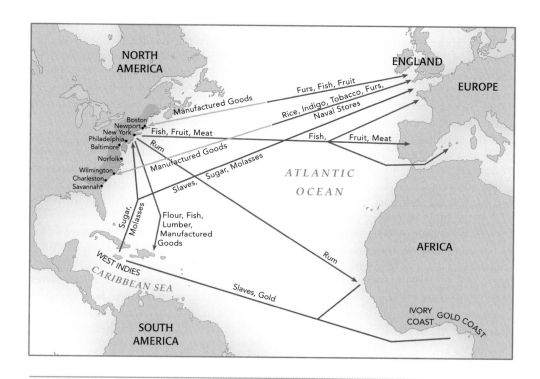

Overseas Trade Networks   *Commercial ties to Spain and Portugal, Africa, and the Caribbean sustained the growth of both seaports and commercial farming regions on the British North American mainland and enabled colonials to purchase an increasing volume of finished goods from England. The proceeds from exports in foodstuffs and lumber to the West Indies and trade in fish to Spain and Portugal enabled northern merchants and farmers to buy hardware and clothing from the mother country. Southern planters financed their consumption of English imports and their investment in African slaves with the profits from the sale of tobacco, rice, and indigo abroad.*

sacrifice, most Americans obeyed imperial regulations. Only sugar, molasses, and tea were routinely smuggled.

Following this policy of **benign neglect** the British empire muddled on to the satisfaction of most people on both sides of the Atlantic. Economic growth and political **autonomy** allowed most Americans to like being English, despite their misgivings about their parent nation. The beauty of it was that Americans could be English in America, enjoying greater economic opportunity and political equality. If imperial arrangements had remained as they were in 1754, the empire might have muddled on indefinitely.

But newcomers continued to arrive in the British colonies, many heading for the backcountry. And the rivalries and shifting alliances among Indians, French, British, and Spanish continued to unsettle peoples across the continent. Under these troubled conditions the British empire began to change in ways that made it increasingly hard for Americans to be English in America.

Toward the Seven Years' War

Three decades after L'Archevêque, the tattooed Frenchman, perished in an imperial skirmish on the Great Plains, two events served as clues of how the competition for power and influence might play out in North America. One was a skirmish much like the one that killed L'Archevêque. The other was a council that brought delegates from seven colonies to Albany, New York, to meet with representatives of the Iroquois Confederacy. Both events took place in the summer of 1754.

The Albany Congress

The British asked for the council meeting with the Iroquois because France had only recently completed a new line of forts stretching from Lake Erie down to the Ohio River. The forts stood directly in the way of the English traders and settlers filtering into the Ohio River Valley. Colonial governors, impressed by the threat, wanted to make sure that they could count on the support of the Iroquois, if yet another war broke out between Britain and France.

The Iroquois had generally remained neutral in this European rivalry, and with good reason. If Britain drove France from North America, English settlers would no doubt spill out onto Indian lands at an even greater rate. And without competition from French traders, English traders would likely raise the prices of the goods they sold. In the end the Iroquois gave only vague promises of loyalty, as they hauled away 30 wagonloads of English presents—diplomatic bribes for favorable treatment.

The most prominent delegate to this Albany Congress, as the meeting became known, was Benjamin Franklin. Franklin had larger aims than negotiations with the Iroquois. He presented the other colonial delegates with a plan for colonial cooperation, in which a federal council made up of representatives from each colony would assume responsibility for a united colonial defense. The Albany delegates were alarmed enough by the wavering Iroquois and the threatening French to accept the idea. But when they brought the proposal home to their respective legislatures, not a single one approved the Albany Plan of Union. "Everyone cries, a union is necessary," Franklin complained, "but when they come to the manner and form of the union, their weak noodles are perfectly distracted."

Franklin's Albany Plan of Union

Washington at Fort Necessity

While the Albany Congress was debating in July 1754, a second event—the skirmish—occurred some 400 miles to the west, beyond the Appalachian Mountains. There, a young Virginian who dreamed of military glory led a company of Virginia militia in an expedition against Fort Duquesne, the newly built French stronghold at the forks of the Ohio River. The militia's leader wanted more than anything to become an officer in the regular British army, but events did not go the way George Washington hoped. A French counterattack forced him to surrender his own makeshift Fort Necessity, thrown together in the woods, and retreat back to Virginia. The disaster dashed any dreams of martial glory. Washington had no future as a soldier.

Backcountry War Turns Global

The French victorious; the British colonies disunited—two telltales in the wind. In the end, though, they were poor predictors of the way events would play out. By the beginning of 1755 the British had determined to renew their war against France, though they wanted a small war. They intended to limit the fighting to the North American backwoods. Those hopes did not last long. By the time the conflict ended seven years later, the contest between France and England had spread across the globe, with battles fought in the Caribbean, in Africa, in India, and even in the Philippines against France's eventual ally, Spain. The war also decided the question of European sovereignty over North America.

Furthermore, despite outward appearances, British colonials did not prove to be hopelessly disunited. The Albany Congress demonstrated that at least a few Americans such as Franklin had seen beyond the diversity of a divided colonial world to the possibility of political union, however strange the idea first seemed. The backcountry war that spread across four continents would also alter the basic relationship between colonials and their parent nation. With this change, an increasing number of Americans began to see in themselves a likeness that was not English.

Significant Events

1689–1697	King William's War (War of the League of Augsburg)
1702	Anne becomes queen of England
1702–1713	Queen Anne's War (War of the Spanish Succession)
1714	George I becomes king of England, beginning Hanover dynasty
1727	George II becomes king of England
1730s–1740s	Rise in importation of black slaves in northern colonies
1739	George Whitefield's first preaching tour in America; Stono Rebellion in South Carolina
1744–1748	King George's War (War of the Austrian Succession)
1751	Franklin's essay on population
1754	The Albany Congress; Washington surrenders at Fort Necessity
1756–1763	Seven Years' War
1760–1769	South Carolina Regulation
1763	Paxton Boys march in Pennsylvania
1766	Tenant rebellion in New York
1766–1771	North Carolina Regulation (Battle of Alamance, 1771)

Chapter Summary

During the eighteenth century, Spain, France, and Great Britain competed for power and influence in North America. Native peoples too played off these shifting alliances, as their cultures were disrupted by epidemics, European settlement, and the arrival of new plants, animals, and technologies. British North Americans grew increasingly diverse, which made the prospect of any future colonial political union appear remote.

- Differences became more pronounced among whites because of the immigration of larger numbers of non-English settlers, the spread of settlement to the backcountry, and the growth of major seaports.

- Although disorder was not uncommon either on the frontier or in cities, the most serious social and political conflict drew its strength from sectional controversies between East and West.

- The South became more embattled, too, as a result of the massive importation of slaves directly from Africa during the first half of the eighteenth century and a rising tide of black resistance to slavery.

- After about 1750 the growth of a native-born population strengthened black communal and family life.

- Religious conflict among colonials was intensified by the spread of Enlightenment ideas and the influence of the first Great Awakening.

- Despite their many differences, a majority of white colonials took pride in their common English ancestry and in belonging to a powerful empire.

- Although the British colonies seemed reluctant in 1754 to unite politically to protect themselves against their French rivals, the looming war for empire eventually created a situation in which British colonials would begin to think themselves better off united and independent.

Additional Reading

Understanding the effects of ethnic and racial diversity is essential to appreciating the dynamism of eighteenth-century colonial society. Some vivid accounts include Bernard Bailyn, *Voyagers to the West* (1986), and Bernard Bailyn and Philip Morgan, eds., *Strangers within the Realm* (1991). Philip Morgan's *Slave Counterpoint* (1998) offers a state-of-the-art overview of African American cultures in the early South. For mounting class, ethnic, and racial tensions in American seaports, consult Jill Lepore, *New York Burning* (2005), and Gary Nash, *The Urban Crucible* (1979).

Nancy Shoemaker, *A Strange Likeness* (2004) and James M. Merrell, *Into the American Woods* (1999), are two compelling accounts of how Indians and white Americans came to perceive one another as different peoples. For the expansion of colonial settlement into the eighteenth-century backcountry, begin with Eric Hinderaker and Peter C. Mancall, *At the Edge of Empire* (2003), and Rachel Klein, *The Unification of a Slave State* (1990). Among the best studies of religion in eighteenth-century society are Rhys Isaac, *The Transformation of Virginia, 1740–1790* (1982); Patricia Bonomi, *Under the Cope of Heaven* (1986); and George Marsden, *Jonathan Edwards* (2003).

For a fuller list of readings, see the Bibliography at www.mhhe.com/davidsonnation6.

A VIEW of the OBELISK erected under LIBERTY-TREE in BOSTON on the Rejoicings for the Repeal

The Joys of Being English

Americans liked being English. They had liked being English from the beginning of colonial settlement, but they liked it more than ever for a few years after 1759. One wonderful day during those years—September 16, 1762—Bostonians turned out to celebrate belonging to the British empire. Soldiers mustered on the Common; bells pealed from the steeples of local churches; the charge of guns fired from the battery resounded through towns; strains of orchestra music from an outdoor concert floated through the city's crowded streets and narrow alleys. As daylight drifted into darkness, bonfires illuminated the city's neighborhoods. Later that evening—having raised many glasses to drink "loyal healths" with his comrades, General John Winslow of Marshfield leapt onto a table and danced to the tinkle of glassware shattering on the tavern floor. No matter. Winslow was a local hero, an officer who had served in the Seven Years' War. Bostonians of all sorts offered toasts to their young king, George III, and in celebration of Britain's glorious victory.

When the great news of that triumph reached the North American mainland in the fall of 1762, similar celebrations broke out all over the colonies. And with good reason. France's empire in America, which only a few years earlier had appeared so formidable, was now vanquished. Great Britain had become master of Canada, thanks to the joint efforts of British and American colonial troops. In 1763 the Treaty of Paris ratified their victories, making Britain the largest and most powerful empire in the Western world. Americans were among His Majesty's proudest subjects.

Thirteen years after the celebration of 1762, Boston was a different place. Pride in belonging to the empire had shriveled to shrill charges that England conspired to enslave its colonies. Massachusetts led the way, drawing other colonies deep into resistance. Bostonians initiated many of the petitions and resolves against British authority. When words did not work, they ignited riots, and in response to this defiance British troops disembarked on Boston's long wharves. Along city streets butchers taunted them, children threw snowballs concealing stones, and mobs destroyed British property. By 1775, once loyal British subjects were laying plans for rebellion against the British empire.

When the Stamp Act was repealed in 1766, Paul Revere constructed an obelisk to stand under Boston's Liberty Tree. The large monument was framed in wood and covered with drawings executed on oiled, semi-transparent paper. Inside was space for 300 lanterns to illuminate the drawings at night. On the far left panel, a threatened Indian represents America being menaced by British officials, including the evil Lord Buta, portrayed as a flying devil carrying the Stamp Act in one claw. In the second panel, the Indian points to his retreating foes, as the Goddess Liberty blows her trumpet. Alas, the oiled paper caught fire, and the obelisk burned down shortly after its construction.

A Process of
Disillusionment

A generation of Americans had loved being English, boasted of their rights as Britons, and celebrated their membership in the all-conquering empire. Ironically, that very pride drove colonials into rebellion, for the men who ran the British empire after 1763 would not allow Americans to be English. Even before the Seven Years' War, some colonials saw that diverging paths of social and political development made them different from the English. After the Seven Years' War, events demonstrated to even more colonials that they were not considered the political equals of the English who lived in England. As their disillusionment with the empire deepened, British North Americans from Massachusetts to Georgia slowly discovered a new identity as Americans and declared their independence from being English.

The Seven Years' War

The Seven Years' War, which actually lasted nine years, pitted Britain and its ally, Prussia, against France, in league with Austria and Spain. The battle raged from 1754 until 1763, ranging over the continent of Europe, the coast of West Africa, India, the Philippines, the Caribbean, and North America.

The Years of Defeat

Braddock's Defeat

The war started in 1754 when Virginia sent George Washington and a company of militia into the Ohio River valley to halt French penetration into the area (see page 139). Washington's surrender at Fort Necessity only stiffened Britain's resolve to assert its own claims to the Ohio country. In the summer of 1755, as two British regiments led

Like a swarm of angry bees, British troops disembark on one of Boston's long wharves in 1768. American colonials who had cheered the triumphs of British soldiers only a few years earlier now complained bitterly at the presence of a standing army designed to intimidate them.

by Major General Edward Braddock approached the French outpost at Fort Duquesne on the forks of the Ohio, they were ambushed and cut to pieces by a party of French and Indians. Washington led the mortally wounded Braddock and the remnants of his army in a retreat. During the summer of Braddock's defeat, New Englanders fared somewhat better against French forces in Nova Scotia and deported 6,000 farmers from that region. The Acadians, as they were known, had their land confiscated, and they were dispersed throughout the colonies.

There followed two disastrous years for Britain and its allies. When England and France formally declared war in May 1756, John Campbell, the Earl of Loudoun, took command of the North American theater. American soldiers and colonial assemblies alike hated Lord Loudoun. They balked at his efforts to take command over colonial troops and dragged their heels at his demands for men and supplies. Meanwhile, the French

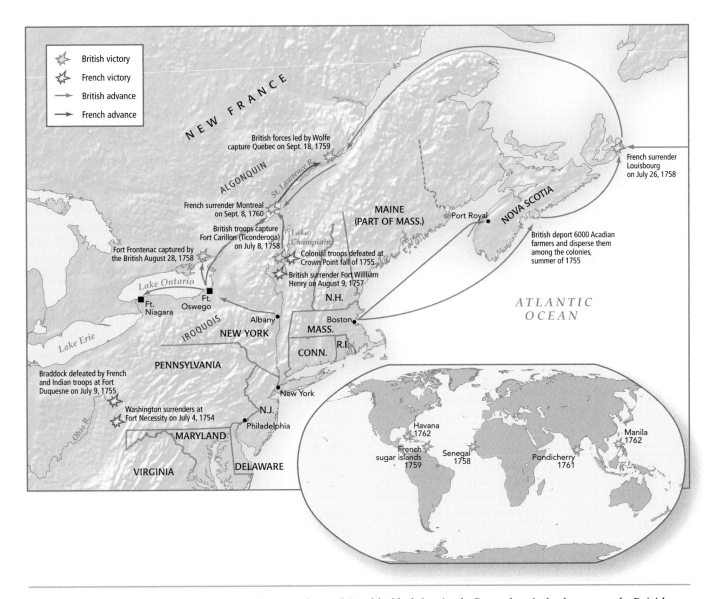

The Seven Years' War   *After Washington's surrender and Braddock's defeat in the Pennsylvania backcountry, the British and French waged their final contest for supremacy in North America in northern New York and Canada. But the rivalry for empire between France and Britain was worldwide, with naval superiority providing the needed edge to Britain. The British navy isolated French forces in India, winning a victory at Pondicherry, while English offensives captured the French sugar islands in the Caribbean and French trading posts along the West African coast. When Spain entered the war on the side of France, British fleets captured both Havana and the strategic port of Manila in the Philippines.*

appointed an effective new commanding general of their forces in Canada, Louis Joseph, the marquis de Montcalm. Montcalm drove southward, capturing key British forts and threatening the security of both New York and New England. While he prospered in America, the British were also taking a beating from the French in Europe and in India.

During the years when the French seemed unstoppable, the British looked for help from the strongest tribes of the interior—the Iroquois in the North and the Creek, Choctaw, and Cherokee in the South. Instead, Benjamin Franklin's worst fears were realized: most tribes adopted neutrality or joined the French. As France seemed certain to carry the continent, Indian attacks on English frontier settlements increased.

The Years of Victory

William Pitt Turns the Tide

British fortunes took a sharp turn for the better when a veteran English politician, William Pitt, came out of retirement to direct the war. Pitt was an odd character. Subject to bouts of depression and loathed for his opportunism and egotism, he was nonetheless buoyed by a strong sense of destiny—his own and that of England. He believed Great Britain must seize the world's trade, because trade meant wealth and wealth meant power. France seemed to him the greatest obstacle to this British destiny—and Pitt returned to the political fray charged with energy. "I know that I can save this country and no one else can," he declared in his usual bold way. Leaving the fighting in Europe to the Prussians, Pitt focused the full strength of the British military on beating the French in America. Pitt also renewed colonial support for the war effort by replacing Lord Loudoun and giving his successor far more limited authority over colonial troops. And Pitt sent requests for men and money directly to each colonial assembly—accompanied by promises of reimbursement in gold and silver.

With Pitt in command, the tide of battle turned. In July of 1758, the British gained control of the St. Lawrence River when the French fortress at Louisbourg fell before the combined force of the Royal Navy and British and colonial troops. In August, a force of New Englanders strangled France's frontier defenses by capturing Fort Frontenac, thereby isolating French forts lining the Great Lakes and the Ohio valley. The Indians, seeing the French routed from the interior, switched their allegiance to the English.

Wolfe and Montcalm Battle for Quebec

The British succeeded even more brilliantly in 1759. In Canada, Brigadier General James Wolfe gambled on a daring stratagem and won Quebec from Montcalm. Under the cover of darkness, naval squadrons landed Wolfe's men beneath the city's steep bluffs, where they scaled the heights to a plateau known as the Plains of Abraham. Montcalm might have won by holding out behind the walls of his fortress and awaiting reinforcements. Instead, he matched Wolfe's recklessness and offered battle. Five days later both Wolfe and Montcalm lay dead, along with 1,400 French soldiers and 600 British and American troops. Quebec had fallen to the British. A year later the French surrender of Montreal ended the fighting in North America, although it continued elsewhere in the world for another two years.

The Treaty of Paris, signed in February 1763, ended the French presence on the continent of North America. The terms confirmed British title to all French territory east of the Mississippi as well as to Spanish Florida. (Spain had made the last-minute mistake of entering the war, against Britain, in 1762.) France ceded to its ally Spain all of its land lying west of the Mississippi, as well as the port of New Orleans.

Postwar Expectations

Colonial Pride and Optimism

Britain's victory gave rise to great expectations among Americans. The end of the war, they were sure, meant the end of high taxes. The terms of the peace, they were confident, meant that the fertile lands of the Ohio valley would be thrown open to English settlement. The prosperity of the war years alone made for a mood of optimism. British military spending and William Pitt's subsidies had made money

The British navy bombarded Quebec, reducing many of the city's buildings to smoldering ruins. The devastation presaged the end of France's empire in North America.

for farmers, merchants, artisans, and anyone else who had anything to do with supplying the army or navy. Colonials also took pride in their contributions of troops and money to the winning of the war. In view of that support, Americans expected to be given more consideration within the British empire. Now, as one anonymous pamphleteer put it, Americans would "not be thought presumptuous, if they consider[ed] themselves upon an equal footing" with English in the parent country.

But most imperial officials in America thought that if Americans took pride in being English, they had done a poor job of showing it. British statesmen complained that colonial assemblies had been tightfisted when it came to supplying the army. British commanders charged that colonial troops had been lily-livered when it came to fighting the French. Such charges were unjust, but they stuck in the minds of many Britons at home. The nation had accumulated a huge debt that would saddle it with high taxes for years to come. To make matters worse, some Britons suspected that, with the French removed from North America, the colonies would move toward independence. As early as 1755, Josiah Tucker, a respected English economist, had warned that "to drive the French out of all North America would be the most fatal step we could take." Ironically, colonial independence entered the minds of some observers in England long before it was ever entertained by Americans.

Americans in 1763 were not, in truth, revolutionaries in the making. They were loyal British subjects in the flush of postwar patriotism. Americans in 1763, deeply divided among themselves, were not even "Americans." But most postwar English colonials did expect to enjoy a more equal status in the empire. And most Britons had no inclination to accord them that equality. The differing expectations of the colonies' place in the empire poised the postwar generation for crisis.

English Resentments

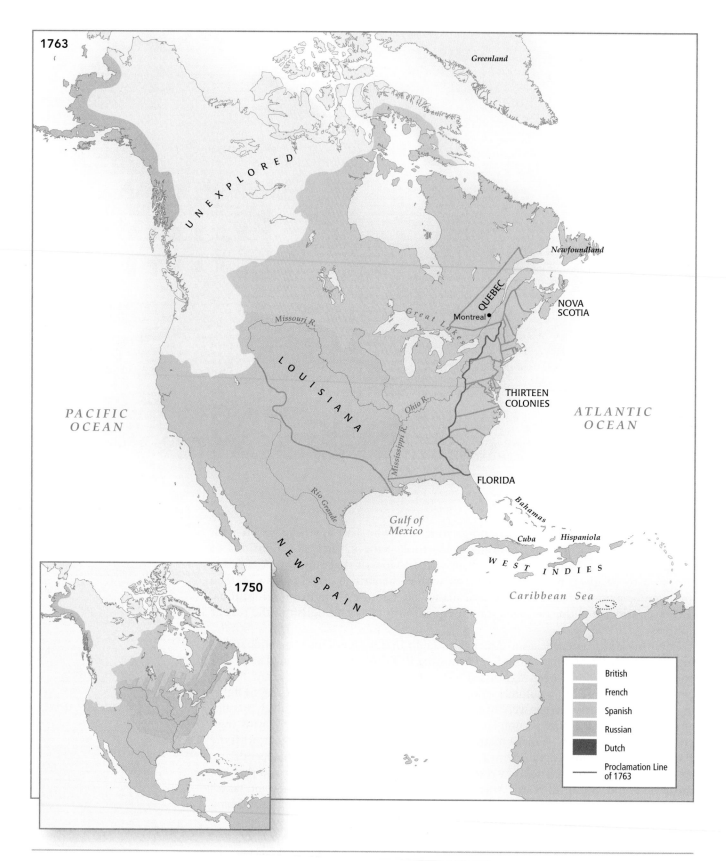

1763

Greenland

UNEXPLORED

Newfoundland

QUEBEC

NOVA
SCOTIA

Montreal •

Great Lakes

Missouri R.

L O U I S I A N A

Ohio R.

THIRTEEN
COLONIES

PACIFIC
OCEAN

ATLANTIC
OCEAN

Mississippi R.

FLORIDA

Rio Grande

Bahamas

N E W   S P A I N

Gulf of
Mexico

Cuba

Hispaniola

W E S T   I N D I E S

Caribbean Sea

1750

	British
	French
	Spanish
	Russian
	Dutch
	Proclamation Line of 1763

European Claims in North America, 1750 and 1763   *The British victory in the Seven Years' War secured Great Britain's title to a large portion of present-day United States and Canada. Colonials hoped to settle the newly won territory, but politicians in London intended to restrict westward movement with the Proclamation of 1763.*

The Imperial Crisis

It was common sense. Great Britain had waged a costly war to secure its empire in America; now it needed to consolidate those gains. The empire's North American territory needed to be protected, its administration tightened, and its colonies made as profitable as possible to the parent nation. In other words, the empire needed to be centralized. That conclusion dictated Britain's decision to leave a standing army of several thousand troops in America after the Seven Years' War. The British army would prevent France from trying to regain its lost territory.

New Troubles on the Frontier

Keeping troops in North America made sense to the British because of the Indians, as well. With the French gone, English traders, speculators, and settlers would swarm into the West. Without the French as trading partners, Indian tribes were in a weaker position to deal with the British. No longer could they count on a steady supply of arms and ammunition from European rivals competing for their furs. The Indians were edgy, expecting the worst, making the British uneasy about peace on the frontier.

Events bore out British fears. In the early 1760s a Lenni Lenape prophet, Neolin, began advising the tribes to return to their native ways and resist the spread of white settlement. Pontiac, an Ottawa chief, embraced Neolin's message of renaissance and rebellion. Other interior tribes joined Pontiac's offensive, and during the summer of 1763 they captured all the British outposts west of Pittsburgh. British troops and American militia finally smothered Pontiac's Rebellion.

Pontiac's Rebellion

Thereafter British administrators discovered another use for troops in America—to enforce the newly issued Proclamation of 1763. That order, issued by England's Board of Trade, prohibited white settlement past the crest of the Appalachian Mountains. Restricting westward movement might ease Indian fears, the British hoped, and so stave off future conflicts. It might also keep the colonials confined to the seaboard, where they were more easily subject to the control of the empire.

Proclamation of 1763

George Grenville's New Measures

A final reason for keeping troops in the colonies occurred to the British by 1764: an armed presence could enforce American acceptance of other new and sensible measures for tightening the empire. Those measures were the solutions of George Grenville, the first lord of the treasury, to the financial problems facing England after the Seven Years' War.

Britain's national debt had doubled in the decade after 1754. Adding to that burden was the drain of supporting troops in the colonies. As matters stood, heavy taxes were already triggering protests among hard-pressed Britons. Americans, in contrast, paid comparatively low taxes to their colonial governments and little in trade duties to the empire. Indeed, Grenville discovered that the colonial customs service paid out four times more in salaries to its collectors than it gathered in duties and was thereby operating at a net loss.

The income from customs duties was slim because colonial merchants evaded the Molasses Act of 1733. That **tariff** imposed a hefty duty of six pence on every gallon of molasses imported from the French and Dutch sugar islands. Parliament had designed the duty to encourage colonists to consume more British molasses, which carried a higher price but came duty-free. New England merchants, who distilled molasses into rum and then traded it to the southern colonies and to West Africa, claimed that the British sugar islands could not satisfy the demands of their distilleries. Regrettably, the merchants were forced to import more molasses from the French and the Dutch. More regrettably, to keep their costs low and the price of their rum competitive, they had to bribe British customs officials. With the going rate for bribes ranging from a halfpenny

Molasses Act of 1733

The Appalachian Frontier, 1750–1775 *Made bold by the presence of British forts and soldiers, land-hungry colonials spilled into the West through the Cumberland Gap, a notch in the chain of mountains stretching the length of the North American interior. Only Indians and some white hunters knew of the Cumberland Gap before it was scouted in 1750 by Dr. Thomas Walker and a party of Virginians on behalf of a company of land speculators. In 1763, Indians led by Pontiac seized eight British forts before troops under Colonel Henry Bouquet stopped the offensive at Bushy Run, Pennsylvania. In 1775 Daniel Boone took the first large party of pioneers through the Cumberland Gap and established a fort at Boonesborough in present-day Kentucky.*

The Line That Wasn't There

The Misplaced Concreteness of Maps

Source: "Cantonment of the Forces in N. America, 1766." Courtesy Clements Library. University of Michigan.

Historians gain their information from the past using not only primary source manuscripts but also maps. This one, from 1766, shows where British troops were located and in addition indicates the bold line established by the Proclamation of 1763, separating British settlements from the also boldly labeled "Lands Reserved for the Indians." Pontiac's show of power prompted Britain to pledge that their troops would protect Indian territories from land-hungry colonial speculators and settlers.

But maps, like diaries or memoirs, are shaped by those who create them. A Proclamation Line in crisp ink drawn in London by the Board of Trade became invisible, or at least unenforceable, thousands of miles away. How were army officers supposed to deal with hunters, speculators, or settlers who refused to leave these Indian lands? The Proclamation gave no hint. And in practice, most British policymakers were more interested in reducing the costs of governing the colonies—or even profiting personally by speculating in lands west of the line. Those tempted found eager allies among wealthy American land speculators and British officials and military commanders in the colonies who had hatched plans for establishing colonies as far west as the Mississippi River. By 1773, the British had abandoned all but three of their forts on the American frontier and had turned over the conduct of Indian affairs to colonial governments dominated by investors in western lands. The Proclamation Line, so firmly etched on this map, proved to be a scribble of ink on parchment, as flimsy and false as the British empire's promise to safeguard Indian territorial claims.

to a penny and a half per gallon, the whole regrettable arrangement made handsome profits for both merchants and customs inspectors.

George Grenville reasoned that if Americans could pay out a little under the table to protect an illegal trade, they would willingly pay a little more to go legitimate. Parliament agreed. In April 1764 it passed the Revenue Act, commonly called the Sugar Act. The legislation actually lowered the duty on foreign molasses from six to three pence a gallon. This time, however, Grenville intended to enforce the new duty and to crack down on smugglers. To do so, the Sugar Act required shipmasters to submit papers listing every item in their cargoes when entering or clearing colonial ports. Even common sailors had to declare the contents of their sea chests. Those caught on the wrong side of the law were to be tried in admiralty courts, where verdicts were handed down by royally appointed judges rather than colonial juries more likely to sympathize with their fellow citizens.

Sugar Act

By tightening customs enforcement, Grenville hoped to raise more revenue from the American trade. Unlike the earlier Navigation Acts, which imposed duties mainly to regulate trade, the Sugar Act's duties were intended mainly to yield revenue. Even so, Grenville regarded his demands as modest: he did not expect colonials to help reduce England's national debt or even to cover the entire cost of their defense.

Grenville made other modest proposals, all approved by Parliament. There was the Currency Act of 1764, which prohibited the colonies from making their paper money legal tender. That prevented Americans from paying their debts to British traders in currency that had fallen to less than its face value. There was the Quartering Act of 1765, which obliged any colony in which troops were stationed to provide them with suitable accommodations. That contributed to the cost of keeping British forces in America. Finally, in March of 1765, Parliament passed the Stamp Act.

The Stamp Act placed **taxes** on legal documents, customs papers, newspapers, almanacs, college diplomas, playing cards, and dice. After November 1, 1765, all these items had to bear a stamp signifying that their possessor had paid the tax. Violators of the Stamp Act, like those disobeying the Sugar Act, were to be tried without juries in admiralty courts. The English had been paying a similar tax for nearly a century, so it seemed to Grenville and Parliament that colonials could have no objections.

Every packet boat from London that brought news of Parliament's passing another one of Grenville's measures dampened postwar optimism. For all the differences between the colonies and England, Americans still held much in common with the English. Those shared ideas included firm beliefs about why the British constitution, British customs, and British history all served to protect liberty and the rights of the empire's freeborn citizens. For that reason the new measures, which seemed like common sense to Grenville and Parliament, did not make sense at all to Americans.

The Beginning of Colonial Resistance

Like other Britons, colonials in America accepted a maxim laid down by the English philosopher John Locke: property guaranteed liberty. Property, in this view, was not merely real estate, or wealth, or material possessions. It was the source of strength for every individual, providing the freedom to think and act independently. Protecting the individual's right to own property was the main responsibility of government, for if personal property was not sacred, then neither was personal liberty.

It followed from this close connection between property, power, and liberty that no people should be taxed without their consent or that of their elected representatives. The power to tax was the power to destroy by depriving a person of property. Yet both the Sugar Act and the Stamp Act were taxes passed by members of Parliament, none of whom had been elected by colonials.

Like the English, colonials also prized the right of trial by jury as one of their basic constitutional liberties. Yet both the Sugar Act and the Stamp Act would prosecute offenders in the admiralty courts, not in local courts, thus depriving colonials of the freedom claimed by all other English men and women.

The concern for protecting individual liberties was only one of the convictions shaping the colonies' response to Britain's new policies. Equally important was their deep suspicion of power itself, a preoccupation that colonials shared with a minority of radical English thinkers. These radicals were known by a variety of names: the Country Party, the Commonwealthmen, and the **Opposition.** They drew their inspiration from the ancient tradition of classical **republicanism,** which held that representative government safeguarded liberty more reliably than either monarchy or oligarchy did. Underlying that judgment was the belief that human beings were driven by passion and insatiable ambition. One person (a monarch), or even a few people (an oligarchy), could not be entrusted with governing, because they would inevitably become corrupted by power and turn into tyrants. Even in representative governments, the people were obliged to watch those in power at all times. The price of liberty was eternal vigilance.

The Opposition believed that the people of England were not watching their rulers closely enough. During the first half of the eighteenth century, they argued, the entire executive branch of England's government— monarchs and their ministers—had been corrupted by their appetite for power. Proof of their ambition was the executive bureaucracy of civil officials and standing armies that steadily grew larger, interfered more with citizens' lives, and drained increasing amounts of money from taxpayers. Even more alarming, in the Opposition's view, the executive branch's bribery of members of Parliament was corrupting the representative branch of England's government. They warned that a sinister conspiracy originating in the executive branch of government threatened English liberty.

Opposition thinkers commanded little attention in England, where they were dismissed as a discontented radical fringe. But they were revered by political leaders in the American colonies. The Opposition's view of politics confirmed colonial anxieties about England, doubts that ran deeper after 1763. Parliament's attempt to tax the colonies and the quartering of a standing army on the frontier confirmed all too well the Opposition's description of how powerful rulers turned themselves into tyrants and reduced the people whom they ruled to slaves.

In sum, Grenville's new measures led some colonials to suspect that ambitious men ruling England might be conspiring against American liberties. At the very least, the new measures implied that colonials were not the political equals of the English living in England. They were not entitled to taxation by consent or to trial by jury. To be treated like second-class citizens wounded colonials' pride and mocked their postwar expectations. The heady dreams of the role that the colonies would play in the British empire evaporated, leaving behind the bitter dregs of disappointment.

Britain's determination to centralize its empire after 1763 was a disaster of timing, not just psychologically but also economically. By then, the colonies were in the throes of a recession. The boom produced in America by government spending during the war had collapsed once subsidies were withdrawn. Colonial merchants were left with stocks full of imported goods gathering dust on their shelves. Farmers lost the brisk and profitable market of the army.

Colonial response to the Sugar Act reflected the painful postwar readjustments. New England merchants led the opposition, objecting to the Sugar Act principally on economic grounds. But with the passage of the Stamp Act, the terms of the imperial debate widened. The Stamp Act hit all colonials, not just New England merchants. It took money from the pockets of anyone who made a will, filed a deed, traded out of a colonial port, bought a newspaper, consulted an almanac, graduated from college, took a chance at dice, or played cards. More important, the Stamp Act served notice that Parliament claimed the authority to tax the colonies directly and for the sole purpose of raising revenue.

Visual imagery brought home the urgency of resistance to Americans who could not read political pamphlets or radical newspapers. This detail from an engraving by Paul Revere includes a liberty tree, from which is hung an effigy of the Boston stamp distributor, and a beast busily destroying the Magna Carta while trampling American colonials. The date on the tree, August 14, 1765, marked the first Stamp Act riot in Boston.

Impact of Postwar Recession

Riots and Resolves

That unprecedented assertion provoked an unprecedented development: the first display of colonial unity. During the spring and summer of 1765, American assemblies passed resolves denying that Parliament could tax the colonies. The right to tax Americans

This idealized likeness of Patrick Henry, painted by Thomas Sully, conveys the subject's intensity. Henry's eloquence and passion as an orator impressed his contemporaries.

belonged to colonial assemblies alone, they argued, by the law of nature and by the liberties guaranteed in colonial charters and in the British constitution.

Virginia's assembly, the House of Burgesses, took the lead in protesting the Stamp Act, prodded by Patrick Henry. Just 29 years old in 1765, Henry had tried his hand at planting in western Virginia before recognizing his real talent—demagoguery. Blessed with the eloquence of an evangelical preacher, the dashing charm of a southern gentleman, and a mind uncluttered by much learning, Henry parlayed his popularity as a smooth-talking lawyer into a place among the Burgesses. He took his seat just 10 days before introducing the Virginia Resolves against the Stamp Act.

The Burgesses passed Henry's resolutions upholding their exclusive right to tax Virginians. They stopped short of adopting those resolves that called for outright resistance. When news of Virginia's stand spread to the rest of the colonies, other assemblies followed suit, affirming that the sole right to tax Americans resided in their elected representatives. But some colonial newspapers deliberately printed a different story—that the Burgesses had approved all of Henry's resolves, including one that sanctioned disobedience to any parliamentary tax. That prompted a few assemblies to endorse resistance. In October 1765 delegates from nine colonies convened in New York, where they prepared a joint statement of the American position and petitioned the king and Parliament to repeal both the Sugar Act and the Stamp Act.

Meanwhile, colonial leaders turned to the press to arouse popular opposition to the Stamp Act. Disposed by the writings of the English Opposition to think of politics in conspiratorial terms, they warned that Grenville and the king's other ministers schemed to deprive the colonies of their liberties by unlawfully taxing their property. The Stamp Act was only the first step in a sinister plan to enslave Americans.

Whether or not fears of a dark conspiracy haunted most colonials in 1765, many resisted the Stamp Act. The merchants of Boston, New York, and Philadelphia agreed to stop importing English goods in order to pressure British traders to lobby for repeal. In every colony, organizations emerged to ensure that the Stamp Act, if not repealed, would never be enforced.

The new resistance groups, which styled themselves the "Sons of Liberty," consisted of traders, lawyers, and prosperous artisans. With great success, they organized the lower classes of seaports in opposition to the Stamp Act. The sailors, dockworkers, poor artisans, apprentices, and servants who poured into the streets resembled mobs that had been organized from time to time earlier in the century. Previous riots against houses of prostitution, merchants who hoarded goods, or supporters of smallpox inoculation had not been spontaneous, uncontrolled outbursts. Crowds chose their targets and their tactics carefully and then carried out the communal will with little violence.

In every colonial city, the mobs of 1765 burnt the stamp distributors in effigy, insulted them on the streets, demolished their offices, and attacked their homes. One hot night in August 1765, a mob went further than the Sons of Liberty had planned. They all but leveled the stately mansion of Thomas Hutchinson, the unpopular lieutenant governor of Massachusetts and the brother-in-law of the colony's stamp distributor. The destruction stunned Bostonians, especially the Sons of Liberty, who resisted Britain in the name of protecting private property. Thereafter they took care to keep crowds under tighter control. By the first of November, the day that the Stamp Act took effect, most of the stamp distributors had resigned.

Repeal of the Stamp Act

Meanwhile, the repeal of the Stamp Act was already in the works back in England. The man who came—unintentionally—to America's relief was George III. The young king was a good man, industrious and devoted to the empire, but he was also immature and not particularly bright. Insecurity made him an irk-some master, and he ran through ministers rapidly. By the end of 1765, George had replaced Grenville with a new first minister, the Marquis of Rockingham. Rockingham had opposed the Stamp Act from the outset, and he had no desire to enforce it. He received support from London merchants, who were beginning to feel the pinch of the American nonimportation campaign, and secured repeal of the Stamp Act in March 1766.

The Stamp Act controversy demonstrated to colonials how similar in political outlook they were to one another and how different they were from the British. Americans had found that they shared the same assumptions about the meaning of representation. To counter colonial objections to the Stamp Act, Grenville and his supporters had claimed that Americans *were* represented in Parliament, even though they had elected none of its members. Americans were virtually represented, Grenville insisted, for each member of Parliament stood for the interests of the whole empire, not just those of the particular constituency that had elected him.

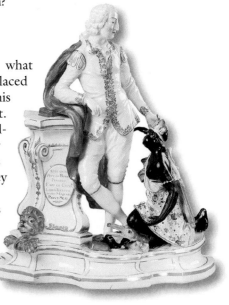

Virtual versus Actual Representation

Colonials could see no virtue in the theory of **virtual representation.** After all, the circumstances and interests of colonials, living an ocean away, were so different from those of Britons. The newly recognized consensus among Americans was that colonials could be truly represented only by those whom they had elected. Their view, known as **actual representation,** emphasized that elected officials were directly accountable to their constituents.

Americans also had discovered that they agreed about the extent of Parliament's authority over the colonies: it did not include the right to tax. Colonials conceded Parliament's right to legislate and to regulate trade for the good of the whole empire. But taxation, in their view, was the free gift of the people through their representatives—who were not sitting in Parliament.

Members of Parliament brushed aside colonial petitions and resolves, all but ignoring these constitutional arguments. To make its own authority clear, Parliament accompanied the repeal of the Stamp Act with a Declaratory Act, asserting that it had the power to make laws for the colonies "in all cases whatsoever." In fact, the Declaratory Act clarified nothing. Did Parliament understand the power of legislation to include the power of taxation?

Declaratory Act

The Townshend Acts

In the summer of 1766 George III—again inadvertently—gave the colonies what should have been an advantage by changing ministers again. The king replaced Rockingham with William Pitt, who enjoyed great favor among colonials for his leadership during the Seven Years' War and for his opposition to the Stamp Act. Almost alone among British politicians, Pitt had grasped and approved the colonists' constitutional objections to taxation. During Parliament's debate over repeal of the Stamp Act, Grenville asked sarcastically, "Tell me when the colonies were emancipated?" Pitt immediately shot back, "I desire to know when they were made slaves!"

If the man who believed that Americans were "the sons not the bastards of England" had been well enough to govern, matters between Great Britain and the colonies might have turned out differently. But almost immediately after Pitt took office, his health collapsed, and power passed into the hands of Charles Townshend, the chancellor of the exchequer, who wished only to raise more revenue from the Americans. In 1767 he persuaded Parliament to tax the lead, paint, paper, glass, and tea that Americans imported from Britain.

In addition, Townshend was determined to curb the power of the upstart American assemblies. To set a bold example, he singled out for punishment the New York legislature, which was refusing to comply with provisions of the Quartering Act of 1765. The troops that were left on the western frontier after the Seven Years' War had been pulled back into colonial seaports in 1766. In part their movement was meant to economize on costs, but royal officials also hoped the troops' presence would help quiet agitation over the Stamp Act. When the largest contingent came to New York, that colony's assembly protested, claiming that the cost of quartering the troops constituted a form of indirect taxation. But Townshend was determined, and Parliament backed him, suspending the New York assembly in 1767 until it agreed to obey the Quartering Act.

This 1766 porcelain of Lord Chatham and America *attests to the popularity of William Pitt, Earl of Chatham, among Americans who resisted the Stamp Act. The artist's representation of "America" as a black kneeling in gratitude echoes the colonists' association of taxation with slavery.*

On the first night of November 1765 the narrow, winding streets of New York glowed with unaccustomed light. The Stamp Act was to have taken effect on that date, but the colony's stampmaster had long since resigned his office. What had frightened him into resignation could be seen in the moving shadows of men, women, and children, hundreds of them. The flaring torches and flickering candles that they carried aloft through the city's crooked byways cast on store-fronts and doorways dark images of a crowd protesting the "death of Liberty."

Bringing up the rear of the procession was a seaman, bearing atop his head an old chair in which was seated a paper effigy. It represented Cadwallader Colden, "the most hated man in the province" and, as New York's temporary governor, the local representative of British authority. The crowd marched to the center of town, shouting insults at Colden's figure and peppering it with pistol shots. When some of the marchers decided that their effigy should evoke the Roman Catholic pope, the chief symbol of tyrannical power to colonial Americans, they broke into Colden's stable and stole his fine coach for a proper papal throne. A second group joined the crowd, bearing its own piece of portable political theater—a gallows illuminated with two lanterns. Hanging from the gallows were effigies of Colden and the devil, the "grand Deceiver of Mankind." The entire assembly climaxed the evening by burning the effigies in a bonfire and then vandalizing the homes of several Stamp Act supporters.

Similar protests were staged in sea-ports all over the colonies. Some crowds held mock trials of unpopular British officials and then tarred and feathered, beat, hung, or burned their effigies. Other crowds enacted mock funerals, parading effigies in carts or coffins as church bells tolled. Certain symbols appeared repeatedly: devils and gallows, lanterns and the paraphernalia of papal authority. The "people-out-of-doors," as such crowds were called in the eigh-teenth century, were making their views known—and their collective power felt.

The frequency and the political focus of street protests were new, the actions taken after 1765 drew on rituals and symbols surrounding traditional forms of protest, punishment, and celebration. For centuries before the Revolution, crowds on both sides of the Atlantic had meted out to prostitutes, adulterers, and hen-pecked husbands punishments known in England as "rough music." After being tarred and feathered, the targets of rough music were often ridden "skimmington": placed on the back of a donkey, pelted with mud and dung, and driven through the streets to the accompaniment of hooting laughter and beating drums.

Townshend also dipped into the revenue from his new tariffs in order to make royal officials less dependent on the assemblies. Governors and other officers such as customs collectors and judges had previously received their salaries from colonial legislatures. The assemblies lost that crucial leverage when Townshend used the revenues to pay those bu-reaucrats directly. Finally, in order to ensure more effective enforcement of all the duties on imports, Townshend created an American Board of Customs Commissioners, who appointed a small army of new customs collectors. He also established three new vice-admiralty courts in Boston, New York, and Charleston to bring smugglers to justice.

The Resistance Organizes

In Townshend's efforts to centralize the administration of the empire, Americans saw new evidence that they were not being treated like the English. A host of newspapers and pamphlets took up the cry against taxation. The most widely read publication, "A Letter from a Farmer in Pennsylvania," was the work of John Dickinson—who was, in fact, a Philadelphia lawyer. He urged Americans to protest the Townshend duties by consuming fewer imported English luxuries. The virtues of hard work, thrift, and home manufacturing, Dickinson argued, would bring about repeal.

John Dickinson and Samuel Adams

As Dickinson's star rose over Philadelphia, the Townshend Acts also shaped the des-tiny of another man, farther north. By the 1760s Samuel Adams was a leader in the Mas-sachusetts assembly. In some ways his rise had been unlikely. Adams's earlier ventures as a merchant ended in bankruptcy; his stint as a tax collector left all of Boston in the red. But he proved a consummate political organizer and agitator. First his enemies and later his friends claimed that Adams had decided on independence for America as early as 1768. In that year he persuaded the assembly to send to other colonial legislatures a circular let-ter condemning the Townshend Acts and calling for a united American resistance.

An even more important inspiration for resistance rituals came from Pope's Day, an elaborate annual outdoor celebration of anti-Catholic sentiment that started in Boston early in the eighteenth century. Craftworkers and apprentices from both the North End and the South End of town fashioned a cart bearing a lantern, effigies of the pope and the devil, and signs reading "The devil take the pope." Local boys with blackened faces and jester's caps played the part of the "devil's imps," taunting the pope's effigy as laboring people from both ends of town paraded their carts through the streets. Each group tried to destroy the other's creation before the final bonfire at the end of the evening.

A Pope's Day parade in mid-eighteenth-century Boston. Dressed as the devil's imps, boys accompany a cart bearing an effigy of the pope.

It was not so great a leap, then, to jump from mocking a pope to vilifying a king. Beginning in 1776 Americans celebrated public readings of the Declaration by parading, burning, and burying effigies of George III. Strangely enough, Americans had converted symbols and ceremonies designed to honor monarchy to represent the killing of a king.

As John Dickinson and Samuel Adams whipped up public outrage, the Sons of Liberty again organized the opposition in the streets. Customs officials, like the stamp distributors before them, became targets of popular hatred. But the customs collectors gave as good as they got. Using the flimsiest excuses, they seized American vessels for violating royal regulations. With cold insolence they shook down American merchants for what amounted to protection money. The racketeering in the customs service brought tensions in Boston to a flash point in June 1768 after officials seized and condemned the *Liberty*, a sloop belonging to one of the city's biggest merchants, John Hancock. Several thousand Bostonians vented their anger in a night of rioting, searching out and roughing up customs officials.

The new secretary of state for the colonies, Lord Hillsborough, responded to the *Liberty* riot by sending two regiments of troops to Boston. In the fall of 1768 the redcoats, like a conquering army, paraded into town under the cover of warships lying off the harbor. (See Paul Revere's illustration on page 136.) In the months that followed, citizens bristled when challenged on the streets by armed soldiers. Even more disturbing to Bostonians was the execution of British military justice on the Common. British soldiers were whipped savagely for breaking military discipline, and desertion was punished by execution.

The *Liberty* riot and the arrival of British troops in Boston pushed colonial assemblies to coordinate their resistance more closely. Most legislatures endorsed the Massachusetts circular letter sent to them by Samuel Adams. They promptly adopted agreements not to import or to consume British goods. The reluctance among some merchants to revive nonimportation in 1767 gave way to greater enthusiasm by 1768, and by early 1769, such agreements were in effect throughout the colonies.

The Stamp Act crisis had also called forth intercolonial cooperation and tactics such as nonimportation. But the protests against the Townshend Acts raised the stakes by creating new institutions to carry forward the resistance. Subscribers to the nonimportation agreements established "committees of inspection" to enforce the ban on trade with Britain. The committees publicly denounced merchants who continued to import, vandalized their warehouses, forced them to stand under the gallows, and sometimes resorted to tar and feathers.

After 1768 the resistance also brought a broader range of colonials into the politics of protest. Artisans, who recognized that nonimportation would spur domestic manu- facturing, began to organize as independent political groups. In many towns, women took an active part in opposing the Townshend duties. The "Daughters of Liberty" took to heart John Dickinson's advice: they wore homespun clothing instead of Eng- lish finery, served coffee instead of tea, and boycotted shops selling British goods.

Daughters of Liberty

The International Sons of Liberty

The resistance after 1768 grew broader in another sense as well. Many of its sup- porters in the colonies felt a new sense of kinship with freedom fighters throughout Europe. Eagerly they read about the doings of men such as Charles Lucas, an Irish newspaper editor and member of the Irish Parliament, and John Wilkes, a London journalist and a leading politician of the Opposition. Both men charged the king's ministers with corrupting the political life of the British Isles. The doings of politi- cal rebels even in distant Poland and Turkey engaged colonial sympathies too. But perhaps the international cause that proved dearest to American lovers of liberty was the fate of Corsica.

Colonials Follow Paoli's Struggle

For years, this tiny island off the coast of Italy had fought for its independence, first from the Italian state of Genoa and then from France, which bought the island in 1768. The leader of the Corsican rebellion, Pascal Paoli, led what one New York newspaper touted as a "glorious struggle." Many in the British empire hoped that England would rally to defend Corsica's freedom, if only to keep France from seizing this strategic point in the Mediterranean. But British statesmen had no intention of going to war with France over mere Corsica, and when French troops routed his rebel army, Paoli fled to exile in England in 1769. Adding insult to injury, this "greatest man of earth," as he was lionized, began to hobnob with British nobles. He even accepted a pension of 1,000 pounds a year from George III. The moral of the sad story, according to more than one colonial newspaper, was that British corruption pervaded not only the empire but all of Europe. Paoli had been "bought"—and if the Corsican sons of liberty could not survive, would their American counterparts manage to remain virtuous for very long?

John Wilkes, an English journalist and member of the Opposition.

The Boston Massacre

Meanwhile, the situation in Boston deteriorated steadily. British troops found themselves regularly cursed by citizens and occasion- ally pelted with stones, dirt, and human excrement. The British reg- ulars were particularly unpopular among Boston's laboring classes because they competed with them for jobs. Off-duty soldiers moon- lighted as maritime laborers, and they sold their services at rates cheaper than the wages paid to locals. By 1769, brawls between British regulars and waterfront workers broke out with unsettling frequency.

With some 4,000 redcoats enduring daily contact with some 15,000 Bostonians under the sway of Samuel Adams, what happened on the night of March 5, 1770, was nearly inevitable. A crowd gathered around the customshouse for the sport of heckling the 10 soldiers who guarded it. The redcoats panicked and fended off insults and snowballs with live fire, hitting 11 rioters and killing 5. Adams and other propagandists seized on the incident. Labeling the bloodshed "the Boston Massacre," they publicized that "atrocity" throughout the colonies. The radical *Boston Gazette* framed its account in an eye-catching black-bordered edition headed with a drawing of five coffins.

While Townshend's policies spurred the resistance in America, the obvious finally dawned on Parliament. They recognized that Townshend's duties only discouraged sales to colonials and encouraged them to manufacture at home. The argument for repeal was overwhelming, and the way had been cleared by the unexpected death of Townshend shortly after Parliament adopted his proposals. In 1770 his successor, Lord North, convinced Parliament to repeal all the Townshend duties except the one on tea, allowing that tax to stand as a source of revenue and as a symbol of Parliament's authority.

Resistance Revived

Repeal of the Townshend duties took the wind from the sails of American resistance for more than two years. But the controversy between England and the colonies had not been resolved. Colonials still paid taxes on molasses and tea, taxes to which they had not consented. They were still subject to trial in admiralty courts, which operated without juries. They still lived with a standing army in their midst. Beneath the banked fires of protest smoldered the live embers of Americans' political inequality. Any shift in the wind could fan those embers into flames.

The wind did shift, quite literally, on Narragansett Bay in 1772, running aground the *Gaspee*, a British naval schooner in hot pursuit of Rhode Island smugglers. Residents of nearby Providence quickly celebrated the *Gaspee*'s misfortune by burning it down to the water line. Outraged British officials sent a special commission to look into the matter, intending once again to bypass the established colonial court system. The arrival of the *Gaspee* Commission reignited the imperial crisis, and in America, once again, resistance flared.

It did so through an ingenious mechanism, the **committees of correspondence.** Established in all the colonies by their assemblies, the committees drew up statements of American rights and grievances, distributed those documents within and among the colonies, and solicited responses from towns and counties. The brainchild of Samuel Adams, the committee structure formed a new communications network, one that fostered an intercolonial agreement on resistance to British measures. The strategy succeeded, and not only among colonies. The committees spread the scope of the resistance from colonial seaports into rural areas, engaging farmers and other country folk in the opposition to Britain.

The committees had much to talk about when Parliament passed the Tea Act in 1773. The law was an effort to bail out the bankrupt East India Company by granting that corporation

A British grenadier

Committees of Correspondence

While the new political activism of some American women merely amused male leaders of the resistance, it inspired the scorn of some partisans of British authority. When the women of Edenton, North Carolina, renounced imported tea, this British cartoon mocked them. Can you find at least five details in the painting used by the artist to insult the Americans?

a monopoly on the tea trade to Americans. Because the company could use agents to sell its product directly, cutting out the middlemen, it could offer a lower price than that charged by colonial merchants. Thus, although the Tea Act would hurt American merchants, it promised to make tea cheaper for ordinary Americans. Still, many colonials saw the act as Parliament's attempt to trick them into accepting its authority to tax the colonies. They set out to deny that power once and for all.

In the early winter of 1773, popular leaders in Boston called for the tea cargoes to be returned immediately to England. On the evening of December 16, thousands of Bostonians, as well as farmers from the surrounding countryside, packed into the Old South Meetinghouse. Some members of the audience knew what Samuel Adams had on the evening's agenda, and they awaited their cue. It came when Adams told the meeting that they could do nothing more to save their country. War whoops rang through the meetinghouse, the crowd spilled onto the streets and out to the waterfront, and the Boston Tea Party commenced. From the throng emerged 50 men dressed as Indians to disguise their identities. The party boarded three vessels docked off Griffin's Wharf, broke open casks containing 90,000 pounds of tea, and brewed a beverage worth 10,000 pounds sterling in Boston harbor.

The Empire Strikes Back

The Boston Tea Party proved to British satisfaction that the colonies aimed at independence. Lord North's assessment was grim: "We are now to dispute whether we have, or have not, any authority in that country." To reassert its authority, Parliament passed the *Coercive Acts*, dubbed in the colonies the "Intolerable Acts." The first of these came in March 1774, two months after hearing of the Tea Party, when Parliament passed the Boston Port Bill, closing that harbor to all oceangoing traffic until such time as the king saw fit to reopen it. And George, Parliament announced, would not see fit until colonials paid the East India Company for their losses.

During the next three months, Parliament approved three other "intolerable" laws designed to punish Massachusetts. The Massachusetts Government Act handed over the colony's government to royal officials. Even convening town meetings would require royal permission. The Impartial Administration of Justice Act permitted any royal official accused of a crime in Massachusetts to be tried in England or in another colony. The Quartering Act allowed the housing of British troops in uninhabited private homes, outlying buildings, and barns—not only in Massachusetts but in all the colonies.

Fear of Conspiracy

Many colonials saw the Coercive Acts as proof of a plot to enslave the colonies. In truth, the taxes and duties, laws and regulations of the past decade *were* part of a deliberate design—a commonsensical plan to centralize the administration of the British empire. But those efforts by the king's ministers and Parliament to run the colonies more efficiently and profitably were viewed by more and more Americans as a sinister conspiracy against their liberties.

For colonials, the study of history confirmed that interpretation, especially their reading of the histories written by the English Opposition. The Opposition's favorite historical subject was the downfall of republics, whether those of ancient Greece and Rome or more recent republican governments in Venice and Denmark. The lesson of their histories was always the same: power overwhelmed liberty, unless the people remained vigilant. The pattern, argued radicals, had been repeated in America over the previous dozen years: costly wars waged; oppressive taxes levied to pay for them; standing armies sent to overawe citizens; corrupt governors, customs collectors, and judges appointed to enrich themselves by enforcing the measures. Everything seemed to fit.

Québec Act

Week after week in the spring of 1774, reports of legislative outrages came across the waters. Shortly after approving the Coercive Acts, Parliament passed the Québec Act, which established a permanent government in what had been French Canada. Ominously, it included no representative assembly. Equally ominous to Protestant colonials, the Québec Act officially recognized the Roman Catholic church and extended the bounds of the province to include all land between the Mississippi and Ohio rivers. Suddenly New York, Pennsylvania, and Virginia found themselves bordering a British colony whose subjects had no voice in their own government.

With the passage of the Coercive Acts, many more colonials came to believe not only that ambitious men plotted to enslave the colonies but also that those conspirators included almost all British political leaders. At the time of the Stamp Act and again during the agitation against the Townshend Acts, most colonials had confined their suspicions to the king's ministers. By 1774 members of Parliament were also implicated in that conspiracy—and a few radicals were wondering aloud about George III.

As alarm deepened in the wake of the Coercive Acts, one colony after another called for an intercolonial congress—like the one that had met during the Stamp Act crisis—to determine the best way to defend their freedom. But many also remained unsettled about where the logic of their actions seemed to be taking them: toward a denial that they were any longer English.

First Continental Congress Called

Toward the Revolution

By the beginning of September 1774, when 55 delegates to the First Continental Congress gathered in Philadelphia, the news from Massachusetts was grim. The colony verged on anarchy, it was reported, as its inhabitants resisted the enforcement of the Massachusetts Government Act.

In the midst of this atmosphere of crisis, the members of Congress also had to take one another's measure. Many of the delegates had not traveled outside their own colonies. (All but Georgia sent representatives.) Although the delegates encountered a great deal of diversity, they quickly discovered that they esteemed the same traits of character, attributes that they called "civic virtue." These traits included simplicity and self-reliance, industry and thrift, and above all, an unselfish commitment to the public good. Most members of the Congress also shared a common mistrust of England, associating the mother country with vice, extravagance, and corruption.

Still, the delegates had some misgivings about those from other colonies. Massachusetts in particular brought with it a reputation—well deserved, considering that Samuel Adams was along—for radical action and a willingness to use force to accomplish its ends.

The First Continental Congress

As the delegates settled down to business, their aim was to reach agreement on three key points. How were they to justify the rights they claimed as American colonials? What were the limits of Parliament's power? And what were the proper tactics for resisting the Coercive Acts? Congress quickly agreed on the first point. The delegates affirmed that the law of nature, the colonial charters, and the British constitution provided the foundations of American liberties. This position was what most colonials had argued since 1765. On the two other issues, Congress charted a middle course between the demands of radicals and the reservations of conservatives.

Since the time of the Stamp Act, most colonials had insisted that Parliament had no authority to tax the colonies. But later events had demonstrated that Parliament could undermine colonial liberties by legislation as well as by taxation. The suspension of the New York legislature, the *Gaspee* Commission, and the Coercive Acts all fell into this category. Given those experiences, the delegates adopted a Declaration of Rights and Grievances on October 14, 1774, asserting the right of the colonies to tax and legislate for themselves. The Declaration of Rights thus limited Parliament's power over Americans more strictly than colonials had a decade earlier.

Samuel Adams, a radical who masterminded colonial resistance tactics.

Joseph Galloway's Plan

By denying Parliament's power to make laws for the colonies, the Continental Congress blocked efforts of the most conservative delegates to reach an accommodation with England. Their leading advocate, Joseph Galloway of Pennsylvania, proposed a plan of union with Britain similar to the one set forth by the Albany Congress in 1754. Under it, a grand council of the colonies would handle all common concerns, with any laws it passed subject to review and veto by Parliament. For its part, Parliament would have to submit for the grand council's approval any acts it passed affecting America. A majority of delegates judged that Galloway's proposal left Parliament too much leeway in legislating for colonials, and they rejected his plan.

Although the Congress denied Parliament the right to impose taxes or to make laws, delegates stopped short of declaring that it had no authority at all in the colonies. They approved Parliament's regulation of trade, but only because of the interdependent economy of the empire. And although some radical pamphleteers were attacking the king for plotting against American liberties, Congress acknowledged the continuing allegiance of the colonies to George III. In other words, the delegates called for a return to the situation that had existed in the empire before 1763, with Parliament regulating trade and the colonies exercising all powers of taxation and legislation.

The Association

On the question of resistance, the Congress satisfied the desires of its most radical delegates by drawing up the Continental Association, an agreement to cease all trade with Britain until the Coercive Acts were repealed. They agreed that their fellow citizens would immediately stop drinking East India Company tea and that by December 1, 1774, merchants would no longer import goods of any sort from Britain. A ban on the export of American produce to Britain and the West Indies would go into effect a year later, during September 1775—the lag being a concession to southern rice and tobacco planters, who wanted to market crops already planted.

Revere and the Suffolk Resolves

The Association provided for the total cessation of trade, but Samuel Adams and other radicals wanted bolder action. They received help from Paul Revere, a Boston silversmith who had long provided newspapers with many lurid engravings showing British abuses. On September 16, Revere galloped into Philadelphia bearing a copy of resolves drawn up by Bostonians and other residents of Suffolk county. The Suffolk Resolves, as they were called, branded the Coercive Acts as unconstitutional and called for civil disobedience to protest them. Congress endorsed the resolves, as Adams had hoped. But it would not approve another part of the radicals' agenda—preparing for war by authorizing proposals to strengthen and arm colonial militias.

Thus the First Continental Congress steered a middle course. Although determined to bring about repeal of the Coercive Acts, it held firm in resisting any revolutionary course of action. If British officials had responded to its recommendations and restored the status quo of 1763, the war for independence might have been postponed—perhaps indefinitely. However, even though the Congress did not go to the extremes urged by the radicals, its decisions drew colonials farther down the road to independence.

The Last Days of the British Empire in America

Most colonials applauded the achievements of the First Continental Congress. They expected that the Association would bring about a speedy repeal of the Coercive Acts. But fear that the colonies were moving toward a break with Britain led others to denounce the doings of the Congress. Conservatives were convinced that if independence were declared, chaos would ensue. Colonials, they argued, would quarrel over land claims and sectional tensions and religious differences, as they had so often in the recent past. Without Britain to referee such disputes, they feared, the result would be civil war, followed by anarchy.

Thomas Gage in Boston

The man in America with the least liking for the Continental Congress sat in the hottest seat in the colonies, that of the governor of Massachusetts. General Thomas Gage now watched as royal authority crumbled in Massachusetts and the rebellion spread to other colonies. In June 1774 a desperate Gage dissolved the Massachusetts legislature, only to see it re-form, on its own, into a Provincial Congress. That new body assumed the government of the colony in October and began arming the militia. Gage then started to fortify Boston and pleaded for more troops—only to find his fortifications damaged by saboteurs and his requests for reinforcements ignored by Britain.

Outside Boston, royal authority fared no better. Farmers in western Massachusetts forcibly closed the county courts, turning out royally appointed justices and establishing their own tribunals. Popularly elected committees of inspection charged with enforcing the Association took over towns everywhere in Massachusetts, not only restricting trade but also regulating every aspect of local life. The committees called on townspeople to display civic virtue by renouncing "effeminate" English luxuries such as tea and fine clothing and "corrupt" leisure activities such as dancing, gambling, and racing. The committees also assigned spies to report on any citizen unfriendly to the resistance. "Enemies of American liberty" risked being roundly condemned in public or beaten and pelted with mud and dung by hooting, raucous mobs.

Collapse of Royal Authority

Throughout the other colonies a similar process was under way. During the winter and early spring of 1775, provincial congresses, county conventions, and local committees of inspection were emerging as revolutionary governments, replacing royal authority at every level. As the spectacle unfolded before General Gage, he concluded that only force could subdue the colonies. It would take more than he had at his command, but reinforcements might be on the way. In February of 1775, Parliament had approved an address to the king declaring that the colonies were in rebellion.

The Fighting Begins

As spring came to Boston, the city waited. A band of artisans, organized as spies and express riders by Paul Revere, watched General Gage and waited for him to act. On April 14 word from Lord North finally arrived: Gage was to seize the leaders of the Provincial Congress, an action that would behead the rebellion, North said. Gage knew better than to believe North—but he also knew that he had to do something.

On the night of April 18 the sexton of Boston's Christ Church hung two lamps from its steeple. It was a signal that British troops had moved out of Boston and were marching toward the arms and ammunition stored by the Provincial Congress in Concord. As the lamps flashed the signal, Revere and a comrade, William Dawes, rode out to arouse the countryside.

When the news of a British march reached Lexington, its Minuteman militia of about 70 farmers, chilled and sleepy, mustered on the Green at the center of the small rural town. Lexington Green lay directly on the road to Concord. About four in the morning 700 British troops massed on the Green, and their commander, Major John Pitcairn, ordered the Lexington militia to disperse. The townsmen, outnumbered and overawed, began to obey. Then a shot rang out—whether the British or the Americans fired first is unknown—and then two volleys burst from the ranks of the redcoats. With a cheer the British set off for Concord, five miles distant, leaving eight Americans dead on Lexington Green.

Lexington and Concord

By dawn, hundreds of Minutemen from nearby towns were surging into Concord. The British entered at about seven in the morning and moved, unopposed, toward their target, a house lying across the bridge that spanned the Concord River. While three companies of British soldiers searched for American guns and ammunition, three others, posted on the bridge itself, had the misfortune to find those American arms—borne by the rebels and being fired with deadly accuracy. By noon, the British were retreating to Boston.

The narrow road from Concord to Boston's outskirts became a corridor of carnage. Pursuing Americans fired on the column of fleeing redcoats from the cover of fences and forests. By the end of April 19, the British had sustained 273 casualties;

the Americans, 95. It was only the beginning. By evening of the next day, some 20,000 New England militia had converged on Boston for a long siege.

Thomas Paine, author of Common Sense

Common Sense

The bloodshed at Lexington Green and Concord's North Bridge committed colonials to a course of rebellion—and independence. That was the conclusion drawn by Thomas Paine, who urged other Americans to join the rebels.

Paine himself was hardly an American at all. He was born in England, first apprenticed as a corsetmaker, appointed later a tax collector, and fated finally to become midwife to the age of republican revolutions. Paine came to Philadelphia late in 1774, set up as a journalist, and made the American cause his own. "Where liberty is, there is my country," he declared. In January 1776 he wrote a pamphlet to inform colonials of their identity as a distinct people and their destiny as a nation. *Common Sense* enjoyed tremendous popularity and wide circulation, selling 120,000 copies within three months of its publication.

After Lexington and Concord, Paine wrote, as the imperial crisis passed "from argument to arms, a new era for politics is struck—a new method of thinking has arisen." That new era of politics for Paine was the age of republicanism. He denounced monarchy as a foolish and dangerous form of government, one that violated the dictates of reason as well as the word of the Bible. By ridicule and remorseless argument, he severed the ties of colonial allegiance to the king. *Common Sense* scorned George III as "the Royal Brute of Britain," who had enslaved the chosen people of the new age—the Americans.

Nor did Paine stop there. He rejected the idea that colonials were or should want to be English. The colonies occupied a huge continent an ocean away from the tiny British Isles—clear proof that nature itself had fashioned America for independence. England lay locked in Europe, doomed to the corruption of an Old World. America had been discovered anew to become an "asylum of liberty."

Conspiracies and Realities

Many Americans had liked being English, but being English hadn't worked. Perhaps that is another way of saying that over the course of nearly two centuries colonial society and politics had evolved in such a way that for Americans an English identity no longer fit.

The radicals in America viewed this change in identity in terms of age-old conspiracies that repeated themselves throughout history. First, the people of a republic were impoverished by costly wars—as the colonists could well appreciate after the Seven Year's War. Then the government burdened the people with taxes to pay for those wars—as in the case of the Sugar Act or the Stamp Act or the Townshend duties. Next those in power stationed a standing army in the country, pretending to protect the people but actually lending military force to their rulers. The rhetoric of the Opposition about ministerial conspiracies gave such talk a fervid quality that, to some modern ears, may seem an exaggeration.

Take away the rhetoric, however, and the argument makes uncomfortable sense. The British administration began its "backwoods" war with France, intending to limit it to the interior of North America. But Pitt's war aims grew with every victory, and he urged war with Spain even as France was looking for peace. Britain had already taken its war in Europe farther afield, driving France out of India. When it declared war against Spain,

British naval forces in India sailed farther east, in a surprise attack on Spain's colony in the Philippines. At the same time another fleet raced toward Spanish Cuba. Peace came only once Britain and the major powers had bankrupted their treasuries. Conspiracy may not have been at the heart of the plan—Pitt, after all, was actually sympathetic to the Americans. But wars must be paid for. And the prevailing assumptions in a monarchy about who should pay led to the effort to regulate and bring order to Britain's "ungrateful" colonies.

In America, colonists were ungrateful precisely because they had established political institutions that made the rights of "freeborn Britons" more available to ordinary citizens than they were in the nation that had created those liberties. Perhaps, in other words, most Americans had succeeded *too* well at becoming English, regarding themselves as political equals entitled to basic constitutional freedoms. In the space of less than a generation, the logic of events made clear that despite all that the English and Americans shared, in the distribution of political power they were fundamentally at odds. And the call to arms at Lexington and Concord made retreat impossible.

On that point Paine was clear. It was the destiny of Americans to be republicans, not monarchists. It was the destiny of Americans to be independent, not subject to British dominion. It was the destiny of Americans to be American, not English. That, according to Thomas Paine, was common sense.

This detail from a satirical cartoon by William Hogarth, done in 1762, shows that some contemporaries were well aware of the drastic consequences of the Seven Year's War. Hogarth's metaphor was a burning London and the globe—literally, in this case—also in flames. As the dove of peace hovers above, King George is represented astride a fire pump trying to put out the conflagration. But William Pitt on stilts, dressed up as King Henry VIII, has a bellows which he uses to blow air toward the blaze, keeping it going.

Significant Events

1755	Braddock defeated by French and Indians
1756	England and France declare war
1759	Decisive English victory at Quebec
1760	George III becomes king of England
1763	Treaty of Paris ends the Seven Years' War; Pontiac's Rebellion; Proclamation prohibits settlement west of the Appalachians
1764	Sugar Act; Currency Act
1765	Stamp Act; Quartering Act
1766	Repeal of the Stamp Act; Declaratory Act
1767	Townshend duties; Parliament suspends New York assembly
1770	Boston Massacre; repeal of most Townshend duties
1772	*Gaspee* Commission
1773	Boston Tea Party
1774	Coercive Acts; First Continental Congress meets at Philadelphia
1775	Battles of Lexington and Concord
1776	Thomas Paine's *Common Sense* published

Chapter Summary

Resistance to British authority grew slowly but steadily in the American colonies during the period following the Seven Years' War.

- The new measures passed by Parliament in the early 1760s—the Proclamation of 1763, the Sugar Act, the Stamp Act, the Currency Act, and the Quartering Act—were all designed to bind the colonies more closely to the empire.

- These new measures deflated American expectations of a more equal status in the empire and also violated what Americans understood to be their constitutional and political liberties—the right to consent to taxation, the right to trial by jury, and the freedom from standing armies.

- Although Parliament repealed the Stamp Act, it reasserted its authority to tax Americans by passing the Townshend Acts in 1767.

- With the passage of the Coercive Acts in 1774, many Americans concluded that all British actions in the past decade were part of a deliberate plot to enslave Americans by depriving them of property and liberty.

- When the First Continental Congress convened in September 1774, delegates resisted both radical demands to mobilize for war and conservative appeals to reach an accommodation.

- The First Continental Congress denied Parliament any authority in the colonies except the right to regulate trade; it also drew up the Continental Association, an agreement to cease all trade with Britain until the Coercive Acts were repealed.

- When General Thomas Gage sent troops from Boston in April 1775 to seize arms being stored at Concord, the first battle of the Revolution took place.

Additional Reading

For comprehensive overviews of the entire revolutionary era, consult Edward Countryman, *The American Revolution* (1985), and Edmund S. Morgan, *Birth of the Republic* (1956). Fred Anderson, *Crucible of War* (2000), offers a magisterial account of the Seven Years' War, and Gregory Evans Dowd, *War Under Heaven* (2002), explores the implications of that conflict for American Indians. *The Stamp Act Crisis* (1953) by Edmund S. Morgan and Helen M. Morgan remains the clearest and most vivid portrayal of the issues, events, and people involved in that defining moment of the imperial crisis. For lively coverage of American resistance after the Stamp Act, see Pauline Maier, *From Resistance to Revolution* (1972), and to understand that struggle as lived and recalled by a Boston artisan, read Alfred F. Young's engaging book, *The Shoemaker and the Tea Party* (1999). Two important interpretations of how the logic of resistance took shape among colonials in Massachusetts and Virginia are Robert Gross, *The Minutemen and Their World*

(1976), and Timothy Breen, *Tobacco Culture* (1985). A more recent study by Breen, *The Marketplace Revolution* (2005), sheds new light on the role of a transatlantic consumer culture in fueling tensions within the British empire.

Bernard Bailyn, *The Ideological Origins of the American Revolution* (1967), remains the classic study of the English Opposition's influence on the evolution of republican political thought in the American colonies. Many fine biographies chronicle the careers of eighteenth-century Americans who led—or opposed—the resistance to Britain and also shed light on the times in which they lived. Of particular interest are Pauline Maier, *The Old Revolutionaries* (1980); Bernard Bailyn, *The Ordeal of Thomas Hutchinson* (1974); and two recent biographies of Thomas Paine (both published in 2006) by Harvey Kaye and Craig Nelson.

For a fuller list of readings, see the Bibliography at www.mhhe.com/davidsonnation6.

CHAPTER 7
The American People:
The American Revolution
1775~1783

BOSTON

CHARLES TOWN

"Will He Fight?"

From a high place somewhere in the city—Beacon Hill, perhaps, or Copse Hill—General Thomas Gage looked down on Boston. Through a spyglass his gaze traveled over the church belfries and steeples, the roofs of brick and white frame houses. Finally he fixed his sights on a figure far in the distance across the Charles River. The man was perched atop a crude fortification on Breed's Hill, an elevation lying just below Bunker Hill on the Charlestown peninsula. Gage took the measure of his enemy: an older man, past middle age, a sword swinging beneath his homespun coat, a broad-brimmed hat shading his eyes. As he passed the spyglass to his ally, an American loyalist, Gage asked Abijah Willard if he knew the man on the fort. Willard peered across the Charles and identified his own brother-in-law, Colonel William Prescott. A veteran of the Seven Years' War, Prescott was now a leader in the rebel army laying siege to Boston.

"Will he fight?" Gage wondered aloud.

"I cannot answer for his men," Willard replied, "but Prescott will fight you to the gates of hell."

Fight they did on June 17, 1775, both William Prescott and his men. The evening before, three regiments had followed the colonel from Cambridge to Breed's Hill—soldiers drawn from the thousands of militia who had swarmed to surround British-occupied Boston after the bloodshed at Lexington and Concord. All through the night, they dug deep trenches and built up high earthen walls atop the hill. At the first light of day, a British warship spotted the new rebel outpost and opened fire. By noon barges were ferrying British troops under Major General William Howe across the half mile of river that separated Boston from Charlestown. The 1,600 raw rebel troops tensed at the sight of scarlet-coated soldiers streaming ashore, glittering bayonets grasped at the ready. The rebels were farmers and artisans, not professional soldiers, and they were frightened out of their wits.

But Prescott and his men held their ground. The British charged Breed's Hill twice, and Howe watched in horror as streams of fire felled his troops. Finally, during the third British frontal assault, the rebels ran out of ammunition and were forced to withdraw. Redcoats poured into the rebel fort, bayoneting its handful of remaining defenders. By nightfall the British had taken Breed's Hill and the rest of the Charlestown peninsula. They had bought a dark triumph at the cost of 228 dead and 800 wounded.

On June 17, 1775 thousands of colonials flocked to the rooftops and upper windows of their Boston homes to witness the British attack on Breed's Hill across the water on nearby Charlestown peninsula. As the British artillery sent shells into the peninsula, houses there caught fire and burst into flames. Then the redcoats, unloaded from their ships, launched their assault on the hill.

Battle of Bunker Hill

The cost came high in loyalties as well. The fighting on Breed's Hill fed the hatred of Britain that had been building since April. Throughout America, preparations for war intensified: militia in every colony mustered; communities stockpiled arms and ammunition. Around Charlestown civilians fled the countryside, abandoning homes and shops set afire by the British shelling of Breed's Hill. "The roads filled with frightened women and children, some in carts with their tattered furniture, others on foot fleeing into the woods," recalled Hannah Winthrop, one of their number.

The bloody, indecisive fight on the Charlestown peninsula known as the Battle of Bunker Hill actually took place on Breed's Hill. And the exchange between Thomas Gage and Abijah Willard that is said to have preceded the battle may not have taken place at all. But the story has persisted in the folklore of the American Revolution. Whether it really happened or not, the conversation between Gage and Willard raised the question that both sides wanted answered. Were Americans willing to fight for independence from British rule? It was one thing, after all, to oppose the British ministry's policy of taxation. It was another to support a rebellion for which the ultimate price of failure was hanging for treason. And it was another matter entirely for men to wait nervously atop a hill as the seasoned troops of their own "mother country" marched toward them with the intent to kill.

Americans React to the Revolution

Indeed, the question "will they fight?" was revolutionary shorthand for a host of other questions concerning how ordinary Americans would react to the tug of loyalties between long-established colonial governments and a long-revered parent nation and monarch. For slaves, the question revolved around their allegiance to masters who spoke of liberty or to their masters' enemies who promised liberation. For those who led the rebels, it was a question of strengthening the resolve of the undecided, coordinating resistance, instilling discipline—translating the *will* to fight into the *ability* to do so. And for those who believed the rebellion was a madness whipped up by artful politicians, it was a question of whether to remain silent or risk speaking out, whether to take up arms for the king or flee. All these questions were raised, of necessity, by the act of revolution. But the barrel of a rifle shortened them to a single, pointed question: will you fight?

Will they fight? This Pennsylvania regimental flag gives one reason why some did.

The Decision for Independence

The delegates to the Second Continental Congress gathered at Philadelphia on May 10, 1775, just one month after the battles at Lexington and Concord. They had to determine whether independence or reconciliation offered the best way to protect the liberties of their colonies.

For a brash, ambitious lawyer from Braintree, Massachusetts, British abuses dictated only one course. "The Cancer [of official corruption] is too deeply rooted," wrote John Adams, "and too far spread to be cured by anything short of cutting it out entire." Yet during the spring and summer of 1775, even strong advocates of independence did not openly seek a separation from Britain. If the radicals' objective of independence was ever to be achieved, greater agreement among Americans had to be attained. Moderates and conservatives harbored deep misgivings about independence: they had to be brought along slowly.

The Second Continental Congress

To bring them along, Congress adopted the "Olive Branch Petition" in July 1775. Drawn up by Pennsylvania's John Dickinson, the document affirmed American loyalty to George III and asked the king to disavow the policies of his principal ministers. At the same time Congress issued a declaration denying that the colonies aimed at independence. Yet, less than a month earlier, Congress had authorized the creation of a rebel military force, the **Continental Army,** and had issued paper money to pay for the troops.

A Congress that sued for peace while preparing for war was a puzzle that British politicians—least of all, Lord George Germain—did not even try to understand. A tough-minded statesman now charged with overseeing colonial affairs, Germain was determined to subdue the rebellion by force. George III proved just as stubborn: he refused to receive the Olive Branch Petition. By the end of that year Parliament had shut down all trade with the colonies and had ordered the Royal Navy to seize colonial merchant ships on the high seas. In November 1775 Virginia's royal governor, Lord Dunmore, offered freedom to any slaves who would join the British. During January of the next year, he ordered the shelling of Norfolk, Virginia, reducing that town to smoldering rubble.

Aggressive British Response

British belligerence withered the cause of reconciliation within Congress and the colonies. Support for independence gained more momentum from the overwhelming reception of Paine's *Common Sense* in January 1776. Radicals in Congress realized that the future was theirs and were ready to act. In April 1776 the delegates opened American trade to every nation in the world except Great Britain; a month later Congress advised the colonies to establish new state governments. And on June 7 Virginia's Richard Henry Lee offered the motion "that these United Colonies are, and of right ought to be, free and independent States . . . and that all political connection between them and the State of Great Britain is, and ought to be, totally dissolved."

The Declaration

Congress postponed a final vote on Lee's motion until July. Some opposition still lingered among delegates from the middle colonies, and a committee appointed to write a declaration of independence needed time to complete its work. That committee included some of the leading delegates in Congress: John Adams, Benjamin Franklin, Connecticut's Roger Sherman, and New York's Robert Livingston. But the man who did most of the drafting was a young planter and lawyer from western Virginia.

Thomas Jefferson was just 33-years-old in the summer of 1776 when he withdrew to his lodgings on the outskirts of Philadelphia, pulled a portable writing desk onto his lap, and wrote the statement that would explain American independence to a "candid world." In the document's brief opening section, Jefferson set forth a general justification of revolution that invoked the "self-evident truths" of human equality and "unalienable rights" to "life, liberty, and the pursuit of happiness." These natural rights had been "endowed" to all persons "by their Creator," the Declaration pointed out; thus there was no need to appeal to the narrower claim of the "rights of Englishmen."

Thomas Jefferson

While the first part of the Declaration served notice that Americans no longer considered themselves English, its second and longer section denied England any authority in the colonies. In its detailed history of American grievances against the British empire, the Declaration referred only once to Parliament. Instead, it blamed George III for a "long train of abuses and usurpations" designed to achieve "absolute despotism." Unlike *Common Sense,* the Declaration denounced only the reigning king of England; it did not attack the institution of monarchy itself. But like *Common Sense,* the Declaration affirmed that government originated in the consent of the governed and upheld the right of the people to overthrow oppressive rule.

Blaming George III

Later generations have debated what Jefferson meant by the "pursuit of happiness" and whether he had either women or black Americans in mind when he wrote the famous phrase "all men are created equal." His own contemporaries in Congress did not pause to consider those questions and surely would have found themselves divided

This detail from a painting, commemorating the signing of the Declaration of Independence, shows Benjamin Franklin (seated center), weighing the consequences of the decisions he and his colleagues are about to undertake. John Hancock, the president of the Congress, is reported to have remarked, "We must be unanimous; there must be no pulling different ways; we must all hang together." Franklin is said to have rejoined, "Yes, we must indeed all hang together, or most assuredly, we shall all hang separately."

if they had. No matter. By firmly grounding the Declaration on the natural rights due all people, Jefferson placed equality at the center of the new nation's identity, setting the framework for a debate that would continue over the next two centuries. Congress adopted the Declaration of Independence on July 4, 1776.

American Loyalists

But the sentiment for independence was not universal. Americans who would not back the rebellion, supporters of the king and Parliament, numbered perhaps one-fifth of the population in 1775. While they proclaimed themselves **loyalists,** their rebel opponents dubbed them "tories"—"a thing whose head is in England, whose body is in America, and whose neck ought to be stretched." That division made the Revolution a conflict pitting Americans against one another as well as the British. In truth, the war for independence was the first American civil war.

Sources of Loyalist Support

Predictably, the king and Parliament commanded the strongest support in colonies that had been wracked by internal strife earlier in the eighteenth century. In New York, New Jersey, Pennsylvania, and the Carolinas, not only did memories of old struggles sharpen worries of future upheaval, but old enemies often took different sides in the Revolution. The Carolina backcountry emerged as a stronghold of loyalist sentiment because of influential local men who cast their lot with Britain. To win support against Carolina's rebels, whose ranks included most wealthy coastal planters, western loyalist leaders played on ordinary settlers' resentments of privileged easterners. Grievances dating back to the 1760s also influenced the revolutionary allegiances of former land rioters of New York and New Jersey. If their old landlord opponents opted for the rebel cause, the tenants took up loyalism.

Patterns of Allegiance
While most New Englanders rallied behind the rebel cause, support for the Revolution was not as widespread in the middle colonies and southern colonies.

Other influences also fostered allegiance to Britain. Government officials who owed their jobs to the empire, major city merchants who depended on British trade, and Anglicans living outside the South retained strong ties to the parent country. Loyalists were also disproportionately represented among recent emigrants from the British Isles. The inhabitants of Georgia, the newest colony, inclined toward the king, as did the Highland Scots, many of whom had arrived in the colonies as soldiers during the Seven Years' War or had worked for a short time in the southern backcountry as tobacco merchants and Indian traders.

Although a substantial minority, loyalists never became numerous enough anywhere to pose a serious menace to the Revolution. A more formidable threat was posed by the British army. And the greatest threat of all was posed by those very Americans who claimed that they wanted independence. For the question remained: would they fight?

The Fighting in the North

In the summer of 1775 Americans who wished to remain neutral probably outnumbered either loyalists or rebels. From the standpoint of mere survival, staying neutral made more sense than fighting for independence. Even the most ardent advocates of American rights had reason to harbor doubts, given the odds against the rebel colonists defeating the armed forces of the British empire.

George Washington, General

Perhaps no friend of American liberty saw more clearly how slim the chances of a rebel victory were than George Washington. But Washington's principles, and his sense of honor, prevailed. June of 1775 found him, then 43-years-old, attending the deliberations of the Second Continental Congress and dressed—a bit conspicuously—in his officer's uniform. The other delegates listened closely to his opinions on military matters, for Washington was the most celebrated American veteran of the Seven Years' War who remained young enough to lead a campaign. Better still, as a southerner he could bring his region into what thus far had remained mostly New England's fight. Congress readily appointed him commander in chief of a newly created Continental Army.

The Two Armies at Bay

Thus did Washington find himself, only a month later, looking to bring some order to the rebel forces massing around Boston. He knew he faced a formidable foe.

Highly trained, ably led, and efficiently equipped, the king's troops were seasoned professionals. Rigorous drills and often severe discipline welded rank-and-file soldiers, men drawn mostly from the bottom of British society, into a savage fighting machine. At the height of the campaign in America, reinforcements brought the number of British troops to 50,000, strengthened by some 30,000 Hessian mercenaries from Germany and the support of half the ships in the British navy, the largest in the world.

"Regulars" versus the Militia

Washington was more modest about the army under his command, and he had much to be modest about. At first Congress recruited his fighting force of 16,600 rebel "regulars," the Continental Army, from the ranks of local New England militia bands. Although enlistments swelled briefly during the patriotic enthusiasm of 1775, for the rest of the war Washington's Continentals suffered chronic shortages of men and supplies. Even strong supporters of the Revolution hesitated to join the regular army, with its low pay and strict discipline and the constant threat of disease and danger. Most men preferred to fight instead as members of local militia units, the "irregular" troops who turned out to support the regular army whenever British forces came close to their neighborhoods.

The general reluctance to join the Continental Army created a host of difficulties for its commander and for Congress. Washington wanted and needed an army whose size and military capability could be counted on in long campaigns. He could not create an effective fighting force out of militias that mustered occasionally or men who enlisted for short stints in the Continental Army. In contrast, most republican leaders feared standing armies and idealized "citizen-soldiers"—men of civic virtue who volunteered whenever needed—as the backbone of the common defense. "Oh, that I was a soldier," chubby John Adams fantasized in 1775. "Everyone must and will and shall be a soldier."

Man or God and How to Tell the Difference

Analyzing a Nation's Mythmaking

Every nation makes its own myths, alongside or intermixed with its history—and historians often analyze the objects of this mythmaking. Unlike most members of the American pantheon Washington attained exalted status during his lifetime. Merely by retiring to private life at the end of the Revolutionary War, he vaulted in the public esteem from a victorious general to a republican saint. Washington had become a self-denying patriot who shunned the temptation to seize political power by exploiting his military glory (though he would eventually come out of retirement to accept the presidency).

Like most of the founders, Washington took care to ensure that his fame would endure. In retirement he sat patiently for a steady stream of visiting artists, among them the French sculptor Jean Antoine Houdon, who cast this bust (*left*) from a life mask in 1785. Even to reproduce Washington in this classical style (note the Greco-Roman clothing) elevates him to the pantheon of Greek and Roman republicans so admired by Enlightenment thinkers. But despite his strivings for immortality, Washington resisted becoming a republican deity. Indeed, nothing would have irked this dignified Virginian of unorthodox re-

ligious views more than the artist Norman Rockwell's cover for this Sears and Roebuck mail-order catalogue in 1932, which depicts a saintly Washington bestowing his blessing on the nation, as a young student composes an essay in his honor.

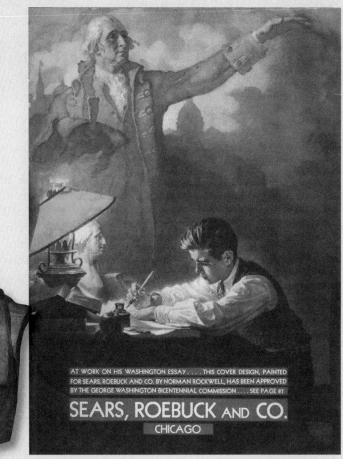

Realistic and romantic images of Washington. LEFT : *the bust by Jean Antoine Houdon, based on the life mask of 1785;* RIGHT : *the Sears, Roebuck catalogue cover by Norman Rockwell, 1932.*

But everyone did not become a soldier, and the dwindling number of volunteers gradually overcame republican fears of standing armies. In September 1776 Congress set terms in the Continental Army at a minimum of three years or for the duration of the war and assigned each state to raise a certain number of troops. They offered every man who enlisted in the army a cash bounty and a yearly clothing issue; enlistees for the duration were offered 100 acres of land as well. Still the problem of recruitment

Women and men of revolutionary America sought to invest themselves with virtue as they escaped British "corruption." The most zealous partisans of colonial rights took that "investiture" to a literal extreme: they made and wore particular clothing as an emblem of political commitment. In the 1760s "homespun," any coarse cloth made in America, became a badge of opposition to British colonial policy.

Clothes sewn from domestic textiles identified the men and women who wore them as friends of liberty, freed from the vanity of British fashion and the humiliating dependence on British imports. As early as 1766 the radical press called for increased domestic industry to offset American reliance on

English cloth. It aimed its pleas particularly at the women who managed colonial households.

By 1769 radical propaganda had produced a new ritual of American resistance, the patriotic spinning competition. Wives and daughters from some of the wealthiest and most prominent families, women who had earlier vied to outdo one another in acquiring the latest English finery, were the featured players in this new form of political theater. Its setting was usually the home of a local minister, where, early in the morning, "respectable" young ladies,

A wheel for spinning flax, made around 1775.

persisted. Less than a year later, Congress recommended that the states adopt a draft, but Congress had no authority to compel the states to meet their troop quotas.

Even in the summer of 1775, before enlistments fell off, Washington was worried. As his inexperienced Continentals laid siege to British-occupied Boston, most officers provided no real leadership, and the men under their command shirked their duties. They slipped away from camp at night; they left sentry duty before being relieved; they took potshots at the British; they tolerated filthy conditions in their camps.

Women of the Army

While Washington strove to impose discipline on his Continentals, he also attempted, without success, to rid himself of "the Women of the Army." When American men went off to fight, their wives usually stayed at home. To women then fell the sole responsibility for running farms and businesses, raising children, and keeping households together. They helped to supply the troops by sewing clothing, making blankets, and saving rags and lead weights for bandages and bullets. Other women on the home front organized relief for the widows and orphans of soldiers and protests against merchants who hoarded scarce commodities.

But the wives of poor men who joined the army were often left with no means to support their families. Thousands of such women—1 for every 15 soldiers—drifted after the troops. In return for half-rations, they cooked and washed for the soldiers; and after battles, they nursed the wounded, buried the dead, and scavenged the field for clothing and equipment. An even larger number of women accompanied the redcoats: their presence was the only thing that Washington did not admire about the British army and could barely tolerate in his own. But the services that they performed were indispensable, and women followed the troops throughout the war.

Laying Strategies

At the same time that he tried to discipline the Continentals, Washington designed a defensive strategy to compensate for their weakness. To avoid exposing raw rebel troops on "open ground against their Superiors in number and Discipline," he planned to fight the British from strong fortifications. With that aim in mind, in March 1776, all dressed in homespun, assembled with their spinning wheels. They spent the day spinning furiously, stopping only to sustain themselves with "American produce . . . which was more agreeable to them than any foreign Dainties and Delicacies" and to drink herbal tea. At the end of the day the minister accepted their homespun and delivered an edifying sermon to all present. That was a large group, often including from 20 to 100 "respectable" female spinners as well as hundreds of other townsfolk who had come to watch the competition or to provide food and entertainment.

Women reveled in the new attention and value that the male resistance movement and the radical press now attached to a common and humdrum domestic task. By the beginning of 1769 New England newspapers were highlighting spinning bees and their female participants, sometimes termed the "Daughters of Liberty." Wives and daughters from families of every rank were made to feel that they could play an important role in the resistance by imitating the elite women showcased in public spinning spectacles.

Spinning bees and "dressing down" in homespun thus contributed to the solidarity of the resistance by narrowing the visible distance between rich and poor Americans. In accounts of spinning competitions, the radical press emphasized that even the daughters of the elite sacrificed for the cause of resistance by embracing domestic economy and simplicity.

American women took pride in the new political importance that radical propaganda attributed to domestic pursuits. Writing to her English cousin, Charity Clarke of New York City cast herself as one of America's "fighting army of amazones . . . armed with spinning wheels."

Washington barricaded his army on Dorchester Heights, an elevation commanding Boston harbor from the south. That maneuver, which allowed American artillery to fire on enemy warships, confirmed a decision already made by the British to evacuate their entire army from Boston and sail for Halifax, Nova Scotia.

Britain had hoped to reclaim its colonies with a strategy of strangling the resistance in Massachusetts. But by the spring of 1776 it saw clearly that more was required than a show of force against New England. Instead Britain's leaders chose to wage a conventional war in America, capturing major cities and crushing the Continental forces in a decisive battle. Military victory, the British believed, would enable them to restore political control and reestablish imperial authority.

The first target was New York City. General William Howe and Lord George Germain, the British officials now charged with overseeing the war, chose that seaport for its central location and—they hoped—its large loyalist population. Howe's army intended to move from New York City up the Hudson River, meeting with British troops under General Sir Guy Carleton coming south from Canada. Either the British drive would lure Washington into a major engagement, crushing the Continentals, or, if unopposed, the British offensive would cut America in two, smothering resistance to the south by isolating New England.

The strategy was sounder than the men placed in charge of executing it. Concern for preserving troops addicted General Howe to caution, when daring more would have carried the day. Howe's brother, Admiral Lord Richard Howe, the head of naval operations in America, also stopped short of pressing the British advantage, owing to his personal desire for reconciliation. The reluctance of the Howe brothers to fight became the formula for British frustration in the two years that followed.

By mid-August, 32,000 British troops, including 8,000 **Hessians,** the largest expeditionary force of the eighteenth century, faced Washington's army of 23,000, which had marched down from Boston to take up positions on Long Island. At dawn on August 22 the Howe brothers launched their offense, easily pushing the rebel army back across the East River to Manhattan. After lingering on Long Island for a month, the Howes again lurched into action, ferrying their forces to Kip's Bay, just a few miles

The British Choose Conventional War

Howe Brothers

The Campaigns in New York and New Jersey

British Capture
New York City

south of Harlem. When the British landed, the handful of rebel defenders at Kip's Bay fled—straight into the towering wrath of Washington, who happened on the scene during the rout. For once the general lost his habitual self-restraint, flogged both officers and men with his riding crop, and came close to being captured himself. But the Howes remained reluctant to hit hard, letting Washington's army escape from Manhattan to Westchester County.

Throughout the fall of 1776 General Howe's forces followed as Washington's fled southward across New Jersey. On December 7, with the British nipping at their heels, the rebels crossed the Delaware River into Pennsylvania. There Howe stopped, pulling back most of his army to winter in New York City and leaving the Hessians to hold the British line of advance along the New Jersey side of the Delaware River.

Rebel Victories at
Trenton and Princeton

Although the retreat had shriveled rebel strength to only 3,000 men, Washington decided that the campaign of 1776 was not over. On a snowy Christmas night, the Continentals floated back across the Delaware, picked their way over roads iced with sleet and finally slid into Hessian-held Trenton at eight in the morning. One thousand German soldiers, still recovering from their spirited Christmas celebration and caught completely by surprise, quickly surrendered. Washington's luck held when, on January 3, 1777, the Continentals defeated British troops on the outskirts of Princeton, New Jersey.

During the winter of 1776–1777 the British lost more than battles: they alienated the very civilians whose loyalties they had hoped to maintain. In New York City the presence of the main body of the British army brought shortages of food and housing and caused constant friction between soldiers and city dwellers. In the New Jersey countryside still held by the Hessians, the situation was more desperate. Forced to live off the land, the Germans aroused resentment among local farmers by seizing "hay, oats, Indian corn, cattle, and horses, which were never or but very seldom paid for," as

At the Battle of Princeton, British troops bayoneted the rebel general Hugh Mercer, an assault later memorialized in this painting by George Washington Parke Custis, the adopted step-grandson of George Washington. This rendering focuses attention not only to Mercer's courage but also to the savagery of the redcoats, both of which helped the rebels gain civilian support.

The Fighting in the North, 1775–1777 *After the British withdrew from Boston in 1775, they launched an attack on New York City the following year. Washington was forced to retreat northward, then across the Hudson and south into New Jersey and Pennsylvania, before surprising the British at Trenton and Princeton. Burgoyne's surrender at Saratoga in 1777 marked a turning point in the war.*

one loyalist admitted. The Hessians ransacked and destroyed homes and churches; they kidnapped and raped young women.

Many repulsed neutrals and loyalists now took their allegiance elsewhere. Bands of **militia** on Long Island, along the Hudson River, and all over New Jersey rallied to support the Continentals.

Capturing Philadelphia

In the summer of 1777 General Howe still hoped to entice the Continentals into a decisive engagement. But he had now decided to goad the Americans into battle by capturing Philadelphia. Rather than risk a march through hostile New Jersey, he sailed his army to Maryland and began a march to Philadelphia, 50 miles away. Washington had hoped to stay on the strategic defensive, holding his smaller army together and harassing the enemy but avoiding full-scale battles. Howe's march on the new nation's capital made that impossible. Washington engaged Howe twice: in September at Brandywine Creek and in October in an early dawn attack at Germantown, but both times the rebels were beaten back. He had been unable to prevent the British occupation of Philadelphia.

Brandywine and Germantown

But in Philadelphia, as in New York, British occupation created hostile feelings, as the flood of troops drove up the price of food, fuel, and housing. While inflation hit hardest at the poor, the wealthy resented British officers who became their uninvited house guests. Philadelphians complained of redcoats looting their shops, trampling their gardens, and harassing them on the streets. Elizabeth Drinker, the wife of a Quaker merchant, confided in her diary that "I often feel afraid to go to bed."

Even worse, the British march through Maryland and Pennsylvania had outraged civilians, who fled before the army and then returned to find their homes and barns bare, their crops and livestock gone. Everywhere Howe's men went in the mid-Atlantic, they left in their wake Americans with compelling reasons to support the rebels. Worst of all, just days after Howe marched his occupying army into Philadelphia in the fall of 1777, another British commander in North America was surrendering his entire army to rebel forces at Saratoga, New York.

Disaster at Saratoga

The calamity that befell the British at Saratoga was the doing of a glorymongering general, John "Gentleman Johnny" Burgoyne. After his superior officer, Sir Guy Carleton, bungled a drive into New York in 1776, Burgoyne won approval to command another attack from Canada. The following summer he set out from Quebec with a force of 9,500 redcoats, 2,000 women and children, and a baggage train that included the commander's silver dining service, his dress uniforms, and numerous cases of his favorite champagne. As Burgoyne's entourage lumbered southward, it was slowed by a winding road that was broken by boulders, felled trees, and ramshackle bridges. Meanwhile, a handful of Continentals and a horde of New England militia assembled several miles below Saratoga at Bemis Heights under the command of General Horatio Gates.

Burgoyne Surrenders at Saratoga

On September 19 Gates's rebel scouts, nested high in the trees, spied the glittering bayonets of Burgoyne's approaching force. Benedict Arnold, a brave young officer, led several thousand rebels into battle at a clearing at Freeman's Farm. At the end of the day British reinforcements finally pushed the rebels back from a battlefield piled high with the bodies of soldiers from both sides. Burgoyne tried to flee to Canada but got no farther than Saratoga, where he surrendered his army to Gates on October 17.

Saratoga changed everything. Burgoyne had not just been nipped in a skirmish; he had lost his entire army. The triumph was enough to convince Britain's old rival France that, with a little help, the Americans might well reap the fruits of victory.

The Turning Point

France had been waiting for revenge against Britain since its humiliating defeat in the Seven Years' War. And for some years a scheme for evening the score had been taking shape in the mind of the French foreign minister, Charles Gravier de Vergennes. He reckoned that France might turn discontented colonials into willing allies against Britain.

The American Revolution Becomes a Global War

Vergennes approached the Americans cautiously. He wanted to make certain that the rift between Britain and its colonies would not be reconciled and that the rebels in

America stood a fighting chance. Although France had been secretly supplying the Continental Army with guns and ammunition since the spring of 1776, Vergennes would go no further than covert assistance.

Congress approached its former French enemies with equal caution. Would France, the leading Catholic monarchy in Europe, make common cause with the republican rebels? A few years earlier American colonials had fought against the French in Canada. Only recently they had renounced a king. For centuries they had overwhelmingly adhered to Protestantism.

The string of defeats dealt the Continental Army during 1776 convinced Congress that they needed the French. In November Congress appointed a three-member commission to negotiate not only aid from France but also a formal alliance. Its senior member was Benjamin Franklin, who enchanted all of Paris when he arrived sporting a simple fur cap and a pair of spectacles (something no fashionable Frenchman wore in public). Hailed as a homespun sage, Franklin played the role of American innocent to the hilt and watched as admiring Parisians stamped his face on everything from the top of snuffboxes to the bottom of porcelain chamber pots.

Still, Franklin understood that mere popularity could not produce the alliance sought by Congress. It was only news that Britain had surrendered an entire army at Saratoga that convinced Vergennes that the rebels could actually win. In February 1778 France signed a treaty of commerce and friendship and a treaty of alliance, which Congress approved in May. Under the terms of the treaties, both parties agreed to accept nothing short of independence for America. The alliance left the British no choice other than to declare war on France. Less than a year later Spain joined France, hoping to recover territory lost to England in earlier wars.

The French public's infatuation with Benjamin Franklin knew no bounds. They particularly delighted in his rustic dress and styled him a representative of "frontier" America. He appears in this guise on a snuffbox along with two revered French philosophers, Voltaire and Rousseau.

Winding Down the War in the North

The Revolution widened into a global war after 1778. Preparing to fight France and Spain dictated a new British strategy in America. No longer could the British concentrate on crushing the Continental Army. Instead they would disperse their forces to fend off challenges all over the world. In May Sir Henry Clinton replaced William Howe as commander in chief and received orders to withdraw from Philadelphia to New York City.

Only 18 miles outside Philadelphia, at Valley Forge, Washington and his Continentals were assessing their own situation. Some 11,000 rebel soldiers had passed a harrowing winter in that isolated spot, starving for want of food, freezing for lack of clothing, huddling in miserable huts, and hating the British who lay so close and yet so comfortably in Philadelphia. The army also cursed their fellow citizens; its misery resulted from congressional disorganization and from civilian indifference. Congress

lacked both money to pay and maintain the army and an efficient system for dispensing provisions to the troops. Most farmers and merchants preferred to supply the British, who could pay handsomely, than to do business with a financially strapped Congress. What little did reach the army often was food too rancid to eat or clothing too rotten to wear. Perhaps 2,500 perished at Valley Forge, the victims of cold, hunger, and disease.

Why did civilians who supported the rebel cause allow the army to suffer? Probably because by the winter of 1777, the Continentals came mainly from social classes that received little consideration at any time. The respectable, propertied farmers and artisans who had laid siege to Boston in 1775 had stopped enlisting. Serving in their

This British cartoon from 1783 evokes the chaos unleashed by the war in the West, but it portrays the Indians as instigators of the violence. In truth, the disorder was as much sparked by the new wave of settlement and pressure on Indians to take sides by European powers and the United States.

stead were single men in their teens and early 20s, some who joined the army out of desperation, others who were drafted, still others who were hired as substitutes for the more affluent. The landless sons of farmers, unemployed laborers, drifters, petty criminals, vagrants, indentured servants, slaves, even captured British and Hessian soldiers—all men with no other means and no other choice—were swept into the Continental Army. The social composition of the rebel rank and file had come to resemble that of the British army. It is the great irony of the Revolution: a war to protect liberty and property was waged by those Americans who were poorest and least free.

The beginning of spring in 1778 brought a reprieve. Supplies arrived at Valley Forge, and so did a fellow calling himself Baron von Steuben, a penniless Prussian soldier of fortune. Although Washington's men had shown spirit and resilience ever since Trenton, they still lacked discipline and training. Those defects and more von Steuben began to remedy. Barking orders and spewing curses in German and French, the baron (and his translators) drilled the rebel regiments to march in formation and to handle their bayonets like proper Prussian soldiers. By the summer of 1778, morale had rebounded.

Spoiling for action after their long winter, Washington's army, now numbering nearly 13,500, harassed Clinton's army as it marched overland from Philadelphia to New York. On June 28 at Monmouth Courthouse a long, confused battle ended in a draw. After both armies retired for the night, Clinton's forces slipped away to safety in New York City. Washington pursued, but he lacked the numbers to launch an all-out assault on New York City.

Army Uprisings

During the two hard winters that followed, resentments mounted among the rank and file over spoiled food, inadequate clothing, and arrears in pay. The army retaliated with mutinies. Between 1779 and 1780 officers managed to quell uprisings in three New England regiments. But in January 1781 both the Pennsylvania and New Jersey lines in an outright **mutiny** marched on Philadelphia, where Congress had reconvened. Order returned only after Congress promised back pay and provisions and Washington put two ringleaders in front of a firing squad.

War in the West

The battles between Washington's Continentals and the British made the war in the West seem, by comparison, a sideshow of attacks and counterattacks that settled little. American fighters such as George Rogers Clark, with great daring, captured outposts such as Kaskaskia and Vincennes, without materially affecting the outcome of the war. Yet the conflict sparked a tremendous upheaval in the West, both from the dislocations of war and from the disease that spread in war's wake.

Indians Caught in a Crossfire

The disruptions were so widespread because the "War for Independence" had also become a war involving the imperial powers of Britain, France, and Spain. The same jockeying for advantage went on in the West as had occurred in previous imperial wars. The United States as well as the European powers pressed Indian tribes to become allies and attacked them when they did not. Caught in the crossfire, some Indian nations were pushed to the brink of their own civil war, splitting into pro-American or British factions. None suffered more than the mighty Iroquois. When days of impassioned speeches failed to secure a unified Iroquois policy regarding the Revolution, the six confederated tribes went their own ways. Most Tuscaroras and Oneidas remained neutral or joined the Americans, whereas Mohawk, Onondaga, Seneca, and Cayuga warriors aided the British by attacking frontier settlements. This pro-British faction rallied around the remarkable Mohawk leader Joseph Brant. Bilingual, literate, and formidable in war, Brant helped lead devastating raids across the frontiers of New York and Pennsylvania. In response Washington dispatched troops into Iroquois country, where they put the torch to 40 towns and destroyed fields and orchards everywhere they went. Many Iroquois perished the following winter—whichever side they had supported in the war—and the confederacy emerged from the revolution with but a shadow of its former power.

The Smallpox Pandemic, 1775–1782 *Smallpox spread across North America beginning late in 1775 as American forces launched an unsuccessful attack on the city of Quebec in Canada. The routes of transmission give only a rough idea of the disease's spread and impact, as it moved down the eastern seaboard and around the Gulf of Mexico, and then penetrated the interior, where the scattered surviving date make the pandemic's progress much harder to track. But the ravages of smallpox, combined with the disruptions sparked by the western raids of the Revolutionary War, placed severe stress on Indian peoples all across the continent. The disruption continued through the end of the eighteenth century.*

Other native peoples switched allegiances more than once. Near St. Louis, a young Kaskaskia chief, Jean Baptiste de Coigne, allied first with the French, then joined the British and briefly threw in his lot with the Spanish, before finally joining the Virginians. Indians understood well that the pressures of war always threatened to deprive them of their homelands. "You are drawing so close to us that we can almost hear the noise of your axes felling our Trees," one Shawnee told the Americans. Another group of Indians concluded in 1784 that the Revolutionary War had been "the greatest blow that could have been dealt us, unless it had been our total destruction." Thousands fled the raids and counter-raids, while whole villages relocated. Hundreds made their way even beyond the Mississippi, to seek shelter in territory claimed by Spain. The aftershocks and dislocations continued for the next two decades; an entire generation of Native Americans grew up with war as a constant companion.

The political instability was vastly compounded by a smallpox epidemic that broke out first among American troops besieging Quebec in 1775. The disease soon spread to Washington's troops in New England, and he was obliged to inoculate them—secretly, for the vaccination left many soldiers temporarily weakened. From New England, the pox spread south along the coast, eventually reached New Orleans and next leapt to Mexico City by the autumn of 1779. From New Orleans it spread via fur traders up the Mississippi River and across the central plains, and from New Spain northward as well. By the time the pandemic burned out in 1782, it had felled over 130,000. By contrast, the Revolutionary War caused the deaths of some 8,000 soldiers while fighting in battle and another 13,000 from disease, including the mortality from smallpox.

Smallpox Pandemic

The Home Front in the North

Although in 1779 most northern civilians on the seaboard enjoyed a respite from the war, the devastation lingered. Refugees on foot and in hastily packed carts filled the roads, fleeing the advancing armies. Those who remained to protect their homes and property might be caught in the crossfire of contending forces or cut off from supplies of food and firewood. Loyalists who remained in areas occupied by rebel troops faced harassment, imprisonment, or the confiscation of their property. Rebel sympathizers met similar fates in regions held by the British.

Women and the War

The demands of war also disrupted family economies throughout the northern countryside. The seasons of intense fighting drew men off into military service just when their labor was most needed on family farms. Wives and daughters were left to assume the work of husbands and sons while coping with loneliness, anxiety, and grief. Two years after she fled before Burgoyne's advance into upstate New York, Ann Eliza Bleecker confessed to a friend, "Alas! the wilderness is within: I muse so long on the dead until I am unfit for the company of the living."

Despite these hardships, many women vigorously supported the revolutionary cause in a variety of ways. The Daughters of Liberty joined in harassing opponents to the rebel cause. One outspoken loyalist found himself surrounded by angry women who stripped off his shirt, covered him with molasses, and plastered him with flower petals. In more genteel fashion, groups of well-to-do women collected not only money but medicines, food, and pewter to melt for bullets.

The Struggle in the South

Britain's Southern Strategy

Despite their armed presence in the North, the British had come to believe by the autumn of 1778 that their most vital aim was to regain their colonies in the mainland South. The Chesapeake and the Carolinas were more profitable to the empire and more strategically important, being so much closer to rich British sugar islands in the West Indies. Inspired by this new "southern strategy," Clinton dispatched forces to the Caribbean and Florida. In addition, the British laid plans for a new offensive drive into the Carolinas and Virginia.

English politicians and generals believed that the war could be won in the South. Loyalists were numerous, they believed, especially in the backcountry, where resentment of the Patriot seaboard would encourage frontier folk to take up arms for the king at the first show of British force. And southern rebels—espeially the vulnerable planters along the coast—could not afford to turn their guns away from their slaves. So, at least, the British theorized. All that was needed, they concluded, was that the British army establish a beachhead in the South and then, in league with loyalists, drive northward, up the coast.

The Siege of Charleston

The southern strategy worked well for a short time in a small place. In November 1778 Clinton sent 3,500 troops to Savannah, Georgia. The resistance in the tiny colony quickly collapsed, and a large number of loyalists turned out to help the British. Encouraged, the army moved on to South Carolina.

During the last days of 1779, an expedition under Clinton himself set sail from New York City. Landing off the Georgia coast, his troops mucked through malarial swamps to the peninsula lying between the Ashley and Cooper rivers. At the tip of that neck of land stood Charleston, and the British began to lay siege. By then, an unseasonably warm spring had set in, making the area a heaven for mosquitoes and a hell for human beings. Sweltering and swatting, redcoats weighted down in their woolen uniforms inched their siege works toward the city. By early May Clinton's army had closed in, and British shelling was setting fire to houses within the city. On May 12 Charleston surrendered.

Clinton sailed back to New York at the end of June 1780, leaving behind 8,300 red-coats to carry the British offensive northward to Virginia. The man charged with leading that campaign was his ambitious and able subordinate, Charles, Lord Cornwallis.

The Partisan Struggle in the South

Cornwallis's task in the Carolinas was complicated by the bitter animosity between rebels and loyalists there. Many Carolinians had taken sides years before Clinton's conquest of Charleston. In the summer and fall of 1775 the supporters of Congress and the new South Carolina revolutionary government mobbed, tortured, and imprisoned supporters of the king in the backcountry. These attacks only hardened loyalist resolve: roving bands seized ammunition, broke their leaders out of jail, and besieged rebel outposts. But within a matter of months, a combined force of rebel militias from the coast and the frontier managed to defeat loyalist forces in the backcountry.

With the fall of Charleston in 1780, the loyalist movement on the frontier returned to life. Out of loyalist vengefulness and rebel desperation issued the brutal civil war that seared the southern backcountry after 1780. Neighbors and even families fought and killed each other as members of roaming rebel and tory militias. The intensity of **partisan warfare** in the backcountry produced unprecedented destruction. Loyalist militia plundered plantations and assaulted local women; rebel militias whipped suspected British supporters and burned their farms; both sides committed brutal assassinations and tortured prisoners. All of society, observed one minister, "seems to be at an end. Every person keeps close on his own plantation. Robberies and murders are often committed on the public roads.... Poverty, want, and hardship appear in almost every countenance."

Rebels and Loyalists Battle for the Backcountry

Cornwallis, when confronted with the chaos, erred fatally. He did nothing to stop his loyalist allies or his own troops from mistreating civilians. A Carolina loyalist admitted that "the lower sort of People, who were in many parts originally attached to the British Government, have suffered so severely ... that Great Britain has now a hundred enemies, where it had one before." Although rebels and loyalists alike plundered and terrorized the backcountry, Cornwallis's forces bore more of the blame and suffered the consequences.

A growing number of civilians outraged by the behavior of the king's troops cast their lot with the rebels. That upsurge of popular support enabled Francis Marion, the "Swamp Fox," and his band of white and black raiders to cut British lines of communication between Charleston and the interior. It swelled another rebel militia led by "the Gamecock," Thomas Sumter, who bloodied loyalist forces throughout the central part of South Carolina. It mobilized the "over-the-mountain men," a rebel militia in western Carolina who claimed victory at the Battle of Kings Mountain in October 1780. By the end of 1780, these successes had persuaded most civilians that only the rebels could restore order.

If rebel fortunes prospered in the partisan struggle, they faltered in the conventional warfare being waged at the same time in the South. In August of 1780 the Continentals commanded by Horatio Gates lost a major engagement to the British force at Camden, South Carolina. In the fall of 1780 Congress replaced Gates with Washington's candidate for the southern command, Nathanael Greene, an energetic 38-year-old Rhode Islander and a veteran of the northern campaigns.

British Victory at Camden

Greene Takes Command

Greene bore out Washington's confidence by grasping the military situation in the South. He understood the needs of his 1,400 hungry, ragged, and demoralized troops

General Nathanael Greene

Cowpens

and instructed von Steuben to lobby Virginia for food and clothing. He understood the importance of the rebel militias and sent Lieutenant Colonel Henry "Lighthorse Harry" Lee to assist Marion's raids. He understood the weariness of southern civilians and prevented his men from plundering the countryside.

Above all, Greene understood that his forces could never hold the field against the whole British army, a decision that led him to break the first rule of conventional warfare: he divided his army. In December 1780 he dispatched to western South Carolina a detachment of 600 men under the command of Brigadier General Daniel Morgan of Virginia.

Back at the British camp, Cornwallis worried that Morgan and his rebels, if left unchecked, might rally the entire backcountry against the British. However, Cornwallis reckoned that he could not commit his entire army to the pursuit of Morgan's men, because then Greene and his troops might retake Charleston. The only solution, unconventional to be sure, was that Cornwallis divide *his* army. That he did, sending Lieutenant Colonel Banastre Tarleton and 1,100 men west after Morgan. Cornwallis had played right into Greene's hands: the rebel troops might be able to defeat a British army split into two pieces. For two weeks Morgan led Tarleton's troops on a breakneck chase across the Carolina countryside. In January 1781 at an open meadow called Cowpens, Morgan routed Tarleton's force.

Now Cornwallis took up the chase. Morgan and Greene joined forces and kept going north until the British army wore out. Cornwallis finally stopped at Hillsboro, North Carolina, but few local loyalists responded to his call for reinforcements. Greene decided to make a show of force near the tiny village of Guilford Courthouse. On a brisk March day the two sides joined battle, each sustaining severe casualties before Greene was forced to retreat. But the high cost of victory convinced Cornwallis that he could not put down the rebellion in the Carolinas. "I am quite tired of marching about the country in quest of adventures," he informed Clinton.

Value of the Militia

Although Nathanael Greene's command provided the Continentals with effective leadership in the South, it was the resilience of rebel militia that thwarted the British

The Fighting in the South, 1780–1781 *In December 1780 Nathanael Greene made the crucial decision to split his army, sending Daniel Morgan west, where he defeated the pursuing Banastre Tarleton at Cowpens. Meanwhile Greene regrouped and replenished at Cheraw, keeping Cornwallis off balance with a raid (dotted line) toward Charleston and the coast. Then, with Cornwallis in hot pursuit, Greene and Morgan rejoined at Salisbury, retreating into Virginia. Cornwallis was worn down in this vain pursuit and lost three-quarters of the troops he began with before finally abandoning the Carolina campaign.*

offensive in the Carolinas. Many Continental Army officers complained about the militia's lack of discipline, its habit of melting away when homesickness set in or harvest approached, and its cowardice under fire in conventional engagements. But when set the task of ambushing supply trains, harrying bands of local loyalists, or raiding isolated British outposts, the militia came through. Many southern civilians refused to join the British or to provide the redcoats with food and information because they knew that once the British army left their neighborhoods, the rebel militia would be back. The Continental Army in the South lost many conventional battles, but the militia kept the British from restoring political control over the backcountry.

African Americans in the Age of Revolution

The British also lost in the Carolinas because they did not seek greater support from those southerners who would have fought for liberty *with* the British—African American slaves.

Black Americans, virtually all in bondage, made up one-third of the population between Delaware and Georgia. Since the beginning of the resistance to Britain, white southerners had worried that the watchwords of *liberty* and *equality* would spread to the slave quarters. Gripped by the fear of slave rebellion, southern revolutionaries began to take precautions. Marylanders disarmed black inhabitants and issued extra guns to the white militia. Charlestonians hanged and then burned the body of Thomas Jeremiah, a free black who was convicted of spreading the word to others that the British "were come to help the poor Negroes."

Southern whites fully expected the British to turn slave rebelliousness to their strategic advantage. As early as 1775, Virginia's royal governor, Lord Dunmore, confirmed white fears by offering to free any slave who joined the British. When Clinton invaded

White Fears of Rebellion

In 1845, painter William Ranney recreated a traditional retelling or account of the Battle of Cowpens recorded in John Marshall's biography of George Washington. According to Marshall, "a waiter, too small to wield a sword" saved the life of a relative of George Washington during the battle. Just as Lieutenant Colonel William Washington, leader of the patriot cavalry, was about to be cut down by a sword, the black man "saved him by wounding the officer with a ball from a pistol." Ranney depicts the unnamed man as a bugler astride a horse, as Morgan and Washington battle three British soldiers.

the South in 1779, he renewed that offer. One North Carolina planter heard that loyalists were "promising every Negro that would murder his master and family he should have his Master's plantation" and that "the Negroes have got it amongst them and believe it to be true."

But in Britain there was overwhelming opposition to organizing support among African Americans. British leaders dismissed Dunmore's ambitious scheme to raise a black army of 10,000 and another plan to create a sanctuary for black loyalists on the southeastern coast. Turning slaves against masters, they recognized, was not the way to conciliate southern whites.

Even so, southern fears of insurrection made the rebels reluctant to enlist black Americans as soldiers. At first, Congress barred African Americans from the Continental Army. But as the rebels became more desperate for manpower, policy changed. Northern states actively encouraged black enlistments, and in the Upper South, some states allowed free men of color to join the army or permitted slaves to substitute for their masters.

African American Quests for Liberty

Slaves themselves sought freedom from whichever side seemed most likely to grant it. Perhaps 10,000 slaves took up Dunmore's offer in 1775 and deserted their masters, and thousands more flocked to Clinton's forces after the fall of Charleston. For many runaways the hope of liberation proved an illusion. Although some served the British army as laborers, spies, and soldiers, many died of disease in army camps (upward of 27,000 by one estimate) or were sold back into slavery in the West Indies. About 5,000 black soldiers served in the revolutionary army in the hope of gaining freedom. In addition, the number of runaways to the North soared during the Revolution. In total, perhaps 100,000 men and women—nearly a fifth of the total slave population—attempted to escape bondage. Their odysseys to freedom took some to far-flung destinations: loyalist communities in Nova Scotia, a settlement established by the British in Sierra Leone on the West African coast, even the Botany Bay penal colony in Australia.

The slave revolts so dreaded by southern whites never materialized. Possibly the boldest slaves were drawn off into the armies; possibly greater white precautions discouraged schemes for black rebellions. In South Carolina, where the potential for revolt was greatest, most slaves chose to remain on plantations rather than risk a collective resistance and escape in the midst of the fierce partisan warfare.

The World Turned Upside Down

Despite his losses in the Carolinas, Cornwallis still believed that he could score a decisive victory against the Continental Army. The theater he chose for that showdown was the Chesapeake. During the spring of 1781, he had marched his army to the Virginia coast and joined forces with the hero of Saratoga and newly turned loyalist, Benedict Arnold. Embarrassed by debt and disgusted by Congress's shabby treatment of the Continental Army, Arnold had started exchanging rebel secrets for British money in 1779 before defecting outright in the fall of 1780. By June of 1781 Arnold and Cornwallis were fortifying a site on the tip of the peninsula formed by the York and James rivers, a place called Yorktown.

Meanwhile, Washington and his French ally, the comte de Rochambeau, met in Connecticut to plan a major attack. Rochambeau urged a coordinated land-sea assault on the Virginia coast. Washington insisted instead on a full-scale offensive against New York City. Just when the rebel commander was about to have his way, word arrived that a French fleet under the comte de Grasse was sailing for the Chesapeake to blockade Cornwallis by sea. Washington's Continentals headed south.

Surrender at Yorktown

By the end of September, 7,800 Frenchmen, 5,700 Continentals, and 3,200 militia had sandwiched Yorktown between the devil of an allied army and the deep blue sea of

On September 30, 1780, a wagon bearing this two-faced effigy was drawn through the streets of Philadelphia. The effigy represents Benedict Arnold, who sits between a gallows and the devil. Note the similarities between this piece of street theater and the demonstrations mounted on Pope's Day several decades earlier, shown on page 151.

French warships. "If you cannot relieve me very soon," Cornwallis wrote to Clinton, "you must expect to hear the worst." The British navy did arrive—but seven days after Cornwallis surrendered to the rebels on October 19, 1781. When Germain carried the news from Yorktown to the king's first minister, Lord North replied, "Oh, God, it is over." Then North resigned, Germain resigned, and even George III murmured something about abdicating.

It need not have ended at Yorktown, but timing made all the difference. At the end of 1781 and early in 1782, the British army received setbacks in the other theaters of the war: India, the West Indies, and Florida. The French and the Spanish were everywhere in Europe as well, gathering in the English Channel, planning a major offensive against Gibraltar. The cost of the fighting was already enormous. British leaders recognized that the rest of the empire was at stake and set about cutting their losses in America.

The Treaty of Paris, signed on September 3, 1783, was a diplomatic triumph for the American negotiators: Benjamin Franklin, John Adams, and John Jay. They dangled before Britain the possibility that a generous settlement might weaken American ties to France. The British jumped at the bait. They recognized the independence of the United States and agreed to ample boundaries for the new nation: the Mississippi River on the west, the 31st parallel on the south, and the present border of Canada on the north. American negotiators then persuaded a skeptical France to approve the treaty by arguing that, as allies, they were bound to present a united front to the British. Spain, the third member of the alliance, settled for retaining Florida and Minorca, an island in the Mediterranean.

If the Treaty of Paris marked both the end of a war and the recognition of a new nation, the surrender at Yorktown captured the significance of a revolution. Those present at Yorktown on that clear autumn afternoon in 1781 watched as the British second in command to Cornwallis (who had sent word that he was "indisposed") surrendered his superior's sword. He offered the sword first, in a face-saving gesture, to the French commander, Rochambeau, who politely refused and pointed to Washington. But the American commander in chief, out of a mixture of military protocol, nationalistic pride, and perhaps even wit, pointed to *his* second in command, Benjamin Lincoln.

Some witnesses recalled that British musicians arrayed on the Yorktown green played "The World Turned Upside Down." Their recollections may have been faulty, but the story has persisted as part of the folklore of the American Revolution—and for good reasons.

Treaty of Paris

The Significance of a Revolution

The world turned upside down: the British lay down their arms at Yorktown.

The world had, it seemed, turned upside down with the coming of American independence. The colonial rebels shocked the British with their answer to the question: would they fight?

The answer had been yes—but on their own terms. By 1777 most propertied Americans avoided fighting in the Continental Army. Yet whenever the war reached their homes, farms, and businesses, many Americans gave their allegiance to the new nation by turning out with rifles or supplying homespun clothing, food, or ammunition. They rallied around Washington in New Jersey, Gates in upstate New York, Greene in the Carolinas. Middle-class American men fought, some from idealism, others out of self-interest, but always on their own terms, as members of the militia. These citizen-soldiers turned the world upside down by defeating professional armies.

Of course, the militia did not bear the brunt of the fighting. That responsibility fell to the Continental Army, which by 1777 drew its strength from the poorest ranks of American society. Yet even the Continentals, for all their desperation, managed to fight on their own terms. Some asserted their rights by raising mutinies, until Congress redressed their grievances. All of them; as the Baron von Steuben observed, behaved differently than European soldiers did. Americans followed orders only if the logic of commands was explained to them. The Continentals, held in contempt by most Americans, turned the world upside down by sensing their power and asserting their measure of personal independence.

Americans of African descent dared as much and more in their quests for liberty. Whether they chose to escape slavery by fighting for the British or the Continentals or by striking out on their own as runaways, their defiance, too, turned the world upside down. Among the tens of thousands of slaves who would not be mastered was one Henry Washington, a native of Africa who became the slave of George Washington in 1763. But Henry Washington made his own declaration of independence in 1776, slipping behind British lines and serving as a corporal in a black unit. Thereafter, like thousands of former slaves, he sought to build a new life elsewhere in the Atlantic world, settling first in Nova Scotia and finally in Sierra Leone. By 1800 he headed a community of former slaves who were exiled to the outskirts of that colony for their determined efforts to win republican self-government from Sierra Leone's white British rulers. Like Thomas Paine, Henry Washington believed that freedom was his only country.

In all those ways, a revolutionary generation turned the world upside down. They were a diverse lot—descended from Indians, Europeans, and Africans, driven by desperation or idealism or greed—but joined, even if they did not recognize it, by their common struggle to break free from the rule of monarchs or masters. What now awaited them in the world of the new United States?

Significant Events

1775	Second Continental Congress convenes at Philadelphia; Congress creates the Continental Army; Battle of Bunker Hill
1775–1782	Smallpox pandemic
1776	Publication of *Common Sense;* British troops evacuate Boston; Declaration of Independence; British occupy New York City, forcing Washington to retreat through New Jersey into Pennsylvania; Washington counterattacks at Battle of Trenton
1777	British summer drive to occupy Philadelphia; battle of Brandywine Creek, Germantown; Burgoyne surrenders at Saratoga; Continental Army encamps for winter at Valley Forge
1778	France allies with rebel Americans; France and Britain declare war; British shift focus to the South; Savannah falls
1780	British occupy Charleston; partisan warfare of Marion, Sumter; rebel victory at King's Mountain, South Carolina; Nathanael Greene takes southern command
1781	Engagements at Cowpens, Guilford Courthouse; Cornwallis surrenders at Yorktown
1783	Treaty of Paris

Chapter Summary

The American Revolution brought independence to Britain's former colonies after an armed struggle that began in 1775 and concluded with the Treaty of Paris in 1783.

- When the Second Continental Congress convened in the spring of 1775, many of the delegates still hoped for reconciliation—even as they approved the creation of the Continental Army.

- The Second Continental Congress adopted the Declaration of Independence on July 4, 1776, hoping that they could count on a majority of Americans to support the Revolution.

- The British scored a string of victories in the North throughout 1776 and 1777, capturing both New York and Philadelphia. Their harsh tactics, however, alienated much of the populace.

- The British suffered a disastrous defeat at the Battle of Saratoga in early 1778, which prompted France to openly ally with the American rebels soon thereafter.

- By 1780 Britain aimed to win the war by claiming the South, and captured both Savannah, Georgia, and Charleston, South Carolina.

- Although the war in the West contributed little to the outcome of the Revolution, the competition for Indian allies among the United States, Britain, France, and Spain sparked two decades of dislocation and conflict across the continent, a situation made worse by a smallpox pandemic.

- The Continental Army in the South, led by Nathanael Greene and aided by guerilla fighters in the partisan struggle, foiled the British strategy, and Cornwallis surrendered to Washington after the Battle of Yorktown in 1781.

- Except during the first year of fighting, the rank and file of the Continental Army were drawn from the poorest Americans, whose needs for food, clothing, and shelter were neglected by the Continental Congress.

Additional Reading

The outstanding military histories of the American Revolution are Don Higginbotham, *The War for American Independence* (1971), and Robert Middlekauff, *The Glorious Cause, 1763 to 1789* (1982). Both provide a wealth of detail about battles, contending armies, and the role of militias and civilian populations in the fighting. For a compelling treatment of the lives of soldiers in the Continental Army, read Caroline Cox, *A Proper Sense of Honor* (2004), and to become better acquainted with their commander-in-chief, turn to *His Excellency: George Washington* (2004) by Joseph Ellis. Colin Calloway, *The American Revolution in Indian Country* (1995), offers a fine summary of the role of American Indians in that conflict, and for a broader historical perspective on the strategies of Indian nations during the decades surrounding the Revolution, see Gregory Evans Dowd, *A Spirited Resistance* (1992). Benjamin Franklin's efforts to secure an alliance with France come in for lively chronicling by Stacy Schiff in *A Great Improvisation* (2005), and the best introductions to the influence of the American Revolution within the wider Atlantic world are Lester Langley, *The Americas in the Age of Revolution, 1750–1850* (1996), and a collection of essays edited by Eliga Gould and Peter Onuf and entitled *Empire and Nation* (2004).

Impressive interpretations of the war's impact on American society include Charles Royster, *A Revolutionary People at War* (1979), and John Shy, *A People Numerous and Armed* (1976). Sylvia Frey offers a thoughtful history of African Americans during this era in *Water from the Rock* (1991), and Cassandra Pybus, *Epic Journeys of Freedom* (2006), recounts the experiences of runaway slaves who seized on the wartime crisis to gain liberty. The role of women in revolutionary America receives excellent coverage in Carol Berkin, *Revolutionary Mothers* (2005), and in Mary Beth Norton's classic study, *Liberty's Daughters* (1980).

For a fuller list of readings, see the Bibliography at www.mhhe.com/davidsonnation6.

CHAPTER 8
Crisis & Constitution
1776~1789

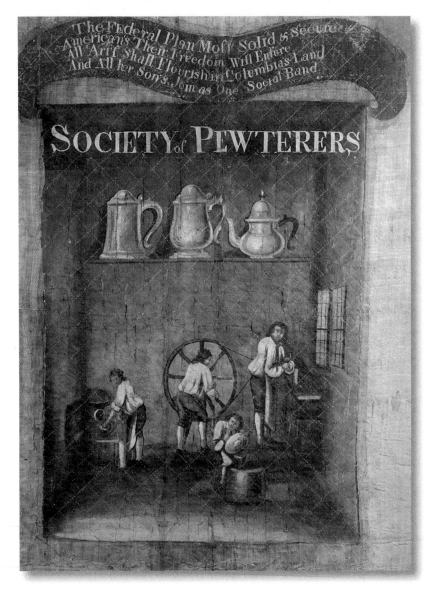

The Revolution instilled in many humble folk a new sense of pride and potential. Typical of such groups were New York's Society of Pewterers. Their banner celebrates "The Federal Plan Most Solid & Secure/Americans Their Freedom Will Ensure/ All Art Shall Flourish in Columbia's Land/And All Her Sons Join as One Social Band."

"These United States"

I am not a Virginian, but an American," Patrick Henry declared in the Virginia House of Burgesses. Most likely he was lying. Certainly no one listening took him seriously, for the newly independent colonists did not identify themselves as members of a nation. They would have said, as did Thomas Jefferson, "Virginia, Sir, is my country." Or as John Adams wrote to another native son, "Massachusetts is our country." Jefferson and Adams were men of wide political vision and experience: both were leaders in the Continental Congress and more inclined than most to think nationally. But like other members of the revolutionary generation, they identified deeply with their home states and even more deeply with their home counties and towns.

It followed that allegiance to the states, not the Union, determined the shape of the first republican political experiments. For a decade after independence, the revolutionaries were less committed to creating an American nation than to organizing 13 separate state republics. The Declaration of Independence referred explicitly not to *the* United States but to *these* United States. It envisioned not one republic so much as a federation of 13.

Only when peace was restored during the decade of the 1780s were Americans forced to face some unanswered questions raised by their revolution. The Declaration proclaimed that these "free and independent states" had "full power to levy war, conclude peace, contract alliances, establish commerce." Did that mean that New Jersey, as a free and independent state, could sign a trade agreement with France, excluding the other states? If the United States were to be more than a loose federation, how could it assert power on a national scale? Similarly, American borderlands to the west presented problems. If these territories were settled by Americans, would they eventually join the United States? Go their own ways as independent nations? Become new colonies of Spain or England?

Such problems were more than political; they were rooted in social realities. For a political union to succeed, the inhabitants of 13 separate states had to start thinking of themselves as Americans. When it came right down to it, what united a Vermont farmer working his rocky fields and a South Carolina gentleman presiding over a vast rice plantation? What bonds existed between a Kentuckian rafting the Ohio River and a Salem merchant sailing to China for porcelain?

The portraits of Captain and Mrs. Samuel Chandler, a New England couple, project the virtuous rectitude of the new republican era. Husband and wife share the same direct, disarming gaze, a mixture of wariness and resolution.

And in a society in which all citizens were said to be "created equal," the inevitable social inequalities had to be confronted. How could women participate in the Revolution's bid for freedom if they were not free to vote or to hold property? How would free or enslaved African Americans live in a republic based on equality? As the British began leaving Yorktown, Charleston, and other ports, they transferred thousands of slaves who had been in their charge to New York City. Southern slaveholders followed, looking to reclaim their bondspeople. "The dreadful rumor" that slave masters were searching for their property "filled us all with inexpressible anguish and horror," reported Boston King, an escaped slave who had fought for the British; ". . . for some days we lost our appetite for food and sleep from our eyes." Repossessing such slaves could be perilous. One master was murdered by "about 12 or 15 of the Ward's blacks" when he came looking. How could black Americans feel a bond with white Americans when so often the only existing bonds had been forged with chains?

How Close a Union?

To such questions there were no final answers in 1781. There was ferment, excitement, and experimentation as 13 states each sought to create their governments anew; as Americans—or rather, Virginians and New Yorkers and Georgians and citizens of other countries—began to imagine how the revolutionary virtue of equality might transform their societies. But as the decade progressed, the sense of crisis deepened.

Republican Experiments

After independence was declared in July 1776, many of America's best political minds turned to drawing up **constitutions** for their individual states. Thomas Jefferson deserted the Continental Congress, leaving the conduct of the war and national affairs to other men, for the more important business of creating Virginia's new government.

In truth, the state constitutions were crucial republican experiments, the first efforts at establishing a government of and by the people. All the revolutionaries agreed that the people—not a king or a few privileged aristocrats—should rule. Yet they were equally certain that republican governments were best suited to small territories. They believed that the new United States was too sprawling and its people too diverse to be safely consolidated into a single national republic. They feared, too, that the government of a large republic would inevitably grow indifferent to popular concerns, being distant from many of its citizens. Without being under the watchful eye of the people, representatives would become less accountable to the electorate and turn tyrannical. A federation of small state republics, they reasoned, would stand a far better chance of enduring.

Belief in the Need for Small Republics

The State Constitutions

The new state constitutions retained the basic form of their old colonial governments, all except Georgia and Pennsylvania providing for a governor and a bicameral legislature. But while most states did not alter the basic structure of their governments, they changed dramatically the balance of power among the different branches of government.

From the republican perspective in 1776, the greatest problem of any government lay in curbing executive power. What had driven Americans into rebellion was the abuse of authority by the king and his appointed officials. To ensure that the executive could never again threaten popular liberty, the new states either accorded almost no power to their governors or abolished that office entirely. The governors had no authority to convene or dissolve the legislatures. They could not veto the legislatures' laws, grant land, or erect courts. Most important from the republican point of view, governors had few powers to appoint other state officials. All these limits were designed to deprive the executive of any patronage or other form of influence over the legislature. By reducing the governors' power, Americans hoped to preserve their states from the corruption that they deplored in British political life.

Curbing Executive Power

What the state governors lost, the legislatures gained. Sam Adams, the Boston rebel leader, expressed the political consensus when he declared that "every legislature of every colony ought to be the sovereign and uncontrollable Power within its own limits of territory." To ensure that those powerful legislatures truly represented the will of the people, the new state constitutions called for annual elections and required candidates for the legislature to live in the districts they represented. Many states even asserted the right of voters to instruct the men elected to office about how to vote on specific issues. Although no state granted universal manhood suffrage, most reduced the amount of property required of qualified voters. Finally, state supreme courts were also either elected by the legislatures or appointed by elected governors.

Strengthening Legislative Powers

By investing all power in popular assemblies, Americans abandoned the British system of mixed government. In one sense, that change was fairly democratic. A majority of voters within a state could do whatever they wanted, unchecked by governors or courts. On the other hand, the arrangement opened the door for legislatures to turn as tyrannical as governors. The revolutionaries brushed that prospect aside: republican theory assured them that the people possessed a generous share of civic virtue, the capacity for selfless pursuit of the general welfare.

In an equally momentous change, the revolutionaries insisted on written state constitutions. Whenever government appeared to exceed the limits of its authority, Americans wanted to have at hand the written contract between rulers and ruled. When eighteenth-century Britons used the word *constitution,* they meant the existing arrangement of government—not an actual document but a collection of parliamentary laws, customs, and precedents. But Americans believed that a constitution should be a written code that stood apart from and above government, a yardstick against

Written Constitutions

Americans responded to independence with rituals of "killing the king," like the one enacted by this New York crowd in 1776 as it pulls down a statue of George III. Americans also expressed their mistrust of monarchs and their ministers by establishing new state governments with weak executive branches.

which the people measured the performance of their rulers. After all, they reasoned, if Britain's constitution had been written down, available for all to consult, would American rights have been violated?

From Congress to Confederation

While Americans lavished attention on their state constitutions, the national government nearly languished during the decade after 1776. With the coming of independence, the Second Continental Congress conducted the common business of the federated states. It created and maintained the Continental Army, issued currency, and negotiated with foreign powers.

But while Congress acted as a central government by common consent, it lacked any legal basis for its authority. To redress that need, in July 1776 Congress appointed a committee to draft a constitution for a national government. The urgent business of waging the war made for delay, but Congress approved the first national constitution in November 1777. It took four more years—until February 1781—for all the states to ratify these Articles of Confederation.

Articles of Confederation

The Articles of Confederation provided for a government by a national legislature—essentially a continuation of the Second Continental Congress. That body had the authority to declare war and make peace, conduct diplomacy, regulate Indian affairs, appoint military and naval officers, and requisition men from the states. In affairs of finance it could coin money and issue paper currency. Extensive as these responsibilities were, Congress could not levy taxes or even regulate trade. The crucial power of the purse rested entirely with the states, as did the final power to make and execute laws. Even worse, the national government had no distinct executive branch. Congressional committees, constantly changing in their membership, not only had to make laws but had to administer and enforce them as well. With no executive to carry out the policies of finance, war, and foreign policy, the federal government's influence was extremely limited.

Those weaknesses appear more evident in hindsight. For Congress in 1777 it was no easy task to frame a new government in the midst of a war. And most American leaders of the 1770s had given little thought to federalism, the means by which political power could be divided among the states and the national government. In any case, to have given significant powers to the national government would have aroused only opposition among the states, each jealous of its independence. Creating a strong national government would also have antagonized many Americans, who after all had just rebelled against the distant, centralized authority of Britain's king and Parliament.

Guided by republican political theory and by their colonial experience, American revolutionaries created a loose confederation of 13 independent state republics under a nearly powerless national government. They succeeded so well that the United States almost failed to survive the first decade of its independence. The problem was that republican theory and lessons from the colonial past were not always useful guides to postwar realities. Only when events forced Americans to think nationally did they begin to consider the possibility of reinventing "these United States"—this time under the yoke of a truly federal republic.

The Temptations of Peace

The surrender of Cornwallis at Yorktown in 1781 marked the end of military crisis in America. But as the threat from Britain receded, so did the source of American unity. The many differences among Americans, most of which lay submerged during the struggle for independence, surfaced in full force. Those domestic divisions, combined with challenges to the new nation from Britain and Spain, created conflicts that neither the states nor the national government proved equal to handling.

The Temptations of the West

The greatest opportunities and the greatest problems for postwar Americans awaited in the rapidly expanding West. With the boundary of the new United States now set at the Mississippi River, more settlers spilled across the Appalachians, planting farmsteads and raw frontier towns throughout Ohio, Kentucky, and Tennessee. By 1790 places that had been almost uninhabited by whites in 1760 held more than 2.25 million people, one-third of the nation's population.

After the Revolution, as before, western settlement fostered intense conflict. American claims that its territory stretched all the way to the Mississippi were by no means taken for granted by European and Indian powers. The West also confronted Americans with questions about their own national identity. Would the newly settled territories enter the nation as states on an equal footing with the original 13 states? Would they be ruled as dependent colonies? Could the federal government reconcile conflicting interests, cultures, and traditions over so great an area? The fate of the West, in other words, constituted a crucial test of whether "these" United States could grow and still remain united.

Foreign Intrigues

Both the British from their base in Canada and the Spanish in Florida and Louisiana hoped to chisel away at American borders. Their considerable success in the 1780s exposed the weakness of Confederation diplomacy.

Before the ink was dry on the Treaty of Paris, Britain's ministers were secretly instructing Canadians to maintain their forts and trading posts inside the United States' northwestern frontier. They reckoned—correctly—that with the Continental Army disbanded, the Confederation could not force the British to withdraw.

The British also made mischief along the Confederation's northern borders, mainly with Vermont. For decades, Ethan Allen and his Green Mountain Boys had waged a war of nerves with neighboring New York, which claimed Vermont as part of its territory. After the Revolution the Vermonters petitioned Congress for statehood, demanding independence from both New York and New Hampshire. When Congress dragged its feet, the British tried to woo Vermont into their empire as a province of Canada. That flirtation with the British pressured Congress into granting Vermont statehood in 1791.

Rivalries flared along the southwestern frontier of the United States as Spain vied to win the allegiance of Indians by supplying them with British trade goods. The Indians welcomed such goods (note the shovel, at left, the plow, center, and European clothing worn by some of the Indians). Here a white man, probably the American Indian agent Benjamin Hawkins, visits an Indian village during the 1790s.

The loyalty of the southwestern frontier was even less certain. By 1790 more than 100,000 settlers had poured through the Cumberland Gap to reach Kentucky and Tennessee. Along with the farmers came speculators, who bought up large tracts of land from the Indians. But the commercial possibilities of the region depended entirely on access to the Mississippi and the port of New Orleans, since it was far too costly to ship southwestern produce over the rough trails east across the Appalachians. And the Mississippi route was still dominated by the Spanish, who controlled Louisiana as well as forts along western Mississippi shores as far north as St. Louis. The Spanish, seeing their opportunity, closed the Mississippi to American navigation in 1784. That action prompted serious talk among southwesterners about seceding from the United States and joining Spain's empire.

Spanish Designs on the Southwest

The Spanish also tried to strengthen their hold on North America by making common cause with the Indians. Of particular concern to both groups was protecting Spanish Florida from the encroachment of American settlers filtering south from Georgia—backwoods folk, Florida's governor complained, who were "nomadic like Arabs and . . . distinguished from savages only in their color, language, and the superiority of their depraved cunning and untrustworthiness." So Spanish colonial officials responded eagerly to the overtures of Alexander McGillivray, a young Indian leader whose mother was of French-Creek descent and whose father was a Scots trader. His efforts brought about a treaty of alliance between the Creeks and the Spanish in 1784, quickly followed by similar alliances with the Choctaws and the Chickasaws. What cemented such treaties were the trade goods that the Spanish agreed to supply the tribes, for, as McGillivray explained, "Indians will attach themselves to and serve them best who supply their necessities." Securing European gunpowder and guns had become essential to southeastern Indians, because their entire economies now revolved around hunting and selling deerskins to white traders. So eager were the Spanish to "serve" the Indians in that matter that they even permitted British merchants, who could command a steady supply of manufactured goods, to monopolize the Indian trade. The largest dealers developed a trading network that reached all the way to the Mississippi by the 1790s. This flood of British merchandise sustained the alliance between the Spanish and the Indians, while British guns enabled the Creeks to defend their hunting territory from American invaders.

Disputes among the States

As if foreign intrigues were not divisive enough, the states continued to argue among themselves over western land claims. The old royal charters for some colonies had extended their boundaries all the way to the Mississippi and beyond. But the charters were

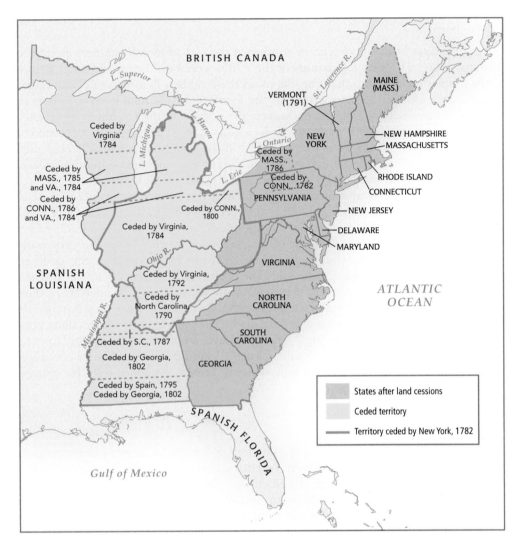

Western Land Claims, 1782–1802 *The Confederation's settlement of conflicting western land claims was an achievement essential to the consolidation of political union. Some states asserted that their original charters extended their western borders to the Mississippi River. A few states, such as Virginia, claimed western borders on the Pacific Ocean.*

often vague, granting both Massachusetts and Virginia, for example, undisputed possession of present-day Wisconsin. In contrast, other charters limited state boundaries to within a few hundred miles of the Atlantic coast. **Landed states** like Virginia wanted to secure control over the large territory granted them by their charters. **Landless states** (which included Maryland, Delaware, Pennsylvania, Rhode Island, and New Jersey) called on Congress to restrict the boundaries of landed states and to convert western lands into a domain administered by the Confederation.

Landed versus Landless States

The landless states argued that the landed states enjoyed an unfair advantage from the money they could raise selling their western claims. That revenue would allow landed states to reduce taxes, and lower taxes would lure settlers from the landless states. Meanwhile, landless states would have to raise taxes to make up for the departed taxpayers, causing even more residents to leave. Speculators were also eager to see Congress control the western lands. Before the Revolution, many prominent citizens of landless Pennsylvania, Maryland, and New Jersey had purchased tracts in the West from Indians. These speculators now also lobbied for congressional ownership of all western lands—except those tracts that they had already purchased from the Indians.

The landless states lost the opening round in the contest over ownership of the West. The Articles of Confederation acknowledged the old charter claims of the landed states. Then Maryland, one of the smallest landless states, retaliated by refusing to ratify the Articles. Since every state had to approve the Articles before they were formally accepted, the fate of the United States hung in the balance. One by one the landed states relented, Virginia being the last. Only then did Maryland ratify the Articles, in February 1781.

The More Democratic West

An even greater bone of contention concerned the sort of men westerners elected to political office. The state legislatures of the 1780s were both larger and more democratic in their membership than the old colonial assemblies. Before the Revolution no more than a fifth of the men serving in the assemblies were middle-class farmers or artisans. Government was almost exclusively the domain of the wealthiest merchants, lawyers, and planters. After the Revolution twice as many state legislators were men of moderate wealth. The shift was more marked in the North, where middle-class men predominated among representatives. But in every state, some men of modest means, humble background, and little formal education attained political power.

Changing Composition of State Legislatures

State legislatures became more democratic in their membership mainly because as backcountry districts grew, so too did the number of their representatives. Since western districts tended to be less developed economically and culturally, their leading men were less rich and cultivated than the eastern seaboard elite. But many of these eastern republican gentlemen, while endorsing government by popular consent, doubted whether ordinary people were fit to rule. The problem, they contended, was that the new western legislators concerned themselves only with the narrow interests of their constituents, not with the good of the whole state. As Ezra Stiles, the president of Yale College, observed, the new breed of politicians were those with "the all-prevailing popular talent of coaxing and flattering," who "whenever a bill is read in the legislature . . . instantly thinks how it will affect his constituents." And if state legislatures could not rise above narrow self-interest, how long would it be before a concern for the general welfare simply withered away?

The Northwest Territory

Such fears of "democratic excess" also influenced policy when Congress finally came to decide what to do with the **Northwest Territory.** Carved out of the land ceded by the states to the national government, the Northwest Territory comprised the present-day states of Ohio, Indiana, Illinois, Michigan, and Wisconsin. With so many white settlers moving into these lands, Congress was faced with a crucial test of its federal system. If an orderly way could not be devised to expand the confederation of states beyond the original 13 colonies, the new territories might well become independent countries or

This sketch of a new cleared farm idealizes many aspects of life on the late-eighteenth-century frontier. Although western farmers first sought to "improve" their acreage by felling trees, as the stumps dotting the landscape indicate, their dwellings were far less substantial than those depicted in the background above. And while Indians sometimes guided parties of white surveyors and settlers into the West, as shown in the foreground, Indians more often resisted white encroachment. For that reason, dogs, here perched placidly in canoes, were trained to alert their white masters to the approach of Indians.

The Ordinance of 1785
Surveyors entered the Northwest Territory in September of 1785, imposing on the land regular grids of six square miles to define new townships, as shown on this range map of a portion of Ohio. Farmers purchased blocks of land within townships, each one mile square, from the federal government or from land speculators. This pattern was followed in mapping and settling public lands all the way to the Pacific coast.

even colonies of Spain or Britain. Congress dealt with the issue of expansion by adopting three ordinances.

The first, drafted by Thomas Jefferson in 1784, divided the Northwest Territory into 10 states, each to be admitted to the Union on equal terms as soon as its population equaled that in any of the existing states. In the meantime, Jefferson provided for democratic self-government of the territory by all free adult males. A second ordinance of 1785 set up an efficient mechanism for dividing and selling public lands. The Northwest Territory was surveyed into townships six miles square. Each township was then divided into 36 lots of one square mile, or 640 acres.

Congress waited in vain for buyers to flock to the land offices it established. The cost of even a single lot—$640—was too steep for most farmers. Disappointed by the shortage of buyers and desperate for money, Congress finally accepted a proposition submitted by a private company of land speculators who offered to buy some 6 million acres in present-day southeastern Ohio. That several members of Congress numbered among the company's stockholders no doubt added to enthusiasm for the deal.

The transaction concluded, Congress calmed the speculators' worries that incoming settlers might enjoy too much self-government by scrapping Jefferson's democratic design and substituting the Northwest Ordinance of 1787. That ordinance provided for a period in which Congress held sway in the territory through its appointees—a governor, a secretary, and three judges. When the population reached 5,000 free adult males, a legislature was to be established, although its laws required the governor's approval. A representative could sit in Congress but had no vote. When the population reached 60,000, the inhabitants might apply for statehood, and the whole Northwest

Jefferson's Plan for the Northwest

Northwest Ordinance

Territory was to be divided into not less than three or more than five states. The ordinance also guaranteed basic rights—freedom of religion and trial by jury—and provided for the support of public education. Equally significant, it also outlawed slavery throughout the territory.

With the Northwest Ordinance in place, Congress had succeeded in extending republican government to the West and incorporating the frontier into the new nation. The Republic now had an orderly way to expand its federation of states in a way that minimized the tensions between the genteel East and the democratic West that had plagued the colonies and the Confederation throughout much of the eighteenth century. Yet ironically, the new ordinance served to heighten tensions in a different way. By limiting the spread of slavery in the northern states, Congress deepened the critical social and economic differences between the North and South, evident already in the 1780s.

The Territorial System and Native Americans

The consequences of the new territorial system were also significant for hundreds of thousands of the continent's other inhabitants. In the short term, the ordinance ignored completely the rights of the Shawnee, Chippewa, and other Indian peoples who lived in the region. In the long term, the system "laid the blueprint," as one historian noted, for bringing new lands into the United States. The ordinance thus accelerated the pressures on Indian lands and aggravated the social and geographic dislocations already set in motion by disease and the western conflicts of the Revolutionary War.

Slavery and Sectionalism

When white Americans declared their independence, they owned nearly half a million black Americans. African Americans of the revolutionary generation, most of them enslaved, constituted 20 percent of the total population of the colonies in 1775, and nearly 90 percent of them lived in the South. Yet few political leaders directly confronted the issue of whether slavery should be permitted to exist in a truly republican society.

Republicanism and Slavery

When political discussion did stray toward the subject of slavery, southerners—especially ardent republicans—bristled defensively. Theirs was a difficult position, riddled with contradictions. On the one hand, they had condemned parliamentary taxation as tantamount to political "slavery" and had rebelled, declaring that all men were "created equal." On the other hand, enslaved African Americans formed the basis of the South's plantation economy. To surrender slavery, southerners believed, would be to usher in economic ruin.

Some planters in the Upper South resolved the dilemma by freeing their slaves. Such decisions were made easier by changing economic conditions in the Chesapeake. As planters shifted from tobacco toward wheat, a crop demanding a good deal less labor, Virginia and Maryland liberalized their manumission statutes, laws providing for freeing slaves. Between 1776 and 1789, most southern states also joined the North in prohibiting the importation of slaves, and a few antislavery societies appeared in the Upper South. But no southern state legally abolished slavery. Masters defended their right to hold human property in the name of republicanism.

Republicanism and Property

Eighteenth-century republicans regarded property as crucial, for it provided a man and his family with security, status, and wealth. More important, it provided a measure of independence: to be able to act freely, without fear or favor of others. People without property were dangerous, republicans believed, because the poor could never be politically independent. Southern defenders of slavery thus argued that free, propertyless black people would pose a political threat to the liberty of propertied white citizens. Subordinating the human rights of blacks to the property rights of whites, southern republicans reached the paradoxical conclusion that their freedom depended on keeping African Americans in bondage.

The North followed a different course. Because its economy depended far less on slave labor, black emancipation did not run counter to powerful economic interests. Antislavery societies, the first founded by the Quakers in 1775, spread throughout the northern states during the next quarter century. Over the same period the legislatures of most northern states provided for the immediate or gradual abolition of slavery. Freedom for most northern African Americans came slowly, but by 1830 there were fewer than 3,000 slaves out of a total northern black population of 125,000.

The Revolution, which had been fought for liberty and equality, did little to change the status of most black Americans. By 1800 more enslaved African Americans lived in the United States than had lived there in 1776. Slavery continued to grow in the Lower South as the rice culture of the Carolinas and Georgia expanded and as the new cotton culture spread westward.

Still, a larger number of slaves than ever before became free during the war and in the following decades, whether through military service, successful escape, manumission, or gradual emancipation. All these developments fostered the growth of free black communities, especially in the Upper South and in northern cities. By 1810 free African Americans made up 10 percent of the total population of Maryland and Virginia.

The composition of the postwar free community changed as well. Before independence most free blacks had been either mulattoes—the offspring of interracial unions—or former slaves too sick or aged to have value as laborers. In contrast, a larger proportion of the free population of the 1780s were darker skinned, younger, and healthier. This group injected new vitality into black communal life, organizing independent schools, churches, and mutual benefit societies for the growing number of "free people of color." Richard Allen and Absalom Jones led the way in these efforts after being ejected from their pews in the midst of prayers one Sunday at St. George **Methodist** Episcopal Church in Philadelphia. Both men ended up founding independent black churches.

After the Revolution slavery ceased to be a national institution. It became the **peculiar institution** of a single region, the American South. The isolation of slavery in one section set North and South on radically different courses of social development, sharpening economic and political divisions.

Growth of the Free Black Community

Negro Methodists Holding a Meeting in a Philadelphia Alley *evokes the vibrancy of African American religious life in the city that became a haven for free blacks.*

Wartime Economic Disruption

With the outbreak of the Revolution, Americans had suffered an immediate economic loss. Formerly, Britain had supplied manufactured goods, markets for American exports, and credit that enabled commerce to flourish. No longer. Hardest hit were southern planters, who had to seek new customers for their tobacco, cotton, and rice as well as find new sources of capital to finance production. Northerners too faced difficulties, for their major seaports were occupied for a time by British troops, whose presence disrupted commercial activity.

Matters did not improve with the coming of peace. France and Britain flooded the new states with their manufactures, and postwar Americans, eager for luxuries, indulged in a most unrepublican spending spree. The flurry of buying left some American merchants and consumers as deeply in debt as their governments. When loans from private citizens and foreign creditors like France proved insufficient to finance the fighting, both Congress and the states printed paper money—a whopping total of $400 million. The paper currency was backed only by the government's promise to redeem the bills with money from future taxes, because legislatures balked at the unpopular alternative of levying taxes during the war. For the bills to be redeemed, the United States had to survive, so by the end of 1776, when Continental forces sustained a series of defeats, paper money started to depreciate dramatically. By 1781 it was virtually without value, and Americans coined the expression "not worth a Continental."

The printing of paper money, combined with a wartime shortage of goods, triggered an inflationary spiral. As goods became scarcer and scarcer, they cost more and more worthless dollars. In this spiral, creditors were gouged by debtors, who paid them back with depreciated currency. At the same time soaring prices for food and manufactured goods eroded the buying power of wage earners and small farmers. And the end of the war brought on demands for prompt repayment from the new nation's foreign creditors as well as from soldiers seeking back pay and pensions.

Congress could do nothing. With no power to regulate trade, it could neither dam the stream of imported goods rushing into the states nor stanch the flow of gold and silver to Europe to pay for these items. With no power to prohibit the states from issuing paper money, it could not halt depreciation. With no power to regulate wages or prices, it could not curb inflation. With no power to tax, it could not reduce the public debt. Efforts to grant Congress greater powers met with determined resistance from the states. They refused Congress any revenue of its own, fearing the first steps toward "arbitrary" government.

Within states, too, economic problems aroused discord. Some major merchants and large commercial farmers had profited handsomely during the war by selling supplies to the American, British, and French armies at high prices. Eager to protect their windfall, they lobbied state legislatures for an end to inflationary monetary policies. They pushed for the passage of high taxes to pay wartime debts, a paper currency that was backed by gold and silver, and an active policy to encourage foreign trade.

Less affluent men fought back, pressing legislatures for programs that met their needs. Western farmers, often in debt, urged the states to print more paper money and to pass laws lowering taxes and postponing the foreclosure of mortgages. Artisans opposed merchants by calling for protection from low-priced foreign imports that competed with the goods they produced. They set themselves against farmers as well by demanding price regulation of the farm products they consumed. In the continuing struggle, the state legislatures became the battleground of competing economic factions, each bent on gaining its own particular advantage.

As the 1780s wore on, conflicts mounted. As long as the individual states remained sovereign, the Confederation was crippled—unable to conduct foreign affairs effectively, unable to set coherent economic policy, unable to deal with discontent in the West. Equally dismaying was the discovery that many Americans, instead of being selflessly concerned for the public good, selfishly pursued their private interests.

Public and Private Debt

Postwar Inflation

Political Divisions over Economic Policy

Republican Society

The war for independence transformed not only America's government and economy but also its society and culture. Inspired by the Declaration's ideal of equality, some Americans rejected the subordinate position assigned to them under the old colonial order. Westerners, newly wealthy entrepreneurs, urban artisans, and women all claimed greater freedom, power, and recognition. The authority of the traditional leaders of government, society, and the family came under a new scrutiny; the impulse to defer to social superiors became less automatic. The new assertiveness demonstrated how deeply egalitarian assumptions were taking root in American culture.

The New Men of the Revolution

The Revolution gave rise to a new sense of social identity and a new set of ambitions among several groups of men who had once accepted a humbler status. The more democratic society of the frontier emboldened westerners to believe themselves the equals of easterners. As one Kentuckian explained to James Madison, the western migrants "must make a very different mass from one which is composed of men born and raised on the same spot. . . . They see none about them to whom or to whose families they have been accustomed to think themselves inferior."

Gilbert Stuart's The Skater *captures one American gentleman's characteristic sense of mastery over himself, nature, and society. But the Revolution gave other republican men a sense of power too, including western backcountry farmers, aspiring entrepreneurs, and urban artisans like the pewterers pictured on page 188.*

Urban Artisans

The war also offered opportunities to aspiring entrepreneurs everywhere, and often they were not the same men who had prospered before the war. At a stroke, independence swept away the political prominence of loyalists, whose ranks included an especially high number of government officials, large landowners, and major merchants. And while loyalists found their properties confiscated by revolutionary governments, other Americans grew rich. Many northern merchants gained newfound wealth from privateering or military contracts. Commercial farmers in the mid-Atlantic states prospered from the high food prices caused by wartime scarcity and army demand.

The Revolution effected no dramatic redistribution of wealth. Indeed, the gap between rich and poor increased during the 1780s. But those families newly enriched by the Revolution came to demand and receive greater social recognition and political influence. The republican ideal of "an aristocracy of merit" justified their ambitions.

City craftworkers pushed for recognition too. Their experience in organizing boycotts against British goods during the imperial crisis gave artisans a greater taste of politics. With the Revolution accomplished, they clamored for men of their own kind to represent them in government. Their assertiveness came as a rude shock to gentlemen like South Carolina's William Henry Drayton, who balked at sharing power with men "who never were in a way to study" anything except "how to cut up a beast in the market to the best advantage, to cobble an old shoe in the neatest manner, or to build a necessary house."

While master craftworkers competed for political office, the laborers who worked for them also exhibited a new sense of independence. As domestic manufacturing expanded after the Revolution, journeymen and even apprentices moved out of their masters' households and away from their masters' supervision. Recognizing that their interests were often distinct from those of masters, journeymen formed new organizations to secure higher wages. Between 1786 and 1816 skilled urban laborers organized the first major strikes in American history.

The New Women of the Revolution

Not long after the fighting with Britain had broken out, Margaret Livingston of New York wrote to her sister Catherine, "You know that our Sex are doomed to be obedient in every stage of life so that we shant be great gainers by this contest." By war's end, however, Eliza Wilkinson from rural South Carolina was complaining boldly to a woman friend: "The men say we have no business with political matters . . . it's not our sphere. . . . [But] I won't have it thought that because we are the weaker Sex (as to bodily strength my dear) we are Capable of nothing more, than minding the Dairy . . . surely we may have enough sense to give our Opinions."

What separated Margaret Livingston's resignation from Eliza Wilkinson's assertion of personal worth and independence was the Revolution. Eliza Wilkinson had managed her parents' plantation during the war and defended it from British marauders. Other women discovered similar reserves of skill and resourcefulness. When soldiers returned home, some were surprised to find their wives and daughters, who had been running family farms and businesses, less submissive and more self-confident.

Exclusion of Women
from Politics

But American men had not fought a revolution for the equality of American women. In fact, male revolutionaries gave no thought whatsoever to the role of women in the new nation, assuming that those of the "weaker sex" were incapable of making informed and independent political decisions. Most women of the revolutionary generation agreed that the proper female domain was the home, not the public arena of politics. Still, the currents of the Revolution occasionally left gaps that allowed women to display their keen political interests. When a loosely worded provision in the New Jersey state constitution gave the vote to "all free inhabitants" owning a specified amount of property, white widows and single women went to the polls. Only in 1807 did the state legislature close the loophole.

Mary Wollstonecraft's *Vindication*

In the wake of the Revolution there also appeared in England a book that would become a classic text of modern feminism, Mary Wollstonecraft's *A Vindication of the Rights of Women* (1792). Attracting a wide, if not widely approving, readership in America as well, it called not only for laws to guarantee women civil and political equality but also for educational reforms to ensure their social and economic equality.

Education as a
Route to Equality

Like many young, single English women with more wit than fortune, Wollstonecraft started her working life as a governess and a school's headmistress. Then she turned to writing for her livelihood, producing book reviews, translations, a novel, and a treatise on women's education before dashing off *Vindication* in six short months. She charged that men deliberately conspired to keep women in "a state of perpetual childhood" by giving them inferior, frivolous educations. That encouraged young girls to fixate on fashion and flirtation and made them "only anxious to inspire love, when they ought to cherish a nobler ambition, and by their abilities and virtues exact respect." Girls, she proposed, should receive the same education as boys, including training that would prepare them for careers in medicine, politics, and business. No woman should have to pin her hopes for financial security on making a good marriage, Wollstonecraft argued. On the contrary, well-educated and resourceful women capable of supporting themselves would make the best wives and mothers, assets to the family and the nation.

Vindication might have been written in gunpowder rather than ink, given the reaction it aroused on both sides of the Atlantic. At first, Wollstonecraft won more than a few defenders among both men and women. This favorable reception ended abruptly after her death in childbirth in 1797, when a memoir written by her husband revealed that she had lived out of wedlock with him—and before him, with another lover. Even so, some of her readers continued to admire her views. The Philadelphia Quaker Elizabeth Drinker confided to her diary that "In very many of her sentiments, [Wollstonecraft] . . . *speaks my mind.*"

Republican Motherhood and Education

Wollstonecraft's ideas also lent support to the leading educational reformers in the revolutionary generation. Her sentiments echo in the writings of Judith Sargent Murray,

Skirting the Issue

Anxieties about Gender in the New Republic

CORNWALLIS turned NURSE, and his MISTRESS a SOLDIER.

A Prifoner from Virginia's coaft,
  Cornwallis has return'd, fir ;
Toolong, toolong he rul'd the roaft
  And for our ruin burn'd, fir.
Before he was, in wretched plight,
  By armed men furrounded,
He fhow'd himfelf a man of might
  And every thing confounded.
But when they thunder'd at his door
  He prov'd by this difafter,
His race was run, his battles done
  And Wafhington his mafter.
His miftrefs in a paffion cry'd,
  She could have acted bolder ;
So put his fword upon her fide,
  His mufquet on her fhoulder.

Like Hercules, renown'd of old,
  The diftaff is his calling ;
And while he hears his miftrefs
  fcold,   [ing.
  He keeps her brat from bawl-
Behold him here and fhed a tear,
  Sir Henry and Knyphaufen ;
And Arnold too may quake with
  fear,
  Whom Satan has his claws on.
Each valiant chief fhall fee with
  grief,
  Their horrid revolution ;
Cornwallis forc'd to fpin for
  bread,
  Burgoyne to thump a cufhion.

Only months after Cornwallis surrendered at Yorktown, this cartoon appeared to razz him. Military defeat has unmanned the British, the poet gloats, and produced a "horrid revolution" in gender roles. While Cornwallis has "turned nurse," other British generals take up women's work—housekeeping ("thumping a cushion"), caring for children, and spinning. Meanwhile, British women like Cornwallis's mistress shoulder muskets and clamor to become soldiers.

The cartoon lampoons the British, but we might as easily note that it reveals American anxieties about the war's effect on gender roles. A few American women—mainly poor free whites and servants and runaway slaves—disguised themselves as men and enlisted in the Continental Army. Other "camp followers" (cooks, washerwomen, and nurses) occasionally manned artillery or stood watch for their husbands or other loved ones. Even more women managed family farms and businesses, while their husbands were off fighting, and might be called on to brandish muskets, axes, and pitchforks to defend their communities against marauding loyalists. Abigail Adams made no idle boast when she wrote to her absent spouse that "If our men are all drawn of[f] and we should be attacked, you would find a Race of Amazons in America." Was that a promise or a threat? In a war that produced new freedoms and opportunities for women, did even the victorious male rebels fear meeting the fate of Cornwallis in the cartoon?

a New Englander who urged the cultivation of women's minds to encourage self-respect and celebrated "excellency in our sex." Her fellow reformer, the Philadelphian Benjamin Rush, agreed that only educated and independent-minded women could raise the informed and self-reliant citizens that a republican government required. Their view, known as **"republican motherhood,"** contributed to the most dramatic change in the lives of women after the war—the spread of female literacy.

Between 1780 and 1830 the number of American colleges and secondary academies rose dramatically, and some of these new institutions were devoted to educating women. Not only did the number of schools for women increase, but these schools also offered a solid academic curriculum. By 1850—for the first time in American history—there were as many literate women as there were men. To counter popular prejudices,

Improved Schooling and Literacy Rates of Women

Contrast the portrait of Mary Wollstonecraft rendered just before her death in 1797 with a strikingly masculinized rendering in a book published in the United States in 1809, which placed her in the company of "actresses, adventurers, authoresses, fortunetellers, gipsies, dwarfs, swindlers, and vagrants."

the defenders of female education contended that schooling for women would produce the ideal republican mother.

Women's Legal Status
The Revolution also prompted some states to reform their marriage laws, making divorce somewhat easier, although it remained extremely rare. But while women won greater freedom to divorce, courts became less concerned with enforcing a widow's traditional legal claim to one-third of her spouse's real estate. And married women still could not sue or be sued, make wills or contracts, or buy and sell property. Any wages that they earned went to their husbands; so did all personal property that wives brought into a marriage; so did the rents and profits of any real estate they owned. Despite the high ideals of republican motherhood, most women remained confined to the domestic sphere of the home and deprived of the most basic legal and political rights.

The Attack on Aristocracy

Why wasn't the American Revolution more revolutionary? Independence secured the full political equality of white men who owned property, but women were still deprived of political rights, African Americans of human rights. Why did the revolutionaries stop short of extending equality to the most unequal groups in American society—and with so little sense that they were being inconsistent?

Republican View of Equality
In part, the lack of concern was rooted in republican ideas themselves. Republican ideology viewed property as the key to independence and power. Lacking property, women and black Americans were easily consigned to the custody of husbands and masters. Then, too, prejudice played its part: the perception of women and blacks as naturally inferior beings.

But revolutionary leaders also failed to press for greater equality because they conceived their crusade in terms of eliminating the evils of a European past dominated by kings and aristocrats. They believed that the great obstacle to equality was monarchy—kings and queens who bestowed hereditary honors and political office on favored individuals and granted legal privileges and monopolies to favored churches and businesses.

These artificial inequalities posed the real threat to liberty, most republicans concluded. In other words, the men of the Revolution were intent on attaining equality by leveling off the top of society. It did not occur to most republicans that the cause of equality could also be served by raising up the bottom—by attacking the laws and prejudices that kept African Americans enslaved and women dependent.

The most significant reform of the republican campaign against artificial privilege was the dismantling of state-supported churches. Most states had a religious establishment. In New York and the South, it was the Anglican church; in New England, the Congregational church. Since the 1740s, dissenters who did not worship at state churches had protested laws that taxed all citizens to support the clergy of established denominations. After the Revolution dissenters argued that equality required ending such privileges. As more dissenters became voters, state legislators gradually abolished state support for Anglican and Congregational churches.

Disestablishment of State-Supported Churches

In the same anti-aristocratic spirit reformers attacked the Society of Cincinnati, a group organized by former officers of the Continental Army in 1783. The society, which was merely a social club for veterans, was forced to disband for its policy of passing on its membership rights to eldest sons. In this way, critics charged, the Cincinnati was creating artificial distinctions and perpetuating a hereditary warrior nobility.

Society of Cincinnati

Today, many of the republican efforts at reform seem misdirected. While only a handful of revolutionaries worked for the education of women and the emancipation of slaves, enormous zeal went into fighting threats from a monarchical past that had never existed in America. Yet the threat from kings and aristocrats was real to the revolutionaries—and indeed remained real in many parts of Europe. Their determination to sweep away every shred of formal privilege ensured that these forms of inequality never took root in America. And if eighteenth-century Americans did not extend equality to women and racial minorities, it was a failure that they shared with later revolutionary movements that promised more.

From Confederation to Constitutions

While Americans in many walks of life sought to realize the republican commitment to equality, Congress wrestled with the problem of preserving the nation itself. With the new republic slowly rending itself to pieces, some political leaders concluded that neither the Confederation nor the state legislatures were able to remedy the basic difficulties facing the nation. But how could the states be convinced to surrender their sovereign powers? The answer came in the wake of two events—one foreign, one domestic—that lent momentum to the cause of strengthening the central government.

The Jay-Gardoqui Treaty

The international episode was a debate over a proposed treaty with Spain. In 1785 southwesterners still could not legally navigate the Mississippi and still were threatening to secede from the union and annex their territory to Spain's American empire. To shore up southwestern loyalties, Congress instructed its secretary of foreign affairs, John Jay, to negotiate an agreement with Spain preserving American rights to navigate on the Mississippi River. But the Spanish emissary, Don Diego de Gardoqui, sweet-talked Jay into accepting a treaty by which the United States would give up all rights to the Mississippi for 25 years. In return, Spain agreed to grant trading privileges to American merchants.

Jay, a New Yorker, knew more than a few northern merchants who were eager to open new markets. But when the proposed treaty became public knowledge, southwesterners denounced it as nothing short of betrayal. The treaty was never ratified, but the hostility stirred up during the debate revealed the strength of sectional feelings.

If God had intended man to drink water, Ben Franklin remarked, he would not have made him with an elbow capable of raising a wineglass. Colonials from all across America agreed with Franklin on the virtues of drink. The ruddy glow of colonial cheeks (still visible in the portraits hung in museums) reflected not only good health but also substantial daily doses of alcohol. Colonials consumed about twice as much alcohol as Americans today, though in different forms. Beer was not popular, the only sort consumed being a weak, homemade "small beer" containing about 1 percent alcohol. Only the wealthy, like Franklin, could afford imported Madeira and port wines. However, the produce of apple orchards allowed Americans northward from Virginia to drink their fill of hard cider. Far and away the most popular distilled liquor was rum, a potent 90 proof beverage (45 percent alcohol) that they sipped straight or mixed with water and sugar to make "toddies."

The liquor flowed freely at special occasions: ministerial ordinations in New England towns, court days in the South, house-raisings, corn-huskings, and quilting bees on the frontier, and weddings, elections, and militia musters everywhere in the colonies. But Americans did not confine their drinking to occasional celebrations. Some, like John Adams, started the day with a tankard of hard cider. Laborers in seaport docks and shipyards, fishermen and sailors at sea, and farm workers in the countryside commonly received a daily allotment of liquor as part of their wages.

New England sea captains in Surinam drink rum the two-handed way—out of a silver bowl.

Only a decade later, when the Senate ratified a treaty negotiated with Spain by Thomas Pinckney in 1796, did Americans gain full access to the Mississippi.

Shays's Rebellion

On the heels of this humiliation by Spain came an internal conflict that challenged the notion that individual states could maintain order in their own territories. The trouble erupted in western Massachusetts, where many small farmers were close to ruin. By 1786 farm wages and prices had fallen sharply and farmers were selling little produce. Yet they still had to pay mortgages on their farms and other debts. In 1786 the lower house of the Massachusetts legislature obliged the farmers with a package of relief measures. But creditors in eastern Massachusetts, determined to safeguard their own investments, persuaded the upper house to defeat the measures.

In the summer of 1786 western farmers responded, demanding that the upper house of the legislature be abolished and that the relief measures go into effect. That autumn 2,000 farmers rose in armed rebellion, led by Captain Daniel Shays, a veteran of the Revolution. They closed the county courts to halt creditors from foreclosing on their farms and marched on the federal arsenal at Springfield. The state militia quelled the uprising by February 1787, but the insurrection left many in Massachusetts and the rest of the country thoroughly shaken.

Response to Agrarian Unrest

Alarmed conservatives saw Shays's Rebellion as the consequence of radical democracy. "The natural effects of pure democracy are already produced among us," lamented one republican gentleman; "it is a war against virtue, talents, and property carried on by the dregs and scum of mankind." He was wrong. The rebels with Daniel Shays were no impoverished rabble. They were reputable members of western communities who wanted their property protected and believed that government existed to provide that protection. The Massachusetts state legislature had been unable to safeguard the property of

Women drank too, although they sometimes explained their use of distilled liquor as serving some "medicinal" purpose. Slaves got around laws restricting their consumption of alcohol by stealing from masters or bartering with white peddlers.

Until the middle of the eighteenth century, most colonials (and Europeans) considered spirits an essential supplement to their diet. They did not condone public drunkenness, but they saw nothing amiss in the regular use of alcohol or even in occasional intoxication.

This easy acceptance of drinking prevailed for two reasons. First, until about the 1760s, frequent access to the strongest spirits, rum, lay beyond the means of most Americans. Second, the leaders of local communities were able to oversee most public drinking and to keep disorder to a minimum. But by the middle of the eighteenth century, some Americans developed misgivings about the drinking culture. Increased production and importation made rum so cheap that an ordinary laborer could earn enough in a day to stay "drunk as a lord" for the rest of the week. Taverns spread, making it impossible for community leaders to monitor the popular consumption of alcohol.

The new concern that the drinking of rum fostered crime and social disruption prompted the first steps toward temperance reform. By the 1770s, Quakers such as Anthony Benezet were urging that alcohol, like slavery, was an "unrepublican vice," for both forms of bondage deprived their victims of liberty and the capacity for rationality and self-control. Some members of the medical profession, most notably Benjamin Rush, also joined early temperance ranks.

Although the advocates of more moderate consumption won some support, most Americans altered their drinking habits by consuming *more* hard liquor as rum, lost much of its ground to a new rival, whiskey. Whiskey was democratic and cheap, for it could be made in the lowliest backcountry farmhouse. It was patriotic, since it did not depend on imports from the Caribbean. Gradually these "spirits of independence" supplanted rum not only in the frontier West but also in the urban East. Consumption of alcohol was on a steady rise that would finally result, half a century after the Revolution, in louder calls for temperance reform.

farmers from the inroads of recession or to protect the property of creditors from the armed debtors who closed the courts. It had failed, in other words, to fulfill the most basic aim of republican government.

What if such violent tactics spread? Other states with discontented debtors feared what the example of western Massachusetts might mean for the future of the Confederation itself. But by 1786 Shays's Rebellion supplied only the sharpest jolt to a movement for reform that was already under way. Even before the rebellion, a group of Virginians had proposed a meeting of the states to adopt a uniform system of commercial regulations. Once assembled at Annapolis in September 1786, the delegates from five states agreed to a more ambitious undertaking. They called for a second, broader meeting in Philadelphia, which Congress approved, for the "express purpose of revising the Articles of Confederation."

Framing a Federal Constitution

It was the wettest spring anyone could remember. The 55 men who traveled over muddy roads to Philadelphia in May 1787 arrived drenched and bespattered. Fortunately, most of the travelers were men in their 30s and 40s, young enough to survive a good soaking. Since most were gentlemen of some means—planters, merchants, and lawyers with powdered wigs and prosperous paunches—they could recover from the rigors of their journey in the best accommodations offered by America's largest city.

The delegates came from all the states except Rhode Island. The rest of New England supplied shrewd backroom politicians—Roger Sherman and Oliver Ellsworth from Connecticut and Rufus King and Elbridge Gerry, Massachusetts men who had learned a trick or two from Sam Adams. The middle states marshaled much of the intellectual might: two Philadelphia lawyers, John Dickinson and James Wilson; one Philadelphia financier, Robert Morris; and the aristocratic Gouverneur Morris. From

Social Profile
of the Delegates

James Madison, the scholar and statesman whose ideas and political skill shaped the Constitution.

New York there was Alexander Hamilton, the mercurial and ambitious young protégé of Washington. South Carolina provided fiery orators Charles Pinckney and John Rutledge.

It was "an assembly of the demi-gods," gushed Thomas Jefferson, who, along with John Adams, was serving as a diplomat in Europe when the convention met. In fact, the only delegate who looked even remotely divine was the convention's presiding deity. Towering a full half foot taller than most of his colleagues, George Washington displayed his usual self-possession from a chair elevated on the speaker's platform in the Pennsylvania State House, where the delegates met. At first glance, the delegate of least commanding presence was Washington's fellow Virginian, James Madison. Short and slightly built, the 36-year-old Madison had no profession except hypochondria; he read a great deal and dressed in black. But he was an astute politician and a brilliant political thinker who, more than anyone else, shaped the framing of the federal Constitution.

The delegates from 12 different states had two things in common. They were all men of considerable political experience, and they all recognized the need for a stronger national union. So when the Virginia delegation introduced Madison's outline for a new central government, the convention was ready to listen.

The Virginia and New Jersey Plans

What Madison had in mind was a truly national republic, not a confederation of independent states. His "Virginia Plan" proposed a central government with three branches: legislative, executive, and judicial. Furthermore, the legislative branch, Congress, would possess the power to veto all state legislation. In place of the Confederation's single assembly, Madison substituted a bicameral legislature, with a lower house elected directly by the people and an upper house chosen by the lower, from nominations made by state legislatures. Representatives to both houses would be apportioned according to population—a change from practice under the Articles, in which each state had a single vote in Congress. Madison also revised the structure of government that had existed under the Articles by adding an executive, who would be elected by Congress, and an independent federal judiciary.

Paterson's New Jersey Plan

After two weeks of debate over the Virginia Plan, William Paterson, a lawyer from New Jersey, presented a less radical counterproposal. Although his "New Jersey Plan" increased Congress's power to tax and to regulate trade, it kept the national government as a unicameral assembly, with each state receiving one vote in Congress under the policy of equal representation. The delegates took just four days to reject Paterson's plan. Most endorsed Madison's design for a stronger central government.

Even so, the issue of apportioning representation continued to divide the delegates. While smaller states pressed for each state's having an equal vote in Congress, larger states backed Madison's provision for basing representation on population. Underlying the dispute over representation was an even deeper rivalry between southern and northern states. While northern and southern populations were nearly equal in the 1780s, and the South's population was growing more rapidly, the northern states were more numerous. Giving the states equal votes would put the South at a disadvantage. Southerners feared being outvoted in Congress by the northern states and felt that only proportional representation would protect the interests of their section.

That division turned into a deadlock as the wet spring burned off into a blazing summer. Delegates suffered the daily torture of staring at a large sun painted on the speaker's chair occupied by Washington. The stifling heat was made even worse because the windows remained shut to keep any news of the proceedings from drifting out into the Philadelphia streets.

The Deadlock Broken

Finally, as the heat wave broke, so did the political stalemate. On July 2 a committee headed by Benjamin Franklin suggested a compromise. States would be equally represented in the upper house of Congress, each state legislature appointing two senators to six-year terms. That satisfied the smaller states. In the lower house of Congress, which alone could initiate money bills, representation was to be apportioned according to population. Every 30,000 inhabitants would elect one representative for a two-year term. A slave was to count as three-fifths of a free person in the calculation of population, and the slave trade was to continue until 1808. That satisfied the larger states and the South.

Compromise over Representation

By the end of August the convention was prepared to approve the final draft of the Constitution. The delegates agreed that the executive, now called the president, would be chosen every four years. Direct election seemed out of the question—after all, how could citizens in South Carolina know anything about a presidential candidate who happened to live in distant Massachusetts, or vice versa? But if voters instead chose presidential electors, those eminent men would likely have been involved in national politics, have known the candidates personally, and be prepared to vote wisely. Thus the Electoral College was established, with each state's total number of senators and representatives determining its share of electoral votes.

Electoral College

An array of other powers ensured that the executive would remain independent and strong. He would have command over the armed forces, authority to conduct diplomatic relations, responsibility to nominate judges and officials in the executive branch, and the power to veto congressional legislation. Just as the executive branch was made independent, so too the federal judiciary was separated from the other two branches of government. Madison believed that this clear **separation of powers** was essential to a balanced republican government.

Separation of Powers

Madison's only real defeat came when the convention refused to give Congress veto power over state legislation. Still, the new bicameral national legislature enjoyed much broader authority than Congress had under the Confederation, including the power to tax and to regulate commerce. The Constitution also limited the powers of state legislatures, prohibiting them from levying duties on trade, coining money or issuing paper currency, and conducting foreign relations. The Constitution and the acts passed by Congress were declared the supreme law of the land, taking precedence over any legislation passed by the states. And changing the Constitution would not be easy. Amendments could be proposed only by a two-thirds vote of both houses of Congress or in a convention requested by two-thirds of the state legislatures. Ratification of amendments required approval by three-quarters of the states.

Amending the Constitution

On September 17, 1787, 39 of the 42 delegates remaining in Philadelphia signed the Constitution. It was fortunate that the signatories included so many lawyers, because the summer's proceedings had been of such dubious legality that many skilled attorneys would be needed to make them seem otherwise. Charged only to revise the Articles, the delegates had instead written a completely new frame of government. And to speed up ratification, the convention decided that the Constitution would go into effect after only nine states had approved it, overlooking the fact that even a revision of the Articles would have required the assent of all state legislatures. They further declared that the people themselves—not the state legislatures—would pass judgment on the Constitution in special ratifying conventions. To serve final notice that the new central government was a republic of the people and not merely another confederation of states, Gouverneur Morris of Pennsylvania hit on a happy turn of phrase to introduce the Constitution. "We the People," the document begins, "in Order to form a more perfect Union..."

A Republic of the People, Not a Confederation of States

Ratification

With grave misgivings on the part of many, the states called for conventions to decide whether to ratify the new Constitution. Those Americans with the gravest misgivings—the Anti-Federalists as they came to be called—voiced familiar republican fears. Older and less cosmopolitan than their **Federalist** opponents, the Anti-Federalists drew upon their memories of the struggle with England to frame their criticisms of the Constitution. Expanding the power of the central government at the expense of the states, they warned, would lead to corrupt and arbitrary rule by new aristocrats. Extending a republic over a large territory, they cautioned, would separate national legislators from the interests and close oversight of their constituents.

Madison responded to these objections in *The Federalist Papers,* a series of 85 essays written with Alexander Hamilton and John Jay during the winter of 1787–1788. He countered Anti-Federalist concerns over the centralization of power by pointing out that each separate branch of the national government would keep the others within the limits of their legal authority. That mechanism of **checks and balances** would prevent the executive from oppressing the people while preventing the people from oppressing themselves.

To answer Anti-Federalist objections to a national republic, Madison drew on the ideas of an English philosopher, David Hume. In his famous tenth essay in *The Federalist Papers,* Madison argued that in a great republic, "the Society becomes broken into a greater variety of interests, of pursuits, of passions, which check each other." The larger the territory, the more likely it was to contain multiple political interests and parties, so that no single faction could dominate. Instead, each would cancel out the others.

The one Anti-Federalist criticism Madison could not get around was the absence of a national bill of rights. Opponents insisted on an explicit statement of rights to secure the freedoms of individuals and minorities from being violated by the federal government. Madison finally promised to place a bill of rights before Congress immediately after the Constitution was ratified.

Ratification of the Constitution

STATE	DATE	VOTE FOR	VOTE AGAINST
Delaware	December 8, 1787	30	9
Pennsylvania	December 12, 1787	46	23
New Jersey	December 18, 1787	38	0
Georgia	January 2, 1788	26	0
Connecticut	January 9, 1788	128	40
Massachusetts	February 16, 1788	187	168
Maryland	April 26, 1788	63	11
South Carolina	May 23, 1788	149	73
New Hampshire	June 21, 1788	57	47
Virginia	June 25, 1788	89	79
New York	July 26, 1788	30	27
North Carolina	November 21, 1789	194	77
Rhode Island	May 29, 1790	34	32

Throughout the early months of 1788, Anti-Federalists continued their opposition. But they lacked the articulate and influential leadership that rallied behind the Constitution and commanded greater access to the public press. In the end, too, Anti-Federalist fears of centralized power proved less compelling than Federalist prophecies of the chaos that would follow if the Constitution were not adopted.

By the end of July 1788 all but two states had voted in favor of ratification. The last holdout—Rhode Island, to no one's surprise—finally came aboard in May 1790, after Madison had carried through on his pledge to submit a bill of rights to the new Congress. Indeed, these 10 amendments—ratified by enough states to become part of the Constitution by the end of 1791—proved to be the Anti-Federalists' most impressive legacy. The bill of rights set the most basic terms for defining personal liberty in the United States. Among the rights guaranteed were freedom of religion, the press, and speech, as well as the right to assemble and petition and the right to bear arms. The amendments also established clear procedural safeguards, including the right to a trial by jury and protection against illegal searches and seizures. They prohibited excessive bail, cruel and unusual punishment, and the quartering of troops in private homes.

Bill of Rights Ratified

Within the life span of a single generation, American had declared their independence twice. In many ways the political freedom claimed from Britain in 1776 was less remarkable than the intellectual freedom from the Old World that Americans achieved by agreeing to the Constitution. The Constitution represented a triumph of the imagination—a challenge to many beliefs long cherished by western Europe's republican thinkers.

Beyond the Ideals of Europe's Republican Thinkers

Revolutionary ideals had been deeply influenced by the conflicts of British politics, in particular the Opposition's warnings about the dangers of executive power. Those concerns at first committed the revolutionaries to making legislatures supreme. In the end, though, Americans ratified a constitution that provided for an independent executive and a balanced government. The Opposition's fears of distant, centralized power had at first prompted the revolutionaries to embrace state sovereignty. But in the Constitution Americans established a national government with authority independent of the states. Finally, the common sense among all of western Europe's republican theorists—that large national republics were an impossibility—was rejected by Americans, making the United States an impossibility that still endures.

What, then, became of the last tenet of the old republican creed—the belief that civic virtue would sustain popular liberty? The hard lessons of the war and the crises of the 1780s withered confidence in the capacity of Americans to sacrifice their private interests for the public welfare. Many came to share Washington's sober view that "the few . . . who act upon Principles of disinterestedness are, comparatively speaking, no more than a drop in the Ocean." The Constitution reflected the new recognition that interest rather than virtue shaped the behavior of most people most of the time and that the clash of diverse interest groups would remain a constant of public life.

Behavior Shaped by Interest Rather Than by Virtue

Yet Madison and many other Federalists did not believe that the competition between private interests would somehow result in policies fostering public welfare. That goal would be met instead by the new national government acting as "a disinterested and dispassionate umpire in disputes between different passions and interests in the State." The

Federalists looked to the national government to fulfill that role because they trusted that a large republic, with its millions of citizens, would yield more of that scarce resource—disinterested gentlemen dedicated to serving the public good. Such gentlemen, in Madison's words, "whose enlightened views and virtuous sentiments render them superior to local prejudices," would fill the small number of national offices.

Not all the old revolutionaries agreed. Anti-Federalists drawn from the ranks of ordinary Americans still believed that common people were more virtuous and gentlemen more interested than the Federalists allowed. "These lawyers and men of learning, and moneyed men, that talk so finely," complained one Anti-Federalist, would "get all the power and all of the money into their own hands, and then they will swallow up all us little folks." Instead of being dominated by enlightened gentlemen, the national government should be composed of representatives from every social class and occupational group.

The narrow majorities by which the Constitution was ratified reflected the continuing influence of such sentiments, as well as fear that the states were surrendering too much power. That fear made Patrick Henry so ardent an Anti-Federalist that he refused to attend the Constitutional Convention in 1787, saying that he "smelt a rat." "I am not a Virginian, but an American," Henry had once declared. Most likely he was lying. Or perhaps Patrick Henry, a southerner and a slaveholder, could see his way clear to being an "American" only as long as sovereignty remained firmly in the hands of the individual states. Henry's convictions, 70 years hence, would rise again to haunt the Union.

Significant Events

1777	Continental Congress approves the Articles of Confederation
1781	Articles of Confederation ratified
1784	Spain closes the Mississippi River to American navigation
1785	Jay-Gardoqui Treaty negotiated but not ratified
1786	Shays's Rebellion; Annapolis convention calls for revising the Articles
1787	Congress adopts the Northwest Ordinance; Constitutional Convention
1787–1788	Publication of *The Federalist Papers*
1788	New Hampshire becomes ninth state to ratify Constitution
1791	Bill of Rights adopted

Chapter Summary

Leading Americans would give more thought to federalism, the organization of a United States, as the events of the post-revolutionary period revealed the weaknesses of the state and national governments.

- For a decade after independence, the revolutionaries were less committed to creating a single national republic than to organizing 13 separate state republics, each dominated by popularly elected legislatures.

- The Articles of Confederation provided for a government by a national legislature but left the crucial power of the purse, as well as all final power to make and execute laws, entirely to the states.

- Many conflicts in the new republic were occasioned by westward expansion, which created both international difficulties with Britain and Spain and internal tensions over the democratization of state legislatures.

- In the wake of the Revolution, ordinary Americans struggled to define republican society; workers began to organize, some women claimed a right to greater political, legal, and educational opportunities, and religious dissenters called for disestablishment.

- The egalitarian principles of the Revolution sparked a debate over slavery that increased the sectional split between northern and southern states. Antislavery societies began to appear in the North; some planters in the Upper South freed their slaves, but no southern state legally abolished slavery.

- In the mid-1780s the political crisis of the Confederation came to a head, prompted by the controversy over the Jay-Gardoqui Treaty and Shays's Rebellion.

- The Constitutional Convention of 1787 produced an entirely new frame of government that established a truly national republic and provided for a separation of powers among a judiciary, a bicameral legislature, and a strong executive.

- The Anti-Federalists, opponents of the Constitution, softened their objections when promised a bill of rights after ratification, which was incorporated into the Constitution by 1791.

Additional Readings

The work of Gordon Wood is indispensable for understanding the transformation of American politics and culture during the 1780s and thereafter; see especially *The Creation of the American Republic* (1969) and *The Radicalism of the American Revolution* (1992). Other good accounts of the Confederation period and the framing of the Constitution include two books by Forrest MacDonald, *E Pluribus Unum* (1965) and *Novus Ordo Seclorum* (1985), and a collection of essays edited by Alfred Young, *Beyond the American Revolution* (1993). To understand the arguments in favor of the Constitution, consult Garry Wills, *Explaining America* (1981), and to appreciate the contributions of its opponents, read Saul Cornell, *The Other Founders* (1999) and the classic writings of Cecilia Kenyon collected in *Men of Little Faith* (2003). The proceedings of the Constitutional Convention receive vivid coverage in Christopher Collier and James Lincoln Collier, *Decision in Philadelphia* (1987) and Clinton Rossiter, *1787: The Grand Convention* (1973).

To explore the meaning of republicanism for American women, see two fine studies by Linda Kerber, *Women of the Republic* (1980) and *No Constitutional Right to Be Ladies* (1998), as well as Rosemarie Zagarri's superb biography of Mercy Otis Warren, *A Woman's Dilemma* (1995). For a vivid sense of how the 1780s transformed local society and politics in one Massachusetts county, read John Brooke, *The Heart of the Commonwealth* (1991), and for a fascinating tale of how the Revolution made one ordinary man's life extraordinary, enjoy Alan Taylor, *William Cooper's Town* (1995). The best accounts of how the Revolution's legacy affected the lives of African Americans in the North include Shane White, *Somewhat More Independent* (1991), and Joan Pope Melish, *Disowning Slavery* (1998).

For a fuller list of readings, see the Bibliography at www.mhhe.com/davidsonnation6.

Historians Reconstruct the Past

White and Black Southerners Worshiping Together

Religious beliefs, gatherings, and rituals reflect some of the deepest human emotions. Often they also lay bare some of society's deepest divisions. For both these reasons and more, historians often study religious institutions and practices to understand how a society functions.

During the 50 years before 1800, evangelicals introduced southerners to new ways of being religious. Those attending their worship services were drawn into the earliest southern Baptist, Methodist, and Presbyterian churches by the First Great Awakening and other revivals that followed. Some of these early services were held in private homes, others in crudely constructed churches, and still others in open fields. As evangelical preachers stressed the importance of being "reborn" by faith in Jesus Christ, some southerners wept, confessed their sins, and encouraged one another with hopeful words and warm embraces. Those who came to such gatherings engaged in the most intimate kind of sharing and self-revelation.

What made the services even more extraordinary is that some participants were white and some black. These religious fellowships were truly biracial and remained so until after the Civil War. That remarkable fact has intrigued historians. In a society increasingly shaped by the institution of slavery, evangelical churches were one of the few southern institutions that brought blacks and whites together rather than keeping them apart. How did members behave toward each other daily?

Were born-again converts from both races treated equally? How was authority within such churches distributed among black and white members?

The questions are tantalizing, but the answers by no means easy to come by. Some letters and diaries survive from the last half of the eighteenth century, among them the daily journals and correspondence of ministers. A few preachers even published autobiographies of their experiences. But even more valuable information can be gathered from what might seem at first a rather drab source. There are scores of church records dating from this period, most kept by Virginia Baptists. The members of each Baptist church elected a clerk, always a white male "brother," whose duty it was to record all the business transacted at their monthly meetings, often in a ledger-sized bound volume called the "church book." Church books provide an insight into relations between whites and blacks in part because their clerks are *not* consciously trying to write about race relations. They are simply recording the everyday business of churches, week in, week out.

Decoding the Church Books

Sometimes practical concerns dominated the meeting. Should the church building be repaired? Who among the brethren will be permitted to preach? (Many Baptist churches boasted several preachers besides the pastor.) On other occasions, members debated about what the Bible taught was the holiest way to govern their churches. But at most meetings, members fixed their attention on admitting new converts to their fellowship and "disciplining" older members suspected of sexual misconduct or theft, slander or swearing, drinking or fighting. Church clerks duly noted all those accepted as new members, as well as the names of wayward brothers and sisters—and whether they were merely scolded for their faults or expelled.

Such records offer the most direct and vivid sense of African Americans' presence and participation in early evangelical churches. First, historians can start by doing a little counting. How many members are white and how many black? The records show that

Churchbook record: "Names of Black Members"
Note the treatment of black names.

positions of authority, to voice their opinions, and to gain leverage over their masters.

Limits of Racial Equality

Yet these same church records also reveal the limits of racial equality among early evangelicals. Like all evidence mined by historians, the sources yield data that are sometimes complex and contradictory.

Records of those meetings at which members discussed the mundane matter of church repair reveal, for example, that the Baptists segregated seating at public worship. African Americans were consigned to the least choice spots at the back of the church or in "sheds" attached to the side. Moreover, when white members filled every available seat, black members were ordered outdoors to listen from underneath open windows. The attitude that such practices convey—that whites regarded African Americans as "second-class" members—is also suggested by the

blacks made up a substantial minority—perhaps one-fifth to one-quarter—of the members in most churches. In a few, they constituted a majority. Many churches, too, authorized at least one African American brother to preach, sometimes permitting him that "liberty" only among other blacks but in other instances allowing him to address racially mixed gatherings. There were even a few predominantly white churches in early Virginia that black preachers served as pastors.

What about voting? In some churches, too, black men and, more rarely, black women were permitted to vote in meetings. In all, African American members could participate in deliberations and give testimony in discipline cases. Indeed, there are several instances of masters being disciplined after slave members complained of being abused. Black members, too, were sometimes charged with wrongdoing, but white men were far more likely than any other group of members to be hauled before the church for reported misdeeds. In short, evangelical churches like these Baptist fellowships were among the most racially egalitarian institutions in early southern society. They offered African Americans unusual opportunities to hold

"Uncle Jack," shown in this 1849 engraving, preaches informally to a white congregation. He began his career as a minister in the 1790s and continued until 1832.

manner in which many clerks recorded new church members. While they always entered the full names of white converts, new African American members were usually listed last and often collectively as "several Negroes."

Church discussions about who might preach also show a growing concern on the part of white members to restrict the activities of black preachers. Increasingly after 1750 those allowed that "liberty" were given ever stricter instructions about whom they might preach to, at which times, and from what texts of the Bible. At meetings in which the rules of conducting church business were discussed, white members also began to express concern about whether African American members should be allowed to vote. Most churches revoked that right before the end of the eighteenth century. Tracing how churches dealt with black members accused of misbehavior suggests a similar anxiety among white members, which increased over time. Although African Americans continued to make up only a tiny minority of church members suspected of misbehavior, those convicted of wrongdoing were far more likely than white members to be expelled rather than to receive a milder punishment.

In other words, a closer inspection of church records suggests that white evangelicals drifted toward more racially restrictive policies over the latter half of the eighteenth century.

Why? The numbers in the church books are suggestive. After the Revolution, increasing numbers of African Americans were entering Baptist (and other evangelical) churches. As the percentage of black members rose, white evangelicals feared that the "freedoms" given to black worshipers might detract from the church's ability to win converts among slaveholders.

Seeking a Separate Way

Clearly, evangelicals were winning converts among African Americans. Yet other evidence suggests that black members were left unsatisfied by their treatment in white churches. The diaries and letters of white evangelicals reveal that many black members of biracial churches had also begun conducting their own separate devotions. Even by the 1790s, African American Christians were meeting nightly in the slave quarters to pray, sing, and hear the sermons of black preachers. Such "shadow churches" served as the crucible of Afro-Christianity, a melding of evangelical Protestant and West African religious traditions. John Antrobus's painting *Plantation Burial* (in a detail shown here, above, and in the full painting shown on page 348) reflects the situation that prevailed by the mid–nineteenth century. Although blacks attended white services in greater numbers, their most vital worship often took place elsewhere.

White masters and preachers were like the shadowy couple Antrobus painted on the right: divorced from the Christian worship of their slaves.

Bibliography Historians disagree about the extent to which early evangelical churches were egalitarian. The strongest arguments in favor are presented by Mechal Sobel, *The World They Made Together* (1987); the most forceful challenge to Sobel is Jewel Spangler, "Salvation Was Not Liberty: Baptists and Slavery in Revolutionary Virginia," *American Baptist Quarterly,* 13 (1994). Other studies that treat the dynamics of these early biracial churches and the experience of the first black southern evangelicals are Albert J. Raboteau, *Slave Religion* (1978), the best introduction to this subject; Sylvia R. Frey, *Water from the Rock* (1991), which usefully updates Raboteau; and, most recently, Christine Leigh Heyrman, *Southern Cross* (1997). The evolving views of race and slavery among early white evangelicals is thoughtfully analyzed in James Essig, *The Bonds of Wickedness* (1982), while the most eloquent descriptions of Afro-Christianity in the slave quarters appear in Eugene Genovese, *Roll, Jordan, Roll* (1972), and Lawrence Levine, *Black Culture and Black Consciousness* (1977).

CHAPTER 9
The Early Republic
1789~1824

"I Felt Myself Mad with Passion"

One spring evening in 1794 General John Neville was riding home from Pittsburgh with his wife and granddaughter. As they went up a hill, his wife's saddle started to slip, so Neville dismounted to tighten the girth. As he adjusted the strap, he heard the clip-clop of an approaching horse. A rider galloped up and in a gruff voice asked, "Are you Neville the excise officer?"

"Yes," Neville replied, without turning around.

"Then I must give you a whipping!" cried the rider and leapt from his horse. He grabbed the startled Neville by the hair and lunged at his throat. Breaking free, Neville finally managed to knock the man down: he recognized his attacker as Jacob Long, a local farmer. After Long fled, Neville resumed his journey, badly shaken.

John Neville was not accustomed to such treatment. As one of the wealthiest men in the area, he expected respect from those of lower social rank. And he had received it—until becoming embroiled in a controversy over the new "whiskey tax" on distilled spirits. In a frontier district such as western Pennsylvania, farmers regularly distilled their grain into whiskey for barter and sale. Not surprisingly, the **excise tax,** passed by Congress in 1791, was notoriously unpopular. Still, Neville had accepted an appointment to be one of the tax's regional inspectors. For three years he had endured threats as he enforced the law, but this roadside assault showed that popular hostility was rising.

As spring turned to summer, the grain ripened, and so did the people's anger. In mid-July, a federal marshal arrived to serve summonses to a number of farmer-distillers who had not paid taxes. One, William Miller, squinted at the paper and was amazed to find the government ordering him to set aside "all manner of business and excuses" and appear in court—hundreds

Wolfing down fresh oysters after enjoying a play at Philadelphia's Chestnut Street Theater (background) was a satisfying experience in the young republic. The market-oriented outlook of urban Americans and commercial farmers contrasted with the semisubsistence lives of many farm families, who grew food primarily for themselves.

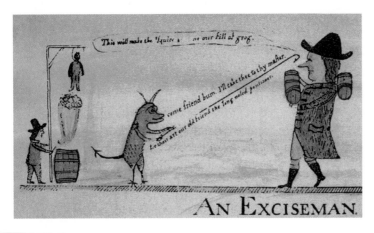

An Exciseman.

In this anti-government cartoon, a devil's imp with horns and barbed tail offers to escort a tax collector—the Exciseman—to his master. Like the Stamp Act riots of the Revolutionary period, protests in western Pennsylviania against the excise tax ritually hanged tax collectors in effigy (left).

of miles away in Philadelphia—in little more than a month. Even worse, the papers claimed he owed $250.

And there, next to this unknown federal marshal, stood the unyielding John Neville.

"I felt myself mad with passion," recalled Miller. "I thought $250 would ruin me; and . . . I felt my blood boil at seeing General Neville along to pilot the sheriff to my very door." Word of the marshal's presence brought 30 or 40 laborers swarming from a nearby field. Armed with muskets and pitchforks, they forced Neville and the marshal to beat a hasty retreat.

Next morning, the local militia company marched to Neville's estate, enraged by what they considered this latest trampling on individual liberty. A battle ensued, and the general, aided by his slaves, beat back the attackers. A larger group, numbering 500 to 700, returned the following day to find Neville fled and his home garrisoned by a group of soldiers from nearby Fort Pitt. The mob burned down most of the outbuildings and, after the soldiers surrendered, torched Neville's elegantly furnished home.

Throughout the region that summer, marauding bands roamed the countryside, burning homes, banishing individuals, and attacking tax collectors. While the greatest unrest flared in western Pennsylvania, farmers in the western districts of several other states also defied federal officials and refused to pay the tax, thus launching a full-scale "Whiskey Rebellion" in the summer of 1794. The whiskey tax had brought the question of the federal government's power quite directly to the attention of the ordinary citizen, and many of them answered with a loud, violent rejection.

Alexander Hamilton, a principal architect of the strong federal government established by the Constitution, knew a challenge to authority when he saw one: "Shall there be a government, or no government?" So did an alarmed George Washington, now president and commander-in-chief of the new republic, who led an army of 13,000 men—larger than that he had commanded at Yorktown against the British—into the Pennsylvania countryside.

That show of force cowed the Pennsylvania protesters, snuffing out the Whiskey Rebellion. But the riots and rebellion deepened fears for the future of the new republic. In the space of only 15 years, Americans had already overturned two governments: England's colonial administration and the Articles of Confederation. As Benjamin Franklin remarked in 1788, Americans were skilled at overthrowing governments, but only time would tell whether they were any good at sustaining them. By 1794 Franklin's warning seemed prophetic.

Federalists such as Washington and Hamilton—supporters of a powerful national government—had high hopes for their newly created republic. Stretching over some 840,000 square miles in 1789, it was approximately four times the size of France, five times the size of Spain, ten times the size of Great Britain. Yet the founders of the republic knew how risky it was to unite such a vast territory. Yankee merchants living along Boston wharves had economic interests and cultural traditions distinct from those of backcountry farmers who raised hogs, tended a few acres of corn, and distilled whiskey. Even among farmers, there was a world of difference between a South Carolina planter who shipped tons of rice to European markets and a New Hampshire family whose stony fields yielded barely enough to survive. Could the new government established by the Constitution provide a framework strong enough to unite such a socially diverse nation? Within a decade national political leaders split into two sharply opposed political parties, drawing ordinary men and women into civic life.

Social and political divisions within the nation were sharpened by currents of global change, both across the Atlantic and westward across the continent. In Europe, traditional rivalries sharpened after 1789 and a far-reaching and increasingly bloody revolution engulfed France. Americans were torn in their loyalties as Europe plunged into war. As Britain fought its archrival France, it also determined to make Americans fight for their independence once again. In the west, Spain and later France pressured white settlers beyond the Appalachians. Indian nations, buffeted themselves by disease and dislocation, sought to unite in a confederacy west of the Appalachian Mountains. Many were determined to push back against American expansion.

International Pressures on the Republic

In short, the early republic was a fragile creation, buffeted by changes beyond its borders and struggling to create a stable government at home. During the nation's first three decades, its survival depended on balancing the interests of a socially and economically diverse population.

1789: A Social Portrait

When the Constitution went into effect, the United States stretched from the Atlantic Ocean to the Mississippi River. The first federal census, compiled in 1790, counted approximately 4 million people, divided about evenly between the northern and southern states. Only about 100,000 settlers lived beyond the Appalachians in the Tennessee and Kentucky territories, which were soon to become states.

Within the Republic's boundaries were two major groups that lacked effective political influence: African Americans and Indians. In 1790 black Americans numbered 750,000, almost one-fifth the total population. More than 90 percent lived in the southern states from Maryland to Georgia; most were slaves who worked on tobacco and rice plantations, but there were free blacks as well. The census did not count the number of Indians living east of the Mississippi. North of the Ohio, the powerful Miami Confederacy discouraged settlement, while to the south, five strong, well-organized tribes—the Creeks, Cherokees, Chickasaws, Choctaws, and Seminoles—dominated the region from the Appalachians to the Mississippi River.

That composition would change as the white population continued to double about every 22 years. Immigration contributed only a small part to this astonishing growth. On average, fewer than 10,000 Europeans arrived annually between 1790 and 1820. The primary cause was natural increase, since, on average, American white women gave birth to nearly eight children each. As a result, the United States had an unusually youthful population: in 1790 almost half of all white Americans were under 16 years old. The age at first marriage was about 25 for men, 24 for women—and three or four years younger in newly settled areas—which contributed to the high birthrate.

Population Growth

This youthful, growing population remained overwhelmingly rural. Only 24 towns and cities boasted 2,500 or more residents, and 19 out of 20 Americans lived outside them. In fact, more than 80 percent of American families in 1800 were engaged in agriculture. In such a rural environment the movement of people, goods, and information was slow. Few individuals used the expensive postal system, and most roads were still little more than dirt paths hacked through the forest. The roads were choked with dust during dry spells and overflowed with mud when it rained. In 1790 the country had 92 newspapers, but they were published mostly in towns and cities along major avenues of transportation. Americans off the beaten path only occasionally heard news of the outside world.

Poor Transportation

Life in isolated regions contrasted markedly with that in bustling urban centers such as New York and Philadelphia. But the most basic division in American society was not between the cities and the countryside, important as that was. What would divide Americans most broadly over the coming decades was the contrast between semisubsistence and commercial ways of life. Semisubsistence farmers lived on the produce of their own land and labor. Americans in the commercial economy were tied more closely to the larger markets of a far-flung world. As the United States began its life under the new federal union, the distinction between a **semisubsistence economy** and a **commercial economy** was a crucial one.

The Semisubsistence Economy of Crèvecoeur's America

Most rural white Americans lived off the produce of their own land in a **barter economy.** It was this world that a French writer, Hector St. John de Crèvecoeur, described so well.

Crèvecoeur arrived in the British colonies in 1759 and almost immediately began wandering: riding over the rutted roads that led to the farms of New England and New York, fording the streams between the scattered settlements of Ohio and Kentucky, knocking the dust of Virginia off his clothes, stopping to talk at taverns along the roads to Philadelphia, and finally settling for a number of years as a farmer in the Hudson River valley. In 1783 he published his *Letters from an American Farmer,* asking in them the question that had so often occurred to him: "What then is the American, this new man?"

Equality   For Crèvecoeur what distinguished American society was the widespread equality of its people, especially the rural farmers. Americans were hostile to social pretensions and anything that smacked of aristocratic privilege. The conditions of the country also promoted equality. Land was abundant and widely distributed, and the population was not divided into the wealthy few and the desperate many. (Like most of his white contemporaries, Crèvecoeur glided quickly over the plight of black slaves.) "We are the most perfect society now existing in the world," he boasted.

Although romantic in his rhetoric, Crèvecoeur painted a reasonably accurate portrait of most of the interior of the northern states and the backcountry of the South. Wealth in those areas, although not distributed equally, was spread fairly broadly. And subsistence remained the goal of most white families. "The great effort was for every farmer to produce anything he required within his own family," one European visitor noted. In such an economy women played a key role. Wives and daughters had to be skilled in making articles such as candles, soap, clothing, and hats, since the cost of buying such items was steep.

With labor scarce and expensive, farmers also depended on their neighbors to help clear fields, build homes, and harvest crops. If a farm family produced a small surplus, it usually exchanged it locally rather than selling it for cash in a distant market. In this barter economy, money was seldom seen and was used primarily to pay taxes and purchase imported goods.

Indians and the Semisubsistence Economy   Indian economies were also based primarily on subsistence. In the division of labor women raised crops, while men fished or hunted—not only for meat but also for skins to make clothing. Because Indians followed game more seasonally than did white settlers, they moved their villages to several different locations over the course of a year. But both whites and Indians in a semisubsistence economy moved periodically to new fields after they had exhausted the old ones. Indians exhausted agricultural lands less quickly because they planted beans, corn, and squash in the same field, a technique that better conserved soil nutrients.

Despite the popular image of both the independent "noble savage" and the self-reliant yeoman farmer, virtually no one in the backcountry operated within a truly self-sufficient economy. Although farmers tried to grow most of the food their families ate, they normally bought salt, sugar, and coffee, and they often traded with their neighbors for food and other items. In addition, necessities such as iron, glass, lead, and gunpowder had to be purchased, and many farmers hired artisans to make shoes and weave cloth. Similarly, Indians were enmeshed in the wider world of European commerce, exchanging furs for iron tools or clothing and ornamental materials.

The Commercial Economy of Franklin's America

Outside the backcountry, Americans were tied much more closely to a commercial economy. Here, merchants, artisans, and even farmers did not subsist on what they produced but instead sold goods or services in a wider market and lived on their earnings. Cities and towns, of course, played a key part in the commercial economy. But so did the agricultural regions near the seaboard and along navigable rivers.

This wooden "moldboard" plow from Maine was a type commonly used in the late eighteenth century. The wood, which did not hold up well when dragged through rough, stony ground, was sometimes reinforced with wrought iron.

For commerce to flourish, goods had to move from producers to market cheaply enough to reap profits. Water offered the only cost-effective transportation over any distance; indeed, it cost as much to ship goods a mere 30 miles over primitive roads as to ship by boat 3,000 miles across the Atlantic to London. Cost-effective transportation was available to the planters of the Tidewater South, and city merchants used their access to the sea to establish trading ties to the West Indies and Europe. But urban artisans and workers were also linked to this market economy, as were many farm families in the Hudson valley, southeastern Pennsylvania, and southern New England. Where transportation was limited or prohibitively expensive, farmers had no incentive to increase production, and an economy of barter and semisubsistence persisted.

Commercial society differed from Crèvecoeur's world in another important way: its wealth was less equally distributed. By 1790, the richest 10 percent of Americans living in cities and in the plantation districts of the Tidewater South owned about 50 percent of the wealth. In the backcountry the top 10 percent was likely to own 25 to 35 percent of the wealth.

Inequality of Wealth

The man who gained international renown as a self-made citizen of commercial America was Benjamin Franklin. In his writings and in the example of his own life, Franklin offered a vision of the new nation that contrasted with Crèvecoeur's ideal of a self-sufficient America. Franklin had arrived in Philadelphia as a runaway apprentice and by hard work and talent rose to be one of the leading citizens of his adopted city. The preface to Franklin's popular *Poor Richard's Almanack,* as well as his countless essays, spelled out simple maxims for Americans seeking the upward path. "The way to wealth is as plain as the way to market," he noted. "It depends chiefly on two words, industry and frugality." Those anxious to succeed should "remember that time is money." The kind of success he preached depended on taking advantage of commerce and a wider market.

Commercial Values

The ethics of Franklin's marketplace, which looked forward to the opening up of opportunity in American society, threatened to destroy Crèvecoeur's egalitarian America. At the time of Franklin's death in 1790, the ideal that Crèvecoeur had so eloquently described still held sway across much of America. But the political debate of the 1790s showed clearly that Franklin's world of commerce and markets was slowly transforming the nation.

The Constitution and Commerce

In many ways the fight over ratification of the Constitution represented a struggle between the commercial and the subsistence-oriented elements of American society.

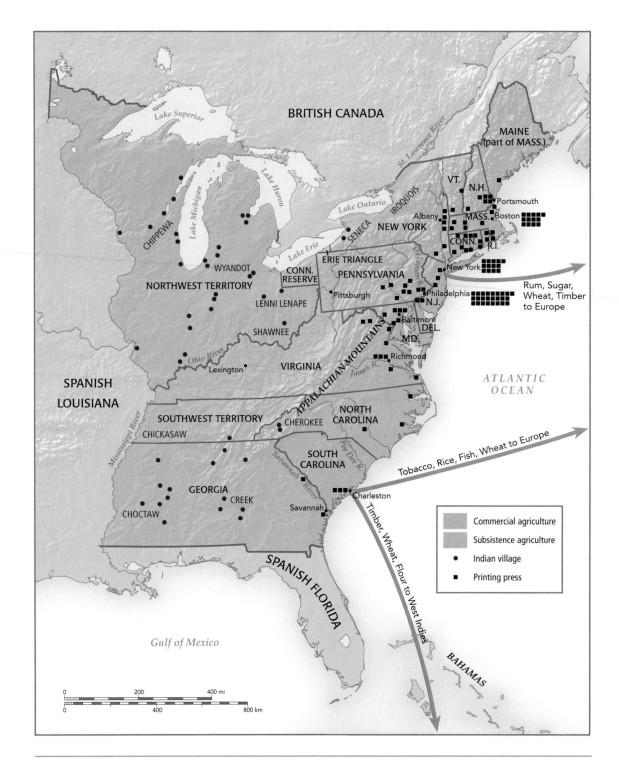

Semisubsistence and Commercial America, 1790   *To prosper, a commercial economy demanded relatively cheap transportation to move goods. Thus in 1790 American commerce was confined largely to settled areas along the coast and to navigable rivers below the fall line. Because commerce depended on an efficient flow of information and goods, newspapers flourished in these areas.*

Urban merchants and workers as well as commercial farmers and planters generally rallied behind the Constitution. They took a broader, more cosmopolitan view of the nation's future, and they had a more favorable view of government power. Franklin, predictably, supported the Constitution. So did Madison and Washington, both planters whose wealth depended on trade and commerce.

Philadelphia was the largest and most prosperous city in the country in 1789. Its growth fueled the development of commercial agriculture in the surrounding countryside, as more and more farmers hauled their surplus to town for sale in the city's busy markets. In this scene, both men and women buy fresh foods on the streets. Indians, pictured here, also participated in the commercial economy.

Americans who remained a part of the semisubsistence barter economy tended to oppose the Constitution. More provincial in outlook, they feared concentrated power, were suspicious of cities and commercial institutions, opposed aristocracy and special privilege, and in general just wanted to be left alone. They were a majority of the population, but they were not easily mobilized, lacked prestigious leaders, and did not have the access to communication that their opponents enjoyed. In defeat they remained suspicious that a powerful government would tax them to benefit the commercial sectors of the economy.

And so in 1789 the United States embarked on its new national course, with two rival visions of the direction that the fledgling Republic should take. Which vision would prevail—a question that was as much social as it was political—increasingly divided the generation of revolutionary leaders in the early republic.

The New Government

Whatever the Republic was to become, Americans agreed that George Washington personified it. When the first Electoral College cast its votes, Washington was unanimously elected, the only president in history so honored. John Adams became vice president.

The Federalists—supporters of the Constitution—called the new government "the great experiment." They were intensely aware that throughout history democratic republics had in the end degenerated into quarreling factions, as with the city-states of ancient Greece, or ushered in dictatorships, as had happened in Cromwell's England. No republic—not England, or Rome, or the Swiss city-states—had stretched over a territory as large as the United States. Loyalty to the new Republic, with its untried form of government and diversity of peoples and interests, rested to a great degree on the trust and respect Americans gave Washington.

Failure of Past Republics

Washington Organizes the Government

George Washington realized that as the first occupant of the executive office, everything he did was fraught with significance. "I walk on untrodden ground," he

Washington's trip from Virginia to New York City to assume the presidency was a triumphant procession as Americans enthusiastically greeted him with cheers and even flowers strewn along his path.

commented. "There is scarcely any part of my conduct which may not hereafter be drawn into precedent."

The Cabinet

The Constitution made no mention of a cabinet. Yet the drafters of the Constitution, aware of the experience of the Continental Congress under the Articles of Confederation, clearly assumed that the president would have some system of advisers. Congress authorized the creation of four departments—War, Treasury, State, and Attorney General—whose heads were to be appointed with the consent of the Senate. Washington's most important choices were Alexander Hamilton as secretary of the treasury and Thomas Jefferson to head the State Department. At first the president did not meet regularly with his advisers as a group, but the idea of a cabinet that met to discuss policy matters eventually evolved. Washington gradually excluded Adams from cabinet discussions, and any meaningful role for the vice president, whose duties were largely undefined by the Constitution, soon disappeared.

The Constitution created a federal Supreme Court but beyond that was silent about the court system. The Judiciary Act of 1789 set the size of the Supreme Court at 6 members; it also established 13 federal district courts and 3 circuit courts of appeal. Supreme Court justices spent much of their time serving on these circuit courts, a distasteful duty whose long hours "riding the circuit" caused one justice to grumble that Congress had made him a "traveling postboy." The Judiciary Act made it clear that federal courts had the right to review decisions of the state courts and specified cases over which the Supreme Court would have original jurisdiction. Washington appointed John Jay of New York, a stanch Federalist, as the first chief justice.

Hamilton's Financial Program

When Congress called on Alexander Hamilton to prepare a report on the nation's finances, the new secretary of the Treasury undertook the assignment eagerly. A brilliant thinker and an ambitious politician, he did not intend to be a minor figure in the new administration.

Convinced that human nature was fundamentally selfish, Hamilton believed that, to succeed, the government needed to appeal to the self-interest of the rich and well-born. He took as his model Great Britain, whose greatness he attributed to its system of public finance and its preeminence in commerce and manufacturing. Thus Hamilton set out to achieve two goals. He intended to use federal power to encourage manufacturing and commerce in order to make the United States economically strong and independent of Europe. And he was determined to link the interests of the wealthy with those of the new government.

Hamilton's Two Goals

Neither goal could be achieved until the federal government solved its two most pressing financial problems: revenue and credit. Without revenue it could not be effective. Without credit—the faith of merchants and other nations that the government would repay its debts—it would lack the ability to borrow. Hamilton proposed that all $52 million of the federal debt, much of it generated by the Revolutionary War, be paid in full (or funded). He also recommended that the federal government assume responsibility for the remaining $25 million in debts that individual states owed—a policy of "assumption." He intended with these twin policies to put the new federal government on a sound financial footing and enhance its power by increasing its need for revenue and making the wealthy look to the national government, not the states. Hamilton also proposed a series of excise taxes, including a controversial 25 percent levy on whiskey, to help meet government expenses.

Funding and Assumption

After heated debate, Congress deadlocked over funding and assumption. Finally, over dinner with Hamilton, Jefferson and James Madison of Virginia agreed to support his proposal if, after 10 years in Philadelphia, the permanent seat of government would be located in the South, on the Potomac River between Virginia and Maryland. Aided by this understanding, funding and assumption passed Congress. In 1791 Congress also approved a 20-year charter for the first Bank of the United States. The bank would hold government deposits and issue banknotes that would be received in payment of all debts owed the federal government. Congress proved less receptive to the rest of Hamilton's program, although a limited tariff to encourage manufacturing and several excise taxes, including the one on whiskey, won approval.

Bank of the United States

Opposition to Hamilton's Program

The passage of Hamilton's program caused a permanent rupture among supporters of the Constitution. Madison, who had collaborated closely with Hamilton in the 1780s, broke with his former ally over funding and assumption. Jefferson finally went over to the opposition when Hamilton announced plans for a national bank. Eventually the two warring factions organized themselves into political parties: the Republicans, led by Jefferson

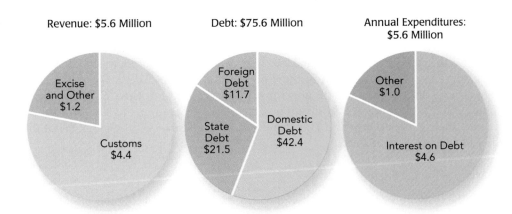

Revenue: $5.6 Million

Excise and Other $1.2

Customs $4.4

Debt: $75.6 Million

Foreign Debt $11.7

State Debt $21.5

Domestic Debt $42.4

Annual Expenditures: $5.6 Million

Other $1.0

Interest on Debt $4.6

Hamilton's Financial System
Under Hamilton's financial system, more than 80 percent of federal revenues went to pay the interest on the national debt. Note that most of the revenue came from tariff duties.

A study in contrasts, Jefferson and Hamilton increasingly came into conflict in Washington's administration. Despite his aristocratic upbringing, Jefferson (left) was awkward, loose-jointed, reserved, and ill at ease in public. Testifying before a congressional committee, he casually lounged in a chair and spoke in a rambling, nonstop manner. "Yet he scattered information wherever he went," conceded Senator William Maclay of Pennsylvania, "and some even brilliant sentiments sparkled from him." Hamilton (right), though short of stature, cut a dashing figure with his erect bearing, strutting manner, meticulous dress, and carefully powdered hair. Declared the wife of the British ambassador: "I have scarcely ever been more charmed with the vivacity and conversation of any man."

and Madison, and the Federalists, led by Hamilton and Adams.* But the division emerged slowly over several years.

Hamilton's program promoted the commercial sector at the expense of semisubsistence farmers. Thus it rekindled many of the concerns that had surfaced during the struggle over ratification of the Constitution. The ideology of the Revolution had stressed that republics inevitably contained groups who sought power in order to destroy popular liberties and overthrow the republic. To some Americans, Hamilton's program seemed a clear threat to establish a privileged and powerful financial aristocracy—perhaps even a monarchy.

Fears of a Financial Aristocracy

Who, after all, would benefit from the funding proposal? During and after the Revolution, the value of notes issued by the Continental Congress dropped sharply. Speculators had bought up most of these notes for a fraction of their face value from small farmers and workers. If the government finally paid back the debt, speculators would profit accordingly. Equally disturbing, members of Congress had been purchasing the notes before the adoption of Hamilton's program. Nearly half the members of the House owned U.S. securities.

---

*The Republican party of the 1790s, sometimes referred to as the Jeffersonian Republicans, is not to be confused with the modern-day Republican party, which originated in the 1850s.

Similarly, the national bank struck its critics as a dangerous mimicking of English corruption. In Great Britain, the Bank of England's loans to many members of Parliament gave it great political influence. Jefferson warned that the same thing would happen in the United States: "paper men" would become rich not by producing anything but by shuffling paper, trading notes, and benefiting from the financial legislation they themselves passed. These fears were heightened because Americans had little experience with banks: only three existed in the country when the Bank of the United States was chartered. One member of Congress expressed a common attitude when he said that he would no more be caught entering a bank than a house of prostitution.

Systems of Corruption

Then, too, banks and commerce were a part of the urban environment that rural Americans so distrusted. Although Hamilton's opponents admitted that a certain amount of commerce was necessary, they believed that it should remain subordinate. Hamilton's program, in contrast, encouraged manufacturing and urbanization, developments that history suggested were incompatible with liberty and equality.

After Congress approved the bank bill, Washington hesitated to sign it. When he consulted his cabinet, Jefferson stressed that the Constitution did not specifically authorize Congress to charter a bank. Both he and Madison upheld the idea of strict construction—that the Constitution should be interpreted narrowly and the federal government restricted to powers expressly delegated to it. Otherwise, the federal government would be the judge of its own powers, and there would be no safeguard against the abuse of power.

Strict Construction of the Constitution

Hamilton countered that the Constitution contained implied as well as enumerated powers. He particularly emphasized the clause that permitted Congress to make all laws "necessary and proper" to carry out its duties. A bank would be useful in carrying out the enumerated powers of regulating commerce and maintaining the public credit; Congress thus had a right to decide whether to establish one. Because the Constitution could not anticipate all future developments, the government needed flexibility to meet its responsibilities. In the end Washington accepted Hamilton's arguments and signed the bill.

Economically Hamilton's program was a success. The government's credit was restored, and the national bank ended the inflation of the previous two decades and created a sound currency. In addition, Hamilton's theory of implied powers and broad construction gave the nation the flexibility necessary to respond to unanticipated crises.

The Emergence of Political Parties

Members of the Revolutionary generation fervently hoped that political parties would not take root in the United States. "If I could not go to heaven but with a party, I would not go at all," remarked Jefferson. Influenced by radical English republican thought, American critics condemned parties as narrow interest groups that placed selfishness and party loyalty above a concern for the public good. Despite Americans' distrust of such institutions, however, the United States became the first nation to establish truly popular parties.

Social conditions encouraged the rise of parties. Because property ownership was widespread, the nation had a broad **suffrage.** During the American Revolution legislatures lowered property requirements in many states, increasing the number of voters still further. If party members hoped to hold office, they had to offer a program attractive to the broader voting public. When parties acted as representatives of economic and social interest groups, they became one means by which a large electorate could make its feelings known. In addition, the United States had the highest literacy rate in the world and the largest number of newspapers, further encouraging political interest and participation. Finally, the fact that well-known patriots of the Revolution headed both the Federalists and the Republicans helped

Social Conditions Encourage Political Parties

The execution of King Louis XVI by guillotine left Americans divided over the French Revolution.

defuse the charge that either party was hostile to the Revolution or the Constitution.

Americans and the French Revolution

While domestic issues first split the supporters of the Constitution, it was a crisis in Europe that pushed Americans toward political parties. Americans had hoped that their revolution would spark similar movements for liberty on the European continent, and in fact the American Revolution was only one of a series of revolutions in the late eighteenth century that shook the Western world, the most important of which began in France in 1789. There a rising population and the collapse of government finances sparked a challenge to royal authority that became a mass revolution. The French revolutionary ideals of "liberty, equality, and fraternity" eventually spilled across the continent, carried by the French army.

Americans first hailed the Revolution as the first stirring of liberty on the European continent. Many rejoiced to learn that the Bastille prison had been stormed in July; the new National Assembly had abolished feudal privileges and adopted the Declaration of the Rights of Man. But by 1793, American enthusiasm for the Revolution had cooled after radical elements instituted a reign of terror, executing the king and queen and many of the nobility. The French republic even outlawed Christianity and substituted the worship of Reason. Finally in 1793 republican France and monarchical England went to war. Americans were deeply divided over whether the United States should continue its old alliance with France or support Great Britain.

Differing Views of the Revolution

Hamilton and his allies viewed the French Revolution as sheer anarchy. Its leaders seemed to be destroying the very institutions that held civilization together: the church, social classes, property, law and order. The United States, Hamilton argued, should renounce the 1778 treaty of alliance with France and side with Britain. By contrast, Jefferson and his followers supported the treaty and regarded France as a sister republic. They believed that despite deplorable excesses, its revolution was spreading the doctrine of liberty. Britain remained repressive and corrupt, presided over by the same tyrannical king who had made war on the colonies. Jefferson insisted that, as neutrals, Americans had every right to trade with France as much as with England.

Washington's Neutral Course

Washington, for his part, was convinced that in order to prosper, the United States must remain independent of European quarrels and wars. Thus he issued a proclamation of American neutrality and tempered Jefferson's efforts to support France.

Neutral Rights

Under international law, neutrals could trade with belligerents—nations at war—as long as the trade had existed before the outbreak of hostilities and did not involve war supplies. But both France and Great Britain refused to respect the rights of neutrals in the midst of their desperate struggle. They began intercepting American ships and confiscating cargoes. In addition, Britain, which badly needed manpower to maintain its powerful navy, impressed into service American sailors it suspected of being British subjects. Britain also continued to maintain the western forts it had promised to evacuate in 1783, and it closed the West Indies, a traditional source of trade, to American ships.

Jay's Treaty

Recognizing that the United States was not strong enough to challenge Britain militarily, Washington sent John Jay to negotiate the differences between the two countries. Although Jay did persuade the British to withdraw their troops from the

Northwest, he could gain no other concessions. Disappointed, Washington nonetheless submitted Jay's Treaty to the Senate. After a bitter debate, the Senate narrowly ratified it in June of 1795.

The Federalists and the Republicans Organize

Thus events in Europe contributed directly to the rise of parties in the United States by stimulating fears over the course of American development. By the mid-1790s both sides were organizing on a national basis. Hamilton took the lead in coordinating the Federalist party, which grew out of the voting bloc in Congress that had enacted his economic program. Increasingly, Washington drew closer to Federalist advisers and policies and became the symbol of the party, although he clung to the vision of a nonpartisan administration.

The guiding genius of the opposition movement was Hamilton's onetime colleague James Madison. Jefferson, who resigned as secretary of state at the end of 1793, became the symbolic head of the party, much as Washington reluctantly headed the Federalists. But it was Madison who orchestrated the Republican strategy and lined up their voting bloc in the House. The disputes over Jay's Treaty and over the whiskey tax in 1794 and 1795 gave the Republicans popular issues, and they began organizing on the state and local levels. Because of broad support for the Constitution, Republican leaders had to be careful to distinguish between opposing the administration and opposing the Constitution. They had to overcome the ingrained idea that an opposition party was seditious. Indeed, it was by no means clear that an opposition party could arise without threatening the government itself.

Republicans in Opposition

As more and more members of Congress allied themselves with one faction or the other, voting became increasingly partisan. By 1796 even minor matters were decided by partisan votes. Gradually, party organization filtered downward to local communities.

The 1796 Election

As long as Washington remained head of the Federalists, they enjoyed a huge advantage. But in 1796 the weary president, stung by the abuse heaped on him by the opposition press, announced that he would not accept a third term. In doing so, he set a two-term precedent that future presidents followed until Franklin Roosevelt. In his Farewell Address Washington warned against the dangers of parties and urged a return to the earlier nonpartisan system. That vision, however, had become obsolete: parties were an effective way of expressing the interests of different social and economic groups within the nation. When the Republicans chose Thomas Jefferson to oppose John Adams, the possibility of a constitutional system without parties ended.

The framers of the Constitution did not anticipate that political parties would run competing candidates for both the presidency and the vice presidency. Thus they provided that, of the candidates running for president, the one with the most electoral votes would win and the one with the second highest number would become vice president. But Hamilton strongly disliked both Adams and Jefferson. Ever the intriguer, he tried to manipulate the electoral vote so that the Federalist vice presidential candidate, Thomas Pinckney of South Carolina, would be elected president. In the ensuing confusion, Adams won with 71 electoral votes, and his rival, Jefferson, gained the vice presidency with 68 votes.

Federalist and Republican Ideologies

The fault line between Federalists and Republicans reflected basic divisions in American life. Geographically, the Federalists were strongest in New England, with its commercial ties to Great Britain and its powerful tradition of hierarchy and order. Moving farther south, the party became progressively weaker. Of the southernmost states, the Federalists enjoyed significant strength only in aristocratic South Carolina. The Republicans won solid support in semisubsistence areas such as the West, where farmers were only weakly involved with commerce. The middle states were closely contested, although the most cosmopolitan and commercially oriented elements remained the core of Federalist strength.

Each party looked both forward and backward: toward certain traditions of the past as well as toward newer social currents that would shape America in the nineteenth century.

Federalist Ideas

Most Federalists viewed themselves as a kind of natural aristocracy making a last desperate stand against the excesses of democracy. They clung to the notion that the upper class should rule over its social and economic inferiors. In supporting the established social order, most Federalists opposed unbridled individualism. In their view, government should regulate individual behavior for the good of society and protect property from the violent and unruly. Federalists were almost obsessed by fear of the "mob": in a republic, they argued, government had to restrain popular power.

Although the Federalists opposed the rising tide of democracy and individualism, they were remarkably forward-looking in their economic ideas. They sensed that the United States would become the major economic and military power of their vision only by prospering through commerce and economic development. The government ought to encourage the growth of commerce and manufacturing, they argued.

Republican Ideas

The Republicans, in contrast, looked backward to the traditional Revolutionary fear that government power threatened liberty. The Treasury, they warned, was corrupting Congress, the army would enslave the people, and broad construction of the Constitution would make the federal government all-powerful. Nor did their economic ideals anticipate future American development. For Republicans, agriculture was the foundation of American liberty and virtue. To be sure, leaders such as Jefferson and Madison recognized that some commercial activity was necessary, especially to sell America's agricultural surplus abroad. But Jefferson and his followers believed that republican values would be preserved only by limiting commerce and promoting household manufacturing instead of industry. Republicans also failed to appreciate the role of financial institutions in promoting economic development. Instead, Republicans focused on the abuses of speculators, bank directors, and holders of the public debt.

Yet the Jeffersonians were more farsighted in matters of equality and personal liberty. Their faith in the people put them in tune with the emerging egalitarian temper of society. They embraced the virtues of individualism, hoping to reduce government to the bare essentials in order to free individuals to develop their potential without interference. And they looked to the West—the land of small farms and a more equal society—as the means to preserve opportunity and American values.

The Presidency of John Adams

As president, John Adams became the head of the Federalists, although in many ways he was out of step with his party. Unlike Hamilton, Adams felt no pressing need to aid the wealthy, nor was he fully committed to Hamilton's commercial-industrial vision. As a crusty revolutionary leader who in the 1780s had served as American minister to England, Adams also opposed any alliance with Britain.

Increasingly Adams and Hamilton clashed over policies and party leadership. Part of the problem stemmed from personalities. Adams was so thin-skinned that it was difficult for anyone to get along with him, and Hamilton's intrigues in the 1796 election had not improved relations between the two men. Although Hamilton had resigned from the Treasury Department in 1795, key members of Adams's cabinet regularly turned to the former secretary for advice. Indeed, they opposed Adams so often that the frustrated president sometimes dealt with them, according to Jefferson, "by dashing and trampling his wig on the floor." The feud between Adams and Hamilton did not bode well for the Federalist party.

The Naval War with France

Adams began his term trying to balance relations with both Great Britain and France. Because the terms of Jay's Treaty were so favorable to the British, the French in retaliation set their navy and privateers to raiding American shipping. To resolve the conflict, Adams dispatched three envoys to France in 1797, but the French foreign minister demanded a bribe before negotiations could even begin. The American representatives refused, and when news of these discussions became public, it became known as the XYZ Affair. (In the official documents the Adams administration substituted the letters X, Y, and Z for the names of the French officials involved.) A tremendous outcry ensued.

XYZ Affair

Confronted with such deeply felt anger, Federalist leaders saw a chance to retain power by exploiting the national emergency and going to war with France. With war fever running high, Congress in 1798 repudiated the French alliance of 1778 and enlarged the army and navy. Republicans suspected that the real purpose of the army was not to fight the French army—none existed in North America—but to crush the opposition party and establish a military despotism. All that remained was for Adams to whip up popular feeling and lead the nation into war.

But Adams hesitated, afraid he would become a scapegoat if his policies failed. Furthermore, he distrusted standing armies and preferred the navy as the nation's primary defense. So an unofficial naval war broke out between the United States and France as ships in each navy raided the fleets of the other, while Britain continued to impress American sailors and seize ships suspected of trading with France.

Suppression at Home

Meanwhile, Federalist leaders attempted to suppress disloyalty at home. In the summer of 1798 Congress passed several measures known together as the Alien and Sedition Acts. The Alien Act authorized the president to arrest and deport aliens suspected of "treasonable" leanings. Although never used, the act directly threatened immigrants who had not yet become citizens, many of whom were prominent Jeffersonians. To limit the number of immigrant voters—again, most of them Republicans—the **Naturalization Act** increased the period of residence required to become a naturalized citizen from 5 to 14 years. But the most controversial law was the Sedition Act, which established heavy fines and even imprisonment for writing, speaking, or publishing anything of "a false, scandalous and malicious" nature against the government or any officer of the government.

Alien and Sedition Acts

Because of the partisan way it was enforced, the Sedition Act quickly became a symbol of tyranny. Federalists convicted and imprisoned a number of prominent Republican editors, and several Republican papers ceased publication. In all, 25 people were arrested under the law and 10 convicted and imprisoned, including Matthew Lyon, a Republican member of Congress from Vermont.

The crisis over the Sedition Act forced Republicans to develop a broader conception of freedom of the press. Previously, most Americans had agreed that newspapers should not be restrained before publication but that they could be punished afterward for sedition. Jefferson and others now argued that the American government was uniquely based on the free expression of public opinion, and thus criticism of the government was not a sign of criminal intent. Only overtly seditious acts, not opinions, should be subject to prosecution. The courts eventually endorsed this view, adopting a new, more absolute view of freedom of speech guaranteed by the First Amendment.

The Republican-controlled legislatures of Virginia and Kentucky each responded to the crisis of 1798 by passing a set of resolutions. Madison secretly wrote those for Virginia, and Jefferson those for Kentucky. These resolutions proclaimed that the Constitution was a compact among sovereign states that delegated strictly limited powers to the federal government. When the government exceeded those limits and threatened the liberties of citizens, states had the right to interpose their authority.

But Jefferson and Madison were not ready to rend a union that had so recently been forged. The two men intended for the Virginia and Kentucky resolutions only to rally public opinion to the Republican cause. They opposed any effort to resist federal authority by force.

The Election of 1800

With a naval war raging on the high seas and the Alien and Sedition Acts sparking debate at home, Adams suddenly shocked his party by negotiating a peace treaty with France. It was a courageous act, for Adams not only split his party in two but also ruined his own chances for reelection by driving Hamilton's pro-British wing of the party into open opposition. But the nation benefited, as peace returned.

With the Federalist party split, Republican prospects in 1800 were bright. Again the party chose Jefferson to run against Adams, along with Aaron Burr for vice president. The Republicans' efficient party organization mobilized supporters, whereas the Federalists' high-handed policies and disdain for the "mob" doomed them in a republic where so many citizens could vote.

Sweeping to victory, the Republicans won the presidency, as well as control of both houses of Congress for the first time. Yet the election again demonstrated the fragility of the fledgling political system. Jefferson and Burr received an equal number of votes, but the Constitution did not distinguish between the votes for president and vice president. With the election tied, the decision lay with the House of Representatives, where each state was allotted one vote. Because Burr refused to step aside for Jefferson, the election remained deadlocked for almost a week, until the Federalists decided that Jefferson represented the lesser of two evils. They allowed his election on

Election of 1800

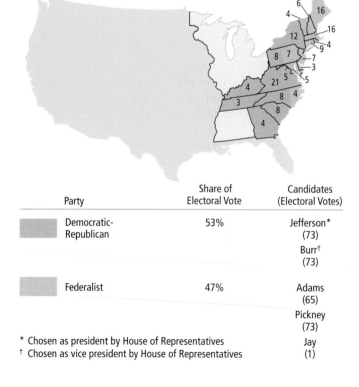

Party	Share of Electoral Vote	Candidates (Electoral Votes)
Democratic-Republican	53%	Jefferson* (73)
		Burr† (73)
Federalist	47%	Adams (65)
		Pickney (73)
		Jay (1)

* Chosen as president by House of Representatives
† Chosen as vice president by House of Representatives

the 36th ballot. In 1804 the Twelfth Amendment corrected the problem, specifying that electors were to vote separately for president and vice president.

John Marshall and Judicial Review

Having lost both the presidency and control of Congress in 1800, the Federalists took steps to shore up their power before Jefferson took office. They did so by expanding the size of the federal court system, the one branch of the federal government that they still controlled. The Judiciary Act of 1801 created 6 circuit courts and 16 new judgeships. Federalists justified these "midnight appointments" (executed by Adams in the last weeks of his term) on the grounds that the expanding nation required a larger judiciary.

Among Adams's last-minute appointments was that of William Marbury as justice of the peace for the District of Columbia. When James Madison assumed the office of secretary of state under the new administration, he found a batch of undelivered commissions, including Marbury's. Wishing to appoint loyal Republicans to these posts, Jefferson instructed Madison not to hand over the commissions, whereupon Marbury sued. The case of *Marbury v. Madison* went directly to the Supreme Court in 1803.

Marbury v. Madison

Chief Justice John Marshall, a Federalist and one of Adams's late-term appointments, actually ruled in favor of Madison—but in a way that strengthened the power of the federal courts. Marshall affirmed the right of the Supreme Court to review statutes and interpret the meaning of the Constitution. "It is emphatically the province of and duty of the judicial department to say what the law is," he wrote in upholding the doctrine of **judicial review.** In Marshall's view, the Court "must of necessity expound and interpret" the Constitution and the laws when one statute conflicted with another or when a law violated the framework of the Constitution.

Marshall and his colleagues later asserted the power of the Court to review the constitutionality not only of federal but also of state laws in *Fletcher v. Peck* (1810). In that dispute it struck down a Georgia law. In fact, during his long tenure as Chief Justice (over 30 years), John Marshall extended judicial review to all acts of government. The power of judicial review became a key element in the American constitutional system.

John Marshall

Federalist Achievements and Disappointments

As John Adams left office, he looked back with mixed feelings on the 12 years that the Federalist party had held power. Under Washington's firm leadership and his own, his party had made the Constitution a workable instrument of government. The Federalists had proved that a republican form of government was compatible with stability and order. They had established economic policies that brought a return of prosperity. Washington had established the principle of American neutrality in foreign affairs, which became an accepted ideal by both parties for decades to come.

But most Federalists took no solace in such reflections, for the forces of history seemed to be running against them. In the election of 1800 they stood as the champions of order and hierarchy, of government by the wellborn, of a society in which social betters guided their respectful inferiors. They had waged one last desperate battle to save their disintegrating world—and had lost. Power had fallen into the hands of the ignorant rabble, led by that demagogue Thomas Jefferson.

The Political Culture of the Early Republic

Such overheated sentiments were a hallmark of the young republic; perhaps understandably so, given the nation's uncertain future. Two distinct parties had emerged during the 1790s, but both longed to reestablish a one-party system. Neither

Federalists nor Republicans could accept the novel idea that political parties might peacefully resolve differences among competing social, geographic, and economic interests. Instead, each party regarded its opponents as a dangerous faction of ambitious men striving to increase their wealth and power at the expense of republican liberty.

What resulted was a political culture marked by verbal and, at times, physical violence. Republicans accused Washington and Hamilton of being British agents and monarchists; Federalists denounced Jefferson as an atheist and his partisans as a pack of "blood-drinking cannibals." The leading Republican newspaper editor in Philadelphia plunged into a street brawl with his Federalist rival; two members of Congress slugged it out on the floor of the House of Representatives. Mobs threatened the leaders of both parties, and at the height of the crisis of 1798–1799, Adams smuggled guns into his home for protection. In this poisonous atmosphere, Jefferson recounted sadly, "men who have been intimate all their lives, cross the streets to avoid meeting."

Popular Participation in Political Festivals

The deepening divisions among national leaders also encouraged ordinary Americans to take an interest in politics. Beginning in the 1790s and for decades thereafter, activists in cities and villages everywhere in the new republic organized grand festivals to celebrate American patriotism and the glories of the Republicans or the Federalists. That grassroots movement democratized the conduct of politics by educating men and women, white and black, voters and nonvoters alike, about the issues of the day. In doing so, such activities encouraged strong partisan loyalties.

Parades and Celebrations

Holidays such as the Fourth of July or Washington's Birthday became prime occasions for local party leaders to rally their fellow-citizens. They hosted celebrations that began with parades in which marchers, hoisting banners to identify their particular trade, militia company, or social club, processed through the main street to a church, meeting hall, or public square. There the assembled throng of marchers and onlookers sang patriotic songs, recited prayers, and listened to the reading of the Declaration of Independence, all capped by a rousing sermon or political oration. Then the party started: in the North, taverns and hotels hosted community banquets; in the South, the crowds flocked to outdoor barbecues. Everywhere the feasts ended with many toasts to the glories of republican liberty and, of course, to the superiority of Federalists or Republicans.

These local celebrations not only made an impact on those who were able to attend the festivities but also reached a wider audience through newspaper accounts. During the 1790s and beyond, the number of local or regional newspapers in the new republic mushroomed, but their coverage was far from objective. Most editors were either staunch Federalists or ardent Republicans, who could be counted on to publish glowing accounts of the festivities sponsored by their party and to instruct a much wider audience about party policies and values.

Women's Participation

These political festivals and newspaper accounts aimed to woo the loyalty of white adult males who held enough property to vote. But they also sought the support of the white women who joined in the crowds and even took part in parades. In one New Jersey village, the folks lining the parade route cheered as "16 young ladies uniformed in white with garlands in their hats" marched past, playing a patriotic anthem on their flutes. Federalists and Republicans alike encouraged women's involvement on these occasions, hoping that displays of approval from "the American Fair" would encourage husbands and male admirers to support their parties. The engagement of white women in these local celebrations at once reflected and encouraged their interest in partisan politics. After all, *The Coquette* (1797), a best-seller (and the first novel written by an American woman, Hannah Webster Foster), affirmed that "truly republican" women should "claim the right of inquiring" into the workings of government and freely discuss politics with men at social gatherings.

Virtue in a Side of Beef

Analyzing the Symbols of Political Culture

Today we tend to focus on parades as celebrations of political or martial events: Fourth of July, Memorial Day, and Veterans Day. But in the early Republic the symbols of political culture extended far beyond narrow politics or commemoration of wars.

This aquatint by Joseph Yeager commemorates the two-mile long "Procession of the Victuallers" held in Philadelphia on March 15, 1821. The victuallers—suppliers of food—hauled over 86,000 pounds of beef, pork, lamb, and other foods to the High Street Market in about 100 carts. The butchers parade proudly in traditional white frocks ahead of a two-story float. In the thriving market economy of urban Philadelphia, butchers eagerly displayed their civic pride at the same time that they advertised and sold their wares.

African-American Celebrations

While white women gained some recognition in early national political culture, African Americans confronted formidable obstacles. They, too, were drawn to political festivals, only to find that whites were determined to keep them away. In the years after 1800, bullies often drove black men and women from Fourth of July celebrations with taunts, threats, and assaults. James Forten, a leading citizen of Philadelphia's African American community, complained that because of the hostility of drunken whites, "black people, upon certain days of public jubilee, dare not to be seen" on the streets after noon.

The growing free black population of northern cities countered that opposition by organizing celebrations to express their own political convictions. The first recorded African American political festival took place in New York City on July 5, 1800, when blacks paraded to celebrate the passage of a state law providing for the gradual emancipation of slaves. (That city's whites refused to allow African Americans to hold their parade on the Fourth of July.) Thereafter, free blacks in other northern cities established annual holidays to celebrate the abolition of the slave trade in Britain and the United States as well as the successful slave revolt in the Caribbean that resulted in the founding of Haiti in 1804 (see page 362). Those acts of defiance—the spectacle of blacks marching down the main streets with banners flying and bands of music playing, and of black men and women hanging on the words of black orators who publicly condemned slavery—only inflamed racial hatred among many whites, who pelted participants with dirt and curses.

But African Americans continued to parade—and to press their demands for full citizenship in the new republic by persuading sympathetic white printers to publish poetry, slave narratives, and pamphlets composed by black authors. The strategy of those

Calling for Full Citizenship

writings was to refute racist notions that people of African descent were inferior to whites by drawing attention to the intelligence, virtue, and patriotism of black American women and men, both free and enslaved. Typical was the autobiography of Venture Smith, the first slave narrative published in the United States (1798), which followed his captivity as a young boy in West Africa through his lifelong struggle in New England to purchase his own freedom and that of his wife and children. Hard-working and thrifty, resourceful and determined to better himself and his family, Venture Smith's story invited white readers to conclude that he was as true a republican and a self-made man as Benjamin Franklin.

Jefferson in Power

The growing political engagement of ordinary white Americans played an important role in electing Thomas Jefferson to the presidency. He later referred to his election as "the Revolution of 1800," asserting that it "was as real a revolution in the principles of our government as that of 1776 was in its form." That claim exaggerates: Jefferson's presidency did little to enhance political rights or social opportunities of white women or African Americans. Even so, during the following two decades Republicans did set the United States on a more democratic course. And in their dealings with Britain and France, as well as with the Indian tribes of the West, Republican administrations defined, for better and for worse, a fuller sense of American nationality.

The New Capital City

Thomas Jefferson was the first president to be inaugurated in the new capital, Washington, D.C. In 1791 George Washington had commissioned Pierre Charles L'Enfant, a French architect and engineer who had served in the American Revolution, to draw up plans for the new seat of government. L'Enfant designed a city with broad avenues, statues and fountains, parks and plazas, and a central mall. Because the Federalists believed that government was the paramount power in a nation, they had intended that the city would be a new Rome—a cultural, intellectual, and commercial center of the Republic.

The new city fell far short of this grandiose dream. It was located in a swampy river bottom near the head of the Potomac, and the surrounding hills rendered the spot oppressively hot and muggy during the summer. The streets were filled with tree stumps and became seas of mud after a rain. Much of the District was wooded, and virtually all of it remained unoccupied. When the government moved to its new residence in 1800, the Senate chamber, where Jefferson took the oath of office, was the only part of the Capitol that had been completed.

This isolated and unimpressive capital reflected the new president's attitude toward government. Distrustful of centralized power of any kind, Jefferson deliberately set out to remake the national government into one of limited scope that touched few people's daily lives. The states rather than the federal government were "the most competent administrators for our domestic concerns," he asserted in his inaugural address. Ever the individualist, he recommended a government that left people "free to regulate their own pursuits of industry and improvement."

Thomas Jefferson's invitations to dinner may strike readers today as formal, but Jefferson was actually attempting to set a tone of democratic informality. One Federalist did not miss the implication and complained, "It is Th: Jefferson *not the* President *that invites—& yet were he not the President I presume I should not be invited."*

Jefferson's Philosophy

Jefferson was a product of the Enlightenment, with its faith in the power of human reason to improve society and decipher the universe. He considered "the will of the majority" to be "the only sure guardian of the rights of man," which he defined as "life, liberty, and the pursuit of happiness." Although he conceded that the masses might err, he was confident they would soon return to correct principles. His faith in human virtue exceeded that of most of the founding generation, yet in good republican fashion, he feared those in power, even if they had been elected by the people. Government seemed to Jefferson a necessary evil at best.

To Jefferson, agriculture was a morally superior way of life. "Those who labour in the earth are the chosen people of God, if ever he had a chosen people," he wrote in *Notes on the State of Virginia* (1787). Like Crèvecoeur, Jefferson praised rural life for nourishing the honesty, independence, and virtue so essential in a republic. Government would "remain virtuous . . . as long as [the American people] are chiefly agricultural," he assured James Madison. Rather than encouraging large-scale factories, Jefferson wanted to preserve small household manufacturing, which was an essential part of the rural economy. He was never able to overcome his belief, rooted in the republican ideology of the Revolution, that cities and commerce promoted speculation, greed, and useless luxury.

Although Jefferson asserted that "the tree of liberty must be refreshed from time to time by the blood of patriots and tyrants," his reputation as a radical was undeserved. While he wanted to extend the suffrage to a greater number of Americans, he clung to the traditional republican idea that voters should own property and thus be economically independent. One of the largest slaveholders in the country, he increasingly muffled his once-bold condemnation of slavery, and in the last years of his life he reproached critics of the institution who sought to prevent it from expanding westward. Nor did his belief in free speech mean that he objected to state governments punishing political criticism.

Slaveholding aristocrat and apostle of democracy, lofty theorist and pragmatic politician, Jefferson was a complex, at times contradictory, personality. But like most politicians, he was flexible in his approach to problems and tried to balance means and ends. And like most leaders, he quickly discovered that he confronted very different problems in power than he had in opposition.

Agrarian Values

Jefferson's Economic Policies

The new president quickly proceeded to cut spending and to reduce the size of the government. He also abolished the internal taxes enacted by the Federalists, including the controversial levy on whiskey, and thus was able to get rid of all tax collectors and inspectors. Land sales and the tariff duties would supply the funds needed to run the scaled-down government.

The most serious spending cuts were made in the military branches. Jefferson slashed the army budget in half, decreasing the army to 3,000 men. In a national emergency, he reasoned, the militia could defend the country. Jefferson reduced the navy even more, halting work on powerful frigates authorized during the naval war with France.

By such steps, Jefferson made significant progress toward paying off Hamilton's national debt. Still, he did not entirely dismantle the Federalists' economic program. Funding and assumption could not be reversed—the nation's honor was pledged to paying these debts, and Jefferson understood the importance of maintaining the nation's credit. The tariff had to be retained as a source of revenue to meet government expenses. More surprising, Jefferson argued that the national bank should be left to run its course until 1811, when its charter would expire. In reality, he expanded the bank's operations and, in words reminiscent of Hamilton, advocated tying banks and members of the business class to the government by rewarding those who supported the Republican party. In effect, practical politics had triumphed over agrarian economics.

Coming to Accept Hamilton's Policies

Whites and Indians in the West

For all his pragmatism, Jefferson still viewed the lands stretching from the Apppalachians to the Pacific through the perspective of his agrarian ideals. America's vast spaces provided enough land to last for a thousand generations, he predicted in his inaugural address, enough to transform the United States into "an empire of liberty."

The Miami Confederacy Resists

That optimistic vision contrasted sharply with the views of most Federalists, who feared the West as a threat to social order and stability. In the 1790s they had good reason to fear. British troops refused to leave their forts in the Northwest, and Indian nations still controlled most of the region. Recognizing that fact, the United States conceded that Indian nations had the right to negotiate as sovereign powers. North of the Ohio, leaders of the Miami Confederacy, composed of eight tribes, stoutly refused to sell their homelands without "the united voice of the confederacy."

Yet white settlers continued to squat on Indian lands, leading to continuing violence. In such borderland clashes, vengeance often seemed brutally personal, as when George Rogers Clark not only took a half dozen Indian captives and "knocked their brains out" but also dipped "his hands in their blood, rubbing it several times on his cheeks, yelping as a Savage," as one observer reported. Similarly enraged Indians dismembered white corpses and distributed pieces among tribes who claimed a part in the revenge. When Indians refused to sell their lands, the Washington administration sent 1,500 soldiers in 1790 under General Josiah Harmar to force the Indians to leave by burning their homes and fields. The Miami Confederacy, led by Blue Jacket and Little Turtle, roundly defeated the whites. Harmar was court-martialed, the nation embarrassed, and a second expedition organized the following year under General Arthur St. Clair. This force of over 2,000 was again routed by Little Turtle, whose warriors killed 600 and wounded another 300. The defeat was the worst in the history of Indian wars undertaken by the United States. (In contrast, General Custer's famous defeat in 1876 counted 264 fatalities.) If the United States could not vanquish what it regarded as "savages," how would the republic prosper?

President Washington dispatched yet another army of 2,000 to the Ohio Valley, commanded by "Mad Anthony" Wayne, an accomplished general. At the Battle of Fallen Timbers in August 1794, Wayne won a decisive victory, breaking the Indians' hold on the Northwest. In the Treaty of Greenville (1795), the tribes **ceded** the southern two-thirds of the area between Lake Erie and the Ohio River, opening it up to white families. Federalists were still not eager to see the land settled. Although they allowed the sale of federal land, they kept the price high, with a required purchase of at least 640 acres—more than four times the size of most American farms.

Once in power, Jefferson and the Republicans encouraged settlement by reducing the minimum tract that buyers could purchase (to 320 acres) and by offering land on credit. Sales boomed. By 1820 more than 2 million whites lived in a region they had first entered only 50 years earlier. From Jefferson's perspective, western expansion was a blessing economically, socially, and even politically, because most of the new westerners were Republican.

Victories of Little Turtle and Blue Jacket

Treaty of Greenville

Doubling the Size of the Nation

With Spain's colonial empire weakening, Americans were confident that before long they would gain control of Florida and the rest of the Mississippi, either through purchase or by military occupation. Spain had already agreed, in Pinckney's Treaty (see page 206), to allow Americans to navigate the lower Mississippi River. In 1802, however, Spain suddenly retracted this right. More alarming, word came that France was about to take control of Louisiana—the territory lying between the Mississippi River and the Rocky Mountains—after a secret agreement with Spain. Under the leadership of Napoleon Bonaparte, France had become the most powerful nation on the European continent, with the military might to protect its new colony and to block American expansion.

Jefferson dispatched James Monroe to Paris to join Robert Livingston, the American minister, in negotiating the purchase of New Orleans and West Florida from the French and thus securing control of the Mississippi. The timing was fortunate: With war looming again in Europe, Napoleon lost interest in Louisiana. He needed money,

The Louisiana Purchase

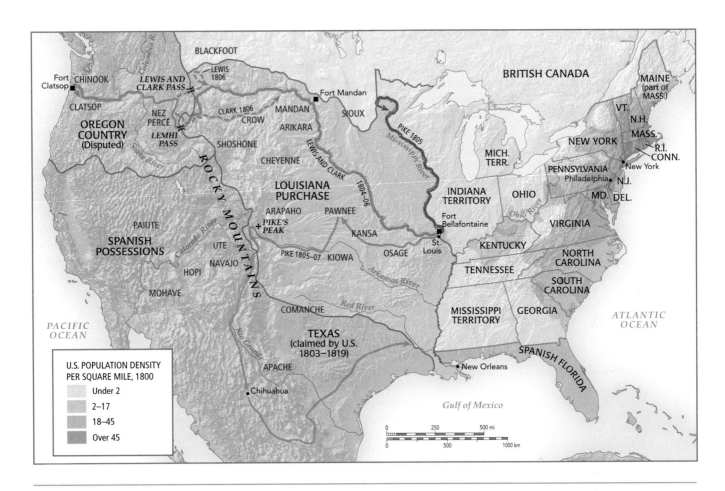

Exploration and Expansion: The Louisiana Purchase *The vast, largely uncharted Louisiana Purchase lay well beyond the most densely populated areas of the United States. The Lewis and Clark expedition, along with Lieutenant Zebulon Pike's exploration of the upper Mississippi River and the Southwest, opened the way for westward expansion.*

and in April 1803 he offered to sell not just New Orleans but all of Louisiana to the United States. This proposal flabbergasted Livingston and Monroe. Their instructions said nothing about acquiring all of Louisiana, and they had not been authorized to spend what the French demanded. But here was an opportunity to expand dramatically the boundaries of the United States. Pressed for an immediate answer, Livingston and Monroe took a deep breath and, after haggling over a few details, agreed to purchase Louisiana for approximately $15 million. In one fell swoop, the American negotiators had doubled the country's size by adding some 830,000 square miles.

While Jefferson was pleased at the prospect of acquiring so much territory, he found the legality of the act troubling. The Constitution, after all, did not authorize the acquisition of territory by treaty. In the end, Jefferson sent the treaty to the Senate for ratification, noting privately, "The less we say about constitutional difficulties the better." Once again pragmatism had triumphed over theory.

Lewis and Clark

Even before the Louisiana Purchase was completed, Congress secretly funded an expedition up the Missouri River to the Pacific. Leading that party were Meriwether Lewis, Jefferson's secretary, and William Clark, a younger brother of Revolutionary War hero George Rogers Clark.

Jefferson instructed Lewis and Clark to recruit a "Corps of Discovery" to map the region and make detailed observations of the soil, climate, rivers, minerals, and plant and animal life. They were also to investigate the practicability of an overland route to the Pacific and engage in diplomacy with the Indians along the way. By pushing onward to the Pacific, Lewis and Clark would strengthen the American title to Oregon, which several nations claimed but none effectively occupied.

In the spring of 1804 Lewis and Clark left St. Louis and headed up the Missouri River with 48 men. They laboriously hauled their boats upstream to present-day North Dakota, where they spent the winter with the Mandan Indians. The next spring, they headed west again. Only with great difficulty did the expedition pass the rugged mountains ahead of the winter snows and then float down first the Snake and then the Columbia River to the Pacific.

A Land Transformed by Change

The western country Lewis and Clark traversed had been shaken by momentous changes over the previous quarter of a century. The trade routes across the plains and through the mountains circulated goods in greater quantities than ever before. Horses and guns in particular upset older Indian ways, making tribes more mobile and more dangerous. Lewis and Clark's expedition spotted Spanish horse gear from Mexico in villages along the upper Missouri River, guns from French traders to the northeast, and British teapots along the Columbia River. In one example of these trading networks at work, members of Lewis and Clark's expedition sold war hatchets to Indians during their winter stay at Fort Mandan. The expedition ran into the same hatchets the following summer in distant Idaho, the trade goods having made their trip across the Plains faster than the expedition.

Disease and Dislocation

Most disruptive to these western lands was smallpox, which had made its way along the same trade routes ever since the pandemic of the 1780s (see page 177). The disease decimated Indian populations and forced many tribes to resettle. The Arikaras, who before 1780 had numbered perhaps 24,000, had dwindled to about 2,000 by the time Lewis and Clark passed through. Portions of tribes to the east had migrated westward, including the Delawares, Shawnees, Miamis, Chickasaws, and Cherokees. Captain Clark, who was present when the Treaty of Greenville was signed in 1795, discovered a Delaware chief he had seen there, along the Missouri, 500 miles west of his earlier home.

After a bleak winter in Oregon, the Corps of Discovery returned home over the Rockies in 1806. It brought back thousands of useful plant and animal specimens and produced a remarkably accurate map of its journey. Lewis and Clark had crossed a continent disrupted by change. In the century to come the changes would only accelerate.

Pressure on Indian Lands and Culture

East of the Mississippi, white settlers continued to flood into the backcountry. Jefferson endorsed the policy that Indian tribes either would have to assimilate into American culture by becoming farmers and abandoning their seminomadic hunting or would have to move west. Jefferson defended these alternatives as in the best interests of the Indians, because he believed that otherwise they faced extermination. But he also recognized that by becoming farmers they would need less land. "While they are learning to do better on less land," he noted, "our increasing numbers will be calling for more land."

Anglo-Americans never doubted the superiority of their ways. As William Henry Harrison, governor of the new Indiana Territory and future president of the United States, confessed in 1801, "A great many of the Inhabitants of the Fronteers consider the murdering of the Indians in the highest degree meritorious." Even a disciple of the Enlightenment such as Jefferson encouraged the policy of selling goods on credit in order to lure Indians into debt. "When these debts get beyond what the individuals can pay," the president observed, "they become willing to lop them off by a cession of lands." Between 1800 and 1810 whites pressed Indians into ceding more than 100 million acres in the Ohio River valley.

The loss of so much land devastated Indian cultures and transformed their environment by reducing hunting grounds and making game and food scarce. "Stop your people from killing our game," the Shawnees complained in 1802 to federal Indian agents. "They would be angry if we were to kill a cow or hog of theirs, the little game that remains is very dear to us." Tribes also became dependent on white trade to obtain blankets, guns, metal utensils, alcohol, and decorative beads. To pay for these goods with furs, Indians often overtrapped, which forced them to invade the lands of neighboring tribes, provoking wars.

The strain produced by white expansion led to alcoholism, growing violence among tribe members, family disintegration, and the collapse of the clan system designed to regulate relations among different villages. The question of how to deal with white culture became a matter of anguished debate. While some Native Americans attempted to take up farming and accommodate to white ways, for most the course of assimilation proved unappealing and fraught with risk.

White Frontier Society

Whites faced their own problems on the frontier. In the first wave of settlement came backwoods families who cleared a few acres of forest by girdling the trees, removing the brush, and planting corn between the dead trunks. Their isolated one-room log cabins were crude, dark, and windowless, with mud stuffed between the chinks; the furniture and utensils were sparse and homemade. Such settlers were mostly squatters without legal title to their land. As a region began to fill up, these pioneers usually sold their improvements and headed west again.

Taking their place, typically, were young single men from the East, who married and started families. Like the pioneers before them, most engaged in semisubsistence agriculture, save for the lucky few whose prime locations allowed them to transport their crops down the Ohio River to the mouth of the Mississippi at New Orleans for shipment to distant markets. But most frontier families struggled to make ends meet. Many moved several times in search of better opportunities but never rose from the ranks of squatters or tenant farmers to become independent landowners. Fledgling western communities lacked schools, churches, and courts, and inhabitants often lived miles distant from even their nearest neighbors.

The Beginnings of the Second Great Awakening

This hardscrabble frontier proved the perfect tinder for sparking a series of dramatic religious revivals in the decades surrounding 1800. What lit the fire were missionary efforts by major Protestant churches—particularly the Baptists and the Methodists—who sent their ministers to travel the countryside on horseback and to preach wherever they could gather a crowd. Often those religious meetings took place outdoors and drew eager hearers from as far as 100 miles away, who camped for several days in makeshift tents to listen to sermons and to share in praying and singing hymns.

Thus was born a new form of Protestant worship, the camp meeting, which drew national notice after a mammoth gathering at Cane Ridge, Kentucky, in August of 1801. (See *Daily Lives*) At a time when the largest city in the state had only 2,000 people, more than 10,000 men, women, and children, white and black, flocked there to hear dozens of ministers preaching the gospel. Many in the crowd were overwhelmed by powerful religious feelings, some shrieking and shaking over guilt for their sins, others laughing and dancing from their high hopes of eternal salvation. No doubt all participants enjoyed the uncommon pleasure of rubbing shoulders with so many other folks: it provided a fleeting release from the lonely struggle to carve a living from the western frontier.

Cane Ridge

The Cane Ridge revival, one of the earliest along the frontier, was a chaotic, disorganized affair. But as western clergy became more experienced with outdoor camp meetings, they standardized the format. About a week in advance, organizers chose a forest clearing, removed nearby underbrush, erected pulpits, and constructed benches. Usually the camp went up near an established church, which provided lodging for the ministers. Since a water supply was essential, camps were located near springs, creeks, or rivers. A good site needed dry ground, shade so worshipers could escape the blazing sun, and pasturage for the horses.

The tents of the worshipers formed a ring around the outdoor auditorium where services were held. At large meetings as many as 200 tents were set up in rows with streets in between to allow easy access. To help people find their lodgings, the streets were sometimes even named. This outer perimeter constituted the meeting's private space. Here,

beneath tents of sailcloth or even shelters patched together from old blankets and sheets, individuals could withdraw from the larger group to find relative solitude, cook meals in front of campfires, and sleep on rude beds of straw or simply on the ground.

Worshipers filled bench after bench in the central public space at the periodic call of a bugle. Rising above the listeners stood the preachers' pulpit. Sometimes it was merely a 10-foot-square platform on stilts; other times it was more elaborate, with several levels and a roof. Services were held in the open, and neither rain nor thunderstorms would interrupt them. At night, the dancing light and shadows produced by the candles, torches, campfires, and fire altars heightened the feeling of awe.

The democracy of the frontier did not automatically break down customary social constraints. For reasons of authority as well as practicality, the ministers' pulpit rose above the congregation. And the audience itself was

segregated: women on one side of the clearing, men on the other. In the South, black worshipers were seated in an area behind the pulpit, where they set up their own camp and conducted separate services.

Since the purpose of camp meetings was to "revive" religion and stir listeners' hearts, several rows of planks were set aside directly in front of the pulpit as an "anxious bench," for those whose souls struggled in the agony of conversion. The design of the space thus focused the attention of both congregation and ministers on the "mourners," who were prayed over in hopes that they would receive a new birth in Christ.

But the social boundaries between public and private, male and female, and even black and white could be broken down. As excitement grew, several services might be held at once, some people praying, others singing, shouting, or listening to ministers who stood on wagons. And when formal services ended, men and women often

Some Protestant ministers denounced the "revival" at Cane Ridge and elsewhere as yet another instance of the ignorance and savagery of westerners. Other ministers were more optimistic: they saw frontier camp meetings as the first sign of a Protestant Christian renewal that would sweep the new republic. Their hopes set the stage for what would come to be called the Second Great Awakening, a wave of religious revivals that spread throughout the nation after 1800. (See Chapter 12.)

The Prophet, Tecumseh, and the Pan-Indian Movement

Native peoples also turned to religion to meet the challenges of the early national frontier. Indeed, in traditional Indian religions, they found the resource to revitalize their cultures by severing all ties with the white world. During the 1790s a revival led by Handsome Lake took hold among the Iroquois, following the loss of most of the Iroquois lands and the collapse of their military power in western New York. Later Lalawethika, also known as the Prophet, sparked a religious renewal among the Shawnees. The Prophet's early life was bleak: he was a poor hunter and as a child accidentally blinded himself in the right eye with an arrow; the ridicule of his fellow tribe members drove him to alcoholism. Suddenly, in April 1805 he lapsed into a trance so deep that he was given up for dead. When he revived, he spoke of being reborn. From this vision and others, he outlined a new creed for the Shawnees.

Taking a new name—Tenskwatawa (Open Door)—he urged the Shawnees to renounce whiskey and white goods and return to their old ways of hunting with bows

Independence from White Society

continued in small groups, searching one another's souls by campfires late into the night. Indeed, the spontaneous excitement was great enough that meeting sponsors quickly learned that supervision was necessary to prevent unseemly activities. The nearby forest and the numerous tents at nightfall all offered temptations for drinking, carousing, or lovemaking. Official patrols regularly investigated suspicious activities.

On the final day white and black worshipers joined in a singing and marching festival before disbanding to their humdrum daily routines. Successful camp meetings depended on more than the talents of the clergy and the enthusiasm of participants. In their layout they were carefully planned and regulated communities in the forest, designed to reduce the distance between public and private space and thereby instill a sense of religion into all the activities that took place in the meeting as well as those that would be resumed in the regular world.

Tents ringed the central area of a camp meeting where benches faced the preachers' platform. What does this illustration of an 1837 camp meeting suggest about gender relations and religious experience?

and arrows, eating customary foods such as corn and beans, and wearing traditional garb. The Shawnee could revitalize their culture, the Prophet insisted, by condemning intertribal violence, embracing monogamous marriage, and rejecting the idea of private instead of communal property. Except for guns, which could be used in self-defense, his followers were to discard all items made by whites. Intermarriage with white settlers was forbidden.

Setting up headquarters in 1808 at the newly built village of Prophetstown in Indiana, Tenskwatawa led a wider revival among the tribes of the Northwest. Just as thousands of white settlers traveled to Methodist or Baptist camp meetings in the woods, where preachers denounced the evils of liquor and called for a return to a purer way of life, so thousands of Indians from northern tribes traveled to the Prophet's village for inspiration. Many were concerned about the threatened loss of Indian lands.

Whereas Tenskwatawa's strategy of revitalization was primarily religious, his older brother Tecumseh turned to political and military solutions. William Henry Harrison described Tecumseh as "one of those uncommon geniuses which spring up occasionally to produce revolutions and overturn the established order of things." Tall and athletic, an accomplished hunter and warrior, Tecumseh became active in 1809, after the Lenni Lenape and Miami tribes ceded yet another 3 million acres in Indiana and Illinois. Traveling throughout the Northwest, he urged tribes to forget ancient rivalries and unite to protect their lands. Tecumseh's confederacy brought together the Wyandot, Chippewa, Sauk and Fox, Winnebago, Potawatomi, and other tribes. Just as Indian nations had in the past, Tecumseh adopted the strategy of uniting in a confederacy, this time on an even larger scale.

Tecumseh's Political Strategy

The Indian Response to White Encroachment   *With land cessions and white western migration placing increased pressure on Indian cultures after 1790, news of the Prophet's revival fell on eager ears. It spread especially quickly northward along the shores of Lake Michigan and westward along Lake Superior and the interior of Wisconsin. Following the Battle of Tippecanoe, Tecumseh eclipsed the Prophet as the major leader of Indian resistance, but his trips south to forge political alliances met with less success.*

Obstacles to a Confederacy

Just as the early American republic found it difficult to unite such a vast region under a single confederation, Tecumseh's campaign for Pan-Indian unity ran into serious obstacles. He asked villages to pay less attention to their local leaders and join his larger movement; he called on tribes to unite with their traditional enemies in a common cause. When Tecumseh headed south in 1811, he encountered greater resistance. Most southern tribes were more prosperous, were more acculturated, and felt less immediate pressure on their land from whites. His southern mission ended largely in failure.

To compound Tecumseh's problems, while he was away a force of Americans under Governor Harrison defeated the Prophet's forces at the Battle of Tippecanoe in

November 1811 and destroyed Prophetstown. As a result, Tecumseh became convinced that the best way to contain white expansion was to play off the Americans against the British, who still held forts in the Great Lakes region. Indeed, by 1811, the two nations were on the brink of war.

The Second War for American Independence

As Tecumseh worked to achieve a Pan-Indian alliance, Jefferson encountered his own difficulties in trying to achieve American political unity. The president hoped to woo all but the most extreme Federalists into the Republican camp. His reelection in 1804 showed how much progress he had made, as he defeated Federalist Charles Cotesworth Pinckney and carried 15 of 17 states. With the Republicans controlling three-quarters of the seats in Congress, one-party rule seemed at hand.

But events across the Atlantic complicated the efforts to unite Americans. Only two weeks after Napoleon agreed to sell Louisiana to the United States, war broke out between France and Great Britain. As in the 1790s, the United States found itself caught between the world's two greatest powers. Jefferson insisted that the nation should remain neutral in a European war. But the policies he proposed to maintain neutrality sparked sharp divisions in American society and momentarily revived the two-party system.

In seeking a common national identity, citizens of the United States often found it easier to define themselves in terms of what they were not. With conflict flaring along the nation's western frontiers, most Americans believed they were not like the Indians, whom they perceived as nomadic and wild. As France and England harassed U.S. ships on the high seas, Americans insisted they should not be like the nations of Europe, where "Favoritism as well as Corruption prevails," as one American diplomat complained. And Americans drew another sharp cultural contrast during these decades: they protested they were not like the "Barbary pirates" of North Africa, who also preyed on American ships.

The Barbary Pirates and Cultural Identities

The Barbary states of North Africa—Algiers, Morocco, Tripoli, and Tunis—lay along the Mediterranean Sea's southern coast. During the seventeenth and eighteenth centuries their light, maneuverable corsairs plundered the cargo of enemy ships and enslaved the crews. In doing so, the Barbary states behaved much like European nations along the Mediterranean, whose ships over the years had swept up North African cargo and crews.

But the Barbary states were Muslim. To American (and European) eyes, that made the tyranny of their rulers particularly objectionable. An American biography of Islam's prophet, Muhammad, condemned Muhammad's teachings as a "system of blasphemy and iniquity" by which the followers of Islam had been "degraded to the rank of brutes." More powerful European nations, such as Britain, France, and Holland, found it convenient to pay tributes to the Barbary states so their ships could sail unmolested. But both Jefferson and John Adams disliked that idea. The "policy of Christendom" of paying tribute, complained Adams, "has made Cowards of all their Sailors before the Standard of Mahomet."

For their part, the Barbary states bore no special hostility toward Americans. Indeed one of them, Morocco, was among the first nations to recognize the new United States. But Congress was so distracted with its own affairs that it could not spare a diplomat to open negotiations. By the time John Adams became president, he had subdued his outrage and agreed to tributes. But when Tripoli increased its demands in 1801, President Jefferson sent a squadron of American ships to force a settlement. In 1803 Tripoli captured the *U.S.S. Philadelphia,* the second largest frigate in the navy. Only the following year did Lieutenant Stephen Decatur repair the situation by sneaking into Tripoli's harbor and burning down the *Philadelphia.* The American blockade

American Perceptions of Islamic Culture

The United States and the Barbary States, 1801–1815
The young United States, like many European powers, found its trading vessels challenged by the Barbary states of Morocco, Algiers, Tunisia, and Tripoli. When the pasha of Tripoli declared war on the United States in 1801, Jefferson dispatched a force that blockaded Tripoli to bring the war to an end in 1805. Tribute paid to the other Barbary States continued until 1816, after a new naval force, led by Captain Stephen Decatur, forced the ruler of Algiers to end the practice.

that followed forced Tripoli to give up its demands for tribute. Even so, the United States continued paying tribute to the other Barbary states until 1816.

The Embargo

At first the war between France and England benefited American trade because it disrupted European agriculture, increasing the demand for American foodstuffs and other raw materials. As the fighting drove most British and French commercial ships from the seas, American foreign trade doubled between 1803 and 1805. But both Britain and France began to raid America's ocean commerce with the other side. Between 1803 and 1807, Britain seized more than 500 American ships; France, more than 300. The British navy also seized and impressed into service thousands of sailors, some who were deserters from England's fleet but others who were native-born Americans.

Yet Jefferson drew back from declaring war. He announced instead a program of "peaceable coercion," designed to protect neutral rights without war. The plan not only prohibited American ships from trading with foreign ports but also stopped the export of all American goods. Jefferson was confident that American exports were so essential to the two belligerents that they would quickly agree to respect American neutral rights. In December 1807 Congress passed the **Embargo Act.**

The president had seriously miscalculated. France did not depend on American trade and so managed well enough, while British ships quickly took over the carrying trade as American vessels lay idle. Under the embargo, American exports plunged from $108 million in 1807 to a mere $22 million a year later. At the same time, imports fell from almost $145 million to about $58 million. As the center of American shipping, New England port cities were hurt the most and protested the loudest. And

Corsairs, light, maneuverable ships sailing out of Barbary ports like Tripoli (shown here), were well fitted for their purpose. As one historian noted, "Like stinging insects, their light, rapid vessels were designed to strike at unarmed or lightly armed merchantmen, while being able to flee very speedily at the mere approach of a warship."

when their merchants were not protesting, they were smuggling behind American officials' backs.

Madison and the Young Republicans

Following Washington's example, Jefferson did not seek a third term. A caucus of Republican members of Congress selected James Madison to run against Federalist Charles Cotesworth Pinckney. Madison triumphed easily, although in discontented New England, the Federalists picked up 24 seats in Congress.

Few men have assumed the presidency with more experience than James Madison. A leading nationalist in the 1780s, the father of the Constitution, a key floor leader in Congress, the founder of the Republican party, Madison had become Jefferson's secretary of state and closest adviser. Yet his tenure as president proved disappointing. Despite his intellectual brilliance, he lacked the force of leadership and the inner strength to impose his will on less capable men.

Madison's Character

With a president reluctant to fight for what he wanted, leadership passed to Congress. The elections of 1810 swept in a new generation of Republicans, led by the magnetic 34-year-old Henry Clay of Kentucky, who gained the rare distinction of being elected Speaker in his first term. These younger Republicans were more nationalistic than the generation led by Jefferson and Madison. They sought an ambitious program of economic development and were aggressive expansionists, especially those from frontier districts. Their willingness to go to war earned them the name of War Hawks. Though they numbered fewer than 30 in Congress, they quickly became the driving force in the Republican party.

War Hawks

The Decision for War

During Jefferson's final week in office in early 1809, Congress repealed the Embargo Act. The following year Congress authorized trade with France and England but decreed that if one of the two belligerents agreed to stop interfering with American shipping, trade with the other would be prohibited.

Given these circumstances, Napoleon outmaneuvered the British by announcing that he would put aside the French trade regulations. Madison took the French emperor at his word and reimposed a ban on trade with England. French raiders continued to seize American ships, but American anger focused on the British, who then seized many more ships and continued to impress American sailors. Finally, on June 16, 1812, the British ministry suspended the searches and seizures of American ships.

The concession came too late. Two days earlier, unaware of the change in policy, Congress granted Madison's request for a declaration of war against Britain. The vote was mostly along party lines, with every Federalist voting against war. As the representatives of commercial interests, Federalists were convinced that war would ruin American commerce.

Supporters of the War

Clearly, the vote for war could not be explained as a matter of outraged Americans protecting neutral rights. On the one hand, the coastal areas, which were most affected, preferred trade over high principle. On the other hand, members of Congress from the South and the West, regions that had a less direct interest in the issue, clamored most strongly for war. Their constituents were consumed with a desire to seize additional territory in Canada or in Florida (owned by Britain's ally Spain). In addition, they accused the British of stirring up hostility among the Indian tribes.

Perhaps most important, the War Hawks were convinced that Britain had never truly accepted the verdict of the American Revolution. To them, American independence—and with it republicanism—hung in the balance. For Americans hungering to be accepted in the community of nations, nothing rankled more than still being treated by the British as colonials.

National Unpreparedness

With Britain preoccupied by Napoleon, the War Hawks expected an easy victory. In truth, the United States was totally unprepared for war. Crippled by Jefferson's cutbacks, the navy was unable to lift the British blockade of the American coast, which bottled up the country's merchant marine and most of its navy. As for the U.S. army, it was small and poorly led. When Congress moved to increase its size to 75,000, even the most hawkish states failed to meet their quotas. Congress was also reluctant to levy taxes to finance the war.

Battle of Lake Erie

A three-pronged American invasion of Canada from Detroit, Niagara, and Lake Champlain failed dismally in 1812. Americans fared better the following year, as both sides raced to build a navy on the strategically located Lake Erie. Led by Commander Oliver Hazard Perry, American forces won a decisive victory at Put-In Bay in 1813. Perry's triumph gave the United States control of Lake Erie and greatly strengthened the American position in the Northwest.

"A Chance Such as Will Never Occur Again"

As the United States struggled to organize its forces, Tecumseh sensed that his long-awaited opportunity had come to drive Americans out of the western territories. "Here is a chance...such as will never occur again," he told a war council, "for us Indians of North America to form ourselves into one great combination." Allying with the British, Tecumseh traveled south in the fall to talk again with his Creek allies. To coordinate an Indian offensive for the following summer, he left a bundle of red sticks with eager Creek soldiers. They were to remove one stick each day from the bundle and attack when the sticks had run out.

Some of the older Creeks were more acculturated and preferred an American alliance. But about 2,000 younger "Red Stick" Creeks launched a series of attacks, climaxed by the destruction of Fort Mims along the Alabama River in August 1813. Once again, the Indians' lack of unity was a serious handicap, as warriors from the

Cherokee, Choctaw, and Chickasaw tribes, traditional Creek enemies, allied with the Americans. At the Battle of Horseshoe Bend in March 1814, General Andrew Jackson and his Tennessee militia soundly defeated the Red Stick Creeks. Jackson promptly dictated a peace treaty under which the Creeks ceded 22 million acres of land in the Mississippi Territory. They and the other southern tribes still retained significant landholdings, but Indian military power had been broken in the South, east of the Mississippi.

Jackson Defeats Creek Indians

Farther north, in October 1813, American forces under General William Henry Harrison defeated the British and their Indian allies at the Battle of the Thames. In the midst of heavy fighting Tecumseh was killed. With him died any hope of a Pan-Indian movement.

Tecumseh's Death

The War of 1812   *After the American victory on Lake Erie and the defeat of the western Indians at the Battle of the Thames, the British adopted a three-pronged strategy to invade the United States, culminating with an attempt on New Orleans. But they met their match in Andrew Jackson, whose troops marched to New Orleans after fighting a series of battles against the Creeks and forcing them to cede a massive tract of land.*

The British Invasion

As long as the war against Napoleon continued, the British were unwilling to divert army units to North America. But in 1814 Napoleon was at last defeated. Free to concentrate on America, the British devised a coordinated strategy to invade the United States in the northern, central, and southern parts of the country. The main army headed south from Montreal but was checked when Americans destroyed the British fleet on Lake Champlain.

Meanwhile, a smaller British force captured Washington and burned several public buildings, including the Capitol and the president's home. To cover the scars of this destruction, the executive mansion was painted with whitewash and became known as the White House. The burning of the capital was a humiliating event: President Madison and his wife, Dolley, were forced to flee. But the defeat had little military significance. The principal British objective was Baltimore, where for 25 hours their fleet bombarded Fort McHenry in the city's harbor. When Francis Scott Key saw the American flag still flying above the fort at dawn, he hurriedly composed the verses of "The Star Spangled Banner," which was eventually adopted as the national anthem.

Jackson's Victory at New Orleans

The third British target was New Orleans, where a formidable army of 7,500 British troops was opposed by a hastily assembled force commanded by Major General Andrew Jackson. The Americans included regular soldiers; frontiersmen from Kentucky and Tennessee; citizens of New Orleans, including several companies of free African Americans; Choctaw Indians; and a group of pirates. Jackson's outnumbered and ill-equipped forces won a stunning victory, which made the general an overnight hero. The Battle of New Orleans enabled Americans to forget the war's many failures and to boast that once again the United States had humbled the world's greatest military power.

The Hartford Convention

In December 1814, while Jackson was organizing the defense of New Orleans, New England Federalists met in Hartford to map strategy against the war. Yankee merchants, contemptuous of "Mr. Madison's War," had continued to trade with the enemy, while New England governors declined to make available the state militias. Finally the Massachusetts legislature called for a convention to discuss New England's grievances. Massachusetts, Connecticut, and Rhode Island sent delegates, but only three counties in New Hampshire and one in Vermont were represented.

Rejecting calls for secession, the delegates proposed a series of amendments to the Constitution that showed their displeasure with the government's economic policies and their resentment of the South's national political power. To their dismay, the committee arrived in Washington to present their demands just as news of Andrew Jackson's victory was being trumpeted on the streets. The nation's pride over Jackson's victory badly undercut the Hartford Convention, as did news from across the Atlantic that American negotiators in Ghent, Belgium, had signed a treaty ending the war. Hostilities had ceased, technically, on Christmas Eve 1814, two weeks before the Battle of New Orleans. Both sides were relieved to end the conflict, even though the Treaty of Ghent left unresolved the issues of impressment, neutral rights or trade. "Nothing was adjusted, nothing was settled," commented John Quincy Adams, who was present at the negotiations.

In truth, Adams' verdict was wide of the mark. From a continental perspective the war's impact was far-reaching. Tecumseh's Pan-Indian confederacy stood in a long tradition of Indian alliances, stretching back to Powhatan's alliance of tribes around seventeenth-century Chesapeake Bay. In 1754, as the English colonies quarreled among themselves at the Albany Congress of 1754, the Iroquois used their confederacy as a significant political counterweight. With Tecumseh's death, the strategy of combination would no longer be used to block white settlement in the west. And with peace reestablished, the United States turned toward the settlement of Jefferson's vast western "empire of liberty." For the continent, the change in orientation was momentous.

America Turns Inward

The return of peace hard on the heels of Jackson's victory sparked a new confidence in many Americans. "We have stood the contest, single-handed, against the conqueror of Europe," wrote Supreme Court justice Joseph Story to a friend, "and we are at peace."

The new nationalism sounded the death knell of the Federalist party, for even talk of secession at the Hartford Convention had tainted the party with disunion and treason. In the 1816 election Madison's secretary of state, James Monroe, resoundingly defeated Federalist Rufus King of New York. Four years later Monroe ran for reelection unopposed.

Collapse of the Federalist Party

Monroe's Presidency

The major domestic challenge that Monroe faced was the renewal of sectional rivalries in 1819, when the Missouri Territory applied for admission as a slave state. Before the controversy over Missouri erupted, slavery had not been a major issue in American politics. Congress had debated the institution when it prohibited the African slave trade in 1808, the earliest year this step could be taken under the Constitution. But lacking any specific federal legislation to stop it, slavery had crossed the Mississippi River into the Louisiana Purchase. Louisiana entered the Union in 1812 as a slave state, and in 1818 Missouri, which had about 10,000 slaves in its population, asked permission to come in too.

In 1818 the Union contained 11 free and 11 slave states. As the federal government became stronger and more active, both the North and the South worried about maintaining their political power. The North's greater population gave it a majority in the House of Representatives, 105 to 81. The Senate, of course, was evenly balanced, because each state had two senators regardless of population. But Maine, which previously had been part of Massachusetts, requested admission as a free state. That would upset the balance unless Missouri came in as a slave state.

Representative James Tallmadge of New York disturbed this delicate state of affairs when in 1819 he introduced an amendment that would establish a program of gradual emancipation in Missouri. For the first time Congress directly debated the morality of slavery, often bitterly. The House approved the Tallmadge amendment, but the Senate refused to accept it, and the two houses deadlocked.

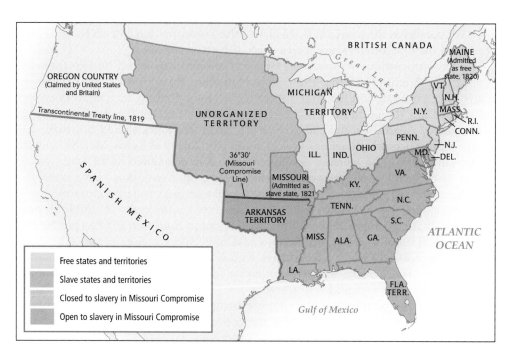

The Missouri Compromise and the Union's Boundaries in 1820

The Missouri Compromise

When Congress reconvened in 1820, Henry Clay of Kentucky promoted what came to be known as the Missouri Compromise. Under its terms Missouri was admitted as a slave state and Maine as a free state. In addition, slavery was forever prohibited in the remainder of the Louisiana Purchase north of 36°30′ (the southern boundary of Missouri). Clay's proposal, the first of several sectional compromises he would engineer in his long career, won congressional approval and Monroe signed the measure, ending the crisis. But southern fears for the security of slavery and northern fears about its spread remained.

The Monroe Doctrine

Monroe's greatest achievements were diplomatic, accomplished largely by his talented secretary of state, John Quincy Adams, the son of President John Adams. An experienced diplomat, Adams thought of the Republic in continental terms and was intent on promoting expansion to the Pacific. Such a vision required dealing with Spain, which had never recognized the legality of the Louisiana Purchase. In addition, between 1810 and 1813 the United States had occupied and unilaterally annexed Spanish West Florida.

But Spain was preoccupied with events farther south in the Americas. In the first quarter of the nineteenth century, its colonies one after another revolted and established themselves as independent nations. These revolutions increased the pressure on the Spanish minister to America, Luis de Onís, to come to terms with the United States. So too did Andrew Jackson, who marched into East Florida and captured several Spanish forts in 1818. Jackson had exceeded his instructions, but Adams understood the additional pressure this aggression put on Onís and refused to disavow it.

Transcontinental Treaty

Fearful that the United States might next invade Texas or other Spanish territory, Spain agreed to the Transcontinental Treaty in February 1819. Its terms set the boundary between American and Spanish territory all the way to the Pacific (map, p. 253). Spain not only gave up its claims to the Pacific Northwest but also ceded Florida. In order to obtain the line to the Pacific, the United States abandoned its contention that Texas was part of the Louisiana Purchase.

More importantly, the United States also came to terms with Great Britain. Following the War of 1812, the British abandoned their connections with the western Indian tribes and no longer attempted to block American expansion to the Rocky Mountains. In a growing spirit of cooperation, the Rush-Bagot Agreement in 1817 limited naval forces on the Great Lakes and on Lake Champlain. In 1818 the countries agreed to the 49th parallel as the northern boundary of the Louisiana Purchase and also to joint control of the Oregon Territory for 10 years, subject to renewal.

In this atmosphere of good will, George Canning, the British foreign secretary, proposed in August 1823 that the United States and Britain issue a joint statement disavowing any expansionist aims in Latin America and opposing the transfer of Spain's colonies to any foreign power. Monroe was inclined to accept the British offer, but John Quincy Adams forcefully argued that the United States should not make any pledge against acquiring territory in the future, particularly in Texas, Mexico, and the Caribbean. Adams also worried that in any joint statement the United States would appear to be merely a junior partner, coming along "as a cock-boat in the wake of a British man-of-war." Monroe finally agreed to make an independent statement.

No Interference in the Western Hemisphere

He included it in his annual message to Congress, on December 2, 1823. Monroe reaffirmed that the United States would not intervene in European affairs, a principle of American foreign policy since Washington's Farewell Address. And he also announced that the United States would not interfere with already established European colonies in the Western Hemisphere. But any intervention in the new republics of Latin America, he warned, would be considered a hostile act: "The American continents . . . are henceforth not to be considered as subjects for future colonization by any European powers." The essence of this policy was the concept of two worlds, one old and one new, each refraining from interfering in the other's affairs.

American public opinion hailed Monroe's statement and then promptly forgot it. Only years later would it be referred to as the Monroe Doctrine. Still, it represented the culmination of the American quest since 1776 for full independence. The very fact that Britain had proposed a joint declaration demonstrated that, at last, the parent nation recognized the United States as a sovereign nation.

The three decades after 1789 demonstrated how profoundly events in the wider world could affect life within the United States, shaping its politics, its boundaries, its economy—its future.

The French Revolution contributed to splintering the once-united leaders of the American Revolution into two rival parties. The wars that followed, between France and England, deepened the divisions between Federalists and Republicans and prompted both parties to mobilize the political loyalties of ordinary white American men and women. Napoleon's ambitions to conquer Europe handed Jefferson the Louisiana Territory, while British efforts to reclaim its American empire tempted some New Enganders to secede from the Union and encouraged Tecumseh's hopes of mounting a pan-Indian resistance on the frontier. The Haitian Revolution in the Caribbean prompted free blacks in northern cities to protest racial inequalities and slavery within the United States.

But by the 1820s, most white Americans paid less attention to events abroad than to expanding across the vast North American continent. The question remained: how would the nation be developed? Jefferson had dreamed of an "empire of liberty," delighting in expansion as the means to preserve a nation of small farmers. Younger, more nationalistic Republicans had a different vision. They spoke of internal improvements, protective tariffs to help foster American industries, better roads and canals to link farmers with towns, cities, and wider markets. The tone of these new Republicans was not aristocratic; they were not like the Federalists of old. Still, their dream of a national, commercial republic resembled Franklin's and Hamilton's more than Jefferson's. They had seen how handsomely American merchants and commercial farmers profited when European wars swelled demand for American wheat and cotton. They looked to profit from speculation in land, the growth of commercial agriculture, and new methods of industrial manufacturing. If they represented the rising generation, what would be the fate of Crèvecoeur's semisubsistence farm communities? The answer was not yet clear.

Significant Events

1789	Washington inaugurated president; French Revolution begins; Judiciary Act passed
1790	Funding and assumption approved
1791	Bank of the United States chartered; Miami Confederacy defeats St. Clair
1793	War breaks out between France and England; Washington proclaims American neutrality
1794	Battle of Fallen Timbers; Whiskey Rebellion

1795	Jay's Treaty ratified; Treaty of Greenville signed
1796	Pinckney's Treaty ratified; first contested presidential election—Adams defeats Jefferson
1798	XYZ Affair; Alien and Sedition Acts passed; Virginia and Kentucky resolutions
1798–1799	Naval war with France
1800	Jefferson defeats Adams
1801	House elects Jefferson president; Cane Ridge religious revival
1803	*Marbury v. Madison;* Louisiana Purchase; war resumes between Great Britain and France
1804	*Decature* burns *U.S.S. Philadelphia* in Tripoli Harbor
1804–1806	Lewis and Clark expedition
1805	Prophet's revivals begin
1807	Embargo Act passed
1808	Madison elected president
1809	Tecumseh's confederacy organized
1810	*Fletcher v. Peck*
1811	Battle of Tippecanoe
1812	War declared against Great Britain
1813	Battle of Lake Erie; Tecumseh killed
1814	Washington burned; Hartford Convention; Treaty of Ghent signed
1815	Battle of New Orleans
1816	Monroe elected president
1818	United States–Canada boundary fixed to the Rockies; joint occupation of Oregon established
1819	Transcontinental Treaty with Spain; United States acquires Florida
1820	Missouri Compromise enacted
1823	Monroe Doctrine proclaimed

Chapter Summary

Basic social divisions between the commercial and semisubsistence regions shaped the politics of the new United States. Between 1789 and the 1820s, the first parties emerged and, along with them, a more popular and participatory political culture. Over the same decades, Indian confederacies mounted a sustained resistance to westward expansion, while events in Europe deepened divisions among Federalists and Repubicans and threatened the very existence of the fledgling American republic.

- The first party to organize in the 1790s was the Federalists, led by Alexander Hamilton and George Washington. Divisions over Hamilton's policies as secretary of the treasury led to the formation of the Republicans, led by James Madison and Thomas Jefferson.

- The commercially minded Federalists believed in order and hierarchy, supported loose construction of the Constitution, and wanted a powerful central government to promote economic growth.

- The Republican party, with its sympathy for agrarian ideals, endorsed strict construction of the Constitution, wanted a less active federal government, and harbored a strong fear of aristocracy.

- The French Revolution, the XYZ Affair, the naval war, and the Alien and Sedition Acts also deepened the partisan division between Federalists and Republicans during the 1790s.

- The Federalists demonstrated that the new government could be a more active force in American society, but their controversial domestic and foreign policies, internal divisions, and open hostility to the masses eventually led to their downfall.

- Before becoming president, Jefferson advocated the principles of agrarianism, limited government, and strict construction of the Constitution. But once in power, he failed to dismantle Hamilton's economic program and promoted western expansion by acquiring Louisiana from France.

- Chief Justice John Marshall proclaimed that the courts were to interpret the meaning of the Constitution (judicial review), a move that helped the judiciary emerge as an equal branch of government.

- Lewis and Clark produced the first reliable information and maps of the Louisiana territory. The lands they passed through had been transformed over the previous 25 years by disease, dislocation, and the arrival of horses and guns.

- The Shawnee prophet Tenskwatawa and his brother Tecumseh organized the most important Indian resistance to the expansion of the new republic, but the movement collapsed with the death of Tecumseh during the War of 1812.

- France and Britain both interfered with neutral rights, and the United States went to war against Britain in 1812.

- In the years after 1815 there was a surge in American nationalism, reflected and reinforced by Britain's recognition of American sovereignty and the Monroe Doctrine's prohibition of European intervention in the Western Hemisphere. But the Missouri crisis was an early indication of growing sectional rivalries.

Additional Reading

Two good overviews of early national politics are Stanley Elkins and Eric McKitrick's *The Age of Federalism* (1993) and James Roger Sharp, *American Politics in the Early Republic* (1993). For a fuller understanding of Federalist political thought, consult Linda Kerber, *Federalists in Dissent* (1970), and David Hackett Fischer, *The Revolution of American Conservatism* (1965); for the Republicans, read Lance Banning, *The Jeffersonian Persuasion* (1978), and Drew R. McCoy, *The Elusive Republic* (1980). Another approach to understanding the politics of this period is to read about the lives of leading political figures: among the best are Joseph Ellis's biographies of John Adams (*Passionate Sage,* 1993) and Thomas Jefferson (*American Sphinx,* rev. ed., 1998) and two biographies of Alexander Hamilton by Ron Chernow and Gerald Stourzh (all cited in the full bibliography). To become better acquainted with the popular political culture of the early republic, consult *Beyond the Founders* (2004), a superb collection of essays edited by Jeffrey Pasley, Andrew W. Robertson, and David Waldstreicher. For an engaging narrative about the political influence exerted by white women, see Catherine Allgor, *Parlor Politics* (2000), and for rich desciptions of the social and political interactions among whites, African Americans, and Indians in the new republic, see Joshua Rothman, *Notorious in the Neighborhood* (2003), and John Wood Sweet, *Bodies Politic* (2003). To gain a fuller understanding of the lives of both Indians and western frontier settlers, rely on Gregory Evans Dowd, *A Spirited Resistance* (1993); Roger Kennedy, *Mr. Jefferson's Lost Cause* (2003); John Mack Faragher's *Sugar Creek* (1986); Adam Rothman, *Slave Country* (2005); Alan Taylor, *William Cooper's Town* (1995); and R. David Edmunds, *The Shawnee Prophet* (1983) and *Tecumseh and the Quest for Indian Leadership* (1984).

For a fuller list of readings, see the Bibliography at www.mhhe.com/davidsonnation6.

Historians Reconstruct the Past

Sally Hemings and Thomas Jefferson

So much goes into the weighing of historical evidence: not only the application of logic and reason, the use of large theories and small inferences, but also the influence of emotion and a culture's prevailing myths. The distortions created by the latter pair come into play especially when topics involving race and sex are involved—as can be seen by following the trail of a story first made public more than two centuries ago.

Some Rumors—and Some Facts

The rumors began in Albemarle County, Virginia, more than 200 years ago; they came to the notice of a contemporary journalist by the name of James Callender. A writer for hire, Callender had once lent his pen to the Republicans but turned from friend into foe when the party failed to reward him with a political appointment. When his story splashed onto the pages of the *Recorder,* a Richmond newspaper, the trickle of rumor turned into a torrent of scandal. Callender alleged that Thomas Jefferson, during his years in Paris as the American minister, had contracted a liaison with one of his own slaves. The woman was the president's mistress even now, he insisted, in 1802. She was kept at Monticello, Jefferson's plantation, and Jefferson had fathered children with her. Her name was Sally Hemings.

Solid information about Sally Hemings is scarce. She was one of six children, we know, born to Betty Hemings and her white master, John Wayles, a Virginia planter whose white daughter, Martha Wayles Skelton, married Jefferson in 1772. We know that Betty Hemings was the child of an African woman and an English sailor, which means Betty's children with Wayles, Sally among them, were quadroons—light-skinned and one-quarter African. We know

that Sally accompanied one of Jefferson's daughters to Paris as her maid in 1787 and that, on returning to Virginia a few years later, she performed domestic work at Monticello. We know that she had six children and that the four who survived to adulthood escaped from slavery into freedom: Jefferson assisted her two eldest children, Beverly and Harriet, in leaving Monticello in 1822, and her two youngest children, Madison and Eston, were freed by Jefferson's will in 1827. We know that shortly after Jefferson's death, his daughter, Martha Jefferson Randolph, freed Sally Hemings and that she lived with her two sons in Charlottesville until her own death in 1835.

Dueling Oral Traditions

We know, too, that Jefferson's white descendants stoutly denied (and, to this day, some still deny) any familial connection with

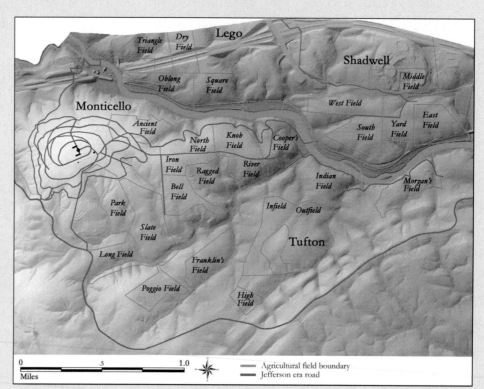

Jefferson owned 5,000 acres of land in Albemarle County, Virginia, his "home farm" of Monticello and three "quarter farms"—Lego, Tufton, and Shadwell. Sally Hemings and her children lived at the Monticello plantation.

This view of Monticello was painted shortly after Jefferson's death. It portrays his white descendants surrounded by a serene landscape.

the descendants of Sally Hemings. Even though Callender's scandal quickly subsided, doing Jefferson no lasting political damage, Jefferson's white grandchildren were still explaining away the accusations half a century later. In the 1850s, Jefferson's granddaughter, Ellen Coolidge Randolph, claimed that her brother, Thomas Jefferson Randolph, had told her that one of Jefferson's nephews, Samuel Carr, fathered Hemings's children. In the 1860s, Henry Randall, an early biographer of Jefferson, recalled a conversation with Thomas Jefferson Randolph in the 1850s in which he attributed paternity to another nephew, Samuel's brother Peter Carr.

Until the end of the twentieth century, most scholars resolved the discrepancy of this dual claim by suggesting that one of the Carr nephews had fathered Sally Hemings's children. And all of Jefferson's most eminent twentieth-century biographers—Douglass Adair, Dumas Malone, John Chester Miller, and Joseph J. Ellis—contended that a man of Jefferson's character and convictions could not have engaged in a liaison with a slave woman. After all, Jefferson was a Virginia gentleman and an American philosophe who believed that reason should rule over passion; he was also an eloquent apostle of equality and democracy and an outspoken critic of the tyrannical power of masters over slaves. And, despite his opposition to slavery, Jefferson argued in his *Notes on the State of Virginia* (1785) for the likelihood that peoples of African descent were inferior intellectually and artistically to those of European descent. Because of that

conviction, he warned of the dire consequences that would attend the mixing of the races.

The official version of events did not go unchallenged. Madison Hemings, a skilled carpenter, in 1873 told an Ohio newspaper reporter of an oral tradition long repeated among his family, that his mother had been Thomas Jefferson's "concubine" and that Jefferson had fathered all of her children. Even so, nearly a century passed before Madison Hemings's claims won wider attention. In 1968, the historian Winthrop Jordan noted that Sally Hemings's pregnancies coincided with Jefferson's stays at Monticello. In 1975, Fawn Brodie's best-selling "intimate history" of Jefferson portrayed his relationship with Sally Hemings as an enduring love affair; four years later, the African American novelist Barbara Chase-Rimboud set Brodie's findings to fiction.

Overturning Cultural Assumptions

An even more powerful case for Jefferson's paternity of all of Hemings's children was made in 1997 by Annette Gordon-Reed, an African American scholar. Gordon-Reed drew on her legal training to subject the handling of the evidence by Jefferson's biographers to a close and telling cross-examination. While they had dismissed Madison Hemings's recollections as mere family lore and wishful thinking, Gordon-Reed argued that such oral testimony was, in fact, no more or less reliable than the oral testimony of Jefferson's white Randolph descendants.

One year later, Gordon-Reed's arguments crested on a tidal wave of new revelations: A team of DNA research scientists headed by Eugene A. Foster discovered an exact match on the Y-chromosome markers between Thomas Jefferson's line and the descendants of Eston Hemings. (Eston was Sally's youngest child and the only one who left male-line descendants whose DNA could be tested.) Since the chance of such a match occurring randomly was less than 1 in 1,000, the DNA evidence made it highly probable that Thomas Jefferson fathered at least one of Sally Hemings's children. In addition, Foster's team found no DNA match between the Hemings line and the Carr family, thus discrediting the assertions of Jefferson's white descendants. Intrigued by these findings, the historian Fraser D. Neiman undertook a sophisticated statistical analysis of Hemings's conceptions and Jefferson's returns to Monticello (where he spent about half his time), which established a 99 percent probability that he had fathered all of Hemings's children.

This new evidence has persuaded most historians that Thomas Jefferson conducted a monogamous liaison with Sally

The names of Sally Hemings and her sons appear on this list of Thomas Jefferson's slaves.

historians should regard the recollections of nonliterate peoples as possessing a superior claim to being accurate recoveries of the past? Gordon-Reed and a host of other historians warn against that conclusion, arguing that all oral testimony must be tested against the findings yielded by the documentary record and scientific research. Their caution is warranted by the fact that the DNA findings to date have failed to show a match between the Jefferson line and that of Thomas Woodson, another Monticello slave whose African American descendants have long cited their own family's oral tradition as evidence of a biological connection to Jefferson.

Hemings over 38 years and that their union produced at least one and most likely all six of her children. As a result, the debate among historians has moved on to explore questions left unresolved by the new scientific findings.

Unresolved Questions

One such question bears on how historians should assess the credibility of their sources. Specifically, how reliable are the oral traditions passed down through families? Both the DNA and the statistical evidence bear out Madison Hemings's recollections. Surely that outcome, as Annette Gordon-Reed has urged, should prompt future historians to scrutinize the oral testimonies of white masters such as the Jeffersons and the Randolphs as closely as they do the narratives of slaves and the oral traditions of their descendants. But does it follow that

An equally intriguing question concerns the character of the relationship between Sally Hemings and Thomas Jefferson. Was it forced and exploitative or consensual and even affectionate? On the one hand, the long duration of their liaison suggests that it may have been based on a shared emotional intimacy. (If Jefferson fathered all of Hemings's children, their involvement began in Paris during the late 1780s and endured at least until the birth of Eston Hemings in 1808.) As Annette Gordon-Reed points out, even stronger support for this interpretation is that Sally Hemings and all her children were the only nuclear slave family at Monticello who finally attained their freedom. Furthermore, biographers have never doubted Jefferson's affection for his first wife, Martha Wayles Skelton, before she died in 1782. Is it not likely that Jefferson felt similarly toward Sally, who was in fact Martha's unacknowledged half-sister?

But the sexual exploitation of black women was common among white masters in the Chesapeake, the Carolinas, and the Caribbean. Like them, Jefferson may have availed himself of the privileges of ownership to compel sexual favors over many years from a slave whom he fancied. Or perhaps Sally Hemings submitted to Jefferson's sexual demands because she hoped to win better treatment—and, in the end, freedom—for herself and her children. Many bondswomen (among them, possibly, Sally's mother, Betty Hemings, and her grandmother) used that strategy to protect their children from the ravages of slavery. What lends added support to either of those interpretations is the testimony of Madison Hemings, who recalled that while Jefferson was affectionate with his white Randolph grandchildren, he was "not in the habit of showing partiality or fatherly affection" to his children with Sally Hemings.

This bell once belonged to Martha Wayles Jefferson, the wife of Thomas Jefferson. According to Hemings family tradition, she gave the bell to Sally Hemings, who was her half-sister.

This painting was discovered on the reverse side of a portrait of a Virginia gentleman. Experts believe that it dates from the early national period and the artist, still unknown, evidently shared Jefferson's criticisms of slavery.

In the last analysis, the significance of Sally Hemings's relationship with Thomas Jefferson may reside in its power to reveal the complexity of southern plantation societies between the American Revolution and the Civil War. In that place and time, the American South was not starkly divided into whites and blacks; instead it was a culture in which the races had been mingling for generations, yielding many people of mixed ancestry such as Sally Hemings. Israel Jefferson, who passed part of his life in slavery at Monticello, remembered her as being "mighty near white," with "long straight hair down her back." Because of their shared bonds of blood, such light-skinned slaves sometimes enjoyed greater privileges and freedoms from their masters, but they also had to negotiate more complicated relationships with them and with less favored members of the slave community.

Bibliography   The best study of the Jefferson-Hemings controversy that predates the DNA discoveries in 1998 is Scot A. French and Edward L. Ayers, "The Strange Career of Thomas Jefferson," in *Jeffersonian Legacies,* ed. Peter S. Onuf (1993). Among those published after the DNA findings, the most informed and comprehensive are a "Forum" piece in the *William and Mary Quarterly,* 57 (2000), entitled "Thomas Jefferson and Sally Hemings Redux" (which includes Fraser D. Neiman's important statistical study); and an anthology of essays edited by Jan Lewis and Peter S. Onuf, *Sally Hemings and Thomas Jefferson* (1999). Readers who wish to pursue the subject in more depth should consult Fawn Brodie's provocative biography, *Thomas Jefferson: An Intimate History* (1974); Annette Gordon-Reed's pathbreaking challenge to the existing scholarship, *Thomas Jefferson and Sally Hemings* (1997); and the November 5, 1998, issue of *Nature,* the British scientific journal in which Eugene A. Foster and his research team first published their DNA findings.

CHAPTER 10
The Opening of America
1815~1850

From Boom to Bust with One-Day Clocks

In the years before the Civil War, the name of Chauncey Jerome could be found traced in neat, sharp letters in a thousand different places across the globe: everywhere from the fireplace mantels of southern planters to the log cabins of Illinois prairie farmers and even in Chinese trading houses in Canton. Chauncey Jerome was a New England clockmaker whose clever, inexpensive, and addictive machines had conquered the markets of the world.

Jerome, the son of a Connecticut blacksmith, at first barely made a living peddling his clocks from farmhouse to farmhouse. Then in 1824 his career took off thanks to a "very showy" bronze looking-glass clock. Between 1827 and 1837 Jerome's factory produced more clocks than any other in the country. But when the Panic of 1837 struck, Jerome had to scramble to avoid financial ruin.

Looking for a new opportunity, he set out to produce an inexpensive brass "one-day" clock—so called because its winding mechanism kept it running that long. Traditionally, the works of these clocks were made of wood, and the wheels and teeth had to be painstakingly cut by hand. Furthermore, wooden clocks could not be exported overseas because the humidity on board ship swelled the wood and ruined them. Jerome's brass version proved more accurate than earlier types and cheaper to boot. Costs came down further when he began to use interchangeable parts and combined his operations for making cases and movements within a single factory in New Haven, Connecticut. By systematically organizing the production process, Jerome brought the price of a good clock within the reach of ordinary people. So popular were the new models that desperate competitors began attaching Jerome labels to their own inferior imitations.

Disaster struck again in 1855, when Jerome went into partnership with several unreliable associates. Within a few years his business faltered, then failed. At the age of 62, the once-prominent business leader found himself working again in a clock factory as an ordinary mechanic. He lived his last years in poverty.

Jerome rose higher than most Americans of his generation, and he fell further. Yet his fellow citizens shared his dreams of success, just as they were haunted by the fear of losing everything. For Jerome, it wasn't only material comforts that

The bustling scene at New York City's South Street, along the East River, provides a sense of the market economy that boomed in the decades following the War of 1812. But while ocean and river transport remained crucial, new methods of moving goods overland—by road, man-made canals, and railroads—allowed the economy to flourish.

vanished; so did respect. "One of the most trying things to me now," he confessed in his autobiography, "is to see how I am looked upon by the community since I lost my property. I never was any better when I owned it than I am now, and never behaved any better. But how different is the feeling towards you, when your neighbors can make nothing more out of you. . . . You are passed by without notice."

As the boom-and-bust economy swirled around him, Jerome sensed that society had taken on a different tone—that the marketplace and its ethos had become dominant. "It is all money and business, business and money which make the man now-a-days," he complained. "Success is every thing, and it makes very little difference how, or what means he uses to obtain it." The United States, according to one foreign traveler, had become "one gigantic workshop, over the entrance of which there is the blazing inscription '*No admission here except on business.*'"

Chauncey Jerome's life spanned the transition from the master-apprentice system of production to the beginnings of mechanization and the rise of the factory system. Crèvecoeur's vision of independent American farmers living mainly on what they themselves produced had, by 1850, become a dream of the past. In its place stood a commercial republic in which a full-blown national market drew together most settled areas of the country.

The concept of the market is crucial here. Americans tied themselves to one another eagerly, even aggressively, through the mechanism of the free market. They sold cotton or wheat and bought manufactured cloth or brass one-day clocks. They borrowed money not merely to buy a house or farm but also to speculate and profit. They relied, even in many rural villages, on cash and paper money instead of bartering for goods and services. American life moved from less to more specialized forms of labor. It moved from face-to-face local dealings to impersonal, distant transactions. It shifted from the mechanically simple to the technologically complex and from less dense patterns of settlement on farms to more complex arrangements in cities and towns. Such were the changes Chauncey Jerome witnessed—indeed, changes he helped to bring about himself, with his clocks that divided the working days of Americans into more disciplined, orderly segments.

Chauncey Jerome's brass clock revolutionized clock-making and made him wealthy. The label displaying Jerome's name, the equivalent of a modern trademark, is visible inside the case.

The Market Revolution

In 1844 John Burrows heard that potatoes were selling for $2.00 a bushel in New Orleans. Potatoes fetched less than 50 cents a bushel in Davenport in the Iowa Territory where Burrows was a small merchant, so he loaded 2,500 bushels on a flatboat and started down the Mississippi River. Along the way, he learned that other merchants, acting on the same information, had done the same and that the market in New Orleans was now glutted with potatoes. When he reached his destination 6 weeks later, he could not sell his load at all. Desperate, he finally swapped his potatoes at 8 cents a bushel, taking a load of coffee in return. He made nothing on the transaction, since it had cost him that much to ship the load to New Orleans.

Burrows's experience demonstrated that a national market economy required not just the efficient movement of goods but also rapid communications. Looking back many years later on the amazing transformation that had occurred in his life-time, Burrows commented, "No one can realize the difficulties of doing a produce business in those days."

A truly national system of markets began to grow following the War of 1812, when the United States entered a period of unprecedented economic expansion. As it grew, the economy became varied enough to sustain and even accelerate its growth. Before the war it had been tied largely to international trade. The United States exported staples like cotton, wheat, tobacco, and timber; if the nations that bought these commodities suddenly stopped doing so, the domestic economy suffered. That happened during the European wars of the 1790s and again after 1803. Because so many Americans remained rural and primarily self-sufficient, they could not absorb any increase in goods produced by American manufacturers.

Growth of a Domestic Market

But the War of 1812 marked the turning point in the creation and expansion of a domestic market. First the embargo and then the war itself stimulated the growth of manufacturing, particularly in textiles. In 1808 the United States had 8000 spindles spinning cotton thread; by the end of the war the number had jumped to around 130,000. In addition, war had also bottled up capital in Europe. When peace was restored, this capital flowed into the United States, seeking investments. Finally, the war experience led the federal government to adopt policies designed to spur economic expansion.

The New Nationalism

After the war with Britain, leadership passed to a new generation of the Republic—younger men like Henry Clay, John C. Calhoun, and John Quincy Adams. All were ardent nationalists eager to use federal power to promote rapid development of the nation. Increasingly dominant within the Republican party, they advocated the "New Nationalism," a set of economic policies designed to foster the prosperity of all regions of the country and bind the nation more tightly together.

National Bank

Even James Madison saw the need for increased federal activity, given the problems the government experienced during the war. The national bank had closed its doors in 1811 when its charter expired. Without it the country had fallen into financial chaos. Madison had opposed Hamilton's national bank in 1791, but now with his approval, Congress in 1816 chartered the Second Bank of the United States for a period of 20 years. Madison also agreed to a mildly protective tariff to aid budding American industries by raising the price of competing foreign goods. Passed in 1816, it set an average duty of 20 percent on imported woolen and cotton cloth, iron, and sugar. The measure enjoyed wide support in the North and West, but a number of southern representatives voted against it because most of its benefits went to northern manufacturers.

Madison also recommended that the government promote internal improvements such as roads, canals, and bridges. The war had demonstrated how cumbersome it was to move troops or supplies overland. Although Madison did not believe that federal funds could be used merely for local projects, he was willing to support projects broader in scope. His successor, James Monroe, approved additional ones.

The Cotton Trade

Cotton proved to be the key to American economic development after 1815. By the end of the eighteenth century, southern planters had discovered that short-fiber cotton would grow in the lower part of the South. But the cotton contained sticky green seeds that could not be easily separated from the lint by hand. The needed breakthrough came in 1793 when Eli Whitney invented the cotton gin, a mechanical device that removed the seeds from the lint. The gin allowed a laborer to clean 50 pounds of cotton a day, compared with only 1 pound by hand. With prices high on the world market, cotton production in the Lower South soared. By 1840 the South produced more than 60 percent of the world supply, which accounted for almost two-thirds of all American exports.

Whitney's cotton gin

Whitney's Cotton Gin   The cotton trade was the major expansive force in the economy until the depression of 1839. Northern factories increasingly made money by turning raw cotton into cloth, while northern merchants reaped profits from shipping the cotton and then reshipping the textiles. Planters used the income they earned to purchase foodstuffs from the West and goods and services from the Northeast.

The Transportation Revolution

To become truly national, a market economy needed an efficient transportation network linking various regions of the nation. The economy had not become self-sustaining earlier partly because the only means of transporting goods cheaply was by water. Thus trade was limited largely to coastal and international markets, for even on rivers, bulky goods moved easily in only one direction—downstream.

All that changed, however, after 1815. From 1825 to 1855—the span of a single generation—the cost of transportation on land fell 95 percent while its speed increased fivefold. As a result, new regions were drawn quickly into the market.

The Canal Age

Erie Canal   Canals attracted considerable investment capital, especially after the success of the wondrous Erie Canal. Built between 1818 and 1825, the canal stretched 364 miles from Albany on the Hudson River to Buffalo on Lake Erie. Its construction by the state was an act of faith, for in 1816 the United States had only 100 miles of canals, none longer than 28 miles. Then, too, the proposed route ran through forests, disease-ridden swamps, and unsettled wilderness. The canal's engineers lacked experience, but they made up for that by sheer ingenuity. Improving on European tools, they devised a cable and screw that allowed one man to pull down even the largest trees and a stump-puller that removed up to 40 stumps a day.

The project paid for itself within a few years. The Erie Canal reduced the cost of shipping a ton of goods from Buffalo to New York City from more than 19 cents a mile to less than 3 cents a mile. By 1860 the cost had fallen to less than a penny a mile. Where its busy traffic passed, settlers flocked, and towns like Rochester and Lockport sprang up and thrived by moving goods and serving markets. "Everything in this bustling place appears to be in motion," wrote one English traveler about Rochester in 1827. The steady flow of goods eastward gave New York City the dominant position in the scramble for control of western trade.

New York's commercial rivals, like Philadelphia and Baltimore, were soon frantically trying to build their own canals to the West. Western states like Ohio and Indiana, convinced that prosperity depended on cheap transportation, constructed canals to link interior regions with the Great Lakes. By 1840 the nation had completed more than 3,300 miles of canals—a length greater than the distance from New York City to Seattle—at a cost of about $125 million. Almost half of that amount came from state governments.

End of Canal Era   By 1850 the canal era was over. The depression of 1839 caused several states to halt or slow their construction, especially since many poorly planned canals lost money. Still, whether profitable or not, canals sharply reduced transportation costs and stimulated economic development in a broad belt along their routes.

Steamboats and Railroads

Because of its vast expanse, the United States was particularly dependent on river transportation. But shipping goods downstream from Pittsburgh to New Orleans took 6 weeks, and the return journey required 17 weeks or more. Steamboats reduced the time of a trip from New Orleans to Louisville from 90 to 8 days while cutting upstream costs by 90 percent.

Although derided as a "big ditch" while it was being built, the Erie Canal proved to be a crucial link in the creation of a national market economy. It promoted urban growth, economic development and feverish activity along its route. Building it required, in some places, an array of hand- and horse-powered hoists as well as back-breaking human labor.

Robert Fulton demonstrated the commercial possibilities of propelling a boat with steam when his ship, the *Clermont,* traveled in 1807 from New York City to Albany on the Hudson River. But steamboats had the greatest effect on transportation on western rivers, where the flat-bottomed boats could haul heavy loads even when the water level was low. The number of steamboats operating in those waters jumped from 17 in 1817 to 727 in 1855. Since steamboats could make many more voyages annually, the carrying capacity on western rivers increased 100-fold between 1820 and 1860. Although railroads would end the steamboat's dominance by 1860, it was the major form of western transportation during the years in which the national market economy grew up, and it proved the most important factor in the rise of manufacturing in the Ohio and upper Mississippi valleys.

Western Steamboats

In 1830 the nation had only 13 miles of railroad track, and most of the lines constructed in the following decade served as feeder lines to canals. But soon enough, cities and towns saw that their economic future depended on having good rail links, so that by 1840 railroad and canal mileage were almost exactly equal (3,325 miles). By 1850, the nation had a total of 8,879 miles of track. Railroad rates were usually higher than canal or steamboat charges, but the new iron roads operated year-round, offered more direct routes, and moved goods about twice as fast. Even so, not until the 1850s did they come to dominate the transportation system.

Railroads' Later Influence

Agriculture in the Market Economy

The new forms of transportation had a remarkable effect on Crèvecoeur's yeoman farm families: they became linked ever more tightly to a national market system. Before the canal era, wheat could be shipped at a profit no farther than 50 miles. But given cheap transportation, farmers eagerly grew more grain and sold the surplus in distant markets.

In this shift toward commercial agriculture, farmers began cultivating more acres, working longer hours, and adopting scientific farming methods, including crop rotation and the use of manures as fertilizer. Instead of bartering goods with friends and neighbors, they more often paid cash or depended on banks to extend them credit. Instead of taking the crops to market themselves, they began to rely on regional merchants, intermediaries in a far-flung distribution system. Like southern planters, western wheat farmers increasingly sold in a world market. Banks and distributors advanced

Commercial Agriculture

Travel Times, 1800 and 1830

credit to farmers, who more and more competed in a market controlled by impersonal forces centered in distant locations.

As transportation and market networks connected more areas of the nation, they encouraged regional specialization. The South increasingly concentrated on staple crops for export, and the West grew foodstuffs, particularly grain. By 1850, Wisconsin and Illinois were major wheat-producing states. Eastern farmers, unable to compete with wheat yields from fertile western farms, shifted to grazing sheep or producing fruits, vegetables, and dairy products for rapidly growing urban areas.

Although foreign commerce expanded too, it was overshadowed by the dramatic growth in domestic markets, which absorbed more and more of the goods and services being produced. The cities of the East no longer looked primarily to the sea for their trade; they looked to southern and western markets. That, indeed, was a revolution in markets.

John Marshall and the Promotion of Enterprise

For a national market system to flourish, a climate favorable to investment had to exist. Under the leadership of Chief Justice John Marshall the Supreme Court became the branch of the federal government most aggressive in protecting the new forms of business central to the growing market economy.

Marshall, who presided over the Court from 1801 to 1835, at first glance seemed an unlikely leader. Informal in manners and almost sloppy in dress, he was nonetheless a commanding figure: tall and slender, with twinkling eyes and a contagious, hearty laugh. His forceful intellect was reinforced by his genial ability to persuade. Time after time he convinced his colleagues to uphold the sanctity of private property and the power of the federal government to promote economic growth.

Constitutionality of the National Bank

In the case of *McCulloch v. Maryland* (1819) the Court upheld the constitutionality of the Second Bank of the United States. Just as Alexander Hamilton had argued in the debate over the first national bank, Marshall emphasized that the Constitution gave Congress the power to make all "necessary and proper" laws to carry out its delegated powers. If Congress believed that a bank would help it meet its responsibilities, such as maintaining the public credit and regulating the currency, then it was constitutional. The bank only had to be useful, not essential. "Let the end be legitimate," Marshall wrote, "let it be within the scope of the Constitution, and all means which are appropriate, which are plainly adapted to that end, which are not prohibited . . . are constitutional." By upholding Hamilton's doctrine of implied powers, Marshall enlarged federal power to an extraordinary degree.

He also encouraged a more freewheeling commerce in *Gibbons v. Ogden* (1824). Under a New York law Aaron Ogden held a monopoly on steamboat traffic on the

Interstate Commerce

The Transportation Network of a Market Economy, 1840 *Canals played their most important role in the Northeast, where they linked eastern cities to western rivers and the Great Lakes. On the Erie Canal, a system of locks raised and lowered boats in a series of steps along the route. Steamboats were most crucial in the extensive river systems of the South and the West.*

Plying the Mississippi River and its tributaries, the steamboat carried both freight and passengers, but it won its greatest fame as a mode of travel. The most luxurious boats, dubbed floating palaces, offered accommodations far beyond the experience of the average American. Steamboats also provided the cheapest form of inland transportation up to the Civil War. By midcentury, cabin passage for the 1,400-mile trip from Louisville to New Orleans was only $12 to $15.

On the earliest steamboats passengers were housed on the main deck along with the cargo, but as the boats became larger, designers added a second, or boiler, deck (which, despite its name, was not where the boilers were located). Eventually a third level was added, the hurricane or texas, with additional accommodations. The boiler deck's saloon was the center of society, with the ladies' parlor at one end and the barroom at the other. Besides serving as a dining room and lounge, the saloon sometimes provided the sleeping quarters for men. Berths were arranged in two tiers on both sides and, at least on the better boats, contained bedding and a mattress. Women entered the saloon only for meals.

Steamboats also offered passage on the main deck for about one-fifth the price of a regular ticket. These passengers received no living quarters or toilet facilities and had to provide their own food. Then, too, boiler explosions, collisions, and sinkings from

Although a steamboat's furnishings in the main saloon often boasted fancy gingerbread trimmings, travelers usually had to make do with primitive facilities.

Hudson River between New Jersey and New York City. Thomas Gibbons, who had a federal license to operate a steamboat, set up a competing line and Ogden sued. The case gave Marshall a chance to define the greatest power of the federal government in peacetime, the right to regulate interstate commerce. In striking down a steamboat monopoly granted by the state of New York, the chief justice gave the term *commerce* the broadest possible definition, declaring that it covered all commercial dealings and that Congress's power over interstate commerce could be "exercised to its utmost extent." The result was increased business competition throughout society.

Protection of Contracts

At the heart of most commercial agreements were private contracts, made between individuals or companies. Marshall took an active role in defining contract law, which was then in its infancy. The case of *Fletcher v. Peck* (1810) showed how far he was willing to go to protect private property. The justices unanimously struck down a Georgia law taking back a land grant that a group of speculators had obtained by bribing members of the legislature. A grant was a contract, Marshall declared, and because the Constitution forbade states to impair "the obligation of contracts," the legislature could not interfere with the grant once it had been made. Although the framers of the Constitution probably meant *contracts* to refer only to agreements between private parties, Marshall made no distinction between public and private agreements, thereby greatly expanding the meaning of the contract clause.

a snag took a much higher loss of life among lower-deck passengers, who were primarily the poor, immigrants, and African Americans. Between 1811 and 1851, 44 steamboats collided, 166 burned, 209 exploded, and 576 hit obstructions and sank, costing thousands of lives.

The steamboat was, as many travelers remarked, a "world in miniature," conveying slaves and planters, farmers and manufacturers, merchants and frontier families, soldiers and Indians, ministers and professional gamblers. As fares steadily dropped, people of widely different wealth and position were thrown together in the main cabin and mingled with democratic familiarity. Women spent their time talking, sewing, caring for children, and strolling the deck. Men passed the time in conversation about politics, the weather, business, and crops. The bar was the center of their social world, and gambling was rife.

The most famous vessels on the rivers boasted intricately carved gingerbread facings, painted a glistening white and trimmed in gold leaf—an architectural style known as "Steamboat Gothic." For all their luxurious veneer, however, steamboats lacked many amenities. Most six-by-six staterooms had two narrow shelves to sleep on and no lighting or heat. The washrooms in the main cabin contained tin basins and pitchers of cold water, a comb and brush, and a communal toothbrush. One traveler complained that there were only two towels for 70 men on one boat. Water, for both drinking and washing, came directly from the river and was laden with silt. Steamboat food was ample but often poorly prepared and saturated with grease. Furthermore, the average riverboat hardly lived up to the standards of the most famous packets. In 1843 John James Audubon journeyed from Louisville to St. Louis on what he described as "the very filthiest of all filthy old rattraps I ever traveled in." He grumbled particularly about a leaky roof, threadbare sheets, and pillows filled with corn husks.

In maintaining law and order, the captain was aided by the passengers, who in the tradition of the frontier sometimes formed their own courts to deal with those charged with minor offenses. Travelers accused of theft, illicit sexual relations, or cheating at gambling might find themselves flogged or put ashore at some desolate spot. In one case, when a young man and woman traveling together as "cousins" aroused suspicion, the passengers insisted on an investigation by the boat's officers, who discovered the pair sharing a berth. At the next stop, while the boat waited, indignant passengers marched the couple ashore, rounded up a minister, and compelled them to get married.

Despite the discomforts of swarming mosquitoes, heat from the boilers, and noisy engines at all hours of the night, observers agreed that journeying by steamboat was far more pleasant than taking a stagecoach, the principal alternative in the West before 1850. With their churning paddlewheels, gingerbread decks, and belching smokestacks, these gaudy vessels became the grandest showpieces of life along the commercial waterways of the Mississippi.

The most celebrated decision Marshall wrote on the contract clause was in *Dartmouth College v. Woodward*, decided in 1819. This case arose out of the attempt by New Hampshire to alter the college's charter granted by George III in 1769. The Court overturned the state law on the grounds that state charters were also contracts and could not be altered by later legislatures. By this ruling Marshall intended to protect corporations, which conducted business under charters granted by individual states.

Thus the Marshall Court encouraged economic risk taking. Its decisions protected property and contracts, limited state interference in business affairs, and created a climate of business confidence.

General Incorporation Laws

Corporations were not new in American business, but as the economy expanded, they grew in numbers. By pooling investors' resources, they also provided a way to raise capital for large-scale undertakings. Then, too, corporations offered the advantage of limited liability: that is, an investor was liable only for the amount he or she had invested. Ventures such as banks, insurance companies, railroads, and manufacturing firms—which all required a large amount of capital—increasingly were incorporated.

Importance of Corporations

271

Originally, state legislatures were required to approve a special charter for each new corporation. Beginning in the 1830s, states adopted general incorporation laws that automatically granted a corporation charter to any applicant who met certain minimum qualifications. This reform made it much easier and faster to secure a charter and stimulated organization of the national market.

A People in Motion

"Eating on the first of May," commented one New York City resident, "is entirely out of the question." That day was "moving day," when all the leases in the city expired. On that date nearly everyone, it seemed, moved to a new residence or place of business. Bedlam prevailed as furniture and personal belongings cluttered the sidewalks and people, movers, and horses crowded the streets. To Frances Trollope, it looked as if the whole population was "flying from the plague." Whereas in Europe millions of ordinary folk had never ventured beyond their local village, a Boston paper commented in 1828, "here, the whole population is in motion."

Like most Europeans, the famous French commentator Alexis de Tocqueville was astonished at the restless mobility of the average American. "Born often under another sky, placed in the middle of an always moving scene, . . . the American . . . grows accustomed only to change, and ends by regarding it as the natural state of man."

A High-Speed Society Surprises Europeans

This emphasis on speed affected nearly every aspect of American life. Americans ate so quickly that one disgruntled European insisted food was "pitchforked down." Steamboat captains risked boiler explosions for the honor of having the fastest boat on the river. American technology emphasized speed over longevity on the assumption that the present design would soon be obsolete. Unlike European railroads, American railroads were lightweight, were hastily constructed, and paid little heed to the safety or comfort of passengers. Even so, Americans quickly embraced this new mode of transportation because of its speed. Eighteen-year-old Caroline Fitch of Boston likened her first ride on a railroad to a "lightning flash": "It was 'whew!' and we were there, and 'whew!' and we were back again."

Even within railroad cars Americans were too fidgety to adapt to the European system of individual passenger compartments. Instead, American cars had a center aisle, allowing ever-restless passengers to wander the length of the train. Riding the rails in Texas, an English visitor was astounded that the passengers were "constantly

Europeans were shocked that Americans bolted their food or gorged themselves on anything within reach, as this English drawing indicates. Such habits reflected both the indifferent preparation of food and the frenetic tempo of American life.

jumping on and off whilst the train is in motion, and larking from one car to the other."

Horatio Greenough, a sculptor who returned to the United States in 1836 after an extended stay abroad, was amazed and a bit frightened by the pace he witnessed. "Go ahead! is the order of the day," he observed. "The whole continent presents a scene of scrambling and roars with greedy hurry." In the economic arena, the growth of a national market increased the sense of motion and restlessness. But social factors also contributed to this high-speed society.

Population Growth

The American population continued to double about every 22 years—more than twice the birthrate of Great Britain. The census, which counted fewer than 4 million Americans in 1790, surpassed 23 million in 1850. Although the birthrate peaked in 1800, it declined only slowly before 1840. During the 1840s, as urban areas grew rapidly, it dropped about 10 percent, the first significant decrease in American history. In cities, families were smaller, in part because the labor of children was not as critical to the family's economic welfare.

At the same time, many basic population characteristics changed little throughout the first half of the nineteenth century. Life expectancy did not improve significantly, the population remained quite young, and early marriage remained the norm, especially in rural areas.

From 1790 to 1820 natural increase accounted for virtually all the country's population growth. But immigration, which had been disrupted by the Napoleonic Wars in Europe, revived after 1815. In the 1830s some 600,000 immigrants arrived, more than double the number in the quarter century after 1790. And these newcomers proved to be merely a foretaste of the flood of immigrants that reached America beginning in the late 1840s.

Immigration Rises After 1830

The Federal Land Rush

The vast areas of land available for settlement absorbed much of the growing population. By 1850 almost half of all Americans lived outside the original 13 states. Well over 2 million lived beyond the Mississippi River. As settlers streamed west, speculation in western lands reached frenzied proportions. In the single year of 1818, at the peak of land-buying fever, the United States sold 3,500,000 million acres of its public domain. (In contrast, only 68,000 acres were sold in 1800.)

The Panic of 1819 sent sales and prices crashing, and in the depression that followed many farmers lost their farms. Congress reacted by abolishing credit sales and demanding payment in cash, but it tempered this policy by lowering the price of the cheapest lands to $1.25 an acre. (The best lands, sold at auction, fetched considerably higher prices, however.) The government also reduced the minimum tract to 80 acres, which meant that an ordinary farm could be purchased for $100.

Even so, speculators purchased most of the public lands sold, since the law put no limit on how many acres an individual or a land company could buy. These land speculators played a leading role in settlement of the West. To hasten sales, they usually sold land partially on credit—a vital aid to poorer farmers. They also provided loans to purchase needed tools and supplies, since the cost of establishing a farm was beyond the means of many young men. Many farmers became speculators themselves, buying up property in the neighborhood and selling it to latecomers at a tidy profit. "Speculation in real estate has been the ruling idea and occupation of the Western mind," one Englishman reported in the 1840s. "Clerks, labourers, farmers, storekeepers merely followed their callings for a living while they were speculating for their fortunes."

Speculators Help Settle Western Lands

Geographic Mobility

On the Road Again

Given such rapid settlement, geographic mobility became one of the most striking characteristics of the American people. The 1850 census revealed that nearly half of all native-born free Americans lived outside the state where they had been born. In Boston from 1830 to 1860 perhaps one-third of the inhabitants changed their place of residence each year. Some owners, dissatisfied with their location, moved their houses instead. An astonished Charles Dickens recounted he once met a house "coming downhill at a good round trot, drawn by some twenty oxen!"

Often, the influence of the market uprooted Americans too. In 1851, a new railroad line bypassed the village of Auburn, Illinois, on the way to Springfield. "It seemed a pity," wrote one resident, "that so pretty a site as that of the old town should be abandoned for so unpromising a one... much of it mere swamp—but railroad corporations possess no bowels of compassion, the practical more than the beautiful being their object." After residents quickly moved to the new town that sprang up around the depot, a neighboring farmer purchased the site and plowed up the streets, and Auburn reverted to a cornfield.

Urbanization

Even with the growth of a national market, the United States remained a rural nation. Nevertheless, the four decades after 1820 witnessed the fastest rate of urbanization in American history. In 1820 there were only 12 cities with a population of more than 5,000; by 1850 there were nearly 150. The 1820 census classified only about 9 percent of the American people as urban (living in towns with a population of 2,500 or more). Forty years later the number had risen to 20 percent. As a result, the ratio of farmers to city dwellers steadily dropped from 15 to 1 in 1800 to 5.5 to 1 in 1850. Improved transportation, the declining productivity of many eastern farms, the beginnings of industrialization, and the arrival of immigrants all stimulated the growth of cities.

St. Louis, a major urban center that developed in the West, depended on the steamboat to sustain its commerce, as this 1859 illustration makes clear.

The most heavily urbanized area of the country was the Northeast, where in 1860 more than a third of the population lived in cities.* The nation's largest city was New York, with more than half a million people, and older cities like Philadelphia, Boston, Baltimore, and New Orleans continued to be major urban centers. Equally significant, important urban centers such as St. Louis and Cincinnati arose in the West. Remarkably, by the century's midpoint, 40 percent of the nation's total urban population resided in interior cities. The South, with only 10 percent of its people living in cities, was the least urbanized region.

All these changes—the growth of the population, the quickening movement westward, and the rising migration to the cities—pointed to a fundamental reorientation of American development.

Urban Centers, Old and New

The Rise of Factories

It was an isolated life, growing up in rural, hilly Vermont. But stories of the textile factories that had sprung up in Lowell and other towns in Massachusetts reached even small villages such as Barnard. Fifteen-year-old Mary Paul was working there as a domestic servant when she asked her father for permission to move to Lowell. "I am in need of clothes which I cannot get about here," she explained. In 1845 two friends from Barnard helped her find a job at the Lowell mills, from which she earned $128 in 11 months. After four years she returned home but now found "countryfied" life too confining. This time she left her rural hometown for good. She moved about and supported herself at several occupations before finally marrying and settling down in nearby Lynn.

Mary Paul was one of thousands of rural Americans whose lives were fundamentally transformed by the market economy. The changes in her lifestyle and her working habits demonstrated that the new factories and industries needed more than technological innovation to run smoothly. Equally crucial, the labor used to manufacture these goods needed to be reorganized.

Technological Advances

Before 1815 manufacturing had been done in homes or shops by skilled artisans. As master craftworkers, they taught their trades to apprentices and **journeymen**. In addition, women often worked in their homes part-time under the putting-out system, making finished articles from raw material supplied by merchant capitalists. After 1815 this older form of manufacturing began to give way to factories with machinery tended by unskilled or semiskilled laborers.

Small-Scale Manufacturing

From England came many of the earliest technological innovations. But Americans often improved on the British machines or adapted them to more extensive uses. In contrast to the more traditional societies of Europe, "everything new is quickly introduced here," one visitor commented in 1820. "There is no clinging to old ways; the moment an American hears the word 'invention' he pricks up his ears." From 1790 to 1860 the United States Patent Office granted more patents than England and France combined.

Acceptance of Technology

To protect their economic advantage, the British forbade the export of any textile machinery or emigration of any craftworker trained in their construction. But in 1790 a mill worker named Samuel Slater slipped past English authorities and built the first textile mill in America. Two decades later, the Boston merchant Francis Cabot Lowell imitated British designs for a power loom and then improved on them.

---

*The Northeast included New England and the mid-Atlantic states (New York, Pennsylvania, and New Jersey). The South comprised the slave states plus the District of Columbia.

Interchangeable Parts

The first machines required highly skilled workers to both build and repair them. Eli Whitney had a better idea. Having won a contract to produce 10,000 muskets for the government, he developed machinery that would mass-produce parts that were interchangeable from one gun to another. Such parts had to be manufactured to rigid specifications that Whitney had difficulty attaining, but once the process was perfected after his death, a worker could assemble a musket quickly with only a few tools. Simeon North applied the same principle to the production of clocks, and Chauncey Jerome followed North's example and soon surpassed him.

Communication

What rail and steam engines did for transportation, Samuel F. B. Morse's telegraph did for communications. Morse patented a device that sent electrical pulses over a wire in 1837, and before long, telegraph lines fanned out in all directions, linking various parts of the country instantaneously. By 1860 more than 50,000 miles of telegraph lines had been laid. The new telegraph sped business information, helped link the transportation network, and allowed newspapers to provide readers with up-to-date news.

Indeed, the invention of the telegraph and the perfection of a power press (1847) by Robert Hoe and his son Richard revolutionized journalism. The mechanical press sharply increased the speed with which sheets could be printed over the old hand method. Mass-produced newspapers, often selling for only a penny, gained huge circulations since ordinary families could afford them. Hoe's press had a similar impact on book publishing, as thousands of copies could be printed at affordable prices.

The Postal System

The development of a national market economy depended on mass communications that transmitted commercial information and brought into contact producers and sellers separated by great distances. While postage was relatively expensive, the American postal system subsidized the distribution of newspapers and spread other information widely. Indeed, in the years before the Civil War, the postal system had more employees than any other enterprise in the country. While the postal system's primary purpose was to promote commerce, it had a profound social impact by accustoming people to long-range and even impersonal communication. By 1840, the post office handled almost 41 million letters and 39 million newspapers.

When traveling in the United States in 1831, Tocqueville was amazed at the scope of the postal system. "There is an astonishing circulation of letters and newspapers among these savage woods," he reported from the Michigan frontier. There was hardly a village or town in the country, no matter how remote, that was not connected with the rest of the country through the postal system. Nothing in Europe, he noted, could match it. While the British and French post offices handled a greater volume of mail, the United States throughout these years had a much more extensive postal system. In 1828, there were almost twice as many post offices in the United States as in Great Britain, and over five times as many as in France.

In the Americas, the Canadian postal system was so limited that merchants and even government officials routinely used the United States postal system to get mail to other provinces, while by midcentury Mexico had only 49 post offices and no regularized service for the whole country. In China, the government maintained a very efficient military-courier system for official communications, but foreigners developed the first private postal system, mainly for business correspondence; it was not until the twentieth century that a mass-based postal system was established. Most countries had no true postal system in these years, since literacy was so limited.

Textile Factories

The factory system originated in the Northeast, where capital, water power, and transportation facilities were available. In New England, as in England, the production of cloth was the first manufacturing process to make significant use of the new technology

Don't Steal This Paper!

Tracing Information Networks in a Market Economy

Today we take information for granted. The Internet, 24-hour television, cell phones, and instant messaging put data of all sorts at our fingers. The situation was much different in 1859, when English artist Lefevre J. Cranstone sketched this hotel scene somewhere along the Ohio River. Clearly Cranstone thought it funny that gentlemen might walk off with newspapers. In any case, what sort of gentlemen blew cigarette smoke insolently and tipped back in his chair? But Cranstone overlooked an important aspect of the "popularity" of newspapers in the United States. In a market economy the movement of information was as crucial as the movement of goods.

Think of the role played by information in the examples already mentioned in this chapter. John Burrows (page 264) lost money trying to ship potatoes to New Orleans because he lacked up-to-date information on prices. Toqueville (page 276) marveled that the backwoods of Michigan possessed 940 miles of mail roads and Arkansas 1,938. Newspapers, mail—*information*—was eagerly in demand.

Historians have paid close attention to the information networks, assembling data to make those links clear. The "time of travel" maps on page 268 are one example. Until 1837 information traveled at the same speed as people. Then Morse's telegraph drastically changed the equation. News on the wire traveled instantly. An eastern farmer selling grain in New York could learn the price asked in Chicago. A western merchant looking for a loan could inquire about the rate of interest in Philadelphia. As historians have discovered, markets in everything from grain to meat to money were becoming national and even international. Out of the ability exchange information efficiently came modern institutions now taken for granted: stock exchanges and commodity markets.

on a large scale. Eventually all the processes of manufacturing cloth were brought together in a single location, from opening the cotton bales to weaving the cloth, and machines did virtually all the work.

In 1820 a group of wealthy Boston merchants known as the Boston Associates set up operations at Lowell, Massachusetts. Intended as a model community, Lowell soon became the nation's most famous center of textile manufacturing.

Its founders sought to avoid the wretched misery that characterized the factory system in England by combining **paternalism** with high profits. Instead of relying primarily on child labor or a permanent working class, the Lowell mills employed daughters of New England farm families. Thus women were the first factory workers in the United States. They lived in company boardinghouses under the watchful eye of a matron. To its many visitors, Lowell presented an impressive sight: huge factories, well-kept houses, bustling shops. Female employees were encouraged to attend lectures and use the library. They even published their own magazine, the *Lowell Offering*.

In reality, however, factory life involved strict rules and long hours of tedious, repetitive work. At Lowell, for example, workers could be fined for lateness or misconduct, including talking on the job. Alcohol, cards, and gambling were forbidden in the shop or mill

Lowell

Hard Work in the Mills

yard. The women's morals in the boardinghouses were strictly guarded; male visitors were supervised, and there was a 10 P.M. curfew. Work typically began at 7 A.M. (earlier in the summer) and continued until 7 at night, six days a week. With only 30 minutes for the noon meal, many workers had to run to the boardinghouse and back to avoid being late. Winter was the "lighting up" season, when work began before daylight and ended after dark. The only light after sunset came from whale oil lamps that filled the long rooms with smoke.

Although the labor was hard, the female operators earned from $2.40 to $3.20 a week, wages that were considered good at the time. (Domestic servants and seamstresses, two of the most common jobs women held, were paid less than a dollar a week.) The average "mill girl," as they were called, was between 16 and 30 years old. Most were not working to support their families back home on the farm; instead they wanted to save some money for perhaps the first time in their lives and sample some of life's pleasures. "I must . . . have something of my own before many more years have passed," Sally Rice wrote in rejecting her parents' request that she return home to Somerset, Vermont. "And where is that something coming from if I go home and earn nothing?"

The sense of sisterhood that united women in the boardinghouses made it easier for farm daughters to adjust to the stress and regimen the factory imposed on them. So did their view of the situation as temporary rather than permanent, for most women worked in the mills no more than five years before getting married.

Mill workers, Lowell

As competition in the textile industry intensified, factory managers sought ways to raise productivity. In the mid-1830s the mills began to increase the workloads and speed up the machinery. Even these changes failed to maintain previous profits, and on several occasions factories cut wages. The ever-quickening pace of work finally provoked resistance among the mill workers. Several times in the 1830s wage cuts sparked strikes in which a minority of workers walked out. Management retaliated by firing strike leaders, hiring new workers, and blacklisting women who refused to return. In the 1840s workers' protests focused on the demand for a 10-hour day.

Transformation of Lowell

The quest for profits also undercut the owners' paternalism. As the mills expanded, a smaller proportion of the workers lived in company boardinghouses and moral regulations were relaxed. But the greatest change was a shift in the workforce from native-born women to Irish immigrants, including men and children. In 1845 the Irish made up only 8 percent of the Lowell workforce; by 1860 they amounted to almost half. Because these new workers were poor and desperate for work, wages declined further. And because they did not view their situation as temporary, a permanent working class began to take shape.

Lowell and the Environment

Lowell was a city built on water power. Early settlers had used the power of the Merrimack River to run mills, but never on the scale used by the new textile factories. As the market spread, Americans came to link progress with the fullest use of the natural resources of the environment. Just as they had done in Lowell itself, the Boston Associates sought to impose a sense of order and regularity on the surrounding physical environment in order to efficiently use its natural resources. In the process, they fundamentally reshaped the area's waterscape.

Reshaping the Area's Waterscape

As more and more mills were built, the Boston Associates sought to harness water for energy. By 1836, Lowell had seven canals, with a supporting network of locks and dams, to govern the Merrimack's flow and distribute water to the city's twenty-six mills. At Lawrence, they constructed the largest dam in the world at the time, a 32-foot-high granite structure that spanned 1,600 feet across the river. But even dammed, the Merrimack's waters proved insufficient. So the Associates gained control of a series of lakes in New Hampshire covering more than 100 square miles that fed into the river system. By damming these lakes, they could provide a regular flow of water down the river, especially in the drier summer months. In the course of establishing this elaborate water-control system, they came to see water as a form of property, divorced from the ownership of land along the river. Water became a commodity that was measured in terms of its power to operate a certain number of spindles and looms.

Damaging Effects

By regulating the river's waters, the Boston Associates made the Merrimack Valley the greatest industrial center in the country in the first half of the nineteenth century. But not all who lived in the valley benefited. By raising water levels, the dams flooded farm lands, blocked the transportation of logs downstream, and damaged mills upstream by reducing the current that powered waterwheels. The dams also devastated the fish population by preventing upstream spawning, while factories routinely dumped their wastes into the river. These wastes, combined with sewage from the growing population, eventually contaminated water supplies. Epidemics of typhoid, cholera, and dysentery occurred with increasing frequency.

In the end, the factory system fundamentally transformed the environment. Far from existing in harmony with its rural surroundings, Lowell, with its clattering

Development of the Lowell Mills   *As more mills were built at Lowell, the demand increased for water to power them. By 1859 the mills drew water from lakes 80 to 100 miles upstream, including Winnipesaukee, Squam, and Newfound. The map at left shows the affected watersheds. In the city of Lowell (right), a system of canals was enlarged over several decades. In the painting (done in 1845), the machine shop can be seen at left, with a row of mills alongside a canal. Rail links tied Lowell and Boston together.*

machines and dammed rivers, presented a glaring contrast to rural life. The founding vision of Lowell had disappeared.

Industrial Work

Artisan System

For most workers, adaptation to the disciplined work routine of the factory did not happen easily. Traditionally, artisans had worked within the home. Apprentices were considered part of the family, and masters were responsible not only for teaching their apprentices a trade but also for providing them some education and for supervising their moral behavior. Journeymen took pride in their work, knowing that if they perfected their skill, they could become respected master artisans with their own shops. Skilled artisans worked not by the clock, at a steady pace, but rather in bursts of intense labor alternating with more leisurely time.

Transformation of Work

The factory changed that. Factory-produced goods were not as finished or elegant as those done by hand, and pride in craftsmanship gave way to rates of productivity. At the same time, workers were required to discard old habits, for industrialism demanded a worker who was sober, dependable, and self-disciplined. The machines, whirring and clacking away, set a strict schedule that had to be followed. Absenteeism, lateness, and drunkenness hurt productivity and, since work was specialized, disrupted the regular factory routine. Thus industrialization not only changed the way work was organized but transformed the very nature of work.

For newcomers to industrial ways, the factory clock became the symbol of the new order. One mill worker who finally quit complained of "obedience to the ding-dong of the bell—just as though we are so many living machines." Along with the loss of personal freedom came the loss of standing in the community. Whereas the master-apprentice relationship was a close bond, factories sharply separated workers from management. Few workers rose through the ranks to supervisory positions, and even fewer could achieve the artisan's dream of setting up one's own business. Even well-paid workers sensed their decline in status.

The Shoe Industry

Shoemaking also illustrated the industrial process at work. Traditionally, a skilled cobbler knew how to judge the quality of leather, cut out the various parts of a shoe, and stitch and glue the parts together. He then sold the shoes in the shop where he and his apprentices made them. Unlike the textile industry, shoemaking was not rapidly transformed in this period by a shift to heavy machinery. Even so, expanding national markets fundamentally altered the business.

Following in his father's footsteps, Micajah Pratt, a cobbler from Lynn, Massachusetts, began selling shoes in 1812 to customers in New England. He found, however, that there were ready markets in the South and West for cheaply made shoes. So he hired workers to produce shoes in larger and larger central shops. Pratt cut costs further by using new production techniques, such as standardized patterns and sole-cutting machines. He eventually employed as many as 500 men and women.

TIME TABLE OF THE LOWELL MILLS,

To take effect on and after Oct. 21st, 1851.

The Standard time being that of the meridian of Lowell, as shown by the regulator clock of JOSEPH RAYNES, 43 Central Street

	From 1st to 10th inclusive.				From 11th to 20th inclusive.				From 21st to last day of month.			
	1st Bell	2d Bell	3d Bell	Eve. Bell	1st Bell	2d Bell	3d Bell	Eve. Bell	1st Bell	2d Bell	3d Bell	Eve. Bell
January,	5.00	6.00	6.50	*7.30	5.00	6 00	6.50	*7.30	5.00	6.00	6.50	*7.30
February,	4.30	5.30	6.40	*7.30	4.30	5.30	6.25	*7.30	4.30	5.30	6.15	*7.30
March,	5.40	6.00		*7.30	5.20	5.40		*7.30	5.05	5.25		6.35
April,	4.45	5.05		6.45	4.30	4.50		6.55	4.30	4.50		7.00
May,	4.30	4.50		7.00	4.30	4.50		7.00	4.30	4.50		7 00
June,	"	"		"	"	"		"	"	"		"
July,	"	"		"	"	"		"	"	"		"
August,	"	"		"	"	"		"	"	"		"
September,	4.40	5.00		6.45	4.50	5.10		6.30	5.00	5.20		*7.30
October,	5.10	5.30		*7.30	5.20	5.40		*7.30	5.35	5.55		*7.30
November,	4.30	5.30	6.10	*7.30	4.30	5.30	6.20	*7.30	5.00	6.00	6.35	*7.30
December,	5.00	6.00	6.45	*7.30	5.00	6.00	6.50	*7.30	5.00	6 00	6.50	*7.30

* Excepting on Saturdays from Sept. 21st to March 20th inclusive, when it is rung at 20 minutes after sunset.

YARD GATES,

Will be opened at ringing of last morning bell, of meal bells, and of evening bells; and kept open Ten minutes.

MILL GATES.

Commence hoisting Mill Gates, Two minutes before commencing work.

WORK COMMENCES,

At Ten minutes after last morning bell, and at Ten minutes after bell which "rings in" from Meals.

BREAKFAST BELLS.

During March "Ring out"........at....7.30 a. m..........."Ring in" at 8·05 a. m.
April 1st to Sept. 20th inclusive.....at....7 00 " " .... " at 7.35 " "
Sept. 21st to Oct. 31st inclusive....at....7.30 " " .... " at 8.05 " "
Remainder of year work commences after Breakfast.

DINNER BELLS.

" Ring out".....................12.30 p. m........."Ring in".... 1.05 p. m.

In all cases, the *first* stroke of the bell is considered as marking the time.

Long hours and punctuality: that is the message of this Lowell timetable. Often accustomed to a less regimented life on a farm, machine operators complained of the pace of the machines and the tyranny of the factory bell that summoned and dismissed them each day.

With the shoe industry booming, Lynn's population doubled every 20 years. Yet so great was the national market that manufacturers could not keep pace with demand. Increasingly they hired nearby farmers, fishermen, and their families to do part-time work at home. Women and girls sewed the upper parts of a shoe, men and boys attached the bottoms. While slow, this mode of production allowed wages to be reduced still further. A few highly paid workers performed critical tasks like cutting the leather, but most work was done either in large central shops or in homes. With workers no longer able to make an entire shoe, in little more than a generation shoemaking ceased to be a craft. Though not organized in a factory setting, it had become essentially an assembly-line process.

Lynn as the Center of Shoemaking

The Labor Movement

In this newly emerging economic order, workers sometimes organized to protect their rights and traditional ways of life. Craftworkers like carpenters, printers, and tailors formed unions, and in 1834 individual unions came together in the National Trades' Union.

Union leaders argued that labor was degraded in America: workers endured long hours, low pay, and low status. Unlike most American social thinkers of the day, a number of labor leaders accepted the idea of conflict between different classes. They did not believe that the interests of workers and employers could be reconciled, and they blamed the plight of labor on monopolies, especially banking and paper money, and on machines and the factory system.

If the unions' rhetoric sounded radical, the solutions they proposed were moderate. Reformers agitated for public education and abolition of imprisonment for debt to provide better opportunities for workers. Leaders saw effective unions and political action as the means to restore labor to its former honored position. Proclaiming the republican virtues of freedom and equality, they attacked special privilege and decried workers' loss of independence.

Emergence of Unions

The labor movement gathered some momentum in the decade before the Panic of 1837, but in the depression that followed, its strength collapsed. During hard times, few workers were willing to strike or engage in collective action. Nor did skilled craftworkers, who spearheaded the union movement, feel a particularly strong bond with semiskilled factory workers and unskilled laborers. More than a decade of agitation did finally gain the 10-hour day for some workers by the 1850s, and the courts also recognized workers' right to strike, but these gains had little immediate impact.

Workers were united in resenting the industrial system and their loss of status. But they found themselves divided by a host of other factors: ethnic and racial antagonisms, gender, conflicting religious perspectives, occupational differences, party loyalties, and disagreements over tactics. For most workers, the factory and industrialism were not agents of opportunity but reminders of their loss of independence and a measure of control over their lives.

Sam Patch and a Worker's "Art"

Some workers fought against the loss of independence in unusual ways. The waterfalls that attracted capitalists looking to build mills also attracted workers in their off hours, coming to picnic, swim, or fish. For those with nerve, the falls provided also a place to show off their skills as waterfall jumpers. Sam Patch was such a young man, known for his daring leaps into the Passaic River at the mills around Paterson, New Jersey.

In 1827 Patch became disgusted by a sawmill owner who was set to open a private park, "Forest Gardens," close to Passaic Falls. The owner said he would charge admission in order to keep out "the lazy, idle, rascally, drunken vagabonds" who might spoil the pleasure of more refined folk come to enjoy the view. Workers who resented this fencing out rejoiced when Patch vowed to spoil Forest Garden's opening-day party. As proper folk gathered, thousands of ordinary laborers crowded along the opposite bank and cheered as Patch leapt 70 feet straight into the foaming water.

Sam Patch's fame led him eventually to the biggest challenge of all: Niagara Falls. Twice he jumped more than 80 feet into the cascade's churning waters. But he drowned a month later when he dared the Genesee Falls in another mill town along the Erie Canal—Rochester, New York. Still, his fame persisted for decades. Leaping waterfalls was "an art which I have knowledge of and courage to perform," he had insisted. In a market economy in which skilled "arts" were being replaced by machine labor, Patch's acts were a defiant protest against the changing times.

Social Structures of the Market Society

American farmers, workers, and merchants were all affected, as individuals, by the revolution in markets. Equally critical, the market revolution restructured American society as a whole. It created greater extremes between the rich and the poor, contributed to the rise of a growing middle class, placed greater emphasis on material goods, and even changed the way Americans thought about time.

Economic Specialization

To begin with, the spread of the market produced greater specialization. As we have seen, transportation networks made it possible for farmers to concentrate on producing certain crops, while factories could focus on making a single item such as cloth or shoes. Within factories, the division of labor broke down the manufacture of an item into smaller, more specialized (and less skilled) tasks.

To be sure, the process evolved at different rates. Large factories were the exception rather than the rule. Much manufacturing was still done in smaller shops with few employees. Even so, the tendency was toward more technology, greater efficiency, and increasing specialization.

Decline of Women's Traditional Work

Specialization had consequences at home as well. The average eighteenth-century American woman produced thread, cloth, clothing, and candles in the home for family use. With the growth of factories, however, household manufacturing all but disappeared. As a result, women lost many of the economic functions they had once performed at home. Again, textiles are a striking example. Between 1815 and 1860, the price of cotton cloth fell from 18 to 2 cents a yard. Because manufactured cloth was also smoother and more brightly colored than homespun, most women purchased cloth rather than making it themselves. Similarly, the new ready-made men's clothing reduced the amount of sewing women did, especially in cities, where more men purchased clothing from retail stores. As Chapter 12 will make clearer, the growth of industry led to an economic reorganization of the family and a new definition of women's role in society.

Materialism

Europeans who visited the United States during these years were struck by how hard Americans worked and how preoccupied they were with material goods and achievements. The new generation did not invent materialism, but the spread of the market after 1815 made it much more evident. And in 1836 the American writer Washington Irving coined the classic phrase that captured the spirit of the age when he spoke, in one of his stories, of "the almighty dollar, that great object of universal devotion throughout the land."

Wealth and Status

In a nation that had no legally recognized aristocracy, no established church, and class lines that were only informally drawn, wealth became the most obvious symbol of status. Dismissing birth as "a mere idea," one magazine explained, "Wealth is something substantial. Everybody knows that and feels it." Materialism reflected more than a desire for goods and physical comfort. It represented a quest for respect and recognition. "Americans boast of their skill in money making," one contemporary observed, "and as it is the only standard of dignity and nobility and worth, they endeavor to obtain it by every possible means." Families were rated by the size, not the source, of their fortunes. Americans also emphasized practicality over theory. The esteem of the founding generation for intellectual achievement was mostly lost in the scramble for wealth that seemed to consume the new generation.

The Emerging Middle Class

In the years after 1815, a new middle class took shape in American society. A small class of shopkeepers, professionals, and master artisans had existed earlier, but the creation of a national market economy greatly expanded its size and influence. As specialization increased, manual and nonmanual labor were more often physically separated. Office work and selling became removed from the production and handling of merchandise. More frequently, businesspeople, professionals, storekeepers, clerks, office workers, and supervisors began to think of themselves as a distinct social group. "In America it is customary to denominate as 'clerk' all young men engaged in commercial pursuits," wrote one observer at midcentury. "Of course, the term is not applied to those engaged in mechanical trades." Members of the growing middle class had access to more education and enjoyed greater social mobility. They were paid not only more but differently. A manual worker might earn $300 a year, paid as wages computed on an hourly basis. White-collar employees received a yearly salary and might make $1000 a year or more.

Separation of Middle Class from Manual Laborers

Middle-class neighborhoods, segregated along income and occupational lines, also began to develop in towns and cities. Moreover, in large urban areas the separation of work from place of residence combined with improvements in transportation made it possible for many middle-class residents to live in surrounding suburbs and travel to work. Leisure also became segregated as separate working-class and middle-class social organizations and institutions emerged.

During these years, a distinct middle-class way of life evolved based in part on levels of consumption. Greater wealth meant the ability to consume more. Someone like Joseph Engles, a Philadelphia publishing agent, might boast a house furnished with not one but two sofas, a looking glass, thirteen chairs, five yards of ingrain carpet on the floors, and even a piano and stool. Material goods became emblems of success and status—as clockmaker Chauncey Jerome sadly discovered when his business failed and his wealth vanished. Indeed, this materialistic ethos was most apparent in the middle class, as they strove to set themselves apart from other groups in society.

Material Goods as Emblems of Success

The rise of a middle class would soon launch far-reaching changes in American society, as we will see in Chapter 12. The middle class came to embrace a new concept of marriage, the family, and the home. Along with occupation and income, moral outlook also marked class boundaries during this period.

The Distribution of Wealth

As American society became more specialized and differentiated, greater extremes of wealth appeared. After 1815, local tax records reveal a growing concentration of wealth at the top of the social pyramid. The concentration was greatest in large eastern cities and in the cotton kingdom of the South, but everywhere the tendency was for the rich to get richer and own a larger share of the community's total wealth. In New York, Brooklyn, Boston, and Philadelphia, the top 1 percent of the wealth holders owned a quarter of the total wealth in 1825; by 1850 they owned half. Similar trends appeared in western cities, such as Cincinnati and St. Louis. By 1860, 5 percent of American families owned more than 50 percent of the nation's wealth.

In contrast, those at the base of the social pyramid held a smaller percentage of a community's wealth. In Connecticut towns between 1831 and 1851 the number of inhabitants listed as having no property increased by 33 percent. In Cincinnati the lower

This traffic jam in New York City conveys the rapid pace and impatient quality of American life in the first half of the nineteenth century. "In the streets all is hurry and bustle," one European visitor to the city reported. "Carts, instead of being drawn by horses at a walking pace, are often met at a gallop, and always in a brisk trot. . . . The whole population seen in the streets seem to enjoy this bustle and add to it by their own rapid pace, as if they were all going to some place of appointment, and were hurrying on under the apprehension of being too late."

half of the city's taxpayers held 10 percent of the wealth in 1817; in 1860 their share had dropped to less than 3 percent.

In a market society, the rich were able to build up their assets because those with capital were in a position to increase it dramatically by taking advantage of new investment opportunities. Although a few men, such as Cornelius Vanderbilt and John Jacob Astor, vaulted from the bottom ranks of society to the top, most of the nation's richest individuals came from wealthy families.

Social Mobility

The existence of great fortunes is not necessarily inconsistent with the idea of **social mobility** or property accumulation. Although the gap between the rich and the poor widened after 1820, even the incomes of most poor Americans rose, because the total amount of wealth produced in America had become much larger. From about 1825 to 1860 the average per capita income almost doubled to $300. Voicing the popular belief, a New York judge proclaimed, "In this favored land of liberty, the road to advancement is open to all."

Limits of Social Mobility   Social mobility existed in these years, but not as much as contemporaries boasted. Most laborers—or more often their sons—did manage to move up the social ladder, but only a rung or two. Few unskilled workers rose higher than to a semiskilled occupation. Even the children of skilled workers normally did not escape the laboring classes and enter the middle-class ranks of clerks, managers, or lawyers. For most workers, improved status came in the form of a savings account or home ownership, which gave them some security during economic downswings and in old age.

A New Sensitivity to Time

It was no accident that Chauncey Jerome's clocks spread throughout the nation along with the market economy. The new methods of doing business involved a new and stricter sense of time. Factory life required a regimented schedule in which work began at the sound of a bell, workers kept machines going at a constant pace, and the day was divided into hours and even minutes.

Clocks began to invade private as well as public space. Before Jerome and his competitors began using standardized parts, only the wealthy owned clocks, but with mass production ordinary families could afford them. Even farmers became more sensitive to time as they became integrated into the marketplace. As one frontier traveler reported in 1844, "In Kentucky, in Indiana, in Illinois, in Missouri, and here in every dale in Arkansas, and in cabins where there was not a chair to sit on, there was sure to be a Connecticut clock."

The Market at Work: Three Examples

To sense how much America was leaving behind Crèvecoeur's vision of a land of subsistence farmers, consider three examples of the new market economy, from a small city on the East Coast to the distant frontier of the Rocky Mountains.

In 1820 Kingston, New York, was a small, rural-oriented community of 1,000 people, located along the Hudson River. But in 1828 the Delaware and Hudson Canal linked Kingston with the Pennsylvania coal fields, jolting the town's economy. The coal trade stimulated commerce and greatly increased the number of banks and the variety of businesses. Life in Kingston now focused on the docks, stores, and canal boats rather than on planting and harvest. By 1850 Kingston had a population of 10,000, ten times that in 1820.

The Market Transforms Kingston, New York

Its landscape changed too. In 1820 most storekeepers and craftworkers conducted business from their homes. By 1850 a commercial district boasted specialized stores, some handling china and glassware, others dry goods, clothing, or jewelry and watches. In addition, most manufacturing facilities were confined to two sections on the city's outskirts. Residential areas were separate from the commercial center and had become segregated along class lines, with different neighborhoods for the elite of the community, for skilled workers, and for unskilled laborers. By midcentury, street signs and gas lamps were going up, and numbers were being assigned to buildings. Kingston had become an urban center.

A thousand miles west lay the small prairie settlement of Sugar Creek, Illinois. The first white settlers had moved to Sugar Creek in 1817, as the market revolution was getting under way. The village's pioneers were primarily concerned about simply surviving. The land they plowed was on the edge of the forest, where girdled trees often remained standing among the crops until they could be cleared. The roads to larger towns like Springfield were mere cart paths, winding hither and yon among the trees.

Sugar Creek, Illinois

By the 1840s and 1850s the market economy had made inroads at Sugar Creek. True, a farmer like Eddin Lewis might still keep an account book noting that James Wilson came by for "six days work planting corn [$]3.00." That was the traditional barter system in action, for no cash actually changed hands. Lewis was simply keeping tabs, noting also when he helped Wilson, so that eventually the account could be balanced. But Lewis had begun to drive hogs to St. Louis, where he received cash in return. By 1848 he was shipping south 6,000 pounds of barreled pork, as well as lard and 350 bushels of corn. Sugar Creek, in other words, was becoming more specialized, more stratified in its wealth, and more tied into regional and national markets.

Mountain Men and the Fur Trade

Another thousand miles west a different sort of American roamed, who might at first seem unconnected to the bustle of urban markets. These were the legendary mountain men. Traveling across the Great Plains, along upland streams, and over the passes of the Rockies, hard-bitten outdoorsmen like Jim Bridger, Jedediah Smith, and James Walker wore buckskin hunting shirts, let their unkempt hair grow to their shoulders, and stuck pistols and tomahawks in their belts. In good times they feasted on raw buffalo liver and roasted hump; when game was scarce, some were not above holding their hands "in an anthill until they were covered with ants, then greedily [licking] them off," as one trapper recalled. Wild and exotic, the mountain men quickly became romantic symbols of the American quest for individual freedom.

Yet these wanderers too were tied to the market. During their heyday, from the mid-1820s to the early 1840s, they trapped beaver, whose pelts were shipped east and turned into fancy hats for gentlemen. The fur trade was not a sporting event but a business, dominated by organizations like John Jacob Astor's American Fur Company, and the trapper was part of a vast economic structure that stretched from the mountains to the eastern cities and on to Europe. The majority of these men went into the wilderness not to flee civilization but to make money. Their ultimate goal was to accumulate capital in order to set themselves up in society. Of those who survived the fur trade, almost none remained permanently outside the bounds of civilization; most returned and took up new careers. Far from repudiating society's values, the mountain men sought respectability and success as defined by the society they had temporarily left. They, like farmers, were expectant capitalists for whom the West was a land of opportunity.

Thomas Hicks's painting, Calculating, *captures the spirit of the United States as the market revolution unfolded. Americans, one foreign visitor reported, were a "guessing, reckoning, expecting and calculating people." During this period the phrase "I calculate" came to mean "I think." The man carefully going over his figures wears a beaver hat, the end product of the fur trade. Indeed, business attitudes shaped and controlled the fur trade, and many mountain men ended up as calculating businessmen.*

Prosperity and Anxiety

As Americans saw their nation's frontiers expand and its market economy grow, many began to view history in terms of an inevitable and continuous improvement. The path of commerce, however, was not steadily upward. Rather it advanced in a series of wrenching **boom-bust cycles**: accelerating growth and overheated expansion, followed by a crash and then depression.

The country remained extraordinarily prosperous from 1815 until 1819, only to sink into a depression that lasted from 1819 to 1823. During the next cycle, slow economic expansion in the 1820s gave way to almost frenzied speculation and investment in the 1830s. Then came the inevitable contraction in 1837, and the country suffered an even more severe depression from 1839 to 1843. The third cycle followed the same pattern: growth during the 1840s, frantic expansion in the 1850s, and a third depression that began in 1857 and lasted until the Civil War. In each "panic," thousands of workers were thrown out of work, overextended farmers lost their farms, and many businesses closed their doors.

In such an environment, prosperity and personal success seemed all too fleeting. Because Americans believed that the good times would not last—that the bubble would burst and another "panic" would set in—their optimism was often tinged by insecurity and anxiety. They knew too many individuals like Chauncey Jerome, who had been rich and then lost all their wealth in a downturn.

Boom-Bust Cycle

Popular Anxiety

The Panic of 1819

The initial shock of this boom-and-bust psychology came with the Panic of 1819, the first major depression in the nation's history. From 1815 to 1818 cotton had commanded fabulous prices on the Liverpool market, reaching 32.5 cents a pound in 1818. In this heady prosperity, the federal government extended liberal credit for land purchases, and the new national bank encouraged merchants and farmers to expand their operations by borrowing in order to catch the rising tide.

But in 1819 the price of cotton collapsed and took the rest of the economy with it. Once the inflationary bubble burst, land values, which had been driven to new heights by the speculative fever, plummeted 50 to 75 percent almost overnight. As the economy went slack, so did the demand for western foodstuffs and eastern manufactured goods and services, pushing the nation into a severe depression. Because the market economy had spread to new areas, the downturn affected not only city folk but rural Americans as well. New cotton planters in the Southwest, who were most vulnerable to the ups and downs of the world market, were especially hard hit.

National Depression

As depression spread in the years following 1819, most Americans could not guess that the ups and downs of the boom-and-bust cycle would continue through the next three decades, their swings made sharper by the growing networks of the market economy. But the interconnections between buyers and sellers did feed both prosperity and panic. Farmers and factories specialized in order to sell goods to distant buyers. Canals and railroads widened the network, speeding products, information, and profits.

As markets tied distant lands more tightly together, international events contributed to the **business cycles.** It was the Liverpool market in England that bid the price of American cotton to its high at over 32 cents; then in 1816 and 1817 English textile manufacturers, looking for cheaper cotton, began to import more cotton from India, sending the price of cotton in New Orleans plummeting to 14 cents. Broader changes also hurt American markets. The French and the British had been at war with one another for decades—more than 100 years, if the imperial wars of the seventeenth and eighteenth centuries were counted. In 1814 and 1815 the major powers of Europe hammered out a peace at the Congress of Vienna, one that lasted, with only minor interruptions, until the coming of World War I in 1914. When Europe had been at war, American farmers had found a ready market abroad. With thousands of European soldiers returning to their usual work as farmers, demand for American goods dropped.

The stresses of the panic of 1819 shook the political system at home too. As the depression deepened and hardship spread, Americans viewed government policies as at least partly to blame. The postwar nationalism, after all, had been based on the belief that government should stimulate economic development through a national bank and protective tariff, by improving transportation, and by opening up new lands. As Americans struggled to make sense of their new economic order, they looked to take more direct control of the government that was so actively shaping their lives. During the 1820s, the popular response to the market and the Panic of 1819 produced a strikingly new kind of politics in the Republic.

Significant Events

1790	Slater's textile mill opens
1793	Eli Whitney invents the cotton gin
1798	Whitney begins work on a system of interchangeable parts
1807	Fulton's *Clermont* begins regular steamboat service on the Hudson River
1810	*Fletcher v. Peck*
1810–1820	Cotton boom begins in the South
1811	First steamboat trip from Pittsburgh to New Orleans
1816	Second Bank of the United States chartered; protective tariff enacted
1819	*Dartmouth College v. Woodward; McCulloch v. Maryland*
1819–1823	Panic and depression
1820	Lowell mills established
1824	*Gibbons v. Ogden*
1825	Erie Canal opened
1825–1850	Canal era
1830	Baltimore and Ohio Railroad begins passenger service
1834	National Trades' Union founded
1837	Panic
1839–1843	Depression
1844	Samuel F. B. Morse sends first intercity telegraphic message
1847	Rotary printing press invented

Chapter Summary

By uniting the country in a single market, the market revolution transformed the United States during the quarter century after 1815.

- The federal government promoted the creation of a market through a protective tariff, a national bank, and internal improvements.

- The development of new forms of transportation, including canals, steamboats, and eventually railroads, allowed goods to be transported cheaply on land.

- The Supreme Court adopted a pro-business stance that encouraged investment and risk taking.

- Economic expansion generated greater national wealth, but it also brought social and intellectual change.

  —Americans pursued opportunity, embraced a new concept of progress, viewed change as normal, developed a strong materialist ethic, and considered wealth the primary means to determine status.

—Entrepreneurs reorganized their operations to increase production and sell in a wider market.

- The earliest factories were built to serve the textile industry, and the first laborers in them were young women from rural families.

  —Factory work imposed on workers a new discipline based on time and strict routine.
  —Workers' declining status led them to form unions and resort to strikes, but the depression that began in 1837 destroyed these organizations.

- The market revolution distributed wealth much more unevenly and left Americans feeling alternately buoyant and anxious about their social and economic status.

  —Social mobility still existed, but it was more limited than popular belief claimed.
  —The economy lurched up and down in a boom-bust cycle.
  —In hard times, such as the Panic of 1819, Americans looked to the government to relieve economic distress.

Additional Reading

For a provocative overview of the economic changes during this period and their impact on society and culture, consult Charles Sellers, *The Market Revolution* (1991). Then dip into two fine anthologies of essays: Melvin Stokes and Stephen Conway, eds., *The Market Revolution in America* (1996), and Scott C. Martin, ed., *Cultural Change and the Market Revolution in America, 1789–1860* (2005). The best recent book on the transportation revolution is John Larson, *Internal Improvements* (2001), and for a fascinating study of the role played by the postal system in linking Americans, see Richard John, *Spreading the News* (1995). There are many fine studies of urban social classes during the first half of the nineteenth century, and among the best are Sean Wilentz, *Chants Democratic* (1984), which traces the formation of New York City's working class, and Stuart Blumin, *The Emergence of the Middle Class* (1989). To understand the market economy's affect on rural society, read John Mack Faragher's vivid account of the transformation of a farming community in frontier Illinois, *Sugar Creek* (1986), and Robert Shalhope, *A Tale of New England* (2003), which traces the fortunes of a Vermont farmer and his family.

There is also no shortage of excellent books exploring the relationship between the market revolution and antebellum American culture. Begin with Karen Halttunen's classic study of middle-class culture, *Confidence Men and Painted Women* (1982), and a more recent study, Thomas Augst, *The Clerk's Tale* (2003), and then turn to Paul Johnson's lively exploration of working-class culture, *Sam Patch, the Famous Jumper* (2003). To celebrate any occasion, treat yourself to Stephen Nissenbaum, *The Battle for Christmas* (1996). And to console yourself in between celebrations, turn to Scott Sandage, *Born Losers: A History of Failure in America* (2005).

For a fuller list of readings, see the Bibliography at www.mhhe.com/davidsonnation6.

CHAPTER 11
The Rise of Democracy
1824~1840

"Wanted: Curling Tongs, Cologne, and Silk-Stockings . . ."

The notice, printed in a local newspaper, made the rounds in the rural Pearl River district of Mississippi. A traveler, the advertisement announced, had lost a suitcase while fording the Tallahala River. The contents included "6 ruffled shirts, 6 cambric handkerchiefs, 1 hair-brush, 1 tooth-brush, 1 nail-brush, . . ."

As the list went on, the popular reaction would inevitably shift from amusement to disdain: "1 pair curling tongs, 2 sticks pomatum . . . 1 box pearl powder, 1 bottle Cologne, 1 [bottle] rose-water, 4 pairs silk stockings, and 2 pairs kid gloves." The howls of derision that filled the air could only have increased on learning that anyone finding said trunk was requested to contact the owner—Mr. Powhatan Ellis of Natchez.

Powhatan Ellis was no ordinary backcountry traveler. Born into a genteel Virginia family, Ellis had moved in 1816 to the raw Southwest to increase his fortune. With his cultivated tastes and careful dress, he upheld the tradition of the gentleman politician. In Virginia he would have commanded respect: indeed, in Mississippi he had been appointed district judge and U.S. senator. But for the voters along the Pearl River, the advertisement for his trunk of ruffled shirts, hair oils, and fancy "skunk-water" proved to be the political kiss of death. His opponents branded him an aristocrat and a dandy, and his support among the piney woods farmers evaporated faster than a morning mist along Old Muddy on a sweltering summer's day.

No one was more satisfied with this outcome than the resourceful Franklin E. Plummer, one of Ellis's political enemies. In truth, while the unfortunate Powhatan Ellis had lost a trunk fording a stream, he had never placed the advertisement trying to locate it. That was the handiwork of Plummer, who well understood the new playing field of American politics in the 1820s. If Powhatan Ellis typified the passing political world of the Revolutionary era, Plummer was a product of the raucous democratic system emerging in its place. Leaving his home in New England during the hard times following the Panic of 1819, Plummer had worked his way downriver to the bustling city of New Orleans, then headed inland to Mississippi. Settling down in a new community, he hung out his shingle as an attorney, complete with a law library of three books. His shrewdness and oratorical talent made up for his lack of legal training, and he was quickly elected to the legislature.

By 1840 the new style of democratic politics was in full swing. This rally in Knoxville, Tennessee, uses a camp meeting–style platform in the woods to rally supporters. The makeup of this audience underscores another feature of Jacksonian democracy: the vote went only to adult white males.

Plummer's ambition soon flowed beyond the state capital. In 1830 he ran for Congress against a wealthy Natchez merchant, military hero, and member of the state's political elite. The uncouth Plummer seemed overmatched against such a distinguished opponent, and at first few observers took his candidacy seriously. In his campaign, however, Plummer portrayed himself as the champion of the people battling against the aristocrats of Natchez. Contrasting his humble background with that of his wealthy opponent, Plummer proclaimed: "We are taught that the highway to office, distinction and honor, is as free to the *meritorious poor* man, as to the *rich;* to the man who has risen from obscurity by his own individual exertions, as to him who has inherited a high and elevated standing in society. . . ." Taking as his slogan "Plummer for the People, and the People for Plummer," he was easily elected.

On the campaign trail Plummer knew how to affect the common touch. Once, while canvassing the district with his opponent, the pair stopped at a farmhouse. When his opponent, seeking the farmer's vote, kissed the daughter, Plummer lifted up a toddling boy and began picking red bugs off him, telling the enchanted mother, "They are powerful bad, and mighty hard on babies." On another occasion, while his opponent slept, Plummer rose at dawn to help milk the family's cow—and won another vote. He was a master at secretly planting false stories attacking himself in the press, and then bringing out the sworn personal testimonials of well-known men defending his character and denouncing the charges against him.

As long as Plummer maintained his image as one of the people, fighting their battles against aristocrats, he remained invincible. But as a candidate for the U.S. Senate in 1835, his touch deserted him. Borrowing money from a Natchez bank, he purchased a stylish coach, put his servant in a uniform, and campaigned across the state. Aghast at such pretensions, his followers promptly abandoned him. He died in 1852 in obscurity and poverty. Ah, Plummer! Even the staunchest of nature's noblemen may stumble, prey to the temptations of power and commerce!

Champion of the People

Franklin Plummer was being pulled two ways by the forces transforming American society. As the previous chapter explained, the growth of commerce and new markets opened up opportunities for more and more Americans in the quarter century after 1815. *Opportunity* was a byword of the age. Through his connections with bankers and the well-to-do, Plummer saw the opportunity to accumulate wealth and to gain status and respect.

Yet at the same time that new markets were producing a more **stratified,** unequal society, the nation's politics were becoming more democratic. The new political system that developed after 1820 differed strikingly from that of the early Republic. Just as national markets linked the regions of America economically, the new system of national politics with its mass electioneering techniques involved more voters than ever before and created a new class of politicians. Plummer's world reflected that new political culture. And its central feature—another byword on everyone's lips—was equality. In truth, the relationship between the new equalities of politics and the new opportunities of the market was an uneasy one.

Equality and Opportunity

Coming from the more stratified society of Europe, middle- and upper-class European visitors to the United States were struck by the "democratic spirit" that had become "infused into all the national habits and all the customs of society" during the 1820s and 1830s.

To begin with, they discovered that only one class of seats was available on stage-coaches and rail cars. These were filled according to the rough-and-ready rule of first come, first served. In steamboat dining rooms or at country taverns, everyone ate at a common table, sharing food from the same serving plates. As one upper-class gentle-man complained, "The rich and the poor, the educated and the ignorant, the polite and the vulgar, all herd on the cabin floor, feed at the same table, sit in each others laps, as it were." Being ushered to bed at an inn, visitors found themselves lodged 10 to 12 people a room, often with several bodies occupying a single bed. Fastidious Europeans were horrified at the thought of sleeping with unwashed representatives of American democracy.

Indeed, the democratic "manners" of Americans seemed positively shocking. In Europe social inferiors would speak only if spoken to. But Americans felt free to strike up a conversation with anyone, including total strangers. Frances Trollope was of-fended by the "coarse familiarity of address" between classes, while another visitor complained that in a nation where every citizen felt free to shake the hand of another, it was impossible to know anyone's social station. This informality—a forward, even *rude* attitude—was not limited to shaking hands. At theaters, it was hard to get patrons to remove their hats so those behind them could see. And American men seemed always to be slouching when they sat, their feet propped up on a nearby stool, legs dangling this way or that, bodies lying full length on a bench; "perfectly indescribable," sniffed Mrs. Trollope. Not only that, they chewed tobacco and spit everywhere: in the national Capitol, in taverns, courts, and hospitals, even in private homes. Fanny Kemble, an English actress, reported that on an American steamboat "it was a perfect shower of saliva all the time."

Americans were self-consciously proud of such democratic behavior, which they viewed as a valued heritage of the Revolution. The keelboaters who carried the future King Louis-Philippe of France on a trip down the Mississippi made their republican feelings plain when the keelboat ran aground. "You kings down there!" bellowed the captain. "Show yourselves and do a man's work, and help us three-spots pull off this bar!" The ideology of the Revolution made it clear that, in the American deck of cards at least, "three-spots" counted as much as jacks, kings, and queens. Kings were not al-lowed to forget that—and neither was Franklin Plummer.

The Tension between Equality and Opportunity

Although Americans praised both opportunity and equality, a fundamental tension existed between the two values. Inevitably, widespread opportunity would produce inequality of wealth. In Crèvecoeur's America, a rough equality of wealth and status had prevailed because of the lack of access to the market. In 1800 shoemakers in Lynn, with no way to ship large quantities of shoes across the country, could not become wealthy. Without steamboats or canals, farmers in Jefferson's day could not market surplus grain for profit. But by the 1820s and 1830s, as the opportunities of the market expanded, wealth became much more unevenly distributed. Thus the new generation had to confront contradictions in the American creed that their parents had been able to conveniently ignore.

By equality, Americans did not mean equality of wealth or property. "I know of no country where profounder contempt is expressed for the theory of permanent equality of property," Alexis de Tocqueville wrote. Nor did equality mean that all citizens had equal talent or capacity. Americans realized that individuals possessed

Opportunity and Inequality of Wealth

Meaning of Equality

The emergence of democracy in American life was accompanied by a dramatic change in men's clothing. In the eighteenth century clothing was a prime indicator of social rank and set members of the upper class apart from ordinary citizens. Only a gentleman could afford ruffled shirts, lace cuffs, silk stockings, decorative garters, and buckled shoes. Because of the cost and extensive labor involved, most Americans owned only a few clothes, and these usually were made out of homespun—cloth woven from thread spun in the household. With a quick glance an observer could tell a person's social rank.

In the Jacksonian era, however, fashionable clothing made from textile mill fabrics became cheaper and much more widely available. As a result dress no longer revealed social standing. "All

As this nattily dressed butcher suggests, clothes were not much help in sorting out social status in America. Although the clothing of the upper class was often made of finer material and was more skillfully tailored, by the 1820s less-prosperous Americans wore similar styles. "The washerwoman's Sunday attire is now as nearly like that of the merchant's wife as it can be," commented one astonished observer.

sorts of cotton fabrics are now so cheap that there is no excuse of any person's

not being well provided," commented *The Young Lady's Friend* in 1836.

The colorful shirts, rude trousers, leather aprons, frocks, and heavy boots and shoes worn by farmers and mechanics while working were readily distinguishable from the coats and trousers of middle-class merchants, professionals, managers, and clerks. Outside the workplace, however, differences in clothing style, if not tailoring quality,

widely differing abilities, which inevitably produced differences in wealth. "Distinctions in society will always exist under every just government," Andrew Jackson declared. "Equality of talents, or education, or of wealth cannot be produced by human institutions."

In the end, what Americans upheld was the equality of opportunity, not equality of condition. "True republicanism requires that every man shall have an equal chance—that every man shall be free to become as unequal as he can," one American commented. In an economy that could go bust as well as boom, Americans agreed that one primary objective of government was to safeguard opportunity. Thus the new politics of democracy walked hand in hand with the new opportunities of the market.

The New Political Culture of Democracy

The stately James Monroe, with his powdered hair and buckled shoes and breeches, was not part of the new politics. In 1824 as he neared the end of his second term, a host of new leaders in the Republican party looked to succeed him. Traditionally, a congressional caucus selected the party's presidential nominee, and the Republican caucus finally settled on Secretary of Treasury William H. Crawford of Georgia. Condemning "King Caucus" as undemocratic, three other Republicans, all ardent nationalists, refused to withdraw from the race: Secretary of State John Quincy Adams; John C. Calhoun, Monroe's secretary of war; and Henry Clay, the Speaker of the House.

Death of the Caucus System

None of these men bargained on the sudden emergence of another Republican candidate, Andrew Jackson, the hero of the Battle of New Orleans. Because of his limited political experience, no one took Jackson's candidacy seriously at first, including Jackson himself. But soon the general's supporters and rivals began receiving reports of his unusual popularity. From Cincinnati an observer wrote, "Strange! Wild! Infatuated!

largely disappeared. British traveler John Fowler in 1831 was amazed to see American workers, decked out in their Sunday best, walking the streets wearing "sleek coats, glossy hats, watchguards, and deerskin gloves!" Unlike men in the eighteenth century, these Americans dressed in somber colors. By the 1830s "black was the prevailing color," one New Yorker recalled. "It was worn for promenade, parlor, church, ball, [or] business."

The emergence after 1840 of the ready-made clothing industry also affected men's fashions. Many men in middle-class positions were anxious to create a proper image but could not afford the expert tailoring required to make a business suit. So tailors developed standardized patterns and a proportional sizing system and began mass-producing affordable ready-made clothing. Decently made suits could be purchased off the rack, and thus clerks began wearing clothing identical in style to that worn by their employer. By eliminating the distinction between homemade apparel and that sewed by a tailor, ready-made clothing further democratized men's attire.

Rather than distinguishing one class from another, democratic fashions increasingly set men apart from women. Fashion came to be considered a female concern, and ornamentation and bright colors now were associated with women's clothing. Ready-made clothing was not available for women, because female apparel required a close fit in the bodice. Nevertheless, the style of women's clothing also became standardized. American women sought to keep abreast of the latest Paris fashions, and if they could not afford a dressmaker's fitting, they sewed their own clothing. Illustrated magazines such as *Godey's Lady's Book* publicized the latest fashions, and even young women working in the mills at Lowell joined together to buy a subscription. Through standardized sizings and the power of the printing press, fashions in Jacksonian America were being made steadily more democratic.

New ways of dressing began with the urban middle class and gradually spread throughout most of society. As one newspaper commented, Americans in the Jacksonian era were citizens of the "plain dark democracy of broadcloth."

All for Jackson!" Savvy politicians soon flocked to his standard, but it was the people who first made Jackson a serious candidate.

The Election of 1824

Calhoun eventually dropped out of the race, but that still left four candidates, none of whom received a majority of the popular vote. Jackson led the field, however, and finished first in the Electoral College with 99 votes. Adams had 84, Crawford 41, and Clay 37. Under the Twelfth Amendment, the House was to select a president from the top three candidates. Clay, though himself eliminated, held enough influence as Speaker of the House to name the winner. After he met privately with Adams, he rallied the votes in the House needed to put Adams over the top.

Two days later, Adams announced that Clay would be his new secretary of state, the usual steppingstone to the presidency. Jackson and his supporters promptly charged that there had been a "corrupt bargain" between Adams and Clay. Before Adams had even assumed office, the 1828 race was under way.

Corrupt Bargain

Even more significant, the election of 1824 shattered the old party system. Henry Clay and John Quincy Adams began to organize a new party, known as the National Republicans, to distinguish it from Jefferson's old party. Jackson's disappointed supporters eventually called themselves Democrats. For the next decade the political system continued to evolve. By the mid-1830s, the National Republicans had given way to the Whigs, a political party that also drew members from another party that flourished briefly, the Anti-Masons. (The Anti-Masons had led a campaign against the Freemasons, or Masons, a fraternal order whose members [including George Washington and Benjamin Franklin] shared the Enlightenment belief in the power of reason but whose secret meetings and rituals seemed aristocratic and undemocratic to many Americans.) The Democrats, as the other major party, came together under the leadership of

Election of 1824

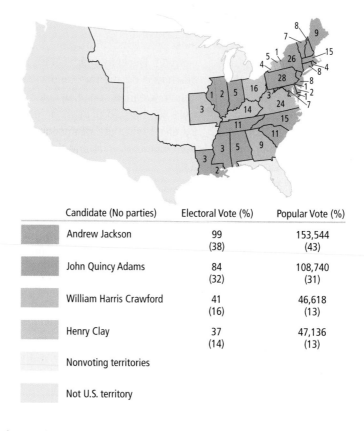

Candidate (No parties)	Electoral Vote (%)	Popular Vote (%)
Andrew Jackson	99 (38)	153,544 (43)
John Quincy Adams	84 (32)	108,740 (31)
William Harris Crawford	41 (16)	46,618 (13)
Henry Clay	37 (14)	47,136 (13)
Nonvoting territories		
Not U.S. territory		

Andrew Jackson. Once established, this second American party system dominated the nation's politics until the 1850s.

Social Sources of the New Politics

New Attitudes Toward Government

Why was it that a new style and new system of politics emerged in the 1820s? We have already seen that a revolution in markets, stimulated by new transportation networks, was under way. We have seen, too, that the scramble to bring western lands into the market generated a speculative land boom that collapsed in the Panic of 1819. The rise of the new **political culture** was rooted in these social conditions. During the sharp depression that followed, many Americans became convinced that government policy had aggravated, if not actually produced, hard times. As a result, they decided that the government had a responsibility to relieve distress and promote prosperity.

For the first time, large numbers of Americans saw politics as relevant to their daily lives. Agitation mounted, especially at the state level, for government to enact relief for those in debt and provide other forms of assistance. Elections soon became the means through which the majority expressed its policy preferences by voting for candidates pledged to specific programs. The older idea that representatives should be independent and vote according to their best judgment gave way to the notion that representatives were to carry out the will of the people, as expressed in the outcomes of elections.

Democratic Reforms

With more citizens championing the "will of the people," pressure mounted to open up the political process. Most states eliminated property qualifications for voting in favor of white manhood suffrage, under which all adult white males were allowed to vote. Similarly, property requirements for officeholders were reduced or dropped.

Presidential elections became more democratic as well. By 1832 South Carolina was the only state in which the legislature rather than the voters still chose presidential electors. The Anti-Masons pioneered a convention as a more democratic method of nominating party candidates and approving a platform, and the other parties soon followed suit. And because a presidential candidate had to carry a number of states in different sections of the country, the backing of a national party, with effective state and local organizations, became essential.

Male Suffrage in Europe and Latin America

These democratic winds of change affected European societies and eventually other areas of the world as well. In no other major country, however, were such reforms achieved as early, and with as little resistance, as in the United States. Suffrage provides a good example. In Britain, in response to growing demonstrations and the cautionary example of the French monarchy's overthrow in 1830, Parliament approved the Reform Bill of 1832, which enfranchised a number of property holders and gave Britain the broadest electorate in Europe. Yet in fact, only about 15 percent of the adult males in Britain enjoyed the right of suffrage after the bill's passage. In France the figure was less than 1 percent.

The democratic revolutions of 1848 championed universal male suffrage in France and Prussia. Yet this ideal soon suffered setbacks. By 1852 the French republic had been replaced by a monarchy under the emperor Louis Napoleon. And in Prussia, the new constitution essentially negated universal male suffrage by dividing the electorate into three classes according to wealth, a formula that enabled 5 percent of the voters to elect one-third of parliament. Belgium, which had the most liberal constitution in Europe, did not approximate manhood suffrage until 1848. Even the second Reform Act (1867) in Britain enfranchised only about one-third of the adult males.

Likewise, the Latin American republics established in the 1820s and 1830s imposed property requirements on voting or, like Uruguay, excluded certain occupational groups such as servants and peasants from the suffrage. One exception was Mexico, where a number of states adopted an extremely broad suffrage. A new constitution in 1836, however, established a much more centralized state and sharply limited voting rights. The most restricted suffrage existed in the republic of Haiti, where only army officers and a few other privileged individuals enjoyed the franchise. When the revolution of 1843 brought a new constitution with mass-based suffrage, it met widespread resistance among elites, and the government quickly failed.

Voter Turnout

As the new reforms went into effect, voter turnout soared. Whereas in the 1824 presidential election only 27 percent of eligible voters bothered to go to the polls, four years later the proportion had more than doubled to 56 percent. In 1840, 78 percent of eligible voters cast ballots, probably the highest turnout in American history.

The Acceptance of Parties

Rise of the Professional Politician

All these developments worked to favor the rise of a new type of politician: one whose life was devoted to party service and who often depended for his living on public office. As the number of state-sponsored internal improvement projects increased during the 1820s, so did the number of government jobs that could support party workers. No longer was politics primarily the province of the wealthy, who spent only part of their time on public affairs. Instead, political leaders were more likely to come from the middle ranks of society, especially outside the South. Many became economically established after entering politics, but as Franklin Plummer demonstrated, large sums of money were not required to conduct a campaign. Indeed, a successful politician now had to mingle with the masses and voice their feelings—requirements that put the wealthy elite at a disadvantage.

Van Buren Champions the Party System

In many ways, Martin Van Buren epitomized the new breed of politician. The son of a New York tavern keeper, Van Buren lacked great oratorical skills or a magnetic personality. But he was a master organizer and tactician, highly skilled at using the new party system. His abilities eventually carried him to the Senate and even the White House. Unlike the older Revolutionary generation, who regarded political parties as dangerous and destructive, Van Buren argued that they were not only "inseparable from free governments" but "in many and material respects . . . highly useful to the country." While conceding that political parties were subject to abuse, he stressed that competing parties would watch each other and check abuses at the same time that they kept the masses informed.

By the mid-1830s, as Americans increasingly came to accept political parties as a positive good, the second party system was falling into place, with Jackson's Democrats facing off against the Whigs.

The Politics of the Common Man

New Style of Politics

Andrew Jackson was one of the first political leaders to grasp the new politics in which the ordinary citizen was celebrated as never before. "Never for a moment believe that the great body of the citizens . . . can deliberately intend to do wrong," he proclaimed. Party leaders everywhere avoided aristocratic airs when on the stump. "I have always dressed chiefly in *Home spun* when among the people," one North Carolina member of Congress explained. "If a Candidate be dressed Farmerlike he is well received and kindly remembered by the inmates of the Log Cabin, and there is no sensation among the children or the *chickens*."

Politics became mass entertainment, in which campaign hoopla often overshadowed the issues. Parades, glee clubs, massive rallies, and barbecues were used to rouse voters, and treating to drinks became an almost universal campaign tactic. ("The way to men's hearts is down their throats," quipped one Kentucky vote-getter.) Although politicians often talked about principles, political parties were pragmatic organizations, intent on gaining and holding power.

Limitations of the Democratic Political System

The Jacksonian era has been called the Age of the Common Man, but such democratic tendencies had distinct limits. Women and slaves were not allowed to vote, nor could free African Americans (except in a few states, primarily in the northeast) and Indians. Nor did the parties always deal effectively with (or even address) basic problems in society. Still, Van Buren's insight was perceptive. Popular political parties provided an essential mechanism for peacefully resolving differences among competing interest groups, regions, and social classes.

Jackson's Rise to Power

The new democratic style of politics first appeared on the state and local levels: Van Buren deftly working behind the scenes in New York; Amos Kendall of Kentucky campaigning in favor of debtor relief; Davy Crockett of Tennessee carefully dressed in frontier garb and offering voters a drink from a jug of whiskey and a chew from a large plug of tobacco. The national implications of these changes, however, were not immediately clear.

John Quincy Adams's Presidency

When he assumed the presidency in 1825, John Quincy Adams might have worked to create a mass-based party. But Adams, a talented diplomat and a great secretary of

"The Will of the People the Supreme Law" reads the banner at this county election. One of the few occasions when most of the men would assemble at the village, Election Day remained an all-male event as well as a time of excitement, heated debate, and boisterous celebration. As citizens give their oath to an election judge, diligent party workers dispense free drinks, solicit support, offer party tickets, and keep a careful tally of who has voted. Liquor and drinking are prominently featured: one elector enjoys another round, a prospective voter who is too drunk to stand is held up by a faithful party member, and on the right a groggy partisan sports a bandage as a result of a political brawl.

state, possessed hardly a political bone in his body. Cold and tactless, he could build no popular support for the ambitious and often farsighted programs he proposed. His plans for the federal government to promote not only manufacturing and agriculture but also the arts, literature, and science left his opponents aghast.

Nor would Adams take any steps to gain reelection, though he earnestly desired it. Despite urgent pleas from Henry Clay and other advisers, he declined to remove from federal office men who actively opposed him. Since Adams refused to be a party leader, Clay undertook to organize the National Republicans. But with a reluctant candidate at the top of the ticket, Clay labored under serious handicaps. The new style of politics came into its own nationally only when Andrew Jackson swept to power at the head of a new party, the Democrats.

Building a new party was a tricky business. Because Jackson's coalition was made up of conflicting interests, "Old Hickory" remained vague about his own position on many issues. Thus the campaign of 1828 soon degenerated into a series of personal

Jackson's Election

Jackson's stubborn determination shows clearly in this portrait by Asher Durand, painted in 1835. "His passions are terrible," Jefferson noted. "When I was President of the Senate, he was Senator, and he could never speak on account of the rashness of his feelings. I have seen him attempt it repeatedly, and as often choke with rage. His passions are, no doubt, cooler now; he has been much tried since I knew him, but he is a dangerous man."

attacks, splattering mud on all involved. Aided by enormous majorities in the South, Jackson won handily.

In one sense, the significance of the election was clear. It marked the beginning of politics as Americans have practiced it ever since, with two disciplined national parties actively competing for votes, an emphasis on personalities over issues, and the resort to mass electioneering techniques. Yet in terms of public policy, the meaning of the election was anything but clear. The people had voted for Jackson as a national hero without any real sense of what he would do with his newly won power.

President of the People

Certainly the people looked for change. "I never saw such a crowd here before," Daniel Webster wrote as inauguration day approached. "Persons have come 500 miles to see General Jackson, and they really seem to think that the country is rescued from some dreadful danger!" Some 15,000 supporters cheered wildly after Jackson was sworn in.

At the White House reception pandemonium reigned as thousands of ordinary citizens pushed inside to catch a glimpse of their idol. The new president had to flee after being nearly crushed to death by well-wishers. The crowd trampled on the furniture, broke glass, smashed mirrors, and ruined carpets and draperies. "It was a proud day for the people," boasted Amos Kendall, one of the new president's advisers. Supreme Court Justice Joseph Story was less thrilled: "I never saw such a mixture. The reign of King Mob seemed triumphant."

Jackson's Character

Whether loved as a man of the people or hated as a demagogue leading the mob, Jackson was the representative of the new democracy. The first president from west of the Appalachians, he moved as a young lawyer to the Tennessee frontier. He had a quick mind but limited schooling and little use for learning; after his death a family friend acknowledged that the general had never believed that the Earth was round. A man of action, his decisiveness served him well as a soldier and also in the booming economy around Nashville, where he established himself as a large landowner and slaveholder. Tall and wiry, with flowing white hair, Jackson carried himself with a soldier's bearing. His troops had nicknamed him Old Hickory out of respect for his toughness, but that strength sometimes became arrogance, and he could be vindictive and a bully. He was not a man to provoke, as his reputation for dueling demonstrated.

For all these flaws, Jackson was a shrewd politician. He knew how to manipulate men and could be affable or abusive as the occasion demanded. He would sometimes burst into a rage to get his way with a hostile delegation, only to chuckle afterward, "They thought I was mad." He also displayed a keen sense of public opinion, skillfully reading the shifting national mood.

Spoils System

As the nation's chief executive, Jackson defended the **spoils system,** under which public offices were awarded to political supporters, as a democratic reform. Rotation in office, he declared, would guard against insensitive bureaucrats who presumed that they held their positions by right. The cabinet, he believed, existed more to carry out his will than to offer counsel, and throughout his term he remained a strong executive who insisted on his way—and usually got it.

The Political Agenda in the Market Economy

Jackson took office at a time when the market economy was spreading through America and the nation's borders were expanding geographically. The three major problems his administration faced were directly caused by the resulting growing pains.

First, the demand for new lands put continuing pressure on Indians, whose valuable cornfields and hunting grounds could produce marketable commodities like cotton and wheat. Second, as the economies of the North, South, and West became more specialized, their rival interests forced a confrontation over the tariff and whether South Carolina could nullify that federal law. And finally, the booming economy focused attention on the role of credit and banking in society and on the new commercial attitudes that were a central part of the developing market economy. The president attacked all three issues in his characteristically combative style.

Democracy and Race

As a planter, Jackson benefited from the international demand for cotton that was drawing new lands into the market. He had gone off to the Tennessee frontier in 1788, a rowdy, ambitious young man who could afford to purchase only one slave. Caught up in the get-rich-quick mania of the frontier, he became a prominent land speculator, established himself as a planter, and by the time he became president owned nearly 100 slaves. His popularity derived not only from defeating the British but also from opening extensive tracts of valuable Indian lands to white settlement. Through military fighting and treaty negotiating, he was personally responsible for obtaining about a third of Tennessee for the United States, three-quarters of Florida and Alabama, a fifth of Georgia and Mississippi, and a tenth of Kentucky and North Carolina.

Even so, in 1820 an estimated 125,000 Indians remained east of the Mississippi River. In the Southwest the Choctaws, Creeks, Cherokees, Chickasaws, and Seminoles retained millions of acres of prime agricultural land in the heart of the cotton kingdom. Led by Georgia, southern states demanded that the federal government clear these titles. In response, Monroe in 1824 proposed to Congress that the remaining eastern tribes be relocated west of the Mississippi River.

As white pressure for removal intensified, a shift in the attitude toward Indians and race increasingly occurred. Previously whites had generally attributed cultural differences among whites, blacks, and Indians to the environment. After 1815 the dominant white culture stressed "innate" racial differences that could never be erased. A growing number of Americans began to argue that the Indian was a permanently inferior savage who blocked progress.

Accommodate or Resist?

The new, more aggressive attitudes among white Americans placed Indians and other minorities in the Old Southwest in a difficult position. During the seventeenth and eighteenth centuries the region reflected a multiracial character because Indians, Spanish, French, and Africans had all settled there. The intermixture of cultures could be seen in the garb of the Creek Indian chief William McIntosh (above), who adopted a style of dress that reflected both his Indian and white heritage. McIntosh's father was a Scot, his mother a Creek, his wife a Cherokee—and McIntosh himself had allied his people with Andrew Jackson's forces during the War of 1812. But not long after he signed a treaty for the cession of Creek lands in 1825, he was murdered

William McIntosh's attire reflects the multicultural nature of the Old Southwest. He wears the ruffled shirt and cravat of a white gentleman, but his robe, sash, leggings, and moccasins display his Creek heritage with pride.

New Attitudes Toward Race

Tan buckskin Cherokee suit, 1820s–1840s. Contrast this more traditional attire with the outfit of William McIntosh, on page 301.

by a rival faction of the tribe, who regarded the cession as an act of betrayal. As southern whites increased their clamor for Indian removal, similar tensions among various tribal factions increased.

Among the Seminoles, mixed-bloods (those with white as well as Indian ancestry) took the lead in urging military resistance to any attempt to expel them. In the Cherokee nation, on the other hand, mixed-bloods led by John Ross advocated a program of accommodation by adopting white ways to prevent removal. After a bitter struggle Ross prevailed, and in 1827 the Cherokees adopted a written constitution modeled after that of the United States. They also enacted the death penalty for any member who sold tribal lands to whites without consent of the governing general council. Developing their own alphabet, they published a bilingual newspaper, the *Cherokee Phoenix*. Similarly, the neighboring Creeks moved to centralize authority by strengthening the power of the governing council at the expense of local towns. They too made it illegal for individual chiefs to sell any more land to whites.

Changing Nature of Cherokee Society

The division between traditionalists and those favoring accommodation reflected the fact that Indians too had been drawn into a web of market relationships. As more Cherokee families began to sell their surplus crops, they ceased to share property communally as in the past. Cherokee society became more stratified and unequal, just as white society had, and economic elites dominated the tribal government. Women's traditional economic role was transformed as well, as men now took over farming operations, previously a female responsibility. As the cotton boom spread, some Cherokees became substantial planters who owned large numbers of black slaves and thousands of acres of cotton land. Largely of mixed ancestry, slaveholders were wealthier, had investments in other enterprises such as gristmills and ferries, raised crops for market, were more likely to read English, and were the driving force behind acculturation.

As cotton cultivation expanded among the Cherokees, slavery became harsher and a primary means of determining status, just as in southern white society. The general council passed several laws forbidding intermarriage with African Americans and excluding African Americans and mulattoes from voting or holding office. Ironically, at the same time that white racial attitudes toward Indians were deteriorating, the Cherokees' racial attitudes toward blacks were also hardening, paralleling the increased racism among white Americans.

Trail of Tears

Pressure for Indian Removal

As western land fever increased and racial attitudes sharpened, Jackson prodded Congress to provide funds for Indian removal. He watched sympathetically as the Georgia legislature overturned the Cherokee constitution, declared Cherokee laws null and void, and decreed that tribal members would be tried in state courts. In 1830 Congress finally passed a removal bill.

But the Cherokees brought suit in federal court against Georgia's actions. In 1832 in the case of *Worcester v. Georgia*, the Supreme Court sided with the Cherokees. Indian tribes had full authority over their lands, wrote Chief Justice John Marshall in the opinion. Thus Georgia had no right to extend its laws over Cherokee territory. Pronouncing Marshall's decision "stillborn," Jackson ignored the Court's edict and went ahead with plans for removal.

Although Jackson assured Indians that they could be removed only voluntarily, he paid no heed when state governments harassed tribes into surrendering lands. Under the threat of coercion, the Choctaws, Chickasaws, and Creeks reluctantly agreed to move to tracts in present-day Oklahoma. In the process, land-hungry schemers cheated tribal members out of as much as 90 percent of their land.

Removal of the Cherokees

The Cherokees held out longest, but to no avail. In order to deal with more pliant leaders of the tribe, Georgia authorities kidnapped Chief John Ross, who led the resistance to relocation, and threw him into jail. Ross was finally released but not allowed to negotiate the treaty, which stipulated that the Cherokees leave their lands no later than 1838. When that time came, most refused to go. In response, President Martin Van Buren had the U.S. Army round up resistant members and force them, at bayonet point, to join the westward march. Of the 15,000 who traveled this Trail of Tears, approximately one-quarter died along the way of exposure, disease, and exhaustion, including Ross's wife. As for the western tracts awaiting the survivors, they were smaller and generally inferior to the rich lands that had been taken from the Cherokees.

Military Resistance

Some Indians chose resistance. In the Old Northwest a group of the Sauk and Fox led by Black Hawk recrossed the Mississippi into Illinois in 1832 and were crushed by federal troops and the militia. More successful was the military resistance of a minority of Seminoles led by Osceola. Despite his death, they held out until 1842 in the Florida Everglades before being subdued and removed. In the end, only a small number of southern tribe members were able to escape removal.

In his Farewell Address in 1837, Jackson defended his policy by piously asserting that the eastern tribes had been finally "placed beyond the reach of injury or oppression, and that [the] paternal care of the General Government will hereafter watch over them and protect them." Indians, however, knew the bitter truth of the matter. Without effective political power, they found themselves at the mercy of the pressures of the marketplace and the hardening racial attitudes of white Americans.

Free Blacks in the North

Unlike Indian removal, the rising discrimination against free African Americans during this period did not depend directly on presidential action. Still, it was Jackson's Democratic party, which was in the vanguard of promoting white equality, that was also the most strongly proslavery and the most hostile to black rights. The intensifying racism that accompanied the emergence of democracy in American life bore down with particular force on free African Americans. "The policy and power of the national and state governments are against them," commented one northerner. "The popular feeling is against them—the interests of our citizens are against them."

Before the Civil War, the free black population remained small: only about 171,000 in the North in 1840, about a quarter of whom were mulattoes. Although those numbers amounted to less than 2 percent of the North's population, most states enacted laws to keep African Americans in an inferior position. (For a discussion of free African Americans in the South, see Chapter 13.)

Discrimination against Free Blacks

Most black northerners lacked meaningful political rights. Black men could vote on equal terms with whites in only five New England states. New York imposed a property requirement only on black voters, which disfranchised the vast majority. Moreover,

Indian Removal *During Jackson's presidency, the federal government concluded nearly 70 treaties with Indian tribes, in the Old Northwest as well as in the South. Under their terms, the United States acquired approximately 100 million acres of Indian land.*

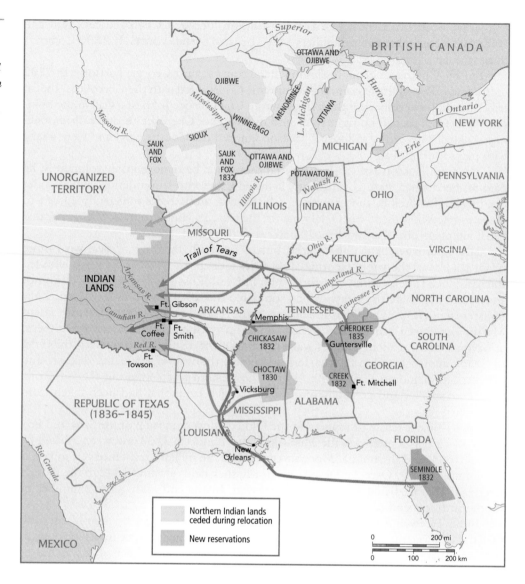

in New Jersey, Pennsylvania, and Connecticut, African American men lost the right to vote after having previously enjoyed that privilege.

Black northerners were also denied basic civil rights that whites enjoyed. Five states prohibited them from testifying against whites, and either law or custom excluded African Americans from juries everywhere except Massachusetts. In addition, several western states passed black exclusion laws prohibiting free African Americans from immigrating into the state. These laws were seldom enforced, but they were available to harass the African American population in times of social stress.

Segregation, or the physical separation of the races, was widely practiced in the free states. African Americans were assigned to separate sections on public transportation. Throughout the North they could not go into most hotels and restaurants, and if permitted to enter theaters and lecture halls, they sat in the corners and balconies. In white churches, they were put in separate pews and took communion after white members. In virtually every community, black children were excluded from the public schools or forced to attend overcrowded and poorly funded separate schools. Commented one English visitor: "We see, in effect, two nations—one white and another black—growing up together . . . but never mingling on a principle of equality."

Black Poverty

Discrimination pushed African American males into the lowest-paying and most unskilled jobs: servants, sailors, waiters, and common laborers. In Philadelphia in 1838,

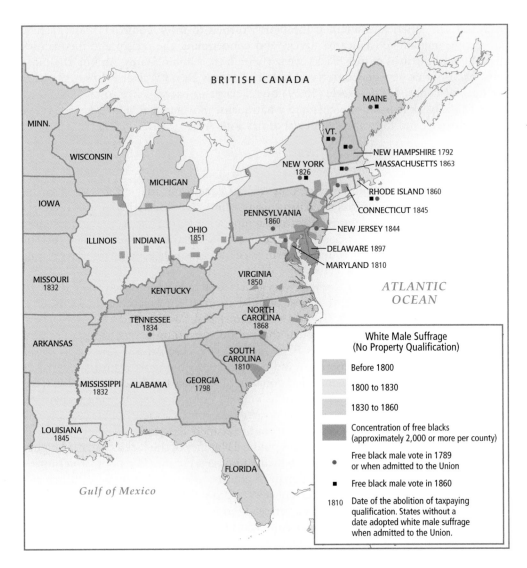

MINN.

WISCONSIN

MICHIGAN

IOWA

ILLINOIS   INDIANA

OHIO
1851

MISSOURI

KENTUCKY

ARKANSAS

TENNESSEE
1834

NORTH
CAROLINA
1868

SOUTH
CAROLINA
1810

MISSISSIPPI
1832   ALABAMA   GEORGIA
1798

LOUISIANA
1845

FLORIDA

Gulf of Mexico

BRITISH CANADA

MAINE

VT.

NEW HAMPSHIRE 1792

MASSACHUSETTS 1863

NEW YORK
1826

RHODE ISLAND 1860

CONNECTICUT 1845

PENNSYLVANIA
1860

NEW JERSEY 1844

DELAWARE 1897

MARYLAND 1810

VIRGINIA
1850

*ATLANTIC
OCEAN*

**White Male Suffrage
(No Property Qualification)**

Before 1800

1800 to 1830

1830 to 1860

Concentration of free blacks
(approximately 2,000 or more per county)

• Free black male vote in 1789
  or when admitted to the Union

■ Free black male vote in 1860

1810   Date of the abolition of taxpaying
  qualification. States without a
  date adopted white male suffrage
  when admitted to the Union.

**The Spread of White
Manhood Suffrage**   *White
manhood suffrage became the
norm during the Jacksonian
era, but in a number of states
free black males who had been
voting by law or by custom lost
the right to vote. After 1821
a $250 property requirement
disfranchised about 90 percent
of adult black males in New
York.*

80 percent of employed black males were unskilled laborers, and three of five black families had less than $60 total wealth. African American women normally continued working after marriage, mostly as servants, cooks, laundresses, and seamstresses, because their wages were critical to the family's economic survival. Blacks were willing strikebreakers, because white workers, fearing economic competition and loss of status, were overtly hostile and excluded them from trade unions. A number of antiblack riots erupted in northern cities during these years. Driven into abject poverty, free blacks in the North suffered from an inadequate diet, were more susceptible to disease, and in 1850 had a life expectancy 8 to 10 years less than that of whites.

"None but those who experience it can know what it is—this constant, galling sense of cruel injustice and wrong," grieved Charlotte Forten, a free African American from Philadelphia.

The African American Community

Free blacks had long suffered from such oppression and injustice. Between the Revolution and the War of 1812, they had responded by founding schools, churches, and mutual aid societies to sustain their communities. Typically, black leaders strove to strike a moderate tone in their published writings, praising whites who embraced the antislavery cause, emphasizing the achievements of black men and women, and even calling for a gradual rather than an immediate abolition of slavery. But by the 1820s, many African American leaders in the North turned to more confrontational tactics, advocating militant resistance to slavery and condemning the racism and inequalities that blighted the lives of free blacks everywhere in the United States. Among the most outspoken of this new generation of black leaders was David Walker, whose *Appeal to the Colored Citizens of the World* (1829) urged slaves to use violence to end bondage. After 1840, black frustration generated a nationalist movement that emphasized racial unity, self-help, and for some, a renewal of ties with Africa.

Racism Strikes a Deeper Root

What prompted greater militancy among African Americans after 1820s was also the growth of an increasingly virulent racism among whites. Ironically, the success of efforts to promote education, religious piety, and temperance within the free black community threatened many lower-class whites and intensified their resentment of African Americans. That animosity found vent in race riots, which erupted in Pittsburgh, Boston, Cincinnati, and New Haven.

Appeal of Minstrelsy

The racist attitudes of the day were very much reflected in popular culture, nowhere more than in minstrel shows, the most popular form of entertainment in Jacksonian America. Originating in the 1830s and 1840s, minstrel shows featured white actors performing in blackface. Although popular throughout the country, minstrelsy's primary audience was in northern cities. Its basic message was that African Americans could not cope with freedom and therefore did not belong in the North. Enslaved African Americans were portrayed as happy and contented, whereas free black Americans were caricatured either as strutting dandies or as helpless ignoramuses. Drawing its patrons from workers, Irish immigrants, and the poorer elements in society, minstrelsy assured these white champions of democracy that they remained superior.

Deepening Racism

The unsettling economic, social, and political changes of the Jacksonian era heightened white Americans' fear of failure, which stimulated racism. The popular yet unrealistic expectation was that any white man might become rich. Yet in fact, 20 percent or more of white adult males of this era never accumulated any property. Their lack of success encouraged them to relieve personal tensions through increased hostility to their black neighbors. Subjecting black Americans to legal disabilities ensured that even the poorest whites would enjoy an advantage in the race for wealth and status. "The prejudice of race appears to be stronger in the states that have abolished slavery than in those where it still exists," Tocqueville noted. The power of racism in Jacksonian

Minstrel sheet music (left) illustrates the racist attitudes that pervaded Jacksonian democracy. Blacks, played by whites, were made to appear ridiculous through grotesque physical features, exaggerated poses, and pretentious airs. In contrast, the confident expression of this African American (right), who had this daguerreotype taken around 1856, evinces the dignity free blacks maintained in the face of unrelenting hostility and discrimination.

America stemmed, at least in part, from the fact that equality remained part of the nation's creed while it steadily receded as a social reality.

The Nullification Crisis

Indian removal and antiblack discrimination provided one answer to the question of who would be given equality of opportunity in America's new democracy. Indians and African Americans would not. The issue of nullification raised a different, equally pressing question. As the market revolution propelled the economies of the North, South, and West toward increased specialization, how would various regions or interest groups accommodate their differences?

The Growing Crisis in South Carolina

South Carolina had been particularly hard hit by the depression of 1819. When prosperity returned to the rest of the nation, many of the state's cotton planters still suffered. With lands exhausted from years of cultivation, they could not compete with the fabulous yields of frontier planters in Alabama and Mississippi.

Increasingly, South Carolinians viewed federal tariffs as the cause of their miseries. When Congress raised the duty rates in 1824, they assailed the tariff as an unfair tax that raised the prices of goods they imported while benefiting other regions of the nation. Other southern states opposed the 1824 tariff as well, though none so vehemently as South Carolina.

The one state in which black inhabitants outnumbered whites, South Carolina had been growing more sensitive about the institution of slavery. In 1822 a slave conspiracy led by Denmark Vesey, a free black carpenter in Charleston, was thwarted only at the last moment. A brilliant leader, literate, and well traveled, Vesey argued that slavery violated the principles of both republicanism and Christianity. He devised a plan to seize control of the city and raise the standard of black liberty, but several slaves betrayed the conspiracy at the last moment. Charleston authorities hurried to arrest Vesey and his lieutenants, who were tried, convicted, and either executed or banished. Even so, white South Carolinians worried that other undetected conspirators lurked in their midst.

Denmark Vesey's Conspiracy

As an additional measure of security, the state's leaders pushed for stronger constitutional protection of slavery. After all, supporters of high tariffs had already claimed that the "implied powers" of the Constitution gave them the right to promote manufacturing. What was to stop this same broad interpretation from being used to end slavery? "In contending against the tariff, I have always felt that we were combatting against the symptom instead of the disease," argued Chancellor William Harper of South Carolina. "Tomorrow may witness [an attempt] to relieve . . . your slaves."

When Congress raised the duty rates still higher in 1828 with the so-called Tariff of Abominations, South Carolina's legislature published the *South Carolina Exposition and Protest*, which outlined for the first time the theory of nullification. Only later was it revealed that its author was Jackson's own vice president, John C. Calhoun.

Calhoun's Theory of Nullification

Educated at Yale and at a distinguished law school, John C. Calhoun was the most impressive intellect of his political generation. During the 1820s the South Carolina leader made a steady journey away from nationalism toward an extreme states' rights position. When he was elected Jackson's vice president, South Carolinians assumed that tariff reform would soon be enacted. But Jackson and Calhoun quarreled, and Calhoun lost all influence in the administration.

In his theory of nullification, Calhoun addressed the problem of how to protect the rights of a minority in a political system based on the rule of the majority. The

Minority Rights Versus Majority Rule

As Daniel Webster outlines his nationalist theory of the Constitution and the Union, Senator Robert Hayne of South Carolina sits (front, left) with his hands together. The Senate gallery is filled, with most of the seats occupied by women, evidence of the widespread interest in politics.

Union, he argued, was a compact between sovereign states. Thus the people of each state, acting in special popular conventions, had the right to nullify any federal law that exceeded the powers granted to Congress under the Constitution. The law would then become null and void in that state. In response, Congress could either repeal the law or propose a constitutional amendment expressly giving it the power in question. If the amendment was ratified, the nullifying state could either accept the decision or exercise its ultimate right as a sovereign state and secede from the Union.

Nationalists' Theory of the Union

When Senator Robert Hayne of South Carolina outlined Calhoun's theory in the Senate in 1830, Senator Daniel Webster of Massachusetts replied sharply that the Union was not a compact of sovereign states. The people and not the states, he argued, had created the Constitution. "It is the people's constitution, the people's government, made for the people, made by the people, and answerable to the people." Webster also insisted that the federal government did not merely act as the agent of the states but had sovereign powers in those areas in which it had been delegated responsibility. Finally, Webster endorsed the doctrine of judicial review, which gave the Supreme Court authority to determine the meaning of the Constitution.

The Nullifiers Nullified

When Congress passed another tariff in 1832 that failed to give the state any relief, South Carolina's legislature called for the election of delegates to a popular convention, which overwhelmingly adopted an ordinance in November that declared the tariffs of 1828 and 1832 "null, void, and no law, nor binding upon this state, its officers or citizens" after February 1, 1833.

Jackson, who had spent much of his life defending the nation, was not about to tolerate any defiance of his authority or the federal government's. In his Proclamation on Nullification, issued in December 1832, he insisted that the Union was perpetual. Under the Constitution, there was no right of secession. To reinforce Jackson's announced determination to enforce the tariff laws, Congress passed the Force Bill, reaffirming the president's military powers. Idea of a Perpetual Union

Yet Jackson was also a skillful politician. At the same time that he threatened South Carolina, he urged Congress to reduce the tariff rates. With no other state willing to follow South Carolina's lead, Calhoun reluctantly agreed to a compromise tariff, which Jackson signed on March 1, 1833, the same day he signed the Force Bill. South Carolina's convention repealed the nullifying ordinance, and the crisis passed. Compromise of 1833

Calhoun's doctrine had proved too radical for the rest of the South. Yet the controversy convinced many southerners that they were becoming a permanent minority. "It is useless and impracticable to disguise the fact," concluded nullifier William Harper, "that we are divided into slave-holding and non-slaveholding states, and this is the broad and marked distinction that must separate us at last." As that feeling of isolation grew, it was not nullification but the threat of secession that ultimately became the South's primary weapon.

The Bank War

Jackson understood well the political ties that bound the nation. He grasped much less firmly the economic and financial connections that linked different regions of the country through banks and national markets. In particular, the president was suspicious of the national bank and the power it possessed. His clash with the Second Bank of the United States brought on the greatest crisis of his presidency.

The National Bank and the Panic of 1819

Chartered by Congress in 1816 for a 20-year period, the Second Bank of the United States suffered initially from woeful mismanagement. At first it helped fuel the speculative pressures in the economy. Then it turned about-face and sharply contracted credit by calling in loans when the depression hit in 1819. To many Americans, the Bank had already become a monster. Monster Bank

The psychological effects of the Panic of 1819 were almost as momentous as the economic. In the midst of dizzying prosperity, Americans were plunged into despair and economic depression. To many uneasy farmers and workers, the hard times seemed like punishment for losing sight of the old virtues of simplicity, frugality, and hard work. For them banks became a symbol of the commercialization of American society and the passing of a simpler way of life.

Biddle's Bank

In 1823 Nicholas Biddle, a rich 37-year-old Philadelphia businessman, became president of the national bank. Biddle was intelligent and thoroughly familiar with the banking system, but he was also impossibly arrogant. Seeking boldly to restore the Bank's reputation, he set out to provide the nation with a sound currency by regulating the amount of credit available in the economy. Function as a Central Bank

Government revenues were paid largely in banknotes (paper money) issued by state-chartered banks. Because the Treasury Department regularly deposited U.S. funds in the national bank, the notes of state banks from all across the Union came into its possession. If Biddle believed that a state bank was overextended and had issued more notes than was safe, he presented them to that bank and demanded they be redeemed in **specie** (gold or silver). Because banks did not have enough specie reserves to back all the paper money they issued, the only way a state bank could continue to redeem its notes was to call in its loans and reduce the amount of its notes in circulation. This action had the effect of lessening the amount of credit in the economy.

On the other hand, if Biddle felt that a bank's credit policies were reasonable, he simply returned the state banknotes to circulation without presenting them for redemption. Being the government's official depository gave Biddle's bank enormous power over state banks and over the economy. As Biddle tactlessly admitted, "There are very few [state banks] which might not have been destroyed by an exertion of the powers of the bank." Under Biddle's direction the Bank became a financial colossus: it had 29 branches and made 20 percent of the country's loans, issued one-fifth of the total banknotes, and held fully a third of all deposits and specie. Yet for the most part, Biddle used the Bank's enormous power responsibly to provide the United States a sound paper currency, which the expanding economy needed.

Opposition to Paper Money

Although the Bank had strong support in the business community, workers complained that they were often paid in **depreciated** state banknotes. Such notes could be redeemed for only a portion of their face value, a practice that in effect cheated workers out of part of their wages. They called for a "hard money" currency of only gold and silver. Hard money advocates viewed bankers and financiers as profiteers who manipulated the paper money system to enrich themselves at the expense of honest, hardworking farmers and laborers.

The Clash between Jackson and Biddle

Jackson's own experiences left him with a deep distrust of banks and paper money. In 1804 his Tennessee land speculations had brought him to the brink of bankruptcy, from which it took years of painful struggle to free himself. Reflecting on his personal situation, he became convinced that banks and paper money threatened to corrupt the Republic.

As president, Jackson called for reform of the banking system from time to time, but Biddle refused even to consider curbing the Bank's powers. Already distracted by the nullification controversy, Jackson warned Biddle not to inject the bank issue into the 1832 campaign. When Biddle went ahead and applied for a renewal of the Bank's charter in 1832, four years early, Jackson was furious. "The Bank is trying to kill me," he stormed to Van Buren, "*but I will kill it.*"

Jackson's Veto

Despite the president's opposition, Congress passed a recharter bill in the summer of 1832. Immediately Jackson vetoed it as unconstitutional (rejecting Chief Justice Marshall's ruling in favor of the Bank in *McCulloch v. Maryland*). Condemning the Bank as an agent of special privilege, the president pledged to protect "the humble members of society—the farmer, mechanics, and laborers. The message completely ignored the Bank's vital services in the economy.

The Bank Destroyed

When Congress failed to override Jackson's veto, the recharter of the Bank became a central issue of the 1832 campaign. Jackson's opponent was Henry Clay, a National Republican who eagerly accepted the financial support of Biddle and the national bank. Clay went down to defeat, and once reelected, Jackson was determined to destroy the Bank. A private corporation should not possess the power to influence government policy and the economy, he believed. And he was justly incensed over the Bank's heavy-handed attempt to influence the election.

Removal of the Deposits

To cripple the Bank, the president simply ordered all the government's federal deposits withdrawn. Because such an act clearly violated federal law, Jackson was forced to transfer one secretary of the treasury and fire another before he finally found in Roger Taney someone willing to take the job and carry out the edict. Taney (pronounced "Taw-ney") began drawing against the government's funds to pay its debts while depositing new revenues in selected state banks.

Biddle fought back by deliberately precipitating a brief financial panic in 1833. "Go to Biddle," Jackson snapped to businesspeople seeking relief. "I never will restore the deposits. I never will recharter the United States Bank, or sign a charter for any other

The Battle between Biddle and Jackson

Decoding a Political Cartoon

Historians often use political cartoons to interpret the currents of American culture. By their nature cartoons deal in visual symbols; to be accessible to their readers, the symbols cannot be subtle. For present-day viewers, however, some decoding is needed. Both the woman holding the bottle of port and the man standing beside the "Old Monongahela Whiskey" (a cat on his head, no less!) look ridiculous. Yet they send contrasting messages in this cartoon, in which Nicholas Biddle and Andrew Jackson square off as bare-knuckled boxers in the war over the Bank.

The woman's fancy flowered bonnet and ruffled collar suggest an aristocratic fussiness—as does the port, which was an imported, upper-class beverage. The plain frontiersman, in contrast, wears simple buckskin and keeps his whiskey—a drink of the masses—close at hand. Just as Franklin Plummer portrayed his Mississippi opponent as a cologne-scented dandy (see page 291), this cartoonist sees Biddle as the aristocrat doing battle with Jackson, defender of the common folk.

bank." Eventually Biddle had to relent, and Jackson's victory was complete. When the Bank's charter expired in 1836, no national banking system replaced it. Instead, Jackson continued depositing federal revenues in selected state banks. A large majority of these "pet banks" were controlled by Democrats.

Jackson's Impact on the Presidency

Jackson approached the end of his administration in triumph. Indian removal was well on its way to completion, the nullifiers of the tariff had been confounded, and the "Monster Bank" had been destroyed. In the process, Jackson immeasurably enlarged the power of the presidency. "The President is the direct representative of the American people," he lectured the Senate when it opposed him. "He was elected by the people, and is responsible to them." With this declaration, Jackson redefined the character of the presidential office and its relationship to the people.

Jackson also converted the veto into an effective presidential power. During his two terms in office, he vetoed 12 bills, compared with only 9 for all previous presidents combined. Moreover, whereas his predecessors had vetoed bills only on strict constitutional grounds, Jackson felt free to block laws simply because he thought them bad policy. The threat of such action became an effective way to shape legislation to his

Strengthening of Presidential Powers

311

liking, which fundamentally strengthened the power of the president over Congress. The development of the modern presidency began with Andrew Jackson.

Van Buren and Depression

With the controls of the national bank removed, state banks rapidly expanded the amount of paper money in circulation. The total value of banknotes jumped from $82 million in January 1835 to $120 million in December 1836. As the currency expanded, so did the number of banks: from 329 in 1829 to 788 in 1837. A spiraling **inflation** set in as prices rose 50 percent after 1830 and interest rates by half as much.

As prices rose sharply, so did speculative fever. By 1836 land sales, which had been only $2.6 million four years earlier, approached $25 million. Almost all these lands were bought entirely on credit with banknotes, many of which had little value. Settlers seeking land poured into the Southwest, and as one observer wryly commented, "under this stimulating process prices rose like smoke." In an attempt to slow the economy, Jackson issued the Specie Circular in July 1836, which decreed that the government would accept only specie for the purchase of public land. Land sales drastically declined, but the speculative pressures in the economy were already too great.

Specie Circular

"Van Ruin's" Depression

Whig Party

During Jackson's second term, his opponents had gradually come together in a new party, the Whigs. Led by Henry Clay, they charged that "King Andrew I" had

This Whig cartoon blames the Democratic party for the depression that began during Van Buren's administration. Barefoot workers go unemployed, and women and children beg and sleep in the streets. Depositors clamor for their money from a bank that has suspended specie payments, while the pawnbroker and liquor store do a thriving business and the sheriff rounds up debtors.

dangerously concentrated power in the presidency. The Whigs also embraced Clay's "American System," designed to spur national economic development and particularly manufacturing. To do this the Whigs advocated a protective tariff, a national bank, and federal aid for internal improvements. In 1836 the Democrats nominated Martin Van Buren, who triumphed over three Whig sectional candidates.

Van Buren had less than two months in office to savor his triumph before the speculative mania collapsed, and with it the economy. After a brief recovery, the bottom fell out of the international cotton market in 1839 and the country entered a serious depression. Arising from causes that were worldwide, the depression demonstrated how deeply the market economy had penetrated American society. It was not until 1843 that the economy revived.

Depression

Public opinion identified hard times with the policies of the Democratic party. Because he strongly opposed a new national bank, Van Buren instead persuaded Congress in 1840 to create an Independent Treasury to keep the government's funds. Its offices were forbidden to accept paper currency, issue any banknotes, or make any loans. The government's money would be safe, but it would also remain unavailable to banks to make loans and stimulate the economy.

Independent Treasury

As the depression deepened, thousands of workers were unemployed and countless businesses failed. Urban workers and their families were among the hardest hit. Nationally wages fell 30 to 50 percent. "Business of all kinds is completely at a stand," wrote one business leader in 1840, "and the whole body politic sick and infirm, and calling aloud for a remedy."

The Whigs' Triumph

With the nation stuck in the worst depression of the century, the Whigs approached the election of 1840 in high spirits. To oppose Van Buren, they turned to William Henry Harrison, the military leader who had won fame defeating the Shawnee Indians at Tippecanoe. Using the democratic electioneering techniques that Jackson's supporters had first perfected, they portrayed Harrison as a man of the people while painting Van Buren as an aristocrat who wore a corset, ate off gold plates with silver spoons, and used cologne. Shades of Franklin Plummer!

First Modern Presidential Campaign

Whig rallies featured hard cider and log cabins to reinforce Harrison's image as a man of the people. Ironically, Harrison had been born into one of Virginia's most aristocratic families and was living in a 16-room mansion in Ohio. But the Whig campaign, by portraying the election as a contest between aristocracy and democracy, was perfectly attuned to the prevailing national spirit.

Both parties used parades, barbecues, liberty pole raisings, party songs, and mass meetings to stir up enthusiasm. But the Whigs pioneered a new aspect of mass political campaigning: they prominently involved women. Deeming themselves the party of morality, Whigs appealed directly to women for support, urging them to become politically informed in order to morally instruct their husbands. Women attended Whig rallies, conducted meetings, made speeches, and wrote campaign pamphlets, activities that before had been solely the duties of men. "I never took so much interest in politics in my life," Mary Steger of Richmond confessed to a friend. Uncertain what to make of this new Whig tactic, one Democrat observed, "This way of making politicians of their women is something new under the sun." Democrats had no choice

Women Take a New Political Role

This Illinois marching club benefited from the support of women.

Election of 1840

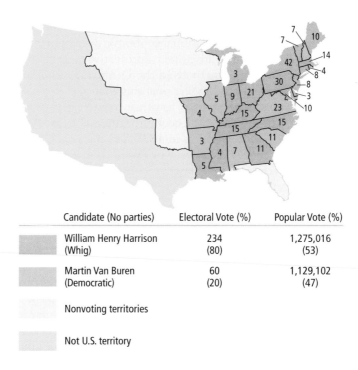

Candidate (No parties)	Electoral Vote (%)	Popular Vote (%)
William Henry Harrison (Whig)	234 (80)	1,275,016 (53)
Martin Van Buren (Democratic)	60 (20)	1,129,102 (47)
Nonvoting territories		
Not U.S. territory		

but to eventually follow suit. Women's role in national politics began in 1840, and within a few years their presence at party rallies was commonplace.

Just as the Panic of 1819 had roused the voters to action, the depression and the two parties' response to it sparked mass interest. The result was a record turnout, as some 900,000 new voters were mobilized between 1836 and 1840 and nearly four-fifths of the eligible voters went to the polls. Although the popular vote was fairly close (Harrison led by about 150,000 votes out of 2.4 million cast), in the Electoral College Harrison won an easy victory, 234 to 60.

The "log cabin" campaign marked the final transition from the deferential politics of the Federalist era to the egalitarian politics that had emerged in the wake of the Panic of 1819. As the *Democratic Review* conceded after the Whigs' victory in 1840, "We have taught them how to conquer us."

The Jacksonian Party System

It is easy, given the hoopla of democratic campaigning, to be distracted from the central fact that the new political system was directly shaped by the social and economic strains of an expanding nation. Whigs and Democrats held different attitudes toward the changes brought about by the market, banks, and commerce.

Democrats, Whigs, and the Market

Democratic Ideology

The Democrats tended to view society as a continuing conflict between "the people"—farmers, planters, and workers—and a set of greedy aristocrats. The latter were not Europe's landed aristocrats, of course, but a "paper money aristocracy" of bankers and investors, who manipulated the banking system for profit. For Democrats, the Bank War became a battle to restore the old Jeffersonian Republic with its values of simplicity, frugality, hard work, and independence.

Jackson understood the dangers that private banks posed to a democratic society. Yet Democrats, in effect, wanted the rewards of the market without sacrificing the features of a simple agrarian republic. They wanted the wealth and goods that the market offered without the competitive, changing society, the complex dealings, the dominance of urban centers, and the loss of independence that came with it.

Whigs, however, were more comfortable with the market. They envisioned no conflict between farmers and mechanics on the one hand and businesspeople and bankers on the other. Economic growth would benefit everyone by creating jobs, stimulating demand for agricultural products, and expanding opportunity. The government's responsibility was to provide a well-regulated economy that guaranteed opportunity for citizens of ability. In such an economy, banks and corporations were not only useful but necessary. "All should be mutual friends and helpers to each other," commented one North Carolina Whig, "and whoever aids and assists his fellow men from good motives, by lending money, by affording employment by precept or example, is a benefactor to his fellow men." *Whig Ideology*

Whigs and Democrats also disagreed over how active government should be. Despite Andrew Jackson's inclination to be a strong president, Democrats as a rule believed in limited government. Government's role in the economy was to promote competition by destroying monopolies and special privileges. *Democrats' Belief in Limited Government*

In *Charles River Bridge v. Warren Bridge* (1837) the Supreme Court strengthened the vision of an expanding capitalistic society undergirded by free competition. The opinion was written by Chief Justice Roger Taney, whom Jackson had appointed in 1835 to succeed John Marshall. At issue was whether in authorizing construction of a free bridge Massachusetts violated the rights of the owners of a nearby toll bridge. Declaring that the public interest was the overriding concern, Taney's opinion struck down the idea of implied monopolies. In this decision, the Court sought to promote equality of opportunity and economic progress. *Opposition to Monopolies*

In keeping with this philosophy of limited government, Democrats also rejected the idea that moral beliefs were the proper sphere of government action. Religion and politics, they believed, should be kept clearly separate, and they generally opposed humanitarian legislation as an interference with personal freedom. On the other hand, they supported debtor relief, which in their view curbed the wealthy aristocrats who tyrannized the common worker.

The Whigs, in contrast, viewed government power positively. They believed that it should be used to protect individual rights and public liberty and that it had a special role where individual effort was ineffective. By regulating the economy and competition, the government could ensure equal opportunity. Indeed, for Whigs the concept that the government would promote the general welfare went beyond the economy. Northern Whigs in particular also believed that government power should be used to foster the moral welfare of the country. They were much more likely to favor temperance or antislavery legislation and aid to education. Whigs portrayed themselves not only as the party of prosperity but also as the party of respectability and proper behavior. *Whigs' Belief in Active Government*

The Social Bases of the Two Parties

In some ways the social makeup of the two parties was similar. To be competitive Whigs and Democrats both had to have significant support among farmers, the largest group in society, and workers. Neither party could carry an election by appealing exclusively to the rich or the poor.

The Whigs, however, enjoyed disproportionate strength among the business and commercial classes, especially following the Bank War. Whigs appealed to planters who needed credit to finance their cotton and rice trade in the world market, to farmers who were eager to sell their surpluses, and to workers who wished to improve their social position. Democrats attracted farmers isolated from the market or uncomfortable with it, workers alienated from the emerging industrial system, and rising entrepreneurs who wanted to break monopolies and open the economy to newcomers like themselves. The Whigs were strongest in the towns, cities, and rural areas that were fully integrated into the market economy, whereas Democrats dominated areas of semisubsistence farming that were more isolated and languishing economically. Attitude toward the market, rather than economic position, was more important in determining party affiliation. *Attitudes toward the Market Economy*

Religion and ethnic identities also shaped partisanship. As the self-proclaimed "party of respectability," Whigs attracted the support of high-status native-born church groups, including the Congregationalists and Unitarians in New England and Presbyterians and Episcopalians elsewhere. The party also attracted immigrant groups that most easily merged into the dominant Anglo-Protestant culture, such as the English, Welsh, and Scots. Democrats, on the other hand, recruited more Germans and Irish, whose more lenient observance of the Sabbath and (among Catholics) use of parochial schools generated native-born hostility. Democrats appealed to the lower-status Baptists and Methodists, particularly in states where they earlier had been subjected to legal disadvantages. Both parties also attracted freethinkers and the unchurched, but the Democrats had the advantage because they resisted demands for temperance and sabbatarian laws, such as the prohibition of Sunday travel. In states where they could vote, African Americans were solidly Whig in reaction to the Democratic party's strong racism and hostility to black rights.

In the Americas as well as in Europe, the rise of democratic governance and the spread of market economies evolved roughly in tandem over the same half-century. Andrew Jackson's triumph, with the common people trampling the White House furniture and Franklin Plummer branding his opponent as a cologne-scented aristocrat, was only the latest in a series of upheavals stretching back to the American and French Revolutions of the eighteenth century. Latin America too experienced democratic revolutions. From 1808 to 1821 Spain's American provinces declared their independence one by one, taking inspiration from the writings of Jefferson and Thomas Paine as well as the French *Declaration of the Rights of Man*. Democracy did not always root itself in the aftermath of these revolutions, but democratic ideology remained a powerful social catalyst.

In the United States, the parallel growth of national markets and democratic institutions was a similarly checkered history. If Jackson championed the cause of the "common people," he also led the movement to displace Indians from their lands. The poorest white American might vote for "Old Hickory," at the same time that he took comfort that African Americans could never rise as high as he in an increasingly racist society. Furthermore, the advance of the market created social strains, including the increasing impoverishment of the labor force in the North and the growing gap in society between the richest and the poorest.

Still, Americans had evolved a system of democratic politics to deal with the conflicts that the new order produced. The new national parties, like the new markets, had become essential structures uniting the American nation. They advanced an ideology of equality and opportunity, competed vigorously with one another, and mobilized large numbers of ordinary Americans in the political process. Along with the market, democracy had become an integral part of American life.

Significant Events

1819–1823	Panic and depression
1822	Denmark Vesey conspiracy
1824	Tariff duties raised; Jackson finishes first in presidential race

1825	House elects John Quincy Adams president
1827	Cherokees adopt written constitution
1828	Tariff of Abominations; *South Carolina Exposition and Protest;* Jackson elected president
1830–1838	Indian removal
1830	Webster-Hayne debate; Indian Removal Act
1832	*Worcester v. Georgia;* Jackson vetoes recharter of the national bank; Jackson reelected; South Carolina nullifies tariff; Jackson's Proclamation on Nullification
1833–1834	Biddle's panic
1833	Force Bill; tariff duties reduced; Jackson removes deposits from the Bank of the United States
1834	Whig party organized
1835–1842	Second Seminole war
1836	Specie Circular; Van Buren elected president
1837	*Charles River Bridge* case; economic panic
1838	Trail of Tears
1839–1843	Depression
1840	Independent Treasury Act; Harrison elected president
1842	First professional minstrel troupe

Chapter Summary

Beginning in the 1820s, the United States experienced a democratic revolution that was identified with Andrew Jackson.

- The rise of democracy was stimulated by the Panic of 1819, which caused Americans to look toward both politicians and the government to address their needs.

- The new political culture of democracy included the use of conventions to make nominations, the adoption of white manhood suffrage, and the acceptance of political parties as essential for the working of the constitutional system.

- The new politics had distinct limits, however. Women were not given the vote, and racism intensified.

  - The eastern Indian tribes were forced to move to new lands west of the Mississippi River.
  - Free African Americans were subject to increasingly harsh discrimination and exclusion.

- Andrew Jackson came to personify the new democratic culture. Through his forceful leadership, he expanded the powers of the presidency.

  - Jackson threatened to use force against South Carolina when it tried to nullify the federal tariff.
  - In response to John C. Calhoun's theory of nullification, nationalists advanced the idea of the perpetual Union.
  - Jackson vetoed a bill to recharter the Second Bank of the United States and destroyed the Bank by removing its federal deposits.

- Under President Martin Van Buren, the nation entered a severe depression.

- Capitalizing on hard times and employing the democratic techniques pioneered by the Democrats, the Whigs gained national power in 1840.

- By 1840 the two parties had developed different ideologies.

  - The Whigs were more comfortable with the mechanisms of the market and linked commerce with progress.
  - The Democrats were uneasy about the market and favored limited government.

Additional Reading

The most comprehensive reinterpretation of antebellum political history from Jackson to Lincoln is Sean Wilentz, *The Rise of Democracy* (2005). For a broader perspective on the evolution of American political culture throughout the nineteenth century, see Glenn Altschuler and Stuart Blumin, *Rude Republic* (2000). A good interpretation of Jacksonian politics is Harry Watson, *Liberty and Power* (1990), and important discussions of party ideologies include Marvin Meyers, *The Jacksonian Persuasion* (1957); Daniel Walker Howe, *The Political Culture of American Whigs* (1979); and Lawrence Frederick Kohl, *The Politics of Individualism* (1988). For the history of the Whig party, the book to read is Michael Holt, *The Rise and Fall of the American Whig Party* (1999).

The best account of the nullification crisis is still William Freehling, *Prelude to the Civil War* (1966), and Robert Remini offers a succinct analysis of the banking controversy in *Andrew Jackson and the Bank War* (1967). Paul Goodman, *Towards a Christian Republic* (1988) is the most valuable study of Anti-Masonry. On Indian removal in the South, see John Ehle, *The Trail of Tears* (1997), and Robert Remini, *Andrew Jackson and His Indian Wars* (2001).

For a fuller list of readings, see the Bibliography at www.mhhe.com/davidsonnation6.

CHAPTER 12
The Fires of Perfection
1820~1850

The Beechers and the Kingdom of God

In 1826 the Reverend Lyman Beecher was probably the most celebrated minister of the Republic, and the pulpit of Hanover Street Church was his to command. Beecher looked and spoke like a pious farmer, but every Sunday he was transformed when he mounted the pulpit of Boston's most imposing church. From there, he would blaze forth denunciations of dancing, drinking, dueling, or "infidelity," all the while punctuating his sermon with pump-handle strokes of the right hand.

Nor were Beecher's ambitions small. His goal was nothing less than to bring the kingdom of Christ to the nation and the world. Like many ministers, Beecher had studied the intriguing final book of the New Testament, the Revelation to John. The Revelation foretold in Latter days of Earth a glorious millennium—a thousand years of peace and triumph—when the saints would rule and evil would be banished from the world. Beecher was convinced that the long-awaited millennium might well begin in the United States.

Personal experience reinforced this optimism. Born to a sturdy line of New England blacksmiths in 1775, Beecher entered Yale College during the high tide of postwar nationalism—and, some said, the lowest ebb of religion among young people. In the revivals of the Second Great Awakening that came to many colleges in 1802, Beecher had been one of those converted.

But he was hardly a stodgy Puritan. Much of Beecher's boundless energy went into raising a family of 11 children, every one of whom he prayed would take leading roles in bringing the kingdom of God to America. He loved to wrestle on the floor with his sons, climb the highest trees, or go "berrying" with his daughters. Still, the religious dimension of their lives was constant. The family attended two services on Sunday, a weekly prayer meeting, and a monthly "concert of prayer," where the devout met to pray for the conversion of the world. Beecher's son Thomas remembered his father commanding: "Overturn and overturn till He whose right it is shall come and reign, King of nations and King of saints."

To usher in the kingdom of God entire communities and even nations would have to be swept with the fire of **millennialism.** Toward that end Beecher joined other Protestant ministers in supporting a host of religious reforms and missionary efforts. In 1810 the American Board of Commissioners for Foreign Missions was established, followed by the American Bible Society (1816) and the American Tract Society (1825), whose Bibles and religious pamphlets blanketed every sleepy hamlet

Revivalist Charles Finney gained fame in New York state's "burned over district," where he led religious revivals in many of the towns along the bustling Erie Canal. As Finney's fame spread, he eventually used a huge tent, 100 feet in diameter, which was able to seat 3,000 worshipers.

321

in the country. Societies sprang up to promote Sunday schools and minister to sailors and the poor. By 1830 the most important of these organizations made up the loosely united "Benevolent Empire." To Beecher these organizations were signs of the coming kingdom.

As the new pastor at Hanover Street, Beecher also directed his righteous artillery on a host of evils that seemed to be obstructing God's kingdom. With scorn he attacked Unitarians, whose liberal, rational creed rejected the divinity of Jesus. In Boston, Unitarians were mainly upper class and cultured. But he also denounced what he viewed as sinful pastimes of the lower class: playing cards, gambling, and drinking. And he denounced Roman Catholic priests and nuns as superstitious, devious agents of "Antichrist."

Beecher's efforts at "moral reform" antagonized many immigrants and other working people who enjoyed liquor or lotteries. Thus, when a blaze broke out in the basement of his church in 1830, unsympathetic local firefighters stood by while the splendid structure burned to the ground. The fires of spiritual reform had been halted, temporarily, by a blaze of a literal sort.

Any fire, real or spiritual, is unpredictable as it spreads from one scrap of tinder to the next. That proved to be the case with reform movements of the 1820s and 1830s, as they moved in diverging, sometimes contradictory, ways. What did it mean, after all, to bring in Christ's kingdom?

The goals of the early reform societies were moral rather than social. Leaders like Beecher sought to convert individuals and to church the unchurched, with the help of religious revivals and benevolent associations. Their conservative aim, as he expressed it, was to restore America to "the moral government of God."

Other Christians, however, began to focus on social issues such as slavery, the inequality of women, and the operation of prisons. To these problems they demanded

Lyman Beecher (center) with his family in 1855. Five of his six sons, all of whom were ministers, stand in back. In front, daughters Catharine (holding his arm to steady it for the long exposure) and Isabella are on the left; Harriet, the author of Uncle Tom's Cabin, *is at the far right.*

more radical solutions. Ironically, many of Beecher's children went well beyond his more conservative strategies for hastening the millennium. They spoke out for abolition, women's rights, and education in ways that left their father distinctly uncomfortable. In their activities the Beechers reflected the diversity of the reform impulse itself.

Revivalism and the Social Order

Society during the Jacksonian era was undergoing deep and rapid changes. The revolution in markets brought both economic expansion and periodic depressions, as its citizens competed—often anxiously—for status and wealth. In a nation where fortunes could be won and lost almost overnight, some reformers sought stability and moral order in religious community. The bonds of unity created by a revival brought a sense of peace in the midst of a society in change. Revivals could reinforce strength and discipline, too, in an emerging industrial culture that demanded sobriety and regular working habits.

Other reformers, however, sought to check the excesses of Jacksonian America by radically remaking institutions or devising utopian, experimental ways of living and working together. The drive for renewal, in other words, led reformers sometimes to preserve social institutions, other times to overturn them. It led them sometimes to liberate, other times to control. And the conflicting ways in which these dynamics operated could be seen in the electric career of Charles Grandison Finney.

Finney's New Measures

In 1821, as a young man, Finney experienced a soul-shattering conversion that led him to give up his law practice to become an itinerant minister. Eventually he was ordained in the Presbyterian church, although he lacked any formal theological training. He first attracted national attention when in the mid-1820s and early 1830s he conducted a series of spectacular revivals in the booming port cities along the new Erie Canal.

Like George Whitefield before him, Finney had an entrancing voice that carried great distances. His power over an audience was such that when he described the descent of a sinner into hell, those in the back of the hall rose to witness the final plunge. His success, however, resulted also from his use of special techniques—"the new measures"—and his casual attitude toward religious doctrine.

These new measures had been developed during the frontier revivals of the Second Great Awakening (see page 243). Finney's contribution was to popularize the techniques and use them systematically. He held "protracted meetings" night after night to build up excitement. Speaking boldly and bluntly, he prayed for sinners by name, encouraged women to testify in public gatherings, and placed those struggling with conversion on the "anxious bench" at the front of the church. "A revival is not a miracle," he coolly declared, "it is a purely scientific result of the right use of constituted means." Like other **evangelical** revivalists Finney looked to help individuals to undergo an emotionally wrenching conversion experience and be reborn.

Charles Finney, about 1834

Free Will and Perfectionism

The Philosophy of the New Revivals

Finney also rejected many religious doctrines of Calvinism, including predestination, which maintained that God had already determined which individuals were destined to be saved or damned and that no human effort could change this decision. But by the 1820s such a proposition seemed unreasonable to a generation that condemned hereditary distinctions, celebrated personal dignity, and praised human ability and activity. Leaving the Lord little role in the drama of human deliverance, Finney

In The Way of Good and Evil *devout Christians are all helped on the path (right) to millennial perfection by the virtues of family, religion, education, and hard work. Sinners on the left, however, take the path of disobedience, intemperance, and lying—straight to hell.*

embraced the doctrine of free will. All men and women who wanted to could be saved. To those anxious about their salvation, he thundered, "Do it!"

With salvation within reach of every individual, what might be in store for society at large? "If the church would do her duty," Finney confidently predicted, "the millennium may come in this country in three years." By the 1830s Finney had taken to preaching not merely faith in human progress but something more—human perfectibility. Embracing this new theology of "perfectionism," he boldly asserted that all Christians should "aim at being holy and not rest satisfied until they are as perfect as God."

By preaching an optimistic message of free will and salvation to all, Finney and his eager imitators transformed Protestantism. But not all clergy applauded. For Lyman Beecher, as well as for many supporters of the Second Great Awakening, Finney's new measures went too far in generating excessive emotionalism, while his theology of perfectionism verged on heresy. Undaunted by such criticism, Finney continued his revivals. As for Lyman Beecher, he decided in 1832 to outflank his adversaries by moving west to become the president of Lane Seminary in Cincinnati. There he planned to train the right sort of revivalists to save the frontier for true religion and to bring about the kingdom of God in America.

Religion and the Market Economy

Revival audiences responded to the call for reform partly because they were unsettled by the era's rapid social changes. In the North, evangelical religion proved strongest not in isolated backwaters but in frontier areas just entering the market economy. Rochester, New York, a booming flour-milling center on the Erie Canal, epitomized that social environment.

When Charles Finney came to town in the winter of 1830–1831, Rochester was a community in crisis. It had grown in a decade and a half from a village of 300 souls to a commercial city of more than 20,000. That wrenching expansion produced sharp divisions among the town's leaders, a large working class that increasingly lived apart from employers and beyond their moral control, and a rowdy saloon culture catering to canal boatmen and other transients. Finney preached almost daily in Rochester for six months, assisted by local ministers. He brought thousands to accept his message of voluntary salvation and doubled church membership. Religion helped bring order to what had been a chaotic and fragmented city.

Revivalism's Appeal to the Middle Class

Although revivals like Finney's Rochester triumph drew converts from all segments of American society, they appealed especially to the middle class. Lawyers, merchants, retailers, and manufacturers all played central roles in the larger market economy and invested in factories and railroads. The market put intense pressure on these upwardly mobile citizens. They viewed success as a reflection of moral character, yet the boom-or-bust economy threatened their security and their wealth. Religion provided a way in which to cope with the tensions and uncertainties of their lives.

Workers, too, were among the converted, especially during the depression that began in 1839. The Methodist church, which lacked the social respectability of some of the other evangelical churches, was particularly important in instilling the values of sobriety, frugality, and hard work in the urban working class.

Among other things, joining a church reflected a desire to get ahead in the new economy by accepting moral self-discipline. To a striking degree, social mobility and church membership were linked. In Rochester two-thirds of the male workers who were church members improved their occupational status in a decade. In contrast, workers who did not join a church rarely stayed in town more than a few years, and those who stayed were likely to decline in status.

Revivalists such as Finney were interested in saving souls, not money, and their converts were most concerned with their spiritual state. Even so, evangelical Protestantism reinforced values needed to succeed in the new competitive economy. Churchgoers embraced the values of hard work, punctuality, and sobriety; they internalized the demand for self-control. In that sense, religion was one means of social control in a disordered society. And many employers put pressure on workers to give up their drinking habits, on and off the job, and to embrace religion.

Workers and Church Membership

The Rise of African American Churches

Independent black churches grew in size and importance as well because African Americans in urban areas increasingly resented being treated as second-class worshipers. In 1787, only a month after the close of the Constitutional Convention in Philadelphia, Richard Allen was praying at St. George's Church. Allen was not only a devout churchgoer but also a popular black preacher. But this Sunday morning his prayers were interrupted. "You must get up—you must not kneel here," a white usher whispered to Allen, who was not in the area reserved for black parishioners. Several white ushers roughly pulled him to his feet. Allen and other black members of the congregation walked out. In 1794 he organized the Bethel Church, where African Americans would be free to worship without discrimination.

In the early nineteenth century, similar tensions led to the formation of black Methodist and Baptist churches in a number of northern and southern cities. The most important was the African Methodist Episcopal (AME) Church, organized in 1816. Growing fears for the security of slavery caused southern white communities, especially in the Deep South, to suppress independent black churches after 1820. But these evangelical churches continued to grow in the North. By 1856 the AME Church boasted some 20,000 members.

St. James AME Zion Church, built in 1833 in Ithaca, New York, became an important transfer point for fugitive slaves heading north. Harriet Tubman visited the church often in her efforts to guide slaves north.

The Significance of the Second Great Awakening

As a result of the Second Great Awakening, the dominant form of Christianity in America became evangelical Protestantism. Membership in the major Protestant churches—Congregational, Presbyterian, Baptist, and Methodist—soared during the first half of the nineteenth century. By 1840 an estimated half of the adult population was connected to some church, with the Methodists emerging as the largest Protestant denomination in both the North and the South.

Evangelicalism was in harmony with the basic values of early-nineteenth-century Americans. Its emphasis on the ability of everyone to bring about his or her salvation upheld the American belief in individualism. By catering to a mass audience without social distinctions, the revivals reinforced the American belief in democracy and equality. And Finney's invincibly optimistic doctrine of perfectionism matched the spirit of the age.

Evangelicalism Bolsters Individualism and Equality

Women's Sphere

Women played a large role in this religious upswing. Indeed, female converts outnumbered males by about three to two. Usually the first convert in a family was a woman, and many men who converted were related to women who had come forward earlier.

Women and Revivalism

Women's Changing Lives

Women played such an important role in the Awakening partly because of changes in their own social universe. Instead of parents arranging the marriages of their children, couples were beginning to wed more often on the basis of affection. Under such conditions, a woman's prospects for marriage became less certain, and in older areas such as New England, the migration of so many young men to the West compounded this uncertainty. Yet marriage was deemed important for a woman's happiness, and it remained essential for her economic security.

The unpredictability of these social circumstances drew young women toward religion. Women between the ages of 12 and 25 were especially susceptible to conversion. Joining a church heightened a young woman's feeling of initiative and gave her a sense of purpose. By establishing respectability and widening her social circle of friends, church membership also enhanced her chances of marriage.

The Ideal of Domesticity

The era's changing economic order brought other pressures to bear on wives and mothers. Most men now worked outside the home, while the rise of factories led to a decline in part-time work such as spinning, which women had once performed to supplement family income. Moreover, except on the frontier, home manufacturing was no longer essential, for the family purchased articles that women previously had made, such as cloth, soap, and candles. "The transition from mother-and-daughter power to water-and-steam power," one New England minister noted, produced "a complete revolution of domestic life."

As business affairs grew increasingly separate from the family in the nineteenth century, the middle-class home became a female domain. A woman's role as a wife and mother was to dispense love and moral guidance to her husband and her children. As this domestic scene makes clear, she was at the very center of the world of the family.

This growing separation of the household from the workplace meant that the home took on a new social identity. It was idealized as a place of "**domesticity,**" a haven away from the competitive, workaday world, with the mother firmly at its center. This new view of women's role was elaborated largely by clergy and female authors in sermons, advice manuals, and pieces of sentimental fiction for an urban middle-class audience. But the ideal's significance and acceptance had far-reaching consequences. The idea of domesticity was based on the notion of separate sexual spheres. If men's sphere was the world of factories, offices, and fields, women's sphere was the home, where they were to dispense love and comfort and teach moral values to husbands and children. "Love is our life our reality, business yours," Mollie Clark told one suitor.

Women, who were considered morally stronger, were also held to a higher standard of sexual purity. A man's sexual infidelity, although hardly condoned, brought no lasting shame. But a woman who engaged in sexual relations before marriage or was unfaithful afterward was threatened with everlasting disgrace. Under this double standard, women were to be passive and submerge their identities in those of their husbands.

The Quaintness of Quilts

Piecing Together Meaning in a Blanket

Today the thought of quilt-making around a living-room fireplace evokes a simpler, less complicated era. But in fact, piecework quilts—sewn together from scraps of cloth to make designs like the one on the right—reflect the coming of the industrial revolution. In the eighteenth century such quilts were rare because the patterned scraps that went into making the designs became available only during the nineteenth century, from machine-produced textiles.

During the colonial period quilts were more likely to be petticoats such as the bright red design below. The crisscross seams sandwiched together a layer of insulation (batting) between wool or silk coverings, but the pieces were not patchwork. Such quilts were also too expensive for most people to own. Only when cheap manufactured cloth produced a wide variety of prints did scrap pieces become available.

Just as the industrial revolution encouraged a cult of domesticity to shelter families from the harsh industrial workplace, so too did factory-made cloth encourage the making of piecework quilts.

No woman played a more important role in creating the ideal of domesticity, than Lyman Beecher's daughter Catharine. Like the earlier advocates of "republican motherhood," Catharine Beecher argued that women exercised power as moral guardians of the nation's future. The proper care of a middle-class household was also a crucial responsibility, and Beecher wrote several books on efficient home management. "There is no one thing more necessary to a housekeeper in performing her varied duties, than a habit of system and order," she told readers. "For all the time afforded us, we must give account to God."

Catharine Beecher was also a leading advocate of giving women greater educational opportunities so that they could become schoolteachers. The school was an extension of the home, she maintained, and teachers, like mothers, should instill sound moral values in children.

Women also exerted their moral authority through the growing number of benevolent organizations, which fostered close friendships. Women gave emotionally much more to other family members than they received in exchange, and they turned to other women for comfort and support. This "sisterhood"—the common sense of identity and shared experiences—helped sustain reform movements launched by women to aid females of the lower classes.

"Sisterhood" and Social Networks

In 1831 Olive Walkley made a significant decision: she moved the bed in which she and her husband, Stephen, slept out of the parlor and replaced it with a carpet. She also had the unfinished upstairs plastered and partitioned into bedrooms for their children. The Walkleys were farmers in Southington, Connecticut, but like middle-class urban families they were influenced by the new movement to separate public and private space in the home.

When the Walkleys were married in 1811, Americans were accustomed to living in close quarters, for most houses had few rooms. Further, the limited light and heat forced members to congregate. Parents and sometimes the entire family slept in the parlor, where visitors were also entertained and where the family's most valuable possessions, including its best bed, were proudly displayed. Even in the wealthiest households, usually only the parents enjoyed separate sleeping quarters, and in most homes beds could be found in virtually every room.

In the years after 1820, however, the American home was reshaped to create specialized regions of privacy, service, and socializing. While houses increasingly faced the road, new designs provided greater privacy by creating an entry hall that served as a transition space from the outside world to the various parts of the house and by separating living and cooking quarters from areas for entertainment.

An architect confers with builders about the plans as a new house goes up in the background

Domesticity in Europe

The ideal of domesticity was not unique to the United States. The middle class became increasingly important in Europe, so that after 1850 it was culturally dominant. Employment opportunities expanded for women as industrialization accelerated, yet the social expectation among the middle class was that women would not be employed outside the home. This redefinition of women's roles was more sweeping in Europe because previously, middle-class women had left the task of child-raising largely to hired nurses and governesses. By midcentury, these mothers devoted much more time to domestic duties, including rearing the children. Family size also declined, both in France and in England. The middle class was most numerous in England; indeed, the importance of the middle class in Britain during Queen Victoria's reign (1837–1901) gave these ideals the label **Victorianism.**

Most white women in the United States hardly had time to make the ideal of domesticity the center of their lives. Farmers' wives had to work constantly, whereas lower-class families could not get by without the wages of female members. Still, many middle-class women tried to live up to the ideal, though many found the effort confining. "The great trial is that I have nothing to do," one complained. "Here I am with abundant leisure and capable, I believe, of accomplishing some good, and yet with no object on which to expend my energies."

Women's socially defined role as guardians of morality helps explain their prominence among revival converts. Religious activity was one way that women could exert influence in society, to say nothing of with their husbands. For some male critics, Finney's policy of giving women a prominent role in revivals threatened to bring about a dangerous equality between the sexes. One unhappy man in Rochester complained about the effect of Finney's visit to his home: "He *stuffed* my wife with tracts, and alarmed her fears, and nothing short of meetings, night and day, could atone for the many fold sins my poor, simple spouse had committed." Then, getting to the heart of the matter, he added, "She made the miraculous discovery, that she had been 'unevenly yoked.' From this unhappy period, peace, quiet, and happiness have fled from my dwelling, never, I fear, to return."

A sitting room was for the family's everyday use, whereas the parlor was reserved for public activity, including receiving company, giving recitals, and performing ceremonies such as weddings and funerals. As Americans developed a new sense of privacy, the parents' bed and the intimate activities associated with it were placed out of sight. In more prosperous homes an upholstered mahogany sofa replaced the bed in the parlor, and the floor was covered with a carpet, as much a symbol of the family's refinement as the mantel clock was of its modern outlook.

Food preparation and domestic work were done in a separate kitchen and adjoining back rooms. While rural families often continued to eat in the sitting room, houses more frequently contained a separate dining room. Stoves, which enlarged usable space by radiating heat, became common in more affluent homes, while the hearth and its fire—once the main source of food, heat, and light—ceased to be the center of the family's life together.

The newer homes projected a sense of order as well, in sharp contrast to the run-down appearance of older houses, especially in the countryside. These were rarely painted, doors often did not fit, and broken windows were patched with rags. Often enough, trash and garbage were simply tossed out the nearest window. However, as middle-class families (especially in the North) became increasingly sensitive to the home's public face, they began to paint their houses and keep them in good repair. They also erected white-washed fences around their front yards, planted ornamental shrubs, and put their refuse in pits.

The new standards of domestic life also emphasized cleanliness and decoration. Lydia Maria Child's popular *The American Frugal Housewife* offered families of modest means numerous tips on cleaning and scouring as well as decorating.

In short, a home's floor plan and furnishings not only determined comfort but also defined a family's status and—increasingly middle-class—aspirations.

The Middle-Class Family in Transition

As the middle-class family adapted to the pressures of competitive society by becoming a haven of moral virtue, it developed a new structure and new set of attitudes closer in spirit to those of the modern family. One basic change was the rise of privacy. The family was increasingly seen as a sheltered retreat from the outside world. (See Daily Lives, "Privacy Begins at Home," pages 328–329.) In addition, the pressures to achieve success led middle-class young adults to delay marriage, since a husband was expected to have the financial means to support his wife.

Smaller family size was a result of the delay in marriage as well, since wives began bearing children later. But especially among the urban middle class, women began to use birth control to space children further apart and minimize the risks of pregnancy. In addition, it has been estimated that before 1860 one abortion was performed for every five or six live births. These practices contributed to a decline in the birthrate, from slightly more than 7 children per family in 1800 to 5.4 in 1850—a 25 percent drop. And over that 50-year period the decline became more abrupt beginning in the 1830s.

Decline in the Birthrate

Family size was directly related to the success ethic. On the farm, children working in the fields and around the house were an economic asset. In the new, market-oriented urban society, in contrast, children needed an extended education and special training in order to succeed. Thus they were a greater financial burden on their parents. With smaller families, however, parents could tend more carefully to their children's success. Increasingly middle-class families took on the expense of additional education to prepare their sons for a career in business. They also frequently equalized inheritances rather than favoring the eldest son or favoring sons over daughters.

American Romanticism

The rational-minded Unitarians in Boston had become accustomed to being attacked by evangelical ministers like Lyman Beecher. They were less prepared to be criticized by one of their own—and on their own home ground, no less. Yet that was what happened when a Unitarian minister named Ralph Waldo Emerson addressed the students of Harvard Divinity School on a warm summer evening in July 1838.

Emerson warned his listeners that the true church seemed "to totter to its fall, almost all life extinct." Outside, nature's world was alive and vibrant: "The grass grows, the buds burst, the meadow is spotted with fire and gold in the tint of flowers." But from the pulpits of too many congregations came lifeless preaching. "In how many churches, by how many prophets, tell me," Emerson demanded, "is man made sensible that he is an infinite Soul?" Leaving the shocked audience to ponder his message, Emerson and his wife drove home beneath a night sky illuminated by the northern lights.

Emerson's Divinity School Address glowed much like that July aurora. The address lacked the searing fire of Finney's revivals, yet in its own bold way it reflected a second major current of thought shaping this era of reform. That current was the intellectual movement known as **Romanticism.**

Romantic Movement

Romanticism began in Europe as a reaction against the Enlightenment. The Enlightenment had placed reason at the center of human achievement; Romanticism instead emphasized the importance of emotion and intuition as sources of truth. It gloried in the unlimited potential of the individual, who might soar if freed from the restraints of institutions. Romanticism extolled humanitarianism and sympathized with the oppressed.

In elevating inner feelings and heartfelt convictions, Romanticism reinforced the emotionalism of religious revivals. Philosophically, its influence was strongest among intellectuals who took part in the Transcendental movement and in the dramatic flowering of American literature. And, like revivalism, Romanticism offered its own paths toward perfectionism.

In the summer of 1858 members of the cultural Saturday Club of Boston made an excursion to the Adirondacks to observe nature. In Philosopher's Camp, *painted by William J. Stillman, who organized the expedition, a group on the left dissects a fish under the supervision of the famous scientist Louis Agassiz, while on the right others practice firing rifles. Symbolically, Ralph Waldo Emerson stands alone in the center of the painting in a contemplative mood.*

Emerson and Transcendentalism

Above all, Romanticism produced individualists. Thus Transcendentalism is difficult to define, because its members resisted being lumped together. It blossomed in the mid-1830s, when a number of Unitarian clergy such as George Ripley and Ralph Waldo Emerson resigned their pulpits, loudly protesting the church's smug, lifeless teachings. The new "Transcendentalist Club" attracted a small following among other discontented Boston intellectuals, including Margaret Fuller, Bronson Alcott, and Orestes Brownson.

Like European Romantics, American Transcendentalists emphasized feeling over reason, seeking a spiritual communion with nature. By *transcend* they meant to go beyond or to rise above—specifically above reason and beyond the material world. As part of creation, every human being contained a spark of divinity, Emerson avowed. Transcendentalists also shared in Romanticism's glorification of the individual. "Trust thyself. Every heart vibrates to that iron string," Emerson advised. If freed from the constraints of traditional authority, the individual had infinite potential. Like the devout at Finney's revivals, who sought to perfect themselves and society, listeners who flocked to Emerson's lectures were infused with the spirit of optimistic reform.

Transcendentalist Ideas

As the currents of Romanticism percolated through American society, the country's literature came of age. In 1820 educated Americans still tended to ape the fashions of Europe and read English books. But as the population grew, education increased, and the country's literary market expanded, American writers looked with greater interest at the customs and character of their own society. Emerson's address "The American Scholar" (1837) constituted a declaration of literary independence. "Our long dependence, our long apprenticeship to the learning of other lands draws to a close," he proclaimed. "Events, actions arise, that must be sung, that will sing themselves."

Emergence of American Literature

The Clash between Nature and Civilization

At the time Emerson spoke, James Fenimore Cooper was already making his mark as the first distinctive American novelist. In the Leatherstocking Tales, a series of five novels written between 1823 and 1841, he focused on the clash between nature and civilization. Cooper clearly admired his hero, Natty Bumppo, a self-reliant frontiersman who represented the nobility and innocence of the wilderness. At the same time, the novels portrayed the culture of the frontier as a threat to the civilization Cooper prized so highly.

Cooper and Wilderness

In one scene in *The Pioneers* (1823), as frontier villagers slaughter thousands of pigeons, Leatherstocking laments the wanton destruction, only to hear a townsman express surprise that anyone would "grumble at the loss of a few pigeons. . . . If you had to sow your wheat twice, and three times, as I have done," he continues, "you wouldn't be so massyfully feeling'd toward the devils." As Americans began to exploit the resources of the hinterlands, many of the country's new Romantic writers betrayed a concern that the advance of civilization, with its market economy and crowded urban centers, might destroy the natural simplicity of the land. Natty Bumppo stood halfway between the savage and civilized worlds, not comfortable embracing either.

Henry David Thoreau, too, used nature as a backdrop to explore the conflict between the unfettered individual and the constraints of society. Thoreau grew up in Concord, Massachusetts, where he became part of Emerson's circle. In 1845 he built a cabin on the edge of Walden Pond, living in relative solitude for 16 months to demonstrate the advantages of self-reliance. His experiences became the basis for one of the classics in American literature, *Walden* (1854).

Thoreau and Individualism

Thoreau argued that only in nature could one find true independence. By living simply, it was possible to master oneself and the world. Thoreau's isolation, to be sure, was less than total. When lonely or hungry, he walked to Emerson's home nearby for conversation and a slice of Lidia Emerson's apple pie. Still, *Walden* eloquently denounced Americans' frantic competition for material goods and wealth. "Money is not required to buy one necessity of the soul," Thoreau maintained. Trapped by property, possessions, and the market, "the mass of men lead lives of quiet desperation."

Thoreau's individualism was so extreme that he rejected any institution that contradicted his personal sense of right. "The only obligation which I have a right to assume, is to do at any time what I think right," he wrote in his essay "On Civil Disobedience." Voicing the anti-institutional impulse of Romanticism, he took individualism to its antisocial extreme.

Songs of the Self-Reliant and Darker Loomings

In contrast to Thoreau's exclusiveness, Walt Whitman was all-inclusive, embracing American society in its infinite variety. A journalist and laborer in the New York City area, Whitman was inspired by the common people, whose "manners, speech, dress, friendships . . . are unrhymed poetry." In taking their measure in *Leaves of Grass* (1855), he pioneered a new, modern form of poetry, unconcerned with meter and rhyme and filled with frank imagery and sexual references.

Conceiving himself the representative of all Americans, Whitman exuberantly titled his first major poem "Song of Myself."

> I am your voice—It was tied in you—In me it began to talk.
> I celebrate myself to celebrate every man and woman alive.

Emerson and other critics were put off by his rough-hewn methods, but Whitman, like the Transcendentalists, exalted the emotions, nature, and the individual. At the same time, he endowed these ideas with a more joyous, democratic spirit.

More brooding in spirit were Nathaniel Hawthorne and Herman Melville, two intellectuals who did not share the Transcendentalists' sunny optimism. Hawthorne wrote of the power of the past to shape future generations and the consequences of pride, selfishness, envy, and secret guilt. In *The Scarlet Letter* (1850), set in New England's Puritan era, Hawthorne searingly portrayed the sufferings of a woman who bore an illegitimate child as well as the hypocrisy of the Puritan neighbors who condemned her.

Herman Melville's dark masterpiece, *Moby-Dick* (1851), drew on his youthful experiences aboard a whaling ship. The novel's Captain Ahab relentlessly drives his ship in pursuit of the great white whale Moby-Dick. In Melville's telling, Ahab becomes a powerful symbol of American character: the prototype of the ruthless businessman despoiling nature's resources in his pursuit of success. Ahab is Emerson's self-reliant man, but in him, self-reliance is transformed into a monomania that eventually destroys his ship, its crew, and himself.

But awash in the many opportunities opening before them, most Americans were not attuned to such searching criticism. They preferred to celebrate, with Emerson, the glories of democracy and the individual's quest for perfection.

The Age of Reform

In the glowing fires of a fervent camp meeting, the quest for perfection often proved hard to control. At the Cane Ridge revival of 1801, the Methodist Peter Cartwright had his hands full trying to stop less orthodox preachers from gathering converts. Quite a few worshipers had joined a group known as the Shakers. Cartwright had to ride around the neighborhood "from cabin to cabin" trying to cure people of the Shaker "delusion."

The Shakers were only one group that demonstrated more radical possibilities for democratic change. While the mainline benevolent societies aimed at a more conservative reformation of individual sinners, the more radical offshoots of Romanticism and perfectionism sought to remake society at large.

Utopian Communities

One radical way of reforming the world was by withdrawing from it, to form a utopian community that would demonstrate the possibilities of perfection. Such communities

Walt Whitman, poet of democracy

Melville and Nature's Destructive Power

Herman Melville

Dancing was an integral part of the Shakers' religion, as this picture of a service at Lebanon, New York, indicates. In worshiping, men and women formed separate lines with their hands held out and moved back and forth in rhythm while singing religious songs. One Shaker hymn proclaimed, "With ev'ry gift I will unite, / And join in sweet devotion / To worship God is my delight, / With hands and feet in motion." Note the presence of African Americans in the community.

looked to replace the competitive individualism of American society with a purer spiritual unity and group cooperation. During the early 1840s, for example, Emerson's friend George Ripley organized Brook Farm, a Transcendentalist community near Boston where members could live "a more wholesome and simple life than can be led amidst the pressure of our competitive institutions." Other utopian communities were more directly linked to religious movements and figures, but, religious or secular, such communities shared the optimism of perfection and millennialism.

Brook Farm

The Shakers proved to be one of the most long-lived utopian experiments. Ann Lee, the illiterate daughter of an English blacksmith, believed that God had a dual nature, part male and part female, and that her own life would reveal the feminine side of the divinity, just as Christ had revealed the masculine. In 1774 she led a small band of followers to America.

The Shakers

The Shaker movement's greatest growth, however, came after Lee's death, when her followers recruited converts at revivals like Cane Ridge. The new disciples founded about 20 communal settlements. The followers of "Mother Ann" sometimes shook in the fervent public demonstration of their faith—hence the name Shakers. Convinced that the end of the world was at hand and that there was no need to perpetuate the human race, Shakers practiced celibacy. Men and women normally worked apart, ate at separate tables in silence, entered separate doorways, and had separate living quarters.

Shakers accorded women unusual authority and equality. Community tasks were generally assigned by gender, with women performing household chores and men laboring in the fields. Leadership of the church, however, was split equally between men and women. By the mid–nineteenth century, a majority of members were female.

Property in Shaker settlements was owned communally and controlled by the church hierarchy. The sect's members worked hard, lived simply, and impressed outsiders with their cleanliness and order. Lacking any natural increase, however, membership began to decline after 1850, from a peak of about 6,000 members.

The Oneida Community, founded by John Humphrey Noyes, also set out to alter the relationship between the sexes, though in a markedly different way. Noyes, a convert of Charles Finney, took the doctrine of perfection to extremes. Whereas Finney argued that men and women should strive to achieve perfection, Noyes announced that he had actually reached this blessed state. Settling in Putney, Vermont, and, after 1848, in Oneida, New York, Noyes set out to create a community organized on his religious ideals.

The Oneida Community and Complex Marriage

The Mormon temple at Nauvoo, Illinois was adorned with this sun stone and other celestial carvings drawn from a dream vision by Joseph Smith. The image resembles some of the astronomical symbols popularized by the Masons (see page 295).

In pursuit of greater freedom, Noyes preached the doctrine of "complex marriage," commune members were permitted to have sexual relations with one another, but only with the approval of the community and after a searching examination of the couple's motives. Noyes eventually undertook experiments in planned reproduction by selecting "scientific" combinations of parents to produce morally perfect children.

Under his charismatic leadership the Oneida Community grew to more than 200 members in 1851. But in 1879 an internal dispute drove him from power, and without his guiding hand the community soon fell apart. In 1881 its members reorganized as a business enterprise.

The Mormon Experience

The Church of Jesus Christ of Latter-day Saints, whose members are generally known as Mormons, was founded by a young man named Joseph Smith in Palmyra, in western New York, where the religious fires of revivalism flared up regularly. The son of a poor farmer, Smith was robust, charming, almost hypnotic in his appeal. In 1827, at the age of only 22, he announced that he had discovered and translated a set of golden tablets on which was written the *Book of Mormon*. The tablets told the story of a band of Hebrews who in biblical times journeyed to America, splitting into two groups, the Nephites and Lamanites. The Nephites established a Christian civilization, only to be exterminated by the Lamanites, whose descendants were said to be the Indians of the Americas. Seeking to reestablish the true church, Smith gathered a group of devoted followers.

Like Charles Finney's more liberal theology, Mormonism proclaimed that salvation was available to all. Moreover, Mormon culture upheld the middle-class values of hard work, thrift, and self-control. It partook of the optimistic, materialist attitudes of American society. And by teaching that Christ would return to rule the earth, it shared in the hope of a coming millennial kingdom.

Movement to Restore the Ancient Church

Mormonism was less an outgrowth of evangelicalism, however, than of the primitive gospel movement, which sought to reestablish the ancient church. In restoring what Smith called "the ancient order of things," he created a **theocracy** uniting church and state, reestablished biblical priesthoods and titles, and adopted temple rituals.

Smith's unorthodox teachings provoked bitter persecution wherever he and his followers went, first to Ohio and then to Missouri. Mob violence finally hounded him out of Missouri in 1839. Smith then established a new holy city, which he named Nauvoo, located on the Mississippi River in Illinois.

City of Zion: Nauvoo

Reinforced by a steady stream of converts from Britain, Nauvoo became the largest city in Illinois, with a population of 10,000 by the mid-1840s. There, Smith introduced the most distinctive features of Mormon theology, including baptism for the dead, eternal marriage, and polygamy, or plural marriage. As a result, Mormonism increasingly diverged from traditional Christianity and became a distinct new religion. To bolster his authority as a prophet, Smith established a theocratic political order under which church leaders controlled political offices and governed the community, with Smith as mayor.

Neighboring residents, alarmed by the Mormons' growing political power and reports that church leaders were practicing polygamy, demanded that Nauvoo's charter be revoked and the church suppressed. In 1844, while in jail for destroying the printing press of dissident Mormons in Nauvoo, Smith was murdered by an anti-Mormon mob. In 1846 the Mormons abandoned Nauvoo, and the following year Brigham Young, Smith's successor, led them westward to Utah.

Socialist Communities

The hardship and poverty that accompanied the growth of industrial factories also inspired utopian communities based on science and reason rather than religion. Robert

Owen, a Scottish industrialist, came to the United States in 1824 committed to creating a society that balanced agriculture and manufacturing. Owen believed that the character of individuals was shaped by their surroundings and that by changing those surroundings, one could change human character.

Unfortunately, most of the 900 or so volunteers who flocked to Owen's community in New Harmony, Indiana, lacked the skills and commitment needed to make it a success. Bitter factions soon split the settlement. Having lost most of his own fortune, Owen dissolved the community in 1827. More than 20 other American communities were founded on Owen's theories, but none was particularly successful.

The experiences of New Harmony and similar communities demonstrated that the United States was poor soil for socialistic experiments. Wages were too high and land too cheap for such experiments to interest most Americans. And individualism was too strong to create a commitment to cooperative action.

Robert Owen and New Harmony

The Temperance Movement

The most significant reform movements of the period sought not to withdraw from society but to change it directly. One of the most determined of these was the temperance movement.

The origins of the campaign against alcohol lay in the era's heavy drinking. Alcohol consumption soared after the Revolution, so that by 1830 the average American consumed four gallons of absolute alcohol a year, the highest level in American history and nearly triple present-day levels. Anne Royale, whose travels took her cross-country by stage, reported, "When I was in Virginia, it was too much whiskey—in Ohio, too much whiskey—in Tennessee, it is too, too much whiskey!" The social costs for such habits were high: broken families, abused and neglected wives and children, sickness and disability, poverty, and crime. The temperance movement undertook to eliminate these problems by curbing drinking.

Attack on Drinking

Led largely by clergy, the movement at first focused on drunkenness and did not oppose moderate drinking. But in 1826 the American Temperance Society was founded, taking voluntary abstinence as its goal. During the next decade approximately 5,000 local temperance societies were founded. As the movement gained momentum, annual per capita consumption of alcohol dropped sharply. By 1845 it had fallen below two gallons a year.

Annual Consumption of Distilled Spirits, per Capita, 1710–1920 *Beginning in 1790, per capita levels of drinking steadily rose, until 1830, when the temperance movement produced a sharp decline over the next two decades.*

The temperance movement lasted longer and attracted many more supporters than other reforms did. It appealed to young and old, to urban and rural residents, to workers and businesspeople. Moreover, it was one of the few reform movements with significant support in the South. Its success came partly for social reasons. Democracy necessitated sober voters; factories required sober workers. In addition, temperance attracted the upwardly mobile—professionals, small businesspeople, and skilled artisans anxious to improve their social standing. Finally, temperance advocates stressed the suffering that men inflicted on women and children, and thus the movement appealed to women as a means to defend the home and carry out their domestic mission.

Educational Reform

In 1800 Massachusetts was the only state that required free public schools supported by community funds. The call for tax-supported education arose first among workers, as a way to restore their deteriorating position in society. But middle-class reformers quickly took control of the movement, looking to uplift the masses, make them responsible citizens, and preserve equal opportunity. Horace Mann, the leading advocate of

Common School Movement

common schools, hailed education as "the great equalizer of the conditions of men" and contended that it would eliminate poverty.

Mann convinced Massachusetts to create a state board of education, which he oversaw from 1837 to 1848. He prodded the state to adopt a minimum-length school year, provide for training of teachers, and include subjects such as history, geography, and various applied skills in the curriculum. Massachusetts also took the lead in requiring every town with a population of 500 or more to establish a high school. This innovation was slow to catch on elsewhere; by 1860 the nation could count only about 300 high schools, fully a third of them in Massachusetts. Moreover, many poor parents out of necessity sent their children to work instead of to school. Still, by the 1850s the number of schools, attendance figures, and school budgets had all increased sharply. School reformers enjoyed their greatest success in the Northeast and the least in the South, where planters opposed paying taxes to educate poorer white children.

Female Education

Educational opportunities for women also expanded. Teachers such as Catharine Beecher and Emma Hunt Willard established private girls' schools, putting to rest the objection of male educators that fragile female minds could not absorb large doses of mathematics, physics, or geography. In 1833 Oberlin became the nation's first coeducational college. Four years later Mary Lyon founded Mount Holyoke, the first American college for women.

The Asylum Movement

After 1820 there was also a dramatic increase in the number of asylums of every sort—orphanages, jails, and hospitals. Advocates of asylums called for isolating and separating the criminal, the insane, the ill, and the dependent from outside society. The goal of care in asylums, which had earlier focused on confinement, shifted to the reform of personal character.

American efforts to rehabilitate prisoners attracted international attention. Pennsylvania and New York developed systems to isolate prisoners, introducing the measures of solitary confinement and absolute silence to give inmates time to reflect on their past errors. The reformers assumed that environment produced criminal behavior and that the new prison routines would rehabilitate criminals. The new measures were not very effective, however, and under the strain of isolation some inmates went insane or committed suicide.

Prison reformers believed that rigid discipline, extensive rules, and (in some programs) solitary confinement were necessary to rehabilitate criminals. Prisoners often had to march lockstep under strict supervision and wear uniforms such as those seen in this photograph from the 1870s.

Dorothea Dix, a Boston schoolteacher, took the lead in advocating state-supported asylums for the mentally ill. Her widely read report detailed the horrors to which the mentally ill were subjected, including being chained, kept in cages and closets, and beaten with rods. In response to her efforts, 28 states maintained mental institutions by 1860.

Dorothea Dix and the Insane

Like other reform movements, the push for new asylums and better educational facilities reflected overtones of both liberation and control. Asylums freed prisoners and the mentally ill from the harsh punishments and abuses of the past, but the new techniques of "rehabilitation" forced prisoners to march in lockstep. Education brought with it the freedom to question, but some reformers hoped that schools would become as orderly as prisons. Louis Dwight, who advocated solitary confinement for prisoners at night and total silence by day, suggested eagerly that such methods "would greatly promote order, seriousness, and purity in large families, male and female boarding schools, and colleges."

Abolitionism

Late in the fall of 1834, Lyman Beecher was in the midst of his continuing efforts to "overturn and overturn" on behalf of the kingdom of God. As planned, he had gone to Cincinnati to assume leadership of Lane Seminary. The school had everything that an institution for training ministers to convert the West needed—everything, that is, except students. In October 1834 all but 8 of Lane's 100 scholars had departed after months of bitter fighting with Beecher and the trustees over the issue of abolition.

Beecher knew the source of his troubles: a scruffy, magnetic student named Theodore Dwight Weld. Weld had been firing up his classmates over the need to end slavery immediately. Beecher was not surprised, for Weld had been converted by that firebrand Finney. He knew, too, that Weld had been influenced by the arguments of William Lloyd Garrison, whose abolitionist writings had sent shock waves across the entire nation. Indeed, Beecher's troubles at Lane Seminary provided only one example of how the flames of reform could spread along paths not anticipated by those who had kindled them.

The Beginnings of the Abolitionist Movement

William Lloyd Garrison symbolized the transition from a moderate antislavery movement to the more militant abolitionism of the 1830s. A sober, religious youngster deeply influenced by his Baptist mother, Garrison in the 1820s edited a newspaper

William Lloyd Garrison (shown, left, at age 30) and Theodore Dwight Weld (right) represented different wings of the abolitionist movement. Garrison's growing radicalism led him to repudiate organized religion in the struggle against slavery. Weld, however, preferred to work through the evangelical churches and cooperate with the clergy.

sympathetic to many of the new reforms. In 1829 he was enlisted in the antislavery cause by Benjamin Lundy, a Quaker who edited a Baltimore antislavery newspaper, *The Genius of Universal Emancipation*. Calling for a gradual end to slavery, Lundy supported colonization, a strategy for overcoming southern fears of emancipation by transporting free black Americans to Africa.

Free Blacks Oppose Colonization

Garrison went to Baltimore to help edit Lundy's paper, and for the first time he encountered the opinions of free African Americans. To his surprise, Garrison discovered that most of them strongly opposed the colonization movement as proslavery and antiblack. "This is our home, and this is our country," a free black convention proclaimed in 1831. "Beneath its sod lie the bones of our fathers; for it some of them fought, bled, and died. Here we were born, and here we will die." Under their influence, Garrison soon developed views far more radical than Lundy's. Within a year of moving to Baltimore, the young firebrand was convicted of libel and imprisoned. On his release Garrison hurried back to Boston, determined to publish a new kind of antislavery journal.

On January 1, 1831, the first issue of *The Liberator* appeared, and abolitionism was born. In appearance, the bespectacled Garrison seemed frail, almost mousy. In print, however, he was abrasive, withering, and uncompromising. "On this subject, I do not wish to think, or speak, or write with moderation," he proclaimed. "I am in earnest—I will not equivocate—I will not excuse—I will not retreat a single inch—

Garrison's Immediatism

AND I WILL BE HEARD." Repudiating gradual emancipation and embracing "immediatism," Garrison insisted that slavery end at once. He denounced colonization as a racist, antiblack movement and upheld the principle of racial equality. To those who suggested that slaveowners should be compensated for freeing their slaves, Garrison was firm. Southerners ought to be convinced by "moral suasion" to renounce slavery as a sin. Virtue was its own reward.

HORRORS OF SLAVERY,
as exemplified by seven figures, being actual likenesses of a slave-owner, a slave-driver, and their victims.

In 1850 the Boston Museum's "New Hall of Wax Statuary" featured seven figures portraying the "Horrors of Slavery," indicating a heightened awareness of the institution's evils on the part of the Northern public.

Garrison attracted the most attention, but other abolitionists spoke with equal conviction. Wendell Phillips, from a socially prominent Boston family, held listeners spellbound with his speeches. Lewis Tappan and his brother Arthur, two New York City silk merchants, boldly placed their wealth behind a number of humanitarian causes, including abolitionism. James G. Birney, an Alabama slaveholder, converted to abolitionism after wrestling with his conscience, and Angelina and Sarah Grimké, the daughters of a South Carolina planter, left their native state to speak against the institution. And there was Angelina's future husband, Theodore Weld, the restless student at Lane Seminary who had fallen so dramatically under Garrison's influence.

To abolitionists, slavery was a moral, not an economic, question. The institution seemed a contradiction of the principle of the American Revolution that all human beings had been created with natural rights. Then, too, it went against the Romantic spirit of the age, which celebrated the individual's freedom and self-reliance. Abolitionists condemned slavery because of the breakup of marriages and families by sale, the harsh punishment of the lash, slaves' lack of access to education, and the sexual abuse of black women. Most of all, they denounced slavery as outrageously contrary to Christian teaching. As one Ohio antislavery paper declared, "We believe slavery to be a sin, always, everywhere, and only, sin—sin, in itself." So persistent were abolitionists in their religious objections that they forced the churches to face the question of slavery head-on. In the 1840s the Methodist and Baptist churches each split into northern and southern organizations over the issue.

The Spread of Abolitionism

After helping organize the New England Anti-Slavery Society in 1832, Garrison joined with Lewis Tappan and Theodore Weld the following year to establish a national organization, the American Anti-Slavery Society. It coordinated a loosely affiliated network of state and local societies. During the years before the Civil War, perhaps 200,000 northerners belonged to an abolitionist society.

Abolitionists were concentrated in the East, especially New England, and in areas that had been settled by New Englanders, such as western New York and northern Ohio. The movement was not strong in cities or among businesspeople and workers. Most abolitionists were young, being generally in their 20s and 30s when the movement began, and had grown up in rural areas and small towns in middle-class families. Intensely religious, many had been profoundly affected by the revivals of the Second Great Awakening. More and more they came to feel that slavery was the fundamental cause of the Republic's degraded condition.

Geography of Abolitionism

Certainly Theodore Weld was cut from this mold. After enrolling in Lane Seminary in 1833, he promoted immediate abolitionism among his fellow students. When Lyman Beecher assumed the Lane presidency a year later, he confronted a student body dominated by committed abolitionists, impatient of any position that stopped short of Garrison's immediatism.

The radicalism of Lane students was also made clear in their commitment to racial equality. Unlike some abolitionists, who opposed slavery but disdained blacks as inferior, Lane students mingled freely with Cincinnati's free black community. Alarmed by rumors in the summer of 1834 that the town's residents intended to demolish the school, Beecher and Lane's trustees forbade any discussion of slavery on campus, restricted contact with the black community, and ordered students to return to their studies. "Who that has an opinion and a soul will enter L. Sem now?" one rebel asked. "Who can do it without degrading himself?" All except a few left the school and enrolled at Oberlin College. That debt-ridden institution agreed to their demands for guaranteeing freedom of speech, admitting black students, and hiring Charles Finney as professor of theology.

Lane Seminary Rebellion

But Finney fared no better than Beecher with the Lane rebels. In the end, he too concluded that reform generated discord, distracting Christians from the greater good of promoting revivals. Both men conceived of sin in terms of individual immorality, not unjust social institutions. To the abolitionists, however, America could never become a godly nation until slavery was abolished. "Revivals, moral Reform, etc. will remain stationary until the temple is cleansed," Weld bluntly concluded.

Free African Americans, who made up the majority of subscribers to Garrison's *Liberator*, provided important support and leadership for the movement. Freder-

Black Abolitionists

Black abolitionist Frederick Douglass (second from left at the podium) was only one of nearly 50 runaway slaves who appeared at an abolitionist convention held in August 1850 in Cazenovia, New York. Other runaways included Emily and Mary Edmonson (both in plaid dresses). When the Edmonsons' attempt at escape failed, Henry Ward Beecher (Lyman Beecher's son) rallied his congregation in Brooklyn to raise the money to purchase the girls' freedom.

ick Douglass assumed the greatest prominence. Having escaped from slavery in Maryland, he became an eloquent critic of its evils. Initially a follower of Garrison, Douglass eventually broke with him and started his own newspaper in Rochester. Other important black abolitionists included Martin Delany, William Wells Brown, William Still, and Sojourner Truth. Aided by many other African Americans, these men and women battled against racial discrimination in the North as well as slavery in the South.

Underground Railroad

A network of antislavery sympathizers also developed in the North to convey runaway slaves to Canada and freedom. While not as extensive or as tightly organized as contemporaries claimed, the Underground Railroad hid fugitives and transported them northward from one station to the next. Free African Americans, who were more readily trusted by wary slaves, played a leading role in the Underground Railroad. One of its most famous conductors was Harriet Tubman, an escaped slave who repeatedly returned to the South and eventually escorted to freedom more than 200 slaves.

Opponents and Divisions

The drive for immediate abolition faced massive obstacles within American society. With slavery increasingly important to the South's economy, Southerners forced opponents of slavery to flee the region. In the North, where racism was equally entrenched, abolitionism provoked bitter resistance. Even abolitionists such as Garrison treated blacks paternalistically, contending that they should occupy a subordinate place in the antislavery movement.

On occasion, northern resistance turned violent. A hostile Boston mob seized Garrison in 1835 and paraded him with a rope around his body before he was finally rescued. Another anti-abolitionist mob burned down the headquarters of the American Anti-Slavery Society in Philadelphia. And in 1837 in Alton, Illinois, Elijah Lovejoy was murdered when he tried to protect his printing press from an angry crowd. The leaders of these mobs were not from the bottom of society but, as one of their victims noted, were "gentlemen of property and standing." Prominent leaders in the community, they reacted vigorously to the threat that abolitionists posed to their power and prosperity and to the established order.

Divisions among Abolitionists

But abolitionists were also hindered by divisions among reformers. At Oberlin College Charles Finney preferred revivalism over Theodore Weld's abolitionism. Within another decade, Lyman Beecher would see his daughter Harriet Beecher Stowe write the most successful piece of antislavery literature in the nation's history, *Uncle Tom's Cabin*. Even the abolitionists themselves splintered, shaken by the opposition they encountered and unable to agree on the most effective response. More conservative reformers wanted to work within established institutions, using the churches and political action to end slavery. But for Garrison and his followers, the mob violence demonstrated that slavery was only part of a deeper national disease, whose cure required the overthrow of American institutions and values.

By the end of the decade, Garrison had worked out a program for the total reform of society. He embraced perfectionism and pacifism, denounced the clergy, urged members to leave the churches, and called for an end to all government. Condemning the Constitution as proslavery—"a covenant with death and an agreement with hell"—he publicly burned a copy one July 4th. No person of conscience, he argued, could vote or otherwise participate in the corrupt political system. This platform was radical enough on all counts, but the final straw for Garrison's opponents was his endorsement of women's rights as an inseparable part of abolitionism.

The Women's Rights Movement

Women faced many disadvantages in American society. They were kept out of most jobs, denied political rights, and given only limited access to education beyond the elementary grades. When a woman married, her husband became the legal representative of the marriage and gained complete control of her property. If a marriage ended in divorce, the husband was awarded custody of the children. Any unmarried woman was made the ward of a male relative.

When abolitionists divided over the issue of female participation, women found it easy to identify with the situation of slaves, since both were victims of male tyranny. Sarah and Angelina Grimké took up the cause of women's rights after they were criticized for speaking to audiences that included men as well as women. Sarah responded with *Letters on the Condition of Women and the Equality of the Sexes* (1838), arguing that women deserved the same rights as men. Abby Kelly, another abolitionist, remarked that women "have good cause to be grateful to the slave," for in "striving to strike his irons off, we found most surely, that we were manacled *ourselves.*"

Two abolitionists, Elizabeth Cady Stanton and Lucretia Mott, launched the women's rights movement after they were forced to sit behind a curtain at a world antislavery convention in London. In 1848 Stanton and Mott organized a conference in Seneca Falls, New York, that attracted about a hundred supporters. The meeting issued a Declaration of Sentiments, modeled after the Declaration of Independence, that began, "All men and women are created equal."

Seneca Falls Convention

The Seneca Falls convention called for educational and professional opportunities for women, laws giving them control of their property, recognition of legal equality, and repeal of laws awarding the father custody of the children in divorce. The most controversial proposal, and the only resolution that did not pass unanimously, was one demanding the right to vote. The Seneca Falls convention established the arguments and the program for the women's rights movement for the remainder of the century.

In response, several states gave women greater control over their property, and a few made divorce easier or granted women the right to sue in courts. But disappointments and defeats outweighed these early victories. Still, many of the important leaders in the crusade for women's rights that emerged after the Civil War had already taken their places at the forefront of the movement. They included Stanton, Susan B. Anthony, Lucy Stone, and—as Lyman Beecher by now must have expected, one of his daughters—Isabella Beecher Hooker.

The Schism of 1840

It was Garrison's position on women's rights that finally split antislavery ranks already divided over other aspects of his growing radicalism. The showdown came in 1840 at the national meeting of the American Anti-Slavery Society, when delegates debated whether women could hold office in the organization. Some of Garrison's opponents favored women's rights but opposed linking the question to the slavery issue, insisting that it would drive off potential supporters. By packing the convention, Garrison carried the day. His opponents, led by Lewis Tappan, resigned to found the rival American and Foreign Anti-Slavery Society.

The schism of 1840 lessened the influence of abolitionism as a reform movement. Although abolitionism heightened moral concern about slavery, it failed to convert the North to its program, and its supporters remained a tiny minority. Despite the considerable courage of its leaders, the movement lacked a realistic, long-range plan for eliminating such a deeply entrenched institution. Abolitionism demonstrated the severe limits of voluntary persuasion and individual conversions as a solution to deeply rooted social problems.

Elizabeth Cady Stanton, one of the instigators and guiding spirits at the Seneca Falls convention, photographed with two of her children about that time.

Reform Shakes the Party System

"What a fog-bank we are in politically. Do you see any head-land or light—or can you get an observation—or soundings?" The words came from a puzzled Whig politician writing a friend after the Massachusetts state elections of 1853. He was in such a confused state because reformers were increasingly entering the political arena to achieve results.

Reform Enters Politics

The crusading idealism of revivalists and reformers inevitably collided with the hard reality that society could not be perfected by converting individuals. Several movements, including those to establish public schools and erect asylums, had operated within the political system from the beginning. But a growing number of other frustrated reformers abandoned the principle of voluntary persuasion and looked to governmental coercion to achieve their goals.

Politicians did not particularly welcome the new interest. Because the Whig and Democratic parties both drew on evangelical and nonevangelical voters, heated moral debates over the harmful effects of drink or the evils of slavery threatened to detach regular party members from their old loyalties and disrupt each party's unity. The strong opposition of German and Irish immigrants to temperance stimulated antiforeign sentiment among reformers and further divided both party coalitions, particularly the Democrats. "The temperance question is playing havock in the old party lines," commented one Indiana politician. The issue of abolition seemed even more disruptive.

Women and the Right to Vote

As the reform impulse shifted toward the political arena, women lost influence. As major participants in the benevolent organizations of the 1820s and 1830s, they had used their efforts on behalf of "moral suasion." But because women could not vote, they felt excluded when the temperance and abolitionist movements turned to electoral action to accomplish their goals. By the 1840s female reformers increasingly demanded the right to vote as the means to change society. Nor were men blind to what was at stake: one reason they so strongly resisted female suffrage was because it would give women real power.

Previously, many female reformers had accepted the right of petition as their most appropriate political activity. But *The Lily,* a women's rights paper, soon changed its tack. "Why shall [women] be left only the poor resource of petition?" it asked. "For even petitions, when they are from women, without the elective franchise to give them backbone, are of but little consequence."

The Maine Law

Struggle over Prohibition

The political parties could resist the women's suffrage movement because most of its advocates lacked the right to vote. Less easily put off were temperance reformers. Although drinking had significantly declined in American society by 1840, it had hardly been eliminated. After 1845 the arrival of large numbers of German and Irish immigrants, who were accustomed to consuming alcohol, made voluntary prohibition even more remote. In response, temperance advocates proposed state laws that would outlaw the manufacture and sale of alcoholic beverages.

Party leaders tried to dodge the question of prohibition, since large numbers of Whigs and Democrats were found on both sides of the issue. Temperance advocates countered by seeking pledges from candidates to support a prohibitory law. To win additional recruits, temperance leaders adopted techniques used in political campaigns, including house-to-house canvasses, parades and processions, bands and singing, banners, picnics, and mass rallies.

The movement's first major triumph came in 1851. The Maine Law, as it was known, authorized search and seizure of private property in that state and provided stiff penalties for selling liquor. In the next few years a number of states enacted similar laws, although most were struck down by the courts or later repealed. Prohibition remained a controversial political issue throughout the century.

Although prohibition was temporarily defeated, the issue badly disrupted the Whig and Democratic parties. It greatly increased party switching and brought to the polls a large number of new voters, including many "wets" who wanted to preserve their right to drink. By dissolving the ties between so many voters and their parties, the temperance issue played a major role in the eventual collapse of the Jacksonian party system in the 1850s.

Abolitionism and the Party System

Abolition was the most divisive issue to come out of the benevolent reform movement. In 1835 abolitionists distributed more than a million pamphlets, mostly in the South, through the post office. A wave of excitement swept the South when the first batches arrived addressed to white southerners. Former senator Robert Hayne led a Charleston mob that burned sacks of U.S. mail containing abolitionist literature, and postmasters in other southern cities refused to deliver the material. The Jackson administration allowed southern states to censor the mail, leading abolitionists to protest that their civil rights had been violated. In reaction, the number of antislavery societies in the North nearly tripled.

Censorship of the Mails

With access to the mails impaired, abolitionists began flooding Congress with petitions against slavery. Asserting that Congress had no power over the institution, angry southern representatives demanded action, and the House in response adopted the so-called gag rule in 1836. It automatically tabled without consideration any petition dealing with slavery. But southern leaders had made a tactical blunder. The gag rule allowed abolitionists not only to attack slavery but also to speak out as defenders of white civil liberties. The appeal of the antislavery movement was broadened, and in 1844 the House finally repealed the controversial rule.

Gag Rule

Many abolitionists outside Garrison's extreme circle began to feel that an antislavery third party offered a more effective means of attacking slavery. In 1840 these political abolitionists founded the Liberty party and nominated for president James Birney, a former slaveholder who had converted to abolitionism. Birney received only 7,000 votes, but the Liberty party was the seed from which a stronger antislavery political movement would grow. From 1840 onward, abolitionism's importance would be in the political arena rather than as a voluntary reform organization.

The ferment of reform during the decades from 1820 to 1850 reflected a multitude of attempts to deal with transformations working through not just the United States but also Europe. Americans crowded the docks of New York City eagerly awaiting the latest installment of Charles Dickens's novels from England, tales often set amid urban slums and dingy factories. European middle classes embraced the home as a domestic refuge, as did their counterparts in America. The "benevolent empire" of American reform organizations drew inspiration from similar British campaigns. Robert Owen launched his utopian reforms in New Lanark, Scotland, before his ideas were tried out at New Harmony, Indiana, and disciples of the French socialist Charles Fourier founded communities in the United States.

Abolition was potentially the most dangerous of these trans-Atlantic reforms because slavery was so deeply and profitably intertwined with the industrial system. Slave labor produced cotton for the textile factories of New England, Great Britain, and Europe; plantation economies supplied the sugar, rice, tea, and coffee that were a part of European and

American diets. Revolutionary France had abolished slavery in 1794, but Napoleon reinstated it, along with the slave trade. Great Britain outlawed the trade in 1808 (as did the United States) and then freed nearly 800,000 slaves in its colonies in 1834.

Any move for emancipation in the United States seemed out of the question and as late as 1840 abolition lacked the power to threaten the political system. Birney's small vote, coupled with the disputes between the two national antislavery societies, encouraged political leaders to believe that the party system had turned back this latest threat of sectionalism. But the growing northern concern about slavery highlighted differences between the two sections. Despite the strength of evangelicalism in the South, the reform impulse spawned by the revivals found little support there, since reform movements were discredited by their association with abolitionism. The party system confronted the difficult challenge of holding together sections that, although sharing much, were also diverging in important ways. To the residents of both sections, the South increasingly appeared to be a unique society with its own distinctive way of life.

Significant Events

1787	First Shaker commune established
1821	New York constructs first penitentiary
1824–1837	Peak of revivals
1824	New Harmony established
1826	James Fenimore Cooper's *The Last of the Mohicans* published; American Temperance Society founded
1829	David Walker's *Appeal to the Colored Citizens of the World* published
1830–1831	Charles Finney's revival at Rochester
1830	*Book of Mormon* published
1831	*The Liberator* established
1833	American Anti-Slavery Society founded; Oberlin College admits women
1834	Lane Seminary rebellion
1835	Abolitionists' postal campaign
1836	Transcendental Club organized; gag rule passed
1837	Massachusetts establishes state board of education; Ralph Waldo Emerson delivers "The American Scholar" address; Mount Holyoke Seminary commences classes; Elijah Lovejoy killed
1839	Nauvoo founded
1840	Schism of American Anti-Slavery Society; Liberty party organized
1841	Brook Farm founded
1843	Dorothea Dix's report on treatment of the insane
1844	Joseph Smith murdered; Congressional gag rule repealed
1848	Oneida Community established; Seneca Falls convention
1850	Nathaniel Hawthorne's *The Scarlet Letter* published
1851	Maine adopts prohibition law; Herman Melville's *Moby-Dick* published
1854	Henry David Thoreau's *Walden* published
1855	Walt Whitman's *Leaves of Grass* published

Chapter Summary

The Jacksonian era produced the greatest number of significant reform movements in American history.

- The movements grew out of the revivals of the Second Great Awakening, which emphasized emotion and preached the doctrines of good works and salvation available to all.
  - Evangelical Protestantism also endorsed the ideals of perfectionism and millennialism.
  - The revival theologies helped people adjust to the pressures in their daily lives created by the new market economy.
- Romanticism, which emphasized the unlimited potential of each individual, also strengthened reform.
- Women's role in society was now defined by the ideal of domesticity—that women's lives should center on the home and the family.

- Middle-class women turned to religion and reform as ways to shape society.
- Utopian communities sought to establish a model society for the rest of the world to follow.
- Humanitarian movements combated a variety of social evils.
  - Crusades for temperance, educational reform, and the establishment of asylums all gained significant support.
  - Abolitionism precipitated both strong support and violent opposition, and the movement split in 1840.
- Temperance, abolitionism, and women's rights movements each turned to political action to accomplish their goals.
- Although it survived, the party system was seriously weakened by these reform movements.

Additional Reading

Good introductions to antebellum evangelical religion and reform include Robert Abzug, *Cosmos Crumbling* (1994); Charles Hambrick-Stowe, *Charles G. Finney and the Spirit of American Evangelicalism* (1996); and Bertram Wyatt-Brown, *Lewis Tappan and the Evangelical War Against Slavery* (1971). For suggestive analyses of the relationship between antebellum evangelicalism and the sweeping changes in economic and political life, consult Richard Carwardine, *Evangelicals and Politics in Antebellum America* (1997); Candy Gunther Brown, *The Word in the World* (2004); and Paul Johnson and Sean Wilentz, *The Kingdom of Matthias* (1994). The best studies of the role of women in evangelical churches and reform societies are Anne Boylan, *The Origins of Women's Activism* (1988); Lori Ginzberg, *Women and the Work of Benevolence* (1990); and Nancy Hewitt, *Women's Activism and Social Change* (1984). To understand the link between reformist activism and the early women's rights movement, begin with Lori Ginzberg, *Untidy*

Origins (2005), and Nancy Isenberg, *Sex and Citizenship in the United States* (1998).

Despite the dominant influence of evangelical Protestants, both Roman Catholics and Mormons attracted a growing number of adherents during the antebellum period. For a fascinating account of the origins and rise of Mormonism, see John Brooke, *The Refiner's Fire* (1996), and for a compelling account of how American Protestants responded to the impressive growth of Roman Catholicism after the 1830s, see Ryan Smith, *Gothic Arches, Latin Crosses* (2006). To explore the reasons why a small but influential minority of nineteenth-century Americans rejected all forms of Christianity in favor of agnosticism or atheism, rely on James Turner, *Without God, Without Creed* (1985).

For a fuller list of readings, see the Bibliography at www.mhhe.com/davidsonnation6.

Where Is the Real South?

The impeccably dressed Colonel Daniel Jordan, master of 261 slaves at Laurel Hill, strolls down his oak-lined lawn to the dock along the Waccamaw River, a day's journey north of Charleston, South Carolina, to board the steamship *Nina*. On Fridays, it is Colonel Jordan's custom to visit the exclusive Hot and Hot Fish Club, founded by his fellow low-country planters, to play a game of lawn bowling or billiards and be waited on by black servants in livery as he sips a mint julep in the refined atmosphere that for him is the South.

Several hundred miles to the west another steamboat, the *Fashion,* makes its way along the Alabama River near the village of Claiborne. One of the passengers is upset by the boat's slow pace. He has been away from his plantation in the Red River country of Texas and is eager to get back. "Time's money, time's money!" he mutters to anyone who will listen. "Time's worth more'n money to me now; a hundred percent more, 'cause I left my niggers all alone; not a damn white man within four mile on 'em." When asked what they are doing, since the cotton crop has already been picked, he says, "I set 'em to clairin', but they ain't doin' a damn thing. . . . I know that as well as you do. . . . But I'll make it up, I'll make it up when I get thar, now you'd better believe." For this Red River planter, time is money and cotton is his world—indeed, cotton is what the South is all about. "I am a cotton man, I am, and I don't care who knows it," he proclaims. "I know cotton, I do. I'm dam' if I know anythin' but cotton."

At the other end of the South, the slave Sam Williams works in the intense heat of Buffalo Forge, an iron-making factory nine miles from Lexington, Virginia, in the Shenandoah Valley. As a refiner, Williams has the most important job at the forge, alternately heating pig iron in the white-hot coals, then slinging the ball of glowing metal on an anvil, where he pounds it with huge, water-powered hammers to remove the impurities. Ambitious and hard working, he earns extra money (at the same rate paid to whites) for any iron he produces beyond his weekly quota. In some years his extra income is more than $100. His wife, Nancy, who is in charge of the dairy, earns extra money as well, and the additional income allows them to buy extra food and items for themselves and their four daughters. More important, it helps keep their family intact in an unstable environment. They know that their owner is very unlikely to sell away slaves who work so hard. For Sam and

This woman sold chicken legs and rolls at the railroad station in Richmond, Virginia. She was sketched in 1860 by Sir Henry Wentworth Acland, a British Traveler.

347

This Louisiana plantation contained the sort of deep woods and bayous to which the slave Octave Johnson fled to escape the harsh life of slavery. In this painting the woods also provide a space apart, where the black community is attending a slave burial.

Nancy Williams, family ties, worship at the local Baptist church, and socializing with their fellow slaves are what make life important.

In the bayous of the Deep South, only a few miles from where the Mississippi delta meets the Gulf, Octave Johnson hears the dogs coming. For over a year Johnson has been a runaway slave. He fled from a Louisiana plantation in St. James Parish when the work bell rang before daybreak and the overseer threatened to whip him for staying in bed. To survive, he hides in the swamps four miles behind the plantation—stealing turkeys, chickens, and pigs and trading with other slaves. As uncertain as this life is, nearly 30 other slaves have joined him over the past year.

The sound of the dogs warns Johnson and his companions that the hound master Eugene Jardeau is out again. This time when the pack bursts upon them, the slaves do not flee but kill as many dogs as possible. Then they plunge into the bayou, and as the hounds follow, alligators make short work of another six. For Octave Johnson the real South is a matter of weighing one's prospects between the uncertainties of alligators and the overseer's whip—and deciding when to say no.

Ferdinand Steel and his family are not forced, by the flick of the lash, to rise at five in the morning. They rise because the land demands it. Steel, in his 20s, owns 170 acres of land in Carroll County, Mississippi. Unmarried, he moved there from Tennessee with his widowed mother, sister, and brother in 1836, only a few years after the Choctaws had been forced to give up the region and march west. His life is one of continuous hard work, caring for the animals and tending the crops. His mother, Eliza, and sister, Julia, have plenty to keep them busy: making soap, fashioning dippers out of gourds, or sewing.

The Steel family grows cotton, too, but not with the single-minded devotion of the planter aboard the *Fashion.* Self-sufficiency and family security always come first, and Steel's total crop amounts to only five or six bales. His profit is never sufficient to consider buying even one slave. In fact, he would have preferred not to raise any cotton—"We are to[o] weak handed," he says—but the five bales mean cash, and cash means that when he goes to market in nearby Grenada, he can buy sugar and coffee, gunpowder and lead, a yard or two of calico, and quinine to treat the malaria that is so common in those parts. Though fiercely independent, Steel and his scattered neighbors help each other raise houses, clear fields, shuck corn, or quilt. They depend on one another and are bound together by blood, religion, obligation, and honor. For small farmers like Ferdinand Steel, these ties constitute the real South.

The portraits could go on and on. Different people, different Souths, all of them real. Such contrasts underscore the difficulty of trying to define a regional identity. Encompassing in 1860 the 15 slave states plus the District of Columbia, the South was a land of great geographic diversity. It extended from the Tidewater coastal plain along the Atlantic seaboard to the prairies of Texas, from the Kentucky bluegrass region to the Gulf coast, from the mountains of western Virginia to the swamps of the Mississippi delta with its semitropical climate. The only geographic feature that separated the North and South was the Ohio River, and it was an avenue of trade rather than a source of division.

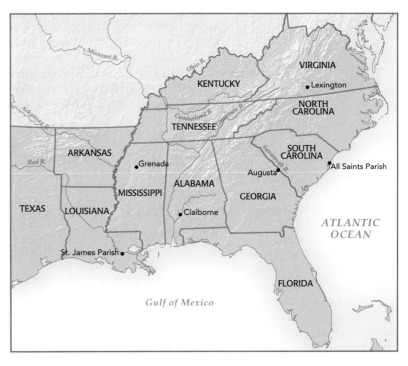

Yet despite its many differences of people and geography, the South was bonded by ties so strong, they eventually outpulled those of the nation itself. At the heart of this unity was an agricultural system that took advantage of the region's warm climate and long growing season. Cotton required 200 frost-free days, and rice and sugar even more, which meant that in the United States these staples could be grown only in the South. Most important, this rural agricultural economy was based on the institution of slavery, which had far-reaching effects on all aspects of southern society. It shaped not only the culture of the slaves but also the lives of their masters and mistresses, and even of farm families and herders in the hills and backwoods who saw few slaves in their day-to-day existence. To understand the Old South, then, we must understand how the southern agricultural economy and the institution of slavery affected the social class structure of both white and black southerners.

The Diverse South *The Old South encompassed a wide variety of social settings. Locate the residences of the five individuals profiled in the chapter introduction on this map.*

The Social Structure of the Cotton Kingdom

We have already seen (in Chapter 10) that the spread of cotton stimulated the nation's remarkable economic growth after the War of 1812. Demand spurred by the textile industry sent the price of cotton soaring on the international market, and white southerners scrambled into the fresh lands of the Southwest to reap the profits to be made in the cotton sweepstakes.

The Boom Country Economy

Cotton Pushes Westward

Letters, newspapers, and word of mouth all brought tales of the black belt region of Alabama, where the dark soil was particularly suited to growing cotton, and of the tremendous yields from the soils along the Mississippi River's broad reaches. "The *Alabama Feaver* rages here with great violence and has *carried off* vast numbers of our Citizens," a North Carolinian wrote in 1817. A generation later, as the removal of the southern Indian tribes opened vast tracts of land to white settlement, immigrants were still "pouring in with a ceaseless tide," one observer reported, "including 'Land Sharks' ready to swallow up the home of the redmen, or the white, as oportunity might offer." By the 1840s planters even began to leave Mississippi and Alabama to head for the new cotton frontier along the Red River and up into Texas. Amazingly, by the eve of the Civil War nearly a third of the total cotton crop came from *west* of the Mississippi River.

Southern Prosperity

As Senator James Henry Hammond of South Carolina boasted in 1858, cotton was king in the Old South. By 1860 the United States produced three-fourths of the world's supply of cotton. This boom fueled the southern economy so strongly that following the depression of 1839–1843, the southern economy grew faster than that in the North. Even so, per capita income in the South remained below that of the free states, and wealth was not as evenly distributed in the plantation South as in northern agricultural areas.

Prosperity masked other basic problems in the economy—problems that would become more apparent after the Civil War. Much of the South's new wealth resulted from migration of its population to more productive western lands. Once that prime

In this romanticized Currier and Ives print of a cotton plantation, field hands are waist-deep in cotton while other slaves haul the picked cotton to be ginned and then pressed into bales. Mounted on a horse, an overseer rides through the field supervising the work while the owner and his wife look on. Picking began as early as August and continued in some areas until late January. Because the bolls ripened at different times, a field had to be picked several times.

agricultural land was settled, the South could not sustain its rate of expansion. Nor did the shift in population alter the structure of the southern economy, stimulate technological change, improve the way goods were produced and marketed, or generate internal markets.

The single-crop agriculture practiced by southern farmers rapidly wore out the soil. Tobacco was a particularly exhaustive crop, and corn also rapidly drained nutrients. To restore their soils, planters and farmers in the **Upper South** increasingly shifted to wheat production, but because they now plowed their fields rather than using a hoe, this shift intensified soil erosion. Destruction of the forests, particularly in the Piedmont, where commercial agriculture now took hold, had the same effect, and many streams quickly silted up and were no longer navigable. Row-crop agriculture made floods and droughts more common. In addition, reliance on a single crop increased toxins and parasites in the soil, making southern agriculture more vulnerable to destruction than varied agriculture was.

Only the South's low population density lessened the impact on the environment. More remote areas remained heavily forested, wetlands were still common, and as late as 1860 eighty percent of the region was uncultivated (cattle and hogs, however, ranged over much of this acreage). Throughout much of the South, farmers fired the woods in the spring to destroy insects, burn off brush, and increase grass for their browsing stock.

Perhaps the most striking environmental consequence of the expansion of southern society was the increase in disease, especially in the **Deep South.** Epidemic diseases such as malaria, yellow fever, and cholera were brought to the area by Europeans. The clearing of land—which increased runoff, precipitated floods, and produced pools of stagnant water—facilitated the spread of these diseases. In notoriously unhealthy areas, such as the coastal swamps of South Carolina's rice district, wealthy whites fled during the sickly summer months.

Environmental Impact of
Single-Crop Agriculture

The Upper South's New Orientation

As cotton transformed the boom country of the Deep South, agriculture in the Upper South also adjusted. Improved varieties and more scientific agricultural practices reversed the decline in tobacco that had begun in the 1790s. More important, however, farmers in the Upper South made wheat and corn their major crops. As early as 1840 the value of wheat grown in Virginia was twice that of tobacco.

Slave Trade

Because the new crops required less labor, planters in the Upper South regularly sold their surplus slaves to cotton and sugar planters in the Deep South. Indeed, some planters in the Upper South maintained a profit margin only by these sales. The demand in the Deep South for field hands drove their price steadily up, so that by the late 1850s a prime field hand, who would have sold for $600 in the early 1840s, commanded $1,500. Even with increased labor costs, southern agriculture flourished.

The Rural South

The Old South, then, was dynamic, expanding, and booming economically. But the region remained overwhelmingly rural, with 84 percent of its labor force engaged in agriculture in 1860, compared with 40 percent in the North. Conversely, the South

Lack of Manufacturing

lagged in manufacturing, producing only 9 percent of the nation's manufactured goods. During the 1850s some southern propagandists urged greater investment in industry to diversify the South's economy. But as long as high profits from cotton continued, these advocates made little headway. With so little industry, few cities developed in the

Cotton and Other Crops of the South   *By 1860, the cotton kingdom extended across the Lower South into the Texas prairie and up the Mississippi River valley. Tobacco and hemp were the staple crops of the Upper South, where they competed with corn and wheat. Rice production was concentrated in the swampy coastal region of South Carolina and Georgia as well as the lower tip of Louisiana. The sugar district was in southern Louisiana.*

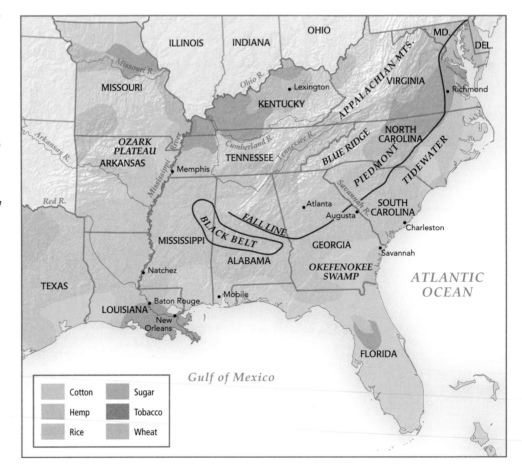

South. New Orleans, with a population of 169,000 in 1860, was the only truly southern city of significant size. Only 1 in 10 southerners lived in cities and towns in 1860, compared with 1 out of 3 persons in the North.

Absence of Cities

As a rural society, the South showed far less interest in education. Southern colleges were inferior to those in the North, and public secondary schools were virtually nonexistent. Wealthy planters, who hired tutors or sent their children to private academies, generally opposed a state-supported school system. Thus free public schools were rare, especially in the rural districts that made up most of the South. Georgia in 1860 had only one county with a free school system, and Mississippi had no public schools outside its few cities. On average southern white children spent only one-fifth as much time in school as did their northern counterparts.

The net result was high illiteracy rates. Among native-born white citizens, the 1850 census showed that 20 percent were unable to read and write. The comparable figure was 3 percent in the middle states and 0.4 percent in New England. In some areas of the South, more than a third of all white residents were illiterate.

Distribution of Slavery

Even more than agrarian ways, slavery set the South apart. Whereas in 1776 slavery had been a national institution, by 1820 slavery was confined to the states south of Pennsylvania and the Ohio River. The South's **"peculiar institution"** bound white and black southerners together in a multitude of ways.

Slaves were not evenly distributed throughout the region. More than half lived in the Deep South, where African Americans outnumbered white southerners in both South Carolina and Mississippi by the 1850s. Elsewhere in the Deep South, the black population exceeded 40 percent in all states except Texas. In the Upper South, on the other hand, whites greatly outnumbered blacks. Only in Virginia and North Carolina did the slave population top 30 percent.

The distribution of slaves showed striking geographic variations within individual states as well. In areas of fertile soil, flat or rolling countryside, and good transportation, slavery and the plantation system dominated. In the pine barrens, areas isolated by lack of transportation, and hilly and mountainous regions, small family farms and few slaves were the rule.

Slave Occupations

Almost all enslaved African Americans, male and female, worked in agricultural pursuits, with only about 10 percent living in cities and towns. On large plantations, a few slaves were domestic servants and others were skilled artisans—blacksmiths, carpenters, or bricklayers—but most toiled in the fields.

Slavery as a Labor System

Slavery was, first and foremost, a system to manage and control labor. The plantation system, with its extensive estates and large labor forces, could never have developed without slavery, nor could it have met the world demand for cotton and other staples. Slaves represented an enormous capital investment, worth more than all the land in the Old South.

Profitability of Slavery

Furthermore, slavery remained a highly profitable investment. The average slaveowner spent perhaps $30 to $35 a year to support an adult slave. Allowing for the cost of land, equipment, and other expenses, a planter could expect one of his slaves to produce more than $78 worth of cotton—which meant that about 60 percent of the wealth produced by a slave's labor was clear profit. For those who pinched pennies and drove slaves harder, the gains were even greater.

Slavery and Aristocratic Values

By concentrating wealth and power in the hands of the planter class, slavery shaped the tone of southern society. Planters were not aristocrats in the European sense of having special legal privileges or formal titles of rank. Still, the system encouraged southern

The Spread of Slavery, 1820–1860 *Between 1820 and 1860, the slave population of the South shifted southward and westward, concentrating especially heavily in coastal South Carolina and Georgia, in the black belt of central Alabama and Mississippi (so named because of its rich soil), and in the Mississippi valley. Small farms with few slaves predominated in cotton-growing areas that lacked good transportation, such as northern Georgia, and in regions with poor soil, such as the piney woods of southern Mississippi.*

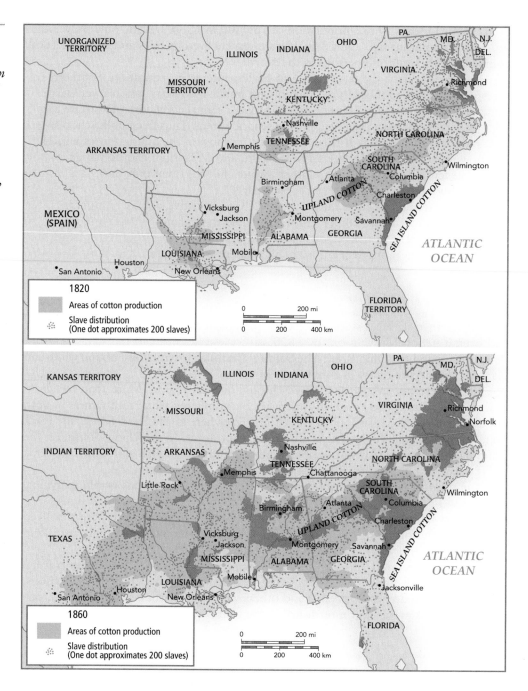

planters to think of themselves as a landed gentry upholding the aristocratic values of pride, honor, family, and hospitality.

Whereas slavery had existed throughout most of the Americas at the beginning of the century, by the 1850s the United States, Cuba, and Brazil were the only slaveholding nations left in the region. Public opinion in Europe and in the North had grown more and more hostile to the peculiar institution, causing white southerners to feel increasingly like an embattled minority. Yet they clung tenaciously to slavery, for it was the base on which the South's economic growth and way of life rested. As one Georgian observed on the eve of the Civil War, slavery was "so intimately mingled with our social conditions that it would be impossible to eradicate it."

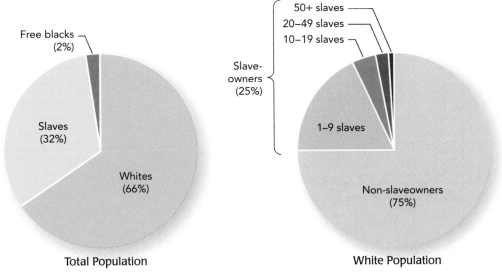

Southern Population, 1860

Free blacks (2%)

Slaves (32%)

Whites (66%)

Total Population

Slave-owners (25%)

50+ slaves
20–49 slaves
10–19 slaves

1–9 slaves

Non-slaveowners (75%)

White Population

Class Structure of the White South

Once a year around Christmastime, James Henry Hammond gave a dinner for his neighbors at his South Carolina plantation, Silver Bluff. The richest man for miles around as well as an ambitious politician, the aristocratic Hammond used these dinners to put his neighbors under personal obligation to him as well as receive the honor and respect he believed his due. Indeed, Hammond's social and political ambitions caused him to carefully cultivate his neighbors, despite his low opinion of them, by hiring them to perform various tasks and by providing them a variety of services such as ginning their cotton and allowing them to use his grist mill. These services enhanced his ethic of paternalism, but his less affluent neighbors also displayed a strong personal pride. After he ungraciously complained about the inconvenience of these services, only three of his neighbors came to his Christmas dinner in 1837, a snub that enraged him. As Hammond's experience demonstrated, class relations among whites in the Old South were a complex blend of privilege, patronage, and equality.

The Slaveowners

In 1860 the region's 15 states had a population of 12 million, of which roughly two-thirds were white, one-third were black slaves, and about 2 percent were free African Americans. Because of the institution of slavery, the social structure of the antebellum South differed in important ways from that of the North. Even so, southern society was remarkably fluid, and as a result, class lines were not rigid.

Of the 8 million white southerners in 1860, only about 2 million (one-quarter) either owned slaves or were members of slaveowning families. Moreover, most slaveowners owned only a few slaves. If one uses the census definition of a planter as a person who owned 20 or more slaves, only about 1 out of every 30 white southerners belonged to families of the planter class.

A planter of consequence, however, needed to own at least 50 slaves, and there were only about 10,000 such families—less than 1 percent of the white population. This privileged group made up the aristocracy at the top of the southern class structure. Owners of large numbers of slaves were very rare; only about 2,000 southerners, such as Colonel Daniel Jordan, owned 100 or more slaves. Although limited in size, the planter class nevertheless owned more than half of all slaves and controlled more than 90 percent of the region's total wealth.

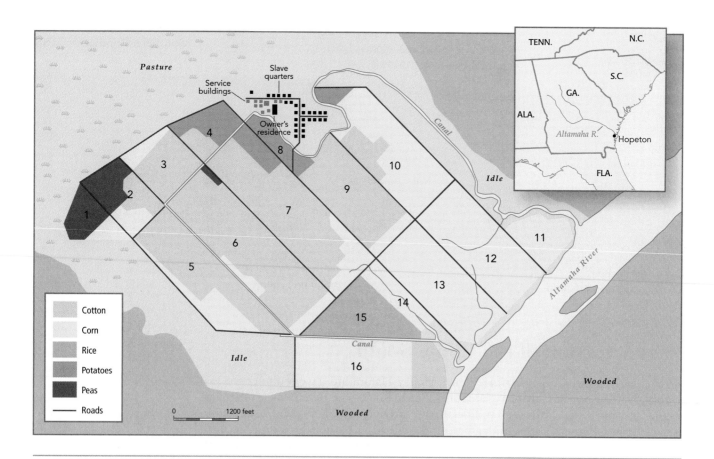

A Plantation Layout, Hopeton, Georgia   *Often covering a thousand acres or more, a plantation was laid out like a small village and contained several fields and usually extensive uncleared woods. Somewhere near the master's "big house" were the quarters—slave cabins clustered along one or more streets. Service buildings might include a smokehouse, stables, a gin house (for cotton) or a rice mill, and an overseer's dwelling. Like most large plantations, Hopeton produced a considerable amount of foodstuffs, but it grew both rice and cotton as staples. Most plantations concentrated on a single cash crop.*

Plantation Administration

The typical plantation had 20 to 50 slaves and 800 to 1,000 acres of land. On an estate larger than that, slaves would have to walk more than an hour to reach the farthest fields, losing valuable work time. Thus larger slaveowners usually owned several plantations, with an overseer to manage the slaves on each while the owner attended to business matters. The slaves were divided into field hands, skilled workers, and house servants, with one or more slaves serving as "drivers" to assist the overseer. Plantations remained labor-intensive operations. Only the production of sugar, among the southern staples, was heavily mechanized.

Tidewater and Frontier

Southern planters shared a commitment to preserve slavery as the source of their wealth and stature. Yet in other ways they were a diverse group. On the one hand, the tobacco and rice planters of the Atlantic Tidewater were part of a settled region and a culture that reached back 150 to 200 years. States such as Mississippi and Arkansas, in contrast, were at or just emerging from the frontier stage, since most residents had arrived after 1815.

Tidewater Society

It was along the Tidewater, especially the bays of the Chesapeake and the South Carolina coast, that the legendary "Old South" was born. Here, masters erected substantial homes, some of them—especially between Charleston and Columbia—the classic white-pillared mansions in the Greek revival style.

The ideal of the Tidewater South was the polished country gentleman of the English tradition. An Irish visitor observed that in Maryland and Virginia the great planters lived in "a style which approaches nearer to that of the English country gentleman than what is to be met with anywhere else on the continent." As in England, in the Tidewater South the local gentry often served as justices of the peace, and the Episcopal church remained the socially accepted road to heaven. Here, too, family names continued to be important in politics.

While the newer regions of the South boasted of planters with cultivated manners, as a group the cotton lords were a different breed. Whatever their background, whether planters, farmers, overseers, or businessmen, these entrepreneurs had moved west for the same reason so many other white Americans had: to make their fortunes. By and large, the cotton gentry were self-made men who through hard work, aggressive business tactics, and good luck had risen from ordinary backgrounds. For them, the cotton boom and the exploitation of enslaved men and women offered the opportunity to move up in a new society that lacked an entrenched elite.

Society in the Cotton Kingdom

"Time's money, time's money." For men like the impatient Texan, time was indeed money, slaves were capital, and cotton by the bale signified cash in hand. This business orientation was especially apparent in the cotton kingdom, where planters sought to maximize their profits and constantly reinvested their returns in land and slaves. As one visitor said of Mississippi slaveholders: "To sell cotton in order to buy negroes—to make more cotton to buy more negroes, 'ad infinitum,' is the aim and direct tendency of all the operations of the thorough-going cotton planter: his whole soul is wrapped up in the pursuit." And indeed there was money to be made. The combined annual income of the richest thousand families of the cotton kingdom approached $50 million, while the wealth of the remaining 666,000 families amounted to only about $60 million.

Slaveholders' Values

Although most planters ranked among the richest citizens in America, their homes were often simple one- or two-story unpainted wooden frame houses, and some were log cabins. A visitor to one Georgia plantation reported that the house did not have a pane of glass in the windows, a door between the rooms, or a ceiling other than the roof. "If you wish to see people worth millions living as [if] they were not worth hundreds," advised one southwestern planter in 1839, "come to the land of cotton and negroes." Practical men, few of the new cotton lords had absorbed the culture and learning of the traditional country gentleman.

This skillful portrait of John Stock, a wealthy South Carolina rice planter, depicts his aristocratic bearing and tastes.

The Master at Home

Whether supervising a Tidewater plantation or creating a cotton estate on the Texas frontier, the master had to coordinate a complex agricultural operation. He gave daily instructions concerning the work to be done, settled disputes between slaves and the overseer, and generally handed out rewards and penalties. In addition, the owner made the critical decisions concerning the planting, harvesting, and marketing of the crops. Planters also watched investments and expenditures, and they often sought to expand their production by clearing additional fields, buying more land or slaves, or investing in machinery such as cotton gins. As in any business, these decisions required a sound understanding of the domestic and international market.

In performing his duties, the plantation owner was supposed to be the "master" of his crops, his family, and his slaves. Defenders of slavery held up this paternalistic ideal—the care and guidance of dependent "children"—maintaining that slavery promoted a genuine affection between caring master and loyal slaves. In real life, however, a concern for money and profits undermined this paternalistic ideal. Some of the most brutal forms of slavery existed on rice tidewater plantations, where the absenteeism of many owners combined with the sheer numbers of slaves made close personal ties impossible.

Paternalism

Except for a few domestic servants, owners of large plantations had little contact with their slaves. Nor could paternalism mask the reality that slavery everywhere rested on violence, racism, and exploitation.

The Plantation Mistress

Upper-class southern white women, like those in the North, grew up with the ideal of domesticity, reinforced by the notion of a paternalistic master who was lord of the plantation. But the plantation mistress soon discovered that, given the demands placed on her, the ideal was hard to fulfill.

In her youth a genteel lady enjoyed a certain amount of leisure. But once she married and became a plantation mistress, a southern woman was often shocked by the size of her responsibilities. Nursing the sick, making clothing, tending the garden, caring for the poultry, and overseeing every aspect of food preparation were all her domain. She also had to supervise and plan the work of the domestic servants and distribute clothing. After taking care of breakfast, one harried Carolina mistress recounted that she "had the [sewing] work cut out, gave orders about dinner, had the horse feed fixed in hot water, had the box filled with cork: went to see the carpenters working on the negro houses . . . now I have to cut out the flannel jackets." Sarah Williams, the New York bride of a North Carolina planter, admitted that her mother-in-law "works harder than any Northern farmer's wife I know."

Unlike female reformers in the North, upper-class southern women did not openly challenge their role, but some found their sphere confining, especially the never-ending task of managing slaves. One southern mistress confessed, "I do not see how I can live my life amid these people! To be always among people whom I do not understand and whom I must guide, and teach and lead on like children. It frightens me." Yet without the labor of slaves, the lifestyle of these women was an impossibility.

Some women drew a parallel between their situation and that of the slaves. Both were subject to male dominance, and independent-minded women found the subordination of marriage difficult. Susan Dabney Smedes, in her recollection of growing up on an Alabama plantation, recalled that "it was a saying that the mistress of a plantation was the most complete slave on it."

Many women were deeply discontented, too, with the widespread double standard for sexual behavior and with the daily reminders of **miscegenation** some had to face. A man who fathered illegitimate children by slave women suffered no social or legal penalties, even in the case of rape (southern law did not recognize such a crime against slave women). In contrast, a white woman guilty of adultery lost all social respectability.

Mary Chesnut, the wife of a South Carolina planter, knew the reality of miscegenation firsthand from her father-in-law's liaisons with slave women. She sneered in her diary at the assumptions of male superiority. "Like the patriarchs of old, our men live all in one house with their wives and concubines; and the mulattoes one sees in every family partly resemble the white children. Any lady is ready to tell you who is the father of all the mulattoes one sees in everybody's household but her own. Those, she seems to think, drop from the clouds. My disgust sometimes is boiling over." One planter's wife spoke of "violations of the moral law that made mulattoes as common as blackberries," and another recalled, "I saw slavery in its bearing on my sex. I saw that it teemed with injustice and shame to all womankind and I hated it."

Mistress' Duties

Sarah Pierce Vick, the mistress of a plantation near Vicksburg, Mississippi, pauses to speak to one of her slaves, who may be holding feed for her horse. A plantation mistress had many duties and, while enjoying the comforts brought by wealth and status, often found her life more difficult than she had anticipated before marriage.

Miscegenation

Still, only a small minority of women questioned either their place in southern society or the corrosive influence of slavery. Racism was so pervasive within American society that the few white southern women who privately criticized the institution displayed little empathy for the plight of slaves themselves, including black women. Whatever the burdens of the plantation mistress, they were hardly akin to the bondage of slavery itself.

Yeoman Farmers

Farmers and Herders

In terms of numbers, yeoman farm families were the backbone of southern society, accounting for more than half the southern white population. They owned no slaves and farmed the traditional 80 to 160 acres, like northern farmers. About 80 percent owned their own land, and the rest were tenant farmers who hoped one day to acquire a homestead. They settled almost everywhere in the South, except in the rice and sugar districts and valuable river bottomlands of the Deep South, which were monopolized by large slaveowners. Like Ferdinand Steel, most were semisubsistence farmers who raised primarily corn and hogs, along with perhaps a few bales of cotton or some tobacco, which they sold to obtain the cash needed to buy items like sugar, coffee, and salt. Some were not so much farmers as herdsmen, who set large herds of scrawny cattle or pigs to forage in the woods until it was time for the annual drive to market. Yeoman farmers lacked the wealth of planters, but they had a pride and dignity that earned them the respect of their richer neighbors.

Southern farmers led more isolated lives than their northern counterparts. Yet the social activities of these people were not much different from those of northern farmers. Religion played an important role at camp meetings held in late summer after the crops were laid by and before harvest time. As in the North, neighbors also met to exchange labor and tools, always managing to combine work with fun. A Tennessee plain farmer recalled that his neighbors "seem to take delight in helping each other sutch as lay[ing] railings, cornshucking and house raising[.] they tried to help each other all they could and dancet all night." Court sessions, militia musters, political rallies—these too were occasions that brought rural folk together.

A FAMILY GROUP IN THE INTERIOR OF THE STATE OF GEORGIA

A majority of white southerners were members of nonslaveholding yeoman farm families. Ruggedly independent, these families depended on their own labor and lived under more primitive conditions than large plantation owners or small farmers in the North. Basil Hall, an Englishman traveling through the South in 1827 and 1828, sketched members of this Georgia family with the aid of a camera lucida, an optical device that projected an image from real life onto paper, where it could be traced with accuracy.

Limits to Economic
Opportunity

Because yeoman farmers lacked cheap slave labor, good transportation, and access to credit, they could not compete with planters in the production of staples. When it came to selling their corn and wheat, small farmers conducted only limited business with planters, who usually grew as many of their own foodstuffs as possible. In the North urban centers became a market for small farmers, but in the South the lack of towns limited this internal market.

Thus while southern yeoman farmers were not poor, they suffered from a chronic lack of money and the absence of conveniences that northern farm families enjoyed, such as cast-iron stoves, sewing machines, specialized tools, and good furniture. A few chafed at the absence of public schools and greater opportunities. Josiah Hinds, who hacked a farm out of the isolated woods of northern Mississippi, worried that his children were growing up "wild." He complained that "education is but little prized by my neighbours," who were satisfied "if the corn and cotton grows to perfection . . . [and] brings a fare price, and hog meat is at hand to boil with the greens."

Absence of Class Conflict

In some ways, then, the worlds of yeoman farmers and upper-class planters were not only different but also in conflict. Still, a hostility between the two classes did not emerge. Yeoman farmers admired planters and hoped that one day they would join the gentry themselves. And even white southerners who owned no slaves accepted slavery as a means of controlling African Americans as members of an inferior social caste based on race. "Now suppose they was free," one poor farmer told Frederick Law Olmsted. "You see they'd all think themselves as good as we." Racism and fear of black people were sufficient to keep nonslaveholders loyal to southern institutions.

Poor Whites

Lives of Poor Whites

The poorest white southerners were confined to land that no one else wanted: the wiregrass region of southeastern Georgia, the sand hills of central South Carolina, the pine barrens of the coastal plains from Virginia to southeastern Mississippi. These southerners lived in rough, unchinked, windowless log cabins located in the remotest areas and were often squatters without title to the land they were on. The men spent their time hunting and fishing, while women did the domestic work and what farming they could manage. Largely illiterate, they suffered from malnutrition stemming from a monotonous diet of corn, pork, and whiskey, and they were afflicted with malaria and hookworm, diseases that sapped their energy. Other white southerners scornfully referred to poor whites as crackers, white trash, sandhillers, and clay eaters. Numbers are hard to come by, but perhaps 5 percent of the white population comprised these poor folk.

Relations with Planters

Because poor whites traded with slaves, exchanging whiskey for stolen goods, contemptuous planters often bought them out simply to rid the neighborhood of them. For their part, poor whites keenly resented planters, but their hostility toward African Americans was even stronger. Poor whites refused to work alongside slaves or perform any work commonly done by them and vehemently opposed ending slavery. Emancipation would remove one of the few symbols of their status—that they were, at least, free.

The Peculiar Institution

Slaves were not free. That overwhelming fact must be understood before anything is said about the kindness or the cruelty that individual slaves experienced; before any consideration of healthy or unhealthy living conditions; before any discussion of how slave families coped with hardship, rejoiced in shared pleasures, or worshiped in prayer. The lives of slaves were affected day in and day out, in big ways and small, by the basic reality that slaves were not their own masters. If a slave's workload was reasonable, it remained so only at the master's discretion, not because the slave determined it to be. If slaves married or visited family or friends on a nearby plantation, they did so only with the master's permission. If they raised a family, they could remain together only as long as the master did not separate them by sale. Whatever slaves wanted to do, they had always to consider the response of their masters.

When power was distributed as unequally as it was between masters and slaves, every action on the part of the enslaved involved a certain calculation, conscious or unconscious. The consequences of every act, of every expression or gesture, had to be considered. In that sense, the line between freedom and slavery penetrated every corner of a slave's life, and it was an absolute and overwhelming distinction.

One other stark fact reinforced the sharp line between freedom and slavery: slaves were distinguished on the basis of color. While the peculiar institution was an economic system of labor, it was also a **caste system** based on race. The color line of slavery made it much easier to brand black people as somehow different. It made it easier to defend the institution and win the support of yeoman farmers and poor white southerners, even though in many ways the system held them back. Hence slavery must be understood on many levels: not only as an economic system but also as a racial and cultural one, not only in terms of its outward conditions of life and labor but also through the inner demands it made on the soul.

Slavery and Race

Work and Discipline

The conditions slaves encountered varied widely, depending on the size of the farm or plantation, the crop being grown, the personality of the master, and whether he was an absentee owner. On small farms slaves worked in the fields with the owners and had much closer contact with whites. On plantations, in contrast, most slaves dealt primarily with the overseer, who was paid by the size of the harvest he brought in and was therefore often harsh in his approach. The largest plantations, which raised rice and sugar, also required the longest hours and the most grueling labor.

House servants and the drivers, who supervised the field hands, were accorded the highest status, and skilled artisans such as carpenters and blacksmiths were also given special recognition. The hardest work was done by the field hands, both men and women, who sometimes were divided into plowhands and hoe gangs. In the summer of 1854 Olmsted watched a group of Mississippi slaves return to work in the fields after a thunderstorm. "First came, led by an old driver carrying a whip, 40 of the largest and strongest women I ever saw together; . . . they carried themselves loftily, each having a hoe over the shoulder, and walking with a free, powerful swing like [soldiers] on the march." Behind them were the plowhands on the mules, "the cavalry, thirty strong, mostly men, but a few of them women." Bringing up the rear was "a lean and vigilant white overseer, on a brisk pony."

Organization of Slave Labor

Some planters organized their slaves by the gang system, in which a white overseer or a black driver supervised gangs of 20 to 25 adults. Although the approach extracted long hours of reasonably hard labor, the slaves had to be constantly supervised and shirkers were difficult to detect. Other planters preferred the task system, under which each slave was given a specific daily assignment to complete, after which he or she was finished for the day. This system allowed slaves to work at their own pace, gave them an incentive to do careful work, and freed overseers from having to closely supervise the work. But, as drivers also discovered, slaves resisted vigorously if masters tried to increase the workload. The task system was most common in the rice fields, whereas the gang system predominated in the cotton districts. Many planters used a combination of the two.

Black slave driver

Toil began just before sunrise and continued until dusk. During cultivation and harvest, slaves were in the field 15 to 16 hours a day, eating a noonday meal there and resting before resuming labor. Work was uncommon on Sundays, and frequently only a half day was required on Saturdays. Even so, the routine was taxing. "We . . . have everybody at work before day dawns," an Arkansas cotton planter reported. "I am never caught in bed after day light nor is any body else on the place, and we continue in the cotton fields when we can have fair weather till it is so dark we can't see to work."

Often masters gave money, additional food, gifts, and time off to slaves who worked diligently, but the threat of punishment was always present. Slaves could be denied passes; their food allowance could be reduced; and if all else failed, they could be sold. The most common instrument of punishment, however, was the whip. The frequency of its use varied from plantation to plantation, but few slaves escaped the lash entirely. "We have to rely more and more on the power of fear," the planter James Henry Hammond acknowledged. "We are determined to continue masters, and to do so we have to draw the rein tighter and tighter day by day to be assured that we hold them in complete check."

Slave Maintenance

Clothing and Housing

Planters generally bought rough, cheap cloth for slave clothing and each year gave adults at most only a couple of outfits and a pair of shoes that were worn out by the end of the year. Few had enough clothing or blankets to keep warm when the weather dipped below freezing. Some planters provided well-built housing, but more commonly slaves lived in cramped, poorly built cabins that were leaky in wet weather, drafty in cold, and furnished with only a few crude chairs, benches and a table, perhaps a mattress filled with corn husks or straw, and a few pots and dishes. To keep medical expenses down, slaveowners treated sick slaves themselves and called in a doctor only for serious cases. Conditions varied widely, but on average, a slaveowner spent less than a dollar a year on medical care for each slave.

Slaves' Lower Life Expectancy

Even so, the United States was the only slave society in the Americas where the slave population increased naturally—indeed, at about the same rate as the white population. Nevertheless, a deficient diet, inadequate clothing and shelter, long hours of hard toil, and poor medical care resulted in a lower life expectancy among slaves.

Resistance

Slave Revolts in Latin America

Given the wide gulf between freedom and slavery, it was only natural that slaves resisted the bondage imposed on them. The most radical form of resistance was rebellion, which occurred repeatedly in slave societies in the Americas. In Latin America, slave revolts were frequent, involving hundreds and even thousands of slaves and pitched battles in which large numbers were killed. The most successful slave revolt occurred in France's sugar-rich colony Saint Domingue (the western part of the Caribbean island of Hispaniola). There, free blacks who had fought in the American Revolution because of France's alliance with the United States brought back the ideals of freedom and equality. Furthermore, the brutally overworked population of half a million slaves was ready to revolt and received further encouragement from the example of the French Revolution. Under the leadership of Toussaint L'Ouverture, rebellion led to the establishment of Haiti in 1804, the second independent republic in the Western Hemisphere.

Elsewhere, Jamaica averaged one significant slave revolt every year from 1731 to 1823, while in 1823 thousands rose in Guiana. Jamaica too witnessed an uprising, of some 20,000 slaves in 1831. These revolts, and ones in 1823 and 1824 in British-controlled Demerara, were savagely suppressed. And in Brazil, which had the largest number of slaves outside the United States, the government took 50 years to suppress with military force a colony of about 20,000 slaves who had sought refuge in the mountains.

Infrequency of Revolts in the United States

In contrast, slave revolts were rare in the United States. Unlike in Latin America, in the Old South whites outnumbered blacks, the government was much more powerful, most slaves were native-born, and family life was much stronger. Slaves recognized the

Steamboat Manifests and Starvation

Estimating Slave Life Expectancies

Historians have for many years combed individual plantation records and the accounts of travelers to judge how long slaves lived and how well they were treated. Such testimony, however, can be impressionistic and inconsistent. More recently some researchers have turned to a different set of data: about 50,000 records collected between 1820 and 1860 from shippers on coastal and inland waterways. To ensure that slaves were not being imported from Africa, merchants were required to record information about slaves traveling on steamboats. The lists include vital data on age, weight, and height.

An analysis of these shipping "manifests" makes clear that slave children in particular faced daunting conditions. On average, they weighed less at birth than white children did and were badly undernourished at least until the age of six. Slave women were worked hard even during the final months of pregnancy; as a result more than half of all conceptions ended in miscarriage or in the infant's early death. For every 1,000 live births among southern slaves, more than 200 died before the age of 5, and fewer than two-thirds of slave children lived to age 10. Those who did had a life expectancy about 8 years less than that of white Americans.

odds against them, and many potential leaders became fugitives instead. In a sense, what is remarkable is that American slaves revolted at all.

Early in the nineteenth century several well-organized uprisings in the United States were barely thwarted. In 1800 Gabriel Prosser, a slave blacksmith, recruited perhaps a couple hundred slaves in a plan to march on Richmond and capture the governor. But a heavy thunderstorm postponed the attack and a few slaves then betrayed the plot. Prosser and other leaders were eventually captured and executed. Denmark Vesey's conspiracy in Charleston in 1822 met a similar fate (see page 307).

The most famous slave revolt, led by a literate slave preacher named Nat Turner, was smaller and more spontaneous. Turner, who lived on a farm in southeastern Virginia, was given unusual privileges by his master, whom he described as a kind and trusting man. Spurred on by an almost fanatic mysticism, Turner became convinced that God intended to punish white people. One night in 1831 following an eclipse of the sun, he and six confederates stole out and murdered Turner's master and family. Gaining some 70 recruits as they went, Turner's band killed 57 white men, women, and children. Along the way, the members voiced their grievances against slavery and announced that they intended to confiscate their masters' wealth.

Nat Turner's Rebellion

Although the uprising was put down and Turner executed, it left white southerners throughout the region with a haunting uneasiness. Nat Turner had seemed a model slave, yet who could read a slave's true emotions behind the mask of obedience?

Day-to-Day Resistance

Beyond outright rebellion, there were other, more subtle, ways of resisting a master's authority. Running away was one. With the odds stacked heavily against them, few runaways escaped safely to freedom except from the border states. More frequently, slaves fled to nearby woods or swamps to avoid punishment or protest their treatment. Some runaways stayed out only a few days; others held out for months.

Many slaves resisted by abusing their masters' property. They mishandled animals, broke tools and machinery, misplaced items, and worked carelessly in the fields. Olmsted observed one field gang that stopped hoeing every time the overseer turned his back. Slaves also sought to trick the master by feigning illness or injury and by hiding rocks in the cotton they picked. Slaves complained directly to the owner about an overseer's mistreatment, thereby attempting to drive a wedge between the two.

The most common form of resistance, and a persistent annoyance to slaveowners, was theft. Slaves took produce from the garden, raided the master's smokehouse, secretly slaughtered his stock, and killed his poultry. "They always told us it was wrong to lie and steal," recalled Josephine Howard, a former slave in Texas, "but why did the white folks steal my mammy and her mammy? They lived over in Africa . . . That's the sinfullest stealing there is."

Slaves' Hidden Feelings

Slaves learned to outwit their masters by wearing an "impenetrable mask" around whites, one bondsman recalled. "How much of joy, of sorrow, of misery and anguish have they hidden from their tormentors." Frederick Douglass, the most famous fugitive slave, explained that "as the master studies to keep the slave ignorant, the slave is cunning enough to make the master think he succeeds."

Slave Culture

Trapped in bondage, faced with the futility of revolt, slaves could at least forge a culture of their own. By the nineteenth century, American slaves had been separated from much of their traditional African heritage, but that did not mean they had fully accepted the dominant white culture. Instead, slaves combined strands from their African past with customs that evolved from their life in America. This slave culture was most distinct on big plantations, where the slave population was large and slaves had more opportunity to live apart from white scrutiny.

The Slave Family

Breakup of Families

Maintaining a sense of family was one of the most remarkable achievements of African Americans in bondage, given the obstacles that faced them. Southern law did not recognize slave marriages as legally binding, nor did it allow slave parents complete authority over their children. Black women faced the possibility of rape by the master or overseer without legal recourse, and husbands, wives, and children had to live with the fear of being sold and separated. From 1820 to 1860 more than 2 million slaves were sold in the interstate slave trade. Perhaps 600,000 husbands and wives were separated by such sales.

Family Ties in Slavery

Despite their vulnerability, family ties remained strong, as slave culture demonstrated. The marriage ceremony among slaves varied from a formal religious service to jumping over a broomstick in front of the slave community to nothing more than the master giving verbal approval. Whatever the ceremony, slaves viewed the ritual as a public affirmation of the couple's commitment to their new responsibilities. Rather than adopting white norms, slaves developed their own moral code concerning sexual relations and marriage. Although young slaves often engaged in premarital sex, they were expected to choose a partner and become part of a stable family. It has been estimated that at

An unknown artist (believed to be European) painted this slave auction in the 1850s, at which a young boy (left) is being examined by a prospective buyer as his mother clings to him. A planter and his wife (perhaps the owners?) look on. Once, while walking with a European visitor, Mary Chesnut, of South Carolina, passed one such slave sale. "If you can stand that," she acidly remarked, "no other Southern thing need choke you."

least one in five slave women had one or more children before marriage, but most of these mothers eventually married. "The negroes had their own ideas of morality, and they held them very strictly," the daughter of a Georgia planter recalled. Black churches played a leading role in condemning adultery.

Gender Roles

The traditional nuclear family of father, mother, and children was the rule, not the exception, among slaves. Within the marriage the father was viewed as the traditional head of the family; wives were to be submissive and obey their husbands. Labor in the quarters was divided according to sex. Women did the indoor work, such as cooking, washing, and sewing, and men performed outdoor chores, such as gathering firewood, hauling water, and tending the animals and garden plots. The men also hunted and fished to supplement the spare weekly rations.

Beyond the nuclear family, slaves developed strong kinship networks that promoted a sense of community. Aunts and uncles were expected to look after children who lost their parents through death or sale. When children were sold to a new plantation, a family in the slave quarters took them in. Thus all members of the slave society drew together in an extended network of mutual obligation.

Slave Songs and Stories

Protest and Celebration

In the songs they sang, slaves expressed some of their deepest feelings about love and work and the joys and pain of life. "The songs of the slave represent the sorrows of his heart," commented Frederick Douglass. Surely there was bitterness as well as sorrow when slaves sang:

> We raise the wheat
> They give us the corn
> We bake the bread
> They give us the crust
> We sift the meal
> They give us the husk

Lewis Miller of York, Pennsylvania, painted this picture of Virginia slaves dancing in 1853. Dancing and music were important components of slave culture and provided a welcome respite from work under slavery. Declared one runaway slave, "The sternest . . . master cannot frighten or whip the fun out of us."

We peel the meat
They give us the skin
And that's the way
They take us in

Yet songs were also central to the celebrations held in the slave quarters: for marriages, Christmas revels, and after harvest time. And a slave on the way to the fields might sing:

Saturday night and Sunday too
Young gals on my mind.
Monday morning 'way 'fore day,
Old master's got me gwine.
Peggy does you love me now?

Folktales

Slaves expressed themselves through stories as well as song. Most often these folktales used animals as symbolic models for the predicaments in which slaves found themselves. In the best known of these, the cunning Brer Rabbit was a weak fellow who defeated larger animals like Brer Fox and Brer Bear by using his wits. Other stories were less symbolic and contained more overt hostility to white people; slaves usually told them only among themselves. But the message, whether direct or symbolic, was much the same: to laugh at the master's shortcomings and teach the young how to survive in a hostile world.

Steal Away to Jesus

At the center of slave culture was religion. The Second Great Awakening, which had begun on the southern frontier, converted many slaves, most of whom joined the Methodist and Baptist churches. Slaves constituted more than a quarter of the members of both of these southern churches.

Slaveowners encouraged a certain amount of religion among slaves as one means of social control. Masters provided slaves with a minister (often white), set the time and place of services, and usually insisted that a white person be present. "Church was what they called it," one former slave protested, "but all that preacher talked about was for us slaves to obey our masters and not to lie and steal." In response, some slaves rejected all religion, while others continued to believe in conjuring, voodoo, and various practices derived from African religion.

Most slaves, however, sought a Christianity firmly their own, beyond the control of the master. On many plantations they met secretly at night, in the quarters or at "hush harbors" in the safety of the woods, where they broke into rhythmic singing and dancing, modeled on the ring shout of African religion. Even regular services were characterized by intense enthusiasm. "The way in which we worshiped is almost indescribable," one slave preacher recalled. "The singing was accompanied by a certain ecstasy of motion, clapping of hands, tossing of heads. . . ." In an environment where slaves, for most of the day, were prevented from expressing their deepest feelings, such meetings served as a satisfying emotional release.

Religion also provided slaves with values and gave them a sense of self-worth. Slaves learned that God would redeem the poor and downtrodden and raise them one day to honor and glory. Rejecting the teaching of some white ministers that slavery was punishment, slave preachers assured their congregations that they were the chosen people of God. "This is one reason why I believe in hell," a former slave declared. "I don't believe a just God is going to take no such man as my former master into His Kingdom."

Again, song played a central role. Slaves sang religious "spirituals" at work and at play as well as in religious services. Seemingly meek and otherworldly, the songs often contained a hidden element of protest. Frederick Douglass disclosed that when slaves sang longingly of "Canaan, sweet Canaan," they were thinking not only of the Bible's Promised Land but also of the North and freedom. When slaves heard "Steal Away to Jesus" sung in the fields, they knew that a secret devotional meeting was scheduled that evening. Songs became one of the few ways that slaves could openly express, in the approved language of Christianity, their yearning for freedom.

Slave Religion

Slave Spirituals

The Slave Community

Although slaves managed with remarkable success to preserve a sense of self-worth in a religion and a culture of their own, the hard reality of slavery made it impossible to escape fully from white control. Even the social hierarchy within the slave quarters never was entirely free from the white world. Slave preachers, conjurers, and herb doctors held status that no white conferred, but the prestige of a slave driver rested ultimately on the authority of the white master. Similarly, skilled slaves and house servants often felt superior to other slaves, an attitude masters consciously promoted. "We house slaves thought we was better'n the others what worked in the field," one personal servant confessed. Light-skinned slaves sometimes deemed their color a badge of superiority. Fanny Kemble recorded that one woman begged to be relieved of field labor, which she considered degrading, "on '*account of her color.*'"

Hierarchy

Lucy Skipworth, who was the daughter of a driver and had been educated by her mistress, was a member of the slave elite on both counts. At Hopewell plantation in Alabama, she was in full charge of the main residence during her master's frequent absences. She ran a plantation school (despite white opposition) and, as a devout Baptist, supervised her fellow slaves' religious life. Eager for her master's approval, Skipworth on several occasions reported slave disobedience, which temporarily estranged her from the slave community. Yet in the end she was always welcomed back. While Skipworth never rebelled or apparently never considered running away, she was far from submissive. She defied white authority, protected her family, and used her influence to get rid of an overseer the slaves disliked. Like many house servants, she lived between two worlds—her master's and the slave quarters—and was never entirely comfortable in either.

Once a week on most plantations, slaves lined up to receive their rations from the master. Each adult could expect to receive about a peck of cornmeal, three or four pounds of bacon or salt pork, and molasses for sweetener. Some masters added vegetables, fruits, or sweet potatoes in season, but only on rare occasions did slaves receive wheat flour, beef, lean meat, poultry, or eggs. Milk, when available at all, was reserved for children and was usually sour.

In terms of simple calories, this ration was ample enough to sustain life. A modern study of the slave diet has concluded that on the eve of the Civil War, adult slaves received almost 5,400 calories, which exceeds today's recommended levels of consumption. More than 80 percent of

On one plantation, slaves working in the field who became thirsty during the heat of the day drank from this canteen. But so did the overseer or plantation owner, who was provided a separate spout. Which spout was for the slaves?

the calories, however, came from corn and pork. This monotonous fare of hog-and-hominy lacked several essential nutrients as well as enough protein, afflicting many slaves with diet-related diseases like pellagra and beriberi. (Although slaveowners and their families enjoyed more variety in their food and better cuts of meat, they too lacked a balanced diet.)

On some plantations masters left all cooking to the slaves, who, before going to work in the morning, would eat breakfast and prepare their noon meal to take with them to eat in the fields. At night, they came home to fix a light supper.

But the realities of slavery and white racism inevitably drove black people closer together in a common bond. New slaves on a plantation were immediately instructed in the mysteries of the quarters, including such vital matters as the best strategies for avoiding punishment. Walled in from the individualistic white society beyond, slaves out of necessity created a community of their own.

Free Black Southerners

Of the 4 million African Americans living in the South in 1860, only 260,000—about 7 percent—were free. More than 85 percent of them lived in the Upper South, with almost 200,000 in Maryland, Virginia, and North Carolina alone. Free black southerners were also much more urban than the southern white and slave populations. As a rule, free African Americans were more literate than slaves, and they were disproportionately female and much more likely to be of mixed ancestry.

Most free black southerners lived in rural areas, although usually not near plantations. A majority eked out a living farming or in low-paying unskilled jobs, but some did well enough to own slaves themselves. In 1830 about 3,600 did, although commonly their "property" was their wives or children, purchased because they could not be emancipated under state laws. A few, however, were full-blown slaveowners.

Between Freedom and Slavery

The boundary sometimes blurred between free and enslaved African Americans. Sally Thomas of Nashville was technically a slave, but in the 1830s and 1840s her owner allowed her to ply her trade as a laundress and keep some of her wages. (She saved some $350, which she used to purchase the freedom of one of her sons.) The boundary stretched especially for African Americans working along rivers and the seashore in the fishing trades, as pilots or seamen, or as "watermen" ferrying supplies and stores in small boats. Under such conditions, laborers preserved more freedom and initiative than did most agricultural workers.

Along Albemarle Sound in North Carolina, free blacks and slaves flocked from miles around to "fisherman's courts," a kind of annual hiring fair. Amid an atmosphere of drinking, carousing, cockfighting, and boxing, men who ran commercial

Other masters established a plantation kitchen where cooks prepared breakfast and dinner, though supper remained the responsibility of the individual slave or family. On these plantations a noon meal was brought to the fields. In general, the quality of food preparation was better under this system because slaves were often too exhausted after work to put much time or care into cooking. Naturally enough, slaves preferred to fix meals according to their own taste and eat as a family in some privacy. Fanny Kemble reported that on her husband's Georgia plantation the slaves sat "on the earth or doorsteps, and ate out of their little cedar tubs or an iron pot, some few with broken iron spoons, more with pieces of wood, and all the children with their fingers."

Wherever their masters permitted it, slaves tended their own vegetable gardens after work or raised chickens and other animals. Not only did this practice provide eggs and other items not included in the weekly rations, but it also enabled slaves to sell their surplus to the master or in town and use their earnings to buy occasional luxuries such as coffee, sugar, and tobacco. Slaves also raided the master's smokehouse, secretly slaughtered his stock and killed his poultry, and stole from neighboring plantations. Richard Carruthers, a former slave, recalled, "If they didn't provision you 'nough, you just had to slip round and get a chicken."

Slaves who worked all day still had plenty of incentive to stir out at night to fish or to hunt raccoon or opossum. "The flesh of the coon is palatable," admitted one slave, "but verily there is nothing in all butcherdom so delicious as a roasted 'possum." Along with such meat might come "hoecakes," a popular dish made by slapping cornmeal dough on the blade of a hoe and holding it over the coals.

On holidays the master usually provided a banquet for all hands on the plantation. Slaves filled up on beef, mutton, roast pig, coffee, wheat bread, pies, and other dishes only rarely tasted. Feasting was one of the slaves' "princi[pal] sources of comfort," one former slave testified. "Only the slave who has lived all the year on his scanty allowance of meal and bacon, can appreciate such suppers."

fishing operations signed up workers. The crews would then go down to the shore in late February or early March to net vast schools of fish, hauling up onto the beach over 100,000 herring in four to seven hours. Women and children then headed, gutted, cleaned, and salted the fish. A good "cutter" might head tens of thousands of herring a day. In such settings African Americans, both free and slave, could share news with folk they did not regularly see.

Following Nat Turner's rebellion of 1831, southern legislatures increased the restrictions on free African Americans. They were forbidden to enter a new state, had to carry their free papers, could not assemble when they wished, were subject to a curfew, often had to post a bond and be licensed to work, and could not vote, hold office, or testify in court against white people.

Free African Americans occupied an uncertain position in southern society, well above black slaves but distinctly beneath even poorer white southerners. They were victims of a society that had no place for them.

Southern Society and the Defense of Slavery

From wealthy planters to yeoman farmers, from free black slaveholders to white mountaineers, from cotton field hands to urban craftworkers, the South was a remarkably diverse region. Yet it was united by its dependence on staple crops and above all by the institution of slavery. As the South's economy became more and more dependent on slave-produced staples, slavery became more central to the life of the South, to its culture and its identity.

This painting shows a free African American market woman in Baltimore. Urban blacks in the South, including slaves, enjoyed greater personal freedom and access to more social activities but had only limited economic opportunity.

369

The Virginia Debate of 1832

At the time of the Revolution, the leading critics of slavery had been southerners—Jefferson, Washington, Madison, and Patrick Henry among them. But beginning in the 1820s, in the wake of the controversy over admitting Missouri as a slave state (see page 253), southern leaders became less apologetic about slavery and more aggressive in defending it. The turning point occurred in the early 1830s, when the South found itself increasingly under attack. It was in 1831 that William Lloyd Garrison began publishing his abolitionist newspaper, *The Liberator.* In that year too Nat Turner launched the revolt that frightened so many white southerners.

Significance of the Virginia Debate

In response to the Turner insurrection, a number of Virginia's western counties, where there were few slaves, petitioned the legislature to adopt a program for gradual emancipation. Between January 16 and 25, 1832, the House of Delegates engaged in a remarkable debate over the merits of slavery. In the end, however, the legislature refused, by a vote of 73 to 58, to consider legislation to end slavery. The debate marked the last significant attempt of white southerners to challenge the peculiar institution.

In its aftermath, most felt that the subject was no longer open to debate. Instead, during the 1830s and 1840s, southern leaders defended slavery as a positive good, not just for white people but for black people as well. As John C. Calhoun proclaimed in 1837, "I hold that in the present state of civilization, where two races . . . distinguished by color and other physical differences, as well as intellectual, are brought together, the relation now existing in the slaveholding states between the two is, instead of an evil, a good—a positive good."

The Proslavery Argument

Religious, Social, and Racial Arguments

Politicians like Calhoun were not alone. White southern leaders justified slavery in a variety of ways. Ministers argued that none of the Biblical prophets or Christ himself had ever condemned slavery. They also pointed out that classical Greece and Rome depended on slavery. They even cited John Locke, that giant of the Enlightenment, who had recognized slavery in the constitution he drafted for the colony of Carolina. African Americans belonged to an intellectually and emotionally inferior race, slavery's defenders argued, and therefore lacked the ability to care for themselves and required white guardianship.

This 1841 proslavery cartoon contrasts the treatment of American slaves, who are allegedly well fed, well clothed, and well cared for, with the plight of English factory workers. Defenders of slavery made the same comparisons to northern laborers.

Proslavery writers sometimes argued that slaves in the South lived better than factory workers in the North. Masters cared for slaves for life, whereas northern workers had no claim on their employer when they were unemployed, old, or no longer able to work. In advancing this argument, white southerners exaggerated the material comforts of slavery and minimized the average worker's standard of living—to say nothing of the psychological value of freedom. Still, to many white southerners, slavery seemed a more humane system of labor relations.

Defenders of slavery did not really expect to influence public opinion in the North. Their target was more often the slaveowners. As one southern editor explained, "We must satisfy the consciences, we must allay the fears of our own people. We must satisfy them that slavery is of itself right—that it is not a sin against God—that it is not an evil, moral or political. In this way only," he went on, "can we prepare our own people to defend their institutions."

Closing Ranks

Not all white southerners could quell their doubts. Still, a striking change in southern opinion seems to have occurred in the three decades before the Civil War. Outside the border states, few white southerners after 1840 would admit even in private that slavery was wrong. Those who continued to oppose slavery found themselves harassed, assaulted, and driven into exile. Southern mobs destroyed the presses of antislavery papers and threatened the editors into either keeping silent or leaving the state. Southern mails were forcibly closed to abolitionist propaganda, and defenders of the South's institutions carefully scrutinized textbooks and faculty members in southern schools.

Increasingly, too, the debate over slavery spread to the national political arena. Before 1836 Andrew Jackson's enormous popularity in the South blocked the formation of a competitive two-party system there. The rise of the abolitionist movement in the 1830s, however, left many southerners uneasy, and when the Democrats nominated the northerner Martin Van Buren in 1836, southern Whigs seized on the issue of the security of slavery and charged that Van Buren could not be counted on to meet the abolitionist threat. The Whigs made impressive gains in the South in 1836, carrying several states and significantly narrowing the margin between the two parties.

During the Jacksonian era, most southern political battles did not revolve around slavery. Even so, southern politicians in both parties had to be careful to avoid the stigma of antislavery, since they were under mounting pressure from John Calhoun and his followers. Frustrated in his presidential hopes by the nullification crisis in 1832–1833 (page 307), Calhoun sought to unite the South behind his leadership by agitating the slavery issue, introducing inflammatory resolutions in Congress, seizing on the abolitionist mailing campaign to demand censorship of the mails, and insisting on a gag rule to block antislavery petitions. During the 1830s and early 1840s, few southern politicians followed his lead, but they did become extremely careful about being in the least critical of southern institutions. They knew quite well that even if their constituents were not as fanatical as Calhoun, southern voters overwhelmingly supported slavery.

As the past several chapters have made clear, two remarkable transformations were sweeping the world in the first half of the nineteenth century. The first was a series of political upheavals leading to increased democratic participation in many nation-states. The second, the industrial revolution, applied machine labor and technological innovation to commercial and agricultural economies.

Although it is common to identify the industrial revolution with New England's factories and the North's cities, that revolution transformed the rural South too. Cotton could not have become king without the demand created by textile factories or without the ability to "gin" the seeds out of cotton by Eli Whitney's invention. Nor could cotton production flourish without industrial advances in transportation, which allowed raw materials to be shipped worldwide. As for democratic change, the suffrage was extended in Britain by the Reform Bill of 1832, and popular uprisings spread across Europe in 1830 and 1848. In the United States white southerners and northerners participated in the democratic reforms of the 1820s and 1830s.

The industrial and democratic revolutions thus transformed the South as well as the North, though in different ways. Increasingly slavery became the focus of disputes between the two sections. The industrial revolution's demand for cotton increased the demand for slave labor and the profits to be gained from it. Yet the spread of democratic ideology worldwide increased pressure to abolish slavery. France and Britain had already done so. In eastern Europe the near-slavery of feudal serfdom was being eliminated as well: in 1848 within the Hapsburg empire; in 1861 in Russia; in 1864 in Romania.

In the mid-1840s the contradictory pressures of the industrial and democratic revolutions would begin to sharpen, as the United States embarked on a new program of westward expansion that thrust the slavery issue into the center of politics. Americans were forced to debate how much of the newly won territory should be open to slavery; and in doing so, some citizens began to question whether the Union could permanently endure, half slave and half free.

Significant Events

1800	Gabriel's rebellion
1815–1860	Spread of the cotton kingdom
1822	Denmark Vesey conspiracy
1830–1840	Proslavery argument developed
1830–1860	Agricultural reform movement in Upper South
1831	Nat Turner's rebellion
1832	Virginia debate on slavery
1844	Methodist church divides into northern and southern organizations
1845	Baptist church divides

Chapter Summary

The Old South was a complex, biracial society that increasingly diverged from the rest of the United States in the years before 1860.

- Southerners placed heavy emphasis on agriculture. Given this rural way of life, few cities and towns developed.

  —Southern commercial agriculture produced staple crops for sale in northern and European markets: tobacco, sugar, rice, and, above all, cotton.
  —As southern agriculture expanded into the fresh lands of the Deep South, the slave population moved steadily westward and southward, and the Upper South became more diversified agriculturally.

- Slavery played a major role in shaping the class structure of the Old South.

  —Ownership of slaves brought privilege and status.
  —Planters on the older eastern seaboard enjoyed a more refined lifestyle than those on the new cotton frontier.

- Most slaveowners, however, owned only a few slaves, and the majority of southern whites were nonslaveowning yeoman farmers.

- The institution of slavery was both a labor system and a social system, regulating relations between the races.

    - Slaves resisted bondage in many ways. Slave revolts, however, were rare.
    - Slaves developed their own culture in which family, religion, and songs all helped cope with the pressures of bondage.

- As slavery came under mounting attack, white southerners developed a set of arguments defending slavery as a positive good.

Additional Reading

The reports of Frederick Law Olmsted, who traveled through the South in the 1850s, make a fascinating jumping-off point for a first look at the region. Much of Olmsted's material is conveniently collected in Lawrence Powell, ed., *The Cotton Kingdom* (1984). A contrasting approach to traveling about is to stay at one plantation, as Erskine Clarke does in his brilliant *Dwelling Place: A Plantation Epic* (2005). Based on meticulous research, this upstairs/downstairs saga profiles the intertwined lives of masters and slaves on a Georgia coastal plantation from 1805–1869. James Oakes, *Slavery and Freedom* (1990), and William W. Freehling, *The Road to Disunion* (1990), are good syntheses that analyze the diversity and the contradictions of the antebellum South.

Although old, Frank Owsley's *Plain Folk of the Old South* (1949), about southern yeoman farmers, is still useful and can be supplemented by Samuel C. Hyde Jr., ed., *Plain Folk of the South Revisited* (1997). The lives of upper-class southern white women and their servants are analyzed in Elizabeth Fox-Genovese, *Within the Plantation Household* (1988), while Victoria E. Bynum, *Unruly Women* (1992), deals with white and black women of lower status.

The best exploration of slavery as a labor system remains Kenneth M. Stampp, *The Peculiar Institution* (1956), but the most perceptive treatment of slave culture is Eugene D. Genovese, *Roll, Jordan, Roll* (1974). Charles Joyner, *Down by the Riverside* (1984), sensitively recreates slave culture in the rice districts, and Wilma A. Dunaway, *The African-American Family in Slavery and Emancipation* (2002), focuses on plantations in the mountain South (and in doing so challenges the prevailing view that slaves carved out a modicum of autonomy within bondage). John Hope Franklin and Loren Schweninger, *Runaway Slaves* (1999), details an important aspect of slave resistance. Walter Johnson, *Soul by Soul: Life Inside the Antebellum Slave Market* (1999), provides a concrete and chilling view of the trade that helped sustain the Peculiar Institution. Ira Berlin, *Slaves Without Masters* (1974), is an excellent account of southern free blacks. As for the political and ideological aspects of slavery, consult Drew Faust, *A Sacred Circle* (1977), and William J. Cooper, Jr., *The Politics of Slavery* (1978).

For a fuller list of readings, see the Bibliography at www.mhhe.com/davidsonnation6.

Soñtag var San Miguel. Santa Fé.
NeuMexico.

Strangers on the Great Plains

At first the Crows, Arapahos, and other Indians of the Great Plains paid little attention to the new people moving out from the forests far to the east. After all, for as long as they could remember, nations such as the Crow had called the plains their own. But the new arrivals were not to be taken lightly. Armed with superior weapons and bringing with them a great many women and children, they seemed to have an unlimited appetite for land. They attacked the villages of the Plains Indians, ruthlessly massacred women and children, and forced defeated enemies to live on reservations and serve their economic interests. In little more than a century and a half—from the first days when only a handful of their hunters and trappers had come into the land—they had become the masters of the northern plains.

The invaders who established this political and military dominance were *not* the strange "white men," who also came from the forest. During the 1830s and early 1840s, whites were still few in number. The more dangerous people—the ones who truly worried the Plains tribes—were the Sioux.

Westward expansion is usually told as a one-dimensional tale, centering on the wagon trains pressing on toward the Pacific. But frontiers, after all, are the transition lines between different cultures or environments, and during the nineteenth century those in the West were constantly shifting and adapting. Frontiers moved not only east to west, as with the white and the Sioux migrations, but also south to north, as Spanish culture diffused, and west to east, as Asian immigrants came to California. Furthermore, frontiers marked not only human but also animal boundaries. Horses, cattle, and pigs, all of which had been imported from Europe, moved across the continent, usually in advance of European settlers. Often they transformed the way Indian peoples lived. Frontiers could also be technological, as in the case of trade goods like firearms. Moreover, as we have already seen, disease moved across the continent with disastrous consequences for natives who had not acquired immunity to European microorganisms.

Three frontiers revolutionized the lives of the Sioux: those of the horse, the gun, and disease. The horse frontier spread ahead of white settlement from the southwest, where horses had first been imported by the Spanish. The Spanish,

Throughout the Spanish and Mexican periods, town life in California, New Mexico, and Texas revolved around central plazas and their churches. One of the first structures built in Santa Fe, the Mission Church of San Miguel (est. c. 1610) is today the oldest church building in the present-day United States. The painting at left, executed in 1882 by the German artist Rudolf Cronau, shows San Miguel in some disrepair but still surrounded by Sunday worshipers.

375

The horse frontier, moving onto the Great Plains from the southwest, and the gun frontier, crossing from the opposite direction in the northeast, contributed to the turbulence of the trans-Mississippi West in the mid-nineteenth century. In 1875 a Kiowa Indian named Koba drew this picture of a Kiowa on horseback. He carries a rifle and the dots surrounding the figure represent musket balls that have been fired.

however—unlike English and French traders—generally refused to sell firearms to Indians, so the gun frontier moved in the opposite direction, from northeast to southwest. The two waves met and crossed along the upper Missouri during the first half of the eighteenth century. For the people that possessed them, horses provided greater mobility, both for hunting bison and for fighting. Guns, too, conferred obvious advantages, and the arrival of these new elements inaugurated an extremely unsettled era for Plains Indian cultures.

The Sioux were first lured from the forest onto the Minnesota prairie during the early 1700s to hunt beaver, whose pelts could be exchanged with white traders for manufactured goods. Having obtained guns in exchange for furs, the Sioux drove the Omahas, Otos, Cheyennes, and Missouris (who had not yet acquired guns) south and west. But by the 1770s their advantage in guns had disappeared, and any farther advance was blocked by powerful tribes such as the Mandans, Hidatsas, and Arikaras. These peoples were primarily horticultural, raising corn, beans, and squash and living in well-fortified towns. They also owned more horses than the Sioux; thus it was easier for them to resist attacks.

But the third frontier, disease, threw the balance of power toward the Sioux after 1779. That year, a continental small-pox pandemic struck the plains via Louisiana. Those who raised crops were hit especially hard because they lived in densely populated villages, where the epidemic spread more easily. The Sioux embarked on a second wave of westward expansion in the late eighteenth century, so that by the time Lewis and Clark came through in 1804, they firmly controlled the upper Missouri as far as the Yellowstone River.

The Sioux's nomadic life, centered on the buffalo hunt, enabled them to avoid the worst ravages of disease, especially the smallpox epidemic of 1837, which reduced the plains population by as much as half. Indeed, the Sioux became the most populous people on the plains and were the only group whose high birthrate approximated that of whites. From an estimated 5,000 in 1804, they grew to 25,000 in the 1850s. Their numbers increased Sioux military power as well as the need for new hunting grounds, and during the first half of the nineteenth century, they pushed even farther up the Missouri, conquered the plains west of the Black Hills, and won control of the hunting grounds on the Platte River.

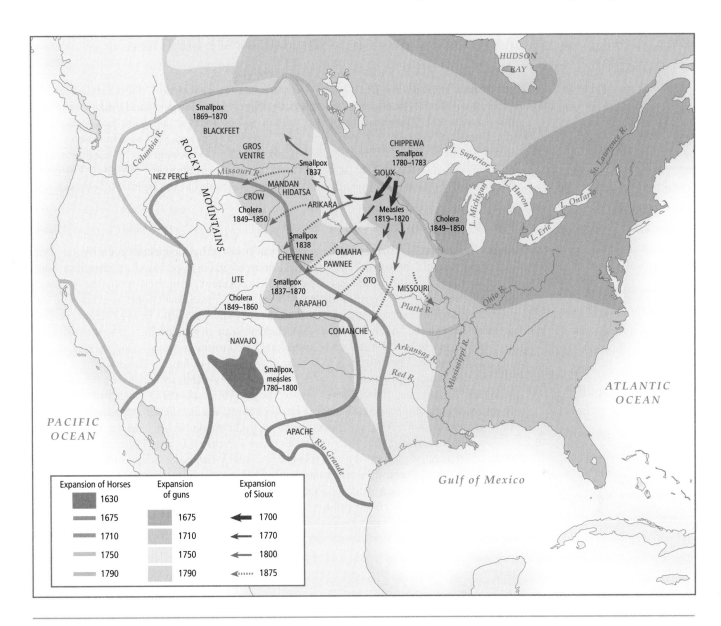

Sioux Expansion and the Horse and Gun Frontiers   *In 1710 the horse and gun frontiers had not yet crossed, but by 1750 the two waves began to overlap. The Sioux pushed west during the early eighteenth century thanks to firearms; they were checked from further expansion until the 1770s, when smallpox epidemics again turned the balance in their favor.*

These shifting frontiers of animals, disease, firearms, and trade goods disrupted the political and cultural life of the Great Plains. And as white Americans moved westward, their own frontier lines produced similar disruptions, not only between white settlers and Indians but also between Anglo-American and Hispanic cultures. The relations between Indian peoples and Mexico were also in flux, as many tribes across the Plains began attacking Mexicans during the 1830s. There would even be a frontier moving west to east, as thousands of Chinese were drawn, as were other immigrants from North and South America, Australia, and Hawaii, to gold fields discovered after 1849.

Ironically, perhaps the greatest instability created by the moving frontiers occurred in established American society. As the political system of the United States struggled to incorporate territories, the North and South engaged in a fierce debate over whether the new lands should become slave or free. Just as the Sioux's cultural identity was brought into question by moving frontiers, so too was the identity of the American Republic.

Cultural Interaction

Manifest (and Not So Manifest) Destiny

Manifest Destiny

"Make way . . . for the young American Buffalo—he has not yet got land enough," roared one American politician in 1844. In the space of a few years, the United States acquired Texas, New Mexico, California, the lower half of the Oregon Territory, and the lands between the Rockies and California: nearly 1.5 million square miles in all. John L. O'Sullivan, a prominent Democratic editor in New York, struck a responsive chord when he declared that it had become the United States' "manifest destiny to overspread the continent allotted by Providence for the free development of our yearly multiplying millions." The cry of **Manifest Destiny** soon echoed in other editorial pages and in the halls of Congress.

The Roots of the Doctrine

Many Americans had long believed that their country had a special, even divine, mission, which could be traced back to the Puritans' attempt to build a "city on a hill." Manifest Destiny also contained a political component, inherited from the ideology of the Revolution. In the mid–nineteenth century, Americans spoke of extending democracy, with widespread suffrage among white males, no king or aristocracy, and no established church, "over the whole North American continent."

Americans believed that their social and economic system, too, should spread around the globe. They pointed to its broad ownership of land, individualism, and free play of economic opportunity as superior features of American life. More importantly, Manifest Destiny was about power, especially economic power. American business interests recognized the value of the fine harbors along the Pacific Coast, which promised a lucrative trade with Asia, and they hoped to make those harbors American.

Racism

Finally, underlying the doctrine of Manifest Destiny was a widespread racism. The same belief in racial superiority that was used to justify Indian removal under Jackson, to uphold slavery in the South, and to excuse segregation in the North also proved handy to defend expansion westward. The United States had a duty to regenerate the backward peoples of America, declared politicians and propagandists. Their reference was not so much to Indians: the forced expulsion of assimilated Cherokees during Indian removal made clear what most American policy makers thought about Indian "regeneration." By

With the Star of Empire blazing from her forehead, the Spirit of Progress dominates John Gast's painting Manifest Destiny. *Indians and wild animals retreat in the face of advancing progress, illustrated by white settlers and farmers, railroads and other forms of transportation, telegraph lines, schools symbolized by a book, and, in the distance, cities. In reality, the movement of the frontier was hardly one-dimensional, as Hispanic, Indian, Asian, and white cultures clashed.*

the 1840s it was rather the Mexicans who had caught the attention of Manifest Destiny's prophets of progress. The Mexican race "must amalgamate and be lost, in the superior vigor of the Anglo-Saxon race," proclaimed O'Sullivan's *Democratic Review,* "or they must utterly perish."

Before 1845 most Americans assumed that expansion would be achieved without international war. American settlement would expand westward, and when the time was right, neighboring provinces, like ripe fruit, would fall naturally into American hands. Texas, New Mexico, Oregon, and California—areas that were sparsely populated and weakly defended—dominated the American expansionist imagination. With time, Americans became less willing to wait patiently for the fruit to fall.

In addition to baptism and an education in certain crafts and skills, Christian missions in California and elsewhere offered native people food, clothing, and sanctuary in a rapidly changing world. Oftentimes missions were also places of harsh discipline, physical coercion, and rampant disease. The Ohlone or Costanoan people pictured here are native to northern California and were drawn or coerced into missions starting in the 1760s.

The Mexican Borderlands

The heart of Spain's American empire was Mexico City, where spacious boulevards spread out through the center of the city and the University of Mexico, the oldest university in North America, had been accepting students since 1553, a full 85 years earlier than Harvard. From the Mexican point of view, the frontier was 1,000 miles to the north, a four-week journey to Texas, another two weeks to New Mexico, and three months by land and sea to the missions of California. Being so isolated, these Mexican provinces developed largely free from royal supervision.

California's settlements were anchored by four coastal *presidios,* or forts, at San Diego, Santa Barbara, Monterey, and San Francisco. Between them lay 21 Catholic missions run by a handful of Franciscans (there were only 36 in 1821). The missions controlled enormous tracts of land on which grazed gigantic herds of cattle, sheep, and horses. The animals and irrigated fields were tended by about 20,000 Indians, who in certain regards lived and worked like slaves.

California Society

When Mexico won its independence from Spain in 1821, California at first was little affected. But in 1833 the Mexican Congress stripped the Catholic church of its vast landholdings. These lands were turned over to Mexican cattle ranchers, usually in massive grants of 50,000 acres or more. The new *rancheros* ruled their estates much like great planters of the Old South. Labor was provided by Indians, who once again were forced to work for little more than room and board. Indeed, the mortality rate of Indian workers was twice that of southern slaves and four times that of the Mexican Californians. At this time the Mexican population of California was approximately 4,000. During the 1820s and 1830s Yankee traders set up shop in California in order to buy cattle hides for the growing shoe industry at Lynn and elsewhere. Still, in 1845 the American population in California amounted to only 700.

Spanish settlement of New Mexico was denser than that of California: the province had about 44,000 Spanish-speaking inhabitants in 1827. But as in California, its society was dominated by *ranchero* families that grazed large herds of sheep along the upper Rio Grande valley between El Paso and Taos. A few individuals controlled most of the wealth, while their workers eked out a meager living. Mining of copper and gold was a side industry, and here too the profits enriched a small upper class. Spain had long outlawed any commerce with Americans, but after Mexico declared its independence in 1821, yearly caravans from the United States began making the long journey along the Santa Fe Trail. Although this trade flourished over the next two decades,

New Mexico

developments in the third Mexican borderland, neighboring Texas, worsened relations between Mexico and the United States.

The Texas Revolution

American Immigration to Texas

At first, the new government in Mexico encouraged American immigration to Texas, where only about 3,000 Mexicans, mostly ranchers, lived. In 1821 Moses Austin, an American, received a grant from the Spanish government to establish a colony. After his death, his son Stephen took over the project, laying out the little town of San Felipe de Austin along the Brazos River and offering large grants of land at almost no cost. By 1824 the colony's population exceeded 2,000. Stephen Austin was only the first of a new wave of American land agents, or *empresarios,* that obtained permission from Mexican authorities to settle families in Texas. Ninety percent of the new arrivals came from the South. Many, intending to grow cotton, brought slaves.

Cultural Conflict

Tensions between Mexicans and American immigrants grew with the Texas economy. Most settlers from the States were Protestant. Although the Mexican government did not insist that all new citizens become Catholic, it did officially bar Protestant churches. In 1829 Mexico abolished slavery, then looked the other way when Texas slaveholders evaded the law. In the early 1830s the Mexican government began to have second thoughts about American settlement and passed laws prohibiting any new immigration. Austin likened the new anti-immigration laws to "trying to stop the Mississippi with a dam of straw." It was an apt metaphor: between 1830 and 1833 illegal American immigrants and their slaves flooded into Mexican Texas, nearly doubling its colonial population.

The Mexican Borderlands

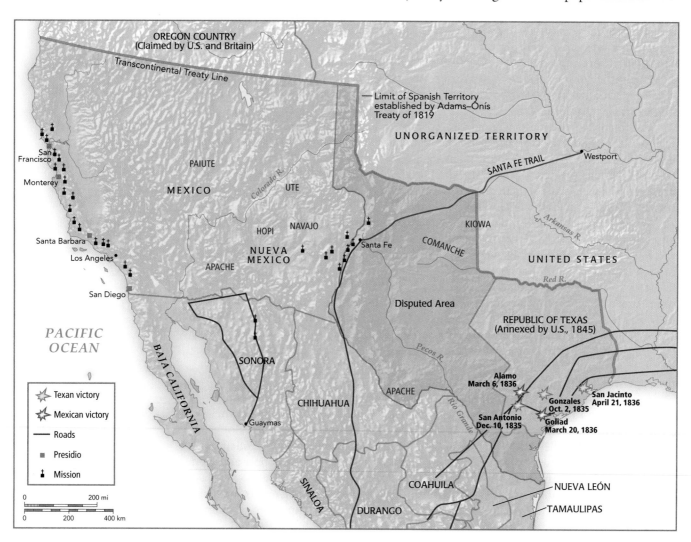

Growing Tensions

Admitting that the new regulations had served only to inflame Texans, Mexico repealed them in 1833. But by then colonial ill-will had ballooned along with the population. By mid-decade the American white population of 40,000 was nearly 10 times the number of Mexicans in the territory. Once again Mexico's government talked of abolishing slavery in Texas. Even more disturbing to the American newcomers, in 1834 President Antonio López de Santa Anna and his allies in the Mexican Congress began passing legislation that took power away from the states and concentrated it in Mexico City. Texans had been struggling for more autonomy, not less. When Santa Anna brutally suppressed an uprising against the central government in the state of Zacatecas, Texans grew all the more nervous. Finally, when conflicts over taxes led Santa Anna to march an army north and enforce his new regime, a ragtag Texas army drove back the advance party and then captured Mexican troops in nearby San Antonio. A full-scale rebellion was under way.

The Texas Republic

As Santa Anna massed his forces, a provisional government on March 2, 1836, proclaimed Texan independence. The document was signed by a number of prominent **Tejanos,** Mexican residents of Texas. The constitution of the new Republic of Texas borrowed heavily from the U.S. Constitution, except that it explicitly prohibited the new Texas Congress from interfering with slavery. Meanwhile, Santa Anna's troops overran a Texan garrison at an old mission in San Antonio, known as the Alamo, and killed all its 187 defenders—including the famous backwoodsman and U.S. congressman, Davy Crockett. The Mexicans, however, paid dearly for the victory, losing more than 1,500 men. The massacre of another force at Goliad after it surrendered further inflamed American resistance.

The Alamo

But anger was one thing; organized resistance was another. The commander of the Texas forces was Sam Houston, a former governor of Tennessee. Physically gifted and something of an eccentric, Houston had a flair for wearing colorful clothing to attract attention. His political career in Tennessee might have continued, except that the failure of his marriage led him to resign abruptly as governor and go live with the Cherokees. Eventually he made his way to Texas, where his intellectual ability and unexcelled talent as a stump speaker propelled him to the forefront of the independence movement. Steadily retreating eastward, Houston tried to discipline his fighting force and wait for an opportunity to counterattack.

Sam Houston

That opportunity came in late April. Reinforced by eager volunteers from the United States, Houston's army surprised Santa Anna's force when spies revealed that they were resting unaware near the San Jacinto River. Admonished to "remember the Alamo," Houston's men burst upon the stunned Mexican force, killing dozens in a brief battle. Driven by revenge, the Texans then pursued the fleeing Mexican soldiers and massacred hundreds. By day's end 630 Mexicans lay dead on the field (compared to only nine Texans), and a humiliated Santa Anna had been taken into custody.

Threatened with execution, the Mexican commander signed treaties recognizing Texan independence and ordering his remaining troops south of the Rio Grande. Texans would later claim that Santa Anna thereby acknowledged the Rio Grande to be Texas's southern boundary. The Mexican Congress repudiated the agreement, especially the claim to the Rio Grande. Over the next decade both sides engaged in low-level border conflict, but neither had the power to mount a successful invasion. In the meantime, Houston assumed office in October 1836 as president of the new republic, determined to bring Texas into the American Union as quickly as possible.

Texan Independence

As an old Tennessee protégé of Andrew Jackson, Houston assumed that the United States would quickly annex such a vast and inviting territory. But Jackson worried that any such move would revive sectional tensions and hurt Martin Van Buren's chances in the 1836 presidential election. Only on his last day in office did he extend formal diplomatic recognition to the Texas Republic. Van Buren, distracted by the economic panic that broke out shortly after he entered office, took no action during his term.

Rebuffed, Texans decided to go their own way. In the 10 years following independence, the Lone Star Republic attracted more than 100,000 immigrants by offering free land to settlers. Mexico refused to recognize Texan independence, and the vast majority of its citizens still wished to join the United States, where most of them, after all, had been born. There matters stood when the Whigs and William Henry Harrison won the presidency in 1840.

The Trek West

As thousands of white Americans were moving into Texas, and increasingly bringing slaves with them, a much smaller trickle headed toward the Oregon country. Since 1818 the United States and Great Britain had occupied that territory jointly, as far north as latitude 54°40′. Although white settlement remained sparse, by 1836 American settlers outnumbered the British in the Willamette valley.

Pushed by the Panic of 1837 and six years of depression and pulled by tales of Oregon's lush, fertile valleys and the healthy, frost-free climate along California's Sacramento River, many American farmers struck out for the West Coast. Missouri was "cleaned" out of money, worried farmer Daniel Waldo, and his wife was even more adamant about heading west: "If you want to stay here another summer and shake your liver out with the fever and ague, you can do it," she announced to her husband, "but in the spring I am going to take the children and go to Oregon, Indians or no Indians." The wagon trains began rolling west.

The Overland Trail

Migration West

Only a few hundred emigrants reached the West in 1841 and 1842, but in 1843 more than 800 followed the Overland Trail across the mountains to Oregon. From then on, they came by the thousands. Every spring brought a new rush of families to Independence or later to St. Joseph, Missouri, or to Council Bluffs, Iowa, where they waited for the spring rains to end and the trails to become passable. The migration was primarily a family enterprise, and many couples had only recently married. Most adults were between 20 and 50 years old; the hard journey discouraged the elderly. Furthermore, a family of four needed about $600 to outfit its journey, an amount that excluded the poor.

Caravans of 20 to 30 wagons were not uncommon the first few years, but after 1845 parties traveled in smaller trains of 8 to 10 wagons. The livestock of large companies ate up the prairie grass quickly, disagreements were more likely, and breakdowns (and hence halts) were more frequent. The trip itself lasted about 6 months, since the wagons normally covered only 15 miles a day, and the weather, repairs, deaths, and other eventualities necessitated occasional halts.

Women on the Overland Trail

The journey west often placed a special strain on women. Few wives were as eager as Daniel Waldo's to undertake the journey. "Poor Ma said only this morning, 'Oh I wish we never had started,'" one daughter reported, "and she looks so sorrowful and dejected." In one study of Oregon-bound parties, three-fourths of the women did not want to make the move.

Breakdown of Women's Traditional Role

At first, parties divided work by gender, as had been done back home. Women cooked, washed, sewed, and took care of the children, while men drove the wagons, cared for the stock, stood guard, and did the heavy labor. Necessity placed new demands on women, however, and eventually altered their roles. Within a few weeks, they found themselves helping to repair wagons and construct bridges. When men became exhausted, sick, or injured, women stood guard and drove the oxen. The change in work assignments proceeded only in one direction, however, for few men undertook "women's work."

As women strove to maintain a semblance of home on the trail, they often experienced a profound sense of loss. Trains often worked or traveled on the Sabbath, which had been ladies' day back home and an emblem of women's moral authority. Women also felt the lack of close companions to whom they could turn for comfort.

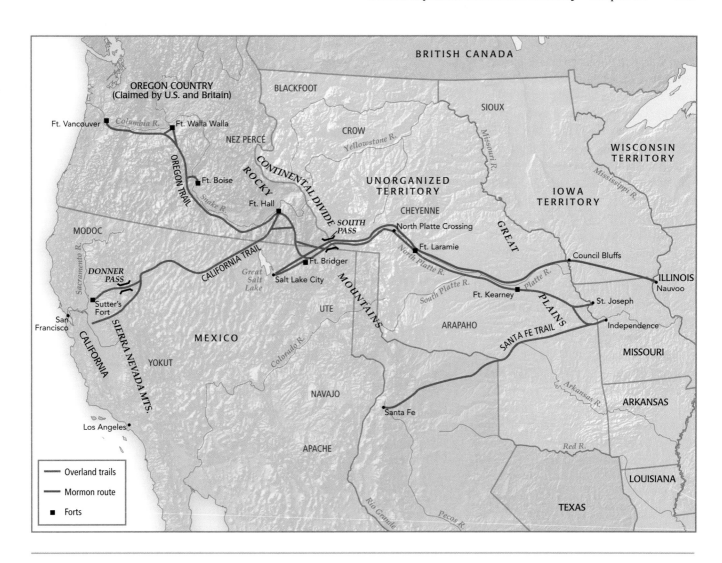

The Overland Trail   *Beginning at several different points, the Overland Trail followed the Platte and Sweetwater rivers across the plains to South Pass, where it crossed the Continental Divide. The trail split again near Fort Hall. Between 1840 and 1860 more than a quarter of a million emigrants made the trek. Following news of the gold strikes in 1848, the flow of westward emigrants increased and shifted toward California.*

One woman, whose husband separated their wagon from the train after a dispute, sadly watched the other wagons pull away: "I felt that indeed I had left all my friends to journey over the dreaded plains without one female acquaintance even for a companion—of course I wept and grieved about it but to no purpose."

Often fatigued, their sense of moral authority eroded, and their ultimate home uncertain, women complained, as one put it, that "we had left all civilization behind us." Civilization to women meant more than law, government, and schools; it also meant their homes and domestic mission. Once settled in the West, they strove to reestablish that order.

Women's Sense of Loss

Indians and the Trail Experience

The nations whose lands were crossed by white wagon trains reacted in a number of ways to the westward tide. The Sioux, who had long been trading with whites, were among the peoples who regularly visited overlanders to trade for blankets, clothes, cows, rifles, and knives. But the white migrants took a heavy toll on the Plains Indians' way of life: emigrant parties scared off game and reduced buffalo herds, overgrazed the grass, and depleted the supply of wood. Having petitioned unsuccessfully in 1846 for government compensation, some Sioux decided to demand payment from

Pressures on the Plains Indians

In an era when traveling circuses proved a welcome though rare attraction, Americans used the expression "I have seen the elephant" to indicate they had gotten all—or considerably more than—they had bargained for. To the quarter of a million men and women who migrated overland to the Pacific coast, "seeing the elephant" meant ceasing to be a greenhorn by overcoming hardship and succeeding. The greeting "Have you seen the elephant?" became the unofficial password of the Overland Trail.

Some walked, rode horseback, or accompanied mule pack trains, but the overwhelming majority of emigrants traveled in wagons. Wagons could haul more pounds per animal, did not have to be packed each day, could carry the sick and injured, and could be arranged in a defensive circle at night. Most often, emigrants modified a common farm wagon, about 10 feet long. The wooden wagon bed, made of seasoned hardwood to withstand

Joseph Goldsborough Bruff, who traveled the Overland Trail to California, drew this picture of a Platte River crossing.

extreme heat, cold, and moisture, was arched over by cloth or waterproofed canvas that could be closed at each end.

Pulled usually by four to six oxen, one wagon could carry provisions and

gear for a family of four. Most farm families were larger, however, and took at least one additional wagon. Packed within was a supply of bacon, breadstuffs (mostly flour), and coffee. For sleeping,

the wagon trains crossing their lands. Whether parties paid or not depended on the relative strength of the two groups, but whites complained bitterly of what seemed to them outright robbery.

Their fears aroused by sensational stories, overland parties were wary of Indians, but this menace was greatly exaggerated, especially on the plains. Few wagon trains were attacked by Indians, and less than 4 percent of deaths on the trail were caused by Indians. In truth, emigrants killed more Indians than Indians killed emigrants. For overlanders the most aggravating problem posed by native peoples was theft of stock. Many companies received valuable assistance from Indians, who acted as guides, directed them to grass and water, and transported stock and wagons across rivers.

As trail congestion and conflict increased, the government constructed a string of protective forts and in 1851 summoned Plains Indians to a conference at Fort Laramie. The U.S. government agreed to make an annual payment as compensation for the damages caused by the wagon trains but also required tribes to confine themselves to areas north or south of a corridor through which the Overland Trail ran. Some tribes were unwilling to surrender their freedom of movement and refused to agree. The Sioux, the most powerful people on the plains, signed and then ignored the terms.

The Political Origins of Expansion

President William Henry Harrison made the gravest mistake of his brief presidential career when he ventured out one raw spring day, bareheaded and without an overcoat, to buy groceries at the Washington markets. He caught pneumonia and died only one month after his inauguration.

families brought blankets and frequently a tent; a well-equipped wagon might have a feather bed laid over the packed possessions in the wagon. Parents normally slept there for privacy while children used the tent.

Before starting, the adult male members of a company elected their leaders and adopted a set of rules of the road. Still, disputes inevitably arose, and leaders were sometimes deposed midjourney. "If you think it's any snap to run a wagon train of 66 wagons with every man in the train having a different idea of what is the best thing to do, all I can say is that some day you ought to try it," commented one traveler.

As the journey settled into a routine, women rose before daybreak to cook breakfast and food for lunch; the men followed around five to care for the animals; the train was off at seven with the call of a bugle. Men and older sons walked alongside the team or herded stock in the rear. Women and children could ride in the wagon as it jolted along, but before long they walked as much as possible to conserve the animals' strength. After a noonday stop for a cold lunch, the journey resumed; by midafternoon the men seemed almost asleep as they plodded under the baking sun beside their teams. At evening camp the men attended to the animals while the women and children collected buffalo dung for fuel and hauled water. Women cooked the evening meal and afterward washed the dishes, took care of the bedding, cleaned the wagons, aired provisions, and mended clothes. After a guard was posted, the exhausted emigrants turned in for the night.

The final third of the route lay across deserts, along twisting rivers with difficult crossings, on paths barely wide enough for a wagon. Wagons had to be double- and triple-teamed up steep grades and hoisted over canyon walls with ropes, chains, and winches. Because most wagons lacked brakes, drivers locked the wheels when going down steep slopes, dragged a weight behind, or lowered the wagon by a rope attached to a tree.

Improvements in the 1850s shortened the trip and reduced the hardships. Still, it required considerable courage to embark on the journey. "To enjoy such a trip," an anonymous overlander testified, "a man must be able to endure heat like a Salamander, . . . dust like a toad, and labor like a jackass. He must learn to eat with his unwashed fingers, drink out of the same vessel with his mules, sleep on the ground when it rains, and share his blanket with vermin. . . . It is a hardship without glory." When they reached their new homes, those who traveled the Overland Trail could boast that they had, indeed, seen the elephant.

Tyler Becomes President

For the first time in the nation's history, a vice president succeeded to the nation's highest office on the death of the president. John Tyler of Virginia had been a Democrat who supported states' rights so strongly that, during the nullification crisis, he was the only senator to vote against the Force Bill (see page 309). After that, Jackson and the Democrats would have nothing to do with him, so Tyler joined the Whigs despite his strict constructionist principles. In 1840 the Whigs put him on the ticket with Harrison in order to balance the ticket sectionally. In the rollicking 1840 campaign, the Whigs sang all too accurately: "And we'll vote for Tyler, therefore, / Without a why or wherefore."

Tyler's Texas Ploy

Tyler Breaks with the Whigs

Tyler's courteous manner and personal warmth masked a rigid mind. Repeatedly, when Henry Clay and the Whigs in Congress passed a major bill, Tyler opposed it. After Tyler twice vetoed bills to charter a new national bank, disgusted congressional Whigs formally expelled their president from the party. Most Democrats, too, avoided him as an untrustworthy "renegade."

Tyler, in short, was a man without a party. Surrounded by a group of flatterers, the president could claim almost no support except among federal officeholders, who could be fired if they did not endorse him. Still, Tyler's ambition led him to believe that he might win another four years in the White House if only he latched onto the right popular issue. Nursing their own personal and political dreams, his advisers began to whisper in his ear that that issue was the annexation of Texas.

The Texas Movement

That advice came mostly from Democrats disgruntled with Martin Van Buren. Jackson's successor was, in their eyes, an ineffective leader who had stumbled through

Election of 1844

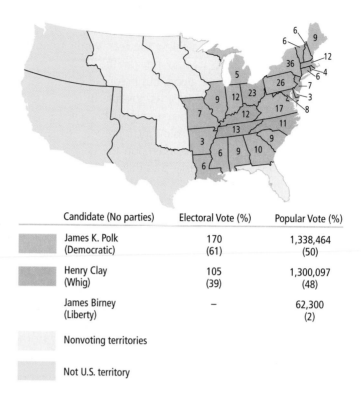

Candidate (No parties)	Electoral Vote (%)	Popular Vote (%)
James K. Polk (Democratic)	170 (61)	1,338,464 (50)
Henry Clay (Whig)	105 (39)	1,300,097 (48)
James Birney (Liberty)	–	62,300 (2)
Nonvoting territories		
Not U.S. territory		

a depression and in 1840 gone down in ignominious defeat. "They mean to throw Van overboard," reported one delighted Whig, who caught wind of the plans. Meanwhile, Tyler's allies launched rumors designed to frighten southerners into pushing for annexation. Britain was ready to offer economic aid if Texas would abolish slavery, they claimed. (The rumor was false.) In April 1844 Tyler sent to the Senate for ratification a treaty he had secretly negotiated to bring Texas into the Union.

Van Overboard

The front runners for the Whig and Democratic presidential nominations were Clay and Van Buren. Although rivals, they were both moderates who feared the slavery issue. Apparently by prearrangement, both men issued letters opposing annexation on the grounds that it threatened the Union and would provoke war with Mexico.

As expected, the Whigs unanimously nominated Clay on a platform that ignored the expansion issue entirely. The Democrats, however, had a more difficult time. Those who opposed Van Buren persuaded the Democratic convention to adopt a rule requiring a two-thirds vote to nominate a candidate. That blocked Van Buren's nomination. *Polk's Nomination* On the ninth ballot the delegates finally turned to James K. Polk of Tennessee, who was pro-Texas. The 1844 Democratic platform called for the "reannexation" of Texas (under the dubious claim it had been part of the Louisiana Purchase) and the "reoccupation" of Oregon, all the way to its northernmost boundary at 54°40′.

Angered by the convention's outcome, Van Buren's supporters in the Senate joined the Whigs in decisively defeating Tyler's treaty of annexation. Tyler eventually withdrew from the race as an independent candidate, but the Texas issue would not go away. Henry Clay found many southerners slipping out of his camp because he opposed annexation; backtracking, he announced that he would be glad to see Texas annexed if it could be done without war or dishonor and without threatening the Union. And in the North, a few antislavery Whigs turned to James G. Birney, running on the Liberty party ticket.

In the end, Polk squeaked through by 38,000 votes out of nearly 3 million cast. If just half of Birney's 15,000 ballots in New York had gone to Clay, he would have carried the state and been narrowly elected president. Indignant Whigs charged that by refusing to support Clay, political abolitionists had made the annexation of Texas, and hence the addition of slave territory to the Union, inevitable. And indeed, Tyler again asked Congress to annex Texas—this time by a joint resolution, which required only a majority in both houses rather than a two-thirds vote for a treaty in the Senate. In the new atmosphere following Polk's victory, the resolution narrowly passed, and on March 3, 1845, his last day in office, Tyler invited Texas to enter the Union.

Election of 1844

To the Pacific

Polk pursued his objectives as president with a dogged determination. Humorless, calculating, and often deceitful, he was not particularly brilliant in his maneuvering. But the life of politics consumed him, he knew his mind, and he could take the political pounding by his opponents. Embracing a continental vision of the United States, Polk not only endorsed Tyler's offer of annexation but also looked beyond, hoping to gain the three best harbors on the Pacific: San Diego, San Francisco, and Puget Sound. That meant wresting Oregon from Britain and California from Mexico.

Claiming that the American title was "clear and unquestionable," the new president brushed aside any notion of continuing joint occupation of Oregon with Britain. To pressure the British, he induced Congress to give the required one-year notice terminating the joint occupation of Oregon. His blustering was reinforced by the knowledge that American settlers in Oregon outnumbered the British 5,000 to 750. On the other hand, Polk hardly wanted war with a nation as powerful as Great Britain. So when the British offered, in June 1846, to divide the Oregon Territory along the 49th parallel, he readily agreed (see map, page 401). Britain retained Vancouver Island, where the Hudson's Bay Company's headquarters was located. But the arrangement gave the United States Puget Sound, which had been the president's objective all along.

James K. Polk, continentalist (detail from an 1846 portrait by George Healy)

Provoking a War

The Oregon settlement left Polk free to deal with Mexico. In 1845 Congress admitted Texas to the Union as a slave state, but Mexico had never formally recognized Texas's independence. Mexico insisted, moreover, that Texas's southern boundary was the Nueces River, not the Rio Grande, 130 miles to the south, as claimed by Texas. In reality, Texas had never controlled the disputed region; the Nueces had always been Texas's boundary when it was a Mexican province; and if taken literally, the Rio Grande border incorporated most of New Mexico, including Santa Fe, Albuquerque, Taos, and other major towns. Few Texans had ever even been to these places. Indeed, the one time Texas tried to exert authority in the region, New Mexicans had to ride out onto the Plains to save the lost and starving expedition, and ultimately sent the men to Mexico City in chains. Nonetheless, Polk was already looking toward the Pacific and thus supported the Rio Grande boundary.

As soon as the Texans entered the union, Mexico broke off diplomatic relations with the United States, and Polk sent American troops under General Zachary Taylor into the newly acquired state. At the same time, knowing that the unstable Mexican government desperately needed money, he attempted to buy territory to the Pacific. Sending John Slidell of Louisiana to Mexico as his special minister, Polk was prepared to offer $2 million in return for clear title to the Rio Grande boundary, $5 million for the remaining part of New Mexico, and up to $25 million for California. But the Mexican public overwhelmingly opposed ceding any more territory to the land-hungry "Yankees" from the United States, and the government refused to receive Slidell. "Depend upon it," reported Slidell, as he departed from Mexico in March 1846, "we can never get along well with them, until we have given them a good drubbing."

Disputed Boundary of Texas

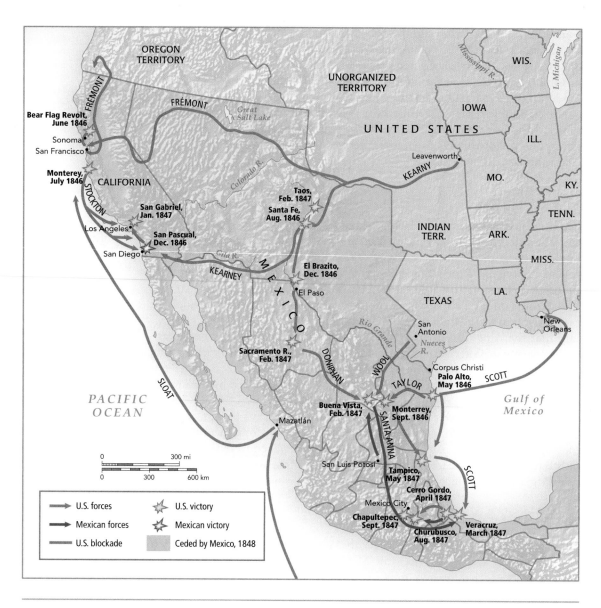

The U.S.–Mexican War

Blocked on the diplomatic front, Polk ordered Taylor, who had already crossed the Nueces with 4,000 troops, to proceed south to the Rio Grande. From the Mexican standpoint, the Americans had invaded their country and occupied their territory. For his part, Polk wanted to be in position to defend the disputed region if the two countries went to war. More importantly, once he realized that Mexico would not cave in to bullying diplomacy, Polk hoped that Taylor's position on the Rio Grande would provoke the Mexican army into starting a war.

By May 9 Polk and his cabinet had lost patience with the plan and decided to submit a war message to Congress without Mexican action. But on that day word arrived that two weeks earlier Mexican forces had crossed the Rio Grande and attacked some of Taylor's troops, killing 11 Americans. The president quickly rewrote his war message, placing the entire blame for the war on Mexico. "Mexico has passed the boundary of the United States, has invaded our territory, and shed American blood upon American soil," he told Congress on May 11. "War exists, and notwithstanding all our efforts to avoid it, exists by the act of Mexico herself." The administration sent a bill to Congress calling for volunteers and requesting money to supply American troops.

Indians and Mexicans

Mexican forces would often outnumber their American enemies in battle, but Mexico nonetheless suffered from critical disadvantages in the war. Chronic instability in its central government left the nation divided against itself in its moment of crisis. An empty national treasury fueled this instability and made it difficult to mobilize an effective response to the U.S. invasion. Mexico was also at a disadvantage in terms of military technology. While Mexican forces had to rely on bulky, fixed cannon, the U.S. army employed new light artillery that could be repositioned quickly as battles progressed. Light artillery would tip the balance in several crucial engagements.

Finally, much of Mexico had to fight two wars at once. While Mexico enjoyed formal diplomatic title to most of the present-day American West, Indians still controlled the vast majority of that territory, and Mexico had seen its relations with these Indians collapse in the 15 years before the U.S. invasion. During the late eighteenth century, Comanches, Navajos, Utes, and several different tribes of Apaches had made peace with Spanish authorities, ending decades of destructive war. Spaniards provided Indian leaders with gifts, guaranteed fair trade, and even handed out rations to minimize the animal thefts that could spark conflict.

This expensive and delicate system began to falter once Mexico achieved independence in 1821. Lacking the finances, the political unity, the stability, and the diplomatic resources of their Spanish predecessors, Mexican authorities watched the peace with northern Indians slip away. By the early 1830s, Native men were traveling hundreds of miles to raid Mexican ranches, haciendas, and towns, killing or capturing the people they found there, and stealing or destroying animals and other property. Whenever they were able, Mexicans did the same things to their Indian enemies. American markets helped drive the increasing violence, as Indian or white traders from the United States eagerly purchased horses and mules stolen from Mexico and supplied the raiders' arms and ammunition in return. By the eve of the U.S. invasion of Mexico the violence encompassed all or parts of nine Mexican states and had claimed thousands of Mexican and Indian lives.

The End of a Fragile Peace

Thus, when American troops invaded northern Mexico they were literally marching in the footsteps of Comanches and Apaches, traversing territory that had already endured more than a decade of war. As Indian peoples pursued their own political, strategic, and economic goals, they made it far easier for the United States to achieve its goals. Impoverished, exhausted, and divided, and facing ongoing Indian raids, few northern Mexicans were willing or able to resist the U.S. conquest and occupation.

The U.S. Mexican War

Opposition to the War

The war with Mexico posed a dilemma for Whigs. They were convinced (correctly) that Polk had provoked the conflict in order to acquire more territory from Mexico, and many northern Whigs accused the president of seeking to extend slavery. But they remembered, too, that the Federalist party had doomed itself to extinction by opposing the War of 1812. Throughout the conflict, they strenuously attacked the conduct of "Mr. Polk's War." But they could not bring themselves to cut off funding for the war.

Pro-war sentiment was strongest in the Old Southwest and most of the Old Northwest. It was much weaker in the East, where antislavery "Conscience Whigs" were prominent. "If I were a Mexican," Senator Thomas Corwin of Ohio affirmed in the Senate, "I would tell you, . . . 'we will greet you with bloody hands and welcome you to hospitable graves.'" With their party deeply divided over the issue of the expansion of slavery, Whigs opposed the acquisition of any territory from Mexico.

The Price of Victory

Even before any word of hostilities arrived in California, a group of impetuous American settlers around Sacramento launched the "Bear Flag Revolt." In June 1846 they

Hide and Go Seek

Reading Geopolitics from an Indian Quiver

Just as native peoples in Eastern North America could tip the balance of power between competing empires in the colonial era, Indians west of the Mississippi continued to exert influence over international events well into the nineteenth century. How can we trace such influence? A few precious sources from the period allow historians to glimpse things from Indian perspectives. Kiowas, for example, kept pictorial calendars painted on buffalo hides that memorialized two key events each year, one for summer and one for winter. The winter of 1840–1841 was memorialized as "Hide-quiver expedition winter" (see the illustration at right).

What was a "hide quiver"? By the 1840s, young Kiowa warriors preferred quivers made from sleek Mexican leather or panther skin to those made from buffalo hide, which only old men used. "Hide-quiver war expedition winter" refers to a campaign comprising older men who headed south into

Mexico. Traditionally Kiowas and Comanches left the older men behind to protect women and children and guard their herds of horses and mules. But in the summer of 1840 a historic peace agreement with their traditional Cheyenne and Arapaho enemies provided the Kiowas and Comanches with a newfound sense of security. When winter came, even aged warriors rode off to steal horses and mules from Mexicans. Bearing their dusky, outmoded quivers made of buffalo hide, they accompanied sons and nephews in raids hundreds of miles below the Rio Grande. Attacks such as these increased over the next several years and indirectly helped the United States win its war against Mexico.

proclaimed California an independent republic. American forces in the area soon put down any Mexican resistance, and by the following January California was safely in American hands.

Conquest of Mexico

Meanwhile, Taylor moved south from the Rio Grande and won several battles. At each town conquered or surrendered he read statements provided in advance by President Polk and the War Department, promising to respect private property and protect the long-suffering residents from Indian attack. Taylor's campaign culminated in a narrow victory over General Antonio López de Santa Anna at Buena Vista in southern Coahuila. Polk had gained the territory he sought to reach the Pacific and wanted an end to the war. But Mexico refused to surrender, so Polk ordered an invasion into the heart of the country.

After an American army commanded by General Winfield Scott captured Mexico City on September 14, 1847, Mexico agreed to come to terms. The two nations ratified a peace treaty in 1848. Including Texas, which Mexico had continued to lay claim to, the Treaty of Guadalupe Hidalgo transferred half of Mexico's territory—more than half a million square miles—to the United States. In return the United States recalled its army and ended its aggressive war. It also assumed all the outstanding claims that U.S. citizens had against Mexico and gave the Mexicans 15 million dollars.

Treaty of Guadalupe Hidalgo

The war had cost the United States $97 million and 13,000 American lives, mostly as a result of disease. Yet the real cost was even higher. By bringing vast new territories into the Union, the war forced the explosive slavery issue to the center of national politics and threatened to upset the balance of power between North and South. Ralph Waldo Emerson had been prophetic: "The United States will conquer Mexico," he

The fortified heights of Chapultepec fell in 1847 to Winfield Scott's invading forces, but not without fierce resistance by young Mexican cadets. Like the partisans of the Alamo, who gained fame in Texas lore, the defenders of Chapultepec won an honored place in Mexican history.

wrote when the U.S.–Mexican War began, "but it will be as the man who swallows the arsenic which brings him down in turn. Mexico will poison us."

The Rise of the Slavery Issue

When the second party system emerged during the 1820s, Martin Van Buren had championed political parties as one way to forge links between North and South that would strengthen the Union. But the Texas movement increased sectional suspicions, and President Polk did nothing to ease this problem.

Polk was a politician to his bones: constantly maneuvering, promising one thing, doing another, making a pledge, taking it back—using any means to accomplish his ends. Discontent over his double-dealing finally erupted in August 1846, when Polk requested $2 million from Congress, as he vaguely explained, to "facilitate negotiations" with Mexico. It was widely understood that the money was to be used to bribe the Mexican government to cede territory to the United States. On August 8 David Wilmot, an obscure Pennsylvania congressman, startled Democratic leaders by introducing an amendment to the bill that barred slavery from any territory acquired from Mexico. The Wilmot Proviso, as the amendment became known, passed the northern-controlled House of Representatives several times, only to be rejected in the Senate, where the South had more power. As such, it revealed mounting sectional tensions.

Northern Discontent

Wilmot Proviso

Wilmot himself was hardly an abolitionist. Indeed, he hoped to keep not only slaves but all black people out of the territories. Denying any "morbid sympathy for the slave," he declared, "I would preserve for white free labor a fair country . . . where the sons of toil, of my own race and color, can live without the disgrace which association with negro slavery brings upon free labor." The Wilmot Proviso aimed not to destroy slavery in the South but to confine the institution to those states where it already existed. Still, abolitionists had long contended that southern slaveholders—the "Slave

Power"—were plotting to extend their sway over the rest of the country. The political maneuverings of slaveholders such as Tyler, and especially Polk, convinced growing numbers of northerners that the Slave Power did indeed exist and that it was aggressively looking to expand its influence.

The status of slavery in the territories became more than an abstract question once the peace with Mexico had been finalized. The United States gained title to an immense territory, including all of what would become the states of California, Nevada, and Utah, nearly all of New Mexico, most of Arizona and Colorado, and parts of Wyoming, Kansas, and Oklahoma. With the United States in control of the Pacific Coast from San Diego to Puget Sound, Polk's continental vision had become a reality. But slavery would once again dominate national politics.

New Societies in the West

As Hispanic, Indian, Asian, and Anglo-American cultures interacted, the patterns of development along the frontier varied widely. Some newcomers recreated the farm economies and small towns of the Anglo-American East; others continued the cattle-ranching life of the Hispanic West. In California the new settlements were overwhelmingly shaped by the rush for gold after 1848. And in the Great Basin around Salt Lake, the Mormons established a society whose sense of religious mission was as strong as that of the Puritans.

Farming in the West

The overlanders expected to replicate the societies they had left behind. When a wagon train arrived at its destination, members had usually exhausted their resources and thus quickly scattered in search of employment or a good farm site. "Friday, October 27.—Arrived at Oregon City at the falls of the Willamette," read one pioneer diary. "Saturday, October 28.—Went to work."

In a process repeated over and over, settlers in a new area set up the machinery of government. Although violence was common on the frontier, farming communities tended to resolve problems by traditional means. Churches took longer to establish, for ministers were hard to recruit and congregations were often not large enough to support a church. As the population grew, however, a more conventional society evolved. Towns and a middle class developed, the proportion of women increased, schools were established, and the residents became less mobile.

Although opportunity was greater on the frontier and early arrivals had a special advantage, more and more the agricultural frontier of the West resembled the older society of the East. With the development of markets and transportation, wealth became concentrated, some families fell to the lower rungs of society, and those who were less successful left, seeking yet another fresh start.

The Gold Rush

In January 1848, while constructing a sawmill along the American River, James Marshall noticed gold flecks in the millrace. More discoveries followed, and when the news reached the East, it spread like wildfire. The following spring the Overland Trail was jammed with eager "forty-niners." Some 80,000 emigrants journeyed to California that year, about 55,000 of whom took the overland route. In only two years, from 1848 to the end of 1849, California's population jumped from 14,000 to 100,000. By 1860 it stood at 380,000.

Among those who went to California was William Swain, a 27-year-old farmer in western New York. Deciding that he had had enough of the hard work of farming, he bid good-bye to his wife and daughter in 1849 and set off for the gold fields to make his fortune. On his arrival in November, he entered a partnership and staked a claim along the Feather River, but after several months of back-breaking work in icy waters, he and his partners discovered that their claim was "worth nothing." He sold out and joined another company, but early rains soon forced them to stop work. In October 1850, after less than a year in the diggings, Swain decided to return home. With only a few hundred dollars to show for his labor, he counted himself one of the vast majority of miners who had seen "their bright daydreams of golden wealth vanish like the dreams of night." He arrived home the following February and resumed farming.

Predictably, mining the miners offered a more reliable road to prosperity. Perhaps half the inhabitants of a mining town were shopkeepers, businesspeople, and professionals who provided services for prospectors. Also conspicuous were gamblers, card sharks, and other outcasts, all bent on separating the miner from his riches.

With their distinctive clothing and bamboo hats, Chinese miners could be seen throughout the diggings. Chinese immigration reached a peak in 1852, when 20,000 arrived in California. In the heyday of the mining camps, perhaps 20 percent of the miners were Chinese. Confronted with intense hostility from other miners, they worked abandoned claims and unpromising sites with primitive and less expensive equipment.

Nativist and Racial Prejudices

More than 80 percent of the prospectors who poured into the gold country were Americans, including free blacks. Mexicans, Australians, Argentinians, Hawaiians, Chinese, French, English, and Irish also came. Observers praised the diggings' democratic spirit. Yet such assertions overlooked strongly held nativist prejudices: when frustrated by a lack of success, American miners directed their hostility toward foreigners. The miners ruthlessly exterminated the Indians in the area, sometimes hunting them for sport. Mob violence drove Mexicans out of nearly every camp, and the Chinese were confined to claims abandoned by Americans as unprofitable. The state eventually enacted a foreign miners' tax that fell largely on the Chinese. Free African Americans felt the sting of discrimination as well, both in the camps and in state law. White American miners proclaimed that "colored men were not privileged to work in a country intended only for American citizens."

Women in the Camps

Only about 5 percent of gold rush emigrants were women or children; given this relative scarcity, men were willing to pay top dollar for women's domestic skills. Women supported themselves by cooking, sewing, and washing, as well as by running hotels and boardinghouses. "A smart woman can do very well in this country," one woman informed a friend in the East. "It is the only country I ever was in where a woman received anything like a just compensation for work." Women went to the mining frontier to be with their husbands, to make money, or to find adventure. But the class most frequently seen in the diggings was prostitutes, who numbered perhaps 20 percent of female Californians in 1850.

Mining's Environmental Legacy

Before long, the most easily worked claims had been played out and large corporations moved in heavy equipment to get at hidden ore. This type of mining left a lasting environmental legacy. Abandoned prospect holes and diggings pockmarked the gold fields and created piles of debris that heavy rains would wash down the valley, choking streams and ruining lands below. Excavation of hillsides, construction of dams to divert rivers, and the destruction of the forest cover to meet the heavy demand for lumber and firewood caused serious erosion of the soil and severe flooding in the spring.

Instant City: San Francisco

When the United States assumed control of California, San Francisco had a population of perhaps 200. But thousands of emigrants took the water route west, passing through San Francisco's harbor on their way to the diggings. By 1856 the city's population had jumped to an astonishing 50,000. In a mere 8 years the city had attained the size New York had taken 190 years to reach.

San Francisco in 1850: Chaos and crowding

San Francisco's Chaotic Growth

The product of economic self-interest, San Francisco developed in helter-skelter fashion. Land prices soared, speculation was rampant, and commercial forces became paramount. Residents lived in tents or poorly constructed, half-finished buildings. To enlarge the commercial district, hills began to be leveled, with the dirt used to fill in the bay (thereby creating more usable land). Since the city government took virtually no role in directing development, almost no land was reserved for public use. Property owners defeated a proposal to widen the streets, prompting the city's leading newspaper to complain, "To sell a few more feet of lots, the streets were compressed like a cheese, into half their width."

The Migration from China

The gold rush that swelled San Francisco's streets was a global phenomenon. Americans predominated in the mining population, but Latin Americans, Europeans, Australians, and Chinese swarmed into California. An amazing assortment of languages could be heard on the city's streets: indeed, in 1860 San Francisco was 50 percent foreign-born.

The most distinctive ethnic group was the Chinese. They had come to Gum San, the land of the golden mountain. Those who arrived in California overwhelmingly hailed from the area of southern China around Canton—and not by accident. Although *Conditions in China* other provinces of China also suffered from economic distress, population pressures, social unrest, and political upheaval, Canton had a large European presence, since it was the only port open to outsiders. That situation changed after the first Opium War (1839–1842), when Britain forced China to open other ports to trade. For Cantonese, the sudden loss of their trade monopoly produced widespread economic hardship. At the same time, a series of religious and political revolts in the region led to severe fighting that devastated the countryside. A growing number of residents concluded that emigration was the only way to survive, and the presence of western ships in the harbors of Canton and nearby Hong Kong (a British possession since 1842) made it easier to migrate to California rather than to southeast Asia.

Between 1849 and 1854, some 45,000 Chinese flocked to California. Among those who went was 16-year-old Lee Chew, who left for California after a man from his village returned with great wealth from the "country of the American wizards." Like the other gold seekers, these Chinese immigrants were overwhelmingly young and male, and they wanted only to accumulate savings and return home to their families. (Indeed, only 16 Chinese women arrived before 1854.) Generally poor, Chinese immigrants arrived already in debt, having borrowed the price of their steamship ticket; they fell further into debt to Chinese merchants in San Francisco, who loaned them money to purchase needed supplies.

When the Chinese were harassed in the mines, many opened laundries in San Francisco and elsewhere, since little capital was required—soap, scrub board, iron, and ironing board. The going rate at the time for washing, ironing, and starching shirts was an exorbitant $8 per dozen. Many early San Franciscans actually found it cheaper to send their dirty laundry to Canton or Honolulu, to be returned several months later. Other Chinese around San Francisco set up restaurants or worked in the fishing industry. In these early years they found Americans less hostile, as long as they stayed away from the gold fields. As immigration and the competition for jobs increased, however, anti-Chinese sentiment intensified.

Occupations

Gradually, San Francisco took on the trappings of a more orderly community. The city government established a public school system, erected streetlights, created a municipal water system, and halted further filling in of the bay. Industry was confined to the area south of the city; several new working-class neighborhoods grew up near the downtown section. Fashionable neighborhoods sprouted on several hills, as high rents drove many residents from the developing commercial center, and churches and families became more common. By 1856, the city of the gold rush had been replaced by a new city whose stone and brick buildings gave it a new sense of permanence.

The Mormons in Utah

The makeshift, often chaotic society spawned by the gold rush was a product of largely uncontrolled economic forces. In contrast, the society evolving in the Great Basin of Utah exhibited an entirely different but equally remarkable growth. Salt Lake City became the center of a religious kingdom established by the Church of Jesus Christ of Latter-Day Saints.

After Joseph Smith's death in 1844 (see page 334), the Mormon church was led by Brigham Young, who lacked Smith's religious mysticism but was a brilliant organizer. Young decided to move his followers to the Great Basin, an isolated area a thousand miles from the settled parts of the United States. In 1847 the first thousand settlers arrived, the vanguard of thousands more who extended Mormon settlement throughout the valley of the Great Salt Lake and the West. Church officials also held the government positions, and Young had supreme power in legislative, executive, and judicial matters as well as religious affairs. In 1849 the state of Deseret was officially established, with Brigham Young as governor. It applied for admission to the Union.

State of Deseret

The most controversial church teaching was the doctrine of polygamy, or plural marriage, which Young finally sanctioned publicly in 1852. Visitors reported with surprise that few Mormon wives seemed to rebel against the practice. Some plural wives developed close friendships; indeed, in one sample almost a third of plural marriages included at least two sisters. Moreover, because polygamy distinguished Mormonism from other religions, plural wives saw it as an expression of their religious faith. "I want to be assured of *position in God's estimation*," one such wife explained. "If polygamy is the Lord's order, we must carry it out."

Polygamy

The Mormons connected control of water to their sense of mission and respect for hierarchy. The Salt Lake valley, where the Mormons established their holy community, lacked significant rivers or abundant sources of water. Thus success depended on irrigating the region, something never before attempted. When the first Mormons arrived from the East, they began constructing a coordinated series of dams, aqueducts, and ditches, bringing life-giving water to the valleys of the region. Fanning out from their original settlement, they founded a series of colonies throughout the West, all tied to Salt Lake City and joined by ribbons of water. Mormon farmers grew corn, wheat, hay, and an assortment of fruits and vegetables. By 1850, there were more than 16,000

Irrigation and Community

Salt Lake City in 1853:
Planned, spacious, and
orderly

irrigated acres in what would eventually become the state of Utah. The Mormons were the first Anglos to extensively use irrigation in North America.

Manipulation of water reinforced the Mormons' sense of hierarchy and group discipline. Centralization of authority in the hands of church officials made possible an overall plan of development, allowed for maximum exploitation of resources, and freed communities from the disputes over water rights that plagued many settlements in the arid West. In a radical departure from American ideals, church leaders insisted that water belonged to the community, not individuals, and vested this authority in the hands of the local bishop. Control of water resources, which were vital for survival in the desert, reinforced the power of the church hierarchy over not just the faithful but dissidents as well. Community needs, as interpreted by church leaders, took precedence over individual rights. Thus irrigation did more than make the desert bloom. By checking the Jeffersonian ideal of an independent, self-sufficient farmer, it also made possible a centralized, well-regulated society under the firm control of the church.

Temple City: Salt Lake City

Salt Lack City's
Orderly Growth

In laying out the Mormons' "temple city" of Salt Lake, Young was also determined to avoid the commercial worldliness and competitive individualism that had plagued the Mormons at Nauvoo. City lots, which were distributed by lottery, could not be subdivided for sale, and real estate speculation was forbidden.

The city itself was laid out in a checkerboard grid well suited to the level terrain. Streets were 132 feet wide (compared with 60 feet in San Francisco), and each square block contained eight home lots of 1.25 acres each. Unlike in early San Francisco, the family was the basic social unit in Salt Lake City, and almost from the beginning the city had an equal balance of men and women. The planners also provided for four public squares in various parts of the city. The city lacked any traditional secular authority: it was divided into 18 wards, each under the supervision of a bishop, who held civil as well as religious power.

As the city expanded, the original plan had to be modified to accommodate the developing commercial district by dividing lots into sizes more suitable for stores. Experience and growth also eventually dictated smaller blocks and narrower streets, but the city still retained its spacious appearance and regular design. Through religious and economic discipline church leaders succeeded in preserving a sense of common purpose.

Shadows on the Moving Frontier

Transformations such as Salt Lake City and San Francisco were truly remarkable. But Americans were not coming into a trackless, unsettled wilderness. As frontier lines crossed, 75,000 Mexicans had to adapt to American rule.

The Treaty of Guadalupe Hidalgo guaranteed Mexicans in the ceded territory "the free enjoyment of their liberty and property." As long as Mexicans continued to be a sizable majority in a given area, their influence remained strong. But wherever Anglos became more numerous, they demanded conformity to American customs. When Mexicans remained faithful to their heritage, language, and religion, these cultural differences worked to reinforce Hispanic powerlessness, social isolation, and economic exploitation.

New Mexico had the largest Hispanic population as well as the fewest Anglos in the Mexican cession. As a result, the upper-class Mexicans who owned the land and employed large numbers of mixed-blood workers on their ranches managed to maintain their position. This class had cultivated American allies during the Santa Fe trade, and their connections grew stronger as American businesspeople slowly entered the territory in the 1850s. Neither group had many qualms about exploiting poorer Hispanics.

The rush of American emigrants quickly overwhelmed Hispanic settlers in California. Even in 1848, before the discovery of gold, Americans in California outnumbered Mexicans two to one, and by 1860 Hispanics amounted to only 2 percent of the population. At the time of the American conquest, the 200 or so *ranchero* families owned about 14 million acres, but changes in California land law required verification of their original land grants by a federal commission. Since the average claim took 17 years to complete and imposed complex procedures and hefty legal fees, many *rancheros* lost large tracts of land to Americans.

Less affluent Mexicans scratched out a bare existence on ranches and farms or in the growing cities and towns. Scorned by the dominant Anglo majority and without marketable skills and resources, they were often reduced to extreme poverty. As the Hispanic population in California became primarily urban, women assumed a larger role in the family. Many men became seasonal workers who were absent part of the year, and thus women played a greater role in sustaining the family economically.

Mexicans in Texas were also greatly outnumbered: they totaled only 6 percent of the population in 1860. Stigmatized and despised by whites as racial inferiors, they were the poorest group in free society. One response to this dislocation, an option commonly taken by persecuted minorities, was social banditry. An example was the folk hero Juan Cortina. A member of a displaced landed family in southern Texas, Cortina was driven into resistance in the 1850s by American harassment. He began stealing from wealthy Anglos to aid poor Mexicans, proclaiming, "To me is entrusted the breaking of the chains of your slavery." Cortina continued to raid Texas border settlements until finally he was imprisoned by Mexican authorities. While failing to produce any lasting change, Cortina demonstrated the depth of frustration and resentment among Hispanics over their abuse at the hands of the new Anglo majority.

Hispanic-Anglo Conflict

Town plazas, such as this one in San Felipe, Coahuila (in Mexico), were commercial centers in the Mexican Southwest. Traders from outlying ranchos *enjoy refreshments while their goods, loaded on oxcarts, await sale.*

Escape from Crisis

Issue of Slavery's Extension

With the return of peace, Congress confronted the problem of whether to allow slavery in the newly acquired territories. David Wilmot, in his controversial proviso, had already proposed to outlaw slavery throughout the Mexican cession. John C. Calhoun, representing the extreme southern position, countered that slavery was legal in all territories. The federal government had acted as the agent of all the states in acquiring the land, he argued, and southerners had a right to take their property there, including slaves. Only when the residents of a territory drafted a state constitution could they decide the question of slavery.

Between these extremes were two moderate positions. One proposed extending the Missouri Compromise line of 36°30′ to the Pacific, which would have continued the earlier policy of dividing the national domain between the North and the South. The other proposal, championed by Senator Lewis Cass of Michigan and Senator Stephen A. Douglas of Illinois, was to allow the people of the territory rather than Congress to decide the status of slavery. This solution, which became known as **popular sovereignty,** was deliberately ambiguous, since its supporters refused to specify whether the residents could make this decision at any time or only when drafting a state constitution, as Calhoun insisted.

When Congress organized the Oregon Territory in 1848, it prohibited slavery there, since even southerners admitted that the region was too far north to grow the South's staple crops. But this seemingly straightforward decision made it impossible to apply the Missouri Compromise line to the other territories. Without Oregon as a part of the package, the bulk of the remaining land would be open to slavery, something at which the North balked. Almost inadvertently, one of the two moderate solutions had been discarded by the summer of 1848.

A Two-Faced Campaign

In the election of 1848 both major parties tried to avoid the slavery issue. The Democrats nominated Lewis Cass, a supporter of popular sovereignty, while the Whigs bypassed all their prominent leaders and selected General Zachary Taylor, who had taken no position on any public issue and who remained silent throughout the campaign. The Whigs adopted no platform and planned instead to emphasize the general's war record.

Free Soil Party

But the slavery issue would not be ignored. A new antislavery coalition, the **Free Soil Party** helped force the issue. Alienated by Polk's policies and still angry over the 1844 convention, northern Democrats loyal to Van Buren spearheaded its creation. They were joined by "Conscience Whigs," who disavowed Taylor's nomination because he was a slaveholder. Furthermore, political abolitionists like Salmon P. Chase left the Liberty party in favor of this broader coalition. To widen its appeal, the Free Soil platform focused on the dangers of extending slavery rather than on the evil of slavery itself. Ironically, the party's convention named as its candidate Martin Van Buren—the man who for years had struggled to keep the slavery issue out of politics.

Election of 1848

With the Free Soilers strongly supporting the Wilmot Proviso, the Whigs and Democrats could not ignore the slavery question. The two major parties responded by running different campaigns in the North and the South. To southern audiences, each party promised that it would protect slavery in the territories; to northern voters, each claimed that it would keep the territories free. In this two-faced, sectional campaign, the Whigs won their second national victory. Taylor held on to the core of Whig voters in both sections (Van Buren and Cass, after all, had long been Democrats). But in the South, where the contest pitted a southern slaveholder against two northerners, Taylor won many more votes than Clay had in 1844. As one southern Democrat complained, "We have lost hundreds of votes, solely on the ground that General Cass was a Northerner and General Taylor a Southern man." Furthermore, Van Buren polled five times as many votes as the Liberty party had four years earlier. It seemed that the national system of political parties was being gradually pulled apart.

The Compromise of 1850

Once he became president, Taylor could no longer remain silent. The territories gained from Mexico had to be organized; furthermore, by 1849 California had gained enough residents to be admitted as a state. In the Senate the balance of power between North and South stood at 15 states each. California's admission would break the sectional balance.

Taylor's Plan

Called "Old Rough and Ready" by his troops, Taylor was a forthright man of action, but he was politically inexperienced and he oversimplified complex problems. Since even Calhoun conceded that entering states had the right to ban slavery, Taylor proposed that the way to end the sectional crisis was to skip the territorial stage by combining all the Mexican cession into two very large states, New Mexico and California. So the president sent agents to California and New Mexico with instructions to set the machinery in motion for both territories to draft constitutions and apply for statehood directly. Even more shocking to southern Whigs, he proposed to apply the Wilmot Proviso to the entire area, since he was convinced that slavery would never flourish there. By the time Congress convened in December 1849, California had drafted a constitution and applied for admission as a free state. Taylor reported that New Mexico

The Great Triumvirate—Clay, Webster, and Calhoun—served together in public life for almost four decades. Clay (left) and Webster (center) supported the Compromise of 1850, whereas in his last speech in the Senate, the dying Calhoun (right) opposed it. By midcentury, power was passing to a new generation of politicians more accustomed to sectional conflict and less amenable to compromise.

(which included most of Arizona, Utah, and Colorado) would soon do the same and recommended that both be admitted as free states. The president's plan touched off the most serious sectional crisis the Union had yet confronted.

Into this turmoil stepped Henry Clay, now 73 years old and nearing the end of his career. A savvy card player all his life, Clay loved politics: the bargaining, the wheeling and dealing, the late-night trade-offs eased along by a bottle of bourbon. Thirty years earlier he had engineered the Missouri Compromise, and in 1833 he had helped defuse the nullification crisis. Clay decided that a grand compromise was needed to save the Union. Already, Mississippi had summoned other southern states to meet in a convention at Nashville to discuss the crisis, and southern extremists were pushing for secession. The points of disagreement went beyond the question of the western territories. Many northerners considered it disgraceful that slaves were bought and sold in the nation's capital, where slavery was still permitted. Southerners complained bitterly that northern states ignored the 1793 fugitive slave law and prevented them from reclaiming runaway slaves.

Clay's compromise, submitted in January 1850, addressed all these concerns. California, he proposed, should be admitted as a free state, which represented the clear wishes of most settlers there. The rest of the Mexican cession would be organized as two territories, New Mexico and Utah, under the doctrine of popular sovereignty. Thus slavery would not be prohibited from these regions. Clay also proposed that Congress abolish the slave trade but not slavery itself in the District of Columbia and that a new, more rigorous fugitive slave law be passed to enable southerners to reclaim runaway slaves. To reinforce the idea that both North and South were yielding ground, Clay combined those provisions that dealt with the former Mexican territory and several others adjusting the Texas–New Mexico boundary into a larger package known as the Omnibus Bill.

With the stakes so high, the Senate debated the bill for six months. Daniel Webster of Massachusetts, always deep-voiced, seemed more somber than usual when he delivered a pro-Compromise speech on the seventh of March. "I wish to speak today not as a Massachusetts man, not as a Northern man, but as an American. . . . I speak today for the preservation of the Union. Hear me for my cause." Calhoun, whose aged, crevassed face mirrored the lines that had been drawn so deeply between the two sections, was near death and too ill to deliver his final speech to the Senate, which a colleague read for him as he listened silently. The "cords of Union," he warned—those ties of interest and affection that held the nation together—were snapping one by one. Only equal rights for the South and an end to the agitation against slavery could preserve the Union.

Clay, wracked by a hacking cough, spent long hours trying to line up the needed votes. But for once, the great card enthusiast had misplayed his hand. The Omnibus Bill required that the components of the compromise be approved as a package. Extremists in Congress from both regions, however, combined against the moderates and rejected the bill.

With Clay exhausted and his strategy in shambles, Democrat Stephen A. Douglas assumed leadership of the pro-Compromise forces. The sudden death in July of President Taylor, who had threatened to veto Clay's plan, aided the compromise movement. One by one, Douglas submitted the individual measures for a vote. Northern representatives provided the necessary votes to admit California and abolish the slave trade in the District of Columbia, while southern representatives supplied the edge needed to organize the Utah and New Mexico territories and pass the new fugitive slave law. On the face of it, everyone had compromised. But in truth, only 61 members of Congress, or 21 percent of the membership, had not voted against some part of the Compromise.

By September 17 all the separate parts of the Compromise of 1850 had passed and been signed into law by the new president, Millard Fillmore. The Union, it seemed, was safe.

Away from the Brink

The general public, both North and South, rallied to the Compromise. At the convention of southern states in Nashville, the fire-eaters—the radical proponents of states' rights and secession—found themselves voted down by more moderate voices. Even in the Deep South, coalitions of pro-Compromise Whigs and Democrats soundly defeated

Clay's Compromise

Passage of the Compromise

Rejection of Secession

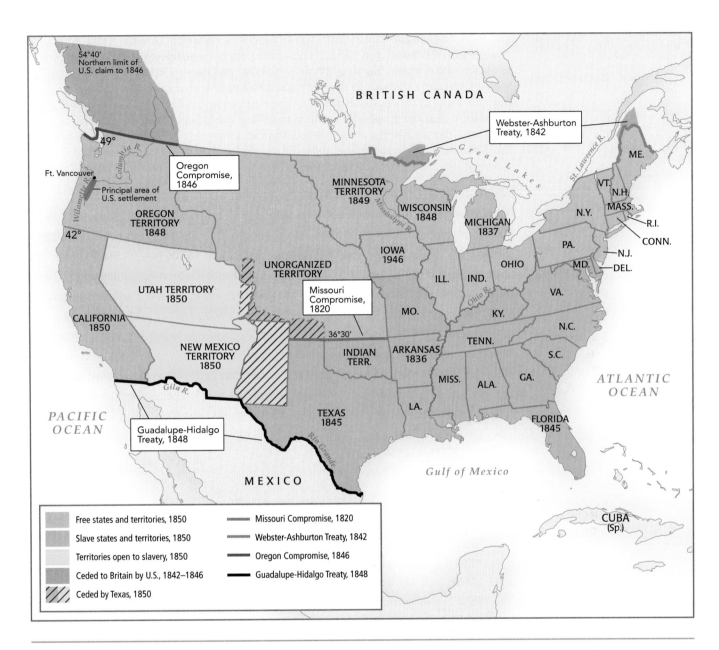

Territorial Growth and the Compromise of 1850   *The Webster-Ashburton Treaty established Maine's northern boundary as well as the American-Canadian boundary west of the Great Lakes.*

secessionists in the state elections that followed. Still, most southerners felt that a firm line had been drawn. With California's admission, they were now outnumbered in the Senate, so it was critical that slaveholders be granted equal legal access to the territories. They announced that any breach of the Compromise of 1850 would justify secession.

The North, for its part, found the new fugitive slave law the hardest measure of the Compromise of 1850 to swallow. The controversial law denied an accused runaway a trial by jury, and it required that all citizens assist federal marshals in its enforcement. Harriet Beecher Stowe's popular novel *Uncle Tom's Cabin* (1852) presented a powerful moral indictment of the law—and of slavery as an institution. Despite sentimental characters, a contrived plot, and clumsy dialect, the book profoundly moved its readers. Emphasizing the duty of Christians toward the downtrodden, it reached a greater audience than any previous abolitionist work and heightened moral opposition to the institution.

In reality, however, fewer than 1,000 slaves a year ran away to the North, many of whom did not succeed. Despite some cases of well-publicized resistance, the 1850 fugitive slave law was generally enforced in the free states. Many northerners did not like the law, but

Fugitive Slave Law

they were unwilling to tamper with the Compromise. Stephen Douglas spoke accurately enough when he boasted in 1851, "The whole country is acquiescing in the compromise measures—everywhere, North and South. Nobody proposes to repeal or disturb them."

And so calm returned. In the lackluster 1852 presidential campaign, both the Whigs and the Democrats endorsed the Compromise. Franklin Pierce, a little-known New Hampshire Democrat, soundly defeated the Whig candidate, Winfield Scott. Even more significant, the antislavery Free Soil candidate received only about half as many votes as Van Buren had four years before. With the slavery issue seemingly losing political force, it appeared that the Republic had weathered the storm unleashed by the Wilmot Proviso.

But the moving frontier had worked many changes during the 1830s and 1840s; and many more upheavals awaited the decade ahead. From a continental point of view, political relations among the United States, Mexico, and the Indian peoples had shifted significantly. Indian attacks on Mexico in the 1820s and 1830s had weakened Mexico's ability to repel an invasion by the United States. And with the treaty of Guadelupe Hidalgo, the United States gained over half a million square miles. Its frontier had leaped from the Mississippi valley to the Pacific, but in between remained territory still unorganized and still controlled by formidable Indian peoples. And as the North became increasingly industrialized and the South more firmly committed to an economy based on cotton and slavery, the movement of Americans into those territories would revive growing conflict between the two sections over slavery. The disputes would shatter the Jacksonian party system, reignite the slavery issue, and shake the Union to its foundation.

Significant Events

1725–1850	Sioux expansion on the Great Plains
1821	Mexico wins independence; Santa Fe trade opens
1823	First American settlers enter Texas
1829	Mexico tries to abolish slavery in Texas
1830	Mexico attempts to halt American migration to Texas
1831	Violence between northern Mexicans and Indians begins to increase dramatically
1835	Texas Revolution
1836	Texas Republic established; Battle of the Alamo; Santa Anna defeated at San Jacinto
1841	Tyler becomes president
1842	Webster-Ashburton Treaty
1843	Large-scale migration to Oregon begins
1844	Polk elected president
1845	United States annexes Texas; phrase *Manifest Destiny* coined
1845–1846	Slidell's unsuccessful mission
1846	War declared against Mexico; Bear Flag Revolt in California; Oregon Treaty ratified; Wilmot Proviso introduced
1847	Mormon migration to Utah; U.S. troops occupy Mexico City
1848	Gold discovered in California; Treaty of Guadalupe Hildalgo approved; Free Soil party founded; Taylor elected president
1849	Gold rush; California drafts free state constitution
1850	Nashville convention; Taylor dies and Fillmore becomes president; Compromise of 1850 enacted

1850–1851	South rejects secession
1852	Harriet Beecher Stowe's *Uncle Tom's Cabin* published; Pierce elected president

Chapter Summary

In the 1840s the United States expanded to the Pacific, a development that required an aggressive war and that led to the rise of the slavery issue in national politics.

- In the 1840s Americans proclaimed that it was the United States' Manifest Destiny to expand across the North American continent.

- Americans in Texas increasingly clashed with Mexican authorities, and in 1836 Texans revolted and established an independent republic.

- Americans headed for Oregon and California on the Overland Trail.

  —The journey put special pressures on women as the traditional division of labor by gender broke down.
  —White migration also put pressure on Plains Indians' grazing lands, wood supplies, and freedom of movement.
  —The gold rush spawned a unique society that was overwhelmingly male, highly mobile, and strongly nativist and racist.
  —Led by Brigham Young, the Mormons established a tightly organized, centrally controlled society in the Great Salt Lake basin.

  —Throughout the Southwest the Hispanic population suffered at the hands of the new Anglo majority, as did the Chinese immigrants who flocked to California.

- President James K. Polk entered office with a vision of the United States as a continental nation.

  —He upheld President John Tyler's annexation of Texas and agreed to divide the Oregon country with Britain.
  —Polk instigated a war with Mexico in order to obtain that country's northern territories.
  —Divided, impoverished, and distracted by ongoing wars with Indians, Mexico was forced to surrender more than half a million square miles of territory in the aftermath of the war.

- The U.S.–Mexican War reinjected the slavery issue into American national politics.

  —The Wilmot Proviso sought to prohibit slavery from any territory acquired from Mexico.
  —The struggle over the Proviso eventually disrupted both major parties.
  —Congress momentarily stilled the sectional crisis with the Compromise of 1850.

Additional Reading

For the Sioux, see the enduring article by Richard White, "The Winning of the West: The Expansion of the Western Sioux in the Eighteenth and Nineteenth Centuries," *Journal of American History* (1978), 319–343. David J. Weber, *The Mexican Frontier, 1821–1846* (1982), is a superb study of the Southwest prior to American control. For a more recent account, with a transnational interpretation of the Texas Rebellion, see Andrés Reséndez, *Changing National Identities at the Frontier* (2005). For the Overland Trail, see John Mack Faragher, *Women and Men on the Overland Trail* (1979). Leonard J. Arrington and Davis Bitton, *The Mormon Experience,* 2nd ed. (1992), is a good survey. Susan Lee Johnson's *Roaring Camp* (2001) explores social interaction during the Gold Rush. Robert V. Hine and John Mack Faragher, *The American West* (2001), is an excellent synthesis of the region's history.

The fullest treatment of American politics in this period is Sean Wilentz's magisterial book *The Rise of American Democracy* (2005). Thomas R. Hietala offers a stimulating analysis of the social roots of expansionism in *Manifest Design* (1985). The drive to annex Texas is carefully untangled in William W. Freehling, *The Road to Disunion* (1990). The best discussions of Polk's handling of the Oregon and Texas issues remain Charles G. Sellers Jr., *James K. Polk, Continentalist, 1843–1846* (1966), and David M. Pletcher, *The Diplomacy of Annexation* (1973). Michael F. Holt presents a powerful analysis of the Whig party's difficulties in this decade in *The Rise and Fall of the American Whig Party* (1999). Howard Lamar's classic account *The Far Southwest* (1966) explores political and economic power in the territories after conquest. For more recent work on the region's postwar history, see Samuel Truett and Elliott Young, *Continental Crossroads* (2004). Holman Hamilton, *Prologue to Conflict* (new ed., 2005), is an excellent study of the Compromise of 1850.

For a fuller list of readings, see the Bibliography at www.mhhe.com/davidsonnation6.

CHAPTER 15
The Union Broken
1850~1861

As Kansas became a battleground over whether slavery would expand into the new territories, pro- and anti-slavery factions armed themselves for open conflict. This free state battery stands ready with its howitzer at the ready.

The Sacking of a Town in Kansas

Into town they rode, several hundred strong, their faces flushed with excitement. They were unshaven, rough-talking men, "armed . . . to the teeth with rifles and revolvers, cutlasses and bowie-knives." At the head of the procession an American flag flapped softly in the warm May breeze. Alongside it was another with a crouching tiger emblazoned on black and white stripes, followed by banners proclaiming "Southern Rights" and "The Superiority of the White Race." At the rear rolled five artillery pieces, which were quickly dragged into range of the town's main street. Watching intently from a window in his office, Josiah Miller, the editor of the Lawrence *Kansas Free State,* predicted, "Well, boys, we're in for it."

For the residents of Lawrence, Kansas, the worst seemed at hand. The town had been founded by the New England Emigrant Aid Company, a Yankee association that recruited settlers in an effort to keep Kansas Territory from becoming a slave state. Accepting Stephen Douglas's idea that the people should decide the status of slavery, the town's residents intended to see to it that under this doctrine of **popular sovereignty** Kansas entered the Union as a free state. Emigrants from the neighboring slave state of Missouri were equally determined that no "abolition tyrants" or "negro thieves" would control the territory. There had been conflict in Kansas almost immediately: land disputes, horse thievery, shootings on both sides.

In the ensuing turmoil, the federal government seemed to back the proslavery forces. In the spring of 1856, a U.S. district court indicted several of Lawrence's leading citizens for treason, and federal marshal Israel Donaldson called for a posse to help make the arrests. Donaldson's posse, swelled by eager volunteers from across the Missouri border, arrived outside Lawrence on the night of May 20.

Meanwhile, Lawrence's "committee of safety" had agreed on a policy of nonresistance. Most of those indicted had fled, but Donaldson arrested two men without incident. Then he dismissed his posse.

The posse, however, was not ready to go home. Already thoroughly liquored up, it marched into town cheering. Ignoring the pleas of some leaders, its members smashed the presses of two newspapers, the *Herald of Freedom* and the *Kansas Free State.* Then the horde unleashed its wrath on the now-deserted Free State Hotel, which more closely resembled a fort. The invaders unsuccessfully attempted to batter it down with cannon fire and blow it up with gunpowder; finally they put a

"Nobody believes this Republican movement can prove the basis of a permanent party," commented one American in the mid-1850s. But the violence in the Kansas Territory over the expansion of slavery dramatically fueled the growth of the new Republican party. By 1860 it was organizing huge marches like this torchlight parade supporting Abraham Lincoln for president.

torch to the building. When the mob finally rode off, it left the residents of Lawrence un-harmed but thoroughly terrified.

Retaliation by free state partisans was not long in coming. Hurrying north along a different road to Lawrence, an older man with a grim face and steely eyes heard the news the next morning that the town had been attacked. "Old Man Brown," as everyone called him, was on his way with several of his sons to provide reinforcements. A severe, God-fearing Calvinist, John Brown was also a staunch abolitionist who had once remarked to a friend that he believed "God had raised him up on purpose to break the jaws of the wicked." Brooding over the failure of the free-staters to resist the "slave hounds" from Missouri, Brown ordered his followers to sharpen their heavy cutlasses. "Caution," he an-nounced, "is nothing but the word of Cowardice."

On the night of May 24, 1856, Brown headed toward Pottawatomie Creek with a half dozen others, including four of his sons. Announcing that they were "the Northern Army" come to serve justice, they burst into the cabin of James Doyle, a proslavery man from Tennessee, with cutlasses drawn. As Brown marched off Doyle and his three sons, Doyle's terrified wife, Mahala, begged him to spare her youngest, and the old man relented. The others were led no more than 100 yards down the road before Owen and Salmon Brown hacked them to death with broadswords. Old Man Brown then walked up to James Doyle's body and put a bullet through his forehead. Before the night was done, two more cabins had been visited and two more proslavery settlers brutally executed. Not one of the five murdered men owned a single slave or had any connection with the raid on Lawrence.

Brown's action precipitated a new wave of fighting in Kansas, and the news of the tumult further angered residents in both sections of the nation. "Everybody here feels as if we are upon a volcano," remarked one congressman in Washington.

Pottawatomie Massacre

The country was indeed atop a smoldering volcano that would finally erupt in the spring of 1861, showering civil war, death and destruction across the land. Popular sovereignty, the last remaining moderate solution to the controversy over the expansion of slavery, had failed dismally in Kansas. The violence and disorder in the territory provided a stark reply to Stephen Douglas's proposition: What could be more peaceable, more fair than the notion of popular sovereignty?

Sectional Changes in American Society

The road to war was not a straight or short one. Six years elapsed between the Compromise of 1850 and the crisis in "Bleeding Kansas." Another five years would pass before the first shot was fired. And the process of separation involved more than ineffective politicians and an unwillingness to compromise. As we have seen, Americans were bound together by a growing transportation network, by national markets, and by a national political system. These social and political ties—the "cords of Union," Calhoun called them—could not be severed all at once. Increasingly, however, the changes occurring in American society heightened sectional tensions. As the North continued to industrialize, its society came into conflict with that of the South. The Old Northwest, which had long been a political ally of the South, became more closely linked to the East. The coming of civil war, in other words, involved social and economic changes as well as political ones.

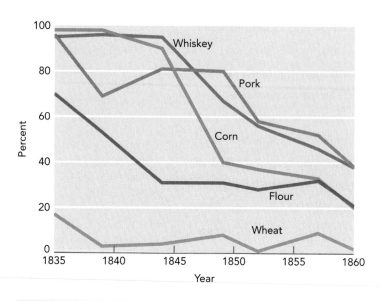

Proportion of Western Exports Shipped via New Orleans, 1835–1860 *In 1835 nearly 100 percent of western exports of corn, pork, and whiskey were being shipped via New Orleans. By 1860 only about 40 percent of pork and whiskey and 20 percent of flour and corn were. The change in shipping patterns weakened the political ties between the South and the Old Northwest.*

Railroads' Impact on the Economy

Reorientation of Western Trade

The Growth of a Railroad Economy

By the time the Compromise of 1850 produced a lull in the tensions between North and South, the American economy had left behind the depression of the early 1840s and was roaring again. Its basic structure, however, was changing. Cotton remained the nation's major export, but it was no longer the driving force for American economic growth. After 1839 this role was taken over by the construction of a vast railroad network covering the eastern half of the continent. By 1850 the United States possessed more than 9,000 miles of track; 10 years later it had over 30,000 miles, more than the rest of the world combined. Much of the new construction during the 1850s occurred west of the Appalachian Mountains.

Because western railroads ran through less settled areas, they were especially dependent on public aid. State and local governments made loans to rail companies and sometimes exempted them temporarily from taxes. About a quarter of the cost of railroad construction came from state and local governments, but federal land grants were crucial, too. By mortgaging or selling the land to farmers, the railroad raised construction capital and also stimulated settlement, which increased its business and profits.

On a national map, the rail network in place by 1860 looked impressive, but these lines were not fully integrated. A few trunk-line roads such as the New York Central had combined a number of smaller lines to facilitate the shipment of freight. But roadbeds had not yet been standardized, so that no fewer than 12 different gauges, or track widths, were in use. Moreover, cities at the end of rail lines jealously strove to maintain their commercial advantages, not wanting to connect with competing port cities for fear that freight would pass through to the next city down the line.

The effect of the new lines rippled outward through the economy. Farmers along the tracks began to specialize in cash crops and market them in distant locations. With their profits they purchased manufactured goods that earlier they might have made at home. Before the railroad reached Athens, Tennessee, the surrounding counties produced about 25,000 bushels of wheat, which sold for less than 50 cents a bushel. Once the railroad came, farmers in these same counties grew 400,000 bushels and sold their crop at a dollar a bushel. Railroads also stimulated other areas of the economy, notably the mining and iron industries.

The new rail networks shifted the direction of western trade. In 1840 most northwestern grain was shipped down the Mississippi River to the bustling port of New Orleans. But low water made steamboat travel risky in summer, and ice shut down traffic in winter. Products such as lard, tallow, and cheese quickly spoiled if stored in New Orleans' sweltering warehouses. Increasingly, traffic from the Midwest flowed west to east, over the new rail lines. Chicago became the region's hub, linking the farms of the upper Midwest to New York and other eastern cities by more than 2,000 miles of track in 1855. Thus, while the value of goods shipped by river to New Orleans continued to increase, the South's overall share of western trade dropped dramatically.

These new patterns of commerce and agriculture weakened the traditional political alliance between the South and the West, which had been based on shared economic interests. "The power of cotton over the financial affairs of the Union has in the last few years rapidly diminished," the *Democratic Review* remarked in 1849, "and bread stuffs will now become the governing power."

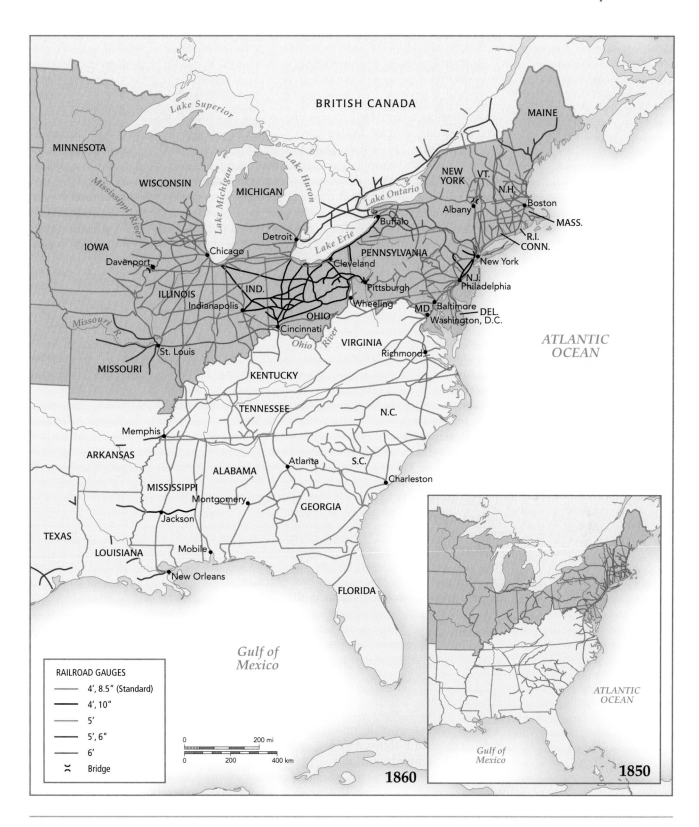

Railroads, 1850 and 1860, with Track Gauges   *During the 1850s a significant amount of railroad track was laid, but total track mileage is misleading, because the United States lacked a fully integrated rail network in 1860. A few trunk-line roads had combined a number of smaller lines into a single system to facilitate shipment. The Pennsylvania Railroad, for example, connected Philadelphia and Pittsburgh. But the existence of five major track gauges as well as minor ones meant that passengers and freight often had to be transferred from one line to the next. And north-south traffic was further disrupted by the lack of bridges over the Ohio River.*

Railroads and the Prairie Environment

As railroad lines fanned out from Chicago, farmers began to acquire open prairie land in Illinois and then Iowa, putting its deep black soil into production. Commercial agriculture transformed this remarkable treeless environment.

To settlers accustomed to woodlands, the thousands of square miles of tall grass were an awesome sight. Indian grass, Canadian wild rye, and native big bluestem all grew higher than a person. In 1838 Edmund Flagg gazed upon "the tall grasstops waving in . . . billowy beauty in the breeze; the narrow pathway winding off like a serpent over the rolling surface, disappearing and reappearing till lost in the luxuriant herbage." Long-grass prairies had their perils too: summer or winter storms sent travelers searching for the shelter of trees along river valleys. Dewitt Smith recalled the fierce green-headed flies awaiting the unsuspecting. "A journey across the big praries was, in the summer time, undertaken only at night," he recalled, "because on a hot summer day horses would be literally stung and worried to death."

Impact of Technology

Because eastern plows could not penetrate the densely tangled roots of prairie grass, the earliest settlers erected farms along the boundary separating the forest from the prairie. In 1837, however, John Deere patented a sharp-cutting steel plow that sliced through the sod without soil sticking to the blade. In addition, Cyrus McCormick refined a mechanical reaper that harvested 14 times more wheat with the same amount of labor. By the 1850s McCormick was selling 1,000 reapers a year and could not keep up with demand, while Deere turned out 10,000 plows annually.

Changes in the Landscape

The new commercial farming fundamentally altered the landscape and the environment. Indians had grown corn in the region for years, but never in such large fields as did white farmers, whose surpluses were shipped east. Prairie farmers also introduced new crops that were not part of the earlier ecological system, notably wheat, along with fruits and vegetables. Native grasses were replaced by a small number of plants cultivated as commodities.

Western farmers also altered the landscape by reducing the annual fires, often set by Indians, that had kept the prairie free from trees. In the fires' absence, trees reappeared on land not in cultivation and, if undisturbed, eventually formed woodlots. The earlier unbroken landscape gave way to independent farms, each fenced in the precise checkerboard pattern established by the Northwest Ordinance. It was an artificial ecosystem of animals, woodlots, and crops whose large, uniform layout made western farms more efficient than the irregular farms in the East.

Railroads and the Urban Environment

Influence on Location of Towns

Railroads transformed the urban environment as well. Communities soon recognized that their economic survival depended on creating adequate rail links to the countryside and to major urban markets. Large cities feared they would be left behind in the struggle to be the dominant city in the region. Smaller communities saw their very survival at stake in the battle for rail connections. When the new railroad line bypassed the prairie village of Auburn, Illinois, its fate was sealed, and residents quickly abandoned it for more promising locations.

Even communities that obtained rail links found the presence of this new technology difficult to adjust to. When a railroad began serving nearby Jacksonville, Illinois, merchants complained about the noise, dirt, and billowing smoke when locomotives hissed through the business district. "Many of the people were as much scared as the horses at the steaming monster," recalled one resident. After a few years, the tracks were relocated on the outskirts of town. Jacksonville's experience became the norm: increasingly communities kept railroads away from fashionable neighborhoods and shopping areas. As the tracks became a physical manifestation of social and economic divisions, the notion of living "on the wrong side of the tracks" became crucial to defining the urban landscape.

Rising Industrialization

On the eve of the Civil War, 60 percent of American laborers worked on farms. In 1860, for the first time, that figure dropped below 50 percent in the North. The expansion of commercial agriculture spurred the growth of industry. Of the 10 leading American industries, 8 processed raw materials produced by agriculture, including flour milling and the manufacture of textiles, shoes, and woolens. (The only exceptions were iron and machinery.) Industrial growth also spurted during the 1850s as water power was increasingly replaced by steam, since there were only a fixed number of water-power sites.

An early locomotive on the Baltimore & Ohio Railroad

Most important, the factory system of organizing labor and the technology of interchangeable parts spread to other areas of the economy. Many industries during the 1850s adopted interchangeable parts. Isaac Singer began using them in 1851 to mass-produce sewing machines, which made possible the ready-made clothing industry, while workers who assembled farm implements performed a single step in the process over and over again. By 1860 the United States had nearly a billion dollars invested in manufacturing, almost twice as much as in 1849.

Immigration

The surge of industry required a large factory labor force. Natural increase helped swell the population to more than 30 million by 1860, but only in part, since the birthrate had begun to decline. On the eve of the Civil War the average white mother bore five children, compared to seven at the turn of the century. It was the beginning of mass immigration to America during the mid-1840s that kept population growth soaring.

In the 20 years from 1820 to 1840, about 700,000 newcomers had entered the United States. That figure jumped to 1.7 million in the 1840s, then to 2.6 million in the 1850s. Though even greater numbers arrived after the Civil War, as a percentage of the nation's total population, the wave from 1845 to 1854 was the largest influx of immigrants in American history. Most newcomers were young people in the prime of life: out of 224,000 arrivals in 1856, only 31,000 were under 10 and only 20,000 were over 40.

Influx of Immigrants

Certainly the booming economy and the lure of freedom drew immigrants, but they were also pushed by deteriorating conditions in Europe. In Ireland, a potato blight in 1846 produced widespread famine. Out of a population of 9 million, as many as a million perished, while a million and a half more emigrated, two-thirds to the United States.

The Irish tended to be poorer than other immigrant groups of the day. Although the Protestant Scots-Irish continued as before to emigrate, the decided majority of the Irish who came after 1845 were Catholic. The newcomers were generally mostly unmarried younger sons and daughters of hard-pressed rural families. Because they were poor and unskilled, the Irish congregated in the cities, where the women performed domestic service and took factory jobs and the men did manual labor.

New Sources of Immigration

Germans and Scandinavians also had economic reasons for leaving Europe. They included small farmers whose lands had become marginal or who had been displaced by landlords, and skilled workers thrown out of work by industrialization. Others fled religious persecution. Some, particularly among the Germans, left after the liberal revolutions of 1848 failed, in order to live under the free institutions of the United States. Since coming to America, wrote a Swede who settled in Iowa in 1850, "I have not been compelled to pay a penny for the privilege of living. Neither is my cap worn out from lifting it in the presence of gentlemen."

Unprecedented unrest and upheaval prevailed in Europe in 1848, the so-called year of revolutions. The famine that had driven so many Irish out of their country

The Revolutions of 1848

Conditions of famine across Ireland led many to buy passage on ships like this one, departing for the United States. New York was the major port of entry for immigrants who surged into the United States during the 1840s and 1850s.

was part of a larger food shortage caused by a series of poor harvests. Mounting unemployment and overburdened relief programs increased suffering. In this situation middle-class reformers, who wanted civil liberty and a more representative government, joined forces with lower-class workers to overthrow several regimes, sometimes by also appealing to nationalist feelings. France, Austria, Hungary, Italy, and Prussia all witnessed major popular uprisings. Although these revolts succeeded at first, they were all crushed by the forces of the old order. Liberal hopes for a more open, democratic society suffered a severe setback.

In the aftermath of this failure, a number of hard-pressed German workers and farmers, as well as disillusioned radicals and reformers, emigrated to the United States, the symbol of democratic liberalism in the world. They were joined by the first significant migration from Asia, as thousands of Chinese headed to the gold rush in California and other strikes (see page 394). This migration was simply part of a century-long phenomenon, as approximately 50 million Europeans, largely from rural areas, would migrate to the Western Hemisphere.

Immigrants and Industrialization   Factories came more and more to depend on immigrant labor, including children, since newcomers would work for lower wages and were less prone to protest harsh working conditions. The shift to an immigrant workforce could be seen most clearly in the textile industry, where by 1860 more than half the workers in New England mills were foreign-born. Tensions between native- and foreign-born workers, as well as among immigrants of various nationalities, made it difficult for workers to unite.

Urban Resources Strained   The sizable foreign-born population in many American cities severely strained urban resources. Immigrants who could barely make ends meet were forced to live in overcrowded, unheated tenement houses, damp cellars, and even shacks—"the hall was dark and reeking with the worst filth," reported one New York journalist; the house was "filled with little narrow rooms, each one having five or six occupants; all very filthy." Urban slums became notorious for crime and drinking, which took a heavy toll on families and the poor. In the eyes of many native-born Americans, immigrants were to blame for driving down factory wages and pushing American workers out of jobs. Overshadowing these complaints was a fear that America might not be able to **assimilate** the new groups, with their unfamiliar social customs, strange languages, and national pride. These fears sparked an outburst of political **nativism** in the mid-1850s.

Southern Complaints

With British and northern factories buying cotton in unprecedented quantities, southern planters prospered in the 1850s. Their operations, like those of northern commercial farmers, became more highly capitalized to keep up with the demand. But instead of machinery, white southerners invested in slaves. During the 1850s, the price of prime field hands reached record levels.

Nonetheless, a number of southern nationalists, who advocated that the South should become a separate nation, pressed for greater industrialization to make the region more independent. "At present, the North fattens and grows rich upon the South," one Alabama newspaper complained in 1851, noting that "we purchase all our luxuries and necessities from the North," including clothing, shoes, implements and machinery, saddles and carriages, and even books. But most southerners ignored such pleas. As long as investments in cotton and slaves absorbed most of the South's capital, efforts to promote southern industry made little headway.

Despite southern prosperity, the section's leaders complained that the North used its power over banking and commerce to convert the South into a colony. In the absence of any significant southern shipping, northern intermediaries controlled the South's commodities through a complex series of transfers from planter to manufacturer. Storage and shipping charges, insurance, port fees, and commissions together added an estimated 20 percent to the cost of cotton and other commodities. These revenues went into the pockets of northern merchants, shippers, and bankers. The idea that the South was a colony of the North was inaccurate, but southern whites found it a convincing explanation of the North's growing wealth. More important, it reinforced their resistance to federal aid for economic development, which they were convinced would inevitably enrich the North at southern expense. This attitude further weakened the South's political alliance with the West, which needed federal aid for transportation.

Southern Economic Dependence

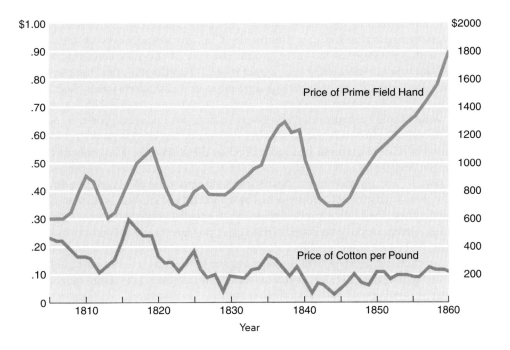

Prices of Cotton and Slaves   *From 1815 to 1850, cotton and slave prices generally moved together, as southerners plowed their profits from growing cotton into buying more land and slaves. During the 1850s, however, the booming southern economy and bumper cotton crops drove the price of slaves steeply upward compared to cotton prices, squeezing slaveowners' profit margins and heightening southern anxieties about the future.*

White southerners also feared that the new tide of immigration would shift the sectional balance of power. Some immigrants did settle in the South's few cities, but most shunned the region because they did not want to compete with cheap slave labor. The lack of industry and the limited demand for skilled labor also shunted immigrants northward. As a result, the North surged even further ahead of the South in population, thereby strengthening its control of the House of Representatives and heightening southern concern that the North would rapidly settle the western territories.

The Political Realignment of the 1850s

When Franklin Pierce (he pronounced it "Purse") assumed the presidency in 1853, he was only 48 years old, the youngest man yet to be elected president. He was also a supporter of the "Young America" movement of the Democratic party, which eagerly looked to spread democracy across the globe by annexing additional territory to the United States.

Gadsden Purchase

The believers in Young America felt it idle to argue about slavery when the nation could be developing new resources. But they failed to appreciate how each new plan for expansion would stir up the slavery issue. In 1853 Pierce did manage to conclude the Gadsden Purchase, thereby gaining control of about 45,000 square miles of Mexican desert that contained the most practical southern route for a transcontinental railroad (see map, page 415).

Ostend Manifesto

Pierce had no success, however, with his major goal, the acquisition of Cuba. Spain rebuffed all efforts to purchase the rich sugar-producing region in which slavery had once been strong and still existed. Then, in 1854, the American ministers meeting at Ostend in Belgium confidentially recommended that if Spain would not sell Cuba, the island should be seized. The contents of the "Ostend Manifesto" soon leaked, and Pierce was forced to renounce any notion of acquiring Cuba by force. In any case the president soon had his hands full with the proposals of another Democrat of the Young America stamp, Senator Stephen A. Douglas of Illinois.

The Kansas-Nebraska Act

Known as the Little Giant, Douglas was ambitious, bursting with energy, and impatient to get things done. As chairman of the Senate's Committee on Territories, he was eager to organize federal lands west of Missouri as part of his program for economic development. And as a citizen of Illinois, he wanted Chicago selected as the eastern terminus of the transcontinental railroad to California. Chicago would never be chosen over St. Louis and New Orleans, however, unless the rest of the Louisiana Purchase was organized, for any northern rail route would have to run through that region.

Repeal of the Missouri Compromise

Under the terms of the Missouri Compromise of 1820, slavery was prohibited in this portion of the Louisiana Purchase. Douglas had already tried in 1853 to organize the area while keeping a ban on slavery—only to have his bill voted down by southern opposition in the Senate. Bowing to southern pressure, the Illinois leader removed the prohibition on slavery that had been in effect for 34 years. The Kansas-Nebraska Act was passed in May 1854.

Popular Sovereignty

The new act created two territories: Kansas, directly west of Missouri, and a much larger Nebraska Territory, located west of Iowa and the Minnesota Territory. The Missouri Compromise was explicitly repealed. Instead, popular sovereignty was to determine the status of slavery in both territories, though it was left unclear whether residents of Kansas and Nebraska could prohibit slavery at any time or only at the time of statehood, as southerners insisted. Still, most members of Congress assumed that Douglas had split the region into two territories so that each section could claim another state: Kansas would be slave and Nebraska free.

The Kansas-Nebraska Act outraged northern Democrats, Whigs, and Free Soilers alike. Critics rejected Douglas's contention that popular sovereignty would keep the

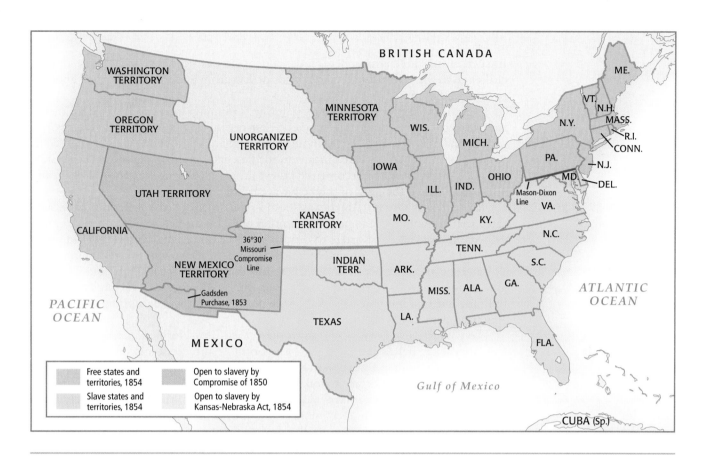

The Kansas-Nebraska Act   *When the Kansas-Nebraska Act of 1854 opened the remaining portion of the Louisiana Purchase to slavery under the doctrine of popular sovereignty, conflict between the two sections focused on control of Kansas, directly west of the slave state of Missouri.*

territories free. As always, most northerners spoke little of the moral evils of slavery; it was the chance that the Slave Power might gain new territory that concerned them. So great was the northern outcry that Douglas joked he could "travel from Boston to Chicago by the light of my own [burning] effigy."

The Collapse of the Second American Party System

The furor over the Kansas-Nebraska Act laid bare the underlying social and economic tensions that had developed between the North and the South. These tensions put mounting pressure on the political parties, and in the 1850s the Jacksonian party system collapsed. Voters who had been loyal to one party for years, even decades, began switching allegiances, while new voters were mobilized. By the time the process of realignment was completed, a new party system had emerged, divided this time along clearly sectional lines.

Political Realignment

In part, the old party system decayed because new problems had replaced the traditional economic issues of both Whigs and Democrats. The Whigs alienated many of their traditional Protestant supporters by openly seeking the support of Catholics and recent immigrants. Then, too, the growing agitation by Protestant reformers for the prohibition of alcohol divided both parties, especially the Whigs. But the Kansas-Nebraska Act provided the final blow, dividing the two major parties along sectional lines. Northern congressional Whigs, who unanimously opposed the bill, found themselves deserted by virtually all their southern colleagues. And fully half the northern Democratic representatives in the House voted against Douglas's bill.

Disillusionment with the Parties

The Know-Nothings

In such an unstable atmosphere, independent parties flourished. The most dramatic challenge to the Whigs and Democrats came first from a movement worried about the recent flood of immigrants.

New York City was the primary gateway for immigrants, and it was here that the American party, a secret nativist society, first organized. Its members were sworn to secrecy and instructed to answer inquiries by replying "I know nothing." In 1853 the Know-Nothings, as they were quickly dubbed, began organizing in several other states; after only a year they had become the fastest-growing party in the nation. Significantly, 1854 also marked the peak of the new wave of immigration.

Nativist Impulse

Taking as its slogan "Americans should rule America," the American party advocated that immigrants be forced to wait not 5 but 21 years before becoming naturalized citizens. It also called on voters to oust from office politicians who openly bid for foreign and Catholic votes. Know-Nothings denounced illegal voting by immigrants, the rising crime and disorder in urban areas, and immigrants' heavy drinking. They were also strongly anti-Catholic, convinced that the "undemocratic" hierarchy of priests, bishops, and archbishops controlled by the pope in Rome was conspiring to undermine American democracy.

To young native-born American workers, the Know-Nothing message was particularly appealing. It was they who bore the brunt of the economic dislocations caused by industrialization and who had to compete with immigrants for jobs. In the 1854 elections, the Know-Nothings won a series of remarkable victories, as former Whigs flocked to the new party in droves. Fueled by its success, the American party turned its attention south, and in a few months it had organized in every state of the Union. With perhaps a million voters enrolled in its lodges in 1855, Know-Nothing leaders confidently predicted that they would elect the next president.

Know-Nothings' Decline

Yet only a year later the party had collapsed as quickly as it had risen. Many Know-Nothing officeholders proved woefully incompetent. Voters deserted them when the party failed to enact its program. But the death knell of the party was rising sectional tensions. In 1856 most northern delegates walked out of the American party's national convention when it adopted a proslavery platform. Significantly, they deserted to the other new party, the Republicans. This party, unlike the Know-Nothings, had no base in the South. It intended to elect a president by sweeping the free states, which controlled a majority of the electoral votes.

In this nativist print, an eagle guards a schoolhouse while a group of Catholic laborers try to undermine its foundation. Directing the work is a priest, who receives instructions from the pope sitting on a throne. Nativist propaganda extolled the importance of public schools in safeguarding democracy and portrayed Catholics as hostile to American institutions.

The Republicans and Bleeding Kansas

Initially, the Republican party made little headway in the North. Many moderate Whigs and Democrats viewed it as too radical. A Democratic newspaper expressed the prevailing view when it declared, "Nobody believes that this Republican movement can prove the basis of a permanent party."

Such predictions, however, did not reckon with the emotions stirred up by developments in Kansas. Most early settlers migrated to Kansas for the same reasons other white Americans headed west—the chance to prosper in a new land. But Douglas's idea of popular sovereignty transformed the process of settlement into a referendum on slavery in the territories. A race soon developed between northerners and southerners to settle Kansas first. To the proslavery residents of neighboring Missouri, free-state communities like Lawrence seemed ominous threats. "We are playing for a mighty stake," former senator David Rice Atchison insisted. "If we win, we carry slavery to the Pacific Ocean; if we fail we lose Missouri, Arkansas and Texas and all the territories; the game must be played boldly."

When the first Kansas elections were held in 1854 and 1855, Missourians poured over the border, seized the polls, and stuffed the ballot boxes. This massive fraud tarnished popular sovereignty at the outset and greatly aroused public opinion in the North. It also provided proslavery forces with a commanding majority in the Kansas legislature, where they promptly expelled the legally elected free-state members and enacted a strict legal code limiting such time-honored rights as freedom of speech, impartial juries, and fair elections. Mobilized into action, the free-staters in the fall of 1855 organized a separate government, drafted a state constitution prohibiting slavery, and asked Congress to admit Kansas as a free state. In such a polarized situation, violence quickly broke out between the two factions, leading to the proslavery attack on Lawrence and to John Brown's reprisals (see page 407).

Turmoil in Kansas

The Caning of Charles Sumner

In May 1856, only a few days before the proslavery attack on Lawrence, Republican Senator Charles Sumner of Massachusetts delivered a scathing speech, "The Crime against Kansas." Sumner not only condemned slavery, but he also deliberately insulted

SOUTHERN CHIVALRY — ARGUMENT versus CLUB'S.

The caning of Senator Charles Sumner of Massachusetts by Representative Preston S. Brooks of South Carolina inflamed public opinion. In this northern drawing, the fallen Sumner, a martyr to free speech, raises his pen against Brooks's club. In the background, several prominent Democrats look on in amusement. Printmakers, rushing to capitalize on the furor, did not know what the obscure Brooks looked like and thus had to devise ingenious ways of portraying the incident. In this print, Brooks's face is hidden by his raised arm.

the state of South Carolina and one of its senators, Andrew Butler. Preston S. Brooks, a South Carolina congressman who was related to Butler, was outraged that Sumner had insulted his relative and mocked his state.

Several days later, Brooks strode into the Senate after it had adjourned, went up to Sumner, who was seated at his desk, and proceeded to beat the Massachusetts leader over the head with his cane. The cane shattered from the violence of the attack, but Brooks, swept up in the emotion of the moment, continued hitting Sumner until the senator collapsed to the floor, drenched in blood.

Significance of the Caning

Northerners were shocked to learn that a senator of the United States had been beaten unconscious in the Senate chamber. But what caused them even greater consternation was southern reaction to Sumner's caning—for in his own region, Preston Brooks was lionized as a hero. Instantly, the Sumner caning breathed life into the fledgling Republican party. Its claims about "Bleeding Kansas" and the Slave Power now seemed credible. Sumner, reelected in 1857 by the Massachusetts legislature, was unable to return to the Senate until 1860, his chair left vacant as a symbol of southern brutality.

The Election of 1856

Given the storm that had arisen over Kansas, Democrats concluded that no candidate associated with the repeal of the Missouri Compromise had a chance to win. So the Democrats turned to James Buchanan of Pennsylvania as their presidential nominee. Buchanan's supreme qualification was having the good fortune to have been out of the country when the Kansas-Nebraska Act was passed. The American party, split badly by the Kansas issue, nominated former president Millard Fillmore. The Republicans chose John C. Frémont, a western explorer who had helped liberate California during the Mexican War. The party's platform denounced slavery as a "relic of barbarism" and demanded that Kansas be admitted as a free state. Throughout the summer the party hammered away on Bleeding Sumner and Bleeding Kansas.

Ideology of the Republican Party

A Campaign badge supporting John C. Frémont

A number of principles guided the Republican party, including the ideal of free labor. Slavery degraded labor, Republicans argued, and would inevitably drive free labor out of the territories. Condemning the South as stagnant, hierarchical, and economically backward, Republicans praised the North as a society of opportunity where enterprising individuals could rise through hard work and self-discipline. Stopping the expansion of slavery, they argued, would preserve this heritage of economic independence for white Americans. Republicans by and large remained blind to ways in which industrialization was closing off avenues of social mobility for poor workers.

Also important was the moral opposition to slavery, which works like Harriet Beecher Stowe's *Uncle Tom's Cabin* had strengthened. Republican speakers and editors stressed that slavery was a moral wrong, that it was incompatible with the ideals of the Republic and Christianity. "Never forget," Republican leader Abraham Lincoln declared on one occasion, "that we have before us this whole matter of the right and wrong of slavery in this Union, though the immediate question is as to its spreading out into new Territories and States."

Concept of the Slave Power

More negatively, Republicans gained support by shifting their attacks from slavery itself to the Slave Power, or the political influence of the planter class. Pointing to the Sumner assault and the incidents in Kansas, Republicans contended that the Slave Power had set out to destroy the liberties of northern whites. "The question has passed on from that of slavery for negro servants, to that of tyranny over free white men," one Republican insisted in the 1856 campaign.

All these fears played on a strong northern attachment to the heritage of the American Revolution. Just as the nation's founders had battled against slavery, tyranny, aristocracy, and minority rule, so the North faced the unrepublican Slave Power. "The liberties of our country are in tenfold the danger that they were at the commencement of the American Revolution," warned one Republican paper. "We then had a distant foe to contend with. Now the enemy is within our borders."

In the election, Buchanan all but swept the South (losing only Maryland to Fillmore) and won enough free states to push him over the top, with 174 electoral votes to Frémont's 114 and Fillmore's 8. Still, the violence in Kansas and Sumner's caning nearly carried Frémont into the presidency. He ran ahead of both Buchanan and Fillmore in the North and won 11 free states out of 16. Had he carried Pennsylvania plus one more state, he would have been elected. For the first time in American history, an antislavery party based entirely in the North threatened to elect a president and snap the bonds of union.

The Worsening Crisis

James Buchanan had spent much of his life in public service: more than 20 years in the House and the Senate, secretary of state under Polk, and minister to Russia and to Great Britain. A tall, heavyset man with flowing white hair, he struck White House visitors as exceptionally courteous: an eye defect caused him to tilt his head slightly forward and to one side, which reinforced the impression of deference and attentiveness. A dutiful party member, he had over the years carefully cultivated wide personal support, yet he was a cautious and uninspiring leader who had a strong stubborn streak and deeply resented opposition to his policies.

Moderates in both sections hoped that the new president would thwart Republican radicals and secessionists of the Deep South, popularly known as "fire-eaters." Throughout his career, however, Buchanan had taken the southern position on sectional matters. Moreover, on March 6, 1857, only two days after Buchanan's inauguration, the Supreme Court gave the new administration an unintended jolt with one of the most controversial decisions in its history.

The *Dred Scott* Decision

The owner of a Missouri slave named Dred Scott had taken him to live for several years in Illinois, a free state, and in the Wisconsin Territory, in what is now Minnesota, where slavery had been banned by the Missouri Compromise. Scott had returned to Missouri with his owner, only to sue eventually for his freedom on the grounds that his residence in a free state and a free territory had made him free. His case ultimately went to the Supreme Court. Two northern justices joined all five southern members of the Court in ruling 7 to 2 that Scott remained a slave. The majority opinion was written by Chief Justice Roger Taney of Maryland, who argued that under Missouri law, which took precedence, Scott was still a slave.

Had the Court stopped there, the public outcry would have been minimal. But the Court majority believed that they had a responsibility to deal with the larger controversy between the two sections. In particular, Chief Justice Taney wanted to strengthen the judicial protection of slavery. Taney, a former Maryland slaveowner who had freed his slaves, ruled that African Americans could not be and never had been citizens of the United States. Instead, he insisted that at the time the Constitution was adopted, they were "regarded as beings of an inferior order, so far inferior that they had no rights which the white man was bound to respect." In addition, the Court ruled that the Missouri Compromise was unconstitutional. Congress, it declared, had no power to ban slavery from *any* territory of the United States.

While southerners rejoiced at this outcome, Republicans denounced the Court. Their platform declared, after all, that Congress ought to prohibit slavery in all territories. "We know the court . . . has often over-ruled its own decisions," Abraham Lincoln

Dred Scott

Chief Justice Roger Taney

observed, "and we shall do what we can to have it over-rule this." But the decision was sobering. If all territories were now open to slavery, how long would it be before a move was made to reintroduce slavery in the free states? For Republicans, the Court's decision foreshadowed the spread of slavery throughout the West and even throughout the nation.

But the decision also threatened Douglas's more moderate solution of popular sovereignty. If Congress had no power to prohibit slavery in a territory, how could it authorize a territorial legislature to do so? Although the Court did not rule on this point, the clear implication of the *Dred Scott* decision was that popular sovereignty was also unconstitutional. The Court, in effect, had endorsed John C. Calhoun's radical view that slavery was legal in all the territories. It had intended to settle the question of slavery in the territories once and for all. Instead the Court succeeded only in strengthening the forces of extremism in American politics.

The Panic of 1857

As the nation grappled with the *Dred Scott* decision, an economic depression aggravated sectional conflict. Once again, boom gave way to bust as falling wheat prices and contracted credit hurt commercial farmers and overextended railroad investors. The Panic of 1857 was nowhere near as severe as the depression of 1837–1843. But the psychological results were far-reaching, for the South remained relatively untouched.

Economic Issues Increase Sectional Tensions

With the price of cotton and other southern commodities still high, southern secessionists hailed the panic as proof that an independent southern nation was economically workable. Insisting that cotton sustained the international economy, James Henry Hammond, a senator from South Carolina, boasted: "What would happen if no cotton was furnished for three years? England would topple headlong and carry the whole civilized world with her save the South. No, you dare not make war on cotton. No power on earth dares to make war on it. Cotton is king."

For their part, northerners urged federal action to spur the economy. Southerners defeated an attempt to increase the tariff duties, at their lowest level since 1815, and Buchanan, under southern pressure, vetoed bills to improve navigation on the Great Lakes and to give free farms to western settlers. Many businesspeople and conservative ex-Whigs condemned these southern actions and now endorsed the Republican party.

The Lecompton Constitution

Although the *Dred Scott* decision and economic depression weakened the bonds of the Union, Kansas remained at the center of the political stage. In June 1857, when the territory elected delegates to draft a state constitution, free-state voters boycotted the election, thereby giving proslavery forces control of the convention that met in Lecompton.

Attempt to Make Kansas a Slave State

The delegates drafted a constitution that made slavery legal. Even more boldly, they scheduled a referendum in which voters could choose only whether to admit additional slaves into the territory. They could not vote against the constitution, and they could not vote to get rid of slavery entirely. Once again, free-staters boycotted the election, and the Lecompton constitution was approved.

As a supporter of popular sovereignty, President Buchanan had pledged a free and fair vote on the Lecompton constitution. But the outcome offered him the unexpected opportunity to satisfy his southern supporters by pushing the Lecompton constitution through Congress. This action was too much for Douglas, who broke party ranks and denounced the Lecompton constitution as a fraud. Nevertheless, the administration prevailed in the Senate. Buchanan now pulled out all the stops to gain the necessary votes in the House to admit Kansas as a slave state. But the House, where northern representation was much stronger, rejected the constitution. In a compromise, Congress, using indirect language, returned the constitution to Kansas for another vote. This time it was decisively defeated, 11,300 to 1,788. No doubt remained that as soon as Kansas had sufficient population, it would come into the Union as a free state.

Defeat of the Lecompton Constitution

The attempt to force slavery on the people of Kansas drove many conservative northerners into the Republican party. And Douglas, once the Democrats' strongest potential candidate in 1860, now found himself assailed by the southern wing of his party. On top of that, in the summer of 1858, Douglas faced a desperate fight in his race for reelection to the Senate against Republican Abraham Lincoln.

The Lincoln-Douglas Debates

"He is the strong man of his party . . . and the best stump speaker, with his droll ways and dry jokes, in the West," Douglas commented when he learned of Lincoln's nomination to oppose him. "He is as honest as he is shrewd, and if I beat him my victory will be hardly won." Tall (6 feet, 4 inches) and gangly, Lincoln had a gaunt face, high cheekbones, deep-socketed gray eyes, and a shock of unruly hair. He appeared awkward as he spoke, never knowing quite what to do with his large, muscular hands. Yet his finely honed logic, his simple, eloquent language, and his sincerity carried the audience with him. His sentences, as spare as the man himself, had none of the oratorical flourishes common in that day. "If we could first know *where* we are, and *whither* we are tending, we could then better judge *what* to do, and *how* to do it," Lincoln began, in accepting his party's nomination for senator from Illinois in 1858. He quoted a proverb from the Bible:

Lincoln's View of the Crisis

> A house divided against itself cannot stand.
>
> I believe this government cannot endure, permanently half *slave* and half *free*.
>
> I do not expect the Union to be *dissolved*—I do not expect the house to *fall*—but I *do* expect it will cease to be divided.
>
> It will become *all* one thing, or *all* the other.
>
> Either the *opponents* of slavery, will arrest the further spread of it, and place it where the public mind shall rest in the belief that it is in course of ultimate extinction; or its *advocates* will push it forward, till it shall become alike lawful in all the States, *old* as well as new—*North* as well as *South*.

The message echoed through the hall and across the pages of the national press.

Born in the slave state of Kentucky, Lincoln had grown up mostly in southern Indiana and central Illinois. He could split rails with the best frontier farmer, loved telling stories, and was at home mixing with ordinary folk. Yet his intense ambition had lifted him above the backwoods from which he came. He compensated for a lack of formal schooling through disciplined self-education, and he became a shrewd courtroom lawyer of respectable social standing. Known for his sense of humor, he was nonetheless subject to chronic depression, and his eyes often mirrored a deep melancholy.

Lincoln's Character

At the age of 25, Lincoln entered the state legislature and soon became an important Whig strategist. After the party's decline, he joined the Republicans and became one of their key leaders in Illinois. In a series of seven joint debates, Lincoln challenged Douglas to discuss the issues of slavery and the sectional controversy. Douglas joined the debate by portraying Lincoln as a radical whose "House Divided" speech preached sectional warfare. The nation *could* endure half slave and half free, Douglas declared, as long as states and territories were left alone to regulate their own affairs. Accusing Lincoln of believing that blacks were his equal, Douglas countered that the American government had been "made by the white man, for the white man, to be administered by the white man."

Douglas and Lincoln on the Slavery Issue

Lincoln responded by denying any intention to interfere with slavery in the South, but he insisted that the spread of slavery to the territories was a blight on the Republic. Douglas could not be counted on to oppose slavery's expansion, Lincoln warned, for he had already admitted that he didn't care whether slavery was voted "down or

Superb debaters, Douglas and Lincoln nevertheless had very different speaking styles. The deep-voiced Douglas was constantly on the attack, drawing on his remarkable memory and showering points like buckshot in all directions. Employing sarcasm and ridicule rather than humor, he never tried to crack a joke. Lincoln, who had a high-pitched voice and a rather awkward platform manner, developed his arguments more carefully and methodically, and he relied on his sense of humor and unmatched ability as a storyteller to drive his points home to the audience.

up." For his part, Lincoln denied any "perfect equality between the negroes and white people" and opposed allowing blacks to vote, hold office, or intermarry with whites. But, he concluded,

> notwithstanding all this, there is no reason in the world why the negro is not entitled to all the natural rights enumerated in the Declaration of Independence, the right to life, liberty and the pursuit of happiness. . . . I agree with Judge Douglas [that the negro] is not my equal in many respects—certainly not in color, perhaps not in moral or intellectual endowment. But in the right to eat the bread, without leave of anybody else, which his own hand earns, *he is my equal and the equal of Judge Douglas, and the equal of every living man.*

Freeport Doctrine

At the debate held at Freeport, Illinois, Lincoln asked Douglas how under the *Dred Scott* decision the people of a territory could lawfully exclude slavery before statehood. Douglas answered, with what became known as the Freeport Doctrine, that slavery could exist only with the protection of law and that slaveowners would never bring their slaves into an area that did not have a slave code. Therefore, Douglas explained, if the people of a territory refused to pass a slave code, slavery would never be established there.

In a close race, the legislature elected Douglas to another term in the Senate.* But Democrats from the South angrily repudiated him and condemned the Freeport Doctrine. Although Lincoln lost, Republicans thought his performance marked him as a presidential contender for 1860.

---

*State legislatures elected senators until 1913, when the Seventeenth Amendment was adopted. While Lincoln and Douglas both campaigned for the office, Illinois voters actually voted for candidates for the legislature who were pledged to one of the senatorial candidates.

The Beleaguered South

While northerners increasingly feared that the Slave Power was conspiring to extend slavery into the free states, southerners worried that the "Black Republicans" would hem them in and undermine their political power. The very factors that brought prosperity during the 1850s stimulated the South's sense of crisis. As the price of slaves rose sharply, the proportion of southerners who owned slaves had dropped almost a third since 1830. Land also was being consolidated into larger holdings, evidence of declining opportunity for ordinary white southerners. Furthermore, California and Kansas had been closed to southern slaveholders—unfairly, in their eyes. Finally, Douglas's clever claim that a territory could effectively outlaw slavery using the Freeport Doctrine seemed to negate the *Dred Scott* decision that slavery was legal in all the territories.

Failed Solutions

The South's growing sense of moral and political isolation made this crisis more acute. By the 1850s slavery had been abolished throughout most of the Americas, and in the United States the South's political power was steadily shrinking. Only the expansion of slavery held out any promise of new slave states needed to preserve the South's political power and protect its way of life. "The truth is," fumed one Alabama politician, ". . . the South is excluded from the common territories of the Union. The right of expansion claimed to be a necessity of her continued existence, is practically and effectively denied the South."

The Road to War

In 1857 John Brown—the abolitionist firebrand—had returned to the East from Kansas, consumed with the idea of attacking slavery in the South itself. With financing from a number of prominent northern reformers, Brown gathered 21 followers, including 5 free blacks, in hope of fomenting a slave insurrection. On the night of October 16, 1859, the group seized the unguarded federal armory at Harpers Ferry in Virginia. But no slaves rallied to Brown's standard: few even lived in the area to begin with. Before long the raiders found themselves holed up in the armory's engine house with hostile townspeople taking potshots at them. Charging with bayonets fixed, federal troops commanded by Colonel Robert E. Lee soon captured Brown and his band.

John Brown's Raid

John Brown

Brown's raid at Harpers Ferry was yet another blow weakening the forces of compromise and moderation at the nation's political center. The invasion itself was a dismal failure, as were most of the enterprises Brown undertook in his troubled life. But the old man knew how to bear himself with a martyr's dignity. "Had I so interfered in behalf of the rich, the powerful, the intelligent, the so-called great," he declared at his trial, ". . . it would have been all right . . . to have interfered as I have done in behalf of [God's] despised poor, is no wrong, but a right." On December 2, 1859, the state of Virginia hanged Brown for treason.

Republicans made haste to denounce Brown's raid, lest they be tarred as radicals, but other northerners were less cautious. Ralph Waldo Emerson described Brown as a "saint, whose martyrdom will make the gallows as glorious as the cross," and on the day of his execution, church bells tolled in many northern cities. Only a minority of northerners endorsed Brown, but southerners were shocked by such public displays of sympathy. And they were firmly convinced that the Republican party was secretly connected to the raid.

Reaction to the Raid

In 1850 theaters remained a controversial if popular form of entertainment. The Puritans had roundly condemned plays of any sort, and many religious critics still frowned on theatergoing. Nevertheless, with the rise of cities the stage became a medium for mass entertainment and increasingly attracted the urban middle class.

In 1852 George C. Howard, the head of the Museum Theater in Troy, New York, was looking for new material. He was attracted to the issue of slavery by a controversial new novel, *Uncle Tom's Cabin*. Written by Harriet Beecher Stowe, one of the Reverend Lyman Beecher's energetic sons and daughters, the book was a runaway bestseller, with more than 300,000 copies printed in the first year.

The book's plot followed a host of characters to a multitude of locales. George and Eliza Harris, a mulatto slave couple, learn that their young son is to be sold. Eliza flees with her child across the ice-choked Ohio River to freedom, while George escapes separately. At the same time, Tom, an older slave and a devout Christian, is sold and taken to Louisiana. He is bought by the father of Evangeline St. Clare, an innocent, golden-haired child who treats Tom kindly, but after both Evangeline and her father die,

In this playbill advertising a dramatic production of Uncle Tom's Cabin, *vicious bloodhounds pursue the light-skinned Eliza, who clutches her child as she frantically leaps to safety across the ice-choked Ohio River.*

A Sectional Election

When Congress convened in December, there were ominous signs everywhere of the growing sectional rift. Intent on destroying Douglas's Freeport Doctrine, southern radicals demanded a congressional slave code to protect slavery in the territories. To northern Democrats, such a platform spelled political death. As one Indiana Democrat put it, "We cannot carry a single congressional district on that doctrine in the state."

Disruption of the Democratic Party

At the Democratic convention in April in Charleston, South Carolina, southern radicals boldly pressed their demand for a federal slave code. After a heated debate, however, the convention adopted the Douglas platform upholding popular sovereignty, whereupon the delegations from eight southern states walked out. Unable to agree on a candidate, the convention finally reassembled two months later in Baltimore and nominated Douglas. At this point most of the remaining southern Democrats left in disgust. Joining with the Charleston seceders, they nominated their own candidate, Vice President John C. Breckinridge of Kentucky, on a platform supporting a federal slave code. The last major national party had shattered.

In May the Republicans met in Chicago, where they turned to Abraham Lincoln, a moderate on the slavery issue who was strong in Illinois and the other northern states the party had lost in 1856. The election that followed was really two contests in one. In the North, which had a majority of the electoral votes, only Lincoln and Douglas had any chance of carrying a state. In the South, the race pitted Breckinridge against John Bell of Tennessee, the candidate of the new conservative Constitutional Union party. Although Lincoln received less than 40 percent of the popular vote and had virtually no support in the South, he won 180 electoral votes, 27 more than needed for election. For the first time, the nation had elected a president

Tom is sold to Simon Legree, a hard-drinking, blasphemous Yankee. When Tom refuses to whip other slaves on the plantation, Legree beats him to death; Tom is a martyr to his faith in God and his love for his fellow man.

Compressing this complex story was not easy. Then, too, no American play on the subject of slavery had been produced before, and many theater managers believed that the public would not accept a black hero. But Howard wanted to cast his four-year-old daughter, Cordelia (already an experienced trouper), as young Eva, and so he produced an adaptation that focused on Tom's experiences in the St. Clare household.

The play's success prompted a sequel based on the Legree section of the novel; finally Howard combined the two plays into a 6-act, 30-scene epic that took an entire evening to perform. From Troy the production moved to New York City, where it ran for an unprecedented 325 performances and then achieved similar triumphs in other northern cities. No play had ever attracted such large audiences.

The production had a good eye for the dramatic: a slave auction, Eva's death after a long illness, and Tom's defiance of Legree when threatened with a whipping. ("My soul a'nt yours, mas'r; you haven't bought it—ye can't buy it.") Eliza's flight across the icy Ohio River—described in two paragraphs in the book—became one of the major scenes, with a pack of bloodhounds added for good measure. As in minstrel shows, blacks were played by whites wearing lampblack.

Howard worked hard to attract a new middle-class audience. He banned the prostitutes who frequented theaters and in the lobby displayed the endorsements of prominent religious leaders and reformers on posters. A further innovation, matinee performances, attracted women and children. Blacks, who normally were barred from New York theaters, were seated in a segregated section.

The play moved audiences of all backgrounds. After wrestling with his religious scruples, John Kirk, a salesman, finally went to see a Chicago production. "The appeals of the dying little Eva to her father, for Uncle Tom's freedom, were overwhelmingly affecting," he testified. "I never saw so many white pocket handkerchiefs in use at the same time . . . I was not the only one in that large audience to shed tears I assure you." Equally striking, the play affected the workers and apprentices who made up the theater's normal clientele. Traditionally hostile to abolitionism, these groups cheered wildly over Eliza's escape. By providing vivid images of the cruelty of slavery, theatrical presentations of *Uncle Tom's Cabin,* even more than the book, heightened the sectional tensions that divided the nation in the 1850s.

who headed a completely sectional party and who was committed to stopping the expansion of slavery.

Secession

Although the Republicans had not won control of either house of Congress, Lincoln's election struck many southerners as a blow of terrible finality. Lincoln had been lifted into office on the strength of the free states alone. With Republicans opposed to slavery's expansion, the South's power base could only shrink. It was not unrealistic, many fire-eaters argued, to believe that Lincoln would use federal aid to induce the border states to voluntarily free their slaves. Once slavery disappeared there, and new states were added, the necessary three-fourths majority would exist to approve a constitutional amendment abolishing slavery. Or perhaps Lincoln might send other John Browns into the South to stir up more slave insurrections. The Montgomery (Alabama) *Mail* accused Republicans of intending "to free the negroes and force amalgamation between them and the children of the poor men of the South."

Southern Fears

Secession seemed the only alternative left to protect southern equality and liberty. South Carolina, which had challenged federal authority in the nullification crisis, was determined to force the other southern states to act. On December 20, 1860, a popular convention unanimously passed a resolution seceding from the Union. The rest of the Deep South followed, and on February 7, 1861, the states stretching from South Carolina to Texas organized the Confederate States of America and elected Jefferson Davis president.

Confederate States of America

But the Upper South and the border states declined to secede, hoping that once again Congress could patch together a settlement. Senator John Crittenden of Kentucky proposed a constitutional amendment extending to California the old Missouri Compromise

Election of 1860 *Although Lincoln did not win a majority of the popular vote, he still would have been elected even if the votes for all three of his opponents had been combined, because he won a clear majority in every state he carried except California, Oregon, and New Jersey (whose electoral votes he split with Douglas).*

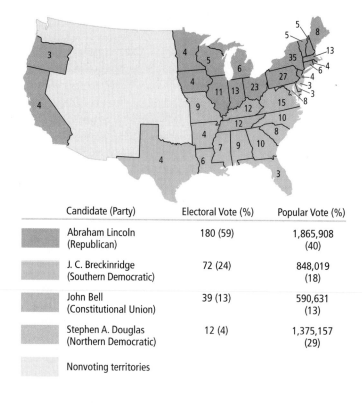

	Candidate (Party)	Electoral Vote (%)	Popular Vote (%)
	Abraham Lincoln (Republican)	180 (59)	1,865,908 (40)
	J. C. Breckinridge (Southern Democratic)	72 (24)	848,019 (18)
	John Bell (Constitutional Union)	39 (13)	590,631 (13)
	Stephen A. Douglas (Northern Democratic)	12 (4)	1,375,157 (29)
	Nonvoting territories		

line of 36°30′. Slavery would be prohibited north of this line and given federal protection south of it in all territories, including any acquired in the future. Furthermore, Crittenden proposed an "unamendable amendment" to the Constitution, forever preserving slavery in states where it already existed.

But the Crittenden Compromise was doomed for the simple reason that the two groups who were required to make concessions—Republicans and secessionists—had no interest in doing so. "The argument is exhausted," representatives from the Deep South announced, even before Crittenden had introduced his legislative package. "We have just carried an election on principles fairly stated to the people," Lincoln wrote in opposing compromise. "Now we are told in advance, the government shall be broken up, unless we surrender to those we have beaten, before we take the offices. If we surrender, it is the end of us, and of the government." Only the unamendable amendment passed, but war ended any possibility that it would be ratified.

Crittenden Compromise Fails

The Outbreak of War

As he prepared to take office, Lincoln pondered what to do about secession. In his inaugural address on March 4, he sought to reassure southerners that he had no intention, "directly or indirectly, to interfere with the institution of slavery in the States where it exists." But he maintained that "the Union of these states is perpetual," echoing Andrew Jackson's Proclamation on Nullification, and that no state could leave the Union by its own action. He also announced that he intended to "hold, occupy and possess" federal property and collect customs duties under the tariff. He closed by calling for a restoration of the "bonds of affection" that united all Americans.

The new president hoped for time to work out a solution, but on his first day in office he was handed a dispatch from Major Robert Anderson, commander of the federal garrison at Fort Sumter in Charleston harbor. Sumter was one of the few remaining federal outposts in the South. Anderson informed the government that he was almost out of food and that, unless resupplied, he would have to surrender in six weeks. For a month Lincoln looked for a way out, but he finally sent a relief expedition. As

Fort Sumter

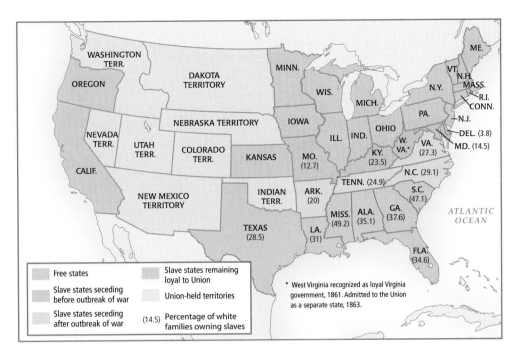

* West Virginia recognized as loyal Virginia
  government, 1861. Admitted to the Union
  as a separate state, 1863.

Free states

Slave states seceding
before outbreak of war

Slave states seceding
after outbreak of war

Slave states remaining
loyal to Union

Union-held territories

(14.5) Percentage of white
families owning slaves

The Pattern of Secession
*Led by South Carolina, the
Deep South seceded between
Lincoln's election in November
and his inauguration in
March. The Upper South
did not secede until after the
firing on Fort Sumter. The
four border slave states never
seceded and remained in the
Union throughout the war. As
the map indicates, secession
sentiment was strongest
in states where the highest
percentage of white families
owned slaves.*

a conciliatory gesture, he notified the governor of South Carolina that supplies were being sent and that if the fleet were allowed to pass, only food, and not men, arms, or ammunition, would be landed.

The burden of decision now shifted to Jefferson Davis. From his point of view, secession was a constitutional right and the Confederacy was a legitimate government. To allow the United States to hold property and maintain military forces within the Confederacy would destroy its claim of independence. Davis therefore instructed the Confederate commander at Charleston to demand the immediate surrender of Fort Sumter and, if refused, to open fire. When Anderson declined the ultimatum, Confederate batteries began shelling the fort on April 12 at 4:30 A.M. Some 33 hours later Anderson surrendered. When in response Lincoln called for 75,000 volunteers to put down the rebellion, four states in the Upper South, led by Virginia, also seceded. Matters had passed beyond compromise.

Upper South Secedes

The Roots of a Divided Society

And so the Union was broken. After 70 years, the forces of sectionalism and separatism had finally outpulled the ties binding "these United States." Why did affairs come to such a pass?

In some ways, as we have seen, the revolution in markets that transformed the nation during these years served to link together northerners and southerners. The cotton planter in Chapter 10 who rode the steamship *Fashion* along the Alabama River ("Time's money! Time's money!") was wearing ready-made clothes manufactured in New York from southern cotton. Chauncey Jerome's clocks from Connecticut were keeping time not only for commercial planters but also for Lowell mill workers like Mary Paul, who learned to measure her lunch break in minutes. Farmers in both Tennessee and Iowa were interested in the price of wheat in New York, for it affected the profits that could be made shipping their grain by the new railroad lines. American society had become far more specialized, and therefore far more interdependent, since the days of Crèvecoeur's self-sufficient farmer of the 1780s.

But a specialized economy had not brought unity. For the North, specialization meant more factories, a higher percentage of urban workers, and a greater number of

*When news of secession spread,
many southern white women
wore decorative cockades
made of woven palmetto
leaves and silk.*

Diverging Economies

States' Rights or Slavery?

Finding the "Lost" Cause of the Civil War

Why did the South secede from the Union? Jefferson Davis, president of the Confederate States, was explicit. The South fought for "the inalienable right of a people to change their government . . . to withdraw from a Union into which they had, as sovereign communities, voluntarily entered." What about slavery? "The existence of African servitude was in no wise the cause of the conflict, but only an incident." Davis's claim is often quoted in defense of "states' rights" as the cause of the war.

Historians, however, are sensitive to chronology and context. Davis made his claim *after* the war had ended and slavery was abolished. *Before* the war, secessionists placed slavery squarely at the center of the dispute. To chart that perspective, one historian retraced the journeys of the Secession Commis-sioners of the Confederacy in 1861. These officials were appointed to visit Southern states that had not yet seceded, to convince them to join the movement. "The conflict between slavery and non-slavery is a conflict for life and death," proclaimed a South Carolina commissioner. "The South cannot exist without African slavery." A commissioner from Alabama asked rhetorically, "Will the South give up the institution of slavery and consent that her citizens be stripped of their property, her civilization destroyed, the whole land laid waste by fire and sword? It is impossible. She cannot; she will not." Sometimes knowing when a statement was made is as important as knowing what was said. What information does the map on secession (see page 427) provide to support the case linking secession and slavery?

cities and towns. Industry affected midwestern farmers as well, for their steel plows and McCormick reapers allowed them to farm larger holdings and required greater capital investment in the new machinery. For its part, the South was transformed by the industrial revolution too, as textile factories made cotton the booming mainstay of its economy. But for all its growth, the region remained largely a rural society. Its prosperity stemmed from expansion westward into new areas of cotton production, not new forms of production or technology. The dominant planter class reinforced its traditional concepts of honor, hierarchy, and deference.

Northerners reacted differently. Envelopes like the one shown here portrayed a secessionist southern preacher inspired by the devil to give "an eloquent discourse" on "Treason" and God's approval of slavery.

AN EMINENT SOUTHERN CLERGYMAN, During an eloquent discourse, is wonderfully assisted in finding scriptural authority for Secession and Treason, and the divine ordination of Slavery.

Above all, the intensive labor required to produce cotton, rice, and sugar made slavery an inseparable part of the southern way of life—"so intimately mingled with our social conditions," as one Georgian admitted, "that it would be impossible to eradicate it." An increasing number of northerners viewed slavery as evil, not so much out of high-minded sympathy toward slaves but as a labor system that threatened the republican ideals of white American society.

Weaknesses of the Political System

It fell to the political system to try to resolve sectional conflict through a system of national parties that represented various interest groups and promoted democratic debate. But the political system had critical weaknesses. The American process of electing a president gave the winning candidate a state's entire electoral vote, regardless of the margin of victory. That procedure made a northern sectional party possible, since the Republicans could never have carried an election on the basis of a popular vote alone. In addition, the four-year fixed presidential term allowed Presidents Pierce and Buchanan to remain in office, pursuing disruptive policies on Kansas even after the voters had rejected those policies in the midterm congressional elections in 1854 and 1858. Finally, since 1844 the Democratic party had required a two-thirds vote to nominate its presidential candidate. Unintentionally, this requirement made it difficult to pick any truly forceful leader and gave the South a veto over the party's candidate. Yet the South, by itself, could not elect a president.

The nation's republican heritage also contributed to the political system's vulnerability. Ever since the Revolution, when Americans accused the king and Parliament of deliberately plotting to deprive them of their liberties, Americans were on the watch for political conspiracies. Such an outlook often stimulated exaggerated fears, unreasonable conclusions, and excessive reactions. For their part, Republicans emphasized the existence of the Slave Power bent on eradicating northern rights. Southerners, on the other hand, accused the Black Republicans of conspiring to destroy southern equality. Each side viewed itself as defending the country's republican tradition from an internal threat.

Belief in Conspiracies Against Liberty

But in the end, the threat to the Union came not from within but from beyond its borders. As the nation expanded in the 1840s, it incorporated vast new territories, becoming a truly continental republic. And that forced the Union, in absorbing new lands, to define itself anew. If the American frontier had not swept so quickly toward the Pacific, the nation might have been able to postpone the day of reckoning on slavery until some form of gradual emancipation could be adopted. But the luxury of time was not available. The new territories became the battlegrounds for two contrasting ways of life, with slavery at the center of the debate. Elsewhere in the world the push toward abolition grew louder, whether of serfdom in eastern Europe or of slavery across the globe. Americans who saw the issue in moral terms joined that chorus. They saw no reason why the abolition of slavery should be postponed.

In 1850, supporters and opponents of slavery were still willing to compromise on how "the peculiar institution" could expand into the new territories. But a decade later, many Americans both North and South had come to accept the idea of an irrepressible conflict between two societies, one based on freedom, the other on slavery, in which only one side could ultimately prevail. At stake, it seemed, was control of the nation's future. Four years later, as a weary Abraham Lincoln looked back to the beginning of the conflict, he noted, "Both parties deprecated war, but one of them would *make* war rather than let the nation survive, and the other would *accept* war rather than let it perish, and the war came."

Significant Events

1834	McCormick patents mechanical reaper
1837	John Deere patents steel plow
1840–1860	Expansion of railroad network
1846–1854	Mass immigration to United States
1849–1860	Cotton boom
1850	Illinois Central is first land-grant railroad
1852	Pierce elected president

1853	Gadsden Purchase
1854	Kansas-Nebraska Act passed; Republican party founded; Ostend Manifesto peak of immigration
1854–1855	Height of Know-Nothings' popularity
1855	Fighting begins in Kansas; Republican party organizes in key northern states
1856	"Sack of Lawrence" in Kansas; caning of Charles Sumner; Pottawatomie massacre; Buchanan elected president
1857	*Dred Scott* decision; Lecompton constitution drafted
1857–1861	Panic and depression
1858	Congress rejects Lecompton constitution; Lincoln-Douglas debates
1859	John Brown's raid on Harpers Ferry
1860	Democratic party ruptures at Charleston; Lincoln elected president; South Carolina secedes
1861	Rest of Deep South secedes; Confederate States of America established; Crittenden Compromise defeated; war begins at Fort Sumter; Upper South secedes

Chapter Summary

In the 1850s, the slavery issue reemerged in national politics and increasingly disrupted the party system, leading to the outbreak of war in 1861.

- Fundamental economic changes heightened sectional tensions in the 1850s.

  —The construction of a vast railroad network reoriented western trade from the South to the East.
  —A tide of new immigrants swelled the North's population (and hence its political power) at the expense of the South, thereby stimulating southern fears.

- The old Jacksonian party system was shattered by the nativist movement and by a renewed controversy of the expansion of slavery.

  —In the Kansas-Nebraska Act, Senator Stephen A. Douglas tried to defuse the slavery debate by incorporating popular sovereignty (the idea that the people of a territory should decide the status of slavery there). This act effectively repealed the Missouri Compromise.
  —Popular sovereignty failed in the Kansas Territory, where fighting broke out between proslavery and antislavery partisans.

- Sectional violence reached a climax in May 1856 with the attack on Lawrence, Kansas, and the caning of Senator Charles Sumner of Massachusetts by Representative Preston S. Brooks of South Carolina.

- Sectional tensions sparked the formation of a new antislavery Republican party, and the party system realigned along sectional lines.

  —The Supreme Court's *Dred Scott* decision, the Panic of 1857, the congressional struggle over the proslavery Lecompton constitution, and John Brown's attack on Harpers Ferry in 1859 strengthened the two sectional extremes.

- In 1860 Abraham Lincoln became the first Republican to be elected president.

  —Following Lincoln's triumph, the seven states of the Deep South seceded.
  —When Lincoln sent supplies to the Union garrison in Fort Sumter in Charleston harbor, Confederate batteries bombarded the fort into submission.
  —The North rallied to Lincoln's decision to use force to restore the Union, and in response the four states of the Upper South seceded.

Additional Reading

The problem of the coming of the Civil War has attracted considerable historical attention over the years. David M. Potter, *The Impending Crisis, 1848–1861* (1976), is a superior political treatment of the period. The political aspects of the conflict also take center stage in Michael F. Holt's brief and incisive work, *The Fate of Their Country: Politicians, Slavery Extension, and the*

Coming of the Civil War (2004). Holt stresses the self-interest of the political leaders and plays down the larger structural economic and social factors. A contrasting and similarly brief study can be found in Don E. Fehrenbacher, *The South and Three Sectional Crises* (1980).

The heavy immigration during these years is described in Philip D. Taylor, *The Distant Magnet* (1971). Michael F. Holt provides the best treatment of the Know Nothing Party, as well as the more general topic of antebellum political realignment, in *The Political Crisis of the 1850s.* (1978).

John McCardell's *The Idea of a Southern Nation* (1979) is a solid, well-written treatment of southern nationalism in this period. The most thorough examination of the blend of factors that produced the Republican party is William E. Gienapp, *The Origins of the Republican Party, 1852–1856* (1987). Eric Foner, in *Free Soil, Free Labor, Free Men* (1970), focuses on the ideas of Republican party leaders. For the turbulent history of Kansas in this period, see James A. Rawley, *Race and Politics* (1969). The critical events of 1857 are the focal point of Kenneth M. Stampp's *America in 1857* (1990). The secession movement has largely been investigated in specific southern states. A particularly good example of this approach is Stephen A. Channing's account of secession in South Carolina, *Crisis of Fear* (1974), although Charles B. Dew provides a regional view by examining the role of the Secession Commissioners appointed by the Confederacy to persuade wavering southerners in *Apostles of Secession* (2001). Kenneth M. Stampp, *And the War Came* (1950), is the best study of northern public opinion during the secession crisis. A sophisticated examination of the war's origins is Gabor S. Boritt, ed., *Why the War Came* (1996). For a discussion of the broader issue of why the South chose secession and fought the Civil War, see Gary W. Gallagher and Alan T. Nolan, eds., *The Myth of the Lost Cause and Civil War History* (2000).

For a fuller list of readings, see the Bibliography at www.mhhe.com/davidsonnation6.

CHAPTER 16
Total War & the Republic
1861~1865

A Rout at Bull Run

The war won't last sixty days!" Of that Jim Tinkham was confident. With dreams of a hero's return, Tinkham quit his job as a grocery store clerk and enlisted for three months in a Massachusetts regiment. Soon he was transferred to Washington as part of the Union army being assembled under General Irvin McDowell. Tinkham was elated when in mid-July the army was finally ordered to march toward the Confederates concentrated at Manassas Junction, 25 miles away. On the way, Tinkham passed carriages carrying members of Congress and other jaunty sightseers, their picnic baskets filled with provisions and fine wines. They too had come to witness the battle that would crush the rebellion.*

The battle began at dawn on July 21, with McDowell commanding 30,000 troops against General Pierre Beauregard's 22,000. Tinkham did not arrive on the field until early afternoon. As his regiment pushed toward the front, he felt faint at his first sight of the dead and wounded, some mangled horribly. But the Massachusetts troops were caught up in the excitement of battle as they charged up Henry Hill. Suddenly the Confederate ranks broke and exuberant Union troops shouted, "The war is over!"

The timely arrival of fresh Confederate troops, however, enabled the rebels to regroup. Among the reinforcements who rushed to Henry Hill was 19-year-old Randolph McKim of Baltimore. A student at the University of Virginia when the war began, McKim joined the First Maryland Infantry as a private when Abraham Lincoln imposed martial law in his home state. "The cause of the South had become identified with liberty itself," he explained. After only a week of drill, McKim boarded a train on July 21 bound for Manassas. When he and his comrades disembarked, they could hear the cannon firing in the distance, so they marched double-quick to the battlefield. The arrival of the First Maryland and other reinforcements in the late afternoon turned the tide of battle. The faltering Confederate line held, then charged, giving full throat for the first time to the famous "rebel yell." "There is nothing like [the yell] this side of the infernal region," explained one Union soldier. "The peculiar sensation that it sends down your backbone under these circumstances can never be told."

---

*The Union and the Confederacy often gave different names to a battle. The Confederates called the first battle Manassas; the Union, Bull Run.

Reveille rouses drowsy Union soldiers on a wintry morning as a drummer boy warms his hands. Instead of the glory they expected, reveille, roll call, and drill constituted Civil War soldiers' usual camp routine. A hired black laborer is already at work as the troops awaken.

The Union troops gave way slowly at first, but discipline dissolved once McDowell ordered a retreat, and the army quickly degenerated into a frightened, stampeding mob. Troops threw away their equipment, shoved aside officers who tried to stop them, and raced frantically past the wagons, artillery pieces, and civilian carriages that clogged the road. Joining the stampede was Jim Tinkham, who confessed he would have continued on to Boston if he had not been stopped by a guard after crossing the Long Bridge into Washington. All the next day in a drizzling rain, mud-spattered troops straggled into the capital in complete disorder.

The rout at Bull Run sobered the North. Gone were dreams of ending the war with one glorious battle. Gone was the illusion that 75,000 volunteers serving three months could crush the rebellion. As one perceptive observer noted, "We have undertaken to make war without in the least knowing how." Having cast off his earlier illusions, a newly determined Jim Tinkham reenlisted for a three-year hitch.

Meaning of Total War

Still, it was not surprising that both sides underestimated the magnitude of the conflict. Previous warfare as it had evolved in Europe consisted largely of maneuverings that took relatively few lives, respected private property, and left civilians largely unharmed. The Civil War, on the other hand, was the first war whose major battles routinely involved more than 100,000 troops. So many combatants could be equipped only through the use of factory-produced weaponry, they could be moved and supplied only with the help of railroads, and they could be sustained only through the concerted efforts of civilian society as a whole. The morale of the population, the quality of political leadership, and the utilization of industrial and economic might were all critical to the outcome. Quite simply, the Civil War was the first total war in history.

The Demands of Total War

When the war began, the North had an enormous advantage in manpower and industrial capacity. The Union's population was 2.5 times larger, and its advantage in white men of military age even greater. The North had a much larger merchant marine; produced more iron, firearms, and textiles; contained more railroad track and rolling stock; and possessed more than ten times the industrial capacity.

Southern Advantages

From a modern perspective, the South's attempt to defend its independence against such odds seems a hopeless cause. Yet this view indicates how much the conception of war has changed. European observers, who knew the strength and resources of the two sides, believed that the Confederacy, with its large area, poor roads, and rugged terrain, could never be conquered. Indeed, the South enjoyed definite strategic advantages. To be victorious, it did not need to invade the North—only to defend its own land and prevent the North from destroying its armies. Southern soldiers knew the topography of their home country better, and a friendly population regularly supplied them with intelligence about Union troop movements.

The North, in contrast, had to invade and conquer the Confederacy and destroy the southern will to resist. To do so, it would have to deploy thousands of soldiers to defend long supply lines in enemy territory, a situation that significantly reduced the northern advantage in manpower. Yet in the end, the Confederacy was not only invaded and conquered but also utterly destroyed. By 1865 the Union forces had penetrated virtually every part of the 500,000 square miles of the Confederacy and were able to move almost at will. The Civil War demonstrated the capacity of a modern society to overcome the problems of distance and terrain with technology.

Resources of the Union and the Confederacy, 1861

	UNION	CONFEDERACY	UNION ADVANTAGE
Total population	23,300,000	9,100,000*	2.5 to 1
White male population (18–45 years)	4,600,000	1,100,000	4.2 to 1
Bank deposits	$207,000,000	$47,000,000	4.4 to 1
Value of manufactured goods	$1,730,000,000	$156,000,000	11 to 1
Railroad mileage	22,000	9,000	2.4 to 1
Shipping tonnage	4,600,000	290,000	16 to 1
Value of textiles produced	$181,000,000	$10,000,000	18 to 1
Value of firearms produced	$2,290,000	$73,000	31 to 1
Pig iron production (tons)	951,000	37,000	26 to 1
Coal production (tons)	13,680,000	650,000	21 to 1
Corn and wheat production (bushels)	698,000,000	314,000,000	2.2 to 1
Draft animals	5,800,000	2,900,000	2 to 1
Cotton production (bales)	43,000	5,344,000	1 to 124

*Slaves accounted for 3,500,000, or 40 percent.

Sources: U.S. Census 1860; E. B. Long, *The Civil War Day by Day* (New York: Doubleday, 1971), p. 723.

Political Leadership

To sustain a commitment to total war required effective political leadership. This task fell on Abraham Lincoln and Jefferson Davis, presidents of the rival governments.

Jefferson Davis grew up in Mississippi accustomed to life's advantages. Educated at West Point, he fought in the Mexican War, served as Franklin Pierce's secretary of war, and became one of the South's leading advocates in the Senate. Although he was hardworking and committed to the cause he led, his temperament was not well suited to his new post. He quarreled tactlessly with generals and politicians and refused to work with those he disliked. "He cannot brook opposition or criticism," one member of the Confederate Congress testified, "and those who do not bow down before him have no chance of success with him." His legalistic approach to problems hurt his efforts to rouse the South.

Yet for all Davis's personal handicaps, he faced an institutional one even more daunting. The Confederacy had been founded on the ideology of states' rights. Yet to meet the demands of total war, Davis would need to increase the authority of the central government beyond anything the South had ever experienced.

When Lincoln took the oath of office, his national experience consisted of one term in the House of Representatives. But Lincoln was a shrewd judge of character and a superb politician. To achieve a common goal, he willingly overlooked withering criticism and personal slights. (The commander of the Union army, General George McClellan, for one, continually snubbed the president and referred to him as "the original Gorilla.") He was not easily humbugged, overawed, or flattered and never allowed personal feelings to blind him to his larger objectives.

"This is essentially a People's contest," Lincoln asserted at the start of the war, and few presidents have been better able to communicate with the average citizen. He reg-

Jefferson Davis

Lincoln's Leadership

Lincoln at the time of the Gettysburg Address

ularly visited Union troops in camp, in the field, and in army hospitals. "The boys liked him," wrote Joseph Twichell, from a Connecticut regiment. "[I]n fact his popularity with the army is and has been universal." Always Lincoln reminded the public that the war was being fought for the ideals of the Revolution and the Republic. It was a test, he remarked in his famous address at Gettysburg, of whether a nation "conceived in Liberty, and dedicated to the proposition that all men are created equal," could "long endure."

Lincoln also proved the more effective military leader. Jefferson Davis took his title of commander in chief literally, interfering with his generals even on the smallest matters. But he failed to formulate an effective overarching strategy. In contrast, Lincoln had a clear grasp of the challenge confronting the Union. He accepted General Winfield Scott's proposal to blockade and surround the Confederacy, cut off its supplies, and slowly strangle it into submission, just as the anaconda snake squeezes its prey. But unlike Scott, he realized that an "anaconda plan" was not enough. The South would also have to be invaded and defeated, not only on an eastern front in Virginia but also in the West, where Union control of the Mississippi would divide the Confederacy fatally. Lincoln understood that the Union's superior manpower and matériel would become decisive only when the Confederacy was simultaneously threatened along a broad front. The Union forces could then break through at the weak points. It took time before the president found generals able to execute this novel strategy.

The Border States

When the war began, only Delaware of the border slave states was certain to remain in the Union. Lincoln's immediate political challenge was to retain the loyalty of Maryland, Kentucky, and Missouri. Maryland especially was crucial, for if it were lost, Washington itself would have to be abandoned.

Suppression in Maryland

The danger became immediately apparent when pro-Confederate forces destroyed the railroad bridges near Baltimore and isolated Washington. Only with difficulty was the administration able to move troops to the city. Once the capital was safe, Lincoln moved vigorously—even ruthlessly—to secure Maryland. He suspended the writ of **habeas corpus,** the right under the Constitution of an arrested person either to be charged with a specific crime or to be released. That done, he held without trial prominent Confederate sympathizers and suppressed pro-Confederate newspapers. Intervention by the army ensured that Unionists won a complete victory in the fall state election. The election ended any possibility that Maryland would join the Confederacy.

Kentucky's Neutrality

At the beginning of the conflict, Kentucky officially declared its neutrality. "I think to lose Kentucky is nearly to lose the whole game," Lincoln wrote with concern. "Kentucky gone, we can not hold Missouri, nor, as I think, Maryland. These all against us, and the job on our hands is too large for us." Union generals requested permission to occupy the state, but the president refused, preferring to act cautiously and wait for Unionist sentiment to assert itself. After Unionists won control of the legislature in the summer election, a Confederate army entered the state, giving Lincoln the opening he needed. He quickly sent in troops, and Kentucky stayed in the Union.

In Missouri, Union forces secured the state only after the Union victory at the Battle of Pea Ridge in March 1862. Even so, guerrilla warfare continued throughout the remainder of the war. In Virginia, internal divisions led to the creation of a new border state, as the hilly western counties, where slavery was not strong, refused to support the Confederacy. West Virginia was formally admitted to the Union in June 1863.

Importance of the Border States

The Union scored an important triumph in holding the border states. The population of all five equaled that of the four states of the Upper South that had joined the Confederacy, and their production of military supplies—food, animals, and minerals—was greater. Furthermore, Maryland and West Virginia contained key railroad lines and were critical to the defense of Washington, while Kentucky and Missouri gave the

Union army access to the major river systems of the western theater, down which it launched the first successful invasions of the Confederacy.

Opening Moves

As with so many Civil War battles, the Confederate victory at Bull Run achieved no decisive military results. But a sobered Congress authorized the enlistment of half a million volunteers to serve for three years. Lincoln named 34-year-old George McClellan, a West Point graduate, to be the new commander of the Union army. Energetic and ambitious, McClellan had been working as a railroad executive when the war began. For the next eight months he appeared the very model of businesslike efficiency as he settled into the much-needed task of organizing and drilling the Army of the Potomac.

Blockade and Isolate

The U.S. Navy began the war with only 42 ships available to blockade 3,550 miles of Confederate coastline. In April 1862 Flag Officer David G. Farragut ran a gauntlet of Confederate shore batteries to capture New Orleans, the Confederacy's largest city and most important port. Memphis, another important river city, fell to Union forces in June.

The blockade was hardly leakproof, and Confederates slipped through it using small, fast ships. Still, southern trade suffered badly. In hopes of lifting the blockade, the Confederacy converted the wooden U.S.S. *Merrimack*, which was rechristened the *Virginia*, into an ironclad gunboat. In March 1862 a Union ironclad, the *Monitor*, battled it to a standoff, and the Confederates were forced to scuttle the *Virginia* when they evacuated Norfolk in May. After that, the Union's naval supremacy was secure.

Ironclads

The South looked to diplomacy as another means to lift the blockade. With cotton so vital to European economies, especially Great Britain's, southerners believed that Europe would formally recognize the Confederacy and come to its aid. The North, for its part, claimed that it was merely putting down a domestic insurrection, but European countries allowed the Confederacy to purchase supplies abroad. As cotton supplies dwindled, France and Great Britain considered recognizing the Confederacy. They never did, however, as new supplies of cotton from Egypt and India enabled the British textile industry to recover. In the end, the South was left to stand or fall on its own resources.

King Cotton Diplomacy

Grant in the West

In the western war theater, the first decisive Union victory was won by a short, shabbily dressed, cigar-chomping general named Ulysses S. Grant. An undistinguished student at West Point, Grant eventually resigned his commission. He failed at everything he tried in civilian life, and when the war broke out he was a store clerk in Galena, Illinois. Almost 39, he promptly volunteered, and two months later became a brigadier general.

Grant's quiet, self-effacing manner gave little indication of his military ability or iron determination. Alert to seize any opening, he remained extraordinarily calm and clear-headed in battle. He absorbed details on a map almost photographically, and in battles that spread out over miles, he was superb at coordinating an attack. He would "try all sorts of cross-cuts," recalled one staff officer, "ford streams and jump any number of fences to reach another road rather than go back and take a fresh start." Grant also took full advantage of the telegraph to track troop movements, stringing new lines as he advanced. (Some of his Union telegraphers were so adept that they could receive messages before a station was set up by touching the end of the wire to their tongues to pick up Morse code.) Most important, Grant grasped that hard fighting, not fancy

Grant's Character

The War in the West, 1861–1862 *Grant's push southward stalled after his costly victory at Shiloh; nevertheless, by the end of 1862 the Union had secured Kentucky and Missouri, as well as most of Confederate Tennessee and the upper and lower stretches of the Mississippi River.*

maneuvering, would bring victory. "The art of war is simple," he once explained. "Find out where your enemy is, get at him as soon as you can and strike him as hard as you can, and keep moving on."

Grant realized that rivers were avenues into the interior of the Confederacy. In February 1862, supported by Union gunboats, he captured Fort Henry on the Tennessee River and Fort Donelson on the Cumberland. These victories forced the Confederates to withdraw from Kentucky and middle Tennessee. Grant continued south with 40,000 men, but he was surprised on April 6 by General Albert Sidney Johnston at Shiloh, just north of the Tennessee-Mississippi border. Johnston was killed in the day's fierce fighting, but by nightfall his army had driven the Union troops back to the Tennessee River, where they huddled numbly as a cold rain fell. William Tecumseh Sherman, one of Grant's subordinates, found the general standing under a dripping tree, his coat collar drawn up against the damp, puffing on a cigar. Sherman was about to suggest retreat, but something in Grant's eyes, lighted by the glow of his cigar, made him hesitate. So he said only, "Well, Grant, we've had the devil's own day, haven't we?" "Yes," the Union commander quietly replied. "Lick 'em tomorrow, though." And he did. With the aid of reinforcements, which he methodically ferried across the river all night, Grant counterattacked the next morning and drove the Confederates from the field.

Victory came at a high price: Shiloh inflicted more than 23,000 casualties. "The scenes on this field would have cured anyone of war," Sherman testified. Grant, who had doubted the commitment of Confederate troops, after Shiloh "gave up all idea of saving the Union except by complete conquest."

Shiloh

Eastern Stalemate

Grant's victories did not silence his critics, who charged he drank too much. But Lincoln was unmoved. "I can't spare this man. He fights." That was a quality in short supply in the East, where General McClellan directed operations.

The short, handsome McClellan looked like a general, but beneath his arrogance and bravado lay a self-doubt that rendered him excessively cautious. As the months dragged on and McClellan did nothing but train and plan, Lincoln's frustration grew. "If General McClellan does not want to use the army I would like to *borrow* it," he remarked sarcastically. In the spring of 1862 the general finally transported his 130,000 troops to the Virginia coast and began inching toward Richmond, the Confederate capital. In May, when McClellan was within five miles of Richmond, General Joseph Johnston suddenly attacked him near Fair Oaks, from which he barely escaped. Worse for McClellan, when Johnston was badly wounded, the formidable Robert E. Lee took command of the Army of Northern Virginia.

Where McClellan was cautious and defensive, the aristocratic Lee was daring and ever alert to assume the offensive. His first name, one of his colleagues commented, should have been Audacity: "He will take more chances, and take them quicker than any other general in this country." Joining Lee was Thomas "Stonewall" Jackson, a deeply religious Calvinist whose rigorous discipline honed his troops to a hard edge. In the Seven Days' battles, McClellan maneuvered brilliantly to parry the attacks of Lee and Jackson; still, he always stayed on the defensive, finally retreating until he was under the protection of the Union gunboats. Frustrated, Lincoln ordered the Peninsula campaign abandoned and formed a new army under John Pope. After Lee

Lincoln Fears "McClellan has the Slows"

Lee's Generalship

With almost 23,000 casualties, Antietam was the bloodiest single day of the war. A group of Confederate soldiers are shown where they fell along the Hagerstown Pike, the scene of some of the heaviest fighting. Said one Union officer of the fighting there: "Men, I cannot say fell; they were knocked out of the ranks by dozens."

badly mauled Pope at the second Battle of Bull Run, Lincoln restored McClellan to command.

Lee's Invasion Fails

Realizing that the Confederacy needed a decisive victory, Lee convinced Davis to allow him to invade the North, hoping to detach Maryland and isolate Washington. But as the army crossed into Maryland, Union soldiers discovered a copy of Lee's orders, accidentally left behind at a campsite by a Confederate officer. From this document McClellan learned that his forces vastly outnumbered Lee's—yet still he hesitated before launching a series of badly coordinated assaults near Antietam Creek on September 17 that Lee barely repulsed. The bloody exchanges horrified both sides for their sheer carnage. Within the space of seven hours, nearly 5,000 soldiers were killed and another 18,000 wounded, making it the bloodiest single day in American history. Two months after McClellan allowed the Confederate army to escape back into Virginia, the president permanently relieved him of command.

The winter of 1862 was the North's Valley Forge, as morale sank to an all-time low. It took General Ambrose Burnside, who assumed McClellan's place, little more than a month to demonstrate his utter incompetence. In December, at the Battle of Fredericksburg, he suffered a disastrous defeat, which prompted Lincoln to put "Fighting Joe" Hooker in charge. In the West, Grant had emerged as the dominant figure, but the Army of the Potomac still lacked a capable commander, the deaths kept mounting, and no end to the war was in sight.

The War in the East, 1861–1862 *McClellan's campaign against Richmond failed when Joseph Johnston surprised him at Fair Oaks. Taking command of the Army of Northern Virginia, Lee drove back McClellan in the Seven Days' battles and then won a resounding victory in the second Battle of Bull Run. He followed this up by invading Maryland, dividing his forces to take advantage of McClellan's caution, and capturing Harpers Ferry. McClellan checked his advance at Antietam. The Army of the Potomac's devastating defeat at Fredericksburg ended a year of frustration and failure for the Union in the eastern theater.*

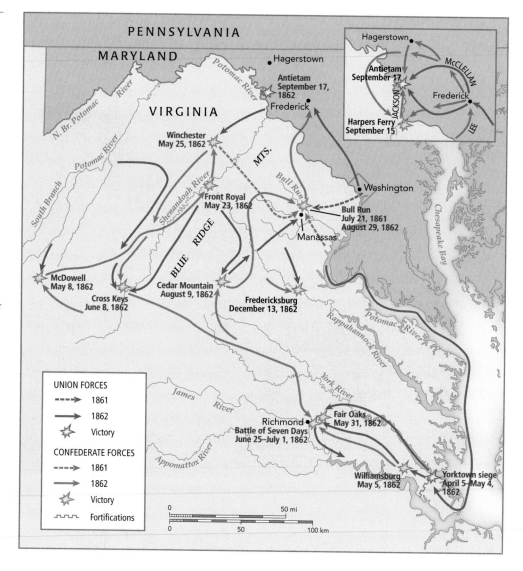

Emancipation

In 1858 Lincoln had proclaimed that an American "house divided" could not stand and that the United States would eventually become either all slave or all free. When the house divided, however, Lincoln hesitated to strike at slavery. He perceived, accurately, that most white northerners were not deeply committed to emancipation. He feared the social upheaval that such a revolutionary step would cause, and he did not want to alarm the wavering border states.

Still, Republican radicals such as Senator Charles Sumner and Horace Greeley pressed Lincoln to adopt a policy of emancipation. Slavery had caused the war, they argued; its destruction would hasten the war's end. Lincoln, however, placed first priority on saving the Union. "My paramount object in this struggle *is* to save the Union, and is *not* either to save or to destroy slavery," he told Greeley in 1862. "If I could save the Union without freeing *any* slave I would do it, and if I could save it by freeing *all* the slaves I would do it, and if I could save it by freeing some and leaving others alone, I would also do that." This statement summarized Lincoln's policy during the first year of the war.

Lincoln Gives Priority to the Union

The Logic of Events

As the Union army began to occupy Confederate territory, slaves flocked to the Union camps. In May 1861 the army adopted the policy of declaring runaway slaves **contraband** of war and refused to return them to their rebel owners. In the Confiscation Act of August 1861, Congress provided that slaves used for military purposes by the Confederacy would become free if they fell into Union hands. For a year Lincoln accepted that position but would go no further. When two of his generals, acting on their own authority, abolished slavery in their districts, he countermanded their orders.

Congressional Attack on Slavery

By the time Congress reconvened in December 1861, opinion was beginning to shift. Congress prohibited federal troops from capturing or returning fugitive slaves and freed the 2,000 slaves living in the District of Columbia with compensation to their owners. In July 1862 it passed the Second Confiscation Act, which declared that the slaves of anyone who supported the rebellion would be freed if they came into federal custody. Unlike the stipulations of the first act, it did not matter whether the slaves had been used for military purposes.

Lincoln signed this bill and then proceeded to ignore it. Instead, he emphasized state action, since slavery was a domestic institution. Twice the president summoned white representatives from the border states and prodded them to support a state-sponsored program of gradual emancipation. Both times they rejected his plea.

So on July 22, 1862, Lincoln presented to his cabinet a proposed proclamation freeing the slaves in the Confederacy. He was increasingly confident that the border states would remain in the Union, and he wanted to strike a blow that would weaken the Confederacy militarily. By making the struggle one of freedom versus slavery, such a proclamation would also undermine Confederate efforts to obtain diplomatic recognition. But Lincoln decided to wait for a Union military victory so that the act would not appear one of desperation.

Lincoln's Decision for Emancipation

The Emancipation Proclamation

On September 22, following the victory at Antietam, Lincoln announced that all slaves within rebel lines would be freed unless the seceded states returned to their allegiance by January 1, 1863. When that day came, the Emancipation Proclamation went formally into effect. Excluded from its terms were the Union slave states, all of Tennessee, and the other areas of the Confederacy that were under Union control. In all, about 830,000 of the nation's 4 million slaves were not covered by its provisions. Because Lincoln justified his actions on strictly military grounds, he believed that there was no legal right to apply the Proclamation to areas not in rebellion.

Terms of the Proclamation

Reaction to the
Proclamation
In the North, Republicans generally favored Lincoln's decision, while the Democrats made it a major issue in the 1862 elections. "Every white man in the North, who does not want to be swapped off for a free Nigger, should vote the Democratic ticket," urged one party orator. Although the Democrats gained ground in the elections the results offered no clear verdict on the Proclamation.

Despite the mixed reaction, the Emancipation Proclamation had immense symbolic importance, for it redefined the nature of the war. The North was fighting not to save the old Union but to create a new nation. The war had become, in Lincoln's words, "remorseless revolution."

African Americans' Civil War

Contrary to white southerners' fears that a race war would erupt behind the lines, the institution of slavery did not explode: it simply disintegrated. Well before federal troops entered an area, slaves took the lead in undermining the institution by openly challenging white authority and claiming greater personal freedom. One experienced overseer reported in frustration that now the "slaves will do only what pleases them, go out in the morning when it suits them, come in when they please, etc." Throughout the Confederacy the vital psychological relationship between master and slave was strained, and sometimes it snapped.

Slaves within Union Lines
Early in the conflict slaves concluded that emancipation would be one consequence of a Union victory. Perhaps as many as half a million—one-seventh of the total slave population of the Confederacy—fled to Union lines, where they faced an uncertain reception since northern troops manifested a deep-seated racism and were often hostile. The ex-slaves, called **freedmen,** ended up living in refugee or contraband camps that were overcrowded and disease-ridden and provided only rudimentary shelter and food. "The poor Negroes die as fast as ever," one northern missionary reported. "The children are all emaciated to the last degree and have such violent coughs and dysenteries that few survive."

Convinced that freed slaves would not work on their own initiative, the U.S. government put some contrabands to work assisting the army as cooks, teamsters, woodchoppers, and other unskilled laborers. Their wages were well below those paid white citizens for the same work. In the Mississippi valley, where two-thirds of the freedpeople under Union control were located, most were forced to work on plantations leased or owned by loyal planters. This policy was officially adopted in the summer of 1863 as a way to free the army from the cost of supporting former slaves and strengthen Unionism in the South. Freedpeople had no say in the contracts negotiated between military authorities and planters, found themselves strictly disciplined, and had so many deductions taken from their wages that in the end most received only room and board. In short, the conditions often approximated slavery.

Black Soldiers

Blacks in Combat
In adopting the policy of emancipation, Lincoln also announced that African Americans would be accepted in the navy and, more controversially, the army. (Throughout its history, the navy had been hard-pressed to get enough recruits, and as a result that service had always included some black sailors.) Resistance to accepting black volunteers in the army remained especially strong in the Midwest. Black northerners themselves were divided over whether to enlist, but Frederick Douglass spoke for the vast majority when he argued that once a black man had served in the army, there was "no power on earth which can deny that he has earned the right of citizenship in the United States."

In the end, nearly 200,000 African Americans served in the Union forces, constituting about 10 percent of the Union's total military manpower. Some, including two of Douglass's sons, were free, but most were former slaves who enlisted after escaping to the Union lines. As a concession to the racism of white troops, blacks served in segregated units under white officers. They were paid only $10 a month, with $3 deducted for clothing. White soldiers, in contrast, received $13 a month plus a $3.50 clothing allowance. Not until June 1864 did Congress finally grant equal pay to black soldiers.

African American recruits to the Union army

At first given undesirable duties such as heavy labor and burial details, black soldiers successfully lobbied for the chance to fight. They impressed white troops with their courage under fire. "I have been one of those men, who never had much confidence in colored troops fighting," one Union officer admitted, "but these doubts are now all removed, for they fought as bravely as any troops in the Fort." In the end 37,000 African American servicemen gave their lives, a rate of loss about 40 percent higher than among white soldiers. Black recruits had good reason to fight fiercely. They knew that the freedom of their race hung in the balance, they hoped to win civil rights at home by their performance on the battlefield, they resented racist sneers about their loyalty and ability, and they knew that capture might mean death.

The Confederate Home Front

"How shall we subsist this winter?" John Jones wondered in the fall of 1862. A clerk in the War Department in Richmond, Jones found it increasingly difficult to make ends meet on his salary. Prices kept going up, essential items were in short supply, and the signs of hardship were everywhere: in the darned and patched clothing, the absence of meat from the market, the desperation on people's faces. Some of the residents of Richmond "look like vagabonds," Jones noted in his diary.

Coffee was a luxury Jones could no longer afford, he sold his watch to buy fuel, and he worried incessantly about being able to feed his family. "I cannot afford to have more than an ounce of meat daily for each member of my family of six," he recorded in 1864. "The old cat goes staggering about from debility, though Fannie [a daughter] often gives him her share. We see neither rats nor mice about the premises now."

Nowhere were the profound effects of war more complete than within the Confederacy. These changes were especially ironic because the southern states had seceded in order to preserve their traditional ways. Not only did the war send hundreds of thousands of "Johnny Rebs" off to the front; it also put extreme burdens on the women and families at home. It fundamentally transformed the southern economy and forced the Confederate government to become more centralized. And, of course, it ended by destroying the institution of slavery, which the South had gone to war to preserve.

The New Economy

With the Union blockade tightening, the production of foodstuffs became crucial to the South's economy. Many men who normally worked in the fields had gone into the army, and with the lessening of discipline, slaves became increasingly assertive and independent. More and more plantations switched from growing cotton to raising grain and livestock. As a result, cotton production dropped from 4.5 million bales in 1861 to 300,000 in 1864. Even so, food production declined. By the last two years of the war, the shortage was serious.

Attempts to Industrialize

The Union blockade also made it impossible to rely on European manufactured goods. So the Confederate War Department built and ran factories, took over the region's mines, and regulated private manufacturers so as to increase the production of war goods. Although the Confederacy never became industrially self-sufficient, it sustained itself far better in industrial goods than it did in agricultural produce. It was symbolic that when Lee surrendered, his troops had sufficient guns and ammunition to continue, but they had not eaten in two days.

New Opportunities for Southern Women

Southern white women took an active role in the war. Some gained notoriety as spies; others smuggled military supplies into the South. Women also spent a good deal of time knitting and sewing clothes for soldiers. "We never went out to pay a visit without taking our knitting along," recalled a South Carolina woman. Perhaps most important, with so many men fighting, women took charge of agricultural production. On a plantation the mistress often supervised the slaves as well as the wrenching shift from cotton to foodstuffs.

"Nannie" McKenzie Semple was one of many southern white women who worked for the Confederate government. Semple's salary, from working as a "Treasury Girl," netted her more than what the average soldier received.

One such woman was 33-year-old Emily Lyles Harris, the wife of a small slaveowner and farmer in upcountry South Carolina. When her husband joined the army in 1862, she was left to care for her seven children as well as supervise the slaves and manage the farm. Despite the disruptions of wartime, she succeeded remarkably, one year producing the largest crop of oats in the neighborhood and always making enough money for her family to live decently. She took little pride, however, in her achievements. "I shall never get used to being left as the head of affairs at home," she wrote on one occasion. "The burden is very heavy, and there is no one to smile on me as I trudge wearily along in the dark with it. . . . I am not an independent woman nor ever shall be." Self-doubt, lack of privacy, and the burdens of responsibility left her depressed, and while she persevered, by 1865 she openly hoped for defeat.

The war also opened up new jobs for women off the farm. Given the manpower shortage, "government girls" became essential to fill the growing Confederate bureaucracy. At first women were paid half the wages of male coworkers, but by the end of the war they had won equal pay. White women also staffed the new factories springing up in southern cities and towns, undertaking even dangerous work that normally would have been considered off-limits. A majority of the workers in the South's munitions factories were women, some of whom lost their lives in accidental explosions.

Confederate Finance and Government

The most serious domestic problem the Confederate government faced was finance, for which officials at Richmond never developed a satisfactory program. The South had few banks and only $27 million in specie when the war began. European governments refused to float major loans, which left taxation as the unappealing alternative. Only in 1863 did the government begin levying a **graduated income tax** (from 1 to 15 percent) and a series of excise taxes. Most controversial, the government resorted to a tax-in-kind on farmers that, after exempting a certain portion, took one-tenth of their agricultural crops. Even more unpopular was the policy of impressment, which allowed the army to seize private property for its own use, often with little or no compensation.

Above all, the Confederacy financed the war effort simply by printing paper money not backed by specie, some $1.5 billion, which amounted to three times more than the federal government issued. The result was runaway inflation, so that by 1865 a Confederate dollar was worth only 1.7 cents in gold and prices had soared to 92 times their prewar base. Prices were highest in Richmond, where flour sold for $275 a barrel by early 1864 and coats for $350. By the end of the war, flour had reached an astronomical $1,000 a barrel. Inflation that ate away at their standard of living was one of the great wartime hardships borne by the southern people.

Soaring Inflation

In politics even more than in finance, the Confederacy exercised far greater powers than those of the federal government before 1861. Indeed, Jefferson Davis strove to meet the demands of total war by transforming the South into a centralized, national state. He sought to limit state authority over military units, and in April 1862 the Confederacy passed the first national **conscription** law in American history, drafting all white males between 18 and 35 unless exempted. As conditions worsened, those age limits widened to 17 and 50, mobilizing virtually the entire military-age white population. Civilians, too, felt the effects of government control, for in 1862 the Congress authorized Davis to invoke martial law and suspend the writ of habeas corpus.

Centralization of Power

Critics protested that Davis was destroying states' rights, the cardinal principle of the Confederacy. Concerned foremost about their states' safety, governors wanted to be able to recall troops if their own territory was threatened. When President Davis suspended the writ of habeas corpus, his vice president, Alexander H. Stephens, accused him of aiming at a dictatorship. Davis used those powers for a limited time, yet in practice it made little difference whether the writ was suspended or not. With disloyalty a greater problem than in the Union, Confederate authorities more stringently regulated civil liberties, and the army arrested thousands of civilians.

Opposition to Davis

But the Confederate draft, more than any other measure, produced an outcry. The law allowed the rich to provide substitutes, at a cost that eventually rose, on the open market, to as much as $6,000. The Confederacy eventually abolished this privilege, but as one Georgia leader complained, "It's a notorious fact if a man has influential friends—or a little money to spare he will never be enrolled." Most controversially, the draft exempted from service one white man on every plantation with 20 or more slaves (later reduced to 15). This law was designed to preserve control of the slave population, but more and more nonslaveholders complained that it was a rich man's war and a poor man's fight. "All they want is to git you pumped up and go to fight for their infernal negroes and after you do their fighting you may kiss their hind parts for all they care," one Alabama farmer complained. In some counties where the draft was unenforceable, conscription officers ventured only at risk to their own safety.

Hostility to Conscription

Hardship and Suffering

By the last year of the conflict, food shortages had become so severe that ingenious southerners concocted various substitutes: parched corn in place of coffee, strained blackberries in place of vinegar. One scarce item for which there was no substitute was salt, which was essential for curing meat. The high prices and food shortages led to riots in several cities, most seriously in Richmond early in April 1863. There, about 300 women and children chanting "Bread!" looted a number of stores.

As always, war corroded the discipline and order of society. With the value of paper money dropping and the future uncertain, many southerners spent money in frenzied haste. Gambling halls were crowded with revelers seeking relief, while soldiers on furlough drank heavily, aware of their increasingly poor chances of survival at the front. Even in the army, theft became common.

The search for escape from the grim reality of the war led to a forced gaiety for those who could afford it. "The cities are gayer than before the war," one refugee reported, "—parties every night in Richmond, suppers costing ten and twenty thousand dollars." Walking home at night after spending several hours at the bedside of a dying soldier, Judith McGuire passed a house gay with laughter, music, and dancing. "The revulsion . . . was sickening," she wrote afterward in her diary. "I thought of the gayety of Paris during the French Revolution, . . . the ball at Brussels the night before the battle of Waterloo, and felt shocked that our own Virginians, at such a time, should remind me of scenes which we were wont to think only belonged to . . . foreign society." The war was a cancer that ate away not only at southern society but at the southern soul itself.

The Union Home Front

Because the war was fought mostly on southern soil, northern civilians rarely felt its effects directly. Yet to be effective, the North's economic resources had to be organized and mobilized.

Government Finances and the Economy

Measures to Raise Money

To begin with, the North required a comprehensive system to finance its massive campaign. Taxing the populace was an obvious means, and taxes paid for 21 percent of Union war expenses, compared with only 1 percent of the Confederacy's. In August 1861 Congress passed the first federal income tax, 3 percent on all incomes over $800 a year. When that, along with increased tariff duties, proved insufficient, Congress enacted a comprehensive tax law in 1862 that for the first time brought the tax collector into every northern household. Excise fees taxed virtually every occupation, commodity, or service; income and inheritances were taxed, as were corporations and consumers. A new bureaucracy, the Internal Revenue Bureau, oversaw the collection process.

The government also borrowed heavily, through the sale of some $2.2 billion in **bonds,** and financed the rest of the war's cost by issuing paper money. In all, the Union printed $431 million in greenbacks (so named because of their color on one side). Although legal for the payment of debts, they could not be redeemed in specie, and therefore their value fluctuated. Also by taxing state banknotes out of circulation, Congress for the first time created a uniform national currency, as well as a national banking system.

Western Development

During the war, the Republican-controlled Congress encouraged economic development. Tariffs to protect industry from foreign competition rose to an average rate of 47 percent, compared to 19 percent in 1860. To encourage development of the West, the Homestead Act of 1862 granted 160 acres of public land—the size of the traditional American family farm—to anyone (including women) who settled and improved the land for five years. Over a million acres were distributed during the war years alone. In addition, the Land Grant College Act of 1862 donated the proceeds from certain land sales to finance public colleges and universities, creating 69 in all, many in the West.

A Rich Man's War

Over the course of the war the government purchased more than $1 billion worth of goods and services. In response to this heavy demand, the economy boomed and business and agriculture prospered. Wages increased 42 percent between 1860 and 1864, but because prices rose faster than wages, workers' real income dropped almost

30 percent, from $363 in 1860 to $261 in 1865. That meant the working class paid a disproportionate share of the war's costs.

Corruption and Fraud

The Republican belief that government should play a major role in the economy also fostered a cozy relationship between business and politics. In the rush to profit from government contracts, some suppliers sold inferior goods at inflated prices. Uniforms made of "shoddy"—bits of unused thread and recycled cloth—were fobbed off in such numbers that the word became an adjective describing inferior quality. Unscrupulous dealers sold clothing that dissolved in the rain, shoes that fell apart, spoiled meat, broken-down horses, and guns that would not fire. At least 20 percent of government expenditures involved fraud.

Stocks and dividends rose with the economy as investors scrambled after profitable new opportunities. An illegal cotton trade flourished in the Mississippi valley, where northern agents bribed military authorities for passes to go through the lines in order to purchase cotton bales from southern planters. The Confederate government quietly traded cotton for contraband such as food, medicine, and enough arms and equipment to maintain an army of 50,000 men.

Speculation during the last two years of the war became particularly feverish, and the fortunes made went toward the purchase of ostentatious luxuries. Like Richmond, Washington became the symbol of this moral decay. Prostitution, drinking, and corruption reached epidemic proportions in the capital, and social festivities became the means to shut out the numbing horror of the casualty lists.

Women and the Workforce

Even more than in the South, the war opened new opportunities for northern women. Countless wives ran farms while their husbands were away at war. One traveler in Iowa reported, "I met more women driving teams on the road and saw more at work in the fields than men." The war also stimulated the shift to mechanization, which made the northern labor shortage less severe. By 1865 three times as many reapers and harvesters were in use as in 1861.

Beyond the farm, women increasingly found work in industry, filling approximately 100,000 new jobs during the war. Like women in the South, they worked as clerks in the expanding government bureaucracy. The work was tedious and the workload heavy, but the new jobs offered good wages, a sense of economic independence, and a pride in having aided the war effort.

The war also allowed women to enter and eventually dominate the profession of nursing. "Our women appear to have become almost wild on the subject of hospital nursing," protested one army physician, who like many others opposed the presence of women in military hospitals. Led by Drs. Emily and Elizabeth Blackwell, Dorothea Dix, and Mary Ann Bickerdyke, women fought the bureaucratic inefficiency of the

A nurse tends a wounded Union soldier in a military hospital in Nashville, Tennessee. Despite the opposition of army doctors, hundreds of female volunteers worked in army hospitals for each side. Nursing became a female profession after the war.

army medical corps. Their service in the wards of the maimed and dying reduced the hostility to women in medicine.

Clara Barton, like so many other nurses, often found herself in battlefield hospitals, amidst massive death and suffering. During the battle of Fredericksburg, she wiped the brows of the wounded and dying, bandaged wounds, and applied tourniquets to stop the flow of blood. She later recalled that as she rose from the side of one soldier, "I wrung the blood from the bottom of my clothing, before I could step, for the weight about my feet." She steeled herself at the sight of amputated arms and legs casually tossed in piles outside the front door as the surgeons cut away, yet she found the extent of suffering overwhelming. She was jolted by the occasional familiar face among the tangled mass of bodies: the sexton of the church in her hometown, his face caked in blood, or a wayward boy she had befriended years ago. Sleeping in a tent nearby, she drove herself to the brink of exhaustion until the last patients were transferred to permanent hospitals. She then returned to her home in Washington, where she broke down and wept.

Before 1861 teaching, too, had been dominated by males, but the shortage of men forced school boards in both sections to turn to women, who were paid half to two-thirds of what men received. After the war teaching increasingly became a female profession, as many women came to see it as a career and not just a temporary occupa-

Women and Teaching

This anti-Republican cartoon from Philadelphia expresses the fears of many Copperhead Democrats that the war for Union had been subverted by becoming a war on slavery. A caricatured black soldier tries to prevent a legless Union veteran from voting for General George McClellan, Lincoln's opponent in the election of 1864. The election clerk beside the stuffed ballot box is told to "pretend you see nothing" of the ballot stuffing.

tion. Women also contributed to the war effort through volunteer work. The United States Sanitary Commission was established in 1861 to provide medical supplies and care. Much of its work was performed by women, who raised funds, collected supplies, and toiled in hospitals alongside paid nurses.

Civil Liberties and Dissent

Suspension of the Writ of Habeas Corpus

In order to mobilize northern society, Lincoln did not hesitate to curb dissenters. Shortly after the firing on Fort Sumter, he suspended the writ of habeas corpus in specified areas, which allowed the indefinite detention of anyone suspected of disloyalty or activity against the war. Although the Constitution permitted such suspension in time of rebellion or invasion, Lincoln did so without consulting Congress (unlike President Davis), and he used his power far more broadly, expanding it in 1862 to cover the entire North for cases involving antiwar activities. The president also decreed that those arrested under its provisions could be tried under the stricter rules of martial law by a military court. Eventually more than 20,000 individuals were arrested, most of whom were never charged with a specific crime or brought to trial.

Democrats attacked Lincoln as a tyrant bent on destroying the Constitution. Among those arrested was Clement Vallandigham, a Democratic member of Congress from Ohio who called for an armistace in May 1963. He was convicted by a military commission and banished to the Confederacy (in 1864 he returned to the North). The Supreme Court refused to review the case, but once the war was over, it ruled in *Ex parte Milligan* (1866) that as long as the regular courts were open, civilians could not be tried by military tribunals.

The Copperheads

Republicans labeled those who opposed the war **Copperheads,** conjuring up the image of a venomous snake waiting to strike the Union. Copperheads constituted the extreme peace wing of the Democratic party. Often they had been hurt by the economic changes of the war, but more crucial was their bitter opposition to emancipation and also the draft, which they condemned as a violation of individual freedom and an instrument of special privilege. According to the provisions enacted in 1863, a person would be exempt from the present (but not any future) draft by paying a commutation fee of $300, about a year's wages for a worker or an ordinary farmer. Or those drafted could hire a substitute, the cost of which was beyond the reach of all but the wealthy. Despite this criticism, in reality poor men also bought their way out of the draft, often by pooling their resources; in addition, the government of some communities paid the commutation fee for any resident who was drafted. In all, approximately 118,000 men provided substitutes, and another 87,000 paid the commutation fee. Perhaps another 160,000 northerners illegally evaded the draft. Only 46,000 men were actually drafted into the Union army, out of more than 2 million who served.

New York City Draft Riot

In July 1863, when the first draftees' names were drawn in New York City, workers in the Irish quarter rose in anger. Rampaging through the streets, the mob attacked draft officials and prominent Republicans, ransacked African American neighborhoods, and lynched black residents who fell into its hands. By the time order was restored four days later, at least 105 people had been killed, the worst loss of life from any riot in American history. (See pages 466–469.)

Gone to Be a Soldier

Marcus Spiegel came to the United States after the revolution of 1848 failed in Germany. The son of a rabbi, Spiegel married an American woman, became a naturalized citizen, and was trying to make it in the warehouse business in Ohio when the war began. As an immigrant, he considered it his duty to preserve the Union for his children, and the regular pay of an officer was also enticing, so he enlisted in November 1861. Eventually he became one the few Jewish colonels in the army. A loyal Democrat, Spiegel did not go to war to end slavery and flatly proclaimed that black people were not "worth fighting for."

By early 1864, however, his views had changed. He had "learned and seen more of what the horrors of Slavery was than I ever knew before," and though he still doubted African Americans' capabilities, he now was "in favor of doing away with the institution of Slavery." He assured his wife that "this is no hasty conclusion but a deep conviction." A few weeks later, Marcus Spiegel died of wounds he received while fighting in Louisiana.

Fervently committed or not, by war's end about 2 million men had served the Union cause and another million, the Confederate. They were mostly young; almost 40 percent of entering soldiers were age 21 or younger. They were not drawn disproportionately from the poor, and in both the North and the South, farmers and farm laborers accounted for the largest group of soldiers. Unskilled workers, who were poorer than other groups, were actually underrepresented in the ranks. It is also a myth that the North hired an army of foreign-born mercenaries. The overwhelming majority of those who wore the blue and the gray were native-born, and the proportion of immigrants in both armies was roughly the same as in the eligible military population.

Most soldiers, like Marcus Spiegel, took patriotism seriously, although officers tended to be more ideological. Chiefly volunteers, enlisted men usually expressed their motivation for fighting in general terms, either to defend the Union or protect the South. Only with time did the majority of Union soldiers, like Spiegel, come to endorse the destruction of slavery as a war aim.

Discipline

The near-holiday atmosphere of the war's early months soon gave way to dull routine. Men from rural areas, accustomed to the freedom of the farm, complained about the endless recurrence of reveille, roll call, and drill. "When this war is over," one Rebel promised, "I will whip the man that says 'fall in' to me." Troops in neither army cared for the spit and polish of regular army men. "They keep us very strict here," noted one Illinois soldier. "It is the most like a prison of any place I ever saw."

By modern standards training was minimal and discipline lax in both armies. Troops from rural families found it harder to adjust to army routine than did urban soldiers, especially factory workers, who were more familiar with impersonal organizations and used to greater social control. Many southerners were "not used to control of any sort," one Rebel noted, "and were not disposed to obey anyone except for good and sufficient reason given." Yanks and Rebs alike complained about officers' privileges and had no special respect for rank. "The boys recognized no superiors, except in the line of legitimate duty," an Indiana private explained. The Union discontinued the election of lower officers, but this tradition was retained in the Confederate army, which further undermined discipline, since those known as strict officers were eventually defeated.

Camp Life

On average, soldiers spent 50 days in camp for every day in battle. Camp life was often unhealthy as well as unpleasant. Poor sanitation, miserable food, exposure to the elements, and primitive medical care contributed to widespread sickness. Officers and men alike regarded army doctors as quacks and tried to avoid them. It was a common belief that if a fellow went to the hospital, "you might as well say good bye." Conditions were even worse in the Confederate hospitals, for the Union blockade produced a shortage of medical supplies. Twice as many soldiers died from dysentery, typhoid, and other diseases as from wounds.

Disease and Medical Care

Treatment at field hospitals was a chilling experience. Ignorance was responsible for the existing conditions and practices, because nothing was known about germs or how wounds became infected. Years later an appalled federal surgeon recounted:

> We operated in old blood-stained and often pus-stained coats. . . . We used undisinfected instruments . . . and still worse, used marine sponges which had been used in prior pus cases and had been only washed in tap water. . . . Our silk to tie blood vessels

"If a person wants to know how to appreciate the value of good vi[c]tuals he had better enlist," a Vermont soldier declared. "I have seen the time when I would have been glad to [have] picked the crusts of bread that mother gives to the hogs." Whether in the field or in quarters, food was generally Johnny Reb's and Billy Yank's first concern.

At the beginning of the war, the prescribed daily allowance for each soldier included 12 ounces of pork or 20 ounces of beef, a pound or more of bread or flour, and ample quantities of rice, beans, sugar, and coffee. In general northern soldiers had more food and greater variety than their opponents. As the war ground on, the Confederacy was forced to reduce sharply the daily ration because of shortages.

Meat, bread, and coffee: these were the soldier's mainstays. The meat was either pork or beef and was usually salted to preserve it. Soldiers, who called salt pork "sowbelly" and pickled beef "salt horse," preferred the former, since the beef was so briny that it was inedible unless thoroughly soaked in water. Many soldiers left salted beef in a creek overnight before they tried to eat it.

Union soldiers normally were given wheat

Hardtack—often dubbed "teeth dullers"

bread or flour, but for Confederates cornbread was the standby. This monotonous fare prompted a Louisiana soldier near the end of the war to grumble, "If any person offers me cornbread after this war comes to a close I shall *probably* tell him to—go to hell." Both armies often replaced bread with hardtack, crackers half an inch thick that were so hard, soldiers dubbed them "teeth-dullers." The crackers became moldy and worm-infested with age, and hence veterans preferred to eat them in the dark.

Coffee was the other main staple, eagerly consumed.

---

was undisinfected. . . . We dressed the wounds with clean but undisinfected sheets, shirts, tablecloths, or other old soft linen rescued from the family ragbag. . . . We knew nothing about antiseptics and therefore used none.

Decline of Morality

The boredom of camp life, the horrors of battle, and the influence of an all-male society all corrupted morals. Swearing and heavy drinking were common, and one Mississippian reported that after payday games of chance were "running night and day, with eager and excited crowds standing around with their hands full of money." Prostitutes flooded the camps of both armies, and an Illinois private stationed in Pulaski, Tennessee, wrote home that the price schedule in each of the brothels in town was quite reasonable. "You may think I am a hard case," he conceded, "but I am as pious as you can find in the army."

With death so near, some soldiers sought solace in religion. Religious fervor was greater in the Confederate camps, and a wave of revivals swept the ranks during the last two winters of the war, producing between 100,000 and 200,000 conversions. Significantly, the first major revivals occurred after the South's twin defeats at Vicksburg and Gettysburg. Then, too, as battle after battle thinned Confederate ranks, the prospect of death became increasingly large.

The Changing Face of Battle

Impact of Technology

As in all modern wars, technology revolutionized the conditions under which Civil War soldiers fought. Smoothbore muskets, which at first served as the basic infantry weapon, gave way to the rifle, so named because of the grooves etched into the barrel to give a bullet spin. A new bullet, the minié ball, allowed the rifle to be easily loaded, and the invention of the percussion cap rendered it serviceable in wet weather. More important, the new weapon had an effective range of 400 yards—five times greater than that of the old musket. As a result, soldiers fought each other from greater distances, and battles took much longer to fight and produced many more casualties.

Strength of the Defense

Under such conditions, the defense became a good deal stronger than the offense. The larger artillery pieces also adopted rifled barrels, but they lacked good fuses and

Because of the Union blockade, the Confederacy could not get enough, and Rebel troops resorted to various unappealing substitutes. Despite official opposition, troops often fraternized during lulls in the fighting, swapping tobacco, which was in short supply on the Union side, for coffee and sugar, which Confederates desired most. When the two armies spent the winter of 1862 camped on opposite sides of the Rappahannock River, enlisted men ferried cargoes of sugar and coffee to one bank and tobacco to the other, using makeshift toy boats.

Members of both armies supplemented their diet by foraging (the army's polite term for stealing), although Union soldiers, being most often in enemy territory, relied more heavily on this tactic. Hungry troops regularly raided pigpens, poultry houses, orchards, gardens, cornfields, and smokehouses.

During training and in winter quarters, cooks normally prepared food for an entire company. Neither army, however, established a cooks' or bakers' school, and troops contended that officers regularly selected the poorest soldiers to be cooks. "A company cook is a most peculiar being," one soldier recalled after the war. "He generally knows less about cooking than any other man in the company. Not being able to learn the drill, and too dirty to appear on inspection, he is sent to the cook house to get him out of the ranks." Once the army went on the march, men usually cooked for themselves or formed a mess of four to eight soldiers, taking turns cooking. Either way, food was rarely prepared with any skill.

By war's end, soldiers on both sides had developed a new appreciation for food. A poetic Yankee summed up the situation succinctly:

> The soldiers' fare is very rough,
> The bread is hard, the beef is tough;
> If they can stand it, it will be,
> Through love of God, a mystery.

accurate sighting devices and could not effectively support attacking troops. They were a deadly defensive weapon, however, that decimated advancing infantry at close range. Confederate general D. H. Hill described the devastating barrage as his men charged the Union line at Malvern Hill: "As each brigade emerged from the woods, from 50 to 100 guns opened upon it, tearing great gaps in its ranks. Most of them had an open field half a mile wide to cross, under the fire of field artillery and heavy ordnance. It was not war—it was murder." More than 100 regiments on both sides suffered in excess of 50 percent casualties in a single battle.

As the haze of gunfire covered the land and the constant spray of bullets mimicked rain pattering through the treetops, soldiers discovered that their romantic notions about war had no place on the battlefield. Men witnessed horrors they had never envisioned as

Soldiers' Hardening Outlook

Soldiers leaving for war often had their pictures taken with their loved ones. The Confederate soldier on the left posed with his two sisters. On the right, a member of the Union forces sits with his family for a farewell portrait. Such photographs are reminders of how much the war and its mounting death toll touched civilians as well as soldiers on both sides.

Battlefield Spin

Assessing the Role of Technology and Warfare

Historians have long noted that wars accelerate social change, both on and off the battlefield. The Civil War's high casualties were caused partly by the increasing use of the minié ball. Soldiers appreciated the new rifles' increased accuracy and range. "We went out the other day to try them," a New Hampshire private wrote. "We fired 600 yds and we put 360 balls into a mark the size of old Jeff." Another innovation, the breech-loading rifle, allowed bullets to be inserted at the rear of the barrel, rather than being painstakingly forced down the mouth.

Yet in the real world, the interactions between human habit and technological change ensured that the transformation to modern warfare moved haltingly. Although breech-loading and repeating rifles became available relatively early in the war, Union Ordinance Bureau Chief James Ripley distrusted them and ordered only small quantities. ("Ripley Van Winkle," his critics called him, complaining that he was asleep on the job.) Lincoln forced Ripley to resign in 1863, but the bureau chief's skepticism may have had merit in the short run. Early in the war soldiers tended to waste ammunition, and quick-loading rifles made that easier to do. Furthermore, time was needed to field-test the weapons, and the wide variety of early models, each requiring different cartridges, would have created supply problems if hundreds of thousands of soldiers had used them. In assessing the role of technology, historians need constantly to weigh the human factor in its adoption.

Minie Ball

Breach-loading rifle

civilians and choked from the stench of decaying flesh and mortal slaughter. They realized that their efforts to convey to those back home the gruesome truth of combat were inadequate. "No tongue can tell, no mind can conceive, no pen portray the horrible sights I witnessed this morning," a Union soldier wrote after Antietam. And still they tried.

An Indiana soldier at Perryville (7,600 casualties): "It was an awful sight to see there men torn all to pieces with cannon balls and bom shells[.] the dead and wounded lay thick in all directions." An Ohio soldier at Antietam (23,000 casualties), two days after the fighting: "The smell was offul . . . there was about 5 or 6,000 dead bodes decaying over the field . . . I could have walked on the boddees all most from one end too the other." A Georgian, the day after Chancellorsville (30,000 casualties): "It looked more like a slaughter pen than anything else. . . . The shrieks and groans of the wounded . . . was heart rending beyond all description." A Maine soldier who fought at Gettysburg (50,000 casualties): "I have Seen . . . men rolling in their own blood, Some Shot in one place, Some another . . . our dead lay in the road and the Rebels in their hast to leave dragged both their baggage wagons and artillery over them and they lay mangled and torn to pieces so that Even friends could not tell them. You can form no idea of a battlefield."

BATTLE OF SHILOH, CIVIL WAR

Snake Creek

Owl Creek

GRANT

BUELL

Pittsburg Landing

TO SAVANNAH, TENN.

U.S. artillery

U.S. gunboats *Tyler* and *Lexington*

Tennessee River

Prentiss surrenders to Confederates

Hornet's Confederate Nest artillery

+ Shiloh Church

+ Johnston killed

TO CORINTH, MISS.

A. S. JOHNSTON BEAUREGARD

BRITISH CANADA

UNITED STATES

Battle of Shiloh Tenn.

MEXICO Battle of Buena Vista

BATTLE OF BUENA VISTA, MEXICAN WAR

TO SALTILLO
Buena Vista

0   1 mi
0   1   2 km

TAYLOR

SANTA ANA

TO SAN LUIS POTOSÍ

| 4,200 total casualties (700 U.S., 3,500 Mexican) | → U.S. forces | ▲▲ U.S. artillery |
| | → Mexican forces | ▲▲ Mexican artillery |

0   1 mi
0   1   2 km

| 23,700 total casualties | → Confederate attack, morning of April 6 | → Union counterattack, morning of April 7 |
| | --- Maximum extent of Confederate advance, evening of April 6 | --- Maximum extent of Union advance, evening of April 7 |

The Changing Magnitude of Battle   *During the Mexican War at Buena Vista, the American army of 4,800 men was overextended trying to defend a two-mile line against 15,000 Mexicans. At Shiloh, in contrast, battle lines stretched almost six miles. (The maps are drawn to the same scale.) Against 40,000 Confederates, Grant galloped back and forth, rallying some 35,000 troops organized under five subordinates and coordinating the overnight reinforcement of 25,000 troops. The size of the armies, the complexity of their organization, the length of battle lines, and the number of casualties all demonstrate the extent to which the magnitude of battle had changed.*

Hardening Attitudes

Throughout the war, soldiers continued to speak in terms of the traditional ideals of duty, honor, and patriotism. Nevertheless, military service profoundly changed them. At first the war seemed a test of courage and manhood, in which the winning side would display superior valor. Expecting a restrained war that would uphold this moral code, volunteers admired the courage of the foe and considered it pointless to kill an isolated soldier.

But the reality of combat did not fit such expectations, and by 1864 the nature of war had been transformed. Soldiers discovered the futility of mass frontal assaults, and under the rain of fire on the battlefield sought cover wherever they could find it. As the fighting intensified, they sought to kill enemy soldiers any way they could in order to hasten the war's end. At the same time, they became indifferent to death and suffering. "The daily sight of blood and mangled bodies," observed a Rhode Island soldier, "so blunted their finer sensibilities as almost to blot out all love, all sympathy from the heart." This hardening of attitudes produced a steady erosion of moral standards. Combatants began taking personal property from the dead and wounded and even prisoners after a battle.

Eroding Moral Values

As they repudiated their earlier moral assumptions, the soldiers in both armies felt increasingly alienated from civilians back home. In reaction, they developed a stronger sense of comradeship with enemy soldiers, based on their belief that only other soldiers could understand what they had gone through and why they acted the way they did. They felt less an actor in the war than an impersonal object caught in a relentless process of destruction.

In the face of what Charles Francis Adams Jr. termed "the carnival of death," soldiers braced themselves with a grim determination to see the war through to the end. Not glorious exploits but endurance became the true measure of heroism.

The Union's Triumph

While talking to a neighbor in Covington, Georgia, Dolly Lunt suddenly saw the blue-coats coming down the road. Thinking to herself, "Oh God, the time of trial has come!" she ran home as fast as she could. William Tecumseh Sherman's dreaded army had arrived at her gate. As the Union troops swarmed over the yard, they cleaned out the smokehouse and dairy, stripped the kitchen and cellar of their contents, and killed her fowl and hogs. They broke open locks, smashed down doors, seized items of no military value such as kitchen utensils and even a doll, and marched off some of the male slaves. Not content with plundering the main house, the troops entered the slave cabins and rifled them of every valuable, even the money some of the slaves had made by doing extra work. Lunt spent a supperless night huddled in the house with her remaining slaves, who were clutching their meager possessions. As darkness descended, she reported, "the heavens from every point were lit up with flames from burning buildings." Total war had come to Dolly Lunt's doorstep.

Confederate High Tide

In the spring of 1863 matters still looked promising for Lee. At the battle of Chancellorsville, he brilliantly defeated Lincoln's latest commander, Joseph Hooker. But during the fighting Stonewall Jackson was accidentally shot by his own men, and he died a few days later—a grievous setback for the Confederacy. Determined to take the offensive, Lee invaded Pennsylvania in June with an army of 75,000. Lincoln's newest general, George Gordon Meade, warily shadowed the Confederates. On the first of July, advance parties from the two armies accidentally collided at the town of Gettysburg, and the war's greatest battle ensued.

The Carnage of Gettysburg

For once it was Lee who had the extended supply lines and was forced to fight on ground chosen by his opponent. After two days of assaults failed to break the Union left or right, Lee made the greatest mistake of his career, sending 14,000 men under General George Pickett in a charge at the center of the Union line on Cemetery Ridge. "Pickett's division just seemed to melt away in the blue musketry smoke which now covered the hill," one Confederate officer wrote. "Nothing but stragglers came back." The Union casualties of more than 23,000 represented a quarter of Meade's effective strength, but Lee lost between 25,000 and 28,000—more than a third of his troops. Never again was he able to assume the offensive.

Lincoln Finds His General

To the west, Grant had been trying for months to capture Vicksburg, a Rebel stronghold on the Mississippi. In a daring maneuver, he left behind his supply lines and marched inland, calculating that he could feed his army from the produce of Confederate farms, weakening southern resistance in the process. These actions were the tactics of total war, and seldom had they been tried before Grant used them. His troops drove the defenders of Vicksburg back into the city and starved them into submission. On July 4, the city surrendered. With the fall of Port Hudson, Louisiana, four days later, the Mississippi was completely in Union hands. Grant had divided the Confederacy and isolated Arkansas, Texas, and part of Louisiana from the rest of the South.

He followed up this victory by rescuing Union forces holed up in Chattanooga. His performance confirmed Lincoln's earlier judgment that "Grant is my man, and I am his the rest of the war." Congress now revived the rank of lieutenant general, held before only by George Washington, which Lincoln bestowed on Grant. In March 1864 Lincoln brought him east and put him in command of all the Union armies.

Grant recognized that the Union possessed the resources to wear down the Confederacy but that its larger armies had "acted independently and without concert, like a balky team, no two ever pulling together." He intended to change that. While he launched a major offensive against Lee in Virginia, William Tecumseh Sherman, who replaced Grant as commander of the western army, would drive a diagonal wedge through the Confederacy from Tennessee across Georgia. Grant's orders to Sherman were as blunt as his response had been that rainy night when the two had conferred at Shiloh: "Get into the interior of the enemy's country so far as you can, inflicting all the damage you can against their war resources."

In May and June 1864 Grant tried to maneuver Lee out of the trenches and into an open battle. But Lee was too weak to win head-on, so he opted for a strategy of attrition, hoping to inflict such heavy losses that the northern will to continue fighting would break. It was a strategy that nearly worked, for Union casualties were staggering. In a month of fierce fighting, the Army of the Potomac lost 60,000 men—the size of Lee's entire army at the beginning of the campaign. Yet at the end of the campaign Grant's reinforced army was larger than when it started, whereas Lee's was significantly weaker.

After especially bloody losses at the battle of Cold Harbor, Grant changed tactics. He marched his army around Richmond and settled into a siege of Petersburg, which guarded Richmond's last remaining rail link to the south. A siege would be agonizingly slow, but he counted on his numerical superiority to eventually stretch Lee's line to the breaking point. In the west, meanwhile, the gaunt and grizzled Sherman fought his way by July to the outskirts of Atlanta, which was heavily defended. "Our all depends on that army at Atlanta," wrote Mary Chesnut in August, based on her conversations with Confederate leaders. "If that fails us, the game is up."

War in the Balance

The game was nearly up for Lincoln as the 1864 election approached. In 1863 the victories at Gettysburg and Vicksburg sparked Republican victories, indicating that public opinion seemed to be swinging toward emancipation. But as the Union war machine swept more and more northerners south to their deaths and as Grant and Sherman bogged down on the Virginia and Georgia fronts, even leaders in Lincoln's own party began to mutter out loud that he was not equal to the task.

Perhaps the most remarkable thing about the 1864 election is that it was held at all. Indeed, before World War II, the United States was the only democratic government in history to carry out a general election in wartime. But Lincoln firmly believed that to postpone it would be to lose the priceless heritage of republicanism itself: "We cannot have free government without elections, and if the rebellion could force us to forego or

Capture of Vicksburg

Grant in Command

Union's Summer Offensive

1864 Election

The War in the East, 1863–1865   *Lee won his most brilliant victory at Chancellorsville, then launched a second invasion of the North, hoping to score a decisive victory. When the two armies accidentally collided at Gettysburg on July 1, 1863, the Union's Army of the Potomac took up a strong defensive position, shaped like a fishhook and anchored by a hill at each end (see map inset). On July 2 the Confederate attack drove back the Union's left flank but failed to dislodge the right. Lee's assault on the center of the Union line on July 3 ended in a shattering defeat, and the Army of Northern Virginia retreated back to Virginia. In 1864 Grant delivered a series of heavy blows against Lee's outnumbered forces in Virginia. Despite staggering losses, Grant relentlessly pressed on. Note the casualties listed for the spring and summer of 1864; from mid-May to mid-June Grant lost nearly 60,000 men, equal to Lee's strength (listed in parentheses). Sheridan's raids against the civilian farms of the Shenandoah Valley helped deprive Lee of desperately needed supplies. In April 1865, too weak to defend Richmond any longer, Lee surrendered at the Appomattox Courthouse.*

postpone a national election, it might fairly claim to have already conquered and ruined us." Exploiting his control of the party machinery, Lincoln easily won the Republican nomination, and he made certain that the Republican platform called for the adoption of a constitutional amendment abolishing slavery. To balance the ticket, the convention selected Andrew Johnson, the military governor of Tennessee and a prowar Democrat, as his running mate. The two men ran under the label of the "Union" party.

The Democrats nominated George McClellan, the former Union commander. Their platform pronounced the war a failure and called for an armistice and a peace conference. Warned that a cessation of fighting would lead to disunion, McClellan partially repudiated this position, insisting that "the Union is the one condition of peace—we ask no more." In private he made it clear that if elected he intended to restore slavery. Late in August, Lincoln was still gloomy about his prospects as well as those of the Union itself. But Admiral David Farragut won a dramatic victory at Mobile Bay, and a few weeks later, in early September, Sherman finally captured Atlanta. As Secretary of State Seward gleefully noted, "Sherman and Farragut have knocked the bottom out of the Chicago [Democratic] nominations."

Confederate flag

Significance of Lincoln's Reelection

Polling an impressive 55 percent of the popular vote, Lincoln won 212 electoral votes to McClellan's 21. Eighteen states allowed soldiers to vote in the field, and Lincoln received nearly 80 percent of their ballots. One lifelong Democrat described the sentiment in the army: "We all want peace, but none any but an honorable one. I had rather stay out here a lifetime (much as I dislike it) than consent to a division of our country." Jefferson Davis remained defiant, but the last hope of a Confederate victory was gone.

Equally important, the election of 1864 ended any doubt that slavery would be abolished in the reconstructed Union. The Emancipation Proclamation had not put an end to the question, for its legal status remained unclear. Lincoln and the Republicans insisted that a constitutional amendment was necessary to secure emancipation. After the election, the president threw all his influence behind the drive to round up the necessary votes, and the measure passed the House on January 31, 1865. By December, enough states had ratified the Thirteenth Amendment to make it part of the Constitution.

Thirteenth Amendment

The abolition of slavery in the United States was part of a worldwide trend. The antislavery movement was spearheaded in Britain, where Parliament abolished slavery in the empire in 1833. The other colonial powers were much slower to act. Portugal did not end slavery in its New World colonies until 1836, Sweden in 1847, Denmark and France in 1848, Holland in 1863, and Spain not until 1886. Most of the Latin American republics had ended slavery when they threw off Spanish or Portuguese control, but the institution remained important in Cuba and Brazil; Spain abolished slavery in Cuba in 1886, and Brazil ended the institution in 1888. European reformers also crusaded against slavery in Africa and Asia, and indeed the antislavery movement increased European presence in Africa. At the same time, European nations ended the medieval institution of serfdom. In Russia, where serfdom had most closely approximated slavery, Czar Alexander II emancipated the serfs in 1861, an act that led him to strongly favor the Union in the American Civil War.

Abolition as a Global Movement

The Twilight of the Confederacy

For the Confederacy, the outcome of the 1864 election had a terrible finality. At the beginning of the war, Vice President Stephens had proclaimed slavery the cornerstone of the Confederacy, but in March 1865 the Confederate Congress authorized recruiting 300,000 slaves for military service. When signing the bill, Davis announced that freedom would be given to those who volunteered and to their families. That same month he offered through a special envoy to abolish slavery in exchange for British diplomatic recognition. A Mississippi paper denounced this proposal as "a total abandonment of the chief object of this war." The British rejected the offer, and the war ended before any slaves were mustered into the Confederate army, but the abandonment of slav-

Confederacy's Abandonment of Slavery

ery surely completed the Confederacy's internal revolution. The demands of total war had forced Confederate leaders to forsake the Old South's fundamental values and institutions.

In the wake of Lincoln's reelection, the Confederate will to resist rapidly disintegrated. White southerners had never fully united behind the war effort, but the large majority had endured great suffering to uphold it. As Sherman pushed deeper into the Confederacy and General Philip Sheridan mounted his devastating raid on the Shenandoah Valley, the war came home to southern civilians as never before. "We haven't got nothing in the house to eat but a little bit o meal," wrote the wife of one Alabama soldier in December 1864. "Try to get off and come home and fix us all up some and then you can go back. . . . If you put off a-coming, 'twont be no use to come, for we'll all . . . [be] in the grave yard." He deserted. In the last months of the fighting, more than half the Confederacy's soldiers were absent without leave.

March to the Sea

After the fall of Atlanta, Sherman gave a frightening demonstration of total war. Imitating Grant's strategy he abandoned his supply lines for an audacious 300-mile march to the sea. Sherman intended to deprive Lee's army of the supplies it desperately needed to continue and to break the southern will to resist. Or as he bluntly put it, "to whip the Rebels, to humble their pride, to follow them to their recesses, and make them fear and dread us."

Moving in four columns, Sherman's army covered about 10 miles a day, cutting a path of destruction 50 miles wide. "We had a gay old campaign," one of his soldiers wrote. "Destroyed all we could not eat, stole their niggers, burned their cotton and gins, spilled their sorghum, burned and twisted their railroads and raised Hell generally." Sherman estimated that his men did $100 million in damage, of which $20 million

General William Sherman demonstrated the tactics of total war in the autumn of 1864. "Destroyed all we could not eat . . . burned their cotton and gins . . . burned and twisted their railroads . . . ," wrote one of Sherman's soldiers. This drawing, done by a Union private, depicts a similar destructive raid on a plantation along Virginia's James River in 1862, and by the spring of 1865, Confederate armies were increasingly unable to resist Union might.

was necessary to supply his army and the rest was wanton destruction. After he captured Savannah in late December, he turned north and wreaked even greater havoc in South Carolina, which Union troops considered the seedbed of the rebellion.

By December the interior of the Confederacy was essentially conquered. Only Lee's army remained, entrenched around Petersburg, Virginia, as Grant relentlessly extended his lines, stretching the Confederates thinner and thinner. On April 2 Confederate forces evacuated Richmond.

Grant doggedly pursued the Army of Northern Virginia westward for another hundred miles. After Union forces captured supplies waiting for Lee at Appomattox Courthouse, the weary gentleman from Virginia asked to see Grant. Lee surrendered on April 9, 1865. As the vanquished foe mounted his horse, Grant saluted by raising his hat; Lee raised his respectfully and rode off at a slow trot. "On our part," one federal officer wrote, there was "not a sound of trumpet . . . nor roll of drum; not a cheer . . . but an awed stillness rather." The guns were quiet.

Lee's Surrender

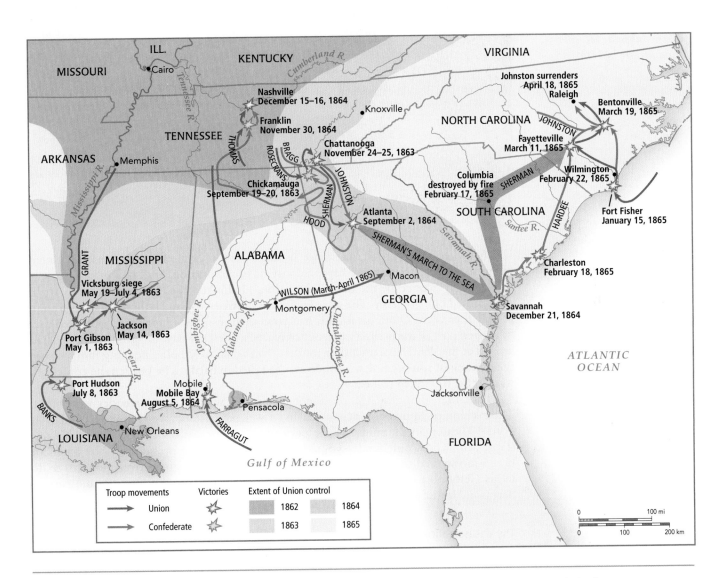

The War in the West, 1863–1865 *The Union continued its war of mobility in the western theater, bringing more Confederate territory under its control. After Grant captured Vicksburg, the entire Mississippi lay in Union hands. His victories at Lookout Mountain and Missionary Ridge, near Chattanooga, ended the Confederate threat to Tennessee. In 1864 Sherman divided the Confederacy by seizing Atlanta and marching across Georgia; then he turned north. When Joseph Johnston surrendered several weeks after Lee's capitulation at Appomattox, the war was effectively over.*

The war's greatest generals, Ulysses S. Grant (left) and Robert E. Lee (right), confronted each other in the eastern theater during the last year of the war. A member of a distinguished Virginia family, the tall, impeccably dressed Lee was every inch the aristocratic gentleman. Grant, a short, slouched figure with a stubby beard, dressed indifferently, often wearing a private's uniform with only the stars on his shoulders to indicate his rank. But his determination is readily apparent in this picture, taken at his field headquarters in 1864.

With Lee's army gone, resistance throughout the Confederacy collapsed within a matter of weeks. Visiting the captured city of Richmond on April 4, Lincoln was enthusiastically greeted by the black population. He looked "pale, haggard, utterly worn out," noted one observer. The lines in his face showed how much the war had aged him in only four years. Often his friends had counseled rest, but Lincoln had observed that "the tired part of me is *inside* and out of reach." Day after day, the grim telegrams had arrived at the War Department, or mothers had come to see him, begging him to spare their youngest son because the other two had died in battle. The burden, he confessed, was almost too much to bear.

Back in Washington the president received news of Lee's surrender with relief. The evening of April 14, Lincoln, seeking a welcome escape, went to see a comedy at Ford's Theater. In the midst of the performance John Wilkes Booth, a mentally unstable actor and Confederate sympathizer, slipped into the presidential box and shot him. Lincoln died the next morning. As he had called upon his fellow Americans to do in his Gettysburg Address, the sixteenth president had given his "last full measure of devotion" to the Republic.

Lincoln's Assassination

The assassination, which capped four years of bloody war, left a tiredness in the nation's bones—a tiredness "inside" and not easily within reach. In every way the conflict had produced fundamental, often devastating changes. There was, of course, the carnage. Approximately 620,000 men on both sides lost their lives, almost as many as in all the other wars the nation has fought from the Revolution through Vietnam combined. In material terms, the conflict cost an estimated $20 billion, or about 10 times the value of all slaves in the country in 1860 and more than 11 times the total amount spent by the federal government from 1789 to 1861. Even without adding the market value of freed slaves, southern wealth declined 43 percent, transforming what had been the richest section in the nation (on a white per capita basis) into the poorest.

The effects of total war, however, went well beyond upheaval and destruction. The Civil War rearranged and reordered not only the national economy but also economic relations worldwide. In the nation, demand for the machines of war stimulated industrialization, especially in the heavy industries of iron and coal, machinery, and agricultural implements. Manufacturers were forced to supply the army on an unprecedented scale over great distances. One consequence was the creation of truly national industries in flour milling, meat packing, clothing and shoe manufacture, and machinery making.

People across the globe felt the effects of the war, particularly due to changes in the cotton trade. By 1860 the South was supplying more than three-quarters of all cotton imported by Britain, France, Germany, and Russia. When the war cut off that supply, manufacturers scrambled to find new sources. India, Egypt, and Brazil all improved their railroad facilities and ports in order to encourage planters to open new cotton fields. The Indian city of Bombay experienced explosive growth handling the flood of new cotton. The effect of the trade on Egypt was so great, historians of that nation rank the American Civil War along with the construction of the Suez Canal as the most crucial events in its nineteenth-century history. In the end, the efforts of cotton merchants, textile operators, and European governments marked the first steps by European powers toward a more aggressive imperialism that flourished in the late nineteenth century.

Politically, the war dramatically changed the balance of power. The South lost its substantial influence, as did the Democratic party, while the Republicans emerged in a dominant position. The Union's military victory also signaled the triumph of nationalism. The war destroyed the idea that the Union was a voluntary confederacy of sovereign states, which theorists like John C. Calhoun had argued, and that the states had the right to secede. The Union was perpetual, as Andrew Jackson had first suggested—truly an indivisible nation. In an important symbolic change, Americans now spoke of the United States in the singular rather than the plural.

In the short run, the price was disillusionment and bitterness. The South had to live with the humiliation of military defeat and occupation, while former slaves anxiously waited to see what freedom would bring them. The war's corrosive effect on morals corrupted American life and politics, destroyed idealism, and severely crippled humanitarian reform. Millennialism and perfectionism were victims of the war's appalling slaughter, forsaken for a new emphasis on practicality, order, materialism, and science. As the war unfolded, the New York *Herald* recognized the deep changes: "All sorts of old fogy ideas, manners, and customs have gone under, and all sorts of new ideas, modes, and practices have risen to the surface and become popular."

George Ticknor, a prominent author and critic who was sensitive to shifting intellectual and social currents, reflected on the changes that had shaken the nation in only a few short years. The war, it seemed to him, had left "a great gulf between what happened before it in our century and what has happened since. . . . It does not seem to me as if I were living in the country in which I was born."

Significant Events

1861	Border states remain in the Union; Union blockade proclaimed; Lincoln suspends writ of habeas corpus in selected areas; Battle of Bull Run; First Confiscation Act
1862	Forts Henry and Donelson captured; *Monitor vs. Virginia (Merrimack)*; Battle of Shiloh; Confederacy adopts conscription; New Orleans captured; Homestead Act; Land Grant College Act; Second Confiscation Act; Union income tax enacted; McClellan's Peninsula campaign fails; Battle of Antietam; preliminary Emancipation Proclamation issued; Lincoln suspends writ of habeas corpus throughout the Union; Battle of Fredericksburg
1863	Emancipation Proclamation issued; National Banking Act; Union institutes conscription; Confederacy enacts general tax laws, initiates impressment; bread riots in the Confederacy; Battle of Chancellorsville; Battle of Gettysburg; Vicksburg captured; New York City draft riots
1864	Grant becomes Union general in chief; Wilderness campaign; siege of Petersburg; fall of Atlanta; Lincoln reelected; Sherman's march to the sea
1865	Congress passes Thirteenth Amendment; Sherman's march through the Carolinas; Lee surrenders; Lincoln assassinated; Thirteenth Amendment ratified
1866	*Ex parte Milligan*

Chapter Summary

For the first total war in history, the Civil War's outcome depended not just on armies but also on the mobilization of each society's human, economic, and intellectual resources.

- Confederate president Jefferson Davis's policy of concentrating power in the government at Richmond, along with the resort to a draft and impressment of private property, provoked strong protests from many southerners.

- Abraham Lincoln's policies, especially his suspension of the writ of habeas corpus and his interference with civil liberties, were equally controversial.

- But Lincoln skillfully handled the delicate situation of the border states in the first year of the war, keeping them in the Union.

- Lincoln at first resisted pressure to make emancipation a Union war aim, but he eventually issued the Emancipation Proclamation, which transformed the meaning of the war.

- African Americans helped undermine slavery in the Confederacy and made a vital contribution to the Union's military victory.

- The war had a powerful impact on the home front.

  - Women confronted new responsibilities and enjoyed new occupational opportunities.
  - In the Confederacy, hardship and suffering became a fact of life.
  - The Confederate government's financial and tax policies and the tightening Union blockade increased this suffering.

- Both societies also experienced the ravages of moral decay.

- The Civil War changed the nature of warfare.

  —Technology, particularly the use of rifles and rifled artillery, revolutionized tactics and strategy.
  —The Union eventually adopted the strategy of attacking the civilian population of the South.
  —Soldiers in both armies suffered from disease and inadequate medical care, poor food, moral corruption, and the mounting death toll.

  —Union soldiers were more accustomed to order and control and adjusted more effectively to the war's demands.

- The war altered the nation's political institutions, its economy, and its values.

Additional Reading

Histories of the Civil War tend to concentrate on either the home front or the military, and on either the Confederacy or the Union. A good single-volume history of the war, up-to-date in its scholarship and balanced in its judgments, covering all these topics is James M. McPherson, *Battle Cry of Freedom* (1988). In recent years military historians have devoted more attention to the relationship between society and the military. An interesting example that traces the evolution of the Union's strategy toward southern civilians is Mark Grimsley, *The Hard Hand of War* (1995).

The best biography of Lincoln, based on extensive research, is David Donald, *Lincoln* (1995). William E. Gienapp, *Abraham Lincoln and Civil War America* (2002), is a concise biography that focuses on the presidential years. Much longer, but vividly written, is Doris Kearns Goodwin's *Team of Rivals: The Political Genius of Abraham Lincoln* (2005). Mark E. Neely has written two innovative studies of civil liberties in wartime: *The Fate of Liberty* (1991) examines the Union and *Southern Rights* (1999) deals with the Confederacy. For the South's bid for independence, Emory M. Thomas, *The Confederate Nation, 1861–1865* (1979), is the standard account. The fullest discussion of southern politics is George C. Rable, *The Confederate Republic* (1994). After years of relative neglect, historians have turned their attention to the vital home front. Drew Faust, *Mothers of Invention* (1996), is an imaginative study of slaveholding women in the Confederacy; Daniel Sutherland, *Seasons of War* (1995), and William Blair, *Virginia's Private War* (1998), analyze the experiences of several Virginian counties in the war; and Stephen V. Ash, *When the Yankees Came* (1995), examines southerners under Union occupation. For the northern home front, see J. Matthew Gallman, *The North Fights the Civil War* (1994). Leon Litwack, *Been in the Storm So Long* (1979), is a gracefully written account of African Americans' experiences during the war, and James L. Roark's *Masters without Slaves* (1977) discusses the collapse of the southern slaveholders' world. Gerald F. Linderman, *Embattled Courage* (1987), presents an interesting assessment of soldiers in both armies. Chandra Manning, in *What This Cruel War Was Over* (2007) argues that early on both Union and Confederate soldiers identified slavery as the roots of the war, and that Union rank-and-file widely believed in emancipation as early as the end of 1861. Two excellent collections of essays that evaluate the war's outcome from various angles are David H. Donald, ed., *Why the North Won the Civil War* (1961), and Gabor S. Boritt, ed., *Why the Confederacy Lost* (1992).

For a fuller list of readings, see the Bibliography at www.mhhe.com/davidsonnation6.

Historians Reconstruct the Past

What Caused the New York Draft Riots?

Making sense out of the chaos of war surely presents one of greatest challenges for historians. Yet amidst the carnage of attack and counterattack, at least officers are working to coordinate troop movements and lines of battle. Civil disturbances, rebellions and riots are even more chaotic, leaving a greater puzzle to decode. How does a historian make sense of the "draft riots" that shook New York City in the summer of 1863?

Observers could hardly have predicted the outburst from the opening day of the Union draft, on Saturday, July 11, 1863. Atop a platform, with a small crowd looking on, a blindfolded man stood beside a cylinder as an attendant cranked it around. When the cylinder stooped, the blindfolded man reached in and pulled out a rolled-up slip of paper with a name on it. In similar fashion the day's selections were made one by one, all without incident.

Monday, however, was another story. Bright and early, hundreds of laborers streamed up Eighth and Ninth avenues. Waving "No Draft" placards, they rousted other workers from the stores and factories that they passed, stopping at last outside the draft office. Someone fired a pistol. Then members of the mob burst in, destroyed the selection cylinder, and set the building afire. Firefighters tried to stop the blaze from spreading, but another angry mob arrived in time to prevent them. All over the city the chaos spread. "Men left their various pursuits," wrote one reporter; store owners "put up their shutters; factories were emptied, conductors or drivers left their cars" until a "concourse of over twelve thousand" men, women, and children were roaming the streets.

Over the next several days, the riots became even more violent. Fires burned out of control, telegraph wires were cut, railroad tracks were torn up, and crowds staged pitched battles with police and troops. Targets of the mob's wrath included both high officials and lowly citizens. Homes of the wealthy were looted and set afire, but so was the Colored Orphan Asylum. Policemen caught by the rioters were stripped of their clothes, and their faces were beaten to bloody pulps. Abraham Franklin, a crippled black coachman, was dragged from his rooms and hung while onlookers cheered for Jefferson Davis. By Friday order was at last restored by troops that had been rushed back from their recent victory at Gettysburg. At least 105 people, mostly rioters, lost their lives, and more than a million dollars in property had been

CHARGE OF THE POLICE ON THE RIOTERS AT THE "TRIBUNE" OFFICE.

destroyed. It was the highest loss of life in any civil disturbance in American history. A month later, the draft resumed in New York City.

Were the Draft Riots About the Draft?

What was the cause of such an immense tumult? "Absolute disloyalty," huffed the Republican New York *Tribune.* "It is absurd . . . to attribute this ruffianism to anything else than sympathy with the Rebels." The Democratic New York *World,* which had condemned the draft beforehand, offered an equally straightforward answer. The riot was a spontaneous protest against Lincoln's "wanton exercise of arbitrary powers." Having perverted the war into a struggle to destroy slavery, the paper complained, the administration was now determined to enforce an unconstitutional conscription law that allowed the rich to escape while sweeping the poor into the army's ranks.

At first glance, the *World's* emphasis on the draft seems sufficient. Rioters, after all, carried "No Draft" placards. They attacked draft officials and, by direct intimidation, forced the government to suspend the draft. Eyewitnesses agreed, moreover, that the rioters were overwhelmingly workers and mostly immigrants. These men certainly could not afford to pay the

SACKING A DRUG STORE IN SECOND AVENUE.

Observers noted that many rioters were boys.

$300 commutation fee to avoid the draft. For them, $300 represented a year's wages or more.

Still, a closer look at the evidence suggests that there was more to these riots than a simple protest of the Union draft. Historians look to put the protest in a broader context by asking questions about the rioters involved. Just who were they? What were their motives for rioting? Do the obvious explanations hold up? To begin with, the draft did not apply to immigrants unless they were naturalized citizens or had declared their intention to be naturalized. Thus many foreign-born rioters were not even eligible. In addition, observers noted that rioters, including some of the most violent, were remarkably young. Dismissing talk of an oppressive conscription law, the New York *Times* asserted that "three-fourths of those who have been actively engaged in violence have been boys and young men under twenty years of age and not at all subject to Conscription." And if the $300 clause was what most angered the mobs, why did they attack free blacks, who were also subject to the draft and almost all of whom were too poor to pay the fee?

Historians who have examined Union conscription records cast further doubt on this explanation. Despite complaints by Democrats that the $300 fee was an instrument of class privilege, in reality poor men as well as wealthy ones bought their way out of the draft. In New York City, the rate of commutation was as high in poorer wards as in wealthy ones. In fact, over the course of the war 98 percent of the men drafted in the Irish districts of the city either paid the fee or provided substitutes. For as little as $10, workers could buy the equivalent of draft insurance by joining commutation clubs, in which members pooled their money to pay the fee for any contributor who was drafted.

If the draft was not the sole cause of the riots, what else was behind the mob's anger? For historians, evidence is not easy to come by. Members of rioting crowds rarely leave written records. More often, descriptions are the work of unsympathetic observers. Still, for historians actions can speak as loudly as words. Look closely at what the mobs did. Whom did they choose as the targets of their violence? Did different mobs express their anger in different ways? By examining the riots as they evolved over several days, it is possible to discover vital evidence concerning motivation. In the New York City disturbances, the makeup of the crowds changed dramatically from one day to the next, and the targets the rioters attacked also varied.

On Monday morning, industrial laborers and skilled workers, especially from the building trades, took a leading role. They were joined by some of the city's fire companies. Although some native-born workers participated, the protesters were largely immigrants, Germans as well as Irish. As they marched to the draft office, they announced a one-day strike in protest against the draft. By noon this throng of workers had halted the selection process.

Other rioters, however, began to attack the police and free blacks. As the mayhem escalated, some members of the morning demonstration, including those from several fire companies, now aided the authorities in trying to restore order. For those who switched sides, opposition to the draft had been paramount, and they were unwilling to sanction looting or murder.

Who Were the Mob's Targets?

When the riots continued on Tuesday and Wednesday, the crowds became much more heavily Irish. German Americans, some of whom were Republicans, no longer joined in. In fact, on several occasions they stepped in to protect free blacks. Skilled workers such as bricklayers, painters, and stonecutters for the most part also held back. Instead, rioters were largely industrial workers and common laborers and included many women and children. Their anger was directed no longer against the draft but against the Republican government and all its policies, including emancipation. Thus they vandalized homes of prominent Republicans, chanted pro-Confederate slogans, and fought pitched battles with the police and soldiers. The offices of Horace Greeley's pro-Republican New York *Tribune* were attacked several times, and Greeley was forced to hide in a nearby restaurant to escape a beating.

For common laborers—longshoremen, street pavers, cartmen—African Americans increasingly became the target of vengeance. Mobs assaulted blacks and lynched at least 12, ransacked businesses that catered to black customers, and destroyed tenements in which African Americans lived. These attacks were designed to purge neighborhoods of any black presence, especially in areas where black workers had been used to break strikes. These common laborers sought to restore the traditional racial order threatened by Republican policies, most notably emancipation.

In contrast, attacks on blacks and black residences were not common in wards where large numbers of industrial workers

Common laborers in particular vented their anger on African Americans. As with colonial mob actions, such protests exhibited ritualistic overtones. The victim here not only is being hanged and burned but is being shot as well.

lived. While heavily Irish, industrial laborers in iron foundries and railroad shops did not work alongside African Americans. Athough hostile to blacks, they aimed their anger more directly at the Republican party. Rather than roaming throughout the city as many common laborers did, industrial workers concentrated on their own neighborhoods, from which they tried to remove all reminders of Republican authority, particularly draft officials, policemen, and soldiers. Although many policemen were not Republicans, the Metropolitan Police had been created by the Republican party in 1857, and its members had been particularly zealous in arresting individuals suspected of disloyalty.

In the end, no single grievance can explain New York's draft riots. Hostility to Republican employers, Protestant reformers, and authorities merged with antiblack racism, fears of job competition, and economic marginality. By itself, opposition to the draft did not produce the escalating violence and extraordinary destruction. But when that inflammatory issue sparked an avalanche of protest, it provided an outlet for more deeply rooted grievances. The result was the most serious civil disturbance of the war.

Bibliography   Iver Bernstein, *The New York City Draft Riots* (1990), does an admirable job of placing the riots within the context of changing class relations and work patterns. Adrian Cook, *The Armies of the Streets* (1974), presents a more straightforward narrative, but it has been superseded by the magisterial study of Barnet Schecter, *The Devil's Own Work* (2005), which sets a gripping account of the riots within the larger context of political, class, ethnic and racial rivalries in the decades preceding the riot, and looks at the riot's consequences for Reconstruction in the decades following the war.

A Secret Sale at Davis Bend

Joseph Davis had had enough. Well on in years and financially ruined by the war, he decided to quit farming. In November 1866, he sold his Mississippi plantations Hurricane and Brierfield to Benjamin Montgomery and his sons. The sale of southern plantations was common enough after the war, but this transaction was bound to attract attention, since Joseph Davis was the elder brother of Jefferson Davis. Indeed, before the war the Confederate president had operated Brierfield as his own plantation, although his brother retained legal title to it. In truth, the sale was so unusual that the parties involved agreed to keep it secret, since the Montgomerys were black, and Mississippi law prohibited African Americans from owning land.

Though a slave, Montgomery had been the business manager of the two Davis plantations before the war. He had also operated a store on Hurricane Plantation for white as well as black customers with his own line of credit in New Orleans. In 1863 Montgomery fled to the North, but when the war was over, he returned to Davis Bend, where the federal government was leasing plots of the land on confiscated plantations, including Hurricane and Brierfield, to black farmers. Montgomery quickly emerged as the leader of the African American community at the Bend.

Then, in 1866, President Andrew Johnson pardoned Joseph Davis and restored his lands. By then Davis was over 80 years old and lacked the will and stamina to rebuild. Yet unlike many ex-slaveholders, he still felt bound by obligations to his former slaves. He was convinced that with proper encouragement African Americans could succeed economically in freedom. Only when the law prohibiting African Americans from owning land was overturned in 1867 did Davis publicly confirm the sale to his former slave.

For his part, Montgomery undertook to create a model society at Davis Bend based on mutual cooperation. He rented land to black farmers, hired others to work his own fields, sold supplies on credit, and ginned and marketed the crops. To the growing African American community, he preached the gospel of hard work, self-reliance, and education.

Various difficulties dogged these black farmers, including the destruction caused by the war, several disastrous floods, insects, droughts, and declining cotton prices. Yet before long, cotton production exceeded that of the prewar years, and in 1870 the black families at Davis Bend produced 2,500 bales. The Montgomerys eventually acquired another plantation and

A black nursemaid holds a baby entrusted to her care in this daguerrotype taken around 1865. After emancipation, freedmen often sought jobs in urban areas, including domestic work for women. But the abolition of slavery inevitably changed relationships as African Americans sought their rights as free citizens and white southerners strove to come to terms with the changed social order.

A Visit from the Old Mistress, *by Winslow Homer, captures the conflicting, often awkward, emotions felt by both races after the war.*

owned 5,500 acres, which made them reputedly the third largest planters in the state. They won national and international awards for the quality of their cotton. Their success demonstrated what African Americans, given a fair chance, might accomplish.

The experiences of Benjamin Montgomery during the years after 1865 were not those of most black southerners, who did not own land or have a powerful white benefactor. Yet Montgomery's dream of economic independence was shared by all African Americans. As one black veteran noted, "Every colored man will be a slave, and feel himself a slave until he can raise him own bale of cotton and put him own mark upon it and say dis is mine!" Blacks could not gain effective freedom simply through a proclamation of emancipation. They needed economic power, including their own land that no one could unfairly take away.

For nearly two centuries the laws had prevented slaves from possessing such economic power. If those conditions were to be overturned, black Americans needed political power too. Thus the Republic would have to be reconstructed to give African Americans political power that they had been previously denied.

War, in its blunt way, had roughed out the contours of a solution, but only in broad terms. Clearly, African Americans would no longer be enslaved. The North, with its industrial might, would be the driving force in the nation's economy and retain the dominant political voice. But beyond that, the outlines of a reconstructed Republic remained vague. Would African Americans receive effective power? How would the North and the South readjust their economic and political relations? These questions lay at the heart of the problem of Reconstruction.

Presidential Reconstruction

Throughout the war Abraham Lincoln had considered Reconstruction his responsibility. Elected with less than 40 percent of the popular vote in 1860, he was acutely aware that once the states of the Confederacy were restored to the Union, the Republicans would be weakened unless they ceased to be a sectional party. By a generous peace, Lincoln hoped to attract former Whigs in the South, who supported many of the Republicans' economic policies, and build up a southern wing of the party.

Lincoln's 10 Percent Plan

Lincoln outlined his program in a Proclamation of **Amnesty** and Reconstruction issued in December 1863. When a minimum of 10 percent of the qualified voters from 1860 took a **loyalty oath** to the Union, they could organize a state government. The new state constitution had to be republican in form, abolish slavery, and provide for black education, but Lincoln did not insist that high-ranking Confederate leaders be barred from public life.

Lincoln indicated that he would be generous in granting pardons and did not rule out compensation for slave property. Moreover, while he privately suggested permitting some black men to vote in the disloyal states, "as for instance, the very intelligent and especially those who have fought gallantly in our ranks," he did not demand social or political equality for black Americans, and he recognized pro-Union governments in Louisiana, Arkansas, and Tennessee that allowed only white men to vote.

The Radical Republicans found Lincoln's approach much too lenient. Strongly antislavery, Radical members of Congress had led the struggle to make emancipation a war aim. Now they were in the forefront in advocating rights for the freed people. Lincoln argued that the executive branch should bear the responsibility for restoring proper relations with the former Confederate states. The Radicals, on the other hand, believed that it was the duty of Congress to set the terms under which states would regain their rights in the Union. Though the Radicals often disagreed on other matters, they were united in a determination to readmit southern states only after slavery had been ended, black rights protected, and the power of the planter class destroyed.

Under the direction of Senator Benjamin Wade of Ohio and Representative Henry Winter Davis of Maryland, Congress formulated a much stricter plan of Reconstruction. It proposed that Confederate states be ruled temporarily by a military governor, required half the white adult males to take an oath of allegiance before drafting a new state constitution, and restricted political power to the hard-core Unionists in each state. When the Wade-Davis bill passed on the final day of the 1864 congressional session, Lincoln exercised his right of a **pocket veto.** Still, his own program could not succeed without the assistance of Congress, which refused to seat Unionist representatives who had been elected from Louisiana or Arkansas. As the war drew to a close, Lincoln appeared ready to make concessions to the Radicals. At his final cabinet meeting, he approved placing the defeated South temporarily under military rule. But only a few days later Booth's bullet found its mark, and Lincoln's final approach to Reconstruction would never be known.

The Mood of the South

In the wake of defeat, the immediate reaction among white southerners was one of shock, despair, and hopelessness. Some former Confederates, of course, were openly antagonistic. A North Carolina innkeeper remarked bitterly that Yankees had stolen his slaves, burned his house, and killed all his sons, leaving him only one privilege: "To hate 'em. I git up at half-past four in the morning, and sit up till twelve at night, to hate 'em." Most Confederate soldiers were less defiant, having had their fill of war. Even among hostile civilians the feeling was widespread that the South must accept northern terms.

Radical Republicans

Wade-Davis Bill

The mood of white southerners at the end of the war was mixed. Many, like the veteran caricatured here by northern cartoonist Thomas Nast, remained hostile. Others, like Texas captain Samuel Foster, came to believe that the institution of slavery "had been abused" and that men "who actually owned and held slaves up to this time,—have now changed in their opinions regarding slavery . . . to see that for a man to have property in man was wrong, and that the 'Declaration of Independence' meant more than they had ever been able to see before."

This psychological moment was critical. To prevent a resurgence of resistance, the president needed to lay out clearly what white southerners had to do to regain their old status in the Union. Any wavering on the peace terms could only increase the likelihood of resistance. Perhaps even a clear and firm policy would not have been enough. But with Lincoln's death, the executive power came to rest in far less capable hands.

Johnson's Program of Reconstruction

Johnson's Character and Values

Andrew Johnson, the new president, had been born in North Carolina and eventually moved to Tennessee, where he worked as a tailor. Barely able to read and write when he married, he rose to political power by portraying himself as the champion of the people against the wealthy planter class. "Some day I will show the stuck-up aristocrats who is running the country," he vowed as he began his political career. He had not opposed slavery before the war—in fact, he hoped to disperse slave ownership more widely in southern society. Although he accepted emancipation as one consequence of the war, Johnson remained a confirmed racist. "Damn the negroes," he said during the war, "I am fighting these traitorous aristocrats, their masters."

Because Johnson disliked the planter class, Republican Radicals in Congress expected him to uphold their views on Reconstruction. In fact, the new president did speak of trying Confederate leaders and breaking up planters' estates. Unlike most Republicans, however, Johnson strongly supported states' rights. Furthermore, his prickly personality made conflict between the president and Congress inevitable. Scarred by his humble origins, Johnson remained an outsider throughout his life. When challenged or criticized, he became tactless and inflexible, alienating even those who sought to work with him.

Johnson's Program

Johnson moved quickly to return the southern states to their place in the Union. He prescribed a loyalty oath that white southerners would have to take to regain their civil and political rights and to have their property, except for slaves, restored. Excluded were high Confederate officials and those with property worth over $20,000, who had to apply for individual pardons. Johnson announced that once a state had drafted a new constitution and elected state officers and members of Congress, he would revoke martial law and recognize the new state government. Suffrage was limited to white citizens who had taken the loyalty oath. This plan was similar to Lincoln's, though more lenient. Only informally did Johnson ask that the southern states renounce their ordinances of secession, repudiate the Confederate debt, and ratify the proposed Thirteenth Amendment abolishing slavery.

The Failure of Johnson's Program

Southern Defiance

The southern delegates who met to construct new governments were in no frame of mind to follow Johnson's recommendations. Several states merely repealed instead of repudiating their ordinances of secession, rejected the Thirteenth Amendment, or refused to repudiate the Confederate debt.

Nor did the new governments allow African Americans any political rights or make any effective provisions for black education. In addition, each state passed a series of laws, often modeled on its old slave code, that applied only to African Americans. These **black codes** did grant African Americans some rights that had not been enjoyed by slaves. They legalized marriages performed under slavery and allowed black southerners to hold and sell property and to sue and be sued in state courts. Yet their primary purpose was to keep African Americans as propertyless agricultural laborers with inferior legal rights. The new **freedmen,** or **freedpeople,** could not serve on juries, testify against whites, or work as they pleased. South Carolina forbade blacks to engage in anything other than agricultural labor without a special license; Mississippi prohibited them from buying or renting farmland. Most states ominously provided that black people who were vagrants could be arrested and hired out to landowners. Many northerners were incensed by the restrictive black codes.

Black Codes

Southern voters under Johnson's plan also defiantly elected prominent Confederate military and political leaders to office, headed by Alexander Stephens, the vice president of the Confederacy, who was elected senator from Georgia. At this point, Johnson could have called for new elections or admitted that a different program of Reconstruction was needed. Instead he caved in. For all his harsh rhetoric, he shrank from the prospect of social upheaval, and he found it enormously gratifying when upper-class planters praised his conduct and requested pardons. As the lines of ex-Confederates waiting to see him lengthened, he began issuing special pardons almost as fast as they could be printed. In the next two years he pardoned some 13,500 former rebels.

In private, Johnson warned southerners against a reckless course. Publicly he put on a bold face, announcing that Reconstruction had been successfully completed. But many members of Congress were deeply alarmed.

Johnson's Break with Congress

The new Congress was by no means of one mind. A small number of Democrats and a few conservative Republicans backed the president's program. At the other end of the spectrum, a larger group of Radical Republicans, led by Thaddeus Stevens, Charles Sumner, Benjamin Wade, and others, was bent on remaking southern society in the image of the North. Reconstruction must "revolutionize Southern institutions, habits, and manners," insisted Representative Stevens, "... or all our blood and treasure have been spent in vain." Unlike Johnson, Radicals championed civil and political rights for African Americans and believed that the only way to maintain loyal governments and develop a Republican party in the South was to give black men the ballot.

As a minority, the Radicals could accomplish nothing without the aid of the moderate Republicans, the largest bloc in Congress. Led by William Pitt Fessenden and Lyman Trumbull, the moderates hoped to avoid a clash with the president, and they had no desire to foster social revolution or promote racial equality in the South. But they wanted to keep Confederate leaders from reassuming power, and they were convinced that the former slaves needed federal protection. Otherwise, Trumbull declared, the freedpeople would "be tyrannized over, abused, and virtually reenslaved."

Moderates agreed that the new southern governments were too harsh toward African Americans, but they feared that too great an emphasis on black civil rights would alienate northern voters.

In December 1865, when southern representatives to Congress appeared in Washington, a majority in Congress voted to exclude them. Congress also appointed a joint committee, chaired by Senator Fessenden, to look into how to implement Reconstruction. The split with the president became clearer when Congress passed a bill extending the life of the Freedmen's Bureau. Created in March 1865, the bureau provided emergency food, clothing, and medical care to war refugees (including white southerners) and took charge of settling freedpeople on abandoned lands. The new bill gave the bureau the added responsibilities of supervising special courts to resolve disputes involving freedpeople and establishing schools for black southerners. Although this bill passed with near unanimous Republican support, Johnson vetoed it. Congress failed to override his veto.

Johnson also vetoed a civil rights bill designed to overturn the most severe provisions of the black codes. The law made African Americans citizens of the United States and granted them the right to own property, make contracts, and have access to courts as parties and witnesses. For most Republicans Johnson's action was the last straw, and in April 1866 Congress overrode his veto, the first major legislation in American history to be enacted over a presidential veto. Congress then approved a slightly revised Freedmen's Bureau bill in July and promptly overrode the president's veto. Johnson's refusal to compromise drove the moderates into the arms of the Radicals.

Thaddeus Stevens, Radical leader in the House

The Fourteenth Amendment

To prevent unrepentant Confederates from taking over the reconstructed state governments and denying African Americans basic freedoms, the Joint Committee on Reconstruction proposed an amendment to the Constitution, which passed both houses of Congress with the necessary two-thirds vote in June 1866. The amendment, coupled with the Freedmen's Bureau and civil rights bills, represented the moderates' terms for Reconstruction.

Provisions of the Amendment

The Fourteenth Amendment put a number of matters beyond the control of the president. The amendment guaranteed repayment of the national war debt and prohibited repayment of the Confederate debt. To counteract the president's wholesale pardons, it disqualified prominent Confederates from holding office and provided that only Congress by a two-thirds vote could remove this penalty. Because moderates, fearful of the reaction of white northerners, balked at giving the vote to African Americans, the amendment merely gave Congress the right to reduce the representation of any state that did not have impartial male suffrage. The practical effect of this provision, which Radicals labeled a "swindle," was to allow northern states to restrict suffrage to whites if they wished, since unlike southern states they had few African Americans and thus would not be penalized.

The amendment's most important provision, Section 1, defined an American citizen as anyone born in the United States or naturalized, thereby automatically making African Americans citizens. Section 1 also prohibited states from abridging "the privileges or immunities" of citizens, depriving "any person of life, liberty, or property, without due process of law," or denying "any person . . . equal protection of the laws." The framers of the amendment probably intended to prohibit laws that applied to one race only, such as the black codes, or that made certain acts felonies when committed by black but not white people, or that decreed different penalties for the same crime when committed by white and black lawbreakers. The framers probably did not intend to prevent African Americans from being excluded from juries or to forbid segregation (the legal separation of the races) in schools and public places.

This politician is literally "waving the bloody shirt"—using the bitter memories of the Civil War to rouse voters to side with Republicans.

Nevertheless, Johnson denounced the proposed amendment and urged southern states not to ratify it. Ironically, of the seceded states only the president's own state ratified the amendment, and Congress readmitted Tennessee with no further restrictions. The telegram sent to Congress by a longtime foe of Johnson announcing Tennessee's approval ended, "Give my respects to the dead dog in the White House." The amendment was ratified in 1868.

The Elections of 1866

When Congress blocked his policies, Johnson undertook a speaking tour of the East and Midwest in the fall of 1866 to drum up popular support. But the president found it difficult to convince northern audiences that white southerners were fully repentant.

Antiblack Riots

News that summer of major race riots in Memphis and New Orleans heightened northern concern. Forty-six African Americans died when white mobs invaded the black section of Memphis, burning homes, churches, and schoolhouses. About the same number were killed in New Orleans when whites attacked both black and white delegates to a convention supporting black suffrage. "The negroes now know, to their sorrow, that it is best not to arouse the fury of the white man," boasted one Memphis newspaper. When the president encountered hostile audiences during his northern campaign, he only made matters worse by trading insults and ranting that the Radicals were traitors. Even supporters found his performance humiliating.

Not to be outdone, the Radicals vilified Johnson as a traitor aiming to turn the country over to rebels and Copperheads. Resorting to the tactic of "waving the **bloody shirt**," they appealed to voters by reviving bitter memories of the war. In a classic example of such rhetoric, Governor Oliver Morton of Indiana proclaimed that "every bounty jumper, every deserter, every sneak who ran away from the draft" was a Democrat; everyone "who murdered Union prisoners. . . . In short, the Democratic party may be described as a common sewer."

Voters soundly repudiated Johnson, as the Republicans won more than a two-thirds majority in both houses of Congress, every northern gubernatorial contest, and control of every northern legislature. The Radicals had reached the height of their power.

Repudiation of Johnson

Congressional Reconstruction

With a clear mandate in hand, congressional Republicans passed their own program of Reconstruction, beginning with the first Reconstruction Act in March 1867. Like all later pieces of Reconstruction legislation, it was repassed over Johnson's veto.

Placing the 10 unreconstructed states under military commanders, the act directed officials to include black adult males as voters but not former Confederates barred from holding office under the Fourteenth Amendment. State conventions would frame constitutions that provided for black suffrage and that disqualified prominent ex-Confederates from office. The first state legislatures to meet under the new constitution were required to ratify the Fourteenth Amendment. Once these steps were completed and Congress approved the new state constitution, a state could send representatives to Congress.

White southerners found these requirements so obnoxious that officials took no steps to register voters. Congress then enacted a second Reconstruction Act, also in March, ordering the local military commanders to put the machinery of Reconstruction into motion. Johnson's efforts to limit the power of military commanders produced a third act, passed in July, that upheld their superiority in all matters. When elections were held to ratify the new state constitutions, white southerners boycotted them in large numbers. Undaunted, Congress passed the fourth Reconstruction Act (March 1868), which required ratification of the constitution by only a majority of those voting rather than those who were registered.

Resistance of Southern Whites

By June 1868 Congress had readmitted the representatives of seven states. Georgia's state legislature expelled its black members once it had been readmitted, granting seats to those barred by Congress from holding office. Congress ordered the military commander to reverse these actions, and Georgia was then admitted a second time in July 1870. Texas, Virginia, and Mississippi did not complete the process until 1869.

Post-Emancipation Societies in the Americas

With the exception of Haiti's revolution (1791–1804), the United States was the only society in the Americas in which the destruction of slavery was accomplished by violence. But the United States, uniquely among these societies, enfranchised former slaves almost immediately after the emancipation. Thus in the United States former masters and slaves battled for control of the state in ways that did not occur in other post-emancipation societies. In most of the Caribbean, property requirements for voting left the planters in political control. Jamaica, for example, with a population of 500,000 in the 1860s, had only 3,000 voters.

Moreover, in reaction to political efforts to mobilize disfranchised black peasants, Jamaican planters dissolved the assembly and reverted to being a Crown colony governed from London. Of the sugar islands, all but Barbados adopted the same policy, thereby blocking the potential for any future black peasant democracy. Nor did any of these societies have the counterparts of the Radical Republicans, a group of outsiders with political power that promoted the fundamental transformation of the

**The Southern States
During Reconstruction**

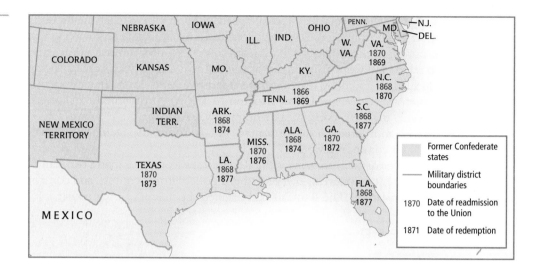

post-emancipation South. These comparisons highlight the radicalism of Reconstruction in the United States, which alone saw an effort to forge an interracial democracy.

The Land Issue

Blacks' Desire for Land

While the political process of Reconstruction proceeded, Congress confronted the question of whether land should be given to former slaves to foster economic independence. At a meeting with Secretary of War Edwin Stanton near the end of the war, African American leaders declared, "The way we can best take care of ourselves is to have land, and till it by our own labor." During the war, the Second Confiscation Act of 1862 had authorized the government to seize and sell the property, including land, of supporters of the rebellion. In June 1866, however, President Johnson ruled that confiscation laws applied only to wartime.

Congress debated land confiscation off and on from December 1865 until early 1867. Thaddeus Stevens, a leading Radical in the House, advocated confiscating 394 million acres of land from about 70,000 of what he termed the "chief rebels" in the South, who made up less than 5 percent of the South's white families. He proposed to give 40 acres to every adult male freedperson and then sell the remaining land, which would amount to nine-tenths of the total, to pay off the public debt, compensate loyal southerners for losses they suffered during the war, and fund Union veterans' pensions. Land, he insisted, would be far more valuable to African Americans than the right to vote.

Failure of Land
Redistribution

But in the end Congress rejected all proposals. Given Americans' strong belief in self-reliance, little sympathy existed for the idea that government should support any group. In addition, land redistribution represented an attack on property rights, another cherished American value. By 1867 land reform was dead.

Few freedpeople acquired land after the war, a development that severely limited African Americans' economic independence and left them vulnerable to white coercion. It is doubtful, however, that this decision was the basic cause of the failure of Reconstruction. In the face of white hostility and institutionalized racism, African Americans probably would have been no more successful in protecting their property than they were in maintaining the right to vote.

Impeachment

Tenure of Office Act

Throughout 1867 Congress routinely overrode Johnson's vetoes. Still, the president had other ways of undercutting congressional Reconstruction. He interpreted the new laws as narrowly as possible and removed military commanders who vigorously enforced them. Congress responded by restricting Johnson's power to issue orders to military commanders in the South. It also passed the Tenure of Office Act, which forbade Johnson to remove any member of the cabinet without the Senate's consent. The intention of this law was to prevent him from firing Secretary of War Edwin Stanton, the only Radical in the cabinet.

When Johnson tried to dismiss Stanton in February 1868, the determined secretary of war barricaded himself in his office (where he remained night and day for about two months). Angrily, the House of Representatives approved articles of impeachment. The articles focused on the violation of the Tenure of Office Act, but the charge with the most substance was that Johnson had conspired to systematically obstruct Reconstruction legislation. In the trial before the Senate, his lawyers argued that a president could be impeached only for an indictable crime, which Johnson clearly had not committed. The Radicals countered that impeachment applied to political offenses and not merely criminal acts. In May 1868 the Senate voted 36 to 19 to convict, one vote short of the two-thirds majority needed. The seven Republicans who joined the Democrats in voting for acquittal were uneasy about using impeachment as a political weapon.

Johnson Acquitted

Reconstruction in the South

The refusal of Congress to convict Johnson sent a clear signal: the power of the Radicals in Congress was waning. Increasingly the success or failure of Reconstruction hinged on developments not in Congress but in the southern states themselves. Power there rested with the new Republican parties, representing a coalition of black and white southerners and transplanted northerners.

Black Office Holding

Almost from the beginning of Reconstruction, African Americans had lobbied for the right to vote. After they received the **franchise,** black men constituted as much as 80 percent of the Republican voters in the South. They steadfastly opposed the Democratic party with its appeal to white supremacy.

Throughout Reconstruction, African Americans never held office in proportion to their voting strength. No African American was ever elected governor, and only in South Carolina, where more than 60 percent of the population was black, did they control even one house of the legislature. During Reconstruction between 15 and 20 percent of the state officers and 6 percent of members of Congress (2 senators and 15 representatives) were black. Only in South Carolina did black officeholders approach their proportion of the population.

Blacks who held office generally came from the top levels of African American society. Among state and federal officeholders, perhaps four-fifths were literate, and more than a quarter had been free before the war, both marks of distinction in the black community.

Background of Black Political Leaders

Their occupations also set them apart: two-fifths were professionals (mostly clergy), and of the third who were farmers, nearly all owned land. Among black members of Congress, all but three had a secondary school education, and four had gone to college. In their political and social values, African American leaders were more conservative than the rural black population was, and they showed little interest in land reform.

White Republicans in the South

Black citizens were a majority of the voters only in South Carolina, Mississippi, and Louisiana. Thus in most of the South the Republican party had to secure white votes to stay in power. Opponents scornfully

Hiram Revels, a minister and educator, became the first African American to serve in the U.S. Senate, representing Mississippi. Later he served as president of Alcorn University.

labeled white southerners who allied with the Republican party **scalawags,** yet an estimated quarter of white southerners at one time voted Republican. Although the party appealed to some wealthy planters, they were outnumbered by Unionists from the upland counties and hill areas who were largely yeoman farmers. Such voters were attracted by Republican promises to rebuild the South, restore prosperity, create public schools, and open isolated areas to the market with railroads.

The other group of white Republicans in the South was known as **carpetbaggers.** Originally from the North, they allegedly had arrived with all their worldly possessions stuffed in a carpetbag, ready to plunder the defeated South. Some did, but northerners moved south for a variety of reasons. Those in political office were especially well educated. Though carpetbaggers made up only a small percentage of Republican voters, they controlled almost a third of the offices. More than half of all southern Republican governors and nearly half of Republican members of Congress were originally northerners.

Divisions Among
Southern Republicans

The Republican party in the South had difficulty maintaining unity. Scalawags were especially susceptible to the race issue and social pressure. "Even my own kinspeople have turned the cold shoulder to me because I hold office under a Republican administration," testified a Mississippi white Republican. As black southerners pressed for greater recognition and a greater share of the offices, white southerners increasingly defected to the Democrats. Carpetbaggers were less sensitive to race, although most felt that their black allies should be content with minor offices. The friction between scalawags and carpetbaggers, which grew out of their rivalry for party honors, was particularly intense.

The New State Governments

New State Constitutions

The new southern state constitutions enacted several reforms. They put in place fairer systems of legislative representation, allowed voters to elect many officials who before had been appointed, and abolished property requirements for officeholding. In South Carolina, for the first time, voters were allowed to vote for the president, governor, and other state officers. (Previously, presidential electors as well as the governor had been chosen by the South Carolina legislature.) The Radical state governments also assumed some responsibility for social welfare and established the first statewide systems of public schools in the South.

Race and Social Equality

All the new constitutions proclaimed the principle of equality and granted black adult males the right to vote. On social relations they were much more cautious. No state outlawed segregation, and South Carolina and Louisiana were the only states that required integration in public schools (a mandate that was almost universally ignored).

Economic Issues and Corruption

The war left the southern economy in ruins, and problems of economic reconstruction were as difficult as those of politics. The new Republican governments encouraged industrial development by providing subsidies, loans, and even temporary exemptions from taxes. These governments also largely rebuilt the southern railroad system, often offering lavish aid to railroad corporations. The investments in the South helped double its manufacturing establishments in the two decades after 1860. Yet the harsh reality was that the South steadily slipped further behind the booming industrial economy of the North. Between 1854 and 1879, 7,000 miles of railroad track were laid in the South, but in the same period 45,000 miles were constructed in the rest of the nation.

Corruption

The expansion of government services offered temptations for corruption. In many southern states, officials regularly received bribes and kickbacks for their award of railroad charters, franchises, and other contracts. By 1872 the debts of the 11 states of the Confederacy had increased by $132 million, largely because of railroad grants and new social services such as schools. The tax rate grew as expenditures went up, so that by the 1870s it was four times the rate of 1860.

THE FIFTEENTH AMENDMENT.
CELEBRATED MAY 19T 1870.

From the beginning of Reconstruction, African Americans demanded the right to vote as free citizens. The Fifteenth Amendment, ratified in 1870, secured that right for black males. In New York, black citizens paraded in support of Ulysses S. Grant for president. Parades played a central role in campaigning: this parade exhibits the usual banners, flags, costumes, and a band. Blacks in both the North and the South voted solidly for the Republican party as the party of Lincoln and emancipation, although white violence in the South increasingly reduced black turnout.

Corruption, however, was not only a southern problem: the decline in morality affected the entire nation. During these years in New York City alone, the Democratic Tweed Ring stole more money than all the Radical Republican governments in the South combined. Moreover, corruption in the South was hardly limited to Republicans. Many Democrats and white business leaders participated in the looting. "Everybody is demoralizing down here. Corruption is the fashion," reported Louisiana governor Henry Warmoth.

Corruption in Radical governments existed, but southern whites exaggerated its extent for partisan purposes. Conservatives just as bitterly opposed honest Radical regimes as they did corrupt ones. In the eyes of most white southerners, the real crime of the Radical governments was that they allowed black citizens to hold some offices and tried to protect the civil rights of African Americans. Race was the conservatives' greatest weapon. And it would prove the most effective means to undermine Republican power in the South.

SAML. DOVE wishes to know of the whereabouts of his mother, Areno, his sisters Maria, Neziah, and Peggy, and his brother Edmond, who were owned by Geo. Dove, of Rockingham county, Shenandoah Valley, Va. Sold in Richmond, after which Saml. and Edmond were taken to Nashville, Tenn., by Joe Mick; Areno was left at the Eagle Tavern, Richmond

Respectfully yours,
SAML. DOVE.

Utica, New York, Aug. 5, 1865–3m

A Tennessee newspaper advertisement seeking a family, 1865.

Black Aspirations

Emancipation came to slaves in different ways and at different times. For some it arrived during the war when Union soldiers entered an area; for others it came some time after the Confederacy's collapse, when Union troops or officials announced that they were free. Whatever the timing, freedom meant a host of precious blessings to people who had been in bondage all their lives.

Experiencing Freedom

The first impulse was to think of freedom as a contrast to slavery. Emancipation immediately released slaves from the most oppressive aspects of bondage—the whippings, the breakup of families, the sexual exploitation. Freedom also meant movement, the right to travel without a pass or white permission. Above all, freedom meant that African Americans' labor would be for their own benefit. One Arkansas freedman, who earned his first dollar working on a railroad, recalled that when he was paid, "I felt like the richest man in the world."

Changing Employment

Freedom included finding a new place to work. Changing jobs was one concrete way to break the psychological ties of slavery. Even planters with reputations for kindness sometimes saw their former hands depart. The cook who left a South Carolina family even though they offered her higher wages than her new job explained, "I must go. If I stays here I'll never know I'm free."

Importance of Names

Symbolically, freedom meant having a full name, and African Americans now adopted last names. More than a few took the last name of some prominent individual; more common was to take the name of the first master in the family's oral history as far back as it could be recalled. Most, however, retained their first name, especially if the name had been given to them by their parents (as most often had been the case among slaves). It had been their form of identity in bondage, and for those separated from their family it was the only link with their parents. Whatever name they took, it was important to black Americans that they make the decision themselves without white interference.

The Black Family

Upholding the Family

African Americans also sought to strengthen the family in freedom. Because slave marriages had not been recognized as legal, thousands of former slaves insisted on being married again by proper authorities, even though a ceremony was not required by law. Blacks who had been forcibly separated in slavery and later remarried confronted the dilemma of which spouse to take. Laura Spicer, whose husband had been sold away in slavery, received a series of wrenching letters from him after the war. He had thought her dead, had remarried, and had a new family. "You know it never was our wishes to be separated from each other, and it never was our fault. I had rather anything to had happened to me most than ever have been parted from you and the children," he wrote. "As I am, I do not know which I love best, you or Anna." Declining to return, he closed, "Laura, truly, I have got another wife, and I am very sorry. . . ."

Like white husbands, black husbands deemed themselves the head of the family and acted legally for their wives. They often insisted that their wives would not work in the fields as they had in slavery, a decision that had major economic repercussions for agricultural labor. In negotiating contracts, a father also demanded the right to control his children and their labor. All these changes were designed to insulate the black family from white control.

The Schoolhouse and the Church

Black Education

In freedom, the schoolhouse and the black church became essential institutions in the black community. Next to ownership of land, African Americans saw education as the best hope for advancement. At first, northern churches and missionaries, working with the Freedmen's Bureau, set up black schools in the South. Tuition represented 10 percent or more of a laborer's monthly wages. Yet these schools were full. Many parents sent their children by day and attended classes themselves at night. Eventually, the Bureau schools were replaced by the new public school systems, which by 1876 enrolled 40 percent of African American children.

Black adults had good reasons for seeking literacy. They wanted to be able to read the Bible, to defend their newly gained civil and political rights, and to protect themselves from being cheated. One elderly Louisiana freedman explained that giving children an education was better than giving them a fortune, "because if you left them even $500, some man having more education than they had would come along and cheat them out of it all."

Teachers in the Freedmen's Bureau schools were primarily northern middle-class white women sent south by northern missionary societies. "I feel that it is a precious privilege," Esther Douglass wrote, "to be allowed to do something for these poor people." Many saw themselves as peacetime soldiers, struggling to make emancipation a reality. Indeed, on more than one occasion, hostile white southerners destroyed black schools and threatened and even murdered white teachers. Then there were the everyday challenges: low pay, dilapidated buildings, lack of sufficient books, classes of 100 or more children, and irregular attendance. Meanwhile, the Freedmen's Bureau undertook to train black teachers, and by 1869 most of the 3,000 teachers in freedmen's schools were black.

Teachers in Black Schools

Before the war, most slaves had attended white churches or services supervised by whites. Once free, African Americans quickly established their own congregations led by black preachers. In the first year of freedom, the Methodist Church South lost fully half of its black members. By 1870 the Negro Baptist Church had increased its membership threefold when compared to the membership in 1850, and the African Methodist Episcopal Church expanded at an even greater rate.

Independent Black Churches

Black churches were so important because they were the only major organizations in the African American community controlled by blacks. Black ministers were respected leaders, and many of the black men elected to office during Reconstruction were preachers. As it had in slavery, religion offered African Americans a place of refuge in a hostile white world and provided them with hope, comfort, and a means of self-identification.

New Working Conditions

As a largely propertyless class, blacks in the postwar South had no choice but to work for white landowners. Except for paying wages, whites wanted to retain the old system of labor, including close supervision, gang labor, and physical punishment. Determined to remove all emblems of servitude, African Americans refused to work under these conditions, and they demanded time off to devote to their own interests. Convinced that working at one's own pace was part of freedom, they simply would not work as long or as hard as they had in slavery. Because of shorter hours and the withdrawal of children and women from the fields, work output declined by an estimated 35 percent in freedom. Blacks also refused to live in the old slave quarters located near the master's house. Instead, they erected cabins on distant parts of the plantation. Wages at first were $5 or $6 a month plus provisions and a cabin; by 1867, they had risen to an average of $10 a month.

These changes eventually led to the rise of sharecropping. Under this arrangement African American families farmed separate plots of land and then at the end of the year split the crop with the white landowner. Sharecropping had higher status and offered greater personal freedom than being a wage laborer. "I am not working for wages," one black farmer declared in defending his right to leave the plantation at will, "but am part owner of the crop and as [such,] I have all the rights that you or any other man has." Although black per capita agricultural income increased 40 percent in freedom,

Sharecropping

On the plantations of the Old South, slaves had lived in cabins along a central path in the shadow of the white master's "big house." These quarters were the center of their community, where marriages and other festivals were celebrated and family life went on. But with the coming of emancipation, freedpeople looked to leave the old quarters, which stood as a symbol of bondage and of close white supervision. African Americans either built new housing or dismantled their old cabins and hauled them to the plots of land they rented as tenants or sharecroppers. Moving enabled them to live on the land they farmed, just as white farmers and tenants did.

Like slave cabins, most sharecroppers' dwellings were one story high, about 16 feet square, and usually built of logs chinked with mud. The few windows had shutters to protect against the weather; glass was rare. Though the inside walls normally lacked plaster or sheeting, they

Chimneys on sharecroppers' cabins were often tilted deliberately so that they could be pushed away from the house quickly if they caught fire.

sharecropping was a harshly exploitative system in which black families often sank into perpetual debt.

The Freedmen's Bureau

The task of supervising the transition from slavery to freedom on southern plantations fell to the Freedmen's Bureau, a unique experiment in social policy supported by the federal

After living for years in a society where teaching slaves to read and write was usually illegal, freedpeople viewed literacy as a key to securing their newfound freedom. Blacks were not merely "anxious to learn," a school official in Virginia reported, they were "crazy to learn."

were given a coat of whitewash annually to brighten the dark interior.

The main room served as kitchen and dining room, parlor, bathing area, and the parents' bedroom. To one side might be a homemade drop-leaf table (essential because of cramped space), which served as a kitchen work counter and a dining table. The other side of the room had a few plain beds, their slats or rope bottoms supporting corn shuck or straw mattresses. The social center of the room was the fireplace, the only source of heat and the main source of light after dark. Pots and pans were hung on the wall near the fireplace, and the mother and daughters did the cooking stooped over an open fire. In the summer, cooking was done outdoors.

The cabin's chimney was made of small logs notched together and covered with several layers of clay to protect it from the heat. Sometimes its height was extended by empty flour barrels. A taller chimney drew better, which kept smoke from blowing back down into the house and kept sparks away from the roof. After the evening meal the family gathered around the fireplace, the children to play with homemade dolls and toys, the mother to sew, and the father perhaps to play the fiddle. At bedtime a trapdoor in the ceiling offered access up a ladder to the loft beneath the gabled roof, where older children slept, usually on pallets on the floor, as had been the case in slavery.

Gradually, as black sharecroppers scraped together some savings, they improved their homes. By the end of the century, frame dwellings were more common, and many older log cabins had been covered with wood siding. The newer homes were generally larger, with wood floors, and often had attached rooms such as a porch or kitchen. In addition, windows had glass panes, roofs were covered with shingles instead of planking, and stone and brick chimneys were less unusual.

Without question, the cabins of black sharecroppers provided more space than the slave quarters had, and certainly more freedom and privacy. Still, they lacked many of the comforts that most white Americans took for granted. Such housing reflected the continuing status of black sharecroppers as poverty-stricken laborers in a caste system based on race.

government. Assigned the task of protecting freedpeople's economic rights, approximately 550 local agents supervised and regulated working conditions in southern agriculture after the war. The racial attitudes of Bureau agents varied widely, as did their commitment and competence. Then, too, they had to depend on the army to enforce their decisions.

Most agents encouraged or required written contracts between white planters and black laborers, specifying not only wages but also the conditions of employment. Although agents sometimes intervened to protect freedpeople from unfair treatment, they also provided important help to planters. They insisted that black laborers not desert at harvest time; they arrested those who violated their contracts or refused to sign new ones at the beginning of the year; and they preached the gospel of work and the need to be orderly and respectful. Given such attitudes, freedpeople increasingly complained that Bureau agents were mere tools of the planter class. "They are, in fact, the planters' guards, and nothing else," claimed the New Orleans *Tribune*, a black newspaper.

Bureau's Mixed Record

The primary means of enforcing working conditions were the Freedmen's Courts, which Congress created in 1866 to avoid the discrimination African Americans received in state courts. These new courts functioned as military tribunals, and often the agent was the entire court. The sympathy black laborers received varied from state to state.

But in 1869, with the Bureau's work scarcely under way, Congress decided to shut it down, and by 1872 it had gone out of business. Despite its mixed record, it was the most effective agency in protecting blacks' civil and political rights. Its disbanding signaled the beginning of the northern retreat from Reconstruction.

End of the Bureau

Planters and a New Way of Life

Planters and other white southerners faced emancipation with dread. "All the traditions and habits of both races had been suddenly overthrown," a Tennessee planter recalled, "and neither knew just what to do, or how to accommodate themselves to the new situation."

The old ideal of a paternalistic planter, which required a facade of black subservience and affection, gave way to an emphasis on strictly economic relationships. Mary

Planters' New Values

Jones, a Georgia slaveholder before the war who did more for her workers than the law required, lost all patience when two workers accused her of trickery and hauled her before a Freedmen's Bureau agent, with whom she won her case. Upon returning home, she announced to the assembled freedpeople that "I have considered them friends and treated them as such but now they were only laborers under contract, and only the law would rule between us." Only with time did planters develop new norms and standards to judge black behavior. What in 1865 had seemed insolence was viewed by the 1870s as the normal attitude of freedom.

Slavery had been a complex institution that welded black and white southerners together in intimate relationships. After the war, however, planters increasingly embraced the ideology of segregation. Because emancipation significantly reduced the social distance between the races, white southerners sought psychological separation and kept dealings with African Americans to a minimum. By the time Reconstruction ended, white planters had developed a new way of life based on the institutions of sharecropping and segregation and undergirded by a militant white supremacy.

Although most planters kept their land, they did not regain the economic prosperity of the prewar years. Rice plantations, unsuitable to tenant farming, largely disappeared after the war. In addition, southern cotton growers faced increased competition from new areas such as India, Egypt, and Brazil. Cotton prices began a long decline, and by 1880 the value of southern farms had slid 33 percent below the level of 1860.

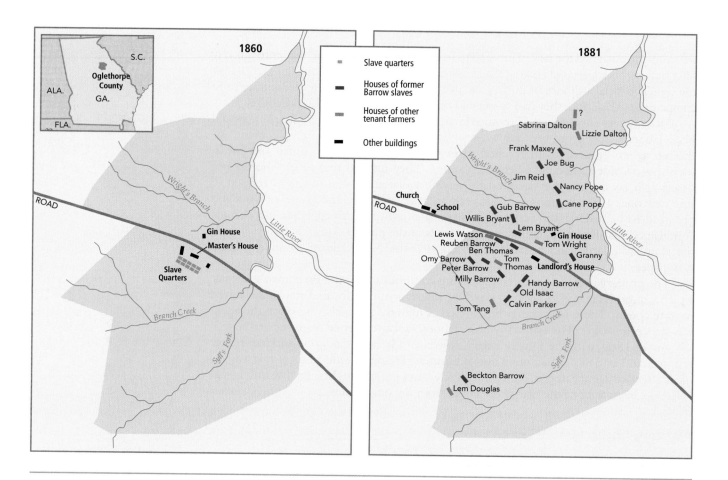

A Georgia Plantation after the War   *After emancipation, sharecropping became the dominant form of agricultural labor in the South. Black families no longer lived in the old slave quarters but dispersed to separate plots of land that they farmed themselves. At the end of the year each sharecropper turned over part of the crop to the white landowner.*

The Abandonment of Reconstruction

On Christmas Day 1875, a white acquaintance approached Charles Caldwell on the streets of Clinton, Mississippi, and invited him into Chilton's store to have a drink to celebrate the holiday. A former slave, Caldwell was a state senator and the leader of the Republican party in Hinds County, Mississippi. But the black leader's fearlessness made him a marked man. Only two months earlier, he had been forced to flee the county to escape a white mob angry about a Republican barbecue he and his fellow Republicans had organized. For four days the mob hunted down and killed nearly 40 Republican leaders for presuming to hold a political meeting. Despite that hostility, Caldwell had returned to vote in the November state election. Even more boldly, he had led a black militia company through the streets to help quell the disturbances. Now, as Caldwell and his "friend" raised their glasses in a holiday toast, a gunshot exploded through the window. Caldwell collapsed, mortally wounded from a bullet to the back of his head. He was taken outside, where his assassins riddled his body with bullets.

Charles Caldwell shared the fate of more than a few southern black Republicans. Southern whites used violence, terror, and political assassination to challenge the federal government's commitment to Reconstruction. If northerners had boldly countered such terrorism, Reconstruction might have ended differently. But in the years following President Johnson's impeachment trial in 1868, the influence of Radical Republicans steadily waned. The Republican party was being drained of the crusading idealism that had stamped its early years.

The Election of Grant

Immensely popular after the war, Ulysses S. Grant was the natural choice of Republicans to run for president in 1868. Although Grant was elected, Republicans were shocked that despite his great military stature, his popular margin was only 300,000 votes. An estimated 450,000 black Republican votes had been cast in the South, which meant that a majority of whites casting ballots had voted Democratic. The 1868 election helped convince Republican leaders that an amendment securing black suffrage throughout the nation was necessary.

In February 1869 Congress sent the Fifteenth Amendment to the states for ratification. It forbade any state to deny the right to vote on grounds of race, color, or previous condition of servitude. Some Radicals had hoped to forbid literacy or property requirements to protect blacks further. Others wanted a simple declaration that all adult male citizens had the right to vote. But the moderates in the party were aware that many northerners were increasingly worried about the number of immigrants who were again entering the country and wanted to be able to restrict their voting. As a result, the final amendment left loopholes that eventually allowed southern states to **disfranchise** African Americans. The amendment was ratified in March 1870, aided by the votes of the four southern states that had not completed the process of Reconstruction and thus were also required to endorse this amendment before being readmitted to Congress.

Proponents of women's suffrage were gravely disappointed when Congress refused to prohibit voting discrimination on the basis of sex as well as race. The Women's Loyal League, led by Elizabeth Cady Stanton and Susan B. Anthony, had pressed for first the Fourteenth and then the Fifteenth Amendment to recognize women's public role. But even most Radicals, contending that black rights had to be ensured first, were unwilling to back women's suffrage. The Fifteenth Amendment ruptured the feminist movement. Although disappointed that women were not included in its provisions, Lucy Stone and the American Woman Suffrage Association urged ratification. Stanton and Anthony, however, broke with their former allies among the Radicals, denounced the amendment, and organized the National Woman Suffrage Association to work for passage of a new amendment giving women the ballot. The division hampered the women's rights movement for decades to come.

Lucy Stone, a major figure in the women's rights movement.

Fifteenth Amendment

Women's Suffrage Rejected

The Grant Administration

Ulysses Grant was ill at ease with the political process. His simple, quiet manner, while superb for commanding armies, did not serve him as well in public life, and his well-known resolution withered when he was uncertain of his goal. Also, he lacked the moral commitment to make Reconstruction succeed.

Corruption under Grant

A series of scandals wracked Grant's presidency. Although Grant did not profit personally, he remained loyal to his friends and displayed little zeal to root out wrongdoing. His relatives were implicated in a scheme to corner the gold market, and his private secretary escaped conviction for stealing federal whiskey revenues only because Grant interceded on his behalf. His secretary of war resigned to avoid impeachment.

Grant swings from a trapeze while supporting a number of associates accused of corruption. Among those holding on are Secretary of the Navy George M. Robeson (top center), who was accused of accepting bribes for awarding navy contracts; Secretary of War William W. Belknap (top right), who was forced to resign for selling Indian post traderships; and the president's private secretary, Orville Babcock (bottom right), who was implicated in the Whiskey Ring scandal. Although not personally involved in the scandals during his administration, Grant was reluctant to dismiss supporters accused of wrongdoing from office.

Nor was Congress immune from the lowered tone of public life. In such a climate ruthless state machines, led by men who favored the status quo, came to dominate the party. Office and power became ends in themselves, and party leaders worked in close cooperation with northern industrial interests. The few Radicals still active in public life increasingly repudiated Grant and the Republican governments in the South. Congress in 1872 passed an amnesty act, removing the restrictions of the Fourteenth Amendment on officeholding except for about 200 to 300 ex-Confederate leaders.

As corruption in both the North and the South worsened, reformers became more interested in cleaning up government than in protecting blacks' rights. These liberal Republicans opposed the continued presence of the army in the South, denounced the corruption of southern governments as well as the national government, and advocated free trade and civil service reform. In 1872 they broke with the Republican party and nominated for president Horace Greeley, the editor of the New York *Tribune*. A onetime Radical, Greeley had become disillusioned with Reconstruction and urged a restoration of home rule in the South as well as adoption of civil service reform. Democrats decided to back the Liberal Republican ticket. The Republicans renominated Grant, who, despite the defection of a number of prominent Radicals, won an easy victory with 56 percent of the popular vote.

Growing Northern Disillusionment

Civil Rights Act of 1875

During Grant's second term, Congress passed the Civil Rights Act of 1875, the last major piece of Reconstruction legislation. This law prohibited racial discrimination in all public accommodations, transportation, places of amusement, and juries. At the same time, Congress rejected a ban on segregation in public schools, which was almost universally practiced in the North as well as the South. Although some railroads, streetcars, and public accommodations in both sections were desegregated after the bill passed, the federal government made little attempt to enforce the law, and it was ignored throughout most of the South. In 1883 the Supreme Court struck down its provisions except the one relating to juries.

Despite passage of the Civil Rights Act, many northerners were growing disillusioned with Reconstruction. They were repelled by the corruption of the southern governments, they were tired of the violence and disorder in the South, and they had little faith in black Americans. "We have tried this long enough," remarked one influential northern Republican of Reconstruction. "Now let the South alone."

As the agony of the war became more distant, the Panic of 1873 diverted public attention from Reconstruction to economic issues. In the severe depression that followed over the next four years, some 3 million people found themselves out of work. Congress became caught up in the question of whether printing greenbacks would help the economy prosper. Battered by the panic and the corruption issue, the Republicans lost a shocking 77 seats in Congress in the 1874 elections, and along with them control of the House of Representatives for the first time since 1861. "The truth is our people are tired out with the worn out cry of 'Southern outrages'!!" one Republican concluded. "Hard times and heavy taxes make them wish the 'ever lasting nigger' were in hell or Africa." Republicans spoke more and more about cutting loose the unpopular southern governments.

Depression and Democratic Resurgence

The Triumph of White Supremacy

As northern commitment to Reconstruction waned, southern Democrats set out to overthrow the remaining Radical governments. White Republicans already in the South felt heavy pressure to desert their party. In Mississippi one party member justified his decision to leave on the grounds that otherwise he would have "to live a life of social oblivion" and his children would have no future.

To poor white southerners who lacked social standing, the Democratic appeal to racial solidarity offered great comfort. As one explained, "I may be poor and my manners may be crude, but . . . because I am a white man, I have a right to be treated with respect by Negroes. . . . That I am poor is not as important as that I am a white man; and no Negro is ever going to forget that he is not a white man." The large landowners and other wealthy groups that led southern Democrats objected less to black southerners voting. These well-to-do leaders did not face social and economic competition from African Americans, and in any case, they were confident that if outside influences were removed, they could control the black vote.

Democrats also resorted to economic pressure to undermine Republican power. In heavily black counties, white observers at the polls took down the names of black residents who cast Republican ballots and published them in local newspapers. Planters were urged to discharge black tenants who persisted in voting Republican. But terror and violence provided the most effective means to overthrow the Radical regimes. A number of paramilitary organizations broke up Republican meetings, terrorized white and black Republicans, assassinated Republican leaders, and prevented black

This campaign badge from 1868 made the sentiments of white Democrats clear.

Racism

Minstrels, Carnivals, and Ghosts

Uncovering the Cultural Roots of a KKK "Performance"

The costumes of Ku Klux Klan night riders—pointed hoods and white sheets—have become a staple of history books. In fact, not all the KKK wore costumes, and those who did sported a variety of outfits. But why use such outlandish, often elaborate disguises? To hide the identity of members, according to some accounts, or to terrorize freedpeople into thinking they were being menaced by Confederate ghosts. But clearly African Americans knew these were living, mortal enemies. Though simpler masks would have hidden identities, the guns that they brandished were far more frightening than any "ghostly" robes.

One historian has suggested that the KKK performances took their cues from traditions already a part of American popular culture: the costumes of Mardi Gras and similar carnivals, as well as the humorous sketches of minstrel shows. In behaving like minstrel performers or carnival revelers, KKK members may have had other audiences in mind. Northerners who read accounts of their doings could be lulled into thinking that the repressive night rides were just humorous pranks, not a threat to Radical rule. For southern Democrats, KKK rituals provided a way to reassert a sense of white supremacy.

Klansmen might have been defeated in war, but their theatrical night rides helped overturn the social order of Reconstruction, just as carousers at carnivals disrupted the night. The ritual garb provided more innocent cover for a campaign of intimidation that often turned deadly.

citizens from voting. The most famous was the Ku Klux Klan, founded in 1866 in Tennessee. It and similar groups functioned as unofficial arms of the Democratic party.

Congress finally moved to break the power of the Klan with the Force Act of 1870 and the Ku Klux Klan Act of 1871. These laws made it a felony to interfere with the right to vote; they also authorized use of the army and suspension of the writ of habeas corpus. The Grant administration eventually suspended the writ of habeas corpus in nine South Carolina counties and arrested hundreds of suspected Klan members throughout the South. Although these actions weakened the Klan, terrorist organizations continued to operate underground.

Mississippi Plan

Then in 1875 Democrats inaugurated what became known as the Mississippi Plan, the decision to use as much violence as necessary to carry the state election. Several local papers trumpeted, "Carry the election peaceably if we can, forcibly if we must." When Republican governor Adelbert Ames requested federal troops to stop the violence, Grant's advisers warned that sending troops to Mississippi would cost the party the Ohio election. In the end the administration told Ames to depend on his own forces. Bolstered by terrorism, the Democrats swept the election in Mississippi. Violence and intimidation prevented as many as 60,000 black and white Republicans from voting, converting the normal Republican majority into a Democratic majority of 30,000. Mississippi had been "redeemed."

The Disputed Election of 1876

With Republicans on the defensive across the nation, the 1876 presidential election was crucial to the final overthrow of Reconstruction. The Republicans nominated Ohio governor Rutherford B. Hayes to oppose Samuel Tilden of New York. Once again, violence prevented many Republican votes, this time an estimated quarter of a million, from being cast in the South. Tilden had a clear majority of 250,000 in the popular vote, but the outcome in the Electoral College was in doubt because both parties claimed South Carolina, Florida, and Louisiana, the only reconstructed states still in Republican hands. Hayes needed all three states to be elected, for even without them, Tilden had amassed 184 electoral votes, one short of a majority. Republican canvassing boards in power disqualified enough Democratic votes to give each state to Hayes.

To arbitrate the disputed returns, Congress established a 15-member electoral commission: 5 members each from the Senate, the House, and the Supreme Court. By a straight party vote of 8–7, the commission awarded the disputed electoral votes—and the presidency—to Hayes.

When angry Democrats threatened a filibuster to prevent the electoral votes from being counted, key Republicans met with southern Democrats on February 26 at the Wormley Hotel in Washington. There they reached an informal understanding, later known as the Compromise of 1877. Hayes's supporters agreed to withdraw federal troops from the South and not oppose the new Democratic state governments. For their part, southern Democrats dropped their opposition to Hayes's election and pledged to respect the rights of African Americans.

Compromise of 1877

Without federal support, the Republican governments in South Carolina and Louisiana promptly collapsed, and Democrats took control of the remaining states of the Confederacy. By 1877, the entire South was in the hands of the **Redeemers,** as they called themselves. Reconstruction and Republican rule had come to an end.

Redeemers Take Control

The Failure of Reconstruction

Reconstruction failed for a multitude of reasons. The reforming impulse that had created the Republican party in the 1850s had been battered and worn down by the war. The new materialism of industrial America inspired in many Americans a jaded cynicism about the corruption of the age and a desire to forget uncomfortable issues. In the South, African American voters and leaders inevitably lacked a certain amount of education and experience; elsewhere, Republicans were divided over policies and options.

Yet beyond these obstacles, the sad fact remains that the ideals of Reconstruction were most clearly defeated by the deep-seated racism that permeated American life. Racism was why the white South so unrelentingly resisted Reconstruction. Racism was why most white northerners had little interest in black rights except as a means to preserve the Union or to safeguard the Republic. Racism was why northerners were willing to write off Reconstruction and with it the welfare of African Americans. While Congress might pass a constitutional amendment abolishing slavery, it could not overturn at a stroke the social habits of two centuries.

Certainly the political equations of power, in the long term, had been changed. The North had fought fiercely during the war to preserve the Union. In doing so, it had secured the power to dominate the

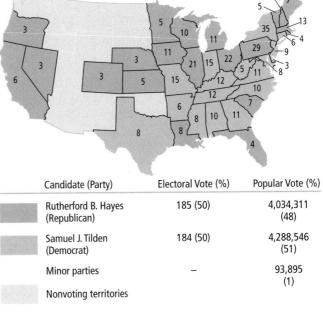

Candidate (Party)	Electoral Vote (%)	Popular Vote (%)
Rutherford B. Hayes (Republican)	185 (50)	4,034,311 (48)
Samuel J. Tilden (Democrat)	184 (50)	4,288,546 (51)
Minor parties	–	93,895 (1)
Nonvoting territories		

Election of 1876

Benjamin Montgomery, together with his sons, purchased Jefferson Davis's plantation along the Mississippi River after the war. A former slave, Montgomery pursued the dream of black economic independence by renting land to black farmers at Davis Bend.

economic and political destiny of the nation. With the overthrow of Reconstruction, the white South had won back some of the power it had lost in 1865. But even with white supremacy triumphant, African Americans did not return to the social position they had occupied before the war. They were no longer slaves, and black southerners who walked dusty roads in search of family members, sent their children to school, or worshiped in churches they controlled knew what a momentous change emancipation was. Even under the exploitative share-cropping system, black income rose significantly in freedom. Then, too, the Fourteenth Amendment principles of "equal protection" and "due process of law" had been written into the Constitution. These guarantees would be available for later generations to use in championing once again the Radicals' goal of racial equality.

End of the Davis Bend Experiment

But this was a struggle left to future reformers. For the time being, the clear trend was away from change or hope—especially for former slaves like Benjamin Montgomery and his sons, the owners of the old Davis plantations in Mississippi. In the 1870s bad crops, lower cotton prices, and falling land values undermined the Montgomerys' financial position, and in 1875 Jefferson Davis sued to have the sale of Brierfield invalidated. A lower court ruled against him, since he had never received legal title to the plantation. Davis appealed to the state supreme court, which, following the overthrow of Mississippi's Radical government, had a white conservative majority. In a politically motivated decision, the court awarded Brierfield to Davis in 1878, and the Montgomerys lost Hurricane as well.

A Wider World

The waning days of Reconstruction were filled with such ironies: of governments "redeemed" by violence and Supreme Court decisions using Fourteenth Amendment rights to protect giant corporations rather than individual African Americans. Increasingly, the industrial North focused on the economic task of integrating the South and West into the Union. Northern factories sought southern and western raw materials (cotton, timber, cattle, and minerals) to produce goods to sell in national and international markets.

This trend was global in scope. During the coming decades European nations also scrambled to acquire natural resources and markets. In the onrushing age of imperialism, Western nations would seek to dominate newly acquired colonies in Africa and Asia. There would be gold rushes in South Africa as well as in the United States, vast cattle ranches in Argentina and Canada as well as across the American Great Plains. Farmers would open up lands in New Zealand and Australia as well as in Oklahoma and Wyoming. And just as racism replaced slavery as the central justification for white supremacy in the South, it promoted the campaigns against Indians and Hispanics in the West and in a belief in "inferior races" to be swept aside by imperialists all across the world. The ideal of a truly diverse and democratic society remained largely unsought and unfulfilled.

Significant Events

1863	Lincoln outlines Reconstruction program
1864	Lincoln vetoes Wade-Davis bill; Louisiana, Arkansas, and Tennessee establish governments under Lincoln's plan
1865–1866	Black codes enacted
1865	Freedmen's Bureau established; Johnson becomes president; presidential Reconstruction completed; Congress excludes representatives of Johnson's governments; Thirteenth Amendment ratified; Joint Committee on Reconstruction established
1866	Civil rights bill passed over Johnson's veto; Memphis and New Orleans riots; Ku Klux Klan organized; Republicans win decisive victory in congressional elections
1867	Congressional Reconstruction enacted; Tenure of Office Act
1868	Johnson impeached but acquitted; Fourteenth Amendment ratified; Grant elected president
1870	Fifteenth Amendment ratified; Force Act passed
1871	Ku Klux Klan Act
1872	General Amnesty Act; Freedmen's Bureau closes down; Liberal Republican revolt
1873–1877	Panic and depression
1875	Civil Rights Act; Mississippi Plan
1876	Disputed Hayes-Tilden election
1877	Compromise of 1877; Hayes declared winner of electoral vote; last Republican governments in South fall

Chapter Summary

Presidents Abraham Lincoln and Andrew Johnson and the Republican-dominated Congress each developed a program of Reconstruction to restore the Confederate states to the Union.

- Lincoln's 10 percent plan required that 10 percent of qualified voters from 1860 swear an oath of loyalty to begin organizing state government.

- Following Lincoln's assassination, Andrew Johnson changed Lincoln's terms and lessened Reconstruction's requirements.

- The more radical Congress repudiated Johnson's state governments and enacted its own program of Reconstruction, which included the principle of black suffrage.

  —Congress passed the Fourteenth and Fifteenth Amendments and also extended the life of the Freedmen's Bureau, a unique experiment in social welfare.
  —Congress rejected land reform, however, which would have provided the freedpeople with a greater economic stake.

  —The effort to remove Johnson from office through impeachment failed.

- The Radical governments in the South, led by black and white southerners and transplanted northerners, compiled a mixed record on matters such as racial equality, education, economic issues, and corruption.

- Reconstruction was a time of both joy and frustration for former slaves.

  —Former slaves took steps to reunite their families and establish black-controlled churches.
  —They evidenced a widespread desire for land and education.
  —Black resistance to the old system of labor led to the adoption of sharecropping.
  —The Freedmen's Bureau fostered these new working arrangements and also the beginnings of black education in the South.

- Northern public opinion became disillusioned with Reconstruction during the presidency of Ulysses S. Grant.

- Southern whites used violence, economic coercion, and racism to overthrow the Republican state governments.

- In 1877 Republican leaders agreed to end Reconstruction in exchange for Rutherford B. Hayes's election as president.

- Racism played a key role in the eventual failure of Reconstruction.

Additional Reading

Historians' views of Reconstruction have dramatically changed over the past half century. Modern studies offer a more sympathetic assessment of Reconstruction and the experience of African Americans. Indicative of this trend is Eric Foner, *Reconstruction* (1988), and his briefer treatment (with photographic essays by Joshua Brown) *Forever Free: the Story of Emancipation and Reconstruction* (2005). Michael Les Benedict treats the clash between Andrew Johnson and Congress in *The Impeachment and Trial of Andrew Johnson* (1973). Political affairs in the South during Reconstruction are examined in Dan T. Carter, *When the War Was Over* (1985), and Thomas Holt, *Black over White* (1977), an imaginative study of black political leadership in South Carolina. Hans Trefousse, *Thaddeus Stevens: Nineteenth-Century Egalitarian* (1997), provides a sympathetic reassessment of the influential Radical Republican.

Leon Litwack, *Been in the Storm So Long* (1979), sensitively analyzes the transition of enslaved African Americans to freedom. Heather Andrea Williams, *Self-Taught: African American Education in Slavery and Freedom* (2005), illustrates the black drive for literacy and education. James L. Roark, *Masters without Slaves* (1977), discusses former slaveholders' adjustment to the end of slavery. The dialectic of black-white relations is charted from the antebellum years through Reconstruction and beyond in Steven Hahn, *A Nation under Our Feet: Black Political Struggles in the Rural South from Slavery to the Great Migration* (2003). Two excellent studies of changing labor relations in southern agriculture are Julie Saville, *The Work of Reconstruction* (1995), and John C. Rodrigue, *Reconstruction in the Cane Fields* (2001). For contrasting views of the Freedman's Bureau see George R. Bentley, *A History of the Freedman's Bureau* (1955)—favorable—and Donald Nieman, *To Set the Law in Motion* (1979)—more critical. "William Gillette, *Retreat from Reconstruction, 1869–1879* (1980) focuses on national politics and the end of Reconstruction, while Michael Perman, *The Road to Redemption* (1984), looks at developments in the South."

For a fuller list of readings, see the Bibliography at www.mhhe.com/davidsonnation6.

The Declaration of Independence

In Congress, July 4, 1776,

THE UNANIMOUS DECLARATION OF THE THIRTEEN UNITED STATES OF AMERICA

When, in the course of human events, it becomes necessary for one people to dissolve the political bands which have connected them with another, and to assume, among the powers of the earth, the separate and equal station to which the laws of nature and of nature's God entitle them, a decent respect to the opinions of mankind requires that they should declare the causes which impel them to the separation.

We hold these truths to be self-evident, that all men are created equal; that they are endowed by their Creator with certain unalienable rights; that among these, are life, liberty, and the pursuit of happiness. That, to secure these rights, governments are instituted among men, deriving their just powers from the consent of the governed; that, whenever any form of government becomes destructive of these ends, it is the right of the people to alter or to abolish it, and to institute a new government, laying its foundation on such principles, and organizing its powers in such form, as to them shall seem most likely to effect their safety and happiness. Prudence, indeed, will dictate that governments long established, should not be changed for light and transient causes; and, accordingly, all experience hath shown, that mankind are more disposed to suffer, while evils are sufferable, than to right themselves by abolishing the forms to which they are accustomed. But, when a long train of abuses and usurpations, pursuing invariably the same object, evinces a design to reduce them under absolute despotism, it is their right, it is their duty, to throw off such government and to provide new guards for their future security. Such has been the patient sufferance of these colonies, and such is now the necessity which constrains them to alter their former systems of government. The history of the present King of Great Britain is a history of repeated injuries and usurpations, all having, in direct object, the establishment of an absolute tyranny over these States. To prove this, let facts be submitted to a candid world:

He has refused his assent to laws the most wholesome and necessary for the public good.

He has forbidden his governors to pass laws of immediate and pressing importance, unless suspended in their operation till his assent should be obtained; and, when so suspended, he has utterly neglected to attend to them.

He has refused to pass other laws for the accommodation of large districts of people, unless those people would relinquish the right of representation in the legislature; a right inestimable to them, and formidable to tyrants only.

He has called together legislative bodies at places unusual, uncomfortable, and distant from the depository of their public records, for the sole purpose of fatiguing them into compliance with his measures.

He has dissolved representative houses repeatedly for opposing, with manly firmness, his invasions on the rights of the people.

He has refused, for a long time after such dissolutions, to cause others to be elected; whereby the legislative powers, incapable of annihilation, have returned to the people at large for their exercise; the state remaining, in the meantime, exposed to all the danger of invasion from without, and convulsions within.

He has endeavored to prevent the population of these States; for that purpose, obstructing the laws for naturalization of foreigners, refusing to pass others to encourage their migration hither, and raising the conditions of new appropriations of lands.

He had obstructed the administration of justice, by refusing his assent to laws for establishing judiciary powers.

He has made judges dependent on his will alone, for the tenure of their offices, and the amount and payment of their salaries.

He has erected a multitude of new offices, and sent hither swarms of officers to harass our people, and eat out their substance.

He has kept among us, in time of peace, standing armies, without the consent of our legislatures.

He has affected to render the military independent of, and superior to, the civil power.

He has combined, with others, to subject us to a jurisdiction foreign to our Constitution, and unacknowledged by our laws; giving his assent to their acts of pretended legislation:

For quartering large bodies of armed troops among us:

For protecting them by a mock trial, from punishment, for any murders which they should commit on the inhabitants of these States:

For cutting off our trade with all parts of the world:

For imposing taxes on us without our consent:

For depriving us, in many cases, of the benefit of trial by jury:

For transporting us beyond seas to be tried for pretended offences:

For abolishing the free system of English laws in a neighboring province, establishing therein an arbitrary government, and enlarging its boundaries, so as to render it at once an example and fit instrument for introducing the same absolute rule into these colonies:

For taking away our charters, abolishing our most valuable laws, and altering, fundamentally, the powers of our governments:

For suspending our own legislatures, and declaring themselves invested with power to legislate for us in all cases whatsoever.

He has abdicated government here, by declaring us out of his protection, and waging war against us.

He has plundered our seas, ravaged our coasts, burnt our towns, and destroyed the lives of our people.

He is, at this time, transporting large armies of foreign mercenaries to complete the works of death, desolation, and tyranny, already begun, with circumstances of cruelty and perfidy scarcely paralleled in the most barbarous ages, and totally unworthy the head of a civilized nation.

He has constrained our fellow citizens, taken captive on the high seas, to bear arms against their country, to become the executioners of their friends, and brethren, or to fall themselves by their hands.

He has excited domestic insurrections amongst us, and has endeavored to bring on the inhabitants of our frontiers, the merciless Indian savages, whose known rule of warfare is an undistinguished destruction of all ages, sexes, and conditions.

In every stage of these oppressions, we have petitioned for redress, in the most humble terms; our repeated petitions have been answered only by repeated injury. A prince, whose character is thus marked by every act which may define a tyrant, is unfit to be the ruler of a free people.

Nor have we been wanting in attention to our British brethren. We have warned them, from time to time, of attempts made by their legislature to extend an unwarrantable jurisdiction over us. We have reminded them of the circumstances of our emigration and settlement here. We have appealed to their native justice and magnanimity, and we have conjured them, by the ties of our common kindred, to disavow these usurpations, which would inevitably interrupt our connections and correspondence. They, too, have been deaf to the voice of justice and consanguinity. We must, therefore, acquiesce in the necessity which denounces our separation, and hold them as we hold the rest of mankind, enemies in war, in peace, friends.

We, therefore, the representatives of the United States of America, in general Congress assembled, appealing to the Supreme Judge of the world for the rectitude of our intentions, do, in the name, and by the authority of the good people of these colonies, solemnly publish and declare, that these united colonies are, and of right ought to be, free and independent states: that they are absolved from all allegiance to the British Crown, and that all political connection between them and the state of Great Britain is, and ought to be, totally dissolved; and that, as free and independent states, they have full power to levy war, conclude peace, contract alliances, establish commerce, and to do all other acts and things which independent states may of right do. And, for the support of this declaration, with a firm reliance on the protection of Divine Providence, we mutually pledge to each other our lives, our fortunes, and our sacred honor.

The foregoing Declaration was, by order of Congress, engrossed, and signed by the following members:

JOHN HANCOCK

New Hampshire	New York	Delaware	North Carolina
Josiah Bartlett	William Floyd	Caesar Rodney	William Hooper
William Whipple	Philip Livingston	George Read	Joseph Hewes
Matthew Thornton	Francis Lewis	Thomas M'Kean	John Penn
	Lewis Morris		

Massachusetts Bay	New Jersey	Maryland	South Carolina
Samuel Adams	Richard Stockton	Samuel Chase	Edward Rutledge
John Adams	John Witherspoon	William Paca	Thomas Heyward, Jr.
Robert Treat Paine	Francis Hopkinson	Thomas Stone	Thomas Lynch, Jr.
Elbridge Gerry	John Hart	Charles Carroll, of Carrollton	Arthur Middleton
	Abraham Clark		

Rhode Island
Stephen Hopkins
William Ellery

Connecticut
Roger Sherman
Samuel Huntington
William Williams
Oliver Wolcott

Pennsylvania
Robert Morris
Benjamin Rush
Benjamin Franklin
John Morton
George Clymer
James Smith
George Taylor
James Wilson
George Ross

Virginia
George Wythe
Richard Henry Lee
Thomas Jefferson
Benjamin Harrison
Thomas Nelson, Jr.
Francis Lightfoot Lee
Carter Braxton

Georgia
Button Gwinnett
Lyman Hall
George Walton

Resolved, That copies of the Declaration be sent to the several assemblies, conventions, and committees, or councils of safety, and to the several commanding officers of the continental troops; that it be proclaimed in each of the United States, at the head of the army.

The Constitution of the United States of America[1]

We the People of the United States, in Order to form a more perfect Union, establish Justice, insure domestic Tranquility, provide for the common defence, promote the general Welfare, and secure the Blessings of Liberty to ourselves and our Posterity, do ordain and establish this CONSTITUTION for the United States of America.

ARTICLE I

Section 1. All legislative Powers herein granted shall be vested in a Congress of the United States, which shall consist of a Senate and House of Representatives.

Section 2. The House of Representatives shall be composed of Members chosen every second Year by the People of the several States, and the Electors in each State shall have the Qualifications requisite for Electors of the most numerous Branch of the State Legislature.

No Person shall be a Representative who shall not have attained to the Age of twenty-five Years, and been seven Years a Citizen of the United States, and who shall not, when elected, be an Inhabitant of that State in which he shall be chosen.

[Representatives and direct Taxes[2] shall be apportioned among the several States which may be included within this Union, according to their respective Numbers, which shall be determined by adding to the whole Number of free Persons, including those bound to Service for a Term of Years, and excluding Indians not taxed, three fifths of all other Persons.][3] The actual Enumeration shall be made within three Years after the first Meeting of the Congress of the United States, and within every subsequent Term of ten Years, in such Manner as they shall by Law direct. The Number of Representatives shall not exceed one for every thirty Thousand, but each State shall have at Least one Representative; and until such enumeration shall be made, the State of New Hampshire shall be entitled to chuse three, Massachusetts eight, Rhode-Island and Providence Plantations one, Connecticut five, New York six, New Jersey four, Pennsylvania eight, Delaware one, Maryland six, Virginia ten, North Carolina five, South Carolina five, and Georgia three.

When vacancies happen in the Representation from any State, the Executive Authority thereof shall issue Writs of Election to fill such Vacancies.

The House of Representatives shall chuse their Speaker and other Officers; and shall have the sole Power of Impeachment.

Section 3. The Senate of the United States shall be composed of two Senators from each State, chosen by the Legislature thereof, for six Years; and each Senator shall have one Vote.

Immediately after they shall be assembled in Consequence of the first Election, they shall be divided as equally as may be into three Classes. The Seats of the Senators of the first Class shall be vacated at the Expiration of the second Year, of the second Class at the Expiration of the fourth Year, and of the third Class at the Expiration of the sixth Year, so that one-third may be chosen every second Year; and if Vacancies happen by Resignation, or otherwise, during the Recess of the Legislature of any State, the Executive thereof may make temporary Appointments until the next Meeting of the Legislature, which shall then fill such Vacancies.

No Person shall be a Senator who shall not have attained to the Age of thirty Years, and been nine Years a Citizen of the United States, and who shall not, when elected, be an Inhabitant of that State for which he shall be chosen.

The Vice President of the United States shall be President of the Senate, but shall have no vote, unless they be equally divided.

The Senate shall chuse their other Officers, and also a President pro tempore, in the absence of the Vice President, or when he shall exercise the Office of President of the United States.

The Senate shall have the sole Power to try all Impeachments. When sitting for that purpose they shall be on Oath or Affirmation. When the President of the United States is tried, the Chief Justice shall preside: And no person shall be convicted without the Concurrence of two thirds of the Members present.

Judgment in Cases of Impeachment shall not extend further than to removal from Office, and disqualification to hold and enjoy any Office of honor, Trust, or Profit

---

[1]This version follows the original Constitution in capitalization and spelling. It is adapted from the text published by the United States Department of the Interior, Office of Education.
[2]Altered by the Sixteenth Amendment.
[3]Negated by the Fourteenth Amendment.

under the United States: but the Party convicted shall nevertheless be liable and subject to Indictment, Trial, Judgment, and Punishment, according to Law.

Section 4. The Times, Places and Manner of holding Elections for Senators and Representatives, shall be prescribed in each State by the Legislature thereof; but the Congress may at any time by Law make or alter such Regulations, except as to the Places of Chusing Senators.

The Congress shall assemble at least once in every Year, and such Meeting shall be on the first Monday in December, unless they shall by Law appoint a different Day.

Section 5. Each House shall be the Judge of the Elections, Returns and Qualifications of its own Members, and a Majority of each shall constitute a Quorum to do Business; but a smaller number may adjourn from day to day, and may be authorized to compel the Attendance of absent Members, in such Manner, and under such Penalties, as each House may provide.

Each House may determine the Rules of its Proceedings, punish its Members for disorderly Behaviour, and, with the Concurrence of two thirds, expel a Member.

Each House shall keep a Journal of its Proceedings, and from time to time publish the same, excepting such Parts as may in their Judgment require Secrecy; and the Yeas and Nays of the Members of either House on any question shall, at the Desire of one fifth of those Present, be entered on the Journal.

Neither House, during the Session of Congress, shall, without the Consent of the other, adjourn for more than three days, nor to any other Place than that in which the two Houses shall be sitting.

Section 6. The Senators and Representatives shall receive a Compensation for their Services, to be ascertained by Law, and paid out of the Treasury of the United States. They shall in all Cases, except Treason, Felony, and Breach of the Peace, be privileged from Arrest during their Attendance at the Session of their respective Houses, and in going to and returning from the same; and for any Speech or Debate in either House, they shall not be questioned in any other Place.

No Senator or Representative shall, during the Time for which he was elected, be appointed to any civil Office under the Authority of the United States, which shall have been created, or the Emoluments whereof shall have been increased, during such time; and no Person holding any Office under the United States shall be a Member of either House during his continuance in Office.

Section 7. All Bills for raising Revenue shall originate in the House of Representatives; but the Senate may propose or concur with Amendments as on other bills.

Every Bill which shall have passed the House of Representatives and the Senate, shall, before it become a Law, be presented to the President of the United States; If he approve he shall sign it, but if not he shall return it, with his Objections, to that House in which it shall have originated, who shall enter the Objections at large on their Journal, and proceed to reconsider it. If after such Reconsideration two thirds of that House shall agree to pass the bill, it shall be sent, together with the objections, to the other House, by which it shall likewise be reconsidered, and if approved by two thirds of that House, it shall become a Law. But in all such Cases the Votes of both Houses shall be determined by Yeas and Nays, and the Names of the Persons voting for and against the Bill shall be entered on the Journal of each House respectively. If any Bill shall not be returned by the President within ten Days (Sundays excepted) after it shall have been presented to him, the Same shall be a Law, in like Manner as if he had signed it, unless the Congress by their Adjournment prevent its Return, in which Case it shall not be a Law.

Every Order, Resolution, or Vote to which the Concurrence of the Senate and House of Representatives may be necessary (except on a question of Adjournment) shall be presented to the President of the United States; and before the Same shall take Effect, shall be approved by him, or being disapproved by him, shall be repassed by two thirds of the Senate and House of Representatives, according to the Rules and Limitations prescribed in the Case of a Bill.

Section 8. The Congress shall have Power To lay and collect Taxes, Duties, Imposts and Excises, to pay the Debts and provide for the common Defence and general Welfare of the United States; but all Duties, Imposts and Excises shall be uniform throughout the United States;

To borrow money on the credit of the United States;

To regulate Commerce with foreign Nations, and among the several States, and with the Indian Tribes;

To establish an uniform rule of Naturalization, and uniform Laws on the subject of Bankruptcies throughout the United States;

To coin Money, regulate the Value thereof, and of foreign Coin, and fix the Standard of Weights and Measures;

To provide for the Punishment of counterfeiting the Securities and current Coin of the United States;

To establish Post Offices and post Roads;

To promote the Progress of Science and useful Arts, by securing for limited Times to Authors and Inventors the exclusive Right to their respective Writings and Discoveries;

To constitute Tribunals inferior to the Supreme Court;

To define and punish Piracies and Felonies committed on the high Seas, and Offenses against the Law of Nations;

To declare War, grant Letters of Marque and Reprisal, and make Rules concerning Captures on Land and Water;

To raise and support Armies, but no Appropriation of Money to that Use shall be for a longer Term than two Years;

To provide and maintain a Navy;

To make Rules for the Government and Regulation of the land and naval forces;

To provide for calling forth the Militia to execute the Laws of the Union, suppress Insurrections and repel Invasions;

To provide for organizing, arming, and disciplining the Militia, and for government such Part of them as may be employed in the Service of the United States, reserving to the States respectively, the Appointment of the Officers, and the Authority of training the Militia according to the discipline prescribed by Congress;

To exercise exclusive Legislation in all Cases whatsoever, over such District (not exceeding ten Miles square) as may, by Cession of particular States, and the acceptance of Congress, become the Seat of the Government of the United States, and to exercise like Authority over all Places purchased by the Consent of the Legislature of the State in which the Same shall be, for the Erection of Forts, Magazines, Arsenals, Dock-yards, and other needful Buildings;—And

To make all Laws which shall be necessary and proper for carrying into Execution the foregoing Powers, and all other Powers vested by this Constitution in the Government of the United States, or in any Department or Officer thereof.

Section 9. The Migration or Importation of such Persons as any of the States now existing shall think proper to admit, shall not be prohibited by the Congress prior to the Year one thousand eight hundred and eight, but a tax or duty may be imposed on such Importation, not exceeding ten dollars for each Person.

The privilege of the Writ of Habeas Corpus shall not be suspended, unless when in Cases of Rebellion or Invasion the public Safety may require it.

No bill of Attainder or ex post facto Law shall be passed.

No capitation, or other direct, Tax shall be laid unless in Proportion to the Census or Enumeration herein before directed to be taken.

No Tax or Duty shall be laid on Articles exported from any State.

No Preference shall be given by any Regulation of Commerce or Revenue to the Ports of one State over those of another: nor shall Vessels bound to, or from, one State, be obliged to enter, clear, or pay Duties in another.

No Money shall be drawn from the Treasury, but in Consequence of Appropriations made by Law; and a regular Statement and Account of the Receipts and Expenditures of all public Money shall be published from time to time.

No Title of Nobility shall be granted by the United States: And no Person holding any Office of Profit or Trust under them, shall, without the Consent of the Congress, accept of any present, Emolument, Office, or Title, of any kind whatever, from any King, Prince, or foreign State.

Section 10. No State shall enter into any Treaty, Alliance, or Confederation; grant Letters of Marque and Reprisal; coin Money; emit Bills of Credit; make any Thing but gold and silver Coin a Tender in Payment of Debts; pass any Bill of Attainder, ex post facto Law, or Law impairing the Obligation of Contracts, or grant any Title of Nobility.

No State shall, without the Consent of the Congress, lay any Imposts or Duties on Imports or Exports, except what may be absolutely necessary for executing its inspection Laws; and the net Produce of all Duties and Imposts, laid by any State on Imports or Exports, shall be for the use of the Treasury of the United States; and all such Laws shall be subject to the Revision and Control of the Congress.

No state shall, without the Consent of Congress, lay any duty of Tonnage, keep Troops, or Ships of War in time of Peace, enter into any Agreement or Compact with another State, or with a foreign Power, or engage in War, unless actually invaded, or in such imminent Danger as will not admit of delay.

ARTICLE II

Section 1. The executive Power shall be vested in a President of the United States of America. He shall hold his Office during the Term of four years, and, together with the Vice President, chosen for the same Term, be elected, as follows:

Each State shall appoint, in such Manner as the Legislature thereof may direct, a Number of Electors, equal to the whole Number of Senators and Representatives to which the State may be entitled in the Congress: but no Senator or Representative, or Person holding an Office of Trust or Profit under the United States, shall be appointed an Elector.

[The Electors shall meet in their respective States, and vote by Ballot for two persons, of whom one at least shall not be an Inhabitant of the same State with themselves. And they shall make a List of all the Persons voted for, and of the Number of Votes for each; which List they shall sign and certify, and transmit sealed to the Seat of the Government of the United States, directed to the President of the Senate. The President of the Senate shall, in the Presence of the Senate and House of Representatives, open all the Certificates, and the Votes shall then be counted. The Person having the greatest Number of Votes shall be the President, if such Number be a Majority of the whole Number of Electors appointed; and if there be more than one who have such Majority, and have an equal Number of Votes, then the House of Representatives shall immediately chuse by Ballot one of them for President; and if no Person have a Majority, then from the five highest on the List the said House shall in like Manner chuse the President. But in chusing the President, the Votes shall be taken by States, the Representation from each State having one Vote; a quorum for this Purpose shall consist of a Member or Members from two-thirds of the States, and a Majority of all the States shall be necessary to a Choice. In every Case, after the Choice of the President, the Person having the greatest Number of Votes of the Electors shall be the Vice President. But if there should remain two or more who have equal votes, the Senate shall chuse from them by Ballot the Vice President.]⁴

The Congress may determine the Time of chusing the Electors, and the Day on which they shall give their Votes; which Day shall be the same throughout the United States.

No person except a natural-born Citizen, or a Citizen of the United States, at the time of the Adoption of this Constitution, shall be eligible to the Office of President; neither shall any Person be eligible to that Office who shall not have attained to the Age of thirty-five years, and been fourteen Years a Resident within the United States.

In Case of the Removal of the President from Office, or of his Death, Resignation, or Inability to discharge the Powers and Duties of the said Office, the same shall devolve on the Vice President, and the Congress may by Law provide for the Case of Removal, Death, Resignation, or Inability, both of the President and Vice President, declaring what Officer shall then act as President, and such Officer shall act accordingly, until the disability be removed, or a President shall be elected.

The President shall, at stated Times, receive for his Services a Compensation, which shall neither be increased nor diminished during the Period for which he shall have been elected, and he shall not receive within that Period any other Emolument from the United States, or any of them.

Before he enter on the execution of his Office, he shall take the following Oath or Affirmation:—"I do solemnly swear (or affirm) that I will faithfully execute the Office of President of the United States, and will, to the best of my Ability, preserve, protect, and defend the Constitution of the United States."

Section 2. The President shall be Commander in Chief of the Army and Navy of the United States, and of the

---

⁴Revised by the Twelfth Amendment.

Militia of the several States, when called into the actual Service of the United States; he may require the Opinion, in writing, of the principal Officer in each of the executive Departments, upon any subject relating to the Duties of their respective Offices, and he shall have Power to Grant Reprieves and Pardons for Offenses against the United States, except in Cases of Impeachment.

He shall have Power, by and with the Advice and Consent of the Senate, to make Treaties, provided two-thirds of the Senators present concur; and he shall nominate, and by and with the Advice and Consent of the Senate, shall appoint Ambassadors, other public Ministers and Consuls, Judges of the supreme Court, and all other Officers of the United States, whose Appointments are not herein otherwise provided for, and which shall be established by Law: but the Congress may by Law vest the Appointment of such inferior Officers, as they think proper, in the President alone, in the Courts of Law, or in the Heads of Departments.

The President shall have Power to fill up all Vacancies that may happen during the Recess of the Senate, by granting Commissions which shall expire at the End of their next Session.

Section 3. He shall from time to time give to the Congress Information of the State of the Union, and recommend to their Consideration such Measures as he shall judge necessary and expedient; he may, on extraordinary occasions, convene both Houses, or either of them, and in Case of Disagreement between them, with respect to the Time of Adjournment, he may adjourn them to such Time as he shall think proper; he shall receive Ambassadors and other public Ministers; he shall take care that the Laws be faithfully executed, and shall Commission all the Officers of the United States.

Section 4. The President, Vice President and all civil Officers of the United States, shall be removed from Office on Impeachment for, and Conviction of, Treason, Bribery, or other high Crimes and Misdemeanors.

ARTICLE III

Section 1. The judicial Power of the United States, shall be vested in one supreme Court, and in such inferior Courts as the Congress may from time to time ordain and establish. The Judges, both of the supreme and inferior Courts, shall hold their Offices during good Behaviour, and shall, at stated Times, receive for their Services, a Compensation, which shall not be diminished during their Continuance in Office.

Section 2. The judicial Power shall extend to all Cases, in Law and Equity, arising under this Constitution, the Laws of the United States, and Treaties made, or which shall be made, under their Authority;—to all

Cases affecting ambassadors, other public ministers and consuls;—to all cases of admiralty and maritime Jurisdiction;—to Controversies to which the United States shall be a Party;—to Controversies between two or more States;—between a State and Citizens of another State;[5]—between Citizens of different States—between Citizens of the same State claiming Lands under Grants of different States, and between a State, or the Citizens thereof, and foreign States, Citizens, or Subjects.

In all Cases affecting Ambassadors, other public Ministers and Consuls, and those in which a State shall be Party, the supreme Court shall have original Jurisdiction. In all the other Cases before mentioned, the supreme Court shall have appellate Jurisdiction, both as to Law and Fact, with such Exceptions, and under such Regulations as the Congress shall make.

The trial of all Crimes, except in Cases of Impeachment, shall be by Jury; and such Trial shall be held in the State where the said Crimes shall have been committed; but when not committed within any State, the Trial shall be at such Place or Places as the Congress may by Law have directed.

Section 3. Treason against the United States, shall consist only in levying War against them, or in adhering to their Enemies, giving them Aid and Comfort. No Person shall be convicted of Treason unless on the Testimony of two Witnesses to the same overt Act, or on Confession in open Court.

The Congress shall have power to declare the Punishment of Treason, but no Attainder of Treason shall work Corruption of Blood, or Forfeiture except during the Life of the Person attainted.

ARTICLE IV

Section 1. Full Faith and Credit shall be given in each State to the public Acts, Records, and judicial Proceedings of every other State. And the Congress may by general Laws prescribe the Manner in which such Acts, Records and Proceedings shall be proved, and the Effect thereof.

Section 2. The Citizens of each State shall be entitled to all Privileges and Immunities of Citizens in the several States.

A Person charged in any State with Treason, Felony, or other Crime, who shall flee from Justice, and be found in another State, shall on demand of the executive Authority of the State from which he fled, be delivered up, to be removed to the State having Jurisdiction of the crime.

No Person held to Service or Labour in one State, under the Laws thereof, escaping into another, shall, in Consequence of any Law or Regulation therein, be discharged from such Service or Labour, but shall be delivered up on Claim of the Party to whom such Service or Labour may be due.

Section 3. New States may be admitted by the Congress into this Union; but no new State shall be formed or erected within the Jurisdiction of any other State; nor any State be formed by the Junction of two or more States, or parts of States, without the Consent of the Legislatures of the States concerned as well as of the Congress.

The Congress shall have Power to dispose of and make all needful Rules and Regulations respecting the Territory or other Property belonging to the United States; and nothing in this Constitution shall be so construed as to Prejudice any Claims of the United States, or of any particular State.

Section 4. The United States shall guarantee to every State in this Union a Republican Form of Government, and shall protect each of them against Invasion; and on Application of the Legislature, or of the Executive (when the Legislature cannot be convened) against domestic Violence.

ARTICLE V

The Congress, whenever two-thirds of both Houses shall deem it necessary, shall propose Amendments to this Constitution, or, on the Application of the Legislatures of two-thirds of the several States, shall call a Convention for proposing Amendments, which, in either Case, shall be valid to all Intents and Purposes, as part of this Constitution, when ratified by the Legislatures of three-fourths of the several States, or by Conventions in three-fourths thereof, as the one or the other Mode of Ratification may be proposed by the Congress; Provided that no Amendment which may be made prior to the Year One thousand eight hundred and eight shall in any Manner affect the first and fourth Clauses in the Ninth Section of the first Article; and that no State, without its Consent, shall be deprived of its equal Suffrage in the Senate.

ARTICLE VI

All Debts contracted and Engagements entered into, before the Adoption of this Constitution, shall be as valid against the United States under this Constitution, as under the Confederation.

This Constitution, and the Laws of the United States which shall be made in Pursuance thereof; and all Treaties made, or which shall be made, under the Authority of the United States, shall be the supreme Law of the Land; and the Judges in every State shall be bound thereby, any Thing in the Constitution or Laws of any State to the Contrary notwithstanding.

---

[5]Qualified by the Eleventh Amendment.

The Senators and Representatives before mentioned, and the Members of the several State Legislatures, and all executive and judicial Officers, both of the United States and of the several States, shall be bound by Oath or Affirmation to support this Constitution; but no religious Tests shall ever be required as a qualification to any Office or public Trust under the United States.

ARTICLE VII

The Ratification of the Conventions of nine States shall be sufficient for the Establishment of this Constitution between the States so ratifying the same.

Done in Convention by the Unanimous Consent of the States present the Seventeenth Day of September in the Year of our Lord one thousand seven hundred and Eighty seven, and of the Independence of the United States of America the Twelfth. In Witness whereof We have hereunto subscribed our Names.[6]

GEORGE WASHINGTON
PRESIDENT AND DEPUTY FROM VIRGINIA

New Hampshire
John Langdon
Nicholas Gilman

New Jersey
William Livingston
David Brearley
William Paterson
Jonathan Dayton

Delaware
George Read
Gunning Bedford, Jr.
John Dickinson
Richard Bassett
Jacob Broom

North Carolina
William Blount
Richard Dobbs Spaight
Hugh Williamson

Massachusetts
Nathaniel Gorham
Rufus King

Connecticut
William Samuel Johnson
Roger Sherman

New York
Alexander Hamilton

Pennsylvania
Benjamin Franklin
Thomas Mifflin
Robert Morris
George Clymer
Thomas FitzSimons
Jared Ingersoll
James Wilson
Gouverneur Morris

Maryland
James McHenry
Daniel of St. Thomas Jenifer
Daniel Carroll

Virginia
John Blair
James Madison, Jr.

South Carolina
John Rutledge
Charles Cotesworth Pinckney
Charles Pinckney
Pierce Butler

Georgia
William Few
Abraham Baldwin

Articles in Addition to, and Amendment of, the Constitution of the United States of America, Proposed by Congress, and Ratified by the Legislatures of the Several States, Pursuant to the Fifth Article of the Original Constitution[7]

[AMENDMENT I]
Congress shall make no law respecting an establishment of religion, or prohibiting the free exercise thereof; or abridging the freedom of speech, or of the press; or the right of the people peaceably to assemble, and to petition the Government for a redress of grievances.

[AMENDMENT II]
A well regulated Militia, being necessary to the security of a free State, the right of the people to keep and bear Arms shall not be infringed.

[AMENDMENT III]
No Soldier shall, in time of peace, be quartered in any house, without the consent of the Owner, nor in time of war, but in a manner to be prescribed by law.

[AMENDMENT IV]
The right of the people to be secure in their persons, houses, papers, and effects, against unreasonable searches and seizures, shall not be violated, and no Warrants shall issue, but upon probable cause, supported by Oath or affirmation, and particularly describing the place to be searched, and the persons or things to be seized.

[AMENDMENT V]
No person shall be held to answer for a capital or otherwise infamous crime, unless on a presentment or indictment of

---

[6]These are the full names of the signers, which in some cases are not the signatures on the document.

[7]This heading appears only in the joint resolution submitting the first ten amendments, known as the Bill of Rights.

a Grand Jury, except in cases arising in the land or naval forces, or in the Militia, when in actual service in time of War or public danger; nor shall any person be subject for the same offence to be twice put in jeopardy of life or limb; nor shall be compelled in any criminal case to be a witness against himself, nor be deprived of life, liberty, or property, without due process of law; nor shall private property be taken for public use, without just compensation.

[AMENDMENT VI]

In all criminal prosecutions, the accused shall enjoy the right to a speedy and public trial, by an impartial jury of the State and district wherein the crime shall have been committed, which district shall have been previously ascertained by law, and to be informed of the nature and cause of the accusation; to be confronted with the witnesses against him; to have compulsory process for obtaining witnesses in his favour, and to have the Assistance of Counsel for his defence.

[AMENDMENT VII]

In suits at common law, where the value in controversy shall exceed twenty dollars, the right of trial by jury shall be preserved, and no fact tried by a jury, shall be otherwise reexamined in any Court of the United States, than according to the rules of the common law.

[AMENDMENT VIII]

Excessive bail shall not be required, nor excessive fines imposed, nor cruel and unusual punishments inflicted.

[AMENDMENT IX]

The enumeration of the Constitution, of certain rights, shall not be construed to deny or disparage others retained by the people.

[AMENDMENT X]

The powers not delegated to the United States by the Constitution, nor prohibited by it to the States, are reserved to the States respectively, or to the people. [Amendments I-X, in force 1791.]

[AMENDMENT XI][8]

The Judicial power of the United States shall not be construed to extend to any suit in law or equity, commenced or prosecuted against one of the United States by Citizens of another State, or by Citizens or Subjects of any Foreign State.

[AMENDMENT XII][9]

The Electors shall meet in their respective States and vote by ballot for President and Vice-President, one of whom, at least, shall not be an inhabitant of the same State with themselves; they shall name in their ballots the person voted for as President, and in distinct ballots the person voted for as Vice-President, and they shall make distinct lists of all persons voted for as President, and of all persons voted for as Vice-President, and of the number of votes for each, which lists they shall sign and certify, and transmit sealed to the seat of the government of the United States, directed to the President of the Senate;—The President of the Senate shall, in the presence of the Senate and House of Representatives, open all the certificates and the votes shall then be counted;—The person having the greatest number of votes for President, shall be the President, if such number be a majority of the whole number of Electors appointed; and if no person have such majority, then from the persons having the highest numbers not exceeding three on the list of those voted for as President, the House of Representatives shall choose immediately, by ballot, the President. But in choosing the President, the votes shall be taken by states, the representation from each state having one vote; a quorum for this purpose shall consist of a member or members from two-thirds of the states, and a majority of all the states shall be necessary to a choice. And if the House of Representatives shall not choose a President whenever the right of choice shall devolve upon them, before the fourth day of March next following, then the Vice-President shall act as President, as in the case of the death or other constitutional disability of the President.—The person having the greatest number of votes as Vice-President, shall be the Vice-President, if such number be a majority of the whole number of Electors appointed, and if no person have a majority, then from the two highest numbers on the list, the Senate shall choose the Vice-President; a quorum for the purpose shall consist of two-thirds of the whole number of Senators, and a majority of the whole number shall be necessary to a choice. But no person constitutionally ineligible to the office of President shall be eligible to that of Vice-President of the United States.

[AMENDMENT XIII][10]

Section 1. Neither slavery nor involuntary servitude, except as a punishment for crime whereof the party shall have been duly convicted, shall exist within the United States, or any place subject to their jurisdiction.

Section 2. Congress shall have power to enforce this article by appropriate legislation.

[AMENDMENT XIV][11]

Section 1. All persons born or naturalized in the United States, and subject to the jurisdiction thereof, are

---

[8]Adopted in 1798.
[9]Adopted in 1804.

[10]Adopted in 1865.
[11]Adopted in 1868.

citizens of the United States and of the State wherein they reside. No State shall abridge the privileges or immunities of citizens of the United States; nor shall any State deprive any person of life, liberty, or property, without due process of law; nor deny to any person within its jurisdiction the equal protection of the laws.

Section 2. Representatives shall be apportioned among the several States according to their respective numbers, counting the whole number of persons in each State, excluding Indians not taxed. But when the right to vote at any election for the choice of electors for President and Vice-President of the United States, Representatives in Congress, the Executive and Judicial officers of a State, or the members of the Legislature thereof, is denied to any of the male inhabitants of such State, being twenty-one years of age, and citizens of the United States, or in any way abridged, except for participation in rebellion, or other crime, the basis of representation therein shall be reduced in the proportion which the number of such male citizens shall bear to the whole number of male citizens twenty-one years of age in such State.

Section 3. No person shall be a Senator or Representative in Congress, or elector of President and Vice-President, or hold any office, civil or military, under the United States, or under any State, who, having previously taken an oath, as a member of Congress, or as an officer of the United States, or as a member of any State legislature, or as an executive or judicial officer of any State, to support the Constitution of the United States, shall have engaged in insurrection or rebellion against the same, or given aid or comfort to the enemies thereof. But Congress may by a vote of two-thirds of each House, remove such disability.

Section 4. The validity of the public debt of the United States, authorized by law, including debts incurred for payment of pensions and bounties for services in suppressing insurrection or rebellion, shall not be questioned. But neither the United States nor any State shall assume or pay any debts or obligation incurred in aid of insurrection or rebellion against the United States, or any claim for the loss or emancipation of any slave; but all such debts, obligations, and claims shall be held illegal and void.

Section 5. The Congress shall have the power to enforce, by appropriate legislation, the provisions of this article.

[AMENDMENT XV][12]

Section 1. The right of citizens of the United States to vote shall not be denied or abridged by the United States or by any State on account of race, color, or previous condition of servitude—

[12]Adopted in 1870.

Section 2. The Congress shall have power to enforce this article by appropriate legislation.

[AMENDMENT XVI][13]

The Congress shall have power to lay and collect taxes on incomes, from whatever source derived, without apportionment among the several States, and without regard to any census or enumeration.

[AMENDMENT XVII][14]

The Senate of the United States shall be composed of two Senators from each State, elected by the people thereof, for six years; and each Senator shall have one vote. The electors in each State shall have the qualifications requisite for electors of the most numerous branch of the State legislatures.

When vacancies happen in the representation of any State in the Senate, the executive authority of such State shall issue writs of election to fill such vacancies: Provided, That the legislature of any State may empower the executive thereof to make temporary appointments until the people fill the vacancies by election as the legislature may direct.

This amendment shall not be so construed as to affect the election or term of any Senator chosen before it becomes valid as part of the Constitution.

[AMENDMENT XVIII][15]

Section 1. After one year from the ratification of this article the manufacture, sale, or transportation of intoxicating liquors within, the importation thereof into, or the exportation thereof from the United States and all territory subject to the jurisdiction thereof for beverage purposes is hereby prohibited.

Section 2. The Congress and the several States shall have concurrent power to enforce this article by appropriate legislation.

Section 3. This article shall be inoperative unless it shall have been ratified as an amendment to the Constitution by the legislatures of the several States, as provided in the Constitution, within seven years from the date of the submission hereof to the States by the Congress.

[AMENDMENT XIX][16]

The right of citizens of the United States to vote shall not be denied or abridged by the United States or by any State on account of sex.

Congress shall have power to enforce this article by appropriate legislation.

[13]Adopted in 1913.
[14]Adopted in 1913.
[15]Adopted in 1918.
[16]Adopted in 1920.

[AMENDMENT XX]^{17}

Section 1. The terms of the President and Vice-President shall end at noon on the 20th day of January, and the terms of Senators and Representatives at noon on the 3d day of January, of the years in which such terms would have ended if this article had not been ratified; and the terms of their successors shall then begin.

Section 2. The Congress shall assemble at least once in every year, and such meeting shall begin at noon on the 3d day of January, unless they shall by law appoint a different day.

Section 3. If, at the time fixed for the beginning of the term of the President, the President elect shall have died, the Vice-President elect shall become President. If a President shall not have been chosen before the time fixed for the beginning of his term or if the President elect shall have failed to qualify, then the Vice-President elect shall act as President until a President shall have qualified; and the Congress may by law provide for the case wherein neither a President elect nor a Vice-President elect shall have qualified, declaring who shall then act as President, or the manner in which one who is to act shall be selected, and such person shall act accordingly until a President or Vice-President shall have qualified.

Section 4. The Congress may by law provide for the case of the death of any of the persons from whom the House of Representatives may choose a President whenever the right of choice shall have devolved upon them, and for the case of the death of any of the persons from whom the Senate may choose a Vice-President whenever the right of choice shall have devolved upon them.

Section 5. Sections 1 and 2 shall take effect on the 15th day of October following the ratification of this article.

Section 6. This article shall be inoperative unless it shall have been ratified as an amendment to the Constitution by the legislatures of three-fourths of the several States within seven years from the date of its submission.

[AMENDMENT XXI]^{18}

Section 1. The eighteenth article of amendment to the Constitution of the United States is hereby repealed.

Section 2. The transportation or importation into any State, Territory, or possession of the United States for delivery or use therein of intoxicating liquors, in violation of the laws thereof, is hereby prohibited.

Section 3. This article shall be inoperative unless it shall have been ratified as an amendment to the Constitution by conventions in the several States, as provided in the Constitution, within seven years from the date of the submission hereof to the States by the Congress.

[AMENDMENT XXII]^{19}

No person shall be elected to the office of the President more than twice, and no person who has held the office of President, or acted as President, for more than two years of a term to which some other person was elected President shall be elected to the office of the President more than once.

But this Article shall not apply to any person holding the office of President when this Article was proposed by the Congress, and shall not prevent any person who may be holding the office of President, or acting as President, during the term within which this Article becomes operative from holding the office of President or acting as President during the remainder of such term.

This article shall be inoperative unless it shall have been ratified as an amendment to the Constitution by the legislatures of three-fourths of the several states within seven years from the date of its submission to the states by the Congress.

[AMENDMENT XXIII]^{20}

Section 1. The District constituting the seat of Government of the United States shall appoint in such manner as the Congress may direct:

A number of electors of President and Vice-President equal to the whole number of Senators and Representatives in Congress to which the District would be entitled if it were a State, but in no event more than the least populous State; they shall be in addition to those appointed by the States, but they shall be considered, for the purpose of the election of President and Vice-President, to be electors appointed by a State; and they shall meet in the District and perform such duties as provided by the twelfth article of amendment.

Section 2. The Congress shall have power to enforce this article by appropriate legislation.

[AMENDMENT XXIV]^{21}

Section 1. The right of citizens of the United States to vote in any primary or other election for President or Vice-President, for electors for President or Vice-President, or for Senator or Representative in Congress, shall not be

---

^{17}Adopted in 1933.
^{18}Adopted in 1933.

^{19}Adopted in 1951.
^{20}Adopted in 1961.
^{21}Adopted in 1964.

denied or abridged by the United States or any state by reason of failure to pay any poll tax or other tax.

Section 2. The Congress shall have the power to enforce this article by appropriate legislation.

[AMENDMENT XXV][22]

Section 1. In case of the removal of the President from office or of his death or resignation, the Vice-President shall become President.

Section 2. Whenever there is a vacancy in the office of the Vice President, the President shall nominate a Vice President who shall take office upon confirmation by a majority vote of both Houses of Congress.

Section 3. Whenever the President transmits to the President Pro Tempore of the Senate and the Speaker of the House of Representatives his written declaration that he is unable to discharge the powers and duties of his office, and until he transmits to them a written declaration to the contrary, such powers and duties shall be discharged by the Vice-President as Acting President.

Section 4. Whenever the Vice-President and a majority of either the principal officers of the executive departments or of such other body as Congress may by law provide, transmit to the President Pro Tempore of the Senate and the Speaker of the House of Representatives their written declaration that the President is unable to discharge the powers and duties of his office, the Vice President shall immediately assume the powers and duties of the office as Acting President.

Thereafter, when the President transmits to the President Pro Tempore of the Senate and the Speaker of the House of Representatives his written declaration that no inability exists, he shall resume the powers and duties of his office unless the Vice President and a majority of either the principal officers of the executive departments or of such other body as Congress may by law provide, transmit within four days to the President Pro Tempore of the Senate and the Speaker of the House of Representatives their written declaration that the President is unable to discharge the powers and duties of his office. Thereupon Congress shall decide the issue, assembling within forty-eight hours for that purpose if not in session. If the Congress, within twenty-one days after receipt of the latter written declaration, or, if Congress is not in session, within twenty-one days after Congress is required to assemble, determines by two-thirds vote of both Houses that the President is unable to discharge the powers and duties of his office, the Vice President shall continue to discharge the same as Acting President; otherwise, the President shall resume the powers and duties of his office.

[AMENDMENT XXVI][23]

Section 1. The right of citizens of the United States, who are eighteen years of age or older, to vote shall not be denied or abridged by the United States or by any State on account of age.

Section 2. The Congress shall have power to enforce this article by appropriate legislation.

[AMENDMENT XXVII][24]

No law, varying the compensation for the services of the Senators and Representatives, shall take effect, until an election of Representatives shall have intervened.

---

[22]Adopted in 1967.

[23]Adopted in 1971.

[24]Adopted in 1992.

Presidential Elections

Year	Candidates	Parties	Popular Vote	% of Popular Vote	Electoral Vote	% Voter Participation
1789	**George Washington**				69	
	John Adams				34	
	Other candidates				35	
1792	**George Washington**				132	
	John Adams				77	
	George Clinton				50	
	Other candidates				5	
1796	**John Adams**	Federalist			71	
	Thomas Jefferson	Dem.-Rep.			68	
	Thomas Pinckney	Federalist			59	
	Aaron Burr	Dem.-Rep.			30	
	Other candidates				48	
1800	**Thomas Jefferson**	Dem.-Rep.			73	
	Aaron Burr	Dem.-Rep.			73	
	John Adams	Federalist			65	
	Charles C. Pinckney	Federalist			64	
	John Jay	Federalist			1	
1804	**Thomas Jefferson**	Dem.-Rep.			162	
	Charles C. Pinckney	Federalist			14	
1808	**James Madison**	Dem.-Rep.			122	
	Charles C. Pinckney	Federalist			47	
	George Clinton	Dem.-Rep.			6	
1812	**James Madison**	Dem.-Rep.			128	
	DeWitt Clinton	Federalist			89	
1816	**James Monroe**	Dem.-Rep.			183	
	Rufus King	Federalist			34	
1820	**James Monroe**	Dem.-Rep.			231	
	John Quincy Adams	Indep.-Rep.			1	
1824	**John Quincy Adams**	Dem.-Rep.	113,122	31.0	84	26.9
	Andrew Jackson	Dem.-Rep.	151,271	43.0	99	
	Henry Clay	Dem.-Rep.	47,136	13.0	37	
	William H. Crawford	Dem.-Rep.	46,618	13.0	41	
1828	**Andrew Jackson**	Democratic	642,553	56.0	178	57.6
	John Quincy Adams	National Republican	500,897	44.0	83	
1832	**Andrew Jackson**	Democratic	701,780	54.5	219	55.4
	Henry Clay	National Republican	484,205	37.5	49	
	William Wirt	Anti-Masonic	101,051	8.0	7	
	John Floyd	Democratic			11	
1836	**Martin Van Buren**	Democratic	764,176	50.9	170	57.8
	William H. Harrison	Whig	550,816	49.1	73	
	Hugh L. White	Whig			26	
	Daniel Webster	Whig			14	
	W. P. Mangum	Whig			11	
1840	**William H. Harrison**	Whig	1,275,390	53.0	234	80.2
	Martin Van Buren	Democratic	1,128,854	47.0	60	

Year	Candidates	Parties	Popular Vote	% of Popular Vote	Electoral Vote	% Voter Participation
1844	**James K. Polk**	Democratic	1,339,494	49.6	170	78.9
	Henry Clay	Whig	1,300,004	48.1	105	
	James G. Birney	Liberty	62,300	2.3		
1848	**Zachary Taylor**	Whig	1,361,393	47.4	163	72.7
	Lewis Cass	Democratic	1,223,460	42.5	127	
	Martin Van Buren	Free Soil	291,263	10.1		
1852	**Franklin Pierce**	Democratic	1,607,510	50.9	254	69.6
	Winfield Scott	Whig	1,386,942	44.1	42	
	John P. Hale	Free Soil	155,825	5.0		
1856	**James Buchanan**	Democratic	1,836,072	45.3	174	78.9
	John C. Fremont	Republican	1,342,345	33.1	114	
	Millard Fillmore	American	871,731	21.6	8	
1860	**Abraham Lincoln**	Republican	1,865,908	39.8	180	81.2
	Stephen A. Douglas	Democratic	1,375,157	29.5	12	
	John C. Breckinridge	Democratic	848,019	18.1	72	
	John Bell	Constitutional Union	590,631	12.6	39	
1864	**Abraham Lincoln**	Republican	2,218,388	55.0	212	73.8
	George B. McClellan	Democratic	1,812,807	45.0	21	
1868	**Ulysses S. Grant**	Republican	3,013,650	52.7	214	78.1
	Horatio Seymour	Democratic	2,708,744	47.3	80	
1872	**Ulysses S. Grant**	Republican	3,598,235	55.6	286	71.3
	Horace Greeley	Democratic	2,834,761	43.9	66	
1876	**Rutherford B. Hayes**	Republican	4,034,311	48.0	185	81.8
	Samuel J. Tilden	Democratic	4,288,546	51.0	184	
1880	**James A. Garfield**	Republican	4,446,158	48.5	214	79.4
	Winfield S. Hancock	Democratic	4,444,260	48.1	155	
	James B. Weaver	Greenback-Labor	308,578	3.4		
1884	**Grover Cleveland**	Democratic	4,874,621	48.5	219	77.5
	James G. Blaine	Republican	4,848,936	48.2	182	
	Benjamin F. Butler	Greenback-Labor	175,370	1.8		
	John P. St. John	Prohibition	150,369	1.5		
1888	**Benjamin Harrison**	Republican	5,443,892	47.9	233	79.3
	Grover Cleveland	Democratic	5,534,488	48.6	168	
	Clinton B. Fisk	Prohibition	249,506	2.2		
	Anson J. Streeter	Union Labor	146,935	1.3		
1892	**Grover Cleveland**	Democratic	5,551,883	46.1	277	74.7
	Benjamin Harrison	Republican	5,179,244	43.0	145	
	James B. Weaver	People's	1,029,846	8.5	22	
	John Bidwell	Prohibition	264,133	2.2		
1896	**William McKinley**	Republican	7,108,480	52.0	271	79.3
	William J. Bryan	Democratic	6,511,495	48.0	176	
1900	**William McKinley**	Republican	7,218,039	51.7	292	73.2
	William J. Bryan	Democratic; Populist	6,358,345	45.5	155	
	John C. Wooley	Prohibition	208,914	1.5		
1904	**Theodore Roosevelt**	Republican	7,626,593	57.4	336	65.2
	Alton B. Parker	Democratic	5,082,898	37.6	140	
	Eugene V. Debs	Socialist	402,283	3.0		
	Silas C. Swallow	Prohibition	258,536	1.9		
1908	**William H. Taft**	Republican	7,676,258	51.6	321	65.4
	William J. Bryan	Democratic	6,406,801	43.1	162	
	Eugene V. Debs	Socialist	420,793	2.8		
	Eugene W. Chafin	Prohibition	253,840	1.7		

Year	Candidates	Parties	Popular Vote	% of Popular Vote	Electoral Vote	% Voter Participation
1912	**Woodrow Wilson**	Democratic	6,293,152	42.0	435	58.8
	Theodore Roosevelt	Progressive	4,119,207	28.0	88	
	William H. Taft	Republican	3,484,980	24.0	8	
	Eugene V. Debs	Socialist	900,672	6.0		
	Eugene W. Chafin	Prohibition	206,275	1.4		
1916	**Woodrow Wilson**	Democratic	9,126,300	49.4	277	61.6
	Charles E. Hughes	Republican	8,546,789	46.2	254	
	A. L. Benson	Socialist	585,113	3.2		
	J. Frank Hanly	Prohibition	220,506	1.2		
1920	**Warren G. Harding**	Republican	16,153,115	60.4	404	49.2
	James M. Cox	Democratic	9,133,092	34.2	127	
	Eugene V. Debs	Socialist	919,799	3.4		
	P. P. Christensen	Farmer-Labor	265,411	1.0		
1924	**Calvin Coolidge**	Republican	15,719,921	54.0	382	48.9
	John W. Davis	Democratic	8,386,704	28.8	136	
	Robert M. La Follette	Progressive	4,831,289	16.6	13	
1928	**Herbert C. Hoover**	Republican	21,437,277	58.2	444	56.9
	Alfred E. Smith	Democratic	15,007,698	40.9	87	
1932	**Franklin D. Roosevelt**	Democratic	22,829,501	57.4	472	56.9
	Herbert C. Hoover	Republican	15,760,684	39.7	59	
	Norman Thomas	Socialist	881,951	2.2		
1936	**Franklin D. Roosevelt**	Democratic	27,757,333	60.8	523	61.0
	Alfred M. Landon	Republican	16,684,231	36.5	8	
	William Lemke	Union	882,479	1.9		
1940	**Franklin D. Roosevelt**	Democratic	27,313,041	54.8	449	62.5
	Wendell L. Wilkie	Republican	22,348,480	44.8	82	
1944	**Franklin D. Roosevelt**	Democratic	25,612,610	53.5	432	55.9
	Thomas E. Dewey	Republican	22,117,617	46.0	99	
1948	**Harry S Truman**	Democratic	24,179,345	50.0	303	53.0
	Thomas E. Dewey	Republican	21,991,291	46.0	189	
	J. Strom Thurmond	States' Rights	1,169,021	2.0	39	
	Henry A. Wallace	Progressive	1,157,172	2.0		
1952	**Dwight D. Eisenhower**	Republican	33,936,234	55.1	442	63.3
	Adlai E. Stevenson	Democratic	27,314,992	44.4	89	
1956	**Dwight D. Eisenhower**	Republican	35,590,472	57.6	457	60.6
	Adlai E. Stevenson	Democratic	26,022,752	42.1	73	
1960	**John F. Kennedy**	Democratic	34,226,731	49.7	303	62.8
	Richard M. Nixon	Republican	34,108,157	49.6	219	
	Harry F. Byrd	Independent	501,643		15	
1964	**Lyndon B. Johnson**	Democratic	43,129,566	61.1	486	61.7
	Barry M. Goldwater	Republican	27,178,188	38.5	52	
1968	**Richard M. Nixon**	Republican	31,785,480	44.0	301	60.6
	Hubert H. Humphrey	Democratic	31,275,166	42.7	191	
	George C. Wallace	American Independent	9,906,473	13.5	46	
1972	**Richard M. Nixon**	Republican	47,169,911	60.7	520	55.2
	George S. McGovern	Democratic	29,170,383	37.5	17	
	John G. Schmitz	American	1,099,482	1.4		
1976	**Jimmy Carter**	Democratic	40,830,763	50.1	297	53.5
	Gerald R. Ford	Republican	39,147,793	48.0	240	

Year	Candidates	Parties	Popular Vote	% of Popular Vote	Electoral Vote	% Voter Participation
1980	**Ronald Reagan**	Republican	43,904,153	51.0	489	52.6
	Jimmy Carter	Democratic	35,483,883	41.0	49	
	John B. Anderson	Independent	5,719,437	7.0	0	
	Ed Clark	Libertarian	920,859	1.0	0	
1984	**Ronald Reagan**	Republican	54,455,075	58.8	525	53.3
	Walter Mondale	Democratic	37,577,185	40.5	13	
1988	**George Bush**	Republican	48,886,097	53.9	426	48.6
	Michael Dukakis	Democratic	41,809,074	46.1	111	
1992	**William J. Clinton**	Democratic	44,908,254	43.0	370	55.9
	George H. Bush	Republican	39,102,343	37.4	168	
	H. Ross Perot	Independent	19,741,065	18.9	0	
1996	**William J. Clinton**	Democratic	45,590,703	49.3	379	49
	Robert Dole	Republican	37,816,307	40.7	159	
	H. Ross Perot	Reform	8,085,294	8.4	0	
2000	**George W. Bush**	Republican	50,456,062	47.9	271	51.2
	Al Gore	Democratic	50,996,582	48.4	266	
	Ralph Nader	Green	2,858,843	2.7	0	
2004	**George W. Bush**	Republican	62,048,610	50.7	286	60.7
	John F. Kerry	Democrat	59,028,444	48.3	251	
	Ralph Nader	Independent	465,650	0.4	0	

Presidential Administrations

The Washington Administration (1789–1797)

Vice President	John Adams	1789–1797
Secretary of State	Thomas Jefferson	1789–1793
	Edmund Randolph	1794–1795
	Timothy Pickering	1795–1797
Secretary of Treasury	Alexander Hamilton	1789–1795
	Oliver Wolcott	1795–1797
Secretary of War	Henry Knox	1789–1794
	Timothy Pickering	1795–1796
	James McHenry	1796–1797
Attorney General	Edmund Randolph	1789–1793
	William Bradford	1794–1795
	Charles Lee	1795–1797
Postmaster General	Samuel Osgood	1789–1791
	Timothy Pickering	1791–1794
	Joseph Habersham	1795–1797

The John Adams Administration (1797–1801)

Vice President	Thomas Jefferson	1797–1801
Secretary of State	Timothy Pickering	1797–1800
	John Marshall	1800–1801
Secretary of Treasury	Oliver Wolcott	1797–1800
	Samuel Dexter	1800–1801
Secretary of War	James McHenry	1797–1800
	Samuel Dexter	1800–1801
Attorney General	Charles Lee	1797–1801
Postmaster General	Joseph Habersham	1797–1801
Secretary of Navy	Benjamin Stoddert	1798–1801

The Jefferson Administration (1801–1809)

Vice President	Aaron Burr	1801–1805
	George Clinton	1805–1809
Secretary of State	James Madison	1801–1809
Secretary of Treasury	Samuel Dexter	1801
	Albert Gallatin	1801–1809
Secretary of War	Henry Dearborn	1801–1809
Attorney General	Levi Lincoln	1801–1805
	Robert Smith	1805
	John Breckinridge	1805–1806
	Caesar Rodney	1807–1809
Postmaster General	Joseph Habersham	1801
	Gideon Granger	1801–1809
Secretary of Navy	Robert Smith	1801–1809

The Madison Administration (1809–1817)

Vice President	George Clinton	1809–1813
	Elbridge Gerry	1813–1817
Secretary of State	Robert Smith	1809–1811
	James Monroe	1811–1817
Secretary of Treasury	Albert Gallatin	1809–1813
	George Campbell	1814
	Alexander Dallas	1814–1816
	William Crawford	1816–1817
Secretary of War	William Eustis	1809–1812
	John Armstrong	1813–1814
	James Monroe	1814–1815
	William Crawford	1815–1817
Attorney General	Caesar Rodney	1809–1811
	William Pinkney	1811–1814
	Richard Rush	1814–1817
Postmaster General	Gideon Granger	1809–1814
	Return Meigs	1814–1817
Secretary of Navy	Paul Hamilton	1809–1813
	William Jones	1813–1814
	Benjamin Crowninshield	1814–1817

The Monroe Administration (1817–1825)

Vice President	Daniel Tompkins	1817–1825
Secretary of State	John Quincy Adams	1817–1825
Secretary of Treasury	William Crawford	1817–1825
Secretary of War	George Graham	1817
	John C. Calhoun	1817–1825
Attorney General	Richard Rush	1817
	William Wirt	1817–1825
Postmaster General	Return Meigs	1817–1823
	John McLean	1823–1825
Secretary of Navy	Benjamin Crowninshield	1817–1818
	Smith Thompson	1818–1823
	Samuel Southard	1823–1825

The John Quincy Adams Administration (1825–1829)

Vice President	John C. Calhoun	1825–1829
Secretary of State	Henry Clay	1825–1829
Secretary of Treasury	Richard Rush	1825–1829
Secretary of War	James Barbour	1825–1828
	Peter Porter	1828–1829
Attorney General	William Wirt	1825–1829
Postmaster General	John McLean	1825–1829
Secretary of Navy	Samuel Southard	1825–1829

The Jackson Administration (1829–1837)

Vice President	John C. Calhoun	1829–1833
	Martin Van Buren	1833–1837
Secretary of State	Martin Van Buren	1829–1831
	Edward Livingston	1831–1833
	Louis McLane	1833–1834
	John Forsyth	1834–1837
Secretary of Treasury	Samuel Ingham	1829–1831
	Louis McLane	1831–1833
	William Duane	1833
	Roger B. Taney	1833–1834
	Levi Woodbury	1834–1837
Secretary of War	John H. Eaton	1829–1831
	Lewis Cass	1831–1837
	Benjamin Butler	1837
Attorney General	John M. Berrien	1829–1831
	Roger B. Taney	1831–1833
	Benjamin Butler	1833–1837
Postmaster General	William Barry	1829–1835
	Amos Kendall	1835–1837
Secretary of Navy	John Branch	1829–1831
	Levi Woodbury	1831–1834
	Mahlon Dickerson	1834–1837

The Van Buren Administration (1837–1841)

Vice President	Richard M. Johnson	1837–1841
Secretary of State	John Forsyth	1837–1841
Secretary of Treasury	Levi Woodbury	1837–1841
Secretary of War	Joel Poinsett	1837–1841
Attorney General	Benjamin Butler	1837–1838
	Felix Grundy	1838–1840
	Henry D. Gilpin	1840–1841
Postmaster General	Amos Kendall	1837–1840
	John M. Niles	1840–1841
Secretary of Navy	Mahlon Dickerson	1837–1838
	James Paulding	1838–1841

The William Harrison Administration (1841)

Vice President	John Tyler	1841
Secretary of State	Daniel Webster	1841
Secretary of Treasury	Thomas Ewing	1841
Secretary of War	John Bell	1841
Attorney General	John J. Crittenden	1841
Postmaster General	Francis Granger	1841
Secretary of Navy	George Badger	1841

The Tyler Administration (1841–1845)

Vice President	None	
Secretary of State	Daniel Webster	1841–1843
	Hugh S. Legaré	1843
	Abel P. Upshur	1843–1844
	John C. Calhoun	1844–1845
Secretary of Treasury	Thomas Ewing	1841
	Walter Forward	1841–1843
	John C. Spencer	1843–1844
	George Bibb	1844–1845
Secretary of War	John Bell	1841
	John C. Spencer	1841–1843
	James M. Porter	1843–1844
	William Wilkins	1844–1845
Attorney General	John J. Crittenden	1841
	Hugh S. Legaré	1841–1843
	John Nelson	1843–1845
Postmaster General	Francis Granger	1841
	Charles Wickliffe	1841–1845
Secretary of Navy	George Badger	1841
	Abel P. Upshur	1841
	David Henshaw	1843–1844
	Thomas Gilmer	1844
	John Y. Mason	1844–1845

The Polk Administration (1845–1849)

Vice President	George M. Dallas	1845–1849
Secretary of State	James Buchanan	1845–1849
Secretary of Treasury	Robert J. Walker	1845–1849
Secretary of War	William L. Marcy	1845–1849
Attorney General	John Y. Mason	1845–1846
	Nathan Clifford	1846–1848
	Isaac Toucey	1848–1849
Postmaster General	Cave Johnson	1845–1849
Secretary of Navy	George Bancroft	1845–1846
	John Y. Mason	1846–1849

The Taylor Administration (1849–1850)

Vice President	Millard Fillmore	1849–1850
Secretary of State	John M. Clayton	1849–1850
Secretary of Treasury	William Meredith	1849–1850
Secretary of War	George Crawford	1849–1850
Attorney General	Reverdy Johnson	1849–1850
Postmaster General	Jacob Collamer	1849–1850
Secretary of Navy	William Preston	1849–1850
Secretary of Interior	Thomas Ewing	1849–1850

The Fillmore Administration (1850–1853)

Vice President	None	
Secretary of State	Daniel Webster	1850–1852
	Edward Everett	1852–1853
Secretary of Treasury	Thomas Corwin	1850–1853
Secretary of War	Charles Conrad	1850–1853
Attorney General	John J. Crittenden	1850–1853
Postmaster General	Nathan Hall	1850–1852
	Sam D. Hubbard	1852–1853

Secretary of Navy	William A. Graham	1850–1852
	John P. Kennedy	1852–1853
Secretary of Interior	Thomas McKennan	1850
	Alexander Stuart	1850–1853

The Pierce Administration (1853–1857)

Vice President	William R. King	1853–1857
Secretary of State	William L. Marcy	1853–1857
Secretary of Treasury	James Guthrie	1853–1857
Secretary of War	Jefferson Davis	1853–1857
Attorney General	Caleb Cushing	1853–1857
Postmaster General	James Campbell	1853–1857
Secretary of Navy	James C. Dobbin	1853–1857
Secretary of Interior	Robert McClelland	1853–1857

The Buchanan Administration (1857–1861)

Vice President	John C. Breckinridge	1857–1861
Secretary of State	Lewis Cass	1857–1860
	Jeremiah S. Black	1860–1861
Secretary of Treasury	Howell Cobb	1857–1860
	Philip Thomas	1860–1861
	John A. Dix	1861
Secretary of War	John B. Floyd	1857–1861
	Joseph Holt	1861
Attorney General	Jeremiah S. Black	1857–1860
	Edwin M. Stanton	1860–1861
Postmaster General	Aaron V. Brown	1857–1859
	Joseph Holt	1859–1861
	Horatio King	1861
Secretary of Navy	Isaac Toucey	1857–1861
Secretary of Interior	Jacob Thompson	1857–1861

The Lincoln Administration (1861–1865)

Vice President	Hannibal Hamlin	1861–1865
	Andrew Johnson	1865
Secretary of State	William H. Seward	1861–1865
Secretary of Treasury	Samuel P. Chase	1861–1864
	William P. Fessenden	1864–1865
	Hugh McCulloch	1865
Secretary of War	Simon Cameron	1861–1862
	Edwin M. Stanton	1862–1865
Attorney General	Edward Bates	1861–1864
	James Speed	1864–1865
Postmaster General	Horatio King	1861
	Montgomery Blair	1861–1864
	William Dennison	1864–1865
Secretary of Navy	Gideon Welles	1861–1865
Secretary of Interior	Caleb B. Smith	1861–1863
	John P. Usher	1863–1865

The Andrew Johnson Administration (1865–1869)

Vice President	None	
Secretary of State	William H. Seward	1865–1869
Secretary of Treasury	Hugh McCulloch	1865–1869
Secretary of War	Edwin M. Stanton	1865–1867
	Ulysses S. Grant	1867–1868
	Lorenzo Thomas	1868
	John M. Schofield	1868–1869
Attorney General	James Speed	1865–1866
	Henry Stanbery	1866–1868
	William M. Evarts	1868–1869
Postmaster General	William Dennison	1865–1866
	Alexander Randall	1866–1869
Secretary of Navy	Gideon Welles	1865–1869
Secretary of Interior	John P. Usher	1865
	James Harlan	1865–1866
	Orville H. Browning	1866–1869

The Grant Administration (1869–1877)

Vice President	Schuyler Colfax	1869–1873
	Henry Wilson	1873–1877
Secretary of State	Elihu B. Washburne	1869
	Hamilton Fish	1869–1877
Secretary of Treasury	George S. Boutwell	1869–1873
	William Richardson	1873–1874
	Benjamin Bristow	1874–1876
	Lot M. Morrill	1876–1877
Secretary of War	John A. Rawlins	1869
	William T. Sherman	1869
	William W. Belknap	1869–1876
	Alphonso Taft	1876
	James D. Cameron	1876–1877
Attorney General	Ebenezer Hoar	1869–1870
	Amos T. Ackerman	1870–1871
	G. H. Williams	1871–1875
	Edwards Pierrepont	1875–1876
	Alphonso Taft	1876–1877
Postmaster General	John A. J. Creswell	1869–1874
	James W. Marshall	1874
	Marshall Jewell	1874–1876
	James N. Tyner	1876–1877
Secretary of Navy	Adolph E. Borie	1869
	George M. Robeson	1869–1877
Secretary of Interior	Jacob D. Cox	1869–1870
	Columbus Delano	1870–1875
	Zachariah Chandler	1875–1877

The Hayes Administration (1877–1881)

Vice President	William A. Wheeler	1877–1881
Secretary of State	William M. Evarts	1877–1881
Secretary of Treasury	John Sherman	1877–1881

Secretary of War	George W. McCrary	1877–1879
	Alex Ramsey	1879–1881
Attorney General	Charles Devens	1877–1881
Postmaster General	David M. Key	1877–1880
	Horace Maynard	1880–1881
Secretary of Navy	Richard W. Thompson	1877–1880
	Nathan Goff Jr.	1881
Secretary of Interior	Carl Schurz	1877–1881

The Garfield Administration (1881)

Vice President	Chester A. Arthur	1881
Secretary of State	James G. Blaine	1881
Secretary of Treasury	William Windom	1881
Secretary of War	Robert T. Lincoln	1881
Attorney General	Wayne MacVeagh	1881
Postmaster General	Thomas L. James	1881
Secretary of Navy	William H. Hunt	1881
Secretary of Interior	Samuel J. Kirkwood	1881

The Arthur Administration (1881–1885)

Vice President	None	
Secretary of State	F. T. Frelinghuysen	1881–1885
Secretary of Treasury	Charles J. Folger	1881–1884
	Walter Q. Gresham	1884
	Hugh McCulloch	1884–1885
Secretary of War	Robert T. Lincoln	1881–1885
Attorney General	Benjamin H. Brewster	1881–1885
Postmaster General	Timothy O. Howe	1881–1883
	Walter Q. Gresham	1883–1884
	Frank Hatton	1884–1885
Secretary of Navy	William H. Hunt	1881–1882
	William E. Chandler	1882–1885
Secretary of Interior	Samuel J. Kirkwood	1881–1882
	Henry M. Teller	1882–1885

The Cleveland Administration (1885–1889)

Vice President	Thomas A. Hendricks	1885–1889
Secretary of State	Thomas F. Bayard	1885–1889
Secretary of Treasury	Daniel Manning	1885–1887
	Charles S. Fairchild	1887–1889
Secretary of War	William C. Endicott	1885–1889
Attorney General	Augustus H. Garland	1885–1889
Postmaster General	William F. Vilas	1885–1888
	Don M. Dickinson	1888–1889
Secretary of Navy	William C. Whitney	1885–1889
Secretary of Interior	Lucius Q. C. Lamar	1885–1888
	William F. Vilas	1888–1889
Secretary of Agriculture	Norman J. Colman	1889

The Benjamin Harrison Administration (1889–1893)

Vice President	Levi P. Morton	1889–1893
Secretary of State	James G. Blaine	1889–1892
	John W. Foster	1892–1893
Secretary of Treasury	William Windom	1889–1891
	Charles Foster	1891–1893
Secretary of War	Redfield Proctor	1889–1891
	Stephen B. Elkins	1891–1893
Attorney General	William H. H. Miller	1889–1893
Postmaster General	John Wanamaker	1889–1893
Secretary of Navy	Benjamin F. Tracy	1889–1893
Secretary of Interior	John W. Noble	1889–1893
Secretary of Agriculture	Jeremiah M. Rusk	1889–1893

The Cleveland Administration (1893–1897)

Vice President	Adlai E. Stevenson	1893–1897
Secretary of State	Walter Q. Gresham	1893–1895
	Richard Olney	1895–1897
Secretary of Treasury	John G. Carlisle	1893–1897
Secretary of War	Daniel S. Lamont	1893–1897
Attorney General	Richard Olney	1893–1895
	James Harmon	1895–1897
Postmaster General	Wilson S. Bissell	1893–1895
	William L. Wilson	1895–1897
Secretary of Navy	Hilary A. Herbert	1893–1897
Secretary of Interior	Hoke Smith	1893–1896
	David R. Francis	1896–1897
Secretary of Agriculture	Julius S. Morton	1893–1897

The McKinley Administration (1897–1901)

Vice President	Garret A. Hobart	1897–1901
	Theodore Roosevelt	1901
Secretary of State	John Sherman	1897–1898
	William R. Day	1898
	John Hay	1898–1901
Secretary of Treasury	Lyman J. Gage	1897–1901
Secretary of War	Russell A. Alger	1897–1899
	Elihu Root	1899–1901
Attorney General	Joseph McKenna	1897–1898
	John W. Griggs	1898–1901
	Philander C. Knox	1901
Postmaster General	James A. Gary	1897–1898
	Charles E. Smith	1898–1901
Secretary of Navy	John D. Long	1897–1901
Secretary of Interior	Cornelius N. Bliss	1897–1899
	Ethan A. Hitchcock	1899–1901
Secretary of Agriculture	James Wilson	1897–1901

The Theodore Roosevelt Administration (1901–1909)

Vice President	Charles Fairbanks	1905–1909
Secretary of State	John Hay	1901–1905
	Elihu Root	1905–1909
	Robert Bacon	1909
Secretary of Treasury	Lyman J. Gage	1901–1902
	Leslie M. Shaw	1902–1907

Position	Name	Term
	George B. Cortelyou	1907–1909
Secretary of War	Elihu Root	1901–1904
	William H. Taft	1904–1908
	Luke E. Wright	1908–1909
Attorney General	Philander C. Knox	1901–1904
	William H. Moody	1904–1906
	Charles J. Bonaparte	1906–1909
Postmaster General	Charles E. Smith	1901–1902
	Henry C. Payne	1902–1904
	Robert J. Wynne	1904–1905
	George B. Cortelyou	1905–1907
	George von L. Meyer	1907–1909
Secretary of Navy	John D. Long	1901–1902
	William H. Moody	1902–1904
	Paul Morton	1904–1905
	Charles J. Bonaparte	1905–1906
	Victor H. Metcalf	1906–1908
	Truman H. Newberry	1908–1909
Secretary of Interior	Ethan A. Hitchcock	1901–1907
	James R. Garfield	1907–1909
Secretary of Agriculture	James Wilson	1901–1909
Secretary of Labor and Commerce	George B. Cortelyou	1903–1904
	Victor H. Metcalf	1904–1906
	Oscar S. Straus	1906–1909
	Charles Nagel	1909

The Taft Administration (1909–1913)

Position	Name	Term
Vice President	James S. Sherman	1909–1913
Secretary of State	Philander C. Knox	1909–1913
Secretary of Treasury	Franklin MacVeagh	1909–1913
Secretary of War	Jacob M. Dickinson	1909–1911
	Henry L. Stimson	1911–1913
Attorney General	George W. Wickersham	1909–1913
Postmaster General	Frank H. Hitchcock	1909–1913
Secretary of Navy	George von L. Meyer	1909–1913
Secretary of Interior	Richard A. Ballinger	1909–1911
	Walter L. Fisher	1911–1913
Secretary of Agriculture	James Wilson	1909–1913
Secretary of Labor and Commerce	Charles Nagel	1909–1913

The Wilson Administration (1913–1921)

Position	Name	Term
Vice President	Thomas R. Marshall	1913–1921
Secretary of State	William J. Bryan	1913–1915
	Robert Lansing	1915–1920
	Bainbridge Colby	1920–1921
Secretary of Treasury	William G. McAdoo	1913–1918
	Carter Glass	1918–1920
	David F. Houston	1920–1921
Secretary of War	Lindley M. Garrison	1913–1916
	Newton D. Baker	1916–1921
Attorney General	James C. McReynolds	1913–1914
	Thomas W. Gregory	1914–1919
	A. Mitchell Palmer	1919–1921
Postmaster General	Albert S. Burleson	1913–1921
Secretary of Navy	Josephus Daniels	1913–1921
Secretary of Interior	Franklin K. Lane	1913–1920
	John B. Payne	1920–1921
Secretary of Agriculture	David F. Houston	1913–1920
	Edwin T. Meredith	1920–1921
Secretary of Commerce	William C. Redfield	1913–1919
	Joshua W. Alexander	1919–1921
Secretary of Labor	William B. Wilson	1913–1921

The Harding Administration (1921–1923)

Position	Name	Term
Vice President	Calvin Coolidge	1921–1923
Secretary of State	Charles E. Hughes	1921–1923
Secretary of Treasury	Andrew Mellon	1921–1923
Secretary of War	John W. Weeks	1921–1923
Attorney General	Harry M. Daugherty	1921–1923
Postmaster General	Will H. Hays	1921–1922
	Hubert Work	1922–1923
	Harry S. New	1923
Secretary of Navy	Edwin Denby	1921–1923
Secretary of Interior	Albert B. Fall	1921–1923
	Hubert Work	1923
Secretary of Agriculture	Henry C. Wallace	1921–1923
Secretary of Commerce	Herbert C. Hoover	1921–1923
Secretary of Labor	James J. Davis	1921–1923

The Coolidge Administration (1923–1929)

Position	Name	Term
Vice President	Charles G. Dawes	1925–1929
Secretary of State	Charles E. Hughes	1923–1925
	Frank B. Kellogg	1925–1929
Secretary of Treasury	Andrew Mellon	1923–1929
Secretary of War	John W. Weeks	1923–1925
	Dwight F. Davis	1925–1929
Attorney General	Henry M. Daugherty	1923–1924
	Harlan F. Stone	1924–1925
	John G. Sargent	1925–1929
Postmaster General	Harry S. New	1923–1929
Secretary of Navy	Edwin Derby	1923–1924
	Curtis D. Wilbur	1924–1929
Secretary of Interior	Hubert Work	1923–1928
	Roy O. West	1928–1929
Secretary of Agriculture	Henry C. Wallace	1923–1924
	Howard M. Gore	1924–1925
	William M. Jardine	1925–1929
Secretary of Commerce	Herbert C. Hoover	1923–1928
	William F. Whiting	1928–1929
Secretary of Labor	James J. Davis	1923–1929

The Hoover Administration (1929–1933)

Vice President	Charles Curtis	1929–1933
Secretary of State	Henry L. Stimson	1929–1933
Secretary of Treasury	Andrew Mellon	1929–1932
	Ogden L. Mills	1932–1933
Secretary of War	James W. Good	1929
	Patrick J. Hurley	1929–1933
Attorney General	William D. Mitchell	1929–1933
Postmaster General	Walter F. Brown	1929–1933
Secretary of Navy	Charles F. Adams	1929–1933
Secretary of Interior	Ray L. Wilbur	1929–1933
Secretary of Agriculture	Arthur M. Hyde	1929–1933
Secretary of Commerce	Robert P. Lamont	1929–1932
	Roy D. Chapin	1932–1933
Secretary of Labor	James J. Davis	1929–1930
	William N. Doak	1930–1933

The Franklin D. Roosevelt Administration (1933–1945)

Vice President	John Nance Garner	1933–1941
	Henry A. Wallace	1941–1945
	Harry S Truman	1945
Secretary of State	Cordell Hull	1933–1944
	Edward R. Stettinius Jr.	1944–1945
Secretary of Treasury	William H. Woodin	1933–1934
	Henry Morgenthau Jr.	1934–1945
Secretary of War	George H. Dern	1933–1936
	Henry A. Woodring	1936–1940
	Henry L. Stimson	1940–1945
Attorney General	Homer S. Cummings	1933–1939
	Frank Murphy	1939–1940
	Robert H. Jackson	1940–1941
	Francis Biddle	1941–1945
Postmaster General	James A. Farley	1933–1940
	Frank C. Walker	1940–1945
Secretary of Navy	Claude A. Swanson	1933–1940
	Charles Edison	1940
	Frank Knox	1940–1944
	James V. Forrestal	1944–1945
Secretary of Interior	Harold L. Ickes	1933–1945
Secretary of Agriculture	Henry A. Wallace	1933–1940
	Claude R. Wickard	1940–1945
Secretary of Commerce	Daniel C. Roper	1933–1939
	Harry L. Hopkins	1939–1940
	Jesse Jones	1940–1945
	Henry A. Wallace	1945
Secretary of Labor	Frances Perkins	1933–1945

The Truman Administration (1945–1953)

Vice President	Alben W. Barkley	1949–1953
Secretary of State	Edward R. Stettinius Jr.	1945
	James F. Byrnes	1945–1947
	George C. Marshall	1947–1949
	Dean G. Acheson	1949–1953
Secretary of Treasury	Fred M. Vinson	1945–1946
	John W. Snyder	1946–1953
Secretary of War	Robert P. Patterson	1945–1947
	Kenneth C. Royall	1947
Attorney General	Tom C. Clark	1945–1949
	J. Howard McGrath	1949–1952
	James P. McGranery	1952–1953
Postmaster General	Frank C. Walker	1945
	Robert E. Hannegan	1945–1947
	Jesse M. Donaldson	1947–1953
Secretary of Navy	James V. Forrestal	1945–1947
Secretary of Interior	Harold L. Ickes	1945–1946
	Julius A. Krug	1946–1949
	Oscar L. Chapman	1949–1953
Secretary of Agriculture	Clinton P. Anderson	1945–1948
	Charles F. Brannan	1948–1953
Secretary of Commerce	Henry A. Wallace	1945–1946
	W. Averell Harriman	1946–1948
	Charles W. Sawyer	1948–1953
Secretary of Labor	Lewis B. Schwellenbach	1945–1948
	Maurice J. Tobin	1948–1953
Secretary of Defense	James V. Forrestal	1947–1949
	Louis A. Johnson	1949–1950
	George C. Marshall	1950–1951
	Robert A. Lovett	1951–1953

The Eisenhower Administration (1953–1961)

Vice President	Richard M. Nixon	1953–1961
Secretary of State	John Foster Dulles	1953–1959
	Christian A. Herter	1959–1961
Secretary of Treasury	George M. Humphrey	1953–1957
	Robert B. Anderson	1957–1961
Attorney General	Herbert Brownell Jr.	1953–1958
	William P. Rogers	1958–1961
Postmaster General	Arthur E. Summerfield	1953–1961
Secretary of Interior	Douglas McKay	1953–1956
	Fred A. Seaton	1956–1961
Secretary of Agriculture	Ezra T. Benson	1953–1961
Secretary of Commerce	Sinclair Weeks	1953–1958
	Lewis L. Strauss	1958–1959
	Frederick H. Mueller	1959–1961
Secretary of Labor	Martin P. Durkin	1953
	James P. Mitchell	1953–1961
Secretary of Defense	Charles E. Wilson	1953–1957
	Neil H. McElroy	1957–1959
	Thomas S. Gates Jr.	1959–1961
Secretary of Health, Education, and Welfare	Oveta Culp Hobby	1953–1955
	Marion B. Folsom	1955–1958
	Arthur S. Flemming	1958–1961

The Kennedy Administration (1961–1963)

Vice President	Lyndon B. Johnson	1961–1963
Secretary of State	Dean Rusk	1961–1963
Secretary of Treasury	C. Douglas Dillon	1961–1963
Attorney General	Robert F. Kennedy	1961–1963
Postmaster General	J. Edward Day	1961–1963
	John A. Gronouski	1963
Secretary of Interior	Stewart L. Udall	1961–1963
Secretary of Agriculture	Orville L. Freeman	1961–1963
Secretary of Commerce	Luther H. Hodges	1961–1963
Secretary of Labor	Arthur J. Goldberg	1961–1962
	W. Willard Wirtz	1962–1963
Secretary of Defense	Robert S. McNamara	1961–1963
Secretary of Health, Education, and Welfare	Abraham A. Ribicoff	1961–1962
	Anthony J. Celebrezze	1962–1963

The Lyndon Johnson Administration (1963–1969)

Vice President	Hubert H. Humphrey	1965–1969
Secretary of State	Dean Rusk	1963–1969
Secretary of Treasury	C. Douglas Dillon	1963–1965
	Henry H. Fowler	1965–1969
Attorney General	Robert F. Kennedy	1963–1964
	Nicholas Katzenbach	1965–1966
	Ramsey Clark	1967–1969
Postmaster General	John A. Gronouski	1963–1965
	Lawrence F. O'Brien	1965–1968
	Marvin Watson	1968–1969
Secretary of Interior	Stewart L. Udall	1963–1969
Secretary of Agriculture	Orville L. Freeman	1963–1969
Secretary of Commerce	Luther H. Hodges	1963–1964
	John T. Connor	1964–1967
	Alexander B. Trowbridge	1967–1968
	Cyrus R. Smith	1968–1969
Secretary of Labor	W. Willard Wirtz	1963–1969
Secretary of Defense	Robert F. McNamara	1963–1968
	Clark Clifford	1968–1969
Secretary of Health, Education, and Welfare	Anthony J. Celebrezze	1963–1965
	John W. Gardner	1965–1968
	Wilbur J. Cohen	1968–1969
Secretary of Housing and Urban Development	Robert C. Weaver	1966–1969
	Robert C. Wood	1969
Secretary of Transportation	Alan S. Boyd	1967–1969

The Nixon Administration (1969–1974)

Vice President	Spiro T. Agnew	1969–1973
	Gerald R. Ford	1973–1974
Secretary of State	William P. Rogers	1969–1973
	Henry A. Kissinger	1973–1974
Secretary of Treasury	David M. Kennedy	1969–1970
	John B. Connally	1971–1972
	George P. Shultz	1972–1974
	William E. Simon	1974
Attorney General	John N. Mitchell	1969–1972
	Richard G. Kleindienst	1972–1973
	Elliot L. Richardson	1973
	William B. Saxbe	1973–1974
Postmaster General	Winton M. Blount	1969–1971
Secretary of Interior	Walter J. Hickel	1969–1970
	Rogers Morton	1971–1974
Secretary of Agriculture	Clifford M. Hardin	1969–1971
	Earl L. Butz	1971–1974
Secretary of Commerce	Maurice H. Stans	1969–1972
	Peter G. Peterson	1972–1973
	Frederick B. Dent	1973–1974
Secretary of Labor	George P. Shultz	1969–1970
	James D. Hodgson	1970–1973
	Peter J. Brennan	1973–1974
Secretary of Defense	Melvin R. Laird	1969–1973
	Elliot L. Richardson	1973
	James R. Schlesinger	1973–1974
Secretary of Health, Education, and Welfare	Robert H. Finch	1969–1970
	Elliot L. Richardson	1970–1973
	Caspar W. Weinberger	1973–1974
Secretary of Housing and Urban Development	George Romney	1969–1973
	James T. Lynn	1973–1974
Secretary of Transportation	John A. Volpe	1969–1973
	Claude S. Brinegar	1973–1974

The Ford Administration (1974–1977)

Vice President	Nelson A. Rockefeller	1974–1977
Secretary of State	Henry A. Kissinger	1974–1977
Secretary of Treasury	William E. Simon	1974–1977
Attorney General	William Saxbe	1974–1975
	Edward Levi	1975–1977
Secretary of Interior	Rogers Morton	1974–1975
	Stanley K. Hathaway	1975
	Thomas Kleppe	1975–1977
Secretary of Agriculture	Earl L. Butz	1974–1976
	John A. Knebel	1976–1977
Secretary of Commerce	Frederick B. Dent	1975–1976
	Rogers Morton	1975–1976
	Elliot L. Richardson	1976–1977
Secretary of Labor	Peter J. Brennan	1974–1975
	John T. Dunlop	1975–1976
	W. J. Usery	1976–1977
Secretary of Defense	James R. Schlesinger	1974–1975
	Donald Rumsfeld	1975–1977

Secretary of Health, Education, and Welfare	Caspar Weinberger	1974–1975
	Forrest D. Mathews	1975–1977
Secretary of Housing and Urban Development	James T. Lynn	1974–1975
	Carla A. Hills	1975–1977
Secretary of Transportation	Claude Brinegar	1974–1975
	William T. Coleman	1975–1977

The Carter Administration (1977–1981)

Vice President	Walter F. Mondale	1977–1981
Secretary of State	Cyrus R. Vance	1977–1980
	Edmund Muskie	1980–1981
Secretary of Treasury	W. Michael Blumenthal	1977–1979
	G. William Miller	1979–1981
Attorney General	Griffin Bell	1977–1979
	Benjamin R. Civiletti	1979–1981
Secretary of Interior	Cecil D. Andrus	1977–1981
Secretary of Agriculture	Robert Bergland	1977–1981
Secretary of Commerce	Juanita M. Kreps	1977–1979
	Philip M. Klutznick	1979–1981
Secretary of Labor	F. Ray Marshall	1977–1981
Secretary of Defense	Harold Brown	1977–1981
Secretary of Health, Education, and Welfare	Joseph A. Califano	1977–1979
	Patricia R. Harris	1979
Secretary of Health and Human Services	Patricia R. Harris	1979–1981
Secretary of Education	Shirley M. Hufstedler	1979–1981
Secretary of Housing and Urban Development	Patricia R. Harris	1977–1979
	Moon Landrieu	1979–1981
Secretary of Transportation	Brock Adams	1977–1979
	Neil E. Goldschmidt	1979–1981
Secretary of Energy	James R. Schlesinger	1977–1979
	Charles W. Duncan	1979–1981

The Reagan Administration (1981–1989)

Vice President	George Bush	1981–1989
Secretary of State	Alexander M. Haig	1981–1982
	George P. Shultz	1982–1989
Secretary of Treasury	Donald Regan	1981–1985
	James A. Baker III	1985–1988
	Nicholas Brady	1988–1989
Attorney General	William F. Smith	1981–1985
	Edwin A. Meese III	1985–1988
	Richard Thornburgh	1988–1989
Secretary of Interior	James Watt	1981–1983
	William P. Clark Jr.	1983–1985
	Donald P. Hodel	1985–1989
Secretary of Agriculture	John Block	1981–1986
	Richard E. Lyng	1986–1989
Secretary of Commerce	Malcolm Baldrige	1981–1987
	C. William Verity Jr.	1987–1989

Secretary of Labor	Raymond Donovan	1981–1985
	William E. Brock	1985–1987
	Ann D. McLaughlin	1987–1989
Secretary of Defense	Caspar Weinberger	1981–1987
	Frank Carlucci	1987–1989
Secretary of Health and Human Services	Richard Schweiker	1981–1983
	Margaret Heckler	1983–1985
	Otis R. Bowen	1985–1989
Secretary of Education	Terrel H. Bell	1981–1985
	William J. Bennett	1985–1988
	Lauro F. Cavazos	1988–1989
Secretary of Housing and Urban Development	Samuel Pierce	1981–1989
Secretary of Transportation	Drew Lewis	1981–1983
	Elizabeth Dole	1983–1987
	James H. Burnley	1987–1989
Secretary of Energy	James Edwards	1981–1982
	Donald P. Hodel	1982–1985
	John S. Herrington	1985–1989

The George H. W. Bush Administration (1989–1993)

Vice President	J. Danforth Quayle	1989–1993
Secretary of State	James A. Baker III	1989–1992
Secretary of Treasury	Nicholas Brady	1989–1993
Attorney General	Richard Thornburgh	1989–1991
	William P. Barr	1991–1993
Secretary of Interior	Manuel Lujan	1989–1993
Secretary of Agriculture	Clayton K. Yeutter	1989–1991
	Edward Madigan	1991–1993
Secretary of Commerce	Robert Mosbacher	1989–1992
	Barbara Franklin	1992–1993
Secretary of Labor	Elizabeth Dole	1989–1991
	Lynn Martin	1991–1993
Secretary of Defense	Richard Cheney	1989–1993
Secretary of Health and Human Services	Louis W. Sullivan	1989–1993
Secretary of Education	Lauro F. Cavazos	1989–1991
	Lamar Alexander	1991–1993
Secretary of Housing and Urban Development	Jack F. Kemp	1989–1993
Secretary of Transportation	Samuel K. Skinner	1989–1992
	Andrew H. Card Jr.	1992–1993
Secretary of Energy	James D. Watkins	1989–1993
Secretary of Veterans Affairs	Edward J. Derwinski	1989–1993

The Clinton Administration (1993–2001)

Vice President	Albert Gore	1993–2001
Secretary of State	Warren Christopher	1993–1997
	Madeleine Albright	1997–2001
Secretary of Treasury	Lloyd Bentsen	1993–1995
	Robert E. Rubin	1995–1999

	Lawrence H. Summers	1999–2001
Attorney General	Janet Reno	1993–2001
Secretary of Interior	Bruce Babbitt	1993–2001
Secretary of Agriculture	Michael Espy	1993–1995
	Dan Glickman	1995–2001
Secretary of Commerce	Ronald Brown	1993–1996
	Mickey Kantor	1996
	William Daley	1997
	Norman Mineta	1997–2001
Secretary of Labor	Robert B. Reich	1993–1997
	Alexis Herman	1997–2001
Secretary of Defense	Les Aspin	1993–1994
	William J. Perry	1994–1997
	William Cohen	1997–2001
Secretary of Health and Human Services	Donna Shalala	1993–2001
Secretary of Housing and Urban Development	Henry G. Cisneros	1993–1997
	Andrew Cuomo	1997–2001
Secretary of Education	Richard W. Riley	1993–2001
Secretary of Transportation	Federico Peña	1993–1997
	Rodney Slater	1997–2001
Secretary of Energy	Hazel R. O'Leary	1993–1997
	Federico Peña	1997
	Bill Richardson	1998–2001
Secretary of Veterans Affairs	Jesse Brown	1993–1998
	Togo D. West Jr.	1998–2001

The George W. Bush Administration (2001–)

Vice President	Richard B. Cheney	2001–
Secretary of State	Colin Powell	2001–2005
	Condoleezza Rice	2005–
Secretary of Treasury	Paul H. O'Neill	2001–2002
	John Snow	2003–2006
	Henry M. Paulson, Jr.,	2006–
Attorney General	John Ashcroft	2001–2005
	Alberto Gonzales	2005–2007
Secretary of Interior	Gale Norton	2001–2006
	Dirk Kempthorne	2006–
Secretary of Agriculture	Ann M. Veneman	2001–2005
	Mike Johanns	2005–
Secretary of Commerce	Don Evans	2001–2005
	Carlos Gutierrez	2005–
Secretary of Labor	Elaine Chao	2001–
Secretary of Defense	Donald Rumsfeld	2001–2006
	Robert M. Gates	2006–
Secretary of Health and Human Services	Tommy G. Thompson	2001–2005
	Michael O. Leavitt	2005–
Secretary of Housing and Urban Development	Melquiades Rafael Martinez	2001–2004
	Alphonso Jackson	2004–
Secretary of Education	Roderick Paige	2001-2005
	Margaret Spellings	2005–
Secretary of Transportation	Norman Y. Mineta	2001–2006
	Mary E. Peters	2006–
Secretary of Energy	Spencer Abraham	2001–2005
	Samuel W. Bodman	2005–
Secretary of Veterans Affairs	Anthony J. Principi	2001–2005
	Jim Nicholson	2005–
Secretary of Homeland Security	Tom Ridge	2001–2005
	Michael Chertoff	2005–

Justices of the Supreme Court

	Term of Service	Years of Service	Life Span
John Jay	1789–1795	5	1745–1829
John Rutledge	1789–1791	1	1739–1800
William Cushing	1789–1810	20	1732–1810
James Wilson	1789–1798	8	1742–1798
John Blair	1789–1796	6	1732–1800
Robert H. Harrison	1789–1790	–	1745–1790
James Iredell	1790–1799	9	1751–1799
Thomas Johnson	1791–1793	1	1732–1819
William Paterson	1793–1806	13	1745–1806
John Rutledge*	1795	–	1739–1800
Samuel Chase	1796–1811	15	1741–1811
Oliver Ellsworth	1796–1800	4	1745–1807
Bushrod Washington	1798–1829	31	1762–1829
Alfred Moore	1799–1804	4	1755–1810
John Marshall	1801–1835	34	1755–1835
William Johnson	1804–1834	30	1771–1834
H. Brockholst Livingston	1806–1823	16	1757–1823
Thomas Todd	1807–1826	18	1765–1826
Joseph Story	1811–1845	33	1779–1845
Gabriel Duval	1811–1835	24	1752–1844
Smith Thompson	1823–1843	20	1768–1843
Robert Trimble	1826–1828	2	1777–1828
John McLean	1829–1861	32	1785–1861
Henry Baldwin	1830–1844	14	1780–1844
James M. Wayne	1835–1867	32	1790–1867
Roger B. Taney	1836–1864	28	1777–1864
Philip P. Barbour	1836–1841	4	1783–1841
John Catron	1837–1865	28	1786–1865
John McKinley	1837–1852	15	1780–1852
Peter V. Daniel	1841–1860	19	1784–1860
Samuel Nelson	1845–1872	27	1792–1873
Levi Woodbury	1845–1851	5	1789–1851
Robert C. Grier	1846–1870	23	1794–1870
Benjamin R. Curtis	1851–1857	6	1809–1874
John A. Campbell	1853–1861	8	1811–1889
Nathan Clifford	1858–1881	23	1803–1881
Noah H. Swayne	1862–1881	18	1804–1884
Samuel F. Miller	1862–1890	28	1816–1890
David Davis	1862–1877	14	1815–1886

*Appointed and served one term, but not confirmed by the Senate.

Note: Chief justices are in italics

	Term of Service	Years of Service	Life Span
Stephen J. Field	1863–1897	34	1816–1899
Salmon P. Chase	1864–1873	8	1808–1873
William Strong	1870–1880	10	1808–1895
Joseph P. Bradley	1870–1892	22	1813–1892
Ward Hunt	1873–1882	9	1810–1886
Morrison R. Waite	1874–1888	14	1816–1888
John M. Harlan	1877–1911	34	1833–1911
William B. Woods	1880–1887	7	1824–1887
Stanley Matthews	1881–1889	7	1824–1889
Horace Gray	1882–1902	20	1828–1902
Samuel Blatchford	1882–1893	11	1820–1893
Lucius Q. C. Lamar	1888–1893	5	1825–1893
Melville W. Fuller	1888–1910	21	1833–1910
David J. Brewer	1890–1910	20	1837–1910
Henry B. Brown	1890–1906	16	1836–1913
George Shiras Jr.	1892–1903	10	1832–1924
Howell E. Jackson	1893–1895	2	1832–1895
Edward D. White	1894–1910	16	1845–1921
Rufus W. Peckham	1895–1909	14	1838–1909
Joseph McKenna	1898–1925	26	1843–1926
Oliver W. Holmes	1902–1932	30	1841–1935
William R. Day	1903–1922	19	1849–1923
William H. Moody	1906–1910	3	1853–1917
Horace H. Lurton	1909–1914	4	1844–1914
Charles E. Hughes	1910–1916	5	1862–1948
Edward D. White	1910–1921	11	1845–1921
Willis Van Devanter	1911–1937	26	1859–1941
Joseph R. Lamar	1911–1916	5	1857–1916
Mahlon Pitney	1912–1922	10	1858–1924
James C. McReynolds	1914–1941	26	1862–1946
Louis D. Brandeis	1916–1939	22	1856–1941
John H. Clarke	1916–1922	6	1857–1945
William H. Taft	1921–1930	8	1857–1930
George Sutherland	1922–1938	15	1862–1942
Pierce Butler	1922–1939	16	1866–1939
Edward T. Sanford	1923–1930	7	1865–1930
Harlan F. Stone	1925–1941	16	1872–1946
Charles E. Hughes	1930–1941	11	1862–1948
Owen J. Roberts	1930–1945	15	1875–1955
Benjamin N. Cardozo	1932–1938	6	1870–1938
Hugo L. Black	1937–1971	34	1886–1971
Stanley F. Reed	1938–1957	19	1884–1980
Felix Frankfurter	1939–1962	23	1882–1965

	Term of Service	Years of Service	Life Span
William O. Douglas	1939–1975	36	1898–1980
Frank Murphy	1940–1949	9	1890–1949
Harlan F. Stone	1941–1946	5	1872–1946
James F. Byrnes	1941–1942	1	1879–1972
Robert H. Jackson	1941–1954	13	1892–1954
Wiley B. Rutledge	1943–1949	6	1894–1949
Harold H. Burton	1945–1958	13	1888–1964
Fred M. Vinson	1946–1953	7	1890–1953
Tom C. Clark	1949–1967	18	1899–1977
Sherman Minton	1949–1956	7	1890–1965
Earl Warren	1953–1969	16	1891–1974
John Marshall Harlan	1955–1971	16	1899–1971
William J. Brennan Jr.	1956–1990	33	1906–1997
Charles E. Whittaker	1957–1962	5	1901–1973
Potter Stewart	1958–1981	23	1915–1985
Bryon R. White	1962–1993	31	1917–2002
Arthur J. Goldberg	1962–1965	3	1908–1990

	Term of Service	Years of Service	Life Span
Abe Fortas	1965–1969	4	1910–1982
Thurgood Marshall	1967–1991	24	1908–1992
Warren C. Burger	1969–1986	17	1907–1995
Harry A. Blackmun	1970–1994	24	1908–1999
Lewis F. Powell Jr.	1972–1987	15	1907–1998
William H. Rehnquist	1972–1986	14	1924–
John P. Stevens III	1975–	–	1920–
Sandra Day O'Connor	1981–2006	24	1930–
William H. Rehnquist	1986–2005	18	1924–2005
Antonin Scalia	1986–	–	1936–
Anthony M. Kennedy	1988–	–	1936–
David H. Souter	1990–	–	1939–
Clarence Thomas	1991–	–	1948–
Ruth Bader Ginsburg	1993–	–	1933–
Stephen Breyer	1994–	–	1938–
John G. Roberts, Jr,	2005–	–	1955–
Samuel A. Alito, Jr.	2006–	–	1950–

A Social Profile of the American Republic

Year	Population	Percent Increase	Population per Square Mile	Population Percent Urban/ Rural	Percent Male/ Female	Percent White/ Nonwhite	Persons per Household	Median Age
1790	3,929,214		4.5	5.1/94.9	NA/NA	80.7/19.3	5.79	NA
1800	5,308,483	35.1	6.1	6.1/93.9	NA/NA	81.1/18.9	NA	NA
1810	7,239,881	36.4	4.3	7.3/92.7	NA/NA	81.0/19.0	NA	NA
1820	9,638,453	33.1	5.5	7.2/92.8	50.8/49.2	81.6/18.4	NA	16.7
1830	12,866,020	33.5	7.4	8.8/91.2	50.8/49.2	81.9/18.1	NA	17.2
1840	17,069,453	32.7	9.8	10.8/89.2	50.9/49.1	83.2/16.8	NA	17.8
1850	23,191,876	35.9	7.9	15.3/84.7	51.0/49.0	84.3/15.7	5.55	18.9
1860	31,443,321	35.6	10.6	19.8/80.2	51.2/48.8	85.6/14.4	5.28	19.4
1870	39,818,449	26.6	13.4	25.7/74.3	50.6/49.4	86.2/13.8	5.09	20.2
1880	50,155,783	26.0	16.9	28.2/71.8	50.9/49.1	86.5/13.5	5.04	20.9
1890	62,947,714	25.5	21.2	35.1/64.9	51.2/48.8	87.5/12.5	4.93	22.0
1900	75,994,575	20.7	25.6	39.6/60.4	51.1/48.9	87.9/12.1	4.76	22.9
1910	91,972,266	21.0	31.0	45.6/54.4	51.5/48.5	88.9/11.1	4.54	24.1
1920	105,710,620	14.9	35.6	51.2/48.8	51.0/49.0	89.7/10.3	4.34	25.3
1930	122,775,046	16.1	41.2	56.1/43.9	50.6/49.4	89.8/10.2	4.11	26.4
1940	131,669,275	7.2	44.2	56.5/43.5	50.2/49.8	89.8/10.2	3.67	29.0
1950	150,697,361	14.5	50.7	64.0/36.0	49.7/50.3	89.5/10.5	3.37	30.2
1960	179,323,175	18.5	50.6	69.9/30.1	49.3/50.7	88.6/11.4	3.33	29.5
1970	203,302,031	13.4	57.4	73.5/26.5	48.7/51.3	87.6/12.4	3.14	28.0
1980	226,545,805	11.4	64.0	73.7/26.3	48.6/51.4	86.0/14.0	2.76	30.0
1990	248,709,873	9.8	70.3	75.2/24.8	48.7/51.3	80.3/19.7	2.63	32.9
2000	281,422,426	13.1	79.6	79.0/21.0	49.0/51.0	81.0/19.0	2.59	35.4

NA = Not available.

Vital Statistics (rates per thousand)						
Year	Births	Year	Births	Deaths*	Marriages*	Divorces*
1800	55.0	1900	32.3	17.2	NA	NA
1810	54.3	1910	30.1	14.7	NA	NA
1820	55.2	1920	27.7	13.0	12.0	1.6
1830	51.4	1930	21.3	11.3	9.2	1.6
1840	51.8	1940	19.4	10.8	12.1	2.0
1850	43.3	1950	24.1	9.6	11.1	2.6
1860	44.3	1960	23.7	9.5	8.5	2.2
1870	38.3	1970	18.4	9.5	10.6	3.5
1880	39.8	1980	15.9	8.8	10.6	5.2
1890	31.5	1990	16.7	8.6	9.8	4.6
		2000	14.7	8.7	8.5	4.2

NA = Not available.
*Data not available before 1900.

Year	Total Population	Life Expectancy (in years)			
		White Females	Nonwhite Females	White Males	Nonwhite Males
1900	47.3	48.7	33.5	46.6	32.5
1910	50.1	52.0	37.5	48.6	33.8
1920	54.1	55.6	45.2	54.4	45.5
1930	59.7	63.5	49.2	59.7	47.3
1940	62.9	66.6	54.9	62.1	51.5
1950	68.2	72.2	62.9	66.5	59.1
1960	69.7	74.1	66.3	67.4	61.1
1970	70.9	75.6	69.4	68.0	61.3
1980	73.7	78.1	73.6	70.7	65.3
1990	75.4	79.3	76.3	72.6	68.4
2000	76.9	80.0	NA	74.8	NA

The Changing Age Structure

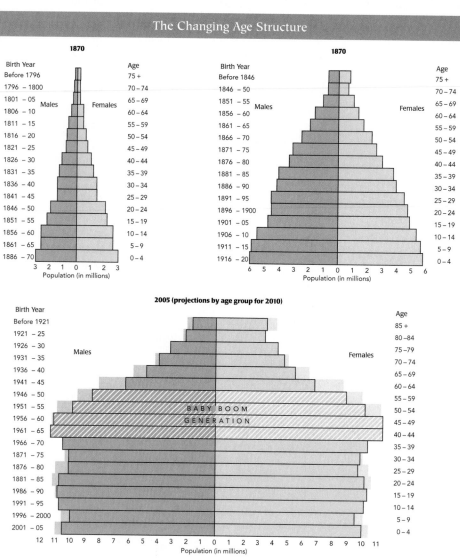

Before the twentieth century, the age distribution of Americans could be charted roughly as a pyramid, as seen in the figures for 1870 and 1920. High birthrates create a broad base at the bottom, while mortality rates winnow the population to a small tip of elderly. But by the year 2000, the pyramid has been transformed more nearly into a cylinder. Over the past two centuries fertility rates have undergone a steady decline, pulling in the base of the pyramid, while higher living standards have allowed Americans to live longer, broadening the top. Only the temporary bulge of the baby boom distorts the shape.

		Regional Origin of Immigrants (percent) EUROPE					
Years	Total Number of Immigrants	Total Europe	North and West	East and Central	South and Other	Western Hemisphere	Asia
1821–1830	143,389	69.2	67.1	–	2.1	8.4	–
1831–1840	599,125	82.8	81.8	–	1.0	5.5	–
1841–1850	1,713,251	93.8	92.9	0.1	0.3	3.6	–
1851–1860	2,598,214	94.4	93.6	0.1	0.8	2.9	1.6
1861–1870	2,314,824	89.2	87.8	0.5	0.9	7.2	2.8
1871–1880	2,812,191	80.8	73.6	4.5	2.7	14.4	4.4
1881–1890	5,246,13	90.3	72.0	11.9	6.3	8.1	1.3
1891–1900	3,687,546	96.5	44.5	32.8	19.1	1.1	1.9
1901–1910	8,795,386	92.5	21.7	44.5	6.3	4.1	2.8
1911–1920	5,735,811	76.3	17.4	33.4	25.5	19.9	3.4
1921–1930	4,107,209	60.3	31.7	14.4	14.3	36.9	2.4
1931–1940	528,431	65.9	38.8	11.0	16.1	30.3	2.8
1941–1950	1,035,039	60.1	47.5	4.6	7.9	34.3	3.1
1951–1960	2,515,479	52.8	17.7	24.3	10.8	39.6	6.0
1961–1970	3,321,677	33.8	11.7	9.4	12.9	51.7	12.9
1971–1980	4,493,300	17.8	4.3	5.6	8.4	44.3	35.2
1981–1990	7,338,000	10.4	5.9	4.8	1.1	49.3	37.3
1991–2000	9,095,417	14.9	4.8	8.6	1.6	49.3	30.7

Dash indicates less than 0.1 percent.

Recent Trends in Immigration (in thousands)					PERCENT		
	1961–1970	1971–1980	1981–1990	1991–2000	1971–1980	1981–1990	1991–2000
All countries	3,321.7	4,493.3	7,338.1	9095.4	100.0	100.0	100.0
Europe	1,123.5	800.4	761.5	1359.7	17.8	10.4	14.9
Austria	20.6	9.5	18.3	15.5	0.2	0.3	0.2
Belgium	9.2	5.3	7.0	7.0	0.1	0.1	0.1
Czechoslovakia	3.3	6.0	7.2	9.8	0.1	0.1	0.1
Denmark	9.2	4.4	5.3	6.0	0.1	0.1	0.1
France	45.2	25.1	22.4	35.8	0.6	1.3	0.4
Germany	190.8	74.4	91.6	92.6	1.7	2.2	1.0
Greece	86.0	92.4	38.3	26.7	2.1	0.4	0.3
Hungary	5.4	6.6	6.5	9.3	0.1	0.1	0.1
Ireland	33.0	11.5	31.9	56.9	0.3	0.9	0.6
Italy	214.1	129.4	67.2	62.7	2.9	0.2	0.7
Netherlands	30.6	10.5	12.2	13.3	0.2	0.1	0.1
Norway	15.5	3.9	4.2	5.1	0.1	1.1	0.5
Poland	53.5	37.2	83.3	163.7	0.8	0.5	1.8
Portugal	76.1	101.7	40.4	22.9	2.3	0.3	0.3
Spain	44.7	39.1	20.4	17.1	0.9	0.2	0.2
Sweden	17.1	6.5	11.0	12.7	0.1	0.1	0.1
Switzerland	18.5	8.2	8.8	11.8	0.2	0.1	0.1
United Kingdom	213.8	137.4	159.2	151.8	3.1	2.2	1.7
USSR	2.5	39.0	57.7	462.8	0.9	0.3	5.1
Yugoslavia	20.4	30.5	18.8	66.5	0.7	0.5	0.7
Other Europe	9.1	18.9	8.2	57.7	0.2	0.0	0.6

Recent Trends in Immigration (in thousands)					PERCENT		
	1961–1970	1971–1980	1981–1990	1991–2000	1971–1980	1981–1990	1991–2000
Asia	427.6	1588.2	2738.1	2795.6	35.2	37.3	30.7
China	34.8	124.3	298.9	419.1	2.8	4.1	4.6
Hong Kong	75.0	113.5	98.2	109.8	2.5	1.3	1.2
India	27.2	164.1	250.7	363.1	3.7	3.4	4.0
Iran	10.3	45.1	116.0	69.0	1.0	1.6	0.8
Israel	29.6	37.7	44.2	39.4	0.8	0.6	0.4
Japan	40.0	49.8	47.0	67.9	1.1	0.6	0.7
Korea	34.5	267.6	333.8	164.2	6.0	4.5	1.8
Philippines	98.4	355.0	548.7	503.9	7.9	7.5	5.5
Turkey	10.1	13.4	23.4	38.2	0.3	0.3	0.4
Vietnam	4.3	172.8	281.0	286.1	3.8	3.8	3.1
Other Asia	36.5	176.1	631.4	735.4	3.8	8.6	8.0
America	1716.4	1982.5	3615.6	4486.8	44.3	49.3	49.3
Argentina	49.7	29.9	27.3	26.6	0.7	0.4	0.3
Canada	413.3	169.9	158.0	192.0	3.8	2.2	2.1
Colombia	72.0	77.3	122.9	128.5	1.7	1.7	1.4
Cuba	208.5	264.9	144.6	169.3	5.9	2.0	1.9
Dominican Rep.	93.3	148.1	252.0	335.3	3.3	3.4	3.7
Ecuador	36.8	50.1	56.2	76.5	1.1	0.8	0.8
El Salvador	15.0	34.4	213.5	215.7	0.8	2.9	2.4
Haiti	34.5	56.3	138.4	179.6	1.3	1.9	2.0
Jamaica	74.9	137.6	208.1	169.2	3.1	2.8	1.9
Mexico	453.9	640.3	1655.7	2249.4	14.3	22.6	24.7
Other America	264.4	373.8	639.3	744.3	8.3	8.7	8.2
Africa	29.0	80.8	176.8	355.0	1.8	2.4	3.9
Oceania	25.1	41.2	45.2	55.8	0.9	0.6	0.6

Figures may not add to total due to rounding.

American Workers and Farmers							
Year	Total Number of Workers (thousands)	Percent of Workers Male/Female	Percent of Female Workers Married	Percent of Workers in Female Population	Percent of Workers in Labor Unions	Farm Population (thousands)	Farm Population as Percent of Total Population
1870	12,506	85/15	NA	NA	NA	NA	NA
1880	17,392	85/15	NA	NA	NA	21,973	43.8
1890	23,318	83/17	13.9	18.9	NA	24,771	42.3
1900	29,073	82/18	15.4	20.6	3	29,875	41.9
1910	38,167	79/21	24.7	25.4	6	32,077	34.9
1920	41,614	79/21	23.0	23.7	12	31,974	30.1
1930	48,830	78/22	28.9	24.8	7	30,529	24.9
1940	53,011	76/24	36.4	27.4	27	30,547	23.2
1950	59,643	72/28	52.1	31.4	25	23,048	15.3
1960	69,877	68/32	59.9	37.7	26	15,635	8.7
1970	82,049	63/37	63.4	43.4	25	9712	4.8
1980	108,544	58/42	59.7	51.5	23	6051	2.7
1990	117,914	55/45	58.4	44.3	16	3871	1.6
2000	135,208	54/46	61.3	45.7	15	3305	1.1

Year	Gross National Product (GNP) (in billions)*	FOREIGN TRADE (in millions)			Federal Budget (in billions)	Federal Surplus/Deficit (in billions)	Federal Debt (in billions)
		Exports	Imports	Balance of Trade			
			The Economy and Federal Spending				
1790	NA	$20	$23	$−3	$0.004	$+0.00015	$0.076
1800	NA	71	91	−20	0.011	+0.0006	0.083
1810	NA	67	85	−18	0.008	+0.0012	0.053
1820	NA	70	74	−4	0.018	−0.0004	0.091
1830	NA	74	71	+3	0.015	+0.100	0.049
1840	NA	132	107	+25	0.024	−0.005	0.004
1850	NA	152	178	−26	0.040	+0.004	0.064
1860	NA	400	362	−38	0.063	−0.01	0.065
1870	$7.4	451	462	−11	0.310	+0.10	2.4
1880	11.2	853	761	+92	0.268	+0.07	2.1
1890	13.1	910	823	+87	0.318	+0.09	1.2
1900	18.7	1499	930	+569	0.521	+0.05	1.2
1910	35.3	1919	1646	+273	0.694	−0.02	1.1
1920	91.5	8664	5784	+2880	6.357	+0.3	24.3
1930	90.7	4013	3500	+513	3.320	+0.7	16.3
1940	100.0	4030	7433	−3403	9.6	−2.7	43.0
1950	286.5	10,816	9125	+1691	43.1	−2.2	257.4
1960	506.5	19,600	15,046	+4556	92.2	+0.3	286.3
1970	992.7	42,700	40,189	+2511	195.6	−2.8	371.0
1980	2631.7	220,783	244,871	+24,088	590.9	−73.8	907.7
1990	5803.2	394,030	495,042	−101,012	1253.1	−220.5	3206.6
2000	9872.9	1,102,900	1,466,900	−364,000	1788.8	+236.4	5629.0

*For 1990 and after, gross domestic product (GDP) is given.

Glossary

actual representation view that the people can be represented only by a person whom they have actually elected to office; this understanding of representation was the consensus among colonials during the imperial crisis and the basis of their objection to the British claim that Americans were virtually represented in Parliament.

affirmative action practice of actively seeking to increase the number of racial and ethnic minorities, women, persons in a protected age category, persons with disabilities, and disabled veterans in a work place or school. Such measures sometimes include the setting of quotas or percentages in hiring.

amnesty general pardon granted by a government, usually for political crimes. Proposals of amnesty were made, with varying degrees of exception for high Confederate officials, by presidents Lincoln and Johnson as well as by Congress in 1872. President Ford offered conditional amnesty in 1974 to draft evaders at the conclusion of the Vietnam war.

anti-Semitism hatred, prejudice, oppression, or discrimination against Jews or Judaism. *Semite* originally referred to the descendents of Shem, which included both Jews and Muslims in the Middle East. More recently the term has come to refer primarily to Jews.

appeasement policy of making concessions to an aggressor nation, as long as its demands appear reasonable, in order to avoid war. Hitler's full conquest of Czechoslovakia, violating his promises given at the Munich Conference in 1938, gave the term its negative connotation.

armistice mutually agreed-on truce or temporary halt in the fighting of a war so that the combatants may discuss peace.

artisan skilled craftworker, such as a blacksmith, a cooper, a miller, or a tailor. Master artisans constituted a large segment of the middle classes in American cities and towns from the beginnings of colonial settlement through the 1820s; they owned their own shops and employed a number of younger journeyman artisans, who owned only their tools, and trained even younger and less skilled apprentices in a craft.

assimilate to absorb a culturally distinct group into the dominant culture. The debate over the process of assimilation, of immigrants "becoming American," has been a persistent fault line in American politics. The debate revolves around what qualities are American and the degree to which a dominant culture should define them. The debate is extremely difficult in a society in which immigration plays a crucial role—in a "nation of nations," as Walt Whitman described the United States.

autonomy condition of being independent or, in the case of a political structure, the right to self-government

balanced constitution view that England's constitution gave every part of English society some voice in the workings of its government. While the Crown represented the monarchy and the House of Lords the aristocracy, the House of Commons represented the ordinary people of England.

barter economy networks of trade based on the mutual exchange of goods and services with little or no use of coin or currency.

behaviorism school of psychology that measures human behavior, believes it can be shaped, and discounts emotion as subjective. Behaviorism was founded by psychologist John Watson and was first presented in his *Psychology as the Behaviorist Views It* (1913).

benign neglect policy also known as "salutary neglect," pursued by the British empire in governing its American colonies until the end of the Seven Years' War.

biocentric life-centered; also a theory of moral responsibility stating that all forms of life have an inherent right to exist and that humanity is not the center of existence.

biogenetic engineering process of changing the DNA of a plant or an animal to produce desirable characteristics. Examples of desirable characteristics include fast growth and unusually large size. Not everyone agrees that the plants and animals that are genetically designed are safe for humans to eat or safe for the environment.

black codes series of laws passed by southern states in 1865 and 1866, modeled on the slave codes in effect before the Civil War. The codes did grant African Americans some rights not enjoyed by slaves, but their primary purpose was to keep African Americans as propertyless agricultural laborers.

bloody shirt political campaign tactic of "waving the bloody shirt," used by Republicans against Democrats; it invoked the tremendous loss of life and casualties from the Civil War as a reason to vote for Republicans as the party of the Union and not to trust Democrats, who had often opposed the war. The tactic continued to work, with diminishing success, throughout Reconstruction.

bonds certificates of debt issued by a government or corporation promising to repay the buyers of the bonds their original investment, plus interest, by a specified date of maturity. Bonds have been traditionally used by governments as a way to raise money during wartime or for large-scale projects.

boom-bust cycle periods of expansion and recession or depression that an economy goes through. Also referred to as *business cycle*. Major downturns in the cycle have occurred in the United States beginning in 1819, 1837, 1857, 1873, 1893, 1907, and 1929, the start of the Great Depression.

bootlegging illegal transport or sale of goods, in this case alcoholic beverages during the 1920s. The term derived from the practice of hiding a container of alcohol in the upper part of a boot.

boycott tactic used by protestors, workers, and consumers to pressure business organizations through a mass refusal to purchase their products or otherwise do business with them.

brinksmanship policy of pushing a critical situation to the edge of catastrophe by using the implicit threat of nuclear war in order to persuade an opponent to back down. The strategy was developed by Secretary of State John Foster Dulles under President Dwight Eisenhower.

bureaucratic state   government run by administrative bureaus or divisions and staffed by nonelected officials.

business cycle   *see* **boom-bust cycle.**

carpetbagger   white Republicans, originally from the North, who came to live in the South after the Civil War. They received their nickname from hostile Southerners who claimed that the newcomers arrived carrying all that they owned stuffed into a carpetbag and eager to get rich by plundering the South.

cartel   organization of private businesses that join together to control production, distribution, and prices.

caste system   system of social stratification separating individuals by various distinctions, among them hereditary, rank, profession, wealth, and race. Slavery as a caste system not only separated whites from blacks but assigned value to people according to shadings of color.

cede   to give up possession of, usually by treaty.

celibate   abstaining from sexual intercourse; also unmarried. Celibacy is the abstention from intercourse, a state often motivated by religious teachings.

charter   document issued by a sovereign ruler, legislature, or other authority creating a public or private corporation. England's rulers issued charters setting forth the authority of corporations or joint stock companies to colonize sections of the Americas; state legislatures have issued charters to corporations; and the British (including American colonials) traced basic rights of representation to the Magna Carta (Great Charter) granted by King John in 1215 C.E.

checks and balances   mechanism by which each branch of government—executive, legislative, and judicial—keeps the others within the bounds of their constitutional authority; James Madison emphasized this feature of the federal constitution to assure the Anti-Federalists.

Columbian exchange   transition of people, plants, insects, and microbes between the two hemispheres, initiated when Columbus reached the Americas in 1492.

commercial economy   economy in which individuals are involved in a network of markets and commercial transactions. Such economies are often urban, where goods and services are exchanged for money and credit; agricultural areas are also commercial when crops and livestock are sold in markets rather than consumed by those who grew or raised them. Commercial economies are less egalitarian, because wealth can be concentrated in the hands of fewer individuals. *See also* **semisubsistence economy.**

committees of correspondence   strategy devised by Samuel Adams in 1772 to rally popular support among American colonials against British imperial policies. The committees of correspondence drew up statements of American rights and grievances, distributed those documents within and among the colonies, and solicited responses from towns and counties. This committee structure formed a new communications network, one that fostered intercolonial agreement on resistance to British measures and spread the resistance from seaports into rural areas.

community action   programs designed to identify and organize local leaders to take steps to alleviate poverty and crime in their neighborhoods. Sociologist Saul Alinsky from Chicago organized the Industrial Areas Foundation to support community action programs in the 1960s.

conformity   degree to which people adjust their behavior, values, and ideas to fit into a group or society.

conglomerate   corporation whose various branches or subsidiaries are either directly or indirectly spread among a variety of industries, usually unrelated to one another. The purpose of a conglomerate is generally to increase shareholder value and ensure against market cycles by spreading its risk, rather than to improve market share or production efficiency by concentrating on excelling within a single industry.

Congregationalists   members of a Protestant denomination that originated in sixteenth-century Britain as part of the Puritan movement. While some early Congregationalists, known as Separatists, concluded that the Church of England was beyond reformation, most strove to reform English religion and society while remaining within the Church of England. Early modern Congregationalists embraced Calvinist theological beliefs and held that each individual congregation should conduct its own religious affairs, answering to no higher authority. The Separatists founded Plymouth, the first northern colony, and the Non-Separating Congregationalists predominated elsewhere in seventeenth-century New England.

conscription   act of compulsory enrollment for military service, as opposed to a voluntary enlistment.

consensus   point of view generally shared by a group, institution, or even a culture. Scholars have analyzed and debated the institutions that contribute to the construction of a consensus viewpoint, ranging from schools and churches to the media in their various forms.

constitution   framework of government establishing the contract between rulers and ruled. American revolutionaries insisted on written constitutions to protect individual rights and liberties; by contrast, Britons understood the term *constitution* to mean the existing arrangement of government—not an actual document but a collection of parliamentary laws, customs, and precedents.

consumer goods   products such as food and clothing that fill the needs and wants of individuals. *Producer* or *capital goods*, in contrast, are the factory equipment and other machines used to manufacture or transport other goods or services.

Continental Army   main rebel military force, created by the Second Continental Congress in July 1775 and commanded by George Washington. After the 1776 campaign, most enlistments came from the poorest and most desperate in American society, and it was they who shouldered the burden of the fighting. During the harsh winter at Valley Forge in 1778/1779, the army acquired greater discipline and expertise and thereafter scored important military victories in the mid-Atlantic and the South.

contraband   goods seized by a government during wartime, when the goods were being used by an enemy nation or being shipped to an enemy nation by a neutral nation. The term was also applied during the Civil War to escaped slaves who fled behind Union lines.

Copperhead derogatory term used by Republicans to label northern Democrats who opposed the war policies of the Lincoln administration and advocated a negotiated peace.

CORE Congress on Racial Equality, an organization founded in Chicago in 1942. The group's inspiration was Krishnalal Shridharani's book *War Without Violence,* which outlined Mohandas K. Gandhi's nonviolent philosophy for action. CORE believed that African Americans could use nonviolent civil disobedience to challenge racial segregation.

corporation business entity that has been granted a charter granting it legal rights, privileges, and liabilities distinct from the individual members that are a part of it. A corporation therefore may survive the death of the individuals who created and run it.

Counter-Reformation reform movement within the Roman Catholic Church in response to the Protestant Reformation, seeking to reform and reinvigorate the Church. Religious orders played a large role in the Counter-Reformation, particularly the Jesuit order, known formally as the Society of Jesus, and founded in 1534 by Ignatius of Loyola.

covert operations military or political actions carried out in secret to allow the responsible government or party to deny its role. Governments have often relied on such operations when overt military force is impractical or dangerous or when public negotiations are likely to fail.

de facto segregation spatial and social separation of populations brought about by social behavior rather than by laws or legal mechanisms. Segregation (especially in schools) has often existed without being sanctioned by law. When the practice is accomplished through explicit legal means, it is known as *de jure segregation.*

debt peonage paying off a debt through labor when the debtor lacks sufficient cash or other assets.

Deep South South Carolina, Georgia, Florida, Alabama, Mississippi, Louisiana, and Texas.

demographic factors relating to the characteristics of populations. Demography is the study of populations, looking at such aspects as size, growth, density, and age distribution.

depreciated decreased in value owing to market conditions. Depreciation in the value of banknotes can occur when too much paper money is put into circulation or when users doubt the ability of the government to back up the paper currency with reserves of gold or silver.

détente relaxation of strained relations between nations, especially among the United States, the Soviet Union, and China in the 1970s and late 1980s. In seeking détente, once-hostile parties begin to emphasize their common interests and reduce their points of conflict.

deterrence prevention of an action by fear of the consequences; during the cold war, the theory that war could be avoided because each side knew that the other possessed large numbers of nuclear weapons. Thus any nuclear exchange threatened the survival of both sides.

disfranchisement denial of a citizen's right to vote.

doctrine of preemption war undertaken in anticipation of imminent attack or invasion by another nation or in hopes of gaining a strategic advantage when war seems unavoidable. In that sense the Japanese government viewed its attack on Pearl Harbor as preemptive.

domesticity devotion to home life, and a woman's place at the center of that life. The ideal of domesticity became popular during the nineteenth century as industrialization was increasingly separating work and home as individual spheres.

dry farming farming system to conserve water in semi-arid regions receiving less than 15 to 20 inches of rain a year. Methods include leaving some fields fallow or unplanted to reduce water use, keeping soil broken to absorb any water, and growing drought-resistant crops.

due process constitutional concept, embodied in the Fifth and Fourteenth Amendments, that no person shall be deprived of life, liberty, or property without legal safeguards such as being present at a hearing, having an opportunity to be heard in court, having the opportunity to confront hostile witnesses, and being able to present evidence.

ecosystem a community and/or region studied as a system of functioning relationships between organisms and their environments.

ecumenism movement encouraging unity among religions, especially among Christian denominations and between Christians and Jews. Ecumenical movements promote cooperation and better understanding among different religious denominations.

egalitarian exhibiting or asserting a belief in the equality of humans in a social, political, or economic context.

elect in theology, those of the faithful chosen, or "elected" by God for eternal salvation.

elites class of people given special social, economic, or intellectual status within society. The singular noun *elite* can also be used as a plural, as in *the colonial elite.*

embargo government act prohibiting trade with a foreign country or countries, usually to exert economic pressure.

enlightenment intellectual movement that flourished in Europe from the mid-1600s through the eighteenth century and stressed the power of human reason to promote social progress by discovering the laws that governed both nature and society. In the American colonies, the Enlightenment's influence encouraged scientists such as Benjamin Franklin to experiment and discover useful scientific knowledge, and it also persuaded a growing minority to accept more liberal religious views, known as "rational Christianity."

escalation process of steady intensification, rather than a sudden or marked increase, applied to the increasing American military presence in Vietnam. The term derives from an escalator, which gradually lifts its cargo to a higher level. Nuclear theorist Herman Kahn used the term geopolitically in his *On Escalation: Metaphors and Scenarios* (1968).

evangelical term that derives from a Greek word meaning the bringing of good news—in this case, the Gospel. Protestant evangelicals stressed the need for individual conversion and rebirth stemming from an awareness of sinful guilt and Christ's act of atoning, through his death, for their sins.

excise tax   internal tax placed on the production or sale of a commodity, usually a luxury item or nonessential.

executive order   declaration issued by the president or by a governor possessing the force of law. Executive orders are usually based on existing statutory authority and require no action by Congress or the state legislature to take effect.

expatriate   one who leaves the country of one's birth or citizenship to live in another, usually out of a sense of alienation. The term is often applied to the group of writers and artists living in self-imposed exile in Paris during the 1920s and sometimes referred to as the "Lost Generation." That term was coined by the writer Gertrude Lawrence, describing the rootless generation of American expatriates who found life in the United States culturally sterile and promises of postwar freedom and democracy empty.

federalism   governing principle established by the Constitution in which the national government and the states divide power. A stronger commitment to federalism as the basis of a national republic replaced the system established by the Articles of Confederation, which granted virtually sovereign power to individual states.

fission   splitting of a nucleus of an atom into at least two other nuclei, accompanied by the release of a relatively large amount of energy. The splitting of the nucleus of the uranium isotope U-235 or its artificial cousin, plutonium, powered the atomic bomb.

franchise   see **suffrage** and **disenfranchisement.**

Free Soil party   antislavery party formed in 1848 by northern Democrats disillusioned with southern Democratic support for slavery. The party tried to widen its appeal by focusing less on outright abolition than on opposing the spread of slavery into the territories (the need to protect "free soil" and "free labor"). The party never gained strength, however, as the Republican Party in the 1850s attracted the greater number of antislavery voters.

freedmen   former slaves; the term came into use during the Civil War, as greater numbers of slaves fled or were freed under the terms of the Emancipation Proclamation, and continued to be widely used during Reconstruction. More recently historians have also used the more gender-neutral term, *freedpeople.*

graduated income tax   tax based on a percentage of an individual's income, the percentage increasing as total income increases. Under such a system, wealthy individuals are taxed at a higher rate than are poorer individuals.

Great Awakening   term used by some historians to describe periods of intense religious piety and commitment among Americans that fueled the expansion of Protestant churches. The First Great Awakening extended from the 1730s to the American Revolution; the Second Great Awakening includes the period from about 1790 to the 1840s; the Third Great Awakening took place during the late nineteenth and early twentieth centuries; the Fourth Great Awakening spans the latter half of the twentieth century.

habeas corpus   Latin phrase meaning, "you have the body." For centuries, the term referred in English law to the right of individuals to be brought before a court and informed of the crime alleged against them. The right of habeus corpus is meant to ensure that the government cannot arbitrarily arrest and imprison a citizen without giving grounds for doing so.

hawks and doves   nicknames for the two opposing positions in American policy during the war in Vietnam. Hawks supported the escalation of the war and a "peace with honor." Doves, the peace faction, argued that the United States had intervened in a civil war and should withdraw its troops.

Hessians   German soldiers who fought with the British Army during the American Revolution. Some Hessians taken as prisoners of war later served in the Continental Army and settled in the United States after the Revolution.

horizontal combination   strategy of business growth (sometimes referred to as "horizontal integration") that attempts to stifle competition by combining more than one firm involved in the same level of production, transportation, or distribution into a single firm.

http://   HyperText Transfer Protocol; abbreviation refers to the Internet rules governing the transfer of data between a server and a computer as well as for exchanging files (text, graphic images, sound, video, and other multimedia files) on the World Wide Web.

impeachment   under the U.S. Constitution, the process by which members of the House of Representatives bring charges against a high government official for "Treason, Bribery, or other high Crimes and Misdemeanors." Once an individual is impeached, he or she must stand trial before the Senate, where a majority vote is required for conviction. Conviction results in removal from office.

imperialism   acquisition of control over the government and the economy of another nation, usually by conquest. The United States became an imperialistic world power in the late nineteenth century by gaining control over the Hawaiian Islands and, after the Spanish American War (1898), Guam, the Philippines, Cuba, and Puerto Rico.

indemnity   compensation for loss or damage.

indentures   contract signed between two parties, binding one to serve the other for a specified period of time. The term originated because two copies of the agreement were made, both indented in the same way at its edges, so that each party was provided an identical record of the agreement.

inflation   increase in the overall price of goods and services over an extended period of time; or a similar decrease over time of the purchasing power of money. The latter situation can be caused by an increase of the amount of currency and credit available in an economy. In such cases, when the perceived value of paper money declines (as often happens in wars, when the government tries to raise revenues by printing money), sellers raise the prices of their goods to compensate.

injunction   court order requiring individuals or groups to participate in or refrain from a certain action.

interstate commerce   trade in goods that crosses state lines. Regulation of interstate commerce is reserved in the Constitution for the federal government and has become the constitutional basis for much of federal regulation of business.

Iroquois League   Indian confederacy, also known as the Five Nations, that exerted enormous influence throughout the region. In 1712, a sixth tribe, the Tuscaroras, joined the confederation.

isolationism   belief that the United States should avoid foreign entanglements, alliances, and involvement in foreign wars. The tradition had its roots in President George Washington's farewell address, which warned in 1796, "It is our true policy to steer clear of permanent alliances with any portion of the foreign world. . . ."

Issei   *see* **Nisei**

itinerant   traveling preacher attached to no settled congregation. Itinerants played an important role in the first Great Awakening, taking their inspiration from George Whitefield, who preached up and down the Atlantic seaboard. In the early nineteenth century, many Protestant denominations—especially the Methodists and the Baptists—made strategic use of itinerants to evangelize settlers on the frontier.

jihad   Arabic term meaning striving or struggling in the way of God. Although broadly the term can indicate a spiritual effort on the part of a Muslim believer to come closer to Allah, the expression is also used to denote a Muslim holy war against unbelievers.

joint stock company   business in which capital is held in transferable shares of stock by joint owners. The joint stock company was an innovation that allowed investors to share and spread the risks of overseas investment. Instead of only a few individuals owning a ship and its cargo—which might sink and bring ruin to its investors—joint stock allowed for smaller sums to be invested in a variety of different ventures.

journeyman   person who has served an apprenticeship in a trade or craft and who is a qualified worker employed by another person.

judicial review   doctrine set out by Chief Justice John Marshall in *Marbury v. Madison*. The decision established that the judicial branch of the federal government possesses the power to determine whether the laws of Congress or the actions of the executive branch violate the Constitution.

laissez faire   a French term ("allow to do") referring to an economic doctrine that advocates holding government interference in the economy to an absolute minimum and ideally having none at all.

landed states and landless states   some of the 13 colonies that became the United States had originally been granted land whose western boundaries were vague or overlapped the land granted to other colonies. During the Confederation period, the so-called "landless" states had boundaries that were firmly drawn on all sides, such as Maryland, New Jersey, and Massachusetts. The so-called "landed" states possessed grants whose western boundaries were not fixed.

libertarian   advocate of a minimalist approach to governing, in which the freedom of private individuals to do as they please ranks paramount. A libertarian philosophy contrasts with the outlook of modern liberals, in which government plays a more active role in meeting the needs of citizens or in managing social and economic life for the common good.

lien   legal claim against property used to obtain a loan, which must be paid when the property is sold. Developing first in the South after the Civil War, the crop-lien system allowed merchants to claim a portion (or all) of current or future crops as payment for loans to farmers for seed, tools, and fertilizer. Merchants often insisted that indebted farmers raise a single cash crop, frequently cotton. That requirement helped to ensnare farmers in a cycle of debt as the price of such crops fell.

loyalists   supporters of the king and Parliament and known to the rebels as "tories." At the outset of the American Revolution, loyalists made up about one-fifth of the white population, but their ranks diminished steadily after about 1777, as the British army alienated many civilians in every region that they occupied.

loyalty oath   oath of fidelity to the state or to an organization. Plans for Reconstruction insisted that southerners returning to the Union take a loyalty oath of some sort, whether that they would be loyal henceforth to the United States or a more strict "ironclad oath" that they never had aided the Confederacy. At other times of stress—as during the Revolutionary era or during the cold war of the 1950s, loyalty oaths and loyalty investigations have been used by groups or governments to enforce obedience to the state or to a revolutionary movement.

managed economy   economy directed by the government with power over prices, allocation of resources, and marketing of goods.

Manifest Destiny   belief, as Democratic editor John L. O'Sullivan put it, that it had become the United States' "manifest destiny to overspread the continent allotted by Providence for the free development of our yearly multiplying millions." The roots of the doctrine were both religious and political. Protestant religious thinkers had long seen American settlement as setting a pious and virtuous example to the rest of the world. The political ideology of the Revolution encouraged the notion that the benefits of democracy would spread along with the political expansion of the nation. Yet Manifest Destiny was also racist in its assumption of the inferiority of other peoples and cultures; and it encompassed a purely economic desire to expand the nation's commerce and power.

"maroon" communities   collective attempts at escape typically undertaken by groups of newly arrived African slaves in the American South. Such slaves fled inland, often to the frontiers of colonial settlement, where they attempted to reconstruct the African villages from which they had been taken captive. Because of their size, such communities proved to be short-lived; they were quickly discovered by white slave patrols or by Indian tribes such as the Cherokees, who profited from returning runaways. "Maroon communities" in the Caribbean proved far more enduring and provided the bases for successful slave rebellions during the eighteenth and early nineteenth centuries.

mass media   forms of communication designed to reach a vast audience, generally a nation state or larger, without personal contact between the senders and receivers. Examples would include newspapers, movies, magazines, radio, television, and—today—some sites on the Internet.

mercantilism European economic doctrine calling for strict regulation of the economy in order to ensure a balance of exports over imports and encrease the amount of gold and silver in a nation's treasury.

merchants of death term popularized in the 1930s to describe American bankers and arms makers whose support for the Allied cause, some historians charged, drew the United States into World War I.

Mesoamerica the area stretching from present-day central Mexico southward through Honduras and Nicaragua, in which pre-Columbian civilizations developed.

Methodist denomination that originated as a reform movement within the Church of England during the mid-eighteenth century, much as the Puritans originated as a reform movement within the English church during the mid-sixteenth century. The distinctive features of early Methodism on both sides of the Atlantic included a strict devotional regimen, an ascetic moral discipline, and an emphasis on evangelical conversion. By the Civil War, Methodists had become the largest Protestant denomination in the United States among both whites and African Americans.

military-industrial complex combination of the U.S. armed forces, arms manufacturers, and associated political and commercial interests, which grew rapidly during the cold war era. It is another term for the mutually supportive relationship of military contractors, the Pentagon, and sympathetic members of Congress, an alliance also known as the "Iron Triangle."

militia local defense band of civilians comprising men between the ages of 16 and 65 whose military training consisted only of occasional gatherings known as musters. Militias were organized in towns and counties throughout the American colonies from the beginnings of settlement, but they played a crucial role in the war for independence by supporting the Continental Army whenever the fighting moved into their neighborhoods.

millennialism belief in the thousand-year reign of Christ predicted in the Bible's final book, the Revelation to John. The belief that dedicated Christians could help bring about this reign of holiness by converting the world to Christianity proved to be a powerful impulse to reform.

miscegenation marriage, cohabitation, or sexual relations between persons of different races. Since race is a socially constructed identifier rather than one with any scientific or genetic basis, *miscegenation* as a term is used only in its historical context.

monoculture growth of a single crop to the virtual exclusion of all others, either on a farm or more generally within a region.

mutiny refusal of rank-and-file soldiers to follow the commands of their superior officers. Mutinies plagued the Continental Army between 1779 and 1781 as resentments mounted among soldiers over spoiled food, inadequate clothing, and back pay.

mutually assured destruction (MAD) national defense strategy in which a nuclear attack by one side would inevitably trigger an equal response leading to the destruction of both the attacker and the defender. Deterrence theory suggested that when both sides possessed the capability to inflict nuclear annihilation, even after being hit by a first strike, neither side would dare use such weapons.

national debt cumulative total of all previous annual *federal deficits* or budget shortfalls incurred each year and owed by the federal government.

nativism outlook championing the supremacy of "native" cultural traits and political rights over those of immigrants from different backgrounds. Nativism flourished during the high immigration of the late 1840s and 1850s, evidenced by the rise of the American ("Know-Nothing") party. In the late nineteenth and early twentieth centuries, nativists pressed for the restriction of immigration and won their biggest victories when Congress enacted the National Origins Acts of 1921 and 1924. As immigrant numbers rose again in the late twentieth century and early twenty-first, the nativist debate again emerged.

naturalization act of granting full citizenship to someone born outside the country.

navalism theories of warfare and trade that rely on a nation's navy as a principal instrument of policy.

neo-isolationist term applied to those who after World War II believed the United States should avoid foreign entanglements. Neo-isolationists especially condemned the United Nations and its supporters, whom they contemptuously referred to as "one-worlders."

"new" immigrants called "new" because they differed substantially from earlier arrivals who had come mostly from Northern and Western Europe; these newcomers came to the United States between 1880 and 1920 from Eastern and Southern Europe. Unlike most earlier immigrants (with the exception of the Irish), these immigrants were non-Protestants: Catholics, Jews, and Russian Orthodox Christians.

Nisei American-born citizens of Japanese ancestry, contrasted with *Issei*, native-born Japanese who had moved to the United States. At the outbreak of World War II, Nisei referred specifically to Japanese Americans who lived on the West Coast (but not in Hawaii or the East Coast), who were interned during the war because of prejudice and the widespread fear that they sympathized with Japan.

nomad a member of a group of people who have no fixed home and who move about, usually seasonally, in pursuit of food, water, and other resources.

normal schools schools that trained teachers, usually for two years and mostly for teaching in the elementary grades.

northwest territory present-day states of Ohio, Indiana, Illinois, Michigan, and Wisconsin. The incorporation of this territory into the United States through the Northwest Ordinance of 1785 marked the major achievement of the national government under the Articles of Confederation.

Opposition diverse group of political thinkers and writers in Great Britain, also known as the Country Party and the Commonwealthmen, who elaborated the tradition of classical republicanism from the late seventeenth century through the eighteenth century. They warned that the executive branch of government (the king and his ministers) was conspiring to corrupt and coopt the legislative branch of government (the House of Commons), thereby endangering popular liberties, and they called for political reforms to make Britain's government more representative of and more accountable to the people. Dismissed in England as a disaffected radical minority, the Opposition exerted a decisive influence on the political thinking of an increasing number of American colonials in the decades leading up to the Revolution.

outsourcing   the contracting of goods or services from outside a company or organization in order to maintain flexibility in the size of the organization's work force. Increasingly outsourcing has used suppliers outside the United States in low-wage countries such as Mexico, India, and China.

pandemic   outbreak of disease that spreads across national boundaries or across the world.

partisan warfare   armed clashes among political rivals, typically involving guerilla fighting and the violent intimidation of civilians by militias. Partisan warfare between loyalists and rebels tore apart communities everywhere in the United States during the war for independence, but the fighting was especially fierce and protracted in the South. The success of rebel insurgencies there ultimately convinced many southern whites to support the cause of independence.

patent   legal document issued by the government giving the holder exclusive rights to use, make, and sell a process, product, or device for a specified period of time. The first patents in America were issued by colonial governments as early as 1641. Congress enacted the first patent law in 1790.

paternalism   attitude or policy of treating individuals or groups in a fatherly manner, by providing for their needs without granting them rights of responsibilities. The relation involves both a dominant and a subordinate party. Sometimes the dominance comes from gender, as in a male patriarchy, whereby females are given subordinate roles. But paternalism can also be expressed in relations between colonial and subject peoples, masters and slaves, or culturally different groups.

pays d'en haut   in the seventeenth century, the lands referred to by the French as the "upper country," the land upriver from Montreal as French fur traders passed into the Great Lakes beyond the southern shores of Lake Ontario. The trading lands stretched all the way to the Mississippi River.

peculiar institution   euphemism for slavery, perhaps revealing in its use. The institution was "peculiar" to the South in that it had been abolished in the North (and other parts of the world, increasingly). *Peculiar* also suggests the contradiction with the ideals of the Declaration of Independence, that "all men are created equal."

per capita income   average yearly income per person in a particular population; it provides one statistical measure of the relative wealth of a region.

pluralism   idea that identity cannot be reduced to a single shared essence. Under such a philosophy, distinct ethnic, cultural, and religious groups are tolerated and affirmed within a society. The philosophy contrasts with the belief, in American politics, that citizens should assimilate into a more uniform cultural identity of shared values. Contrasting metaphors portray an assimilationist United States as a melting pot versus a pluralist mixing bowl.

plurality   in elections, a candidate who receives a plurality wins more votes than any other candidate but less than half of all votes cast. Receiving more than half of the votes cast is called a *majority.*

pocket veto   means of vetoing a bill without formally doing so. Normally, if a president does not veto or sign a bill within 10 days of receiving it, the bill automatically becomes law. If it is received, however, within 10 days of Congress's adjournment, the president can simply "pocket" the bill unsigned, until Congress adjourns, and it does not go into effect.

political culture   patterns, habits, institutions, and traits associated with a political system. The political culture of the Jacksonian era, for example, was marked by a number of innovations: political nominating conventions, torchlight parades, campaign songs, badges, and other souvenirs.

political machine   hierarchical political organization developed in the nineteenth century that controlled the activities of a political party and was usually headed by a political boss.

popular sovereignty   doctrine that a territory could decide by vote whether or not to permit slavery within its boundaries. The doctrine was devised by Senator Stephen Douglas of Illinois as a way to placate southerners who wanted slavery permitted within Kansas Territory, forbidden under the Missouri Compromise. Meant as a compromise measure, the doctrine only inflamed the situation, as both sides worked to win a vote over slavery.

Populism   political outlook that supports the rights and powers of the common people in opposition to the interests of the privileged elite. The Populist Party evolved out of the economic distress of the 1890s among farmers and focused its anger against the era's large industrial corporations, railroad monopolies, and banks. But populism as an outlook and philosophy persisted long after the party had dissolved.

pragmatism   philosophical movement, led by philosophers Charles S. Peirce and William James, that stressed the visible, real-world results of ideas. Pragmatism was embraced by many progressives who wanted to promote the possibilities of change by abandoning the old notion that events were predetermined and inevitable.

predestination   basis of Calvinist theology and a belief that holds that God has ordained the outcome of all human history before the beginning of time, including the eternal fate of every human being. Believers in this doctrine found comfort and meaning from its assurance that God was directing the fate of nations, individuals, and all of creation toward his divine purposes.

Presbyterians   members of a Protestant denomination that originated in sixteenth-century Britain as part of the Puritan movement. Like their fellow Puritan reformers, the **Congregationalists,** the Presbyterians embraced Calvinist theology beliefs; but unlike the Congregationalists, Presbyterians favored a more hierarchical form of church governance, a system in which individual congregations were guided by presbyteries and synods comprising both laymen and ministers.

presidio military garrison; as Spanish colonizers moved north from central Mexico in the sixteenth and seventeenth century, they constructed presidios to consolidate claims over new territory. Presidios often encouraged the growth of nearby towns and ranches and were probably more important as sites of diplomacy with Indians than as centers of military power. Poor funding and political instability led to the decline of the presidios after Mexican independence in 1821.

privatize transferral of an economic enterprise or public utility from the control of the government into private ownership. The Bush plan for Social Security reform sought to place retirement contributions into investment accounts managed privately, rather than into a fund managed by the Social Security Administration.

producer goods goods, such as heavy machinery, used to manufacture other goods, often consumer goods.

psychedelic characterized by or generating shifts in perception and altered states of awareness, often hallucinatory, and usually brought on by drugs such as LSD, mescaline, or psilocybin. Advocates of the psychedelic state spoke of euphoria, mystic visions, and philosophic insights produced. Critical observers pointed to the potential not only of inducing hallucinations but sometimes psychoses.

public works government-financed construction projects, such as highways and bridges, for use by the public.

Puritans members of a reform movement within the Church of England that originated in the sixteenth century and that ultimately formed the Congregationalist and Presbyterian churches. Calvinist in their theology, the Puritans strove to reform English religion, society, and politics by restricting church membership to the pious and godly, by according the laity greater power in church governance, and by enlisting the state to enforce a strict moral code that prohibited drunkenness, gambling, swearing, and attending the theater.

Quakers Protestant sect, also known as the Society of Friends, founded in mid-seventeenth century England. The Quakers believed that the Holy Spirit dwelt within each human being and that religious conviction was the source of their egalitarian social practices, which included allowing women to speak in churches and to preach in public gatherings. Quakers settled the mid-Atlantic colonies in large numbers and founded the colony of Pennsylvania.

racialism see *racism*.

racism form of discrimination based on the belief that one race is superior to another. Racism may be expressed individually and consciously, through explicit thoughts, feelings, or acts; it can be codified into a theory that claims scientific backing for its tenets. It can also be expressed socially and unconsciously, through institutions that promote inequality between races. In the early twentieth century, when racism became much more pronounced, the term *racialism* was also coined.

reconquista military reconquest of the Iberian peninsula from Islamic Moors of Africa by European Christian rulers. The campaign lasted on and off from 718 to 1492 C.E.

Redeemers southerners who came to power in southern state governments from 1875 to 1877, claiming to have "redeemed" the South from Reconstruction. The Redeemers looked to undo many of the changes wrought by the Civil War. Their goals included minimizing the role of African Americans in government and reducing their economic independence and strengthening the "New South" through industrial development.

red-light district area in cities reserved for prostitutes. The term, first employed in the United States, resulted from the use of red lights to show that prostitutes were open for business.

repatriation act of returning people to their nation of origin. The term often refers to the act of returning soldiers or refugees to their birth country.

republican motherhood redefinition of the role of women promoted by many American reformers in the 1780s and 1790s, who believed that the success of republican government depended on educated and independent-minded mothers who would raise children to become informed and self-reliant citizens. The ideal of republican motherhood fostered improvements in educational opportunities for women and accorded them an important role in civic life, but it also reinforced the notion that women should confine the sphere of their activities to home and family.

republicanism belief that representative government safeguards popular liberties more reliably than does either monarchy or oligarchy and that all citizens must practice vigilance and self-denying virtue to prevent their rulers from succumbing to the temptations of power and becoming tyrants. This "classical republicanism" profoundly influenced the political views of many Americans from the middle of the eighteenth century to the middle of the nineteenth century.

Romanticism intellectual and artistic movement that arose in the early nineteenth century out of a rejection of the Enlightenment values of reason and balance. Romanticism emphasized the individual's expression of emotion and intuition.

sagebrush rebels group of western cattlemen, loggers, miners, developers, and others who argued that federal ownership of huge tracts of land and natural resources violated the principle of states' rights. This group demanded that government transfer control to individual states, in respect of their right to make decisions about the management of both the land and the natural resources.

scalawag white southerners who supported the Republican party. The derisive nickname was given by their opponents. Perhaps a quarter of all white southerners voted Republican at some time during Reconstruction.

scientific management system of factory production that stresses efficiency. The system was pioneered by American engineer Frederick Winslow Taylor. In *The Principles of Scientific Management* (1911), his most famous work, he emphasized time-and-motion studies to enhance productivity. The book became the bible of efficiency experts and Taylor the "Father of Scientific Management."

sedition words or actions that incite revolt against the law or duly constituted government.

segregation system, imposed through law and custom, of separating people by race; first enacted into law in Tennessee

(1875) with a statute separating blacks from whites on trains, one of the most prevalent public spaces for racial mingling.

self-determination principle in international law that people have a right to determine their own form of government free from outside control. The principle contrasts with colonialism and imperialism, under which people are subject to foreign rulers.

semisubsistence economy economy in which individuals and families produce most of what they need to live on. Such economies are overwhelmingly rural and also egalitarian, in that wealth is distributed fairly broadly. During the colonial period and early republic, much of the American economy was semisubsistence. *See also* **commercial economy.**

separate but equal rationale for a policy of segregation granting equal facilities and services to African American and whites in schools, hospitals, transportation and lodging facilities, and other public places. The Supreme Court upheld such laws in *Plessy v. Ferguson* (1896). In practice such facilities were separate but seldom equal.

separation of Church and State principle that religious institutions and their representatives should exercise no civil or judicial powers and that civil governments should give no official sanction, privileges, or financial support to any religious denomination or organization.

separation of powers principle that each branch of government—the legislature (Congress), the executive (the President), and the judiciary (the Supreme Court)—should wield distinct powers independent from interference or infringement by other branches of government. During the debates of the Constitutional Convention in 1797, James Madison successfully argued that this separation of powers was essential to a balanced republican government.

settlement house social reform effort that used neighborhood centers in which settlement house workers lived and worked among the poor, often in slum neighborhoods. The first settlement house, Toynbee Hall in London, was founded in 1884. The first settlement house in the United States (The Neighborhood Guild, later University Settlement House) was built in 1886 in New York City and was founded by Stanton Coit.

Shi'ite and Sunni two major branches of Islam, a division not unlike the Protestant-Catholic split in Christianity. After the death of the Prophet Muhammad followers disagreed over who should be his successor. Most believers accepted the tradition of having their leader chosen by community consensus (the Sunni branch), but a minority supported the claim of Ali, the Prophet's cousin. Over the years theological differences have separated Shi'ite and Sunni Muslims as well. Today the Shi'ites are dominant largely in Iran and southeastern Iraq.

silent majority phrase coined by President Richard Nixon in a 1969 speech, referring to the large number of Americans who supported his policies but did not express their views publicly.

sit-in form of direct action in which protesters nonviolently occupy and refuse to leave an area. Mahatma Gandhi employed the tactic during the Indian independence movement, and autoworkers used it in Flint, Michigan, in the late 1930s. Student movements around the world widely adopted the tactic in the 1960s.

social mobility movement of individuals from one social class to another. In general, the stronger the barriers of class, race, gender or caste, the less social mobility exhibited by a society.

socialism philosophy of social and economic organization in which the means of producing and distributing goods is owned collectively or by government.

sociological jurisprudence legal theory that emphasizes the importance not merely of precedent but of contemporary social context in interpreting the law.

specie coined money of gold or silver. Also referred to as hard money or hard currency. In contrast, banknotes or notes are paper money or paper currency.

sphere of influence geographic region beyond its border over which a nation exerts political or economic control.

spoils system practice of rewarding loyal party members with jobs in government. Known more formally as "patronage," the practice drew its name from the old saying, "To the victor belong the spoils," in this instance meaning the rewards of election victories.

steerage least expensive accommodation on a passenger ship, located below decks and often used by immigrants for passage to the United States in the late nineteenth and early twentieth centuries.

stock exchange market at which shares of ownership in corporations are bought and sold. The creation of what were markets for investment capital made it easier to raise the large sums of money needed for large industrial projects.

stratified layered; in this case according to class or social station. A highly stratified society has a greater variety of social levels, from the richest or most socially esteemed to the poorest or least socially approved. A society can be stratified according to wealth, race, religion, or a number of other social markers.

subsistence farming see **semisubsistence economy**.

subversive one who seeks the destruction or overthrow of a legally constituted government; also used as an adjective (for example, *subversive conduct*) to refer more generally to behavior undermining the established social order.

suffrage right to vote; also referred to as the franchise. To *disfranchise* is to take away the right to vote.

sun belt areas of the southern and western parts of the United States that experienced significant economic and population growth since World War II. That growth has been a contrast to the relative decline of the *rust belt*, the older industrial area from New England to the mid-Atlantic region across the upper-Middle West.

supply-side economics theory that emphasizes tax cuts and business incentives to encourage economic growth rather than deficit spending to promote demand. Businesses and individuals, the theory assumes, will use their tax savings to create new businesses and expand old businesses, which in turn will increase productivity, employment, and general well-being.

tariff duty on trade, the purpose of which is primarily to regulate the flow of commerce rather than to raise a revenue. The Molasses Act of 1733, for example, imposed a hefty customs duty on molasses imported from non-British Caribbean islands to encourage American distillers to purchase molasses exclusively from the British West Indies.

task system way of organizing slave labor in the South Carolina low country during the eighteenth century. Masters and overseers of rice and indigo plantations assigned individual slaves a daily task, and after its completion, slaves could spend the rest of the day engaged in pursuits of their own choosing. Gang labor, the system practiced in the Chesapeake, afforded slaves less opportunity for freedom within slavery.

taxes duty on trade (known as external taxation) or a duty on items circulating within a nation or a colony (known as internal taxation) intended primarily to raise a revenue rather than to regulate the flow of commerce. The Sugar Act of 1764 was an external tax, whereas the Stamp Act of 1765 was an internal tax.

Tejano Texan of Hispanic descent. In the early stages of the rebellion against Santa Anna, more than a few Tejanos supported the Texan drive for independence. But as Americans continued to arrive in Texas in large numbers, many viewed Tejanos with suspicion and they were marginalized in Texan society.

temperance movement reform movement, begun in the 1820s, to temper or restrain the sale and use of alcohol. It achieved its greatest success when the Eighteenth Amendment took effect in 1920, outlawing the manufacture, sale, transportation, and importation of alcohol. The amendment was repealed in 1933.

tenement building, often in disrepair and usually five or six stories in height, in which cheap apartments were rented to tenants. Such dilapidated housing sprang up in cities across the United States in the late nineteenth and early twentieth centuries to lodge the growing numbers of immigrants, African Americans, and other poor populations moving to urban centers.

theocracy system of government dominated by the clergy.

totalitarian government system in which the state controls all aspects of economic, political, and even social life, usually through some form of dictatorship. Nazi Germany under Adolf Hitler and the Soviet Union under Joseph Stalin are examples of totalitarian regimes.

trade association organization of individuals and firms in a given industry that provides statistical, lobbying, and other services to members.

trust business arrangement in which owners of shares in a business turn over their shares "in trust" to a board with power to control those businesses for the benefit of the trust. Following the example set by John D. Rockefeller and Standard Oil, trusts blossomed in the late nineteenth century as a means of consolidating power over production, marketing, and pricing, often crowding out other competitors."

union organization of workers designed to improve their economic status and working conditions. Such organizations come in two varieties: the horizontal union, in which all members share a common skill or craft, and the vertical union, composed of workers from all across the same industry.

Upper South the border states (Delaware, Maryland, Kentucky, and Missouri) and Virginia, North Carolina, Tennessee, and Arkansas.

vertical integration strategy of business growth that attempts to reduce costs by gaining control of the successive stages of a business operation, incorporating into a single firm several firms involved in all aspects of the manufacture of a product—from exploiting raw materials to manufacturing and distribution.

Victorianism constellation of middle-class values attributed to the proper virtues of Britain's Queen Victoria. Victorianism responded to the instabilities of an industrial age in which factory work dominated the lives of struggling workers and middle-class clerks as well as down-at-the-heels landed gentry. The culture's emphasis on "refinement" and "manners" established a social hierarchy offering some sense of stability.

virgin soil epidemic epidemic in which the populations at risk have had no previous contact with the diseases that strike them and are therefore immunologically almost defenseless.

virtual representation view that representation is not linked to election but rather to common interests; for example, during the imperial crisis the British argued that Americans were virtually represented in Parliament, even though colonials elected none of its members, because each member of Parliament stood for the interests of the whole empire. See also **actual representation.**

"watered" stock stock issued in excess of the assets of a company. The term derived from the practice of some ranchers who made their cattle drink large amounts of water before weighing them for sale.

welfare capitalism business practice of providing welfare—in the form of pension and profit-sharing programs, subsidized housing, personnel management, paid vacations, and other services and benefits—for workers. The practice was pioneered by Henry Ford under the philosophy that businesses in a capitalist economy should act for the common good of their workers. The philosophy, if not the business-wide practice, became popular in the 1920s as a way of reducing high rates of turnover among employees and integrating technological change into the workplace.

Wisconsin idea series of progressive reforms at the state level promoted by Robert LaFollette during his governorship of Wisconsin (1901–1906). They included primary elections, corporate property taxes, regulation of railroads and public utilities, and supervision of public resources in the public interest. A nonpartisan civil service group, recruited mostly from faculty at the University of Wisconsin, provided a cadre of expert bureaucrats to run the new programs.

yellow journalism brand of newspaper reporting that stresses excitement and shock over even-handedness and dull fact. The term "yellow journalism" derived from the color of the ink used to print the first comic strip, which appeared in William Randolph Hearst's *New York Journal* in 1895. Hearst's newspaper specialized in yellow journalism and is often credited with igniting public passions for war with Spain in 1898.

Credits

Index